GHOST WARS

'No one else I know of has been able to bring such a broad perspective to bear on the rise of bin Laden . . . it's an inside account written by an outsider, the most objective history I have read of the many failures of the CIA and US government in the region' *New York Review of Books*

'Coll's access to senior officials of all the principal countries involved is nothing short of astounding . . . a powerful indictment of strategic short-sightedness' *Globe and Mail*

'A powerful book, impeccably reported, containing hundreds of interviews with the principals in the US intelligence and national security establishments . . . goes a long way toward explaining the systemic errors that caused the United States, through five administrations, to fail in its most important foreign policy challenge since World War II' *Newsday*

'Coll's riveting narrative makes the reader want to rip the page and yell at the American counterterrorism officials he describes . . . and tell them to watch out' *The New York Times Book Review*

'An important work . . . truly a page turner . . . of the more than one hundred published books dealing with the September 11th attacks . . . none approach Coll's work for clarity and insight into the agency itself' *New York Sun*

'A gripping new history of the events leading up to September 11th, 2001 . . . Coll never simplifies a complex situation' *Seattle Times*

ABOUT THE AUTHOR

Winner of a 1990 Pulitzer Prize for explanatory journalism, Steve Coll has been managing editor of *The Washington Post* since 1998 and covered Afghanistan as the *Post*'s South Asia bureau chief between 1989 and 1992. Coll is the author of four books, including *On the Grand Trunk Road* and *The Taking of Getty Oil*. He lives with his wife and three children in Maryland.

Ghost Wars won the 2005 Pulitzer Prize for General Non-Fiction.

GHOST WARS

The Secret History of the CIA, Afghanistan, and bin Laden,
from the Soviet Invasion to September 10, 2001

STEVE COLL

PENGUIN BOOKS

PENGUIN BOOKS

Published by the Penguin Group
Penguin Books Ltd, 80 Strand, London WC2R 0RL, England
Penguin Group (USA) Inc., 375 Hudson Street, New York, New York 10014, USA
Penguin Group (Canada), 10 Alcorn Avenue, Toronto, Ontario, Canada M4V 3B2
(a division of Pearson Penguin Canada Inc.)
Penguin Ireland, 25 St Stephen's Green, Dublin 2, Ireland (a division of Penguin Books Ltd)
Penguin Group (Australia), 250 Camberwell Road,
Camberwell, Victoria 3124, Australia (a division of Pearson Australia Group Pty Ltd)
Penguin Books India Pvt Ltd, 11 Community Centre,
Panchsheel Park, New Delhi – 110 017, India
Penguin Group (NZ), cnr Airborne and Rosedale Roads, Albany,
Auckland 1310, New Zealand (a division of Pearson New Zealand Ltd)
Penguin Books (South Africa) (Pty) Ltd, 24 Sturdee Avenue,
Rosebank 2196, South Africa

Penguin Books Ltd, Registered Offices: 80 Strand, London WC2R 0RL, England

www.penguin.com

First published in the United States of America by The Penguin Press,
a member of Penguin Group (USA) Inc. 2004
Published in Penguin Books 2005

14

ISBN-13: 978–0–141–02080–8
ISBN-10: 0–141–02080–6

www.greenpenguin.co.uk

Penguin Books is committed to a sustainable future
for our business, our readers and our planet.
The book in your hands is made from paper
certified by the Forest Stewardship Council.

For Susan,
who understood

AUTHOR'S NOTE

Griff Witte, a 2000 graduate in history from Princeton University and a former reporter for the *Miami Herald,* worked for more than a year as my assistant on this book. He was a full partner in every respect. He contributed research, reporting, writing, editing, and ideas. He traveled to Afghanistan, Dubai, and across the United States to conduct interviews with dozens of sources. He wrote outstanding first drafts of chapters six and seventeen. His intelligence, persistence, resourcefulness, and high standards strengthened the book elsewhere in countless ways. He was an ideal collaborator and essential to the entire project.

CONTENTS

LIST OF MAPS

PRINCIPAL CHARACTERS

The Central Intelligence Agency

FRANK ANDERSON, Director, Afghanistan Task Force, 1987–1989; Chief, Near East Division, Directorate of Operations, 1991–1994

MILTON BEARDEN, Chief of Station, Islamabad, 1986–1989

J. COFER BLACK, Chief of Station, Khartoum, 1993–1995; Director, Counterterrorist Center, 1999–2002

WILLIAM J. CASEY, Director, 1981–1987

DUANE R. "DEWEY" CLARRIDGE, Director, Counterterrorist Center, 1986–1988

JOHN DEUTCH, Director, 1995–1997

ROBERT GATES, Director, 1991–1993

HOWARD HART, Chief of Station, Islamabad, 1981–1984

JEFF O'CONNELL, Director, Counterterrorist Center, 1997–1999

JAMES PAVITT, Deputy Director, Operations, 1999–

WILLIAM PIEKNEY, Chief of Station, Islamabad, 1984–1986

PAUL PILLAR, Senior Analyst, later Deputy Director, Counterterrorist Center, 1993–1999

RICH, Chief, Bin Laden Unit, Counterterrorist Center, 1999–2001

MICHAEL F. SCHEUER, Chief, Bin Laden Unit, Counterterrorist Center, 1996–1999

GARY SCHROEN, Case Officer, Islamabad, 1978–1980; Chief of Station–designate, Kabul, 1988–1990; Chief of Station, Islamabad, 1996–1999; Deputy Chief, Near East Division, Directorate of Operations, 1999–2001

GEORGE J. TENET, Director, 1997–
THOMAS TWETTEN, Deputy Director, Operations, 1991–1993
HARRY, Chief of Station, Islamabad, 1989–1992
JAMES WOOLSEY, Director, 1993–1995

The White House

SAMUEL L. "SANDY" BERGER, Deputy National Security Adviser,
    1993–1997; National Security Adviser, 1997–2000
ZBIGNIEW BRZEZINSKI, National Security Adviser, 1977–1980
RICHARD CLARKE, Counterterrorism Coordinator, National Security
    Council, 1998–2001
ANTHONY "TONY" LAKE, National Security Adviser, 1993–1997

Department of State

MADELEINE ALBRIGHT, Secretary of State, 1997–2000
KARL F. "RICK" INDERFURTH, Assistant Secretary for South Asia,
    1997–2000
EDMUND MCWILLIAMS, Special Envoy to the Afghan resistance,
    1988–1989
WILLIAM MILAM, Ambassador to Pakistan, 1998–2001
ROBERT OAKLEY, Ambassador to Pakistan, 1988–1991
TOM PICKERING, Undersecretary of State, 1997–2000
ROBIN RAPHEL, Assistant Secretary for South Asia, 1993–1997
GEORGE SHULTZ, Secretary of State, 1982–1989
TOM SIMONS, Ambassador to Pakistan, 1996–1998
PETER TOMSEN, Special Envoy to the Afghan resistance, 1989–1992

In Afghanistan

ABDULLAH, foreign policy aide to Ahmed Shah Massoud
MOHAMMED ATEF, Egyptian-born military commander in bin Laden's
    al Qaeda
ABDULLAH AZZAM, Palestinian-born spiritual leader, headed al Qaeda pre-
    cursor group until 1989

ABURRASHID DOSTUM, former communist, Uzbek militia leader, sometime ally of Massoud

MOHAMMED FAHIM, intelligence and military aide to Massoud

ABDUL HAQ, Afghan Pashtun tribal and guerrilla leader, breaks with CIA during late 1980s

JALLALADIN HAQQANNI, radical Afghan Islamist guerrilla leader, successful military commander, CIA and Saudi intelligence ally during 1980s, joins Taliban during 1990s

GULBUDDIN HEKMATYAR, radical Afghan Islamist guerrilla leader, rival of Massoud

HAMID KARZAI, Afghan Pashtun tribal leader and political activist, initially backs Taliban, later joins Pashtun opposition to Taliban

MASSOUD KHALILI, schoolmate and close aide to Ahmed Shah Massoud

OSAMA BIN LADEN, Saudi-born leader of al Qaeda after 1989

AHMED SHAH MASSOUD, Tajik guerrilla commander, leads anti-Soviet resistance in northern Afghanistan, later forms Northern Alliance, leads opposition to Taliban

PRESIDENT NAJIBULLAH, Soviet-backed Afghan communist leader

MULLAH MOHAMMED OMAR, supreme leader of the Taliban; after 1996, self-declared emir of Afghanistan

BURHANUDDIN RABBANI, Cairo-trained Islamist scholar, political leader of Massoud's party

MULLAH MOHAMMED RABBANI, Taliban leader favored by Saudi Arabia, seen as possible moderate

AMRULLAH SALEH, intelligence aide to Massoud

ABDURRAB RASUL SAYYAF, Cairo-trained Islamist scholar, Saudi-backed guerrilla leader

AYMAN AL-ZAWAHIRI, Egyptian-born leader of Islamic Jihad, close ally of bin Laden after 1998

In Pakistan

GEN. MAHMOUD AHMED, Director-General, Inter-Services Intelligence, 1999–2001

BENAZIR BHUTTO, Prime Minister, 1988–1990; 1993–1996

GEN. ASAD DURRANI, Director-General, Inter-Services Intelligence, 1990–1992

GEN. HAMID GUL, Director-General, Inter-Services Intelligence, 1987–1989

COLONEL (LATER BRIGADIER) IMAM, Afghan Bureau, Inter-Services Intelligence, 1980s through mid-1990s

GEN. PERVEZ MUSHARRAF, Chief of Army Staff, 1998–1999; military leader of Pakistan, 1999–2001

GEN. JAVED ASHRAF QAZI, Director-General, Inter-Services Intelligence, 1993–1995

GEN. AKHTAR ABDUR RAHMAN, Director-General, Inter-Services Intelligence, 1978–1987

GEN. NASEEM RANA, Director-General, Inter-Services Intelligence, 1995–1998

NAWAZ SHARIF, Prime Minister, 1990–1993; 1997–1999

BRIGADIER MOHAMMED YOUSAF, Afghan Bureau, Inter-Services Intelligence, 1983–1987

GEN. KHWAJA ZIAUDDIN, Director-General, Inter-Services Intelligence, 1998–1999

GEN. MOHAMMED ZIA-UL-HAQ, military leader of Pakistan, 1977–1988

In Saudi Arabia

CROWN PRINCE ABDULLAH, de facto ruler of Saudi Arabia, 1996–

AHMED BADEEB, Prince Turki's Chief of Staff, 1979–1997

SAEED BADEEB, Ahmed's brother, director of analysis, Saudi intelligence, approximately 1983–2001

PRINCE BANDAR, Saudi Ambassador to the United States, 1983–

KING FAHD, ruler of Saudi Arabia, 1982–

KING FAISAL, ruler of Saudi Arabia, 1964–1975, father of Prince Turki

PRINCE SAUD AL-FAISAL, Saudi Foreign Minister, 1975–

PRINCE TURKI AL-FAISAL, chief of Saudi intelligence, 1977–2001

KING ABDUL AZIZ IBN SAUD, founding ruler of modern Saudi Arabia, 1901–1953

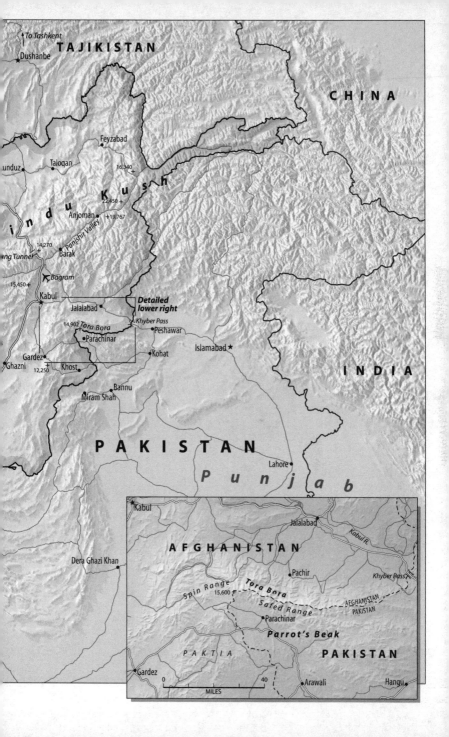

ACCOUNTS RECEIVABLE

September 1996

I N THE TATTERED, cargo-strewn cabin of an Ariana Afghan Airlines passenger jet streaking above Punjab toward Kabul sat a stocky, broad-faced American with short graying hair. He was a friendly man in his early fifties who spoke in a flat midwestern accent. He looked as if he might be a dentist, an acquaintance once remarked. Gary Schroen had served for twenty-six years as an officer in the Central Intelligence Agency's clandestine services. He was now, in September 1996, chief of station in Islamabad, Pakistan. He spoke Persian and its cousin, Dari, one of Afghanistan's two main languages. In spy terminology, Schroen was an operator. He recruited and managed paid intelligence agents, conducted espionage operations, and supervised covert actions against foreign governments and terrorist groups. A few weeks be-fore, with approval from CIA headquarters in Langley, Virginia, he had made contact through intermediaries with Ahmed Shah Massoud, the celebrated anti-Soviet guerrilla commander, now defense minister in a war-battered Afghan government crumbling from within. Schroen had requested a meet-ing, and Massoud had accepted.[1]

They had not spoken in five years. During the late 1980s and early 1990s, as allies battling Soviet occupation forces and their Afghan communist proxies, the CIA had pumped cash stipends as high as $200,000 a month to Massoud and his Islamic guerrilla organization, along with weapons and other supplies. Between 1989 and 1991, Schroen had personally delivered some of the cash. But the aid stopped in December 1991 when the Soviet Union dissolved. The United States government decided it had no further interests in Afghanistan.

Meanwhile the country had collapsed. Kabul, once an elegant city of broad streets and walled gardens tucked spectacularly amid barren crags, had been pummelled by its warlords into a state of physical ruin and human misery that compared unfavorably to the very worst places on Earth. Armed factions within armed factions erupted seasonally in vicious urban battles, blasting down mud-brick block after mud-brick block in search of tactical advantages usually apparent only to them. Militias led by Islamic scholars who disagreed profoundly over religious minutia baked prisoners of war to death by the hundreds in discarded metal shipping containers. The city had been without electricity since 1993. Hundreds of thousands of Kabulis relied for daily bread and tea on the courageous but limited efforts of international charities. In some sections of the countryside thousands of displaced refugees died of malnutrition and preventable disease because they could not reach clinics and feeding stations. And all the while neighboring countries—Pakistan, Iran, India, Saudi Arabia—delivered pallets of guns and money to their preferred Afghan proxies. The governments of these countries sought territorial advantage over their neighbors. Money and weapons also arrived from individuals or Islamic charities seeking to extend their spiritual and political influence by proselytizing to the destitute.

Ahmed Shah Massoud remained Afghanistan's most formidable military leader. A sinewy man with a wispy beard and penetrating dark eyes, he had become a charismatic popular leader, especially in northeastern Afghanistan. There he had fought and negotiated with equal imagination during the 1980s, punishing and frustrating Soviet generals. Massoud saw politics and war as intertwined. He was an attentive student of Mao and other successful guerrilla leaders. Some wondered as time passed if he could imagine a life without guerrilla conflict. Yet through various councils and coalitions, he had also proven able to acquire power by sharing it. During the long horror of the Soviet occupation, Massoud had symbolized for many Afghans—especially his own Tajik people—the spirit and potential of their brave resistance. He was above all an independent man. He surrounded himself with books. He prayed piously, read Persian poetry, studied Islamic theology, and immersed himself in the history of guerrilla warfare. He was drawn to the doctrines of revolutionary and political Islam, but he had also established himself as a broad-minded, tolerant Afghan nationalist.

That September 1996, however, Massoud's reputation had fallen to a low ebb. His passage from rebellion during the 1980s to governance in the 1990s had evolved disastrously. After the collapse of Afghan communism he had joined Kabul's newly triumphant but unsettled Islamic coalition as its defense minister. Attacked by rivals armed in Pakistan, Massoud counterattacked, and as he did, he became the bloodstained power behind a failed, self-immolating government. His allies to the north smuggled heroin. He was unable to unify or pacify the country. His troops showed poor discipline. Some of them mercilessly massacred rivals while battling for control of Kabul neighborhoods.[2]

Promising to cleanse the nation of its warlords, including Massoud, a new militia movement swept from Afghanistan's south beginning in 1994. Its turbaned, eye-shadowed leaders declared that the Koran would slay the Lion of Panjshir, as Massoud was known, where other means had failed.

They traveled behind white banners raised in the name of an unusually severe school of Islam that promoted lengthy and bizarre rules of personal conduct. These Taliban, or students, as they called themselves, now controlled vast areas of southern and western Afghanistan. Their rising strength shook Massoud. The Taliban traveled in shiny new Toyota double-cab pickup trucks. They carried fresh weapons and ample ammunition. Mysteriously, they repaired and flew former Soviet fighter aircraft, despite only rudimentary military experience among their leaders.

The U.S. embassy in Kabul had been shut for security reasons since January 1989, so there was no CIA station in Afghanistan from which to collect intelligence about the Taliban or the sources of their newfound strength. The nearest station, in Islamabad, no longer had Afghanistan on its Operating Directive, the official list of intelligence-gathering priorities transmitted each year to CIA stations worldwide.[3] Without the formal blessing of the O.D., as it was called, a station chief like Gary Schroen lacked the budgetary resources needed to recruit agents, supply them with communications gear, manage them in the field, and process their intelligence reports.

The CIA maintained a handful of paid agents in Afghanistan, but these were dedicated to tracking down Mir Amal Kasi, a young and angry Pakistani who on January 25, 1993, had opened fire on CIA employees arriving at the agency's Langley headquarters. Kasi had killed two and wounded three, and then fled to Pakistan. By 1996 he was believed to be moving back and forth to

Afghanistan, taking refuge in tribal areas where American police and spies could not operate easily.

The CIA's Kasi-hunting agents did not report on the Taliban's developing war against Ahmed Shah Massoud except in passing. The job of collecting intelligence about political and military developments in Afghanistan had been assigned to CIA headquarters in faraway Virginia, lumped in with the general responsibilities of the Near East Division of the Directorate of Operations.[4]

This was hardly an unusual development among U.S. government agencies. The U.S. Agency for International Development had shut down its Afghan humanitarian assistance program in 1994. The Pentagon had no relationships there. The National Security Council at the White House had no Afghan policy beyond a vague wish for peace and prosperity. The State Department was more involved in Afghan affairs, but only at the middle levels of its bureaucracy. Secretary of State Warren Christopher had barely commented about Afghanistan during his four years in office.[5]

MASSOUD SENT a close adviser named Massoud Khalili to escort Gary Schroen into Kabul. To make room for cargo desperately needed in the landlocked capital, Ariana Afghan had ripped most of the passenger seats out of their airplanes to stack the aisles with loose boxes and crates, none of them strapped down or secured. "It's never crashed before," Khalili assured Schroen.

Their jet swept above barren russet ridges folded one upon the other as it crossed into Afghanistan. The treeless land below lay mottled in palettes of sand brown and clay red. To the north, ink black rivers cut plunging gorges through the Hindu Kush Mountains. To the south, eleven-thousand-foot peaks rose in a ring above the Kabul valley, itself more than a mile high. The plane banked toward Bagram, a military air base north of Kabul. Along the surrounding roads lay rusting carcasses of tanks and armored personnel carriers, burned and abandoned. Fractured shells of fighter aircraft and transport planes lined the runway.

Officers in Massoud's intelligence service met the plane with four-wheel-drive vehicles, packed their American visitor inside, and began the bone-jarring drive across the Shomali Plains to Kabul. It amazed some of them that Schroen had turned up with just a small bag tossed over his shoulder—no communications gear, no personal security. His relaxed demeanor, ability to speak Dari, and detailed knowledge of Afghanistan impressed them.

Then, too, Schroen had been known to turn up in the past with bags full of American dollars. In that respect he and his CIA colleagues could be easy men for Afghan fighters to like. For sixteen years now the CIA had routinely pursued its objectives in Afghanistan with large boxes of cash. It frustrated some of Massoud's intelligence officers that the CIA always seemed to think Massoud and his men were motivated by money.

Their civil war might be complex and vicious, but they saw themselves as fighters for a national cause, bleeding and dying by the day, risking what little they had. Enough untraceable bills had flowed to Massoud's organization over the years to assure their comfortable retirements if they wished. Yet many of them were still here in Kabul, still at Massoud's side, despite the severe risks and deprivations. Some of them wondered resentfully why the CIA often seemed to treat them as if money mattered more than kin and country. Of course, they had not been known to refuse the cash, either.

They delivered Gary Schroen to one of the half-dozen unmarked safehouses Massoud maintained in Kabul. They waited for the commander's summons, which came about an hour before midnight. They met in a house that had once been the residence of Austria's ambassador, before rocketing and gun battles had driven most of Europe's diplomats away.

Massoud wore a white Afghan robe and a round, soft, wool Panjshiri cap. He was a tall man, but not physically imposing. He was quiet and formal, yet he radiated intensity.

His attendant poured tea. They sat in dim light around a makeshift conference table. Massoud chatted in Dari with Khalili about their visitor, his background, what Khalili knew of him.

Massoud sounded skeptical about the CIA's request for this meeting. The agency had ignored what Massoud and his men saw as the rising threat posed by the radical Taliban. There were some in Massoud's circle who suspected that the CIA had secretly passed money and guns to the Taliban. America had been a friend to Massoud over the years, but a fickle friend. What did the agency want now?

"You and I have a history, although we never met face to face," Schroen began, as he recalled it. He was not going to make accusations, but in truth, it was not an altogether happy history.

In the winter of 1990, Schroen reminded Massoud, the CIA had been working closely with the commander. Massoud operated then in the mountains of northeastern Afghanistan. Kabul was controlled by President Najibullah, a beefy, mustached former secret police chief and communist who clung to power despite the withdrawal of Soviet troops in 1989. Moscow backed Najibullah; U.S. policy sought his defeat by military force. The Soviets supplied vast amounts of military and economic aid to their client by road and air. Working with Pakistan's military intelligence service, the CIA had come up with a plan that winter to launch simultaneous attacks on key supply lines around Afghanistan. CIA officers had mapped a crucial role for Massoud because his forces were positioned near the Salang Highway, the main north-south road leading from the Soviet Union to Kabul.

In January 1990, Gary Schroen had traveled to Peshawar, Pakistan. One of Massoud's brothers, Ahmed Zia, maintained a compound there with a radio connection to Massoud's northeastern headquarters. Schroen spoke on the radio with Massoud about the CIA's attack plan. The agency wanted Massoud to drive west and shut down the Salang Highway for the winter.

Massoud agreed but said he needed financial help. He would have to purchase fresh ammunition and winter clothing for his troops. He needed to move villagers away from the area of the attacks so they would not be vulnerable to retaliation from the regime's forces. To pay for all this, Massoud wanted a large payment over and above his monthly CIA stipend. Schroen and the commander agreed on a onetime lump sum of $500,000 in cash. Schroen soon delivered the money by hand to Massoud's brother in Peshawar.

Weeks passed. There were a few minor skirmishes, and the Salang Highway closed for a few days, but it promptly reopened. As far as the CIA could determine, Massoud had not put any of his main forces into action as they had agreed he would. CIA officers involved suspected they had been ripped off for half a million dollars. The Salang was a vital source of commerce and revenue for civilians in northern Afghanistan, and Massoud in the past had been reluctant to close the road down, fearing he would alienate his local followers. Massoud's forces also earned taxes along the road.

In later exchanges with CIA officers, Massoud defended himself, saying his subcommanders had initiated the planned attacks as agreed that winter, but they had been stalled by weather and other problems. The CIA could find no evidence to support Massoud's account. As far as they could tell, Massoud's commanders had chosen to sit out the battles along the Salang.

Schroen now reminded Massoud about their agreement six years earlier, and he mentioned that he had personally handed over $500,000 to Massoud's brother.

"How much?" Massoud asked.

"Five hundred thousand," Schroen replied, as he recalled.

Massoud and his aides began to talk among themselves. One of them quietly said in Dari, "We didn't get $500,000."

Massoud repeated his earlier defense to Schroen. The weather in that winter of 1990 had been awful. He couldn't move his troops as successfully as he had hoped. He lacked adequate ammunition, despite the big payment.

"That's all history," Schroen finally said.

Massoud voiced his own complaints. He was a deliberate, cogent speaker, clear and forceful, never loud or demonstrative. The CIA and the United States had walked away from Afghanistan, leaving its people bereft, he said. Yes, Massoud and his colleagues were grateful for the aid the CIA had provided during the years of Soviet occupation, but now they were bitter about what they saw as an American decision to abandon their country.

"Look, we're here," Schroen said. "We want to reopen the relationship. The United States is becoming more and more interested in Afghanistan." It may be a year, Schroen told them, or maybe two years, but the CIA was going to return. That's the way things are moving, he said. One concern in particular was now rising: terrorism.

FOUR MONTHS EARLIER, in May 1996, Osama bin Laden, the seventeenth son of a Saudi Arabian billionaire, had flown into Afghanistan on his own Ariana Afghan Airlines jet. Unlike the CIA, bin Laden could afford to charter a plane for personal use. He brought with him scores of hardened Arab radicals fired by visions of global Islamic war. He arrived initially in Jalalabad, a dust-blown Afghan provincial capital east of Kabul, where he was welcomed by local warlords who had known bin Laden as a rebel philanthropist and occasional fighter during the anti-Soviet jihad.[6]

He had returned to Afghanistan this time because he had little choice. He had been living in Sudan during the previous four years, but now that government had expelled him. The United States, Egypt, and Algeria, among others, complained that bin Laden financed violent Islamic terrorist groups across the Middle East. To win international favor, the Sudanese told bin Laden to get out. His native country of Saudi Arabia had stripped him of citizenship. Afghanistan was one of the few places where he could find asylum. Its government barely functioned, its Islamist warlords marauded independently, and its impoverished people would welcome a wealthy sheikh bearing gifts.

These were much rougher accommodations than the urban compounds and air-conditioned business offices that bin Laden had enjoyed in Khartoum, and when he arrived in Afghanistan he seemed to be in a foul mood, angry at those he held responsible for his exile. That summer bin Laden for the first time publicly sanctioned large-scale violence against Americans.

In August he issued an open call for war titled "The Declaration of Jihad on the Americans Occupying the Country of the Two Sacred Places," meaning Saudi Arabia, where more than five thousand U.S. soldiers and airmen were based. Bin Laden asked his followers to attack Israelis and Americans and cause them "as much harm as can be possibly achieved."

Bin Laden also released a poem he had written, addressed to the U.S. secretary of defense, William Perry:

O William, tomorrow you will be informed
As to which young man will face your swaggering brother
A youngster enters the midst of battle smiling, and
Retreats with his spearhead stained with blood

He signed the document "From the Peaks of the Hindu Kush, Afghanistan."[7]

The CIA had been tracking bin Laden for several years. When he lived in Sudan, a team of CIA officers working from the U.S. embassy in Khartoum had surveilled him. The agency at that time assessed bin Laden mainly as a financier of other terrorists.[8] In January 1996 the CIA had recommended closing the U.S. embassy in Khartoum because of fears that bin Laden's group might attack CIA officers or U.S. diplomats. As the embassy shut, the CIA opened a new Virginia-based unit to track the Saudi.[9]

After bin Laden published his bloodcurdling poetry from Afghanistan, CIA headquarters and its Islamabad station traded cables about whether a meeting in Kabul with Massoud might help, among other things, to reestablish intelligence collection against bin Laden now that he had set himself up in "the Peaks of the Hindu Kush."

There were reasons to be skeptical about the value of such a liaison with Massoud. Most CIA officers who knew Afghanistan admired Massoud's canniness and courage. But episodes such as the $500,000 Salang Highway payment signaled that Massoud's innate independence could make him an unpredictable ally. Also, while Massoud was not a radical Islamist of bin Laden's type, he had welcomed some Arab fighters to his cause and maintained contacts in extremist networks. Could Massoud and his intelligence service become reliable partners in tracking and confronting bin Laden? Opinion within the CIA was divided in September 1996. It would remain divided for five years to come, even as the agency's secret collaborations with Massoud deepened, until a further September when Massoud's fate and America's became fatally entwined.

Langley had provided Gary Schroen with no money or formal orders to open a partnership with Massoud on terrorism. The CIA unit that worked on bin Laden had supported his visit, and its officers encouraged Schroen to discuss the terrorism issue with Massoud. But they had no funding or legal authority to do more. Schroen did have another way, however, to revive the agency's relationship with Massoud: Stinger missiles.

The Stinger had first been introduced to the Afghan battlefield by the CIA in 1986. It was a portable, shoulder-fired weapon that proved durable and easy to use. Its automated heat-seeking guidance system worked uncannily. CIA-supplied Afghan rebels used Stingers to down scores of Soviet helicopters and transport aircraft between 1986 and 1989. The missile forced Soviet generals to change air assault tactics. Its potency sowed fear among thousands of Russian pilots and troops.

After Soviet troops left, the CIA fretted that loose Stingers would be bought by terrorist groups or hostile governments such as Iran's for use against American civilian passenger planes or military aircraft. Between 2,000 and 2,500 missiles had been given away by the CIA to Afghan rebels during the war. Many had gone to commanders associated with anti-American radical Islamist leaders. A few missiles had already been acquired by Iran.

President George H. W. Bush and later President Bill Clinton authorized a highly classified program that directed the CIA to buy back as many Stingers as it could from anyone who possessed them. Congress secretly approved tens of millions of dollars to support the purchases. The program was administered by the Near East Division of the CIA's Directorate of Operations, which oversaw the Islamabad station. Detailed record-keeping based on missile serial numbers had allowed the CIA to keep fairly close count of the Stingers it handed out. But once the weapons reached Afghanistan, they were beyond auditing. In 1996 the CIA estimated that about six hundred Stingers were still at large.[10]

The agency's repurchase program had evolved into a kind of post–Cold War cash rebate system for Afghan warlords. The going rate per missile ranged between $80,000 and $150,000. Pakistan's intelligence service handled most of the purchases on a subcontract basis for the CIA, earning an authorized commission for each missile collected.[11] In part because airpower did not figure much in the grinding civil war then being fought in Afghanistan, commanders holding the missiles proved willing to sell. The total cash spent by the CIA on Stinger repurchases during the mid-1990s rivaled the total cash donations by other sections of the U.S. government for humanitarian assistance in Afghanistan during those years. The Stinger repurchases may have improved aviation security, but they also delivered boxes of money to the warlords who were destroying Afghanistan's cities and towns.

Ahmed Shah Massoud had yet to turn over any missiles and had not received any funds. The CIA now hoped to change that. This was a key aspect of Gary Schroen's mission to Kabul that September. If Massoud would participate in the Stinger roundup, he could earn cash by selling his own stockpiles and also potentially earn commission income as a middleman. This revenue, some CIA officers hoped, might also purchase goodwill from Massoud for joint work in the future on the bin Laden problem.

IN THEIR DIM MEETING ROOM, Schroen handed Massoud a piece of paper. It showed an estimate of just more than two thousand missiles provided by the CIA to Afghan fighters during the jihad.[12]

Massoud looked at the figure. "Do you know how many of those missiles I received?" He wrote a number on the paper and showed it to Schroen. In a very neat hand Massoud had written "8." "That was all," Massoud declared, "and only at the end of the fight against the communist regime."

Later, after Schroen reported his conversations by cable to several departments at headquarters, the CIA determined that Massoud was correct. It seemed incredible to some who had lived through the anti-Soviet Afghan war that Massoud could have received so few. He had been one of the war's fiercest commanders. Yet for complicated reasons, Pakistan's intelligence service, the CIA's partner in supplying the anti-Soviet rebels, distrusted Massoud and continually tried to undermine him. Massoud also had shaky relations with the Islamist political party that helped channel supplies to him. As a result, when the war's most important weapon system had been distributed to Afghan commanders, Massoud had received less than 1 percent, and this only in 1991.

The CIA now wanted Massoud to sell back his own stored missiles; he still had all eight of them. They also wanted him to act as an intermediary with other commanders across the north of Afghanistan. The Pakistani intelligence service had few connections in the north and had repurchased few Stingers there. Schroen told Massoud that they could use his help.

He agreed to take part. He would sell back his stockpile and begin seeking Stingers from subcommanders and other Afghan fighters he knew, he told Schroen. He suspected that some of his allied commanders would be willing to sell for the prices on offer. Schroen and Massoud worked out a logistics plan: The Stingers would be gathered initially under Massoud's control, and when enough had accumulated to justify a trip, the CIA would arrange for a C-130 transport plane to fly out clandestinely to pick them up.

They discussed bin Laden. Massoud described the Saudi's puritanical, intolerant outlook on Islam as abhorrent to Afghans. Bin Laden's group was just one dangerous part of a wider movement of armed Islamic radicalism then gathering in Afghanistan around the Taliban, Massoud said. He described this movement as a poisonous coalition: Pakistani and Arab intelligence agencies; impoverished young students bused to their deaths as volunteer fighters from Pakistani religious schools; exiled Central Asian Islamic radicals trying to establish bases in Afghanistan for their revolutionary movements; and wealthy sheikhs and preachers who jetted in from the Persian Gulf with money, supplies, and inspiration. Osama bin Laden was only the most ambitious and media-conscious of these outside sheikhs.

The eastern area of Jalalabad where bin Laden had initially arrived had now fallen into turmoil. By one account the Afghan warlord who had greeted bin Laden's plane in May had been assassinated, leaving the Saudi sheikh without a clear Afghan sponsor.[13] Meanwhile, the Taliban had begun to move through Jalalabad, overthrowing the warlords there who had earlier been loosely allied with Massoud. It was a volatile moment.

Schroen asked Massoud if he could help develop reliable sources about bin Laden that might benefit them both. The CIA hoped Massoud could reach out to some of the commanders they both knew from the 1980s who were now operating in the eastern areas where bin Laden and his Arab followers had settled. Massoud said he would try. This is a beginning, Schroen told him. He did not have funds at this stage to support these intelligence collection efforts, but he said that others in the CIA would want to follow up and deepen cooperation.

The meeting broke up around two in the morning. The next day Schroen took a sightseeing drive to the Salang Tunnel, a vivid rock passage between Kabul and northern Afghanistan, eleven thousand feet above sea level. His bumpy four-hour journey took him along sections of the road that he had spent the CIA's $500,000 in a futile effort to close.

Massoud's aides saw him off on his return Ariana Afghan flight, his small bag slung on his shoulder. They were glad he had come. Few Americans took the trouble to visit Kabul, and fewer still spoke the language or understood Afghanistan's complexities as Schroen did, Massoud's intelligence officers believed. Uncertain about where this CIA initiative had come from so suddenly, they speculated that Schroen had planned his own mission, perhaps in defiance of headquarters.

Still, if it was a beginning, Massoud's advisers thought, it was a very small one. They were in a brutal, unfinished war and felt neglected by the United States. They needed supplies, political support, and strong public denunciations of the Taliban. Instead, the CIA proposed a narrow collaboration on Stinger missile recovery.

One of Massoud's advisers involved in the meeting with Schroen would later recall an Afghan phrase that went, roughly translated, "Your mouth cannot be sweet when you talk about honey; you must have honey in your mouth." CIA officers might speak promisingly about a new clandestine relationship with Massoud focused on Stingers and terrorism, but where was the honey?

AHMED SHAH MASSOUD suffered the most devastating defeat of his military career less than a week after Schroen's departure.

Taliban forces approached from Jalalabad, apparently rich with cash from bin Laden or elsewhere. On September 25 the key forward post of Sarobi fell to white-turbaned mascara-painted Taliban who sped and zigzagged in new four-wheel-drive pickup trucks equipped with machine guns and rockets. At 3 P.M. on September 26, at a meeting with senior commanders at his armored division headquarters on Kabul's northern outskirts, Massoud concluded that his forces had been encircled and that he had to withdraw to avoid destruction.[14] His government forces retreated to the north in a rush, dragging along as much salvageable military equipment as they could. By nightfall the Taliban had conquered Kabul. A militia whose one-eyed emir believed that he had been selected by God to prepare pious Muslims for glory in the afterlife now controlled most of Afghanistan's territory, most of its key cities, and its seat of government.

In Washington a spokesperson for the State Department, Glyn Davies, announced the official American reaction from a briefing room podium: "We hope this presents an opportunity for a process of national reconciliation to begin," he said. "We hope very much and expect that the Taliban will respect

the rights of all Afghans and that the new authorities will move quickly to restore order and security and to form a representative government on the way
to some form of national reconciliation." Asked if the United States might
open diplomatic relations with the Taliban government, Davies replied, "I'm
not going to prejudge where we're going to go with Afghanistan."[15]

It was the sort of pablum routinely pronounced by State Department
spokesmen when they had no real policy to describe. Outside a few small
pockets of Afghan watchers in government and out, there was barely a ripple
about the fall of Kabul in Washington. Bill Clinton had just begun campaigning in earnest for reelection, coasting against the overmatched Republican
nominee, Bob Dole. The Dow Jones Industrial Average stood at 5,872, up
nearly 80 percent in four years. Unemployment was falling. American and Soviet nuclear arsenals, which had once threatened the world with doomsday,
were being steadily dismantled. The nation believed it was at peace.

In Afghanistan and neighboring countries such as Pakistan, Davies's words
and similar remarks by other State Department officials that week were interpreted as an American endorsement of Taliban rule.

The CIA had not predicted the fall of Kabul that September.[16] To the contrary, a station chief had been permitted to fly solo into the capital several
days before it was about to collapse, risking entrapment. Few CIA officers in
the field or at Langley understood Massoud's weakening position or the Taliban's strength.

Just a few years before, Afghanistan had been the nexus of what most CIA
officers regarded as one of the proudest achievements in the agency's history:
the repulsion of invading Soviet forces by covert action. Now, not only in lit-
eral terms but in a far larger sense, Afghanistan was not part of the agency's
Operating Directive.

THE DOWNWARD SPIRAL following the Cold War's end was no less steep
in, say, Congo or Rwanda than it was in Afghanistan. Yet for Americans on
the morning of September 11, it was Afghanistan's storm that struck. A war
they hardly knew and an enemy they had barely met crossed oceans never traversed by the German Luftwaffe or the Soviet Rocket Forces to claim several
thousand civilian lives in two mainland cities. How had this happened?

In history's long inventory of surprise attacks, September 11 is distinguished in part by the role played by intelligence agencies and informal secret
networks in the preceding events. As bin Laden and his aides endorsed the

September 11 attacks from their Afghan sanctuary, they were pursued secretly by salaried officers from the CIA. At the same time, bin Laden and his closest allies received protection, via the Taliban, from salaried officers in Pakistan's Inter-Services Intelligence Directorate.

This was a pattern for two decades. Strand after strand of official covert action, unofficial covert action, clandestine terrorism, and clandestine counterterrorism wove one upon the other to create the matrix of undeclared war that burst into plain sight in 2001.

America's primary actor in this subterranean narrative was the CIA, which shaped the anti-Soviet jihad in Afghanistan during the 1980s and then waged a secret campaign to disrupt, capture, or kill Osama bin Laden after he returned to Afghanistan during the late 1990s. In the two years prior to September 11, the CIA's Counterterrorist Center worked closely with Ahmed Shah Massoud and other Afghans against bin Laden. But the agency was unable to persuade most of the rest of the U.S. government to go as far as Massoud and some CIA officers wanted.

In these struggles over how best to confront bin Laden—as in previous turning points in the CIA's involvement with Afghanistan—the agency struggled to control its mutually mistrustful and at times toxic alliances with the intelligence services of Saudi Arabia and Pakistan. The self-perpetuating secret routines of these official liaisons, and their unexamined assumptions, helped create the Afghanistan that became Osama bin Laden's sanctuary. They also stoked the rise of a radical Islam in Afghanistan that exuded violent global ambitions.

The CIA's central place in the story is unusual, compared to other cataclysmic episodes in American history. The stories of the agency's officers and leaders, their conflicts, their successes, and their failures, help describe and explain the secret wars preceding September 11 the way stories of generals and dog-faced GIs have described conventional wars in the past. Of course other Americans shaped this struggle as well: presidents, diplomats, military officers, national security advisers, and, later, dispersed specialists in the new art termed "counterterrorism."

Pakistani and Saudi spies, and the sheikhs and politicians who gave them their orders or tried in vain to control them, joined Afghan commanders such as Ahmed Shah Massoud in a regional war that shifted so often, it existed in a permanent shroud. Some of these local powers and spies were partners of the CIA. Some pursued competing agendas. Many did both at once. The story of September 11's antecedents is their story as well. Among them swirled the fluid networks of stateless Islamic radicals whose global revival after 1979 eventually birthed bin Laden's al Qaeda, among many other groups. As the years passed, these radical Islamic networks adopted some of the secret deception-laden tradecraft of the formal intelligence services, methods they sometimes acquired through direct training.

During the 1980s, Soviet conscripts besieged by CIA-supplied Afghan rebels called them *dukhi,* or ghosts. The Soviets could never quite grasp and hold their enemy. It remained that way in Afghanistan long after they had gone. From its first days before the Soviet invasion until its last hours in the late summer of 2001, this was a struggle among ghosts.

PART ONE

BLOOD BROTHERS

November 1979 to February 1989

1

"We're Going to Die Here"

IT WAS A SMALL RIOT in a year of upheavals, a passing thunderclap disgorged by racing skies.

When the mob broke in, William Putscher, a thirty-two-year-old American government auditor, was eating a hot dog. He had decided to lunch in the club by the swimming pool of the serene thirty-two-acre United States embassy compound in Islamabad, Pakistan. The embassy employed about 150 diplomats, spies, aid workers, communications specialists, assorted administrators, and a handful of U.S. Marines. "Carter dog!" the rioters shouted, referring to the American president Jimmy Carter. "Kill the Americans!" Putscher abandoned his meal and hid in a small office until the choking fumes of smoke and gasoline drove him out. A raging protestor threw a brick in his face as he emerged. Another hit him on the back of his head with a pipe. They stole two rings and his wallet, hustled him into a vehicle, and took him three miles away to concrete dormitories at Quaid-I-Azam University. There, student leaders of Pakistan's elite graduate school, fired by visions of a truer Islamic society, announced that Putscher would be tried for crimes "against the Islamic movement." It seemed to Putscher that he "was accused of just being an American."[1]

It was November 21, 1979. As the riot erupted in Pakistan, forty-nine Americans sat imprisoned in the United States embassy in Tehran, trapped by Islamic radical students and Iranian revolutionary militia who announced that day a plan to murder the hostages by suicide explosions if any attempt was made to rescue them. In Mecca, Saudi Arabia, the holiest city in the Islamic world, Saudi national guardsmen encircled the Grand Mosque in pursuit of a failed theology student who had announced that he was the Mahdi, or Savior, dispatched to Earth by Allah as forecast in the Koran. To demonstrate their faith, the aspiring Mahdi's followers had opened fire on worshipers with automatic weapons. Just outside Washington, President Jimmy Carter prepared for Thanksgiving at Camp David. By day's end he would have endured the first death by hostile fire of an American soldier during his presidency.[2]

Inside the CIA station on the clean and carpeted third floor of the Islamabad embassy, the deputy chief of station, Bob Lessard, and a young case officer, Gary Schroen, checked the station's incinerator and prepared to burn classified documents. For situations like this, in addition to shredders, the station was equipped with a small gas-fed incinerator with its own chimney. Lessard sorted through case files and other classified materials, preparing if necessary to begin a burn.

Lessard and Schroen were both Persian-speaking veterans of service in Iran during the 1970s. Schroen, who had grown up in East St. Louis, the son of a union electrician, was the first member of his family to attend college. He had enlisted in the army in 1959 and was discharged honorably as a private. "I have a problem with authority," he told friends by way of explanation of his final rank. He kicked around odd jobs before joining the CIA in 1969, an agency full of people who had problems with authority. As deputy chief of station, Bob Lessard was Schroen's boss, but they dealt with each other as colleagues. Lessard was a tall, athletic, handsome man with thinning hair and long sideburns. He had arrived at the Islamabad station feeling as if his career was in the doghouse. He had been transferred from Kabul, where an operation to recruit a Soviet agent had gone sour. An intermediary in the operation had been turned into a double agent without Lessard's knowledge, and the recruitment had been blown. Lessard had been forced to leave Afghanistan, and while the busted operation hadn't been his fault, he had landed in Islamabad believing he needed to redeem himself.

Life undercover forced CIA case officers into friendships with one another. These were the only safe relationships—bound by membership in a private society, unencumbered by the constant need for secrecy. When officers spoke the same foreign languages and served in the same area divisions, as Lessard and Schroen did, they were brought into extraordinarily close contact. To stay fit, Lessard and Schroen ran together through the barren chaparral of the hills and canyons around Islamabad. In the embassy they worked in the same office suite. Watching television and reading classified cables, they had monitored with amazement and dismay the takeover of the American embassy in Iran a few weeks earlier. Together they had tracked rumors of a similar impending attack on the U.S. embassy in Islamabad. That Wednesday morning they had driven together into the Pakistani capital to check for gathering crowds, and they had seen nothing to alarm them.

Now, suddenly, young Pakistani rioters began to pour across the embassy's walls.

The Islamabad CIA station chief, John Reagan, had gone home for lunch, as had the American ambassador to Pakistan, Arthur Hummel. They missed the action inside the embassy that afternoon but soon began to rally support from a command post at the British embassy next door.

Looking out windows, Schroen and Lessard could see buses pulling up before the main gate. Hundreds of rioters streamed out and jumped over sections of the embassy's perimeter protected by metal bars. One gang threw ropes over the bars and began to pull down the entire wall.

A group of hardcore student protestors carried Lee Enfield rifles and a few pistols on the lawns fronting the embassy's redbrick facade. One rioter tried to imitate Hollywood films by shooting an embassy gate lock with a pistol. As the American side later reconstructed events, the bullet ricocheted and struck protestors in the crowd. The rioters now believed they were being fired upon by U.S. Marines posted on the roof. They began to shoot. Under their rules of engagement, the six Marine guards at the embassy that day could only fire their weapons to save lives. They were overwhelmed quickly and outnumbered massively.

The Marines had always considered Islamabad a quiet posting. From the embassy's roof they could watch cows grazing in nearby fields. Master Gunnery Sergeant Lloyd Miller, a powerfully built Vietnam veteran who was the only member of his family to leave his small hometown in California, had seen nothing since his arrival in Pakistan a year earlier that even remotely compared to the battlefields around Danang. In July there had been a protest, but it wasn't much of one: "They sang a few songs and chucked a few rocks. Then they went away." To pass the time, Miller and the Marines under his command drilled regularly. They practiced keeping modest-sized crowds out of the embassy compound and even rehearsed what would happen if one or two intruders found their way inside the building. But they had no way of preparing for what they now faced: wave upon wave of armed rioters charging directly toward their post in the lobby. Miller could see bus after bus pulling up near what was left of the front gates, but with only two security cameras on the grounds, he could not assess just how pervasive the riot had become. He sent two of his Marines to the roof to find out.

Inside the embassy hallways only minutes later, shouts went up: "They shot a Marine!" In the CIA station Lessard and Schroen grabbed a medical kit and ran up the back stairway near the embassy's communications section. On the roof a cluster of embassy personnel knelt over the prone six-foot-six-inch figure of blond twenty-year-old Corporal Stephen Crowley of Port Jefferson Station, Long Island, New York, a chess enthusiast and cross-country runner who had enlisted in the Marines two years before. Miller organized a makeshift stretcher from a slab of plywood lying close by. Crouched down low to avoid bullets that whizzed overhead, they lifted Crowley onto the plywood and scampered toward the stairs. The CIA men held Crowley's head. The wound was life-threatening, but he might still be saved if they could get him out of the embassy and into a hospital. The stretcher bearers reached the third floor and headed toward the embassy's secure communications vault where the State Department and the CIA each had adjoining secure code rooms to send cables and messages to Washington and Langley. Emergency procedures dictated that in a case like this embassy personnel should lock themselves behind the communications vault's steel-reinforced doors to wait for Pakistani police or army troops to clear the grounds of attackers. It was now around one o'clock in the afternoon. The riot had been raging for nearly an hour. Surely Pakistani reinforcements would not be long coming.[3]

QUAID-I-AZAM UNIVERSITY'S campus lay in a shaded vale about three miles from the American embassy. A four-cornered arch at the entrance pointed to a bucolic expanse of low-slung hostels, classrooms, and small mosques along University Road. A planned, isolated, prosperous city laid out on geometrical grids, Islamabad radiated none of Pakistan's exuberant chaos. A Greek architect and Pakistani commissioners had combined to design the capital during the 1960s, inflicting a vision of shiny white modernity on a government hungry for recognition as a rising nation. Within Islamabad's antiseptic isolation, Quaid-I-Azam University was more isolated still. It had been named after the affectionate title bestowed on Pakistan's founding father, Mohammed Ali Jinnah, the "Father of the Nation." Its students plied walkways shaded by weeping trees beneath the dry, picturesque Margalla Hills, several miles from Islamabad's few shops and restaurants. During much of the 1970s the university's culture had been Western in many of its leanings. Women could be seen in blue jeans, men in the latest sunglasses and leather jackets. Partly this reflected Pakistan's seeming comfort in an era of growing international crosscurrents. Partly, too, it reflected the open, decorative cultural styles of Pakistan's dominant ethnic Punjabis. In Lahore and Rawalpindi, hotels and offices festooned in electric lights winked at passersby. Weddings rocked wildly through the night with music and dance. While the ethnic mix was different, in coastal Karachi social mores were perhaps even more secular, especially among the country's business elites. For the most part, Quaid-I-Azam's students expressed the fashion-conscious edges of this loose, slightly licentious stew of Islamic tradition and subcontinental flair.

More recently, however, an Islamist counterforce had begun to rise at the university. By late 1979 the student wing of a conservative Islamic political party, Jamaat-e-Islami (the Islamic Group or, alternatively, the Islamic Society) had taken control of Quaid-I-Azam's student union.[4] The Jamaat student activists, while a minority, intimidated secular-minded professors and students, and shamed women who adopted Western styles or declined to wear the veil. Like their elder political leaders, Jamaat students campaigned for a moral transformation of Pakistani society through the application of Islamic law. Their announced aim was a pure Islamic government in Pakistan. The party had been founded in 1941 by the prominent Islamic radical writer Maulana Abu Ala Maududi, who advocated a Leninist revolutionary approach to Islamic politics, and whose first book, published in the late 1920s, was titled *Jihad in Islam*. Despite its leaders' calls to arms, Jamaat had mainly languished on the fringes of Pakistani politics and society, unable to attract many votes when elections were held and unable to command much influence during periods of military rule, either. Maududi had died just weeks earlier, in September 1979, his dream of an Islamic state in Pakistan unrealized. Yet at the hour of his passing, his influence had reached a new peak and his followers were on the march. The causes were both international and local.

Because it had long cultivated ties to informal Islamic networks in the Persian Gulf and elsewhere, Jamaat-e-Islami found itself afloat during the 1970s on a swelling tide of what the French scholar Gilles Kepel would later term "petro dollar Islam," a vast infusion of proselytizing wealth from Saudi Arabia arising from the 1973 oil boycott staged by the Organization of Petroleum Exporting Countries (OPEC). The boycott sent global oil prices soaring. As angry Americans pumped their Chevrolets with dollar-a-gallon gasoline, they filled Saudi and other Persian Gulf treasuries with sudden and unimagined riches. Saudi Arabia's government consisted of an uneasy alliance between its royal family and its conservative, semi-independent religious clergy. The Saudi clergy followed an unusual, puritanical doctrine of Islam often referred to as "Wahhabism," after its founder, Mohammed ibn Abdul Wahhab, an eighteenth-century desert preacher who regarded all forms of adornment and modernity as blasphemous. Wahhabism's insistent severity stood in opposition to many of the artistic and cultural traditions of past Islamic civilizations. But it was a determined faith, and now overnight an extraordinarily wealthy one. Saudi charities and proselytizing organizations such as the Jedda-based Muslim World League began printing Korans by the millions as the oil money gushed. They endowed mosque construction across the world and forged connections with like-minded conservative Islamic groups from southeast Asia to the Maghreb, distributing Wahhabi-oriented Islamic texts and sponsoring education in their creed.

In Pakistan, Jamaat-e-Islami proved a natural and enthusiastic ally for the Wahhabis. Maududi's writings, while more antiestablishment than Saudi Arabia's self-protecting monarchy might tolerate at home, nonetheless promoted many of the Islamic moral and social transformations sought by Saudi clergy.

By the end of the 1970s Islamic parties like Jamaat had begun to assert themselves across the Muslim world as the corrupt, failing reigns of leftist Arab nationalists led youthful populations to seek a new cleansing politics. Clandestine, informal, transnational religious networks such as the Muslim Brotherhood reinforced the gathering strength of old-line religious parties such as Jamaat. This was especially true on university campuses, where radical Islamic student wings competed for influence from Cairo to Amman to Kuala Lumpur.[5] When Ayatollah Khomeini returned to Iran and forced the American-backed monarch Shah Mohammed Reza Pahlavi to flee early in 1979, his fire-breathing triumph jolted these parties and their youth wings, igniting campuses in fevered agitation. Khomeini's minority Shiite creed was anathema to many conservative Sunni Islamists, especially those in Saudi Arabia, but his audacious achievements inspired Muslims everywhere.

On November 5, 1979, Iranian students stormed the U.S. embassy in Tehran, sacked its offices, and captured hostages. The next morning in Islamabad's serene diplomatic quarter near the university, local Iranians draped their embassy with provocative banners denouncing the United States and calling for a global Islamic revolution against the superpowers. The student leaders of Jamaat were enthusiastic volunteers. Although the party's older leaders had always focused their wrath on India—motivated by memories of the religious violence that accompanied Pakistan's birth—the new generation had its sights on a more distant target: the United States. Secular leftist students on campus also denounced America. Kicking the American big dog was an easy way to unite Islamist believers and nonbelievers alike.

Jamaat's student union leaders enjoyed an additional pedigree: They had lately emerged as favored political protégés of Pakistan's new military dictator, General Mohammed Zia-ul-Haq. The general had seized power in July 1977 from the socialist politician Zulfikar Ali Bhutto, father of future prime minister Benazir Bhutto. Despite personal appeals for clemency from President Carter and many other world leaders, Zia sent Zulfikar Ali Bhutto to the gallows in April 1979. Around the same time American intelligence analysts announced that Pakistan had undertaken a secret program to acquire nuclear weapons. Zia canceled elections and tried to quell domestic dissent. Shunned abroad and shaky at home, he began to preach political religion fervently, strengthening Jamaat in an effort to develop a grassroots political base in Pakistan. In the years to come, engorged by funds from Saudi Arabia and other Gulf emirates, Jamaat would become a vanguard of Pakistan's official and clandestine Islamist agendas in Afghanistan and, later, Kashmir.

On October 21, 1979, Zia announced that he intended to establish "a genuine Islamic order" in Pakistan. Earlier in the year he had approved Islamic punishments such as amputations for thieves and floggings for adulterers. These turned out to be largely symbolic announcements since the punishments were hardly ever implemented. Still, they signaled a new and forceful direction for Pakistan's politics. Conveniently, since he had just aborted national polls, Zia noted that "in Islam there is no provision for Western-type elections."[6] Jamaat's leaders defended him, and its student wing, an eye cocked at the celebrated violence of Iranian student radicals, prepared to demonstrate its potency.

IN THIS INCENDIARY SEASON arrived a parade of apparent mourners wearing red handbands and shouldering coffins at Mecca's holy Grand Mosque, in the western deserts of Saudi Arabia. The picture they presented to fellow worshipers at dawn on Tuesday, November 20, was not an uncommon one because the mosque was a popular place to bless the dead. There would soon be more to bless. The mourners set their coffins down, opened the lids, and unpacked an arsenal of assault rifles and grenades.

Their conspiracy was born from an Islamic study group at Saudi Arabia's University of Medina during the early 1970s. The group's leader, Juhayman al-Utaybi, had been discharged from the Saudi national guard. He persuaded several hundred followers—many of them Yemenis and Egyptians who had been living in Saudi Arabia for years—that his Saudi brother-in-law, Mohammed Abdullah al-Qahtani, who had once studied theology, was the Savior returned to Earth to save all Muslims from their depredations. Juhayman attacked the Saudi royal family. Oil-addled royal princes had "seized land" and "squandered the state's money," he proclaimed. Some princes were "drunkards" who "led a dissolute life in luxurious palaces." He had his facts right, but his prescriptions were extreme. The purpose of the Mahdi's return to Earth was "the purification of Islam" and the liberation of Saudi Arabia from the royal family. Signaling a pattern of future Saudi dissent, Juhayman was more puritan than even Saudi Arabia's officially sanctioned puritans. He sought bans on radio, television, and soccer. That November morning, impatient with traditional proselytizing, he chained shut the gates to the Grand Mosque, locking tens of thousands of stunned worshipers inside. The mosque's imam declined to ratify the new savior. Juhayman and his gang began shooting. Dozens of innocent pilgrims fell dead.[7]

Saudi Arabia did little in the early hours of this bizarre uprising to clarify for the Islamic world who was behind the assault. Every devout Muslim worldwide faced Mecca's black, cube-shaped Kaaba five times a day to pray. Now it had been captured by usurping invaders. But who were they, and what did they want? Saudi Arabia's government was disinclined to publicize its crises. Saudi officials were themselves uncertain initially about who had sponsored the attack. Fragmented eyewitness accounts and galloping rumors leaped from country to country, continent to continent. In Washington, Secretary of State Cyrus Vance dispatched an overnight cable to U.S. embassies worldwide on that Tuesday night, urging them to take precautions as the Mecca crisis unfolded. The State Department had painfully learned only weeks earlier about the vulnerability of its compounds and the speed at which American diplomats could face mobs inflamed by grievances real and imagined.

Ambassador Hummel in Islamabad sorted through these cabled cautions the next morning. He did not regard Islamic radicalism as a significant threat to Americans in Pakistan. It never had been before. Still, the Islamabad CIA station had weeks earlier picked up indications from its sources that students at Quaid-I-Azam might be planning demonstrations at the embassy in support of the Iranian hostage takers in Tehran. As a result, Hummel had requested and received a small contingent of about two dozen armed Pakistani police, over and above the embassy's normal security force.

That squad was in place on Wednesday morning when rumors began to circulate in Islamabad, and later on local radio stations, that the United States and Israel stood behind the attack at the Grand Mosque. The rumor held that Washington and Tel Aviv had decided to seize a citadel of Islamic faith in order to neutralize the Muslim world. Absurd on its face, the rumor was nonetheless received as utterly plausible by thousands if not millions of Pakistanis. The Voice of America reported that as the riot in Mecca raged, President Carter had ordered U.S. Navy ships to the Indian Ocean as a show of force against the hostage takers in Tehran. With a little imagination it wasn't hard to link the two news items. As the students at Quaid-I-Azam made their protest plans, *The Muslim,* an Islamabad daily, published a special edition that referred to the "two hostile actions against the Muslim world . . . by the Imperialists and their stooges."[8]

General Zia had plans that day to promote civic advancement through Islamic values. He had decided to spend most of the afternoon in teeming Rawalpindi, adjacent to Islamabad, riding about on a bicycle. Zia intended to hand out Islamic pamphlets and advertise by example the simple virtues of self-propelled transport. And, of course, where the military dictator went, so went most of Pakistan's military and security establishment. When the first distress calls went out from the U.S. embassy later that day, much of Pakistan's army brass was unavailable. They were pedaling behind the boss on their bicycles.

GARY SCHROEN stood by the window of his office preparing to close the curtains when a Pakistani rioter below raised a shotgun at him and blasted out the plate glass. He and a young Marine beside him had spotted the shooter just early enough to leap like movie stuntmen beyond the line of fire. The shotgun pellets smashed into the CIA station's plaster walls. They had no time now to destroy classified documents. Schroen and Lessard locked their case files and disguise materials in the station suite behind a vault door, grabbed a pair of pump-action Winchester 1200 shotguns from a Marine gun case, and headed to the third-floor code room vault.

By about 2 P.M., 139 embassy personnel and Pakistani employees had herded themselves inside, hoping for shelter from the mob. Within the vault a young political officer had cleared off a desk and was busy writing by hand the FLASH cable that would announce the attack to Washington. As he wrote, embassy communications officers destroyed cryptography packages one by one to prevent them from falling into the hands of rioters. The vault echoed with the sound of a sledgehammer rhythmically descending on CIA code equipment.

The wounded Marine, Stephen Crowley, lay unconscious and bleeding on the floor, tended by an embassy nurse. He was breathing with help from an oxygen tank. Crowley had been shot in the riot's early moments, and by now the protestors had swollen in number and anger, and had begun to rampage through every corner of the compound. They hurled Molotov cocktails into the chancery's lower offices, setting files and furniture on fire. Entire wings of the building leaped in flames, particularly the paper-laden budget and finance section located directly underneath the communications vault, which began to cook like a pot on a bonfire. Onlookers at the British embassy estimated that at the height of the action, fifteen thousand Pakistani rioters swarmed the grounds.

Marine Master Gunnery Sergeant Miller—or the Gunney, as he was called—directed the defense from his post in the lobby. There he watched as rioters rushed through the now mangled front door no more than fifteen feet away. They scurried into the lobby carrying bundles of wood, buckets of gasoline, and matches. Miller repeatedly requested permission for his men to fire on the arsonists, but each time the embassy's administrative counselor, David Fields, denied the request on the grounds that shooting would only further incite the riot. Miller had to content himself with rolling out more tear gas canisters as fire engulfed the building he was sworn to protect.

When the lobby had completely filled with smoke, the Marines retreated upstairs to join the rest of the embassy staff in the third-floor vault. Just before going in, they dropped a few final tear gas canisters down each of the stairwells in the hope that would dissuade the rioters from climbing to the embassy's last remaining refuge.

Outside at the motor pool the rioters poured gasoline into embassy cars and set them burning one after another; in all, more than sixty embassy vehicles would go up in flames. Some rioters attacked the embassy residences, a cluster of modest brick town houses that were home to midlevel American personnel and their families. Quaid-I-Azam University student leaders rounded up a group of hostages from these quarters and announced their intention to drive them to the campus to put them on trial as American spies. An enterprising Pakistani police lieutenant, one of the few guards who had refused to surrender his weapon to the mob in the riot's earliest moments, pretended to go along with the students' plan, loaded the hostages into a truck, and promptly drove them off to safety. He was not the only Pakistani to risk himself for the Americans. At the American School in Islamabad several miles away from the embassy, a retired army colonel armed an impromptu squad of Pakistani guards with cricket bats and broomsticks. They successfully beat off rioters who attacked the school while children lay cowering in locked rooms. Although these and other individuals acted heroically, Pakistan's government did not. Despite dozens of pleas from Arthur Hummel, the ambassador, and John Reagan, the CIA station chief, hour after hour passed and still no Pakistani troops or police arrived to clear the rioters. By midafternoon enormous black clouds of gasoline-scented smoke poured out from the American compound, visible from miles away.

Many of the rioters joined the melee spontaneously, but as the rampage unfolded, it also revealed evidence of substantial coordinated planning. On the embassy grounds CIA personnel spotted what appeared to be riot organizers wearing distinctive sweater vests and carrying weapons. Some were Arabs, likely members of the sizable Palestinian population at Quaid-I-Azam. The speed with which so many rioters descended on the embassy also suggested advanced preparation. Thousands arrived in government-owned Punjab Transport Corporation buses. Rioters turned up nearly at once at multiple American locations: the embassy compound, the American School, American information centers in Rawalpindi and Lahore, and several American businesses in Islamabad. Professors at Quaid-I-Azam later reported that some students had burst into classrooms very early in the morning, before the rumor about American involvement in the Grand Mosque uprising had spread very far, shouting that students should attack the embassy to take vengeance in the name of Islam.

Around 4 P.M. Pakistani army headquarters finally dispatched a helicopter to survey the scene. It flew directly above the embassy, its whirring rotors fanning flames that raked the building. Then the helicopter flew away. Zia's spokesmen later said the smoke had been too thick to make a visual assessment. The CIA reported that its sources in Zia's circle told a different story. When the helicopter returned to base, the crew advised Zia that the fire in the embassy was so hot and so pervasive that there was no way the American personnel inside could have survived. Since it seemed certain that the Americans had all been killed, there was no sense in risking further bloodshed—and a possible domestic political cataclysm—by sending army troops to forcibly confront the Islamist rioters. According to the CIA's later reports, Zia decided that since he couldn't save the Americans inside the embassy anyway, he might as well just let the riot burn itself out.[9]

By this time the Americans and Pakistanis in the vault were nearing the end of their tolerance. They had been inside for more than two hours, and there was no rescue in sight. In the State Department's chamber they lay drenched with sweat and breathing shallowly through wet paper towels. Tear gas had blown back to the third floor, and some were gagging and vomiting. Temperatures rose as fires in the offices below burned hotter. Carpet seams burst from the heat. Floor tiles blistered and warped.

In the adjacent CIA code room, Miller, Schroen, Lessard, and a crew of CIA officers and Marine guards stared at a bolted hatch in the ceiling that led up to the roof. They wondered if they should try to force the hatch open and lead everyone to the fresh air above. A previous Islamabad station chief had installed the hatch for just this purpose. But about an hour into the attack, the rioters had discovered the passageway. They pounded relentlessly on the iron lid with pieces of a brick wall they had torn apart, hoping to break in. Some rioters poked their rifles into nearby ventilation shafts and shot. The sound of bullets crashing down from above was occasionally punctuated by even more jolting explosions as the fire crept up on oxygen tanks stored elsewhere in the building.

The group in the code room listened to the metallic clanging on the hatch for about an hour. Then one of the CIA communications specialists, an engineer of sorts, came up with a plan to wire a heavy-duty extension cord into the iron cover. "Those guys up there, I'm going to electrocute them!" he announced gleefully, as Gary Schroen later recalled it. He stripped to the waist and began to sweat as he attached large alligator clips to the hatch. "Now I'm going to plug this baby in, and the electricity's going to kill them." He was filthy and covered with bits of shredded documents. He thrust the plug into the wall. Four hundred volts of current seemed to fly up to the hatch, bounce off, and fly right back into the wall, where it exploded in sparks and smoke. "Goddamn it! The resistance is too much!"

The idea had seemed dubious from the beginning—the device wasn't even grounded properly—and there was laughter for the first time all afternoon when it failed. But what other options did they have? The heat had grown unbearable inside the vault. "What are we going to do?" they asked. "They're up there. What are we going to do?"

Another hour passed. Slowly the hatch bent under the rioters' bricks. The concrete around it began to crumble into the code room. The CIA officers and Marines estimated they had about thirty minutes before the cover collapsed. But suddenly the banging stopped and the voices on the roof quieted. After a few minutes of silence the Gunney decided: "Let's open the hatch and we'll face what happens," he said. The ambassador had given them the go-ahead to fire first to maintain security in the vault, and they had enough weaponry to make it a battle if it came to that.

Lessard and Schroen climbed ladders and popped the hatch halfway off. Half a dozen colleagues crouched below, shotguns primed, as Schroen recalled it, ready to shoot as soon as the rioters poured in.

"Guys, guys! When we open the hatch, if somebody's up there, we're going to drop down. Then shoot! Don't shoot first!" They worked out a plan for sequential firing.

Schroen looked across the ladder at Lessard. "We're going to die here if anybody—"

"Yeah, I think so, Gary."

But they couldn't open the hatch. They beat on the bolt, but the contraption was now so bent and warped that it wouldn't pop. They pushed and pushed, but there was nothing they could do.

The sun set on Islamabad, and the noises outside began to drift off into the chilly November air. It was now about 6:30 P.M. Maybe the rioters were gone, or maybe they were lying in wait for the Americans to try to escape. David Fields, the administrative counselor, decided it was time to find out. He ordered the Gunney to lead an expedition out the third-floor hallway and up onto the roof. Fields told them they had the authority to fire on any rioters who got in their way.

Miller and his team of five sneaked out of the vault and into a hallway thick with smoke. They ran their hands along the curved hallway wall to keep track of their position and felt their way to the end where a staircase led to the roof. The locked metal door normally guarding access to the stairs had been torn off its hinges. The rioters had already been here.

With shotguns and revolvers locked and loaded, Miller cautiously guided his team up the stairs. As he poked his head out onto the roof, he fully expected a shoot-out. Instead, he saw a single Pakistani running toward him with hands raised high in the air and yelling, "Friend! Friend!" Miller gave the man a quick pat-down and found a copy of *Who's Who in the CIA* stuffed in one of his pockets, suggesting that student leaders had planned, Tehran-style, to arrest their own nest of spies. Miller took the book and told the straggler to get lost. The Gunney would not fire his weapon that day, nor would any of the Marines under his command.[10] The riot had finally dissipated. During the last hour it had degenerated gradually into a smoky, sporadic carnival of looting.

A few minutes after the expedition party set out, those still inside the vault heard the sound of the hatch being wrenched from above. An enormous U.S. Marine with hands like mallets ripped it off its moorings. Soon everyone from the CIA code room was up on the roof and staring over the chancery walls. Through the halo of smoke that ringed the building they looked across the embassy grounds and saw bright leaping flames where some of their homes had once stood. All of the embassy compound's six buildings, constructed at a cost of $20 million, had been torched beyond repair.

Using bicycle racks stacked end to end, the Marines set up makeshift ladders and led the large group huddled in the vault to safety. It was now dark and cold, and the footing was precarious. Vehicle lights and embers from fires illuminated the ground in a soft glow. Some Pakistani army troops had finally arrived. They were standing around inside the compound, mostly watching.

When the last of those in the vault had been helped down, the Gunney turned to climb the ladder. The CIA men asked where he was going. "I've got to go get Steve," he said. "I'm not going to leave my man up there."

Minutes later he emerged with Crowley's inert form wrapped in a blanket, slung across his shoulder. Crowley had died when the oxygen supply in the vault ran out. In flickering light the Gunney carried the body down the ladder to the ground.

"ALL REPORTS INDICATE all of the people in the compound have been removed and taken to safety thanks to the Pakistani troops," State Department spokesman Hodding Carter told reporters in Washington later that day. In a telephone call, President Carter thanked Zia for his assistance, and Zia expressed regret about the loss of life. The Pakistani ambassador in Washington accepted the Americans' gratitude and noted that Pakistani army troops had reacted "promptly, with dispatch." Secretary of State Cyrus Vance hurriedly summoned ambassadors from thirty Islamic countries to discuss the Pakistan embassy attack and its context. Asked about the recent wave of Islamic militancy abroad, Vance said, "It's hard to say at this point whether a pattern is developing."[11]

It took a day or two to sort out the dead and missing. Putscher, the kidnapped auditor, was released by the students at Quaid-I-Azam around midnight. They had called him "an imperialist pig" and found America guilty "of the trouble in Mecca and all the world's problems," but they decided in the end that he was personally innocent. He wandered back to the embassy, wounded and shaken.

Rescue workers found two Pakistani employees of the embassy in a first-floor office. They had died of apparent asphyxiation, and their bodies had been badly burned. In the compound's residential section, workers found an American airman, Brian Ellis, twenty-nine, lying dead on the floor of his fire-gutted apartment. A golf club lay beside him; he had apparently been beaten unconscious and left to burn.

On Friday, a Pan American Airlines jumbo jet evacuated 309 nonessential personnel, dependents, and other Americans from Pakistan and back to the United States.

Saudi Arabian soldiers and French commandos routed the armed attackers at the Grand Mosque on Saturday in a bloody gun battle. The Saudis never provided an accounting of the final death toll. Most estimates placed it in the hundreds. Saudi interior minister Prince Naif downplayed the uprising's significance, calling the Saudi renegades "no more than a criminal deviation" who were "far from having any political essence." Surviving followers of the Mahdi, who had been shot dead, fled to the mosque's intricate network of basements and underground tunnels. They were flushed out by Saudi troops after a further week of fighting. The building contractor who had originally reconstructed the mosque for the Saudi royal family reportedly supplied blueprints that helped security forces in this final phase of the battle. The Bin Laden Brothers for Contracting and Industry were, after all, one of the kingdom's most loyal and prosperous private companies.[12]

The American treasury secretary, William Miller, flew into the kingdom amid the turmoil. He hoped to reassure Saudi investors, who had about $30 billion on deposit in U.S. banks, that America would remain a faithful ally. He also urged the Saudi royal family to use their influence with OPEC to hold oil prices in check.[13] Rising gasoline prices had stoked debilitating inflation and demoralized the American people.

Saudi princes feared the Mecca uprising reflected popular anxiety about small Westernizing trends that had been permitted in the kingdom during recent years. They soon banned women's hairdressing salons and dismissed female announcers from state television programs. New rules stopped Saudi girls from continuing their education abroad. Prince Turki al-Faisal, the Saudi intelligence chief, concluded that the Mecca uprising was a protest against the conduct of all Saudis—the sheikhs, the government, and the people in general. There should be no future danger or conflict between social progress and traditional religious practices, Turki told visitors, as long as the Saudi royal family reduced corruption and created economic opportunities for the public.

In Tehran, the Ayatollah Khomeini said it was "a great joy for us to learn about the uprising in Pakistan against the U.S.A. It is good news for our oppressed nation. Borders should not separate hearts." Khomeini theorized that "because of propaganda, people are afraid of superpowers, and they think that the superpowers cannot be touched." This, he predicted, would be proven false.[14]

The riot had sketched a pattern that would recur for years. For reasons of his own, the Pakistani dictator, General Zia, had sponsored and strengthened a radical Islamic partner—in this case, Jamaat and its student wing—that had a virulently anti-American outlook. This Islamist partner had veered out of control. By attacking the American embassy, Jamaat had far exceeded Zia's brief. Yet Zia felt he could not afford to repudiate his religious ally. And the Americans felt they could not afford to dwell on the issue. There were larger stakes in the U.S. relationship with Pakistan. In a crisis-laden, impoverished Islamic nation like Pakistan, on the verge of acquiring nuclear weapons, there always seemed to be larger strategic issues for the United States to worry about than the vague, seemingly manageable dangers of political religion.

On the night of the embassy's sacking, Zia gently chided the rioters in a nationally broadcast speech. "I understand that the anger and grief over this incident were quite natural," he said, referring to the uprising in Mecca, "but the way in which they were expressed is not in keeping with the lofty Islamic traditions of discipline and forbearance."[15] As the years passed, Zia's partnership with Jamaat would only deepen.

The CIA and State Department personnel left behind in Islamabad felt deeply embittered. They and more than one hundred of their colleagues had been left to die in the embassy vault; it had taken Pakistani troops more than five hours to make what was at maximum a thirty-minute drive from army headquarters in Rawalpindi. Had events taken a slight turn for the worse, the riot would have produced one of the most catastrophic losses of American life in U.S. diplomatic history.

The CIA's Islamabad station now lacked vehicles in which to meet its agents. The cars had all been burned by mobs. Gary Schroen found a Quaid-I-Azam University jeep parked near the embassy, a vehicle apparently left behind by the rioters. Schroen hot-wired it so that he could continue to drive out at night for clandestine meetings with his reporting agents. Soon university officials turned up at the embassy to ask after the missing jeep—the university now wanted it back. Schroen decided that he couldn't afford to drive around Islamabad in a vehicle that was more or less reported as stolen. He drove the jeep one night to a lake on Islamabad's outskirts. There he got out and rolled it under the water. Small satisfaction, but something.

2

"Lenin Taught Us"

YURI ANDROPOV was a rising force within the gray cabal that circled the Kremlin's listless don, the hound-faced Leonid Brezhnev, general secretary of the Communist Party of the Soviet Union. At sixty-five, Andropov knew—or thought he knew—how to smother a rebellion. As a young communist apparatchik he had soared to prominence as ambassador to Budapest when Soviet troops crushed the 1956 Hungarian uprising. He became KGB chief a decade later, managing the vast apparatus of Soviet internal security and external espionage. He was the leading spy in a political system constructed on deception. From his service's headquarters in the Lubyanka on Moscow's Dzerzhinsky Square, Andropov oversaw KGB foreign covert operations, attempted penetrations of the CIA, and campaigned to suppress dissent within the Soviet Union. Ashen-faced, he conformed outwardly to the drab personal norms of collective leadership. Because he also read Plato, led drives against Soviet corruption, and mentored younger reformers such as Mikhail Gorbachev, a few Kremlin watchers in the West saw tiny glimmers of enlightenment in Andropov, at least in comparison to decaying elder statesmen such as foreign minister Andrei Gromyko or defense minister Dimitri

Ustinov.[1] Yet Andropov's KGB remained ruthless and murderous at home and abroad. In Third World outposts such as Kabul, his lieutenants tortured and killed with impunity. Communist allies who fell out of favor were murdered or exiled. Political detainees languished by the hundreds of thousands in cruel gulags.

Neither Andropov nor the KGB saw Afghanistan's anticommunist revolt coming. The first sharp mutiny erupted in Herat in March 1979, soon after Kabul's recently installed Marxists announced a compulsory initiative to teach girls to read. Such literacy drives were a staple of red-splashed Soviet propaganda posters shipped by the trainload to Third World client states. *Women workers on the march:* muscled and unsmiling, progressive and determined, chins jutted, staring into the future. Earlier in the century, as the Bolsheviks swept through the republics that became Soviet Central Asia—Uzbekistan, Tajikistan, Kazakhstan—they had transformed pastoral Islamic societies into insistently godless police states. Women poured into factories and onto collective farms. So it would be in neighboring Afghanistan, the KGB's political specialists believed.

For nearly two decades the KGB had secretly funded and nurtured communist leadership networks at Kabul University and in the Afghan army, training and indoctrinating some 3,725 military personnel on Soviet soil. Afghan president Mohammed Daoud played Moscow and Washington against each other during the 1970s, accepting financial aid and construction projects from each in a precarious balancing act. In April 1978, Daoud fell off his beam. He arrested communist leaders in Kabul after they staged a noisy protest. Soviet-backed conspirators seeded within the Afghan army shot him dead days later in a reception room of his tattered palace. Triumphant Afghan leftists ripped down the green-striped national flag and unfurled red banners across a rural and deeply religious nation barely acquainted with industrial technology or modernism. Hundreds of Soviet military and political advisers were barracked in Afghan cities and towns to organize secret police networks, army and militia units, small factories, and coeducational schools. Advised by the KGB, Kabul's Marxists launched a terror campaign against religious and social leaders who might have the standing to challenge communist rule. By 1979 about twelve thousand political prisoners had been jailed. Systematic executions began behind prison walls.[2]

No less than America's modernizing capitalists, Russia's retrenching communists underestimated the Iranian revolution. They failed initially to detect the virus of Islamist militancy spreading north and east from Tehran through informal underground networks. The Kremlin and its supporting academies possessed few experts on Islam.[3] The Soviet Union's closest allies in the Middle East were secular regimes such as Syria and Iraq. Like the Americans, the Soviets had directed most of their resources and talent toward the ideological battlefields of Europe and Asia during the previous two decades.

In the early spring of 1979 religious activists inspired by Khomeini's triumphant return carried their defiant gospel across Iran's open desert border with Afghanistan, particularly to Herat, an ancient crossroads on an open plain long bound to Iran by trade and politics. A Persian-accented desert town watered by the Hari Rud River, Herat's traditional cultures and schools of Islam—which included prominent strains of mysticism—were not as severe toward women as in some rural areas of Afghanistan to the east. Yet it was a pious city. Its population included many followers of Shiism, Iran's dominant Islamic sect. And as elsewhere, even non-Shias found themselves energized in early 1979 by Khomeini's religious-political revival. Oblivious, Kabul's communists and their Soviet advisers pressed secular reforms prescribed in Marxist texts. In addition to their literacy campaigns for girls they conscripted soldiers and seized lands previously controlled by tribal elders and Islamic scholars. They abolished Islamic lending systems, banned dowries for brides, legislated freedom of choice within marriages, and mandated universal education in Marxist dogma.

A charismatic Afghan army captain named Ismail Khan called for jihad against the communist usurpers that March and led his heavily armed Herat garrison into violent revolt. His followers hunted down and hacked to death more than a dozen Russian communist political advisers, as well as their wives and children.[4] The rebels displayed Russian corpses on pikes along shaded city streets. Soviet-trained pilots flew bomber-jets out of Kabul in vengeful reply, pulverizing the town in remorseless waves of attack. By the time the raids were finished, on the eve of its first anniversary in power, the Afghan communist government had killed as many as twenty thousand of its own citizenry in Herat alone. Ismail Khan escaped and helped spread rebellion in the western countryside.

As Herat burned, KGB officers seethed. "Bearing in mind that we will be labeled as an aggressor, but in spite of that, under no circumstances can we lose Afghanistan," Andropov told a crisis session of the Soviet Politburo meeting secretly behind Moscow's Kremlin ramparts on March 17, 1979.[5]

Records of the Kremlin's private discussions in Moscow that spring, unavailable to Americans at the time, depict a Soviet leadership dominated by KGB viewpoints. Andropov was a rising figure as Brezhnev faded. His Kabul outpost, the KGB Residency, as it was called, maintained many of the contacts and financial relationships with Afghan communist leaders, bypassing Soviet diplomats.

The Afghans were confusing and frustrating clients, however. Andropov and the rest of Brezhnev's lieutenants found their Afghan communist comrades dense, self-absorbed, and unreliable. The Afghan Marxists had taken their Moscow-supplied revolutionary textbooks much too literally. They were moving too fast. They had split into irreconcilable party factions, and they argued over petty privileges and arid ideology.

"The problem," noted Ustinov at a March 18 Politburo meeting, "is that the leadership of Afghanistan did not sufficiently appreciate the role of Islamic fundamentalists."

"It is completely clear to us that Afghanistan is not ready at this time to resolve all of the issues it faces through socialism," Andropov acknowledged. "The economy is backward, the Islamic religion predominates, and nearly all of the rural population is illiterate. We know Lenin's teaching about a revolutionary situation. Whatever situation we are talking about in Afghanistan, it is not that type of situation."[6]

The group dispatched former premier Alexei Kosygin to telephone the Afghan communist boss, Nur Mohammed Taraki, an inexperienced thug, to see if they could persuade him to steer a more measured course. Taraki had spent the first year of the Afghan communist revolution constructing a personality cult. He had printed and tacked up thousands of posters that displayed his photograph and described him as "The Great Teacher." As his countrymen rose in mass revolt, Taraki maneuvered Afghan communist rivals into exile. He had confided at a Kabul reception for a KGB delegation that he saw himself directly following Lenin's example, forswearing any compromises with noncommunist Afghans and seizing the early period of his revolution to establish a "dictatorship of the proletariat, based on the Soviet model." The murders of political prisoners under way in Kabul jails might be severe, Taraki once told his KGB handlers, but "Lenin taught us to be merciless towards the enemies of the revolution and millions of people had to be eliminated in order to secure the victory of the October Revolution" in the Soviet Union in 1917.

Kosygin placed the call to Taraki on March 18, in the midst of the Politburo's crisis sessions. "The situation is bad and getting worse," Taraki admitted. Herat was falling to the newly emerging Islamic opposition. The city was "almost wholly under the influence of Shiite slogans."

"Do you have the forces to rout them?" Kosygin asked.

"I wish it were the case," Taraki said.

The Afghan communists desperately needed direct Soviet military assistance, Taraki pleaded.

"Hundreds of Afghan officers were trained in the Soviet Union. Where are they all now?" an exasperated Kosygin inquired.

"Most of them are Muslim reactionaries. . . . What else do they call themselves—the Muslim Brotherhood," Taraki said. "We are unable to rely on them. We have no confidence in them."

Taraki had a solution, however. Moscow, he advised, should secretly send in regiments of Soviet soldiers drawn from its Central Asian republics. "Why can't the Soviet Union send Uzbeks, Tajiks, and Turkmens in civilian clothing?" Taraki pleaded. "No one will recognize them. . . . They could drive tanks, because we have all these nationalities in Afghanistan. Let them don Afghan costume and wear Afghan badges, and no one will recognize them." Iran and Pakistan were using this clandestine method, Taraki believed, to foment the Islamic revolution, infiltrating into Afghanistan their own regular troops disguised as guerrillas.

"You are, of course, oversimplifying the issue," Kosygin sniffed. Afghanistan's rising Islamic rebellion, he told Taraki, presented "a complex political and international issue."[7]

THE CIA SENT its first classified proposals for secret support to the anticommunist Afghan rebels to Jimmy Carter's White House in early March 1979, just as the revolt in Herat began to gather force. The options paper went to the Special Coordination Committee, an unpublicized Cabinet subgroup that oversaw covert action on the president's behalf. The CIA's covering memo reported that Soviet leaders were clearly worried about the gathering Afghan revolt. It noted that Soviet-controlled media had launched a propaganda campaign to accuse the United States, Pakistan, and Egypt of secretly backing the Afghan Islamic insurgents. In fact, the United States had not done so until now. Perhaps this would be a good time to begin.[8]

The upheaval in Iran had created new vulnerabilities for the United States in the Middle East. The KGB might seek to exploit this chaos. Here was an opportunity to deflect some of the fire spreading from Khomeini's pulpit away from the United States and toward the Soviet Union. A sustained rebellion in Afghanistan might constrain the Soviets' ability to project power into Middle Eastern oil fields. It also might embarrass and tie down Afghan and perhaps Soviet forces as they attempted to quell the uprising. Still, this was a risky course. The Soviets might retaliate if they saw an American hand in their Afghan cauldron. Carter's White House remained undecided about the CIA's initial options paper. On March 6 the Special Coordination Committee asked the CIA to develop a second round of proposals for covert action.

The CIA's chief analyst for Soviet affairs, Arnold Hoelick, wrote a worried memo to Admiral Stansfield Turner, the CIA's director. Hoelick feared that Taraki's communist regime might disintegrate, prompting the Soviets to intervene. A Soviet incursion might lead Pakistan, Iran, and perhaps China to augment secret support to the Afghan rebels. General Mohammed Zia-ul-Haq in Pakistan might then ask the United States to openly oppose or deter any Soviet military thrust across Pakistan's border. Here was a scenario for the outbreak of World War III, with all of its horrifying potential for nuclear escalation. As to Moscow's attitude toward the floundering Kabul communists, Hoelick concluded that in at least some scenarios "the Soviets may well be prepared to intervene on behalf of the ruling group."[9]

As the CIA and KGB hurtled forward that spring, each had glimpses of the other's motivations, but neither fully understood the other's calculus.

From CIA headquarters at Langley clandestine service officers in the Near East Division reached out to Pakistani and Saudi contacts to explore what might be done on the ground inside Afghanistan. At last, some of the CIA officers felt, the agency was taking initiative. The exploration of an Afghan covert action plan, however tentative, seemed to these Near East hands a rare exception to what had become a dismal, defensive, passive period at the CIA.

Widely publicized congressional hearings a few years before had exposed agency assassination plots in Cuba, rogue covert operations in Latin America, and other shocking secrets. An American public and Congress already outraged about governmental abuses of power after Watergate had turned on the CIA, creating a hostile political environment for agency operations. Assassinations had been formally and legally banned by executive order. New laws and procedures had been enacted to ensure presidential and congressional control over CIA covert actions. Inside Langley the reforms produced anger and demoralization among the professional spy cadres, and even among those who welcomed some of the changes. The CIA had only been doing its job, following presidential directives, sometimes at great personal risk to the officers involved, many at Langley felt. Now there was a sense in Washington that the agency had all along been a kind of criminal organization, a black hole of outrageous conspiracies. By 1979 the public and congressional backlash far exceeded the scale of the original abuses, many career CIA officers believed. Meanwhile Jimmy Carter had sent a team of brass-polish outsiders, led by Navy Admiral Turner, to whip them into shape. To cut the CIA's budget Turner had issued pink slips to scores of clandestine service case officers, the first substantial layoffs in the agency's history. Inside the Directorate of Operations it felt as if they had hit rock bottom.[10]

As they probed for options in Afghanistan that spring, officers in the CIA's Near East Division reported that General Zia in Pakistan might be willing to step up his existing low-level clandestine support for the Afghan insurgents. The general was concerned, however, that unless the United States committed to protect Pakistan from Soviet retaliation, they "could not risk Soviet wrath" by increasing support to the anticommunist rebels too much, the CIA officers reported.[11]

Diplomatic relations between the United States and Pakistan had reached a nadir in 1979, but the CIA had kept its liaison channels in Islamabad open. Zia understood that no matter how sternly Jimmy Carter might denounce him in public because of his poor human rights record or his secret nuclear program, he had backdoor influence in Washington through the CIA. Khomeini's victory early in the year had led to the loss of vital American electronic listening stations based in Iran and trained on the Soviet Union. Zia had accepted a CIA proposal to locate new facilities in Pakistan. For decades there had been these sorts of layers within layers in the U.S.-Pakistani relationship. During the 1960s the first American U-2 spy planes had flown secretly out of Peshawar air bases. During the early 1970s Henry Kissinger had used Pakistani intermediaries to forge his secret opening to China. For his part, Zia saw covert operations as the most prudent way to pursue his regional foreign policy and military objectives. Pakistan had lost half its territory in a war with India eight years earlier. It was too small and too weak a country to openly challenge its neighbors with military force. Zia preferred to strike and hide.

Jimmy Carter's deputy national security adviser, David Aaron, chaired a second secret session of the Special Coordination Committee on March 30 to consider direct American covert aid to the Afghan rebellion. It was just two weeks after Kosygin's stalemated telephone conversation with Taraki. The State Department's David Newsom explained to the group that the Carter administration now sought "to reverse the current Soviet trend and presence in Afghanistan, to demonstrate to the Pakistanis our interest and concern about Soviet involvement, and to demonstrate to the Pakistanis, Saudis, and others our resolve to stop extension of Soviet influence in the Third World." But what steps, exactly, should they take? Should they supply guns and ammunition to defecting Afghan army units? How would the Soviets react?

Aaron posed the central question: "Is there interest in maintaining and assisting the insurgency, or is the risk that we will provoke the Soviets too great?"

They decided to keep studying their options.[12]

Within days Afghan army officers in Jalalabad followed Ismail Khan's example and mutinied against the communists, murdering Soviet advisers. Afghan commanders climbed into their tanks and rumbled over to the rebel lines, declaring themselves allies of the jihad. To Jalalabad's north, in a village of Kunar province known as Kerala, Afghan government forces accompanied by Soviet advisers carried out a massacre of hundreds of men and boys. As word of this and other executions spread in the Afghan countryside, defections and desertions from government army units mounted. Week by week that spring the communist-led army melted with the snow, its conscripts sliding away into the rock canyons and pine-forested mountains where mujahedin ("holy warrior") rebel units had begun to acquire large swaths of uncontested territory.[13]

Most analysts at CIA and other American intelligence agencies continued to predict that the Soviet forces would not invade to quell the rebellion. As summer neared, the CIA documented shipments of attack helicopters from the Soviet Union to Afghanistan and described increasing involvement by Soviet military advisers on the ground. But Langley's analysts felt the Politburo would try to minimize direct involvement. So did the U.S. embassy in Moscow. "Under foreseeable circumstances," predicted a Secret cable from the embassy on May 24, the Soviet Union "will probably avoid shouldering a substantial part of the anti-insurgency combat."[14]

The cable accurately reflected the mood inside the Kremlin. The KGB's Andropov—along with Gromyko and Ustinov—formed a working group that spring to study the emerging crises in Afghan communism. None of their options seemed attractive. They completed a top-secret report for Brezhnev on June 28. The Afghan revolution was struggling because of "economic backwardness, the small size of the working class," and the weakness of the local Communist Party, as well as the selfishness of its Afghan leaders, they concluded.[15]

Andropov's team drafted a letter to Great Teacher Taraki urging him to stop squabbling with his rivals. They instructed him to involve more comrades in revolutionary leadership and soften his stance toward Islam. They advised him to work at recruiting mullahs onto the communist payroll and "convincing the broad number of Muslims that the socioeconomic reforms . . . will not affect the religious beliefs of Muslims." For his part, Taraki preferred guns. He still wanted Soviet troops to confront the rebels.[16]

In Washington that week, National Security Adviser Zbigniew Brzezinski, the son of a Polish diplomat whose family was forced into exile by the Nazi invasion and later by Soviet occupation, recommended that President Carter endorse "non-lethal" covert support for the Afghan rebels. There were too few opportunities to embarrass the Soviets in the Third World, Brzezinski believed. One had now presented itself in Afghanistan. The risks could be managed. Brzezinski's plan was a compromise that bridged unresolved arguments within the Special Coordination Committee. The CIA would funnel support to the Afghan insurgents, but no weapons would be supplied for now.

On July 3, 1979, Carter scrawled his name on a presidential "finding" required under a recent law intended to ensure White House control over CIA operations.[17] Under the new system, if the CIA intended to undertake "special activities" designed to influence political conditions abroad—as opposed to its more routine work of espionage, or stealing secrets—the president had to "find" or declare formally and in writing that such covert action promoted American national security. The president also had to notify a handful of congressional leaders of his decision.[18]

Carter's finding authorized the CIA to spend just over $500,000 on propaganda and psychological operations, as well as provide radio equipment, medical supplies, and cash to the Afghan rebels.[19] Using intermediaries in Germany and elsewhere to disguise their involvement, CIA officers from the Near East Division began that summer to ship medical equipment and radios to Pakistan, where they were passed to Zia's intelligence service for onward distribution to the Afghan guerrillas.

It seemed at the time a small beginning.

DESPITE MOSCOW'S PLEAS for common sense, Kabul's Marxist leaders began to consume themselves. By late summer Great Teacher Taraki had become locked in deadly rivalry with a party comrade, Hafizullah Amin, a former failed graduate student at Columbia University in New York and a leading architect of Afghanistan's 1978 communist revolution. Each soon concluded that the other had to go. Amin managed to oust Taraki from office in September. A few weeks later he ordered Taraki's death; the Great Teacher perished in a fusillade of gunfire inside a barricaded Kabul compound.

Hafizullah Amin's ascension launched a tragicomedy of suspicion and miscalculation within the KGB. KGB handlers working out of the Kabul Residency had kept both Taraki and Amin on their payroll for years, sometimes meeting their clients secretly in parked cars on the city's streets.[20] After Amin gained power, however, he became imperious. Among other transgressions he sought authority from the KGB to withdraw funds from Afghanistan's foreign bank accounts, which had about $400 million on deposit, according to KGB records. Frustrated and hoping to discredit him, the KGB initially planted false stories that Amin was a CIA agent.

In the autumn these rumors rebounded on the KGB in a strange case of "blowback," the term used by spies to describe planted propaganda that filters back to confuse the country that first set the story loose. For reasons that remain unclear, Amin held a series of private meetings in Kabul that fall with American diplomats. When the KGB learned of these meetings, its officers feared that their own false rumors about Amin might be true. A document from India circulating that autumn noted that when he lived in New York, Amin had been affiliated with the Asia Foundation, which had a history of contacts with the CIA. As the weeks passed, some KGB officers examined the possibility that Amin might be an American plant sent to infiltrate the Afghan Communist Party. They also picked up reports that Amin might be seeking a political compromise with Afghanistan's Islamic rebels. Of course, this was the approach the KGB itself had been urging on Taraki from Moscow earlier in the year. Now, suddenly, it looked suspicious. KGB officers feared Amin might be trying to curry favor with America and Pakistan.[21]

The KGB sent a written warning to Brezhnev about Amin in November. The Kabul Residency feared "an intended shift" of Afghan foreign policy "to the right," meaning into closer alignment with the United States. Amin "has met with the U.S. chargé d'affaires a number of times, but he has given no indication of the subject of these talks in his meetings with Soviet representatives."[22]

For their part, the Americans in Kabul regarded Amin as a dangerous tyrant. They held Amin partly responsible for the murder of Adolph Dubs, the American ambassador to Afghanistan, who had been kidnapped and shot to death in a Kabul hotel room earlier in 1979. Still, U.S. diplomats inside the embassy were aware of the rumors that Amin was a CIA agent. There was enough concern and confusion about this question among State Department diplomats in the embassy that before his murder, Ambassador Dubs had asked his CIA station chief point-blank whether there was any foundation to the rumors. He was told emphatically that Amin had never worked for the CIA, according to J. Bruce Amstutz, who was Dubs's deputy at the time and became U.S. chargé d'affaires after his death. Officers in the Near East Division of the CIA, who would have handled Amin if he were on the agency payroll, also said later that they had no contacts with him when he lived in New York or later, other then casual discussions at diplomatic receptions. No evidence has yet surfaced to contradict these assertions.[23]

That fateful autumn, however, Amstutz did meet five times with Amin in private. Their discussions were stilted and unproductive, Amstutz recalled years later. Far from tilting toward the United States, Amstutz found the Afghan communist leader uncompromisingly hostile. Amin had twice failed his doctoral examination at Columbia, and in Amstutz's estimation, this humiliation left him angry and resentful toward Americans.

CIA officers working in the Kabul station concentrated most of their efforts on Soviet targets, not Afghan communists. Their principal mission in Kabul for years had been to steal Soviet military secrets, especially the operating manuals of new Soviet weapons systems, such as the MiG-21 fighter jet. They also tried to recruit KGB agents and communist bloc diplomats onto the agency's payroll. Toward this end the CIA case officers joined a six-on-six international soccer league for spies and diplomats sponsored by the German Club in Kabul. The officers spent comparatively little time cultivating Afghan sources or reporting on intramural Afghan politics. As a result the CIA had failed to predict Afghanistan's initial 1978 communist coup.[24] The agency still had relatively few Afghan sources. "What Are the Soviets Doing in Afghanistan?" asked a Top Secret/Codeword memorandum sent to National Security Adviser Brzezinski by Thomas Thornton in September 1979 that drew on all available U.S. intelligence. "Simply, we don't know," the memo began.[25]

The KGB fared no better in assessing American intentions. Knowing that Amin had been meeting with U.S. diplomats in secret but unable to learn the content of those discussions, KGB officers concluded that the CIA had begun to work with Amin to manipulate Kabul's government. The KGB officers in Afghanistan then convinced their superiors in Moscow that drastic measures had to be undertaken: Amin should be killed or otherwise removed from office to save the Afghan revolution from CIA penetration.

In a personal memorandum to Brezhnev, KGB chief Andropov explained why. "After the coup and the murder of Taraki in September of this year, the situation in the party, the army and the government apparatus has become more acute, as they were essentially destroyed as a result of the mass repressions carried out by Amin. At the same time, alarming information started to arrive about Amin's secret activities, forewarning of a possible political shift to the West." These included, Andropov wrote, "contacts with an American agent about issues which are kept secret from us." In Andropov's fevered imagination, the CIA's recruitment of Amin was part of a wider unfolding plot by the agency "to create a 'New Great Ottoman Empire' including the southern republics of the Soviet Union." With a base secured in Afghanistan, the KGB chief feared, as he wrote confidentially, that the United States could point Pershing nuclear missiles at the Soviet Union's southern underbelly, where its air defenses were weak. Iran and Pakistan might go nuclear as well with American support and push into Central Asia. To prevent this, Andropov advised, the Soviet Union must act decisively to replace Amin and shore up Afghan communism.[26]

In the end Andropov and the rest of Brezhnev's inner circle concluded the best way to achieve these goals would be to assassinate Amin and mount a military invasion of Afghanistan, installing new and more responsive Afghan communist leaders. KGB fears about Amin's reliability were by no means the only factor in this decision. Without direct military support from Moscow, the broader Afghan government faced collapse because of desertions from its army. If communism in Afghanistan was to be saved, Moscow had to act decisively. Yet Politburo records also make clear that KGB fears about Amin's loyalty played a role in this analysis. The questions about Amin accelerated the timetable for decision-making, encouraged the Politburo's inner circle to think they faced devious CIA intrigues in Kabul, and helped convince them that only drastic measures could succeed.

Meeting in Moscow, the Politburo's inner circle made the first tentative decision to invade on November 26, 1979, just five days after the Jamaat student mob had sacked the U.S. embassy in Islamabad and three weeks after Iranian students had seized hostages at the besieged American embassy in Tehran.

Clandestine Soviet military and KGB units began to infiltrate Afghanistan early in December to prepare for the assault. On December 7, Babrak Karmal, the exiled Afghan communist selected by the KGB to replace Amin, secretly arrived at Bagram air base on a Tu-134 aircraft, protected by KGB officers and Soviet paratroopers. KGB assassins began to case Amin's residence. Operatives first sought to poison Amin by penetrating his kitchen, but Amin had by now grown so paranoid that he employed multiple food tasters, including members of his family. According to KGB records, the poisoning attempt succeeded only in sickening one of Amin's nephews. The next day a sniper shot at Amin and missed. Frustrated, the KGB fell back on plans to stage a massive frontal assault on Amin's residence once the broader Soviet military invasion began.[27]

The CIA had been watching Soviet troop deployments in and around Afghanistan since the summer, and while its analysts were divided in assessing Soviet political intentions, the CIA reported steadily and accurately about Soviet military moves. By mid-December ominous large-scale Soviet deployments toward the Soviet-Afghan border had been detected by U.S. intelligence. CIA director Turner sent President Carter and his senior advisers a classified "Alert" memo on December 19, warning that the Soviets had "crossed a significant threshold in their growing military involvement in Afghanistan" and were sending more forces south. Three days later deputy CIA director Bobby Inman called Brzezinski and Defense Secretary Harold Brown to report that the CIA had no doubt the Soviet Union intended to undertake a major military invasion of Afghanistan within seventy-two hours.[28]

Antonov transport planes loaded with Soviet airborne troops landed at Kabul's international airport as darkness fell on Christmas Eve. Pontoon regiments working with the Soviet Fortieth Army laid floating bridges across the Amu Darya River near Termez in the early hours of Christmas morning, and the first Soviet tanks rolled across the border. As regular Soviet forces fanned out, more than seven hundred KGB paramilitaries dressed in Afghan army uniforms launched an operation to kill Hafizullah Amin and his closest aides, and to install new leadership in the Afghan Communist Party. Dozens of KGB officers were killed before they finally battled their way inside Amin's Kabul palace and gunned him down.[29]

FROM THE VERY FIRST HOURS after cables from the U.S. embassy in Kabul confirmed that a Soviet invasion had begun, Zbigniew Brzezinski, Jimmy Carter's most determined cold warrior, wondered if this time the Soviets had overreached. Brzezinski and his colleagues knew nothing about the KGB's fears of CIA plotting. They interpreted the invasion as a desperate act of support for the Afghan communists and as a possible thrust toward the Persian Gulf. As he analyzed American options, Brzezinski was torn. He hoped the Soviets could be punished for invading Afghanistan, that they could be tied down and bloodied the way the United States had been in Vietnam. Yet he feared the Soviets would crush the Afghans mercilessly, just as they had crushed the Hungarians in 1956 and the Czechs in 1968.

In a discursive memo to Carter written on the day after Christmas, classified Secret and titled "Reflections on Soviet Intervention in Afghanistan," Brzezinski worried that the Soviets might not be plagued by the self-doubts and self-criticisms that had constrained American military tactics in Vietnam. "We should not be too sanguine about Afghanistan becoming a Soviet Vietnam," he wrote. "The guerrillas are badly organized and poorly led. They have no sanctuary, no organized army, and no central government—all of which North Vietnam had. They have limited foreign support, in contrast to the enormous amount of arms that flowed to the Vietnamese from both the Soviet Union and China. The Soviets are likely to act decisively, unlike the U.S. which pursued in Vietnam a policy of 'inoculating' the enemy.

"What is to be done?" Brzezinski then asked. He sketched out a new Afghan policy, much of it to be carried out in secret. He drew on the plans developed earlier in the year at the White House and CIA to channel medical kits and other aid to the Afghan rebels. "It is essential that Afghanistan's resistance continues," he wrote. "This means more money as well as arms shipments to the rebels, and some technical advice. To make the above possible we must both reassure Pakistan and encourage it to help the rebels. This will require a review of our policy toward Pakistan, more guarantees to it, more arms aid, and, alas, a decision that our security policy toward Pakistan cannot be dictated by our nonproliferation policy. We should encourage the Chinese to help the rebels also. We should concert with Islamic countries both in a propaganda campaign and in a covert action campaign to help the rebels."[30]

Disguised KGB paramilitaries were still chasing Hafizullah Amin through the hallways of his Kabul palace, Soviet tanks had barely reached their first staging areas, and Brzezinski had already described a CIA-led American campaign in Afghanistan whose broad outlines would stand for a decade to come.

"Our ultimate goal is the withdrawal of Soviet troops from Afghanistan," Brzezinski wrote in a Top Secret memo a week later. "Even if this is not attainable, we should make Soviet involvement as costly as possible."[31]

Anti-Soviet fever swept Washington, arousing support for a new phase of close alliance between the United States and Pakistan. Together they would challenge the Soviets across the Khyber Pass, much as the British had challenged czarist Russia on the same Afghan ground a century before.

Yet for the American staff left behind to work near the charred campus of the U.S. embassy in Islamabad, half a day's drive from the Khyber, the Soviet invasion was a doubly bitter turn of events. They were shocked by Moscow's hegemonic violence and at the same time angry that Pakistani dictator Zia-ul-Haq would benefit.

The diplomats and CIA officers in Islamabad had spent much of December burning compromised documents and reorganizing their shattered offices in makeshift quarters at a U.S. Agency for International Development (AID) compound near the burned embassy grounds. Worried about another attack on their offices by rioters, the CIA had shipped back to Langley decades' worth of index cards filled with names and details of contacts and agents.

It took more diplomatic fortitude than many of them possessed to suddenly embrace Zia as a strategic partner. As many inside the embassy saw it, the Pakistani general had left them for dead on that Wednesday afternoon in November. As Soviet armor rolled into Afghanistan, there were sarcastic suggestions from the Islamabad CIA station of an alternative new American policy toward Pakistan: the secret export of hundreds of thousands of Russian dictionaries and phrase books to Islamabad for government use after the Soviet regional occupation was complete. They might be able to use a few of those Russian phrase books over at the student union of Quaid-I-Azam University, too.

"Go Raise Hell"

H OWARD HART STOOD ALONE in Peshawar's cold, smoky night
air. He tried to appear inconspicuous. He was a tall, bespectacled American shuffling his feet on a darkened road in an arid frontier city teeming with
Afghan refugees, rebel fighters, smugglers, money changers, poets, proselytizers, prostitutes, and intriguers of every additional stripe. Hart had arrived in
Pakistan in May 1981 as the CIA's chief of station. He ran the agency's clandestine program to arm anti-Soviet guerrillas in Afghanistan. A colleague
from the MI6, the British secret service, had arranged an introduction to a
young, bluff, confident Afghan rebel commander named Abdul Haq. The Islamabad CIA station ran some Pakistani agents, but it had very few Afghan
contacts. Hart had scheduled his nighttime meeting with Haq to coincide with
a money drop he had to make to an Indian agent. He carried a small bag with
a couple hundred thousand Indian rupees inside. Earlier that day he had
driven the hundred miles from Islamabad down the raucous Grand Trunk
Road toward the baked, treeless hills that rose to Afghanistan. He had woven
beneath the ramparts of Bala Hissar fort and through the city's ballet of horse
carts, wheeled fruit stands, diesel rickshaws, motorcycles, and painted trucks.
He did not want to register at a Peshawar hotel because guest passports were

routinely copied and passed to Pakistani intelligence. He stood exposed now beside a dim street, waiting, aware that an Afghan guerrilla's sense of time might not conform to his own.

Down the road rumbled a large, loud motorcycle driven by a man wearing the unmistakable pressure suit, coat, and helmet of a Soviet fighter pilot. Soviet soldiers or airmen were not supposed to be on Pakistani territory, but occasionally Soviet special forces ran small raids across the Afghan border. A CIA case officer's great fear was being kidnapped by the Afghan communist secret service or the KGB. The motorcycle stopped beside him, and the figure waved for Hart to get on the back. He could only stare in disbelief. Finally the man pulled off his helmet and revealed a beard as bushy as a lumberjack's. It was Abdul Haq. His fighters had shot down a Soviet plane and then peeled a pressure suit off the pilot's corpse. The suit fit Haq and kept him warm on winter nights. He did not mind looking like an Afghan Buck Rogers. Hart climbed on the motorcycle and bump, bump, bump, off they drove through muddy rutted lanes. "We had a lovely evening," Hart would say later. He did tell his new Afghan contact, "Don't ever do that to me again."[1]

It was the beginning of a long and tumultuous relationship between Abdul Haq and the CIA. Courageous and stubbornly independent, Haq was "very certain about everything, very skeptical about everybody else," Hart recalled. "At the ripe old age—he was probably twenty-seven then—he had been through it all." Scion of a prominent Pashtun tribal family with roots near the eastern Afghan city of Jalalabad, Abdul Haq had raised a fighting force soon after the Soviet invasion and mounted raids against communist forces around Kabul. When the CIA began shipping guns, Haq became an intermediary between the agency, MI6, and the Kabul front. He was not an especially religious fighter. He espoused none of the anti-American rhetoric of the Muslim Brotherhood–influenced Afghan guerrillas often favored by Pakistani intelligence. Haq grew to become Howard Hart's most important Afghan guide to the anti-Soviet war. They were two boisterous, adventurous men who rubbed some of their colleagues the wrong way. They were bound by a driving passion that defined the early years of the CIA's Afghan jihad: They wanted to kill Soviet soldiers.

Howard Hart had spent the first years of his life in a Japanese internment camp in the Philippines. His father had gone to Manila in the late 1930s as a banker and had been trapped when Japan invaded as World War II began. The Hart family spent three years in a Japanese garrison with about two thousand other Americans, Europeans, and Australians. In early 1945, when Japan's military collapsed, the camp commander decided to commence executions and ordered adult men to dig trenches in the parade ground to receive the dead. General Douglas MacArthur ordered airborne troops to liberate the prisoners. Hart recalled being carried across a Philippine beach under the left arm of a young American paratrooper who held a tommy gun in his right hand. Hart's mother jogged behind. They were loaded into a landing craft and pushed out to sea. He was five years old.

Later his father took up banking again, moving first to Calcutta and then back to Manila. Hart grew up with Filipino boys whose fathers had fought the Japanese in the jungles. In his childhood games, guerrilla warfare figured as baseball did for other American kids.

He studied Asian politics and learned to speak Hindi and Urdu at American universities, completing graduate school as the Vietnam War swelled in 1965. He thought about enlisting in the Marines but chose the CIA. At "the Farm" at Camp Peary, Virginia, the agency gave Hart the standard two-year course for career trainees, as aspiring case officers were called: how to run a paid agent, how to surveil targets and avoid being surveilled, how to manage codebooks, how to jump out of airplanes. Upon graduation Hart joined the Directorate of Operations, the clandestine service. He was posted to Calcutta, scene of his youth. Later he served in Bahrain and Tehran. When Iranian students seized the American embassy, he was assigned as a country and paramilitary operations specialist to the secret team that attempted a rescue. The mission, called Desert One, ended catastrophically when sand-blown helicopters crashed at a desert staging area far from Tehran on April 24, 1980.

Although young, he was a natural choice to run the Islamabad station in 1981 because of his passion for weapons and paramilitary tactics. He collected knives, pistols, rifles, assault guns, machine guns, bullets, artillery shells, bazookas, and mortars. Eventually he would accumulate in his home one of the CIA's largest private collections of antique and modern American weaponry. In Islamabad he would act as a quartermaster for the Afghan mujahedin. He ordered guns from CIA headquarters, helped oversee secret training programs for the mujahedin in Pakistani camps, and evaluated weapons to determine which ones worked for the rebels and which did not.

The CIA had no intricate strategy for this war. "You're a young man; here's your bag of money, go raise hell" was the way Hart understood his orders. "Don't fuck it up, just go out there and kill Soviets, and take care of the Pakistanis and make them do whatever you need to make them do."[2]

At Langley a new generation of case officers was coming of age. Many were Vietnam-era military veterans and law enforcement officers. Their influence within the CIA now competed with the Kennedy-era, northeastern, Ivy League officers who had dominated the agency during the 1950s and early 1960s. "The tennis players were being replaced by the bowlers," as one of the self-styled bowlers put it.

By the early 1980s many Ivy League graduates sought Wall Street wealth, not a relatively low-paid civil service career. American liberals saw the CIA as discredited. Instead of prep school graduates came men like Gary Schroen, working-class midwesterners who had enlisted in the army when others their age were protesting the Vietnam War. They acquired their language skills in CIA classrooms, not on Sorbonne sabbaticals. Many were Republicans or independents. Ronald Reagan was their president. A few of this group inside the Directorate of Operations saw themselves as profane insurgents waging culture and class war against the old CIA elite. Yet as Hart arrived in Islamabad the CIA was still led by the generation of elite clandestine officers, many of them Democrats from the northeast, whose outlook had been shaped by the idealism of the early Cold War and the cultural styles of the Kennedys. Hart's supervisor in Langley, for instance, was Charles Cogan, a Francophile, polo-playing Harvard graduate who wore an Errol Flynn mustache and read history like a scholar. When he served as station chief in Paris, Cogan "spent his free time riding in the Bois de Boulogne with his French aristocratic friends," as a colleague put it. Rising beside him in the D.O.'s leadership was Clair George. He was a postman's son who had grown up in working-class Pennsylvania but had adopted the manners of an East Coast Democrat with country club élan. Thomas Twetten was soon to become the overall head of the clandestine service. After his retirement Twetten became an antique bookseller in Vermont. None of these men bowled regularly.[3]

Howard Hart did not fall neatly into either camp. He read deeply about British colonial experience in Afghanistan, especially about the tribal complexities of the Pashtuns, to prepare himself for the Islamabad station. He saw himself as an intellectual activist. But he was also a blunt, politically conservative gun afficionado who favored direct paramilitary action against the Soviets. He had little time for subtle political manipulations among the Afghans. He wanted to get on with the shooting.

In Tehran and then while working on the Iran account at headquarters Hart had alienated some of his colleagues, who saw him as unreliable and self-aggrandizing. Because of its intensity and claustrophobic secrecy, the CIA sometimes engenders bitter office politics, the kinds of eyeball-tearing rivalries that develop among roommates or brothers. Hart's opponents included Bob Lessard, who had been deputy station chief during the sacking of the Islamabad embassy in 1979. Lessard had returned to teach at Camp Peary, convinced that his career was in shards—not only because he and Hart didn't get along but because of his earlier troubles with the double agent in Kabul. Few within the Near East Division understood how deeply depressed Lessard had become. On Christmas morning 1980, in his CIA quarters at the Farm, he committed suicide with a shotgun.[4]

Hart arrived in May 1981 at an Islamabad embassy still under reconstruction. The CIA station was crammed into the old U.S. AID building. It was a relatively small station—a chief, a deputy, and three or four case officers. Fearing another Pakistani riot, Hart announced that he wanted a nearly "paperless station." Typed classified documents would be burned immediately if at all possible. To retain a small number of records, Hart showed his team a secret writing method. They were to place a standard piece of wax paper over their blank sheets and type. To read it later, the case officers were to sprinkle it with cinnamon powder and then blow; the cinnamon would stick to the wax and illuminate the text. "This is the best headquarters could do for me," Hart told them sheepishly.

Hart's instructions emphasized the clandestine Afghan war and espionage directed at Pakistan's nuclear program. He announced that the Islamabad station would not collect intelligence on internal Pakistani politics. The State Department's diplomats could handle that subject.

Like dozens of nineteenth-century British colonial political agents before him—some of whose memoirs he had read—Hart regarded the Afghans as charming, martial, semicivilized, and ungovernable. Any two Afghans created three factions, he told his colleagues. "Every man will be king," Hart believed of the Afghans. This political tendency could not be overridden by American ingenuity, he thought. Hart sought to encourage the mujahedin to fight the Soviets in small, irregular bands of fifty or one hundred men. He did not want to plan the rebels' tactics or field operations. "One of the ways to manage a war properly is don't worry about the little details," he said later.

There might be twenty thousand to forty thousand war-fighting mujahedin guerrillas in the field at any one time, Hart figured. Hundreds of thousands more might be visiting family in Pakistani refugee camps, farming, smuggling, or just hanging around until the weather improved. The disorganized, part-time character of the mujahedin didn't bother Hart. His strategy was to supply hundreds of thousands of rifles and tens of millions of bullets en masse to the guerrillas and then sit back in Islamabad and watch. The Afghans had ample motivation to fight the Soviets, he thought. They would make effective use of the weapons against Soviet and Afghan communists in their own way, on their own timetables.[5]

In any event, policy makers back in Washington did not believe the Soviets could be defeated militarily by the rebels. The CIA's mission was spelled out in an amended Top Secret presidential finding signed by President Carter in late December 1979 and reauthorized by President Reagan in 1981. The finding permitted the CIA to ship weapons secretly to the mujahedin. The document used the word *harassment* to describe the CIA's goals against Soviet forces. The CIA's covert action was to raise the costs of Soviet intervention in Afghanistan. It might also deter the Soviets from undertaking other Third World invasions. But this was not a war the CIA was expected to win outright on the battlefield. The finding made clear that the agency was to work through Pakistan and defer to Pakistani priorities. The CIA's Afghan program would not be "unilateral," as the agency called operations it ran in secret on its own. Instead the CIA would emphasize "liaison" with Pakistani intelligence.[6]

The first guns shipped in were single-shot, bolt-action .303 Lee Enfield rifles, a standard British infantry weapon until the 1950s. With its heavy wooden stock and antique design, it was not an especially exciting weapon, but it was accurate and powerful. Hart regarded it as a far superior weapon to the flashier communist-made AK-47 assault rifle, which looked sleek and made a lot of noise but was less powerful and more difficult to aim. CIA logistics officers working from Langley secretly purchased hundreds of thousands of the .303 rifles from Greece, India, and elsewhere, and shipped them to Karachi. They also bought thousands of rocket-propelled grenade launchers from Egypt and China. The RPG-7, as it was called, was cheap, easy to carry, and could stop a Soviet tank.[7]

As battlefield damage assessments poured in from the CIA's Kabul station and from Afghan liaisons such as Abdul Haq, Hart began to think that the jihad had greater potential than some of the bureaucrats back in Langley realized. The initial popular Afghan reaction to invading Soviet troops had been broad and emotional. In Kabul at night tens of thousands gathered on their rooftops and sang out the Muslim call to prayer, "Allahu Akbar" (God is Great), in eerie and united defiance. Soviet tanks and troops had killed hundreds of Afghan civilians to quell street demonstrations. As the months passed, Afghan intellectuals, civil servants, and athletes defected to the mujahedin. By late 1981 the rebels roamed freely in nearly all of Afghanistan's twenty-nine provinces. They mounted frequent ambushes on Soviet convoys and executed raids against cities and towns. The pace of their attacks was escalating.[8]

Hart concluded within months of his arrival that the war should be expanded. In the fall of 1981 he attended a regional conference of CIA station chiefs in Bangkok. On a piece of paper in his back pocket he had hand-scrawled a new list of weapons that would make the mujahedin more effective. The questions debated at Bangkok included "What would the Pakistanis tolerate? What will the Soviets tolerate before they start striking at Pakistan?" Officers from Langley worried that they might go too far, too fast.

Back in Islamabad, Hart sat in his house at night and drafted long cables to Langley on yellow legal pads, describing a Soviet convoy of tanks destroyed here, a helicopter shot down there. With CIA help the mujahedin were crippling heavily equipped Soviet detachments, Hart wrote, while using dated weaponry and loose guerrilla tactics. In January 1982, Hart cabled headquarters to ask again for more and better weapons.[9]

Hart and other case officers involved sometimes reflected that it might have been a relatively uncomplicated war, if only the CIA had been able to run it on its own. But the United States did not own a subcontinental empire, as the British had a century before. If the CIA wanted to pump more and better weapons into Afghanistan, it had to negotiate access to the Afghan frontier through the sovereign nation of Pakistan. When the jihad began to gather strength by 1982, Hart found himself increasingly forced to reckon with Pakistan's own agenda in the war. This meant reckoning with the personal goals of the Pakistani dictator, General Zia-ul-Haq. It also meant accommodating Zia's primary secret service, Inter-Services Intelligence, or ISI.

After Vietnam and the stinging Washington scandals of the 1970s, many case officers feared local political entanglements, especially in violent covert operations. Many of them had vowed after Vietnam that there would be no more CIA-led quixotic quests for Third World hearts and minds. In Afghanistan, they said, the CIA would stick to its legal authority: mules, money, and mortars.[10]

For many in the CIA the Afghan jihad was about killing Soviets, first and last. Hart even suggested that the Pakistanis put a bounty out on Soviet soldiers: ten thousand rupees for a special forces soldier, five thousand for a conscript, and double in either case if the prisoners were brought in alive.[11] This was payback for Soviet aid to the North Vietnamese and the Vietcong, and for many CIA officers who had served in that war, it was personal. Guns for everyone! was Howard Hart's preference. Langley's D.O. leaders did not want to organize exiled Afghan political parties on Pakistani soil. They did not want to build a provisional anticommunist Afghan government. They did not even like to help choose winners and losers among the jihad's guerrilla leaders. Let the Pakistanis fuss over Afghan politics to the extent that it was necessary at all.

This indirect approach was beginning to work, Hart believed. Yet as the mujahedin resistance grew and stiffened, the agency's passivity about who led the Afghan rebels—who got the most guns, the most money, the most power—helped ensure that Zia-ul-Haq's political and religious agenda in Afghanistan gradually became the CIA's own.

MOHAMMED ZIA-UL-HAQ was a young captain in a Punjabi unit of Britain's colonial army when London's exhausted government finally quit India in 1947. He had been born and raised on the Indian side of the new border with Pakistan, a line soon drawn in the blood of Hindu-Muslim religious riots. His father had been an Anglophilic civil servant but also a pious lay Islamic teacher. His family spoke in British accents and bandied slang as if in a Wiltshire country house.

As with millions of Punjabi Muslims, the religious violence at Pakistan's birth seared Zia's memory. While escorting a train of refugees on a weeklong journey from northern India to Pakistan in 1947, he witnessed a nightmarish landscape of mutilated corpses. "We were under constant fire. The country was burning until we reached Lahore. Life had become so cheap between Hindu and Muslim." Once in Pakistan, he said later, he "realized that we were bathed in blood, but at last we were free citizens."[12]

British-trained Punjabi Muslim army officers such as Zia became one of the new nation's most powerful ruling groups. Three wars with India anointed them as Pakistan's supreme guardians. Battlefield experience coalesced them into a disciplined brotherhood. Failed civilian governments and a series of army-led coups d'état conditioned rising young generals to see themselves as politicians.

The nation had been created in Islam's name, yet it lacked confidence about its identity. Mohammed Ali Jinnah, Pakistan's founder, belonged to a movement of secular, urban Muslim intellectuals. They saw Islam as a source of culture but not as a proselytizing faith or a basis of political order. Jinnah attempted to construct for Pakistan a secular democratic constitution tinted with Islamic values. But he died while the nation was young, and his successors failed to overcome Pakistan's obstacles: divided territory, a weak middle class, plural ethnic traditions, an unruly western border facing Afghanistan, a hostile India, and vast wealth gaps.

As Zia rose to his generalship, he embraced personal religious faith to a greater degree than many of his comrades in arms. He also believed that Pakistanis should embrace political Islam as an organizing principle. "We were *created* on the basis of Islam," Zia said. He compared his country to Israel, where "its religion and its ideology are the main sources of its strength." Without Islam, he believed, "Pakistan would fail."[13]

After 1977 he reigned as a dictator and ceded few political privileges to others. But he did not decorate himself in ornate trappings of power. He was a courteous man in private, patient with his handicapped child, and attentive to visitors and guests. He wore his hair slicked down with grease, neatly parted in the style of film actors of a bygone era, and his mustache was trimmed and waxed. His deferential manner was easily underestimated. Zulfikar Ali Bhutto had promoted him to army chief of staff apparently in the belief that Zia would be compliant. Zia not only overthrew Bhutto but hanged him.

In the context of 1979's upheavals Zia was not a radical. He declared Pakistan an Islamic state but did not move as forcefully as Khomeini did in Iran. He created no Pakistani religious police fashioned on the Saudi Arabian model. He did not bring Pakistan's Islamic clergy to power. Zia believed deeply in the colonial-era army's values, traditions, and geopolitical mission—a thoroughly British orientation. "Devout Muslim, yes, but too much a politician to have the fundamentalist's fervor," as an ISI brigadier put it. "Without Zia there could have been no successful jihad, but behind all the public image there was always the calculating politician who put his own position foremost." He also sought to safeguard Pakistan, and at times he showed himself willing to compromise with the Soviets over Afghanistan, through negotiations.[14]

Yet Zia strongly encouraged personal religious piety within the Pakistan army's officer corps, a major change from the past. He encouraged the financing and construction of hundreds of *madrassas,* or religious schools, along the Afghan frontier to educate young Afghans—as well as Pakistanis—in Islam's precepts and to prepare some of them for anticommunist jihad. The border *madrassas* formed a kind of Islamic ideological picket fence between communist Afghanistan and Pakistan. Gradually Zia embraced jihad as a strategy. He saw the legions of Islamic fighters gathering on the Afghan frontier in the early 1980s as a secret tactical weapon. They accepted martyrdom's glories. Their faith could trump the superior firepower of the godless

Soviet occupiers. "Afghan youth will fight the Soviet invasion with bare hands, if necessary," he assured President Reagan in private.[15]

He feared that Kabul's communists would stir up Pashtun independence activists along the disputed Afghanistan-Pakistan border. Pashtuns comprised Afghanistan's dominant ethnic group, but there were more Pashtuns living inside Pakistan than inside Afghanistan. A successful independence campaign might well shatter Pakistan once and for all. Within a year of the Soviet invasion, about one million Afghan refugees had poured into Pakistan, threatening social unrest. Soviet and Afghan secret services had begun to run terrorist operations on Pakistani soil, as far inland as Sind province. A stronghold of the Bhutto family, Sind was a hotbed of opposition to Zia. The KGB's Afghan agents set up shop in Karachi, Islamabad, Peshawar, and Quetta. They linked up with one of the hanged Bhutto's sons, Murtaza, and helped him carry out hijackings of Pakistani airliners.[16] Zia suspected that India's intelligence service was involved as well. If Soviet-backed communists took full control in Afghanistan, Pakistan would be sandwiched between two hostile regimes— the Soviet empire to the west and north, and India to the east. To avoid this, Zia felt he needed to carry the Afghan jihad well across the Khyber Pass, to keep the Soviets back on their heels. A war fought on Islamic principles could also help Zia shore up a political base at home and deflect appeals to Pashtun nationalism.

Zia knew he would need American help, and he milked Washington for all he could. He turned down Carter's initial offer of $400 million in aid, dismissing it as "peanuts," and was rewarded with a $3.2 billion proposal from the Reagan administration plus permission to buy F-16 fighter jets, previously available only to NATO allies and Japan.[17] Yet as he loaded up his shopping cart, Zia kept his cool and his distance. In private meetings with President Reagan, Vice President Bush, Secretary of State Shultz, and others, Zia lied brazenly about Pakistan's secret efforts to develop nuclear weapons. Reagan had come into office criticizing Carter for alienating American allies by harping on human rights. The new president assured Zia that Washington would now be a more faithful friend. "Given the uncertainty and sensitivity surrounding certain areas of our relationship," Shultz wrote in a classified memo as the Pakistani general prepared to visit Washington late in 1982, President Reagan should "endeavor to convince Zia of his personal interest in these concerns and his sensitivity to Zia's views." Shultz added, "We must remember that without Zia's support, the Afghan resistance, key to making the Soviets pay a heavy price for their Afghan adventure, is effectively dead."[18]

Zia sought and obtained political control over the CIA's weapons and money. He insisted that every gun and dollar allocated for the mujahedin pass through Pakistani hands. He would decide which Afghan guerrillas benefited. He did not want Langley setting up its own Afghan kingmaking operation on Pakistani soil. Zia wanted to run his own hearts-and-minds operation inside Afghanistan. As it happened, this suited the Vietnam-scarred officers at Langley just fine.[19]

For the first four years of its Afghan jihad, the CIA kept its solo operations and contacts with Afghans to a minimum. That was why Hart had sneaked into Peshawar for his initial contact with Abdul Haq. Such direct encounters between CIA officers and Afghan rebels were officially forbidden by Zia's intelligence service. The CIA held the meetings anyway but limited their extent. The agency's main unilateral operations early in the war were aimed at stealing advanced Soviet weaponry off the Afghan battlefield and shipping it back to the United States for examination.

To make his complex liaison with the CIA work, Zia relied on his chief spy and most trusted lieutenant, a gray-eyed and patrician general, Akhtar Abdur Rahman, director-general of ISI. Zia told Akhtar that it was his job to draw the CIA in and hold them at bay. Among other things, Zia felt he needed time. He did not want to take big risks on the Afghan battlefield—risks that might increase Soviet-backed terrorism in Pakistan or prompt a direct military attack. Again and again Zia told Akhtar: "The water in Afghanistan must boil at the right temperature." Zia did not want the Afghan pot to boil over.[20]

ABOUT EVERY OTHER MONTH Howard Hart drove the dozen miles from Islamabad to Rawalpindi to have a meal with General Akhtar at ISI headquarters and catch up on the Afghan jihad. They would talk in Akhtar's office or in a small dining room, attended by servants in starched uniforms. Outside, gardeners trimmed shrubbery or washed sidewalks. Pakistan's army bases were the cleanest and most freshly painted places in the country, conspicuous sanctuaries of green lawns and whitewashed walls.

ISI and the CIA had collaborated secretly for decades, yet mutual suspicion reigned. Akhtar laid down rules to ensure that ISI would retain control over contacts with Afghan rebels. No American—CIA or otherwise—would be permitted to cross the border into Afghanistan. Movements of weapons within Pakistan and distributions to Afghan commanders would be handled strictly by ISI officers. All training of mujahedin would be carried out solely by ISI in camps along the Afghan frontiers. No CIA officers would train Afghans directly, although when new and complex weapons systems were introduced, ISI would permit the CIA to teach its own Pakistani instructors.

Akhtar banned social contact between ISI officers and their CIA counterparts. His men weren't allowed to attend diplomatic functions. ISI officers routinely swept their homes and offices for bugs and talked in crude codes on the telephone. Howard Hart was "H2." Certain weapons in transit might be "apples" or "oranges." The CIA was no more trusting. When Akhtar and his aides visited CIA training facilities in the United States, they were forced to wear blindfolds on the internal flight to the base.[21]

Akhtar himself kept a very low profile. He rarely surfaced on the Islamabad social circuit. He met Hart almost exclusively on ISI's grounds.

He was the son of a Pathan medical doctor from Peshawar, on the Afghan frontier. (*Pathan* is the term used by Pakistanis to refer to members of the Afghan Pashtun tribes that straddle the Afghanistan-Pakistan border.) He had joined the British colonial army in Punjab just before independence, as Zia had done. They had risen through the ranks together, and Zia trusted him. As a young artillery officer Akhtar had been a champion boxer and wrestler. He had grown over the years into a vain, difficult, self-absorbed general who operated within the Pakistani army as Zia's most loyal cohort. "If Zia said, 'It is going to rain frogs tonight,' Akhtar would go out with his frog net," Hart recalled. Zia had appointed him to run ISI in June 1979; Akhtar would hold the position for eight influential years.

"His physique was stocky and tough, his uniform immaculate, with three rows of medal ribbons," recalled an ISI colleague, Mohammed Yousaf. "He had a pale skin, which he proudly attributed to his Afghan ancestry, and he carried his years well. . . . He hated to be photographed, he had no real intimates, and nobody in whom to confide. . . . He was a tough, cold, and a hard general who was sure he knew wrong from right. . . . In fact many of his subordinates disliked him as a martinet."[22]

Hart found Akhtar stubborn and unimaginative, but also quite likable. Akhtar's "self-image was sort of a cross between Genghis Khan and Alexander the Great." The success of Hart's tour as CIA station chief depended on his ability to work effectively with the ISI chief. In spy parlance, Hart sought to recruit Akhtar—not formally, as a paid agent is recruited with money, but informally, as a friend and professional ally.

As the months passed, Hart would ask the colonel who took notes at all of Akhtar's private meetings to leave them alone for what Hart called "executive sessions." Gradually the meetings grew less formal. The core questions they discussed were almost always the same: How much CIA weaponry for the Afghan rebels would Moscow tolerate? How much would Zia tolerate?

ISI's treasury began to swell with CIA and Saudi Arabian subsidies. Head-quartered in an unmarked compound in Rawalpindi, ISI was a rising force across Pakistan. Among other things, the service enforced Zia's ironfisted martial law regime. Its missions included domestic security, covert guerrilla operations, and espionage against India. ISI functioned as a quasi-division of the Pakistan army. It was staffed down the line by army officers and enlisted men. But because ISI's spies were always watching out for troublemakers and potential coup makers within the army, many regular officers regarded the agency with disdain. Akhtar's bullying personality exacerbated its unpopularity within the ranks.

ISI's Afghan bureau, overseen by several brigadiers, managed Pakistan's support for the mujahedin day to day. By 1983 the bureau employed about sixty officers and three hundred noncommissioned officers and enlisted men. It often recruited Pathan majors and colonels who spoke the eastern and southern Afghan language of Pashto. These Pakistani officers belonged to border-straddling tribes and could operate undetected in civilian dress along the frontier or inside Afghan territory. Some officers, especially these Pathans, would make decades-long careers within ISI's Afghan bureau, never transferring to other army units. The bureau was becoming a permanent secret institution.[23]

At their liaison sessions Hart and Akhtar often traded bits of intelligence. Hart might offer a few CIA intercepts of Soviet military communications or reports on battlefield damage in Afghanistan obtained from satellite photography. Akhtar, who had excellent sources inside the Indian government, would half-tease Hart by telling him how, in private, the Indians espoused their disgust with America. "You should hear what they're saying about you," he would say, reading from a tattered folder.

Much of their work involved mundane details of shipping and finance. Congress authorized annual budgets for the CIA's Afghan program in each of the October-to-October fiscal years observed by the U.S. government. The amounts approved soared during Hart's tour in Islamabad, from about $30 million in fiscal 1981 to about $200 million in fiscal 1984. Under an agreement negotiated between the Saudi royal family and President Reagan—designed to seal the anticommunist, oil-smoothed alliance between Washington and Riyadh—Saudi Arabia effectively doubled those numbers by agreeing to match the CIA's aid dollar for dollar. (Still, the CIA's Afghan program paled beside the Soviet Union's aid to Kabul's communists, which totaled just over $1 billion in 1980 alone and continued to grow.[24]) Hart consulted with Akhtar as each new fiscal year approached. They would draw up lists of weapons needed by the Afghan rebels, and Hart would cable the orders to Langley. Their careful plans were often overtaken by obscure funding deals struck secretly in Congress just as a fiscal year ended. Suddenly a huge surge of weapons would be approved for Pakistan, taxing ISI's storage and transport capabilities. Hart's case officers and their ISI counterparts had to get the weapons across to the Afghan frontier.

New and more potent weapons began to pour in. From hundreds of thousands of Lee Enfield .303s they branched out to Chinese-made AK-47s, despite Hart's reservations about the rifle. They bought RPG-7s in vast quantities, 60-millimeter Chinese mortars, and 12.7-millimeter heavy machine guns in batches of two thousand or more. Hart bought ISI a fleet of trucks to roll at night down the Grand Trunk Road from Rawalpindi depots to warehouses along the Afghan frontier.

There was so much cash washing through the system by 1983 that it was hard for Hart to be sure who was making a reasonable profit and who was ripping off the CIA. The headquarters task force that made the purchases prided itself on buying communist weapons through global arms markets and putting them into the hands of anticommunist Afghans. Dissident Polish army officers accepted payoffs to sell surplus Soviet weaponry in secret to the CIA. The agency then shipped the Polish guns to Afghanistan for use against Soviet troops. The Chinese communists cleared huge profit margins on weapons they sold in deals negotiated by the CIA station in Beijing. Tens of millions of dollars in arms deals annually cemented a growing secret anti-Soviet collaboration between the CIA and Chinese intelligence. (The Chinese communists had broken with the Soviet communists during the early 1960s and were now mortal rivals. "Can it possibly be any better than buying bullets from the Chinese to use to shoot Russians?" asked one CIA officer involved in the Afghan program.) American allies in the Third World jumped in just to make a buck. The Egyptians were selling the CIA junky stores of old weapons previously sold to them by the Soviets. Turkey sold sixty thousand rifles, eight thousand light machine guns, ten thousand pistols, and 100 million rounds of ammunition—mainly of 1940–42 vintage. ISI logistics officers grumbled but accepted them.[25]

Hart knew the Pakistanis were stealing from the till but thought the thefts were modest and reasonable. The Pakistani army was perhaps the least corrupt organization in the country, which might not be saying a lot, but it was some solace. Anyway, Hart felt there was little choice but to hand over unaccountable cash in a covert program like this one. Either you thought the larger goals of the program justified the expense or you didn't; you couldn't fuss over it like a bank auditor. ISI needed money to run training programs for the mujahedin, for example. Zia's government was genuinely strapped. If the CIA wanted thousands of Afghan rebels to learn how to use their new weapons properly, there had to be stipends for Pakistani trainers, cooks, and drivers. The CIA could hardly set up this kind of payroll itself. By 1983, Hart and his supervisors in Langley felt they had no choice but to turn millions of dollars over to Akhtar and then monitor the results at the training camps themselves, hoping that the "commission" stripped from these training funds by the ISI was relatively modest. Saudi Arabia was pumping cash into ISI as well, and the Saudis were even less attentive to where it ended up.

To try to detect any large-scale weapons thefts, the CIA recruited Abdul Haq and a few other Afghan contacts to monitor gun prices in the open markets along the Afghan frontier. If .303 or AK-47 prices fell dramatically, that would indicate that CIA-supplied weapons were being dumped for cash.

Still, the Pakistanis beat the CIA's systems. In Quetta in 1983, ISI officers were caught colluding with Afghan rebels to profit by selling off CIA-supplied weapons. In another instance, the Pakistan army quietly sold the CIA its own surplus .303 rifles and about 30 million bullets. A ship registered in Singapore picked up about 100,000 guns in Karachi, steamed out to sea, turned around, came back to port, and off-loaded the guns, pretending they had come from abroad. The scheme was discovered—the bullets were still marked "POF," for "Pakistan Ordnance Factory." ISI had to pay to scrub the Pakistani bullets of their markings, so if they were used in Afghanistan and picked up by the Soviets, they couldn't be exploited by the communists as evidence of Pakistani support for the mujahedin.[26]

Akhtar, who seemed embarrassed about the scale of the skimming, told Hart that he was going to organize a more formal system of weapons distribution, using ISI-backed Afghan political parties to hand them out. That way ISI could hold the Afghan party leaders accountable. It was also a way for ISI to exercise more control over which Afghan guerrilla leaders would receive the most weaponry and become the most powerful.

Many of ISI's favored Afghan leaders, such as Gulbuddin Hekmatyar, were Muslim Brotherhood–linked Islamists. Especially after 1983, Akhtar and his colleagues tended to freeze out traditional Afghan royalty and tribal leaders, depriving them of weapons. Akhtar told Hart this was because the Pashtun royalists didn't fight vigorously enough. As with every other facet of the covert war, the CIA accepted ISI's approach with little dissent. Hart and his colleagues believed the policy not only agreed with Zia's personal faith, but it weakened the Afghan rebels most likely to stir up Pashtun nationalism inside Pakistani territory.[27]

Hart wanted the CIA's supplies to reach Afghan commanders who would fight the Soviets hard, whatever their religious outlook. "Have you ever met anyone who could unite them all?" Hart asked Akhtar, as Hart recalled it. "You're going to try to bring your power of the purse, meaning guns and some money, to force them into something? Fine, if you can, but don't put too much reliance on it."

By 1983 some diplomats within the U.S. embassy in Islamabad had begun to worry that the CIA's dependence on ISI was creating disunity within the Afghan resistance. "A change in approach would probably require some differentiation of our policy from that of Pakistan," a Secret cable from the embassy to the State Department reported. "Since the Soviet invasion of Afghanistan, we have largely been content to follow Pakistan's lead."[28]

But few within the U.S. government could see any reason to question the CIA's heavy dependence on ISI. The Soviets were becoming bogged down in Afghanistan. The war continued to embarrass Moscow internationally. And by 1983 the CIA's covert action program had become cost effective, according to Hart's calculations, which he cabled to Langley. The money allocated secretly by Congress each year for weapons for the mujahedin was destroying Soviet equipment and personnel worth eight to ten times that amount or more, Hart reported.

"Howard, how can you help these people when, in the end, they will all be killed or destroyed by the Soviets?" Senator Daniel Patrick Moynihan asked Hart during a visit to Pakistan.

"Senator," Hart replied, "what they are saying to us is Winston Churchill: 'Give us the tools and we will do the job.'"

HART DECIDED to see Afghanistan for himself. Strictly speaking, this was illegal. Hart knew he would be reprimanded or fired if he was caught, but this was the sort of thing a proper CIA station chief just up and did on his own. It was part of the D.O.'s culture. Hart had gotten close to Abdul Haq since their initial meeting in Peshawar, and Haq assured him that they could make a quick tour inside with very little risk. Abdul Haq's guerrillas ruled the roads and the footpaths, especially in the mountain ravines just above Peshawar. They traveled in Toyota Land Cruisers in heavily armed groups. At night they were especially secure because the Soviets rarely operated in the dark.

Hart worked out a plan to leave his deputy in charge of the station for a few days. He headed toward the frontier in Abdul Haq's jeep, armed. He would be introduced to other Afghans as a Canadian journalist. Hart worked out his excuses to CIA headquarters in advance: He was traveling up *near* the border with Abdul Haq to inspect weapons supplies. The terrain was unmarked, and accidentally, regrettably, they had strayed into Afghanistan.

He traveled several miles across the border with a group of about fifty well-equipped mujahedin. They camped at night and met visiting rebel delegations. The conversation was all in Pashto or Dari and had to be translated for Hart's benefit. Sitting on a rock while bearded, turbaned rebels chattered all around, Hart felt as if he were in some sort of movie. He marveled at the lines of Afghan men wandering past in the cold, shuffling in groups of ten or twenty, barely covered against the chill, some confessing quietly that they had not eaten in two days.

Soviet aerial bombing and road attacks meant it was difficult for the mujahedin to secure steady food supplies, Hart learned. There were few markets outside of the main cities, and the rebels had little cash. "I remember I was terribly embarrassed that night, because they all looked at me, and they thought I was a newspaper man, so they just ignored me. . . . I really wanted to give the guys some money, because they had nothing. They had been walking for weeks."

The mujahedin exploited the darkness to move in and out of Pakistan, and to set up ambushes. They lit no fires. The bread and tea were cold. This was the real war, Hart reflected, the war so many Afghans knew, a brutal grassroots national struggle fought among rocks and boulders. It was a war fueled by the two superpowers but also indifferent to them.

For a D.O. case officer, Hart's Islamabad tour was about as good as it got. There had been no public scandals. He had worked Akhtar and the ISI liaison successfully. In Langley his career would get a lift from an excellent report card. "Howard's relations with General Akhtar are close and productive concerning Afghanistan," Ambassador Dean Hinton, Spiers's successor, wrote in a classified evaluation letter as Hart prepared to go. "On the other hand, Howard runs an extraordinary intelligence collection operation against Pakistan. . . . His collection efforts on the Pakistani effort to develop nuclear weapons is amazingly successful and disturbing. I would sleep better if he and his people did not find out so much about what is really going on in secret and contrary to President Zia's assurances to us."[29]

Ship after ship, truck convoy after truck convoy, the CIA's covert supplies to the Afghan frontier had surged to unprecedented levels during Hart's tour. The program was hardly a secret anymore, either. President Reagan had begun to hint openly that America was aiding the Afghan "freedom fighters." Journalists from the United States and Europe traveled inside Afghanistan with mujahedin escorts. Their stories made clear that the rebels were receiving substantial outside help.

Still, Zia maintained his public denials. In private he continued to fear Soviet retaliation against Pakistan. Hardly a meeting with Hart or other CIA officers could pass without the dictator bringing up his metaphor about the need to keep the Afghan pot simmering at just the right temperature—to prevent it from boiling over. At their liaison meetings at ISI headquarters Hart and Akhtar began to turn the metaphor into a private joke. More wood on the fire! they would say to each other as they scrawled out weapons orders on their requisition forms.

Hart now believed the Soviets were not prepared to reinforce their occupying forces in Afghanistan enough to make a serious thrust into Pakistan. "The fuckers haven't got the balls, they aren't going to do it," he concluded. "It is not going to happen, boys and girls, so don't worry about it." The CIA was winning. It could afford to press its advantage.

4

"I Loved Osama"

I T WAS BRAND NEW, imported from the United States in wooden boxes, and it was very heavy. Along with his personal luggage, Ahmed Badeeb checked about $1.8 million in American cash on a Saudia Airlines commercial flight to Karachi, and as soon as he collected his bags in Pakistan, he regretted the absence of a trusted porter. He felt his muscles bulging under the strain. To reach Islamabad, Badeeb had to transfer to a domestic Pakistan International Airlines flight. Customs officials and security guards wanted to search his bags by hand. He was a lively man who was quick with an off-color joke, and he began to filibuster in front of the security tables. *These are very important documents; I cannot show them to anyone.* Fine, the guards said. We'll put the boxes through the X-ray machine. Fearing the consequences of exposure—for himself and for the cash if it was discovered by poorly paid Pakistani customs officers—Badeeb began chattering again. *I have very important films in here; if you put them in the X-ray, they will burn.* Finally, they let him pass. He heaved his boxes across the check-in counter. Landing in Islamabad, he was relieved to see that his mission had attracted a high-ranking reception party. General Akhtar Abdur Rahman, the ISI chief, welcomed Badeeb as he came off the plane.

In his midthirties when the anti-Soviet jihad gathered force in the early 1980s, Ahmed Badeeb was a desert-born Saudi Arabian who had attended an American college in the snow-swept plains of North Dakota. He had worked for a time as a teacher employed by the Saudi ministry of education. One of his pupils had been an earnest young man named Osama bin Laden. They had become friends. Ahmed Badeeb was a stout, bearded man with dark skin and a natural, boisterous confidence. By dint of luck, family connections, and the generous machinery of Saudi government patronage, he had lately graduated from academia to become chief of staff to the director of the General Intelligence Department of the Kingdom of Saudi Arabia.[1]

Soon after the Soviet invasion of Afghanistan, Prince Turki al-Faisal, the chief of Saudi intelligence, dispatched Badeeb to Pakistan with the kingdom's calling card: cash dollars. The Saudi intelligence service—along with Saudi charities whose funds the spy agency sometimes directed—was becoming ISI's most generous patron, even more so than the CIA.

Akhtar led Ahmed Badeeb to a meeting with President Zia in Rawalpindi. Badeeb announced that Saudi Arabia had decided to supply cash to ISI so that the Pakistani intelligence service could buy precision-made rocket-propelled grenade launchers from China, among other weapons. Badeeb's cash would be the first of many installments.

As Zia and Badeeb talked that night, five ISI generals pried open Badeeb's boxes in an adjoining room and began to count the money, as Badeeb recalled it. He tried to keep half an eye on them while maintaining polite conversation with the Pakistani president. "Excuse me, Mr. President, I have to see if the generals are . . ."

"It's counted!" he told them in the other room, half-joking. "It's brand new! The serial numbers are there!"

A Saudi spy quickly became accustomed to being treated like a bank teller. "We don't do operations," Prince Turki once told a CIA colleague from the D.O.'s Near East Division. "We don't know how. All we know how to do is write checks."[2]

As it did in Langley, the Soviet invasion of Afghanistan had a galvanizing impact in the headquarters of the Saudi General Intelligence Department, or GID, the desert kingdom's main external spy service. Saudi Arabia's deeply religious Bedouin royal family viewed Soviet communism as heresy. A Soviet drive toward the Persian Gulf threatened the Saudi elite's oil wealth. Leading Saudi princes embraced the American view of Pakistan as a frontline state in the worldwide effort to contain Soviet ambitions. And beyond statecraft, Turki and Akhtar "both believed fervently in the importance of an Islamic brother-hood which ignored territorial frontiers," as one of Akhtar's senior aides put it. After the upheavals of 1979, Crown Prince Fahd, soon to become king, saw Pakistan as Saudi Arabia's most muscular, reliable ally on its eastern flank. He authorized his intelligence service to open its bountiful treasury to Akhtar's ISI.[3]

The clandestine alliance between Saudi Arabia and Pakistan was grounded in history. Each was a young, insecure nation that saw Islam as central to its identity. Pakistani troops had been hired by the Saudis in the past for security deployments in the kingdom. The Saudi air force had secretly provided air cover over Karachi during Pakistan's 1971 war with India.[4]

Until the early 1980s, the Saudi spy service played a limited role. The General Intelligence Department had been for many years a weak and unprofessional organization. It had been built around royal family connections. Modern Saudi Arabia's founding monarch, King Abdul Aziz ibn Saud, who had forty-one children by seventeen wives and reigned from 1902 until his death in 1953, at one stage dispatched one of his older sons, Faisal, to Turkey to evaluate a marriageable woman with royal lineage. Faisal ended up marrying the woman himself. His new wife's wealthy Turkish half-brother, Kamal Adham, who had connections across the Arab world, was appointed during the 1960s as Saudi Arabia's founding spy chief. Adham opened GID offices in embassies abroad. He was fired during the mid-1970s and replaced by his worldly young nephew, Prince Turki al-Faisal. It was an appointment typical of Saudi politics, where maintaining balance among restive royal family clans was imperative.[5] From this semiaccidental beginning Prince Turki went on to hold the GID directorship for more than two decades, becoming one of the longest-serving and most influential intelligence operatives on the world stage.

As much as any individual, Prince Turki became an architect of Afghanistan's destiny—and of American engagements with Islamic radicalism—in the two decades after 1979. He picked winners and losers among Afghan commanders, he funded Islamist revolutionaries across the Middle East, he created alliances among these movements, and he paid large subsidies to the Pakistan intelligence service, aiding its rise as a kind of shadow government.

A champion of Saudi Arabia's austere Islam, a promoter of women's rights, a multimillionaire, a workaholic, a pious man, a sipper of banana daiquiris, an intriguer, an intellectual, a loyal prince, a sincere friend of Americans, a generous funder of anti-American causes, Prince Turki embodied Saudi Arabia's cascading contradictions. His spy agency became an important liaison as the CIA confronted communism and, later, militant Islam. At least as much as Pakistan's ISI, the Saudi intelligence agency that Prince Turki built became the chalice—sometimes poisoned, sometimes sweet—from which the CIA's Near East and counterterrorist officers believed they had no choice but to drink.

PRINCE TURKI AL-FAISAL was born in the Kingdom of Saudi Arabia on February 15, 1945, the day after Saudi King Abdul Aziz boarded an American warship anchored in the Red Sea to meet for the first time the president of the United States, Franklin Roosevelt, who was returning from Yalta.

The Bedouin king brought aboard his own herd of sheep so that he could slaughter them at mealtimes. He watched newsreels of American soldiers in action and befuddled his hosts by then sleeping for long and unpredictable

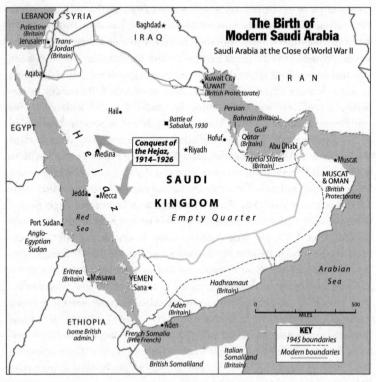

Credit: Richard Furno

hours. Yet Roosevelt, who even before the Nazi surrender sought allies for the postwar world, made a favorable impression on him. They discussed Palestine and oil. Abdul Aziz knew relatively little of the world, but he identified with the Arab struggle against the Zionists. Roosevelt's agents on the Arabian peninsula, some of them oil prospectors, had begun to glimpse the vast wealth sloshing beneath the sands. They had urged their president to embrace the Saudi royals before the British wheedled in, and Roosevelt did, flattering Abdul Aziz as best he could and winning limited pledges of military and economic cooperation.

The al-Sauds, the royal family Abdul Aziz led, had largely evaded colonial subjugation. They lived in an area so bleak and isolated that it did not interest European powers. They first burst out of the hot empty deserts of the central Nejd region in the eighteenth century to wage tribal war. The Arabian peninsula then was a severe, poor, sparsely inhabited wasteland of camel-breeding nomads. The nearest thing to civilization was Jedda, a desultory trading port of the Ottoman Empire that had become a modest prize in colonial competitions. Few of its urbane residents dared to venture far from the Red Sea. The interior lands were scorching, and the local tribes were unforgiving. Muslim pilgrims did flock inland each year to Mecca and Medina, but they had to beware of robbery and extortion on the roads.

The al-Sauds were but one militia among many until they forged a fateful alliance with an austere and martial desert preacher, Mohammed ibn Abdul Wahhab. The decorous, arty, tobacco-smoking, hashish-imbibing, music-happy, drum-pounding Egyptian and Ottoman nobility who traveled across Arabia to pray at Mecca each year angered Wahhab deeply. In his personal reading of the Koran, the Ottoman pilgrims were not the Muslims they claimed to be but were blasphemous polytheists, worshipers of false idols. Local Arabs also aggravated Wahhab by honoring saints with monuments or decorated gravestones, and by mixing Islam with animist superstitions. All this Wahhab denounced as *bida,* forbidden by God. People who worshiped graven images lived outside Allah's true community. They were Allah's enemies, and they should be converted or destroyed. Wahhab won the allegiance of the al-Saud tribes to his theology—or they won him to their political cause, depending on which family recounts the history. Either way, Wahhab's proselytizing merged with the al-Sauds' military ambition. When the united religious militia overran an oasis, they destroyed grave markers and holy trees and spread the unforgiving word of Allah as interpreted by Wahhab. At one point Wahhab came across a woman accused of fornication and ordered her stoned to death. The preacher's fearsome legend spread.

Honored with great tracts of land for his righteousness, Wahhab ultimately retreated to a life of religious contemplation and multiple marriages. After his death the Egyptians surged onto the peninsula and pushed his descendants— and the al-Saud tribes—back into the empty Nejd. (The vengeance-minded Egyptians executed one of Wahhab's grandsons after forcing him to listen to music from a one-stringed violin.) There the Saudis languished for most of the nineteenth century, herding animals and nursing grievances.

They roared back to the Red Sea when the Ottoman Empire collapsed amid the chaos of World War I. The al-Sauds were led this time by their extraordinary commander Abdul Aziz, a laconic and skillful emir who united the peninsula's fractious Bedouin tribes through military courage and political acumen. "His deliberate movements, his slow, sweet smile, and the contemplative glance of his heavy-lidded eyes, though they add to his dignity and charm, do not accord with the Western conception of a vigorous personality," wrote a British traveler who encountered the king. "Nevertheless, report credits him with powers of physical endurance rare even in hard-bitten Arabia."[6] Abdul Aziz embraced Wahhabi doctrine. He sponsored a new, fierce, semi-independent vanguard of *Ikhwan,* or Brothers, war-fighting believers who dressed in distinctive white turbans and trimmed their beards and mustaches to express Islamic solidarity. The Ikhwan conquered village after village, town after town. In Wahhab's name they enforced bans on alcohol, tobacco, embroidered silk, gambling, fortune-telling, and magic. They denounced telephones, radios, and automobiles as affronts to God's law. When a motor truck first appeared in their territory, they set it on fire and sent its driver fleeing on foot.

Abdul Aziz skillfully employed the Ikhwan to capture Mecca, Medina, and Jedda between 1914 and 1926. But the king soon felt threatened by the brotherhood's unquenchable radicalism. The Ikhwan revolted, and Abdul Aziz put them down with modern machine guns. To outflank the brotherhood's popular appeal to Islamic righteousness, Abdul Aziz founded the Saudi religious police, organized eventually as the Ministry for the Propagation of Virtue and the Prevention of Vice. The king delared that his royal family would govern strictly by the doctrines of Wahhab, enforcing a severe and patriarchal piety shorn of adornment.

It was the debut of a strategy employed by the Saudi royal family throughout the twentieth century: Threatened by Islamic radicalism, they embraced it, hoping to retain control. The al-Sauds' claims to power on the Arabian peninsula were weak and grew largely from conquests made by allied jihadists. They now ruled the holiest shrines in worldwide Islam. There seemed to them no plausible politics but strict official religiosity. Many among the royal family were themselves true believers. Theirs was, after all, the only modern nation-state created by jihad.[7]

Prince Turki al-Faisal, the future spy chief, grew up less than a generation after the Saudi nation's awkward blood-soaked birth. He came of age before the kingdom's great boom in oil revenues, before its accompanying modernization drives, before the hastily laid ribbons of California-style freeways and the indoor shopping malls. In the mid-1950s, when Turki was a boy, two-thirds of Saudi Arabians were still nomads or semi-nomads. Less than a quarter lived in cities or towns. Even in the mid-1960s half of Saudi Arabians earned their living from animal husbandry. Slavery was banned only in 1962. Africans and Asians continued to be indentured informally in Saudi households for years afterward. Traditional Bedouin nomad culture viewed settled labor with contempt. Americans and other foreigners were beginning to drill for oil in the eastern provinces, and the first investments in roads and telephone lines had begun, but the kingdom of Turki's childhood was still largely an impoverished land of wanderers, tent-dwellers, camel-breeders, and preaching mullahs, all ruled by a shaky alliance between a privileged royal family and its righteous *ulama,* or senior Islamic clergy.[8]

In this unmodern landscape Prince Turki's father, Prince Faisal, was a relatively modern man. He was a hardworking nationalist, well read, and a leading technocrat and government reformer among Abdul Aziz's older sons, some of whom had little education and sybaritic appetites. Prince Faisal believed in balanced budgets, social investments, and the benefits of technology. He also embraced Wahhabi Islam and argued that the kingdom should pursue social change slowly and carefully. An experienced provincial governor, he seemed destined for the Saudi throne and expected his sons to prepare for serious lives. This meant an American education.

Faisal dispatched Prince Turki at age fourteen to Lawrenceville School, a preparatory and boarding school for wealthy boys in New Jersey. To call the young Turki's transition to prep school a culture shock would hardly do it justice. "I was alone," Turki recalled years later. "I was extremely nervous. . . . As I entered the dormitory, I felt somebody's hand slapping me on my backside." A young man called out to him, "Hi. My name is Steve Callahan. Who are you?" Turki stood in stunned silence "because in Saudi Arabia, you never hit anybody on the backside." Finally he offered his name. Callahan replied, "Oh. Like a Thanksgiving turkey?"[9]

In later years Turki rarely spoke in public, and more rarely still did he speak of his inner life, so it is difficult to know what impressions he had of America, traumatic or favorable or both, from Lawrenceville. Barely an adolescent, Turki had been sent oceans away from home, catapulted from an isolated kingdom of austere Islamic ritual to an American world of football, sex, and beer. At least his fellow Lawrenceville students had wealth, as he did. There were some other foreign students as well; Turki's prep school classmates included a future president of Honduras.

Back in the kingdom, his father entered a tenacious struggle with his older half-brother, Saud, the first of Abdul Aziz's sons to succeed to the throne after the great patriarch's death. By taking many wives and siring many sons Abdul Aziz created multiple competing branches within the royal family. Confused power struggles erupted as soon as he was gone. Saud's spendthrift ways exacerbated the trouble. The oil bubbled and the dollars began to flow, but Saud and his retainers managed to spend it all and then some on palaces, shopping sprees, and poorly managed development projects. In search of order, the family arranged for Prince Faisal's appointment as crown prince. But Saud resented him, and in frustration Faisal resigned his office while Turki was still at Lawrenceville.

Prepped in the American East Coast manner, Turki matriculated at Georgetown University in Washington, D.C., in 1964, a member of the same class as an ambitious, talkative boy from Hope, Arkansas, named Bill Clinton. In a rare breakdown of Clinton's networking radar, he failed to seek out and befriend a rich crown prince's son destined for power. (The pair met for the first time at the White House soon after Clinton became president.) Years later Turki told a reunion at Georgetown, referring to Clinton's infamous claim that he had tried marijuana but never inhaled, "It wasn't just the class that didn't inhale. It was the class that tried to smoke banana peels. Do you remember that? I promise you, can anybody imagine smoking a banana peel? But those were the days."[10]

On campus someone approached Turki during his freshman year and asked, "Did you hear the news?" Turki said he had not. "Oh, your father has become king."

Saud had finally relinquished his crown. Georgetown's dean called Turki in and asked if he wanted a security detail. Turki declined because, as he later put it wryly, "I'd never have anybody following me in those days, especially at Georgetown."[11]

He left the university after his junior year. He said later it was because he was upset and disillusioned by the Arab defeat by Israel in the Six Day War of 1967. "You can't imagine the state of total depression and sense of failure that struck the Arab world." A few years later he finished his education in England. Turki found employment as a counselor in a government ministry before following his uncle as director of the GID.

By then Turki's father lay dead of an assassin's bullet. Two years after he shocked America by leading the anti-Israel oil boycott that sent global energy prices soaring, King Faisal was murdered by an aggrieved, deranged cousin. His killing had roots in the kingdom's struggles over modernization. In 1965, Saudi television debuted, and Wahhabi radicals stormed a government studio in violent protest. One of the protestors, a cousin of King Faisal, died in the shootout. A decade later, on March 25, 1975, the victim's brother leveled a pistol at the king during a local festival and shot him to death in apparent revenge. Turki had lost his father to a terrorist act at least partially derived from Saudi Arabia's attempt to marry postindustrial development with regressive Islamic orthodoxy. "It was," Turki said later, without elaborating, "the most painful thing."[12]

As PRINCE TURKI took charge in the late 1970s, the Saudi intelligence service was in the throes of a massive expansion. Gushing oil revenue poured into every bureaucratic nook and cranny in the kingdom. Saudi Arabia's five-year government budget from 1969 to 1974 was $9.2 billion. During the next five years it was $142 billion. Just a generation removed from nomadic poverty, the kingdom was on a forced march to the computer age. Turki wired up the General Intelligence Department offices inside the kingdom and in thirty-two embassies and consulates abroad. All the software, however, failed to detect the violent plot by the crazed Juhayman al-Utaybi to seize Mecca in November 1979. With its echoes of the Ikhwan revolt put down by Abdul Aziz, the Mecca uprising rattled all of the Saudi security agencies. It also helped convince the royal family that it needed to invest heavily in spies and police.[13]

Not only the Saudis worried. After the Shah of Iran's fall, the American intelligence community feared the Saudi royal family might be next. The CIA station in Jedda tried to improve its reporting on the kingdom's opaque internal politics. The Mecca uprising only emphasized how little the agency knew about Islamic radicalism on the peninsula. One way to deepen access was to cozy up to the Saudi spy service by providing technical assistance. After 1979 the CIA's station in Saudi Arabia redoubled its efforts to recruit sources in the kingdom unilaterally. At the same time, as part of its official liaison, the CIA helped GID with its computer system and also with a sensitive program to capture electronic intercepts from Soviet sources.[14]

Turki and his aides traveled to Langley as well as European and Arab capitals to study how other intelligence agencies were organized. As he built GID, he copied the CIA's blueprint. Prince Turki was the agency's non-cabinet-level director. Immediately beneath him were half a dozen directorates. As at Langley, one of these was the Directorate of Operations, which carried out covert action and liaisons with foreign intelligence agencies. Turki also organized a Directorate of Intelligence, which produced classified reports for the Saudi royal family about security issues. His Directorate of Intelligence even circulated a daily intelligence digest for the Saudi king and crown prince, mirroring the President's Daily Brief circulated at the White House by the CIA.[15]

His impeccable English, his polite manner, his sly humor, his elegant taste for luxury, his serious reading of history, and, above all, his rare ability to navigate between Saudi Arabia and the West—and to interpret each for the other—helped ingratiate Prince Turki with the Americans. He was an unassuming man who spoke softly but with a sweeping, cogent confidence. One Arabic-speaking CIA officer who worked with him described Turki as the most accomplished, nuanced interpreter of the English language into Arabic that he had ever met. Turki consumed Western news sources voraciously. He became a regular delegate to the annual gatherings of the international elite in Davos, Switzerland, and other off-the-record conferences devoted to finance, strategy, and the global balance of power. At the same time some at the CIA recognized that Turki was a master manipulator. "He was deceitful," recalled Clair George, a senior officer in the CIA's clandestine service who eventually ran the agency's Directorate of Operations. The scale of wealth Turki seemed to acquire on the job stunned his American counterparts. As George put it, "You're not going to find somebody to run their intelligence service who hasn't stolen a lot of money." Of course, in the Saudi system, there were no clear lines between government funds, royal wealth, and private wealth. All the senior princes in the kingdom enriched themselves. Turki used GID's funds not only to live well but to recruit American and European friends willing to defend Saudi interests. When CIA station chiefs, State Department diplomats, or MI6 officers with experience in Saudi Arabia retired or left government service, many landed on the GID payroll as Turki's well-paid private consultants, his eyes and ears in Washington, London, and elsewhere. Turki also systematically subsidized intelligence services in poorer Arab countries, buying information and allies.[16]

Ahmed Badeeb and his brother Saeed were two of Turki's key aides. Their father had been a modestly successful merchant in Jedda. Ahmed Badeeb was an energetic operator, working as Turki's advance man, bag man, and operational surrogate. Saeed was milder, bespectacled, and bookish. He earned a Ph.D. at George Washington University in Washington, D.C., during the early 1980s and then returned to his post as chief of the GID's Directorate of Intelligence. He wrote his doctoral thesis on Saudi relations with Yemen and Egypt, and published a book about Saudi relations with Iran. Both Badeeb brothers interacted regularly with CIA counterparts.[17]

The Saudi royals, so hostile to Marxist atheism that they did not even maintain diplomatic relations with the Soviets, had quietly collaborated with the CIA against Moscow for decades. During the annual *hajj* season (the pilgrimage to Mecca made in the twelfth month of the Muslim year), the Saudis arranged for CIA officers to interview Muslim pilgrims from Soviet Central Asia about conditions back home. During the 1970s, when CIA covert operations were inhibited by scandals in Congress and caution at the White House, Turki's GID joined Britain, France, Morocco, and Iran to form a "Safari Club" that worked covertly against Soviet-backed Marxist movements in Africa.[18]

When the Soviets invaded Afghanistan, Turki quickly reached out to Pakistan. The ISI's Akhtar flew to the kingdom within weeks and met with Turki and Ahmed Badeeb at a restaurant in Riyadh. Akhtar carried a message from President Zia warning that Saudi Arabia itself faced danger if the Soviet incursion wasn't checked. Soon Badeeb began his shuttle to Islamabad and Peshawar, sometimes hauling his wooden boxes of cash.

Turki believed that the Soviet invasion signaled a drive by Moscow to establish strategic parity with the United States in the Middle East. Until recently arms sales had been the communists' primary calling card in the Arab world. Now the Soviet Union was looking to gain more influence over oil prices and supplies. Occupying Afghanistan was not per se a Soviet objective, he concluded, but a step toward increasing its power in the region through proxy communist parties and leftist movements. Geographically, Turki thought, Pakistan offered the best path to confront Soviet ambitions. Aid to the Afghan rebels channeled through Pakistan's army and intelligence service would also helpfully strengthen Pakistan as a regional ally after the devastation of its war with India in 1971.[19]

Turki reached a formal agreement with the CIA in July 1980 to match U.S.

congressional funding for the Afghan rebels. Each year the Saudis sent their part of the money to their embassy in Washington. The Saudi ambassador in Washington, Bandar bin Sultan, then transferred the funds to a Swiss bank account controlled by the CIA. The agency used its Swiss account to make its covert purchases on the international arms markets. Langley's Near East Division, which handled the Saudi liaison, had to continually haggle with Turki's GID over late payments. Once the money was pried out of Riyadh's treasury and transferred to Washington, Bandar would often hold on to the funds for weeks. Near East Division officers speculated that Bandar used the delays to enrich his embassy or himself with "the float," the millions of dollars of interest that piled up daily from the Saudis' enormous mujahedin-bound bank deposits.[20]

Turki took a personal interest in the Afghan program, traveling to Pakistan up to five times a month. Turki "did not object [to] entering into Afghanistan," Ahmed Badeeb recalled. The Saudi prince made a favorable impression on Pakistan's ISI brigadiers, his main partners on the Afghan frontier. "Although his character was formed by his aristocratic upbringing, he was the most humble and modest Arab prince I ever met," recalled Mohammed Yousaf, who directed ISI operations for four years during the mid-1980s. "His education and experience in the West made him completely free of the common Arab prejudices toward non-Arabs."[21]

ABDURRAB RASUL SAYYAF became the Saudis' most important client among the mujahedin rebels. A hulking former professor of Islamic law at Kabul University who maintained a long white-flecked beard, Sayyaf had lived for years in Cairo, where he acquired florid and impeccable Arabic. Crackdowns by the Afghan secret police, including a lengthy prison sentence, forced him into exile in Pakistan.

As Prince Turki's GID began to penetrate the Afghan jihad in 1980, the Organization of the Islamic Conference, an alliance of Muslim governments, held a major summit in Saudi Arabia, in the resort town of Taif. The Saudis wanted the conference to condemn Soviet interference in Afghanistan. Yasser Arafat, then backing many leftist causes, planned to speak in Moscow's defense. Afghan rebel leaders flew in from Peshawar to appeal for their cause. Ahmed Badeeb was assigned to select just one of the mujahedin leaders to make a speech, right after Arafat, attacking the Soviet invasion as an affront to Islam.

Several Afghan rebel leaders spoke passable Arabic, but Badeeb found that Sayyaf, then an assistant to another leader, was by far the most fluent and effective. "We chose him to give the speech," Badeeb recalled later. Immediately, however, the Afghan leaders began to "fight among themselves. Unbelievable guys. . . . Everyone was claiming that he represents the Afghans and he should give the speech." The scene became so unruly that Badeeb decided to lock all of them in a Taif prison until they agreed on a single speaker.

After six hours of jailhouse debate, the Afghans accepted Sayyaf. Badeeb then decided that his client needed a better stage name. As he recalled it, Sayyaf had been introduced to him as "Abdul Rasur Sayyaf." The first two names, he said, translated to Saudis as "Slave of the Prophet," suggesting that Sayyaf's ancestors had been indentured servants. By adding "Abdur" to the name Badeeb altered its meaning to "Slave of the God of the Prophet," suggesting religious devotion, not low social status. For years Badeeb was proud that Saudi intelligence had literally given Sayyaf his name.[22]

An emboldened Sayyaf returned to Peshawar and formed his own Afghan rebel party, drawing on Saudi cash. Sayyaf promoted Wahhabi doctrine among the rebels and provided GID with access to the war independent of ISI control.

Sayyaf also offered GID a means to compete for Afghan influence against Saudi Arabia's wealthy Wahhabi clerics. Sheikh Abdul bin Baz, the head of the kingdom's official religious establishment and a descendant of the Wahhabi sect's founder, had his own mujahedin clients. Bin Baz managed charities that sent millions of dollars and hundreds of volunteer Arab fighters to help an austere Afghan religious leader, Jamil al-Rahman, who had set up a small Wahhabi-inspired "emirate" in an isolated valley of Afghanistan's Kunar province. Badeeb saw Sayyaf as the GID-backed alternative to this and other rival Wahhabi groups.

The Saudi spy service's murky mix of alliance and rivalry with the kingdom's Islamic *ulama* (scholars of Islamic law) became a defining feature of the Afghan jihad as it swelled during the 1980s.

Middle-class, pious Saudis flush with oil wealth embraced the Afghan cause as American churchgoers might respond to an African famine or a Turkish earthquake. Charity is a compulsion of Islamic law. The money flowing from the kingdom arrived at the Afghan frontier in all shapes and sizes: gold jewelry dropped on offering plates by merchants' wives in Jedda mosques; bags of cash delivered by businessmen to Riyadh charities as *zakat*, an annual Islamic tithe; fat checks written from semiofficial government accounts by minor Saudi princes; bountiful proceeds raised in annual telethons led by Prince Salman, the governor of Riyadh; and richest of all, the annual transfers from GID to the CIA's Swiss bank accounts.

Prince Turki said years later that GID often controlled who among the Afghans was authorized to receive the semiofficial and unofficial charity funds, but it was never clear how effectively the spy service oversaw the *ulama*-run charities. There was relatively little supervision during the early and mid-1980s, a lack of control that Badeeb later regretted.[23]

Even more ambiguous than the money trail was the legion of Saudis flocking to join or support the Afghan jihad. It was rarely clear who was acting as a formal agent of the kingdom's intelligence service and who was acting as an independent religious volunteer. To the Pakistani generals and American intelligence officers who came to know of him, no Saudi more embodied that mystery than Ahmed Badeeb's former pupil from Jedda, Osama bin Laden.

MOHAMMED BIN LADEN migrated to Jedda in 1931 from a harsh, impoverished valley in Yemen. He arrived just a few years after Abdul Aziz and his fierce Ikhwan took control of the Red Sea coastline. Talented, ambitious, frugal, and determined, bin Laden cobbled together a construction business one project at a time during the sparse years of the 1930s and 1940s. He built houses, roads, offices, and hotels, and he began to cultivate the Saudi royal clan. In the tradition of Saudi and Yemeni sheikhs, bin Laden took multiple young wives. He ultimately fathered about fifty children. By the time his seventeenth son, Osama, was born in 1957 to a young Syrian wife, Mohammed bin Laden had established himself in Jedda, Medina (where Osama lived as a boy), and Riyadh. First under King Saud and then especially under Crown Prince and King Faisal, bin Laden's construction firm became the kingdom's lead contractor for such ambitious and politically sensitive projects as a new highway from Jedda to Taif and the massive refurbishment of the holy cities of Mecca and Medina.[24]

Prince Turki's father and Osama bin Laden's father were friends, business partners, and political allies. Mohammed bin Laden "was a worthy man," as Prince Turki recalled. "He was truly a genuine hero in the eyes of many Saudis, including the royal family, because of what he did for the kingdom. But he was always the construction man. When there was a job to be done, bin Laden would do it."[25] King Faisal appointed Mohammed bin Laden as his minister of public works. The king's patronage crowned the bin Laden family with open royal support and ensured that their construction fortune would grow into the billions of dollars as the Saudi treasury reaped the oil profits stoked by Faisal's OPEC gambits.

As a child Osama rode his father's bulldozers and wandered his teeming construction sites in the boomtowns of the Hejaz, as the region around the Red Sea is known. But he hardly knew his father. In 1967, just three years into Faisal's reign, Mohammed bin Laden died in a plane crash. Faisal intervened to establish a trust to oversee the operations of the bin Laden construction firm. He wanted to guarantee its stability until the older bin Laden sons, led by Osama's half-brother Salem, could grow up and take charge. In effect, because of the initiative of Prince Turki's father, the bin Laden boys became for a time wards of the Saudi kingdom.

Salem and other bin Ladens paid their way into elite British boarding schools and American universities. On the wings of their wealth many of them moved comfortably and even adventurously between the kingdom and the West. Salem married an English aristocrat, played the guitar, piloted airplanes, and vacationed in Orlando. A photograph of the bin Laden children snapped on a cobbled Swedish street during the early 1970s shows a shaggy, mod clan in bell-bottoms. Perhaps because his mother was not one of Mohammed's favored wives, or because of choices she made about schooling, or because of her boy's own preferences, Osama never slipped into the jetstream that carried his half-brothers and half-sisters to Geneva and London and Aspen. Instead he enrolled in Jedda's King Abdul Aziz University, a prestigious school by Saudi standards but one isolated from world affairs and populated by Islamist professors from Egypt and Jordan—some of them members of the Muslim Brotherhood or connected to its underground proselytizing networks.

Osama bin Laden was an impressionable college sophomore on a $1 million annual allowance during the first shocking upheavals of 1979. His teachers in Jedda included Abdullah Azzam, a Palestinian who would become a spiritual founder of Hamas, the Palestinian branch of the Muslim Brotherhood, the Islamist rival to the secular-leftist Palestine Liberation Organization. Another of bin Laden's teachers was Mohammed Qutb, the brother of Sayyed Qutb, an Egyptian Islamic radical executed in 1966 for advocating his secular government's violent overthrow. In these classrooms bin Laden studied the imperatives and nuances of contemporary Islamic jihad.[26]

Exactly when bin Laden made his first visit to Pakistan to meet leaders of the Afghan mujahedin isn't clear. In later interviews bin Laden suggested that he flew to Pakistan "within weeks" of the Soviet invasion. Others place his first trip later, shortly after he graduated from King Abdul Aziz University with a degree in economics and public administration, in 1981. Bin Laden had met Afghan mujahedin leaders at Mecca during the annual *hajj*. (The Afghan guerrillas with Saudi connections quickly learned they could raise enormous sums outside of ISI's control by rattling their tin cups before wealthy pilgrims.) According to Badeeb, on bin Laden's first trip to Pakistan he brought donations to the Lahore offices of Jamaat-e-Islami, Zia's political shock force. Jamaat was the Pakistani offshoot of the Muslim Brotherhood; its students had sacked the U.S. embassy in Islamabad in 1979. Bin Laden did not trust the official Pakistan intelligence service, Badeeb recalled, and preferred to funnel his initial charity through private religious and political networks.

From the beginning of the Afghan jihad, Saudi intelligence used religious charities to support its own unilateral operations. This mainly involved funneling money and equipment to favored Afghan commanders outside ISI or CIA control. Badeeb established safehouses for himself and other Saudi spies through Saudi charities operating in Peshawar. Badeeb also stayed frequently at the Saudi embassy in Islamabad. "The humanitarian aid—that was completely separate from the Americans," Badeeb recalled. "And we insist[ed] that the Americans will not get to that, get involved—especially in the beginning," in part because some of the Islamist mujahedin objected to direct contacts with Western infidels.[27]

With Zia's encouragement, Saudi charities built along the Afghan frontier hundreds of *madrassas,* or Islamic schools, where they taught young Afghan refugees to memorize the Koran. Ahmed Badeeb made personal contributions to establish his own refugee school along the frontier. He did insist that his school's curriculum emphasize crafts and practical trade skills, not Koran memorization. "I thought, 'Why does everybody have to be a religious student?'"[28]

In spy lexicon, each of the major intelligence agencies working the Afghan jihad—GID, ISI, and the CIA—began to "compartment" their work, even as all three collaborated with one another through formal liaisons. Working together they purchased and shipped to the Afghan rebels tens of thousands of tons of weapons and ammunition. Separately they spied on one another and pursued independent political agendas. Howard Hart, the CIA station chief in Islamabad until 1984, regarded it as "the worst kept secret in town" that the Saudis were privately running guns and cash to Sayyaf.

The Saudis insisted that there be no interaction in Pakistan between the

CIA and the GID. All such contact was to take place in Riyadh or Langley. GID tried to keep secret the subsidies it paid to the ISI outside of the arms-buying program. For their part, CIA officers tried to shield their own direct contacts with Afghan commanders such as Abdul Haq.[29]

Bin Laden moved within Saudi intelligence's compartmented operations, outside of CIA eyesight. CIA archives contain no record of any direct contact between a CIA officer and bin Laden during the 1980s. CIA officers delivering sworn testimony before Congress in 2002 asserted there were no such contacts, and so did multiple CIA officers and U.S. officials in interviews. The CIA became aware of bin Laden's work with Afghan rebels in Pakistan and Afghanistan later in the 1980s but did not meet with him even then, according to these record searches and interviews. If the CIA did have contact with bin Laden during the 1980s and subsequently covered it up, it has so far done an excellent job.[30]

Prince Turki and other Saudi intelligence officials said years later that bin Laden was never a professional Saudi intelligence agent. Still, while the exact character and timeline of his dealings with GID remains uncertain, it seems clear that bin Laden did have a substantial relationship with Saudi intelligence. Some CIA officers later concluded that bin Laden operated as a semiofficial liaison between GID, the international Islamist religious networks such as Jamaat, and the leading Saudi-backed Afghan commanders, such as Sayyaf. Ahmed Badeeb describes an active, operational partnership between GID and Osama bin Laden, a relationship more direct than Prince Turki or any other Saudi official has yet acknowledged. By Badeeb's account, bin Laden was responsive to specific direction from both the Saudi and Pakistani intelligence agencies during the early and mid-1980s. Bin Laden may not have been paid a regular stipend or salary; he was a wealthy man. But Badeeb's account suggests that bin Laden may have arranged formal road-building and other construction deals with GID during this period—contracts from which bin Laden would have earned profits. Badeeb's account is incomplete and in places ambiguous; he is known to have given only two interviews on the subject, and he does not address every aspect of his history with bin Laden in depth. But his description of the relationship, on its face, is one of intimacy and professional alliance. "I loved Osama and considered him a good citizen of Saudi Arabia," Badeeb said.

The Badeeb family and the bin Ladens hailed from the same regions of Saudi Arabia and Yemen, Badeeb said. When Ahmed Badeeb first met Osama at school in Jedda, before Badeeb became Turki's chief of staff, bin Laden had "joined the religious committee at the school, as opposed to any of the other many other committees," Badeeb recalled. "He was not an extremist at all, and I liked him because he was a decent and polite person. In school and academically he was in the middle."[31]

As the Afghan jihad roused Saudis to action, bin Laden met regularly in the kingdom with senior princes, including Prince Turki and Prince Naif, the Saudi minister of the interior, "who liked and appreciated him," as Badeeb recalled it. And as he shuttled back and forth to Afghanistan, bin Laden developed "strong relations with the Saudi intelligence and with our embassy in Pakistan." The Saudi embassy in Islamabad had "a very powerful and active role" in the Afghan jihad. The ambassador often hosted dinner parties for visiting Saudi sheikhs or government officials and would invite bin Laden to attend. He "had a very good rapport with the ambassador and with all the Saudi ambassadors that served there."[32]

Prince Turki has acknowledged meeting bin Laden "several times" at these embassy receptions in Islamabad. "He seemed to be a relatively pleasant man," Turki recalled, "very shy, soft spoken, and as a matter of fact, he didn't speak much at all." But Turki has suggested these meetings were passing encounters of little consequence. He has also said they were his only dealings with bin Laden during the early and mid-1980s.[33]

Badeeb has said that he met with bin Laden only "in my capacity as his former teacher." Given that Badeeb was working full-time as the chief of staff to the director of Saudi intelligence, this description strains credulity. Badeeb described a relationship that was far more active than just a series of casual chats at diplomatic receptions. The Saudi embassy in Islamabad "would ask [bin Laden] for some things, and he would respond positively," Badeeb recalled. Also, "The Pakistanis saw in him one who was helping them do what they wanted done there." As Badeeb organized safehouses through Saudi religious charities, bin Laden's "role in Afghanistan—and he was about twenty-four, twenty-five years old at the time—was to build roads in the country to make easy the delivery of weapons to the mujahedin." The Afghans regarded bin Laden as "a nice and generous person who has money and good contacts with Saudi government officials."

The chief of staff to the director of Saudi intelligence put it simply: "We were happy with him. He was our man. He was doing all what we ask him."[34]

For now.

5

"Don't Make It Our War"

I N JANUARY 1984, CIA director William Casey briefed President Reagan and his national security cabinet about the progress of their covert Afghan war. It had been four years since the first Lee Enfield rifles arrived in Karachi. Mujahedin warriors had killed or wounded about seventeen thousand Soviet soldiers to date, by the CIA's classified estimate. They controlled 62 percent of the countryside and had become so effective that the Soviets would have to triple or quadruple their deployments in Afghanistan to put the rebellion down. Soviet forces had so far lost about 350 to 400 aircraft in combat, the CIA estimated. The mujahedin had also destroyed about 2,750 Soviet tanks and armored carriers and just under 8,000 trucks, jeeps, and other vehicles. The war had already cost the Soviet government about $12 billion in direct expenses. All this mayhem had been purchased by U.S. taxpayers for $200 million so far, plus another $200 million contributed by Prince Turki's GID, Casey reported. Islamabad station chief Howard Hart's argument that covert action in Afghanistan was proving cost effective had never been laid out so starkly for the White House.[1]

By early 1984, Casey was among the most ardent of the jihad's true believers. After arriving at CIA headquarters in a whirlwind of controversy and ambition in 1981, it had taken Casey a year or two to focus on the details of the Afghan program. Now he was becoming its champion. Hopping oceans in his unmarked C-141 Starlifter to meet with Turki, Akhtar, and Zia, Casey cut deals that more than doubled CIA and Saudi GID spending on the Afghan mujahedin by year's end. And he began to endorse or at least tolerate provocative operations that skirted the edges of American law. Outfitted with mortars, boats, and target maps, Afghan rebels carrying CIA-printed Holy Korans in the Uzbek language secretly crossed the Amu Darya River to mount sabotage and propaganda operations inside Soviet Central Asia. The incursions marked the first outside-sponsored violent guerrilla activity on Soviet soil since the early 1950s. They were the kind of operations Casey loved most.[2]

He faced resistance within the CIA. His initial deputy, Bobby Ray Inman, saw covert action as a naïve quick fix. After Inman left, Casey's second deputy director, John McMahon, a blunt Irish veteran of the agency's spy satellite division, worried continually that something in the Afghan covert program was going to go badly wrong and that the agency was going to be hammered on Capitol Hill. He wondered about the purpose of the U.S. covert war in Afghanistan, whether it could be sustained, and whether the Reagan administration was putting enough emphasis on diplomacy to force the Soviets to leave. McMahon wanted to manage the Afghan arms pipeline defensively, sending only basic weapons, preserving secrecy to the greatest possible extent. "There was a concern between what I call the sensible bureaucrats, having been one of them, and the rabid right," recalled Thomas Twetten, one of McMahon's senior colleagues in the clandestine service. Also, the CIA's analysts in the Soviet division of the Directorate of Intelligence told Casey that no amount of aid to the mujahedin was likely to force a Soviet withdrawal from Afghanistan. In one classified assessment they predicted that the Soviet military would pressure the Afghan rebels until "the cost of continued resistance [was] too high for the insurgents to bear." These career analysts regarded Soviet economic and military power as vast and unshakable. Casey, too, saw the Soviet Union as a mighty giant, but he wanted to confront the communists where they were weakest—and Afghanistan was such a place.[3]

Reagan's election had brought to power in Washington a network of conservatives, Casey among them, who were determined to challenge Soviet power worldwide. Their active, risk-taking vision embraced the full range of competition between the superpowers. They endorsed a "Star Wars" missile defense to nullify the threat of Soviet nuclear missiles. They backed the deployment of new medium-range Pershing missiles to Europe to raise the stakes of a Soviet invasion there. Led by Reagan himself, they spoke of the Soviet Union not in the moderating language of détente, but in a religious vocabulary of good and evil. They were prepared to launch covert action wherever it might rattle Soviet power: to support the Solidarity labor movement in Poland, and to arm anticommunist rebels in Central America and Africa. The Afghan theater seemed especially compelling to Casey and his conservative allies because of the stark aggression of the Soviet invasion, the direct use of Soviet soldiers, and their indiscriminate violence against Afghan civilians.

By 1984 some in Congress wanted the CIA to do more for the Afghan rebels. Compared to the partisan controversies raging over Nicaragua, the Afghan covert action program enjoyed a peaceful consensus on Capitol Hill. The program's maniacal champion was Representative Charlie Wilson, a tall, boisterous Texas Democrat in polished cowboy boots who was in the midst of what he later called "the longest midlife crisis in history." An alcoholic, Wilson abused government privileges to travel the world first class with former beauty queens who had earned such titles as Miss Sea and Ski and Miss Humble Oil. Almost accidentally (he preferred to think of it as destiny), Wilson had become enthralled by the mujahedin. Through a strange group of fervently anticommunist Texas socialites, Wilson traveled often to meet Zia and to visit the Khyber Pass overlooking Afghanistan. He had few Afghan contacts and knew very little about Afghan history or culture. He saw the mujahedin through the prism of his own whiskey-soaked romanticism, as noble savages fighting for freedom, as almost biblical figures. Wilson used his trips to the Afghan frontier in part to impress upon a succession of girlfriends how powerful he was.

The former Miss Northern Hemisphere, also known as Snowflake, recalled a trip to Peshawar: It was "just very, very exciting to be in that room with those men with their huge white teeth," and "it was very clandestine."[4]

Beginning in 1984, Wilson began to force more money and more sophisticated weapons systems into the CIA's classified Afghan budget, even when Langley wasn't interested. Goaded by small but passionate anticommunist lobbies in Washington, Wilson argued that the CIA's lukewarm attitude toward the jihad, exemplified by McMahon, amounted to a policy of fighting the Soviets "to the last Afghan." The agency was sending just enough weaponry to ensure that many brave Afghan rebels died violently in battle, but not enough to help them win. As a resolution pushed through Congress by Wilson put it, "It would be indefensible to provide the freedom fighters with only enough aid to fight and die, but not enough to advance their cause of freedom." He told congressional committee members on the eve of one crucial funding vote: "The U.S. had nothing whatsoever to do with these people's decision to fight. They made this decision on Christmas Eve and they're going to fight to the last, even if they have to fight with stones. But we'll be damned by history if we let them fight with stones."[5]

Those arguments resonated with William Casey. The jowly grandson of an Irish saloon keeper, Casey was a seventy-one-year-old self-made multimillionaire whose passionate creeds of Catholic faith and anticommunist fervor distinguished him from many of the career officers who populated Langley. The professionals in the clandestine service were inspired by Casey's enthusiasm for high-rolling covert action, but like McMahon, some of them worried that he would gamble the CIA's credibility and lose. Still, they loved his energy and clout. By the mid-1980s, Casey had established himself as perhaps the most influential man in the Reagan administration after the president; he was able to shape foreign policy and win backing even for high-risk schemes. Reagan had broken precedent and appointed Casey as a full member of his Cabinet. It was already becoming clear that Casey would be the most important CIA director in a generation.

An eclectic crusader in his life's twilight, he bullied opponents and habitually evaded rule books. He was fixated on the Soviet Union. He believed that the epochal conflict between the United States and the Soviets would not be settled by a nuclear arms race or by war in Europe. Casey's reading of Soviet doctrine and history convinced him that Andropov's aging KGB-dominated Politburo intended to avoid an apocalyptic nuclear exchange with the West. Instead they would pursue the Brezhnev doctrine by waging a slow campaign—across generations if necessary—to surround and undermine America's capitalist democracy by sponsoring Marxists in wars of "national liberation" waged in the Third World. Casey saw himself as about the only person in Reagan's Cabinet who fully understood this tenacious Soviet strategy. He was prepared to confront the communists on their chosen ground.

He was a Catholic Knight of Malta educated by Jesuits. Statues of the Virgin Mary filled his mansion, Maryknoll, on Long Island. He attended Mass daily and urged Christian faith upon anyone who asked his advice. Once settled at the CIA, he began to funnel covert action funds through the Catholic Church to anticommunists in Poland and Central America, sometimes in violation of American law. He believed fervently that by spreading the Catholic church's reach and power he could contain communism's advance, or reverse it.[6]

Casey shared with Reagan a particular emphasis on the role of Christian faith in the moral mission to defeat communism, yet he was a more obvious pragmatist than the president. He had run spies behind enemy lines during World War II and had built a business through crafty deals and cold-eyed lawsuits. He was surrounded at Langley by legions of Henry Kissinger's *realpolitik* disciples. Casey was an excitable gunrunner *and* a profoundly devoted Catholic. He saw no conflict; he was bending rules for the greater good.

If anything, Casey's religiosity seemed to bind him closer to his proselytizing Islamic partners in the Afghan jihad. Many Muslims accounted for Christianity in the architecture of their faith and accepted some of its texts as God's word. There were Catholic schools in Pakistan, and Zia grudgingly tolerated the country's Christian minority. Saudi Arabia's Wahhabis were less relaxed. Once, while traveling secretly to Saudi Arabia to negotiate with Prince Turki, Casey asked his station chief to find a Catholic Mass for him to attend in Riyadh on Easter Sunday. The chief tried to talk him out of it; formal Christian worship in the kingdom was banned. But Casey insisted, and Prince Turki scrambled to arrange a private service.[7] The Saudi *ulama* rejected religious pluralism, but many in the Saudi royal family, including Prince Turki, respected unbending religious faith even when it was Christian. Casey won the GID's personal loyalty to the extent that Saudi intelligence, with permission from King Fahd, agreed to secretly fund Casey's riskiest anticommunist adventures in Central America.

More than any other American, it was Casey who welded the alliance among the CIA, Saudi intelligence, and Zia's army. As his Muslim allies did, Casey saw the Afghan jihad not merely as statecraft, but as an important front in a worldwide struggle between communist atheism and God's community of believers.

CASEY'S CLASSMATES were the sons of New York City policemen and firemen. Almost 60 percent were Irish Catholic, and many others were Italian. Casey rode the bus to Fordham University in the Bronx from his family's modest suburban home in Queens. In the early 1930s, the Depression's shocking deprivations caused many young Americans in the lower middle classes to be drawn to radicals who preached socialist equity or even communist unity. Not William Joseph Casey. His father was a clerk in the city sanitation department, one of tens of thousands of Irishmen who owed their government jobs to the city's Democratic patronage machine. But Casey would break early with his family's liberal political inheritance. Fordham's Jesuit teachers filled his mind with rigorous, rational arguments that Catholicism was truth. The Jesuits "let him know who he was," his wife said later. He was no renunciant. At Fordham he guzzled bootleg beer and gin with his friends and bellowed Irish Republican Army songs as he staggered home.[8]

On July 12, 1941, five months before Pearl Harbor, President Franklin Roosevelt created the Office of the Coordinator of Information, America's first independent civilian intelligence agency focused on overseas threats. He named as its first director William Joseph Donovan, a wealthy Irish Catholic corporate lawyer from New York. Donovan had run two private fact-finding missions for Roosevelt in Europe and had urged the president to create a spy service outside of the military or the FBI. A year after its founding Roosevelt renamed the agency the Office of Strategic Services, or OSS.

In September 1943, Casey, a Navy lieutenant, junior grade, was a landing craft production coordinator shuffling papers around a stifling Washington office. He had resolved not "to spend this war goosing ship builders," and he had heard through his office grapevine about the outfit usually referred to as "Oh So Secret." Casey knew a lawyer who knew Donovan, and he pushed himself forward. He was interviewed, lobbied as best he could, and within weeks was in the presence of Donovan himself, a paunchy, blue-eyed, white-haired teetotaler with red cheeks and an appetite for new ideas. Fearless in battle against rivals and relentless in the task of building his government empire, Donovan had won Roosevelt's personal loyalty. He had recruited to his fledgling spy service du Ponts, Morgans, Mellons, and what a Washington newspaper columnist called "ex-polo players, millionaires, Russian princes, society gambol boys, and dilettante detectives." With the war raging in North Africa and the Pacific, the OSS had swelled to fifteen thousand employees. Casey won a job in headquarters. It changed his life and his destiny.[9]

"I was just a boy from Long Island," Casey said later. "Never had I been in personal contact with a man of Donovan's candlepower. He was bigger than life. . . . I watched the way he operated, and after a while, I understood. You didn't wait six months for a feasibility study to prove that an idea could work. You gambled that it might work."[10]

Casey shipped out to London. Nineteen days after D-Day he rode an amphibious truck onto Normandy's Omaha Beach. The British had forbidden the OSS from running its own spy operations in Europe. They especially regarded running spies on German soil a doomed mission, needlessly wasteful of agent lives. After the Normandy invasion the British relented. In September 1944, Casey wrote Donovan a classified cable titled "An OSS Program Against Germany." He noted that hundreds of thousands of foreign-born guest workers in Germany—Russians, Poles, Belgians, and Dutch—moved freely in and out of the country with proper papers. Exiles from those countries could be equipped as agents and placed behind Nazi lines under cover as workers. In December, Donovan told Casey, "I'm giving you carte blanche. . . . Get us into Germany."[11]

As he recruited and trained agents, Casey reluctantly concluded that he needed to work with communists. They were the ones ardent enough in their beliefs to endure the enormous risks. Donovan had taught Casey that the perfect should not be the enemy of the good, Casey said later. In Hitler he was fighting a greater evil, and he would recruit unsavory allies if they were needed.

Casey had parachuted fifty-eight two-man teams into Germany by the end of April 1945. He would see them off at night from unmarked airstrips in Surrey, England. Some died in plane crashes; one team was dropped by error in sight of an SS unit watching an outdoor film; but many others survived and flourished as Germany crumbled. Ultimately Casey judged in a classified assessment that about 60 percent of his missions succeeded. He had sent men to their deaths in a righteous cause. He did not make large claims about his agent penetrations, saying later, "We probably saved some lives." Their greatest value may have been that "for the first time, we operated under our own steam." He concluded that the OSS probably could have run agents in Germany successfully a year earlier. The British ban on such operations bothered him for years afterward. Who knew what lives they might have saved?[12]

After the war Casey earned a fortune in New York by analyzing tax shelters and publishing research newsletters. He dabbled in Republican politics and accepted a tour under President Nixon as chairman of the Securities and Exchange Commission. There he cut secret deals, obfuscated about his investments, and barely escaped Washington with his reputation. As he aged, he hankered again for high office and respectability. He was invited into Ronald Reagan's presidential campaign as its manager and helped pull out a famous 1980 primary victory over George H. W. Bush in New Hampshire. After the triumph over Jimmy Carter, he moved to Washington to join the Cabinet. His first choice was the State Department, but when the offer to run the CIA came through, Casey's history with Donovan and the OSS made it impossible to resist. He would take on the Soviet empire in many of the same ways he had taken on Germany, and in the same spirit.

Perched on a rise above the Potomac River, CIA headquarters sprawled across a wooded campus behind a chain-link fence laced with barbed wire. But for the satellite dishes and antennae sprouting from every rooftop, the compound would be indistinguishable from the headquarters of a pharmaceutical company. The director's office, which was on the seventh floor of a bland concrete and glass building near the center of the campus, overlooked a bucolic wood. It was a large office but not ornate and had its own private elevator, dining room, and bathroom with shower. Casey moved in and began banging about the place as if he owned it. At 9 A.M. meetings three times a week he exhorted his fourteen top deputies to action.

The CIA "had been permitted to run down and get too thin in top-level people and capabilities," he wrote Reagan early on. As Casey's executive assistant Robert Gates put it, telling the new director what he wanted to hear, "The CIA is slowly turning into the Department of Agriculture." Casey wanted more human agents working outside of embassies, using what the agency called "nonofficial cover" as businessmen or academics, and he wanted to draw more heavily on American immigrant communities to find agents who could penetrate foreign societies. He came across as a whirlwind. Gates recalled of their first encounter: "The old man, nearly bald, tall but slightly hunched, yanked open his office door and called out to no one in particular, 'Two vodka martinis!'" There was "panic in the outer office" because the director's suite had been dry under Stansfield Turner. This was Casey, Gates reflected. "He would demand something be done immediately which the agency no longer had the capability to do. He would fire instructions at the closest person regardless of whether that person had anything to do with the matter at hand. And he would not wait around even for confirmation that anyone heard him."[13]

Perhaps that was because he was so difficult to hear. Casey mumbled. In business his secretaries refused to take dictation because they couldn't understand what he was saying. He had taken a blow to the throat while boxing as a boy and he had a thick palate; between these two impediments the words refused to flow. Ahmed Badeeb, Turki's chief of staff, called him "the Mumbling Guy." Attempting to translate during meetings with Crown Prince Fahd, Badeeb could only shrug. Even President Reagan couldn't understand him. During an early briefing Casey delivered to the national security cabinet, Reagan slipped Vice President Bush a note: "Did you understand a word he said?" Reagan later told William F. Buckley, "My problem with Bill was that I didn't understand him at meetings. Now, you can ask a person to repeat himself once. You can ask him twice. But you can't ask him a third time. You start to sound rude. So I'd just nod my head, but I didn't know what he was actually saying." Such was the dialogue for six years between the president and his intelligence chief in a nuclear-armed nation running secret wars on four continents. Casey was sensitive about the problem. "I can tell you that mumbling is more in the mind of the listener than in the mouth of the speaker," he said. "There are people who just don't want to hear what the Director of Central Intelligence sees in a complex and dangerous world."[14]

Casey believed that his mentor, Donovan, had left the CIA to the United States "as a legacy to ensure there will never be another Pearl Harbor." Since Casey could envision only the Soviets as the authors of a surprise attack on Pearl Harbor's scale, he focused almost entirely on Moscow's intentions. Spy satellites and signals collection had made it likely that the United States would have advanced warning of a Soviet military strike, Casey conceded; in that sense, Donovan's goal had been achieved. But Casey thought the CIA had to do much more than just watch the Soviets or try to steal their secrets. "The primary battlefield" in America's confrontation with Marxism-Leninism, Casey said, "is not on the missile test range or at the arms control negotiating table but in the countryside of the Third World." The Soviets were pursuing a strategy of "creeping imperialism," and they had two specific targets: "the isthmus between North and South America" and "the oil fields of the Middle East, which are the lifeline of the Western alliance." The latter target explained the Soviet invasion of Afghanistan, Casey believed.[15]

In 1961, Nikita Khrushchev had laid out Soviet plans to gain ground worldwide by aiding leftists in wars of national liberation, and the next generations of Soviet leaders had reaffirmed his doctrine. Just as European leaders had failed to understand that Hitler meant exactly what he said when he announced in *Mein Kampf* that he planned to conquer his neighbors, so the United States had placed itself at risk by failing to grasp and respond to the Soviet Union's announced ambitions. The CIA's role now, Casey said, was to demonstrate "that two can play the same game. Just as there is a classic formula for communist subversion and takeover, there also is a proven method of overthrowing repressive government that can be applied successfully in the Third World." It was in Afghanistan that he was beginning to make this "proven method" of anticommunist guerrilla war work. As his classified briefings to Reagan proved, "Far fewer people and weapons are needed to put a government on the defensive than are needed to protect it," Casey said. He boasted on another occasion: "Afghan freedom fighters have made it as dangerous for a Russian soldier or a Soviet convoy to stray off a main road as it was for the Germans in France in 1944."[16]

Casey saw political Islam and the Catholic Church as natural allies in the "realistic counter-strategy" of covert action he was forging at the CIA to thwart Soviet imperialism. Robert Ames, one of the CIA's leading Middle East analysts, influenced Casey's thinking about the role of religion in this campaign. Ames told Casey in 1983 about cases such as South Yemen where the Soviets manipulated the education of young people to suppress religious values in order to soften the ground for communist expansion. The Soviets were pursuing their aims in the Islamic world by recruiting "young revolutionaries" who would change their nation's education systems in order to "uproot and ultimately change the traditional elements of society," Ames said, as Casey recalled it. "This meant undermining the influence of religion and taking the young away from their parents for education by the state." Religious education such as Casey himself had enjoyed could counter this Soviet tactic— whether the education was in Islamic or Christian beliefs. Because the Soviets saw all religious faith as an obstacle, they suppressed churches and mosques alike. To fight back, militant Islam and militant Christianity should cooperate in a common cause.[17]

MUCH OF A CIA DIRECTOR'S travel involved schmoozing with counterparts. Casey's manners were rough. He was poor at small talk, and as a colleague put it, he always "ate like he was hungry," sometimes dripping food onto his chest. But he worked his accounts tirelessly. For global tours his black Starlifter transport came outfitted with a windowless VIP compartment secured in the vast cargo bay. Inside were couches, a bed, worktables, and a liquor cabinet. For security he would depart and arrive at night when possible, and he pushed himself on a schedule that would exhaust younger men.

Casey's Afghanistan-focused trips usually brought him first to Saudi Arabia. He met regularly with Prince Turki, sometimes with Interior Minister Naif, and usually with the crown prince or the king. Saudi ministers often worked at night, when the temperatures in the desert cooled, and by aristocratic habit they kept even important visitors waiting for long stretches in the gilded, overstuffed waiting rooms of their palaces and offices. Casey grumbled and mumbled impatiently. King Khalid once summoned him to see his dairy herd, managed by an Irish family, and then sent him in a jeep to view herds of royal camels. Casey barely tolerated these sorts of tours, and he blanched when the king thrust a glass of warm camel's milk at him.

Casey knew that the Soviet economy depended on hard currency revenue from oil exports. He urged the Saudis to use their power in the oil markets to moderate prices and deprive the Soviets of any OPEC-generated windfalls. Of course, lower oil prices would aid the American economy, too. The Saudis understood their leverage over both the Soviets and the Americans, and they traded oil favors with a merchant's cold eye.[18]

In Pakistan, Casey's Starlifter touched down in darkness at the Islamabad civil-military airport. Akhtar and the station chief would be on the tarmac to meet him. There were formal liaison meetings at ISI headquarters where the two intelligence teams would review details about shipments to the mujahedin. The ISI generals saw Casey as a forgiving ally, always focused on the big picture, content to let ISI make the detailed decisions on the ground, even when working-level CIA case officers disagreed. Casey explained that Akhtar "is completely involved in this war and certainly knows better than anyone else about his requirements. We simply have to support him." On one trip Akhtar presented Casey with a $7,000 carpet.[19]

"Here's the beauty of the Afghan operation," Casey told his colleagues. "Usually it looks like the big bad Americans are beating up on the natives. Afghanistan is just the reverse. The Russians are beating up on the little guys. We don't make it our war. The mujahedin have all the motivation they need. All we have to do is give them help, only more of it."[20]

Casey's visits usually included dinner with Zia at Army House in Rawalpindi, where to Casey's dismay servants filled the wineglasses with Coke and 7-UP. Casey seemed genuinely surprised by Zia's politeness and by the general's easy warmth. They talked about golf and Zia's short iron game, but it was geopolitics that animated them most.

Casey and Zia both emphasized that Soviet ambitions were spatial. For them, Soviet strategy echoed the colonial era's scrambles among European powers for natural resources, shipping lanes, and continental footholds. Pakistan's generals, stepchildren of imperial mapmakers, understood this competition all too well. Separately, Casey and Zia each had developed a presentation for visitors about Soviet expansionism involving red-colored maps. Zia used his to drive home his belief that Moscow had invaded Afghanistan in order to push toward the Middle East's oil. He displayed a regional map and then pulled out a red triangular celluloid template to illustrate the Soviets' continuing southwestern thrust toward warm water ports and energy resources. In one meeting he told Casey that the British colonialists had drawn a firm line across northern Afghanistan during the nineteenth century to halt Russian encroachments, and as a result the Russians hadn't moved south for ninety years. Now the United States had a "moral duty" to enforce a line against the

Soviets. Casey had developed a similar briefing about Soviet geopolitical ambitions, only on a global scale. He had ordered the CIA's Office of Global Issues in the Directorate of Intelligence to draw a map of the world that showed Soviet presence and influence. It was splotched in six different shades to depict the categories of Soviet imperial accomplishment: eight countries totally dominated by the Soviets; six that were Soviet proxies; eighteen that had been significantly influenced by Moscow; twelve that confronted Soviet-backed insurgencies; ten that had signed treaties of friendship and cooperation; and three more that were highly unstable. A second annotated map showed how the Soviets, using the KGB as well as economic and military aid, had increased their influence in country after country between 1970 and 1982.[21]

A pink-tinted country in Casey's red-splattered world was India, which had signed wide-ranging treaty agreements with Moscow even while it maintained its democratic independence. Casey briefed Zia periodically on Indian military movements. Zia often lectured that India was the region's true danger. The Americans might be reliable allies against communism, but they had proven fickle about the Indo-Pakistani conflict. Zia told Casey that being an ally of the United States was like living on the banks of an enormous river. "The soil is wonderfully fertile," he said, "but every four or eight years the river changes course, and you may find yourself alone in a desert."[22]

ISI tried to keep CIA officers away from the border camps where Afghan rebels trained, but Casey insisted that he be allowed to visit. In early 1984, the first time he asked, the panicked Pakistanis turned to the Islamabad CIA station for help in dissuading him. Soviet special forces had become active across the Pakistani borders, and ISI feared the Russians might pick up word of Casey's movements or accidentally encounter him in an ambush. It was hard to imagine a more nightmarish scenario for Pakistan's national security than the prospect, however slim, that the CIA director might be kidnapped by the KGB on Pakistani soil. But Casey refused to be put off. In the end ISI collaborated with the Islamabad station to set up a temporary—essentially fake—mujahedin training camp in the hills that sprawled to the north behind Islamabad, far away from the Afghan border. They loaded Casey in a jeep at night, declined at least initially to tell him where they were going, and bumped in circles along rough roads for about the time that would be required to reach the Afghan frontier. Then they unpacked him from the convoy and showed him a small crew of Afghans training on 14.5-millimeter and 20.7-millimeter antiaircraft guns. The Afghans made a lot of noise, and Casey wept tears of joy at the sight of his freedom fighters.[23]

Back in Washington that summer he heard more and more complaints from Congress and from ideological conservatives that the CIA's cautious, hands-off approach to the Afghan war was hurting the rebel cause. Spurred by Charlie Wilson's romanticized tales and envious of his battlefield souvenirs, more and more congressional delegations toured Pakistan and the frontier. Visiting congressmen heard complaints from Afghan commanders such as Abdul Haq about ISI corruption, ISI control over weapon distribution, and the erratic quality of the weapons themselves. They lobbied Casey for more sophisticated arms and more direct American involvement in the jihad. At Langley, McMahon balked. Case officers in the Near East Division detected the birth of a classic Washington syndrome: When any government program is going well, whether a foreign covert action or a domestic education plan, every bureaucrat and congressman in town wants to horn in on it. Suddenly CIA officers began to hear whispers from the Pentagon that perhaps the mujahedin would be more effective if the U.S. military played a greater role. Casey's CIA colleagues spit nails over such gambits, but he hardly cared at all. He thought the critics of CIA caution were probably right. On July 28, 1984, Casey told McMahon by memo that with all the new money beginning to wash into the Afghan pipeline and because of the rising complaints, "a thorough review and reevaluation of the Afghan program is in order."[24]

Casey appointed a new station chief to succeed Howard Hart in Islamabad. William Piekney rotated to Pakistan that summer from Paris, where he had been deputy. A former officer in the Navy and a veteran of CIA stations in Tunisia and Guinea, Piekney was a smoother, more cerebral spy than Hart. He had none of Hart's sharp elbows and none of his fascination with antique weaponry. Nor was he a firebrand conservative. He saw McMahon as the victim of right-wing baiting and sympathized with his colleague's frustrations. Piekney was a balancer, a fine-tuner, a team-builder. He would take visiting congressmen and senators into the Islamabad embassy's secure "bubble" and deliver an articulate briefing about the war's hidden course and the punishment being inflicted on the Soviets. As more and more Pentagon visitors began to turn up in Pakistan, rubbing their hands and asking to help, Piekney tried to smother them with kindness while keeping them well away from the CIA's business. Dealing with the Pentagon was always a tricky equation for the agency. The Pentagon dwarfed the CIA in resources. The CIA's annual budget was a Pentagon rounding error. It was in the CIA's interest, Piekney believed, to try to keep the relationship balanced.[25]

With the Pentagon's acquiescence, Casey helped arrange an annual feat of budgeting gimmickry that siphoned Defense Department money to pump up the funds available for Afghan covert action. As each fiscal year ended in October, mujahedin sympathizers in Congress, led by Wilson, scrutinized the Pentagon's massive treasury for money allocated the year before but never spent. Congress would then order some of those leftover sums—tens of millions of dollars—transferred to the Afghan rebels. Charles Cogan, the old-school spy who ran the Near East Division, resisted accepting these new funds, but as Gates recalled, "Wilson just steamrolled Cogan—and the CIA for that matter."[26]

The funding surge in October 1984 was so huge that it threatened to change the very nature of the CIA's covert action in Afghanistan. Congress that month shoveled another enormous injection of leftover Pentagon money to the CIA for use in support of the mujahedin, bringing the total Afghan program budget for 1985 up to $250 million, about as much as all the previous years combined. If Saudi Arabia's GID matched that allocation, that would mean the CIA could spend $500 million on weapons and supplies for the mujahedin through October 1985, an amount so large in comparison to previous budgets that it was hard to contemplate. In late October, Casey cabled the Saudis and the Pakistanis to say that the United States planned to commit $175 million immediately and place another $75 million in reserve, pending further discussions with them. Under Wilson's spur, Casey had tripled funding for the Afghan covert war in a matter of weeks.

Casey wanted to stretch the war's ambitions to a similar degree. "Unless U.S. policy is redesigned to achieve a broader attack on Soviet vulnerabilities it cannot restore independence to Afghanistan," Casey wrote in a classified memo to McMahon and other senior CIA officers on December 6, 1984. "Continuation of the current U.S. program will allow the Soviets to wear down the Afghan resistance at a cost affordable and tolerable to themselves." He insisted that the CIA take a close look at the Pentagon's latest proposals to provide satellite intelligence about Soviet targets in Afghanistan. Casey concluded: "In the long run, merely increasing the cost to the Soviets of an Afghan intrusion, which is basically how we have been justifying the activity when asked, is not likely to fly."[27]

Casey was rewriting his own presidential authority. "Restoring independence to Afghanistan" was not a goal spelled out for CIA covert action in the January 1980 presidential finding renewed by President Reagan. Nor was it a possibility deemed plausible by many of Casey's own Soviet analysts. No longer would the CIA be content to tie the Soviets down, Casey was saying. They were going to drive them out.

He flew back to Pakistan late in 1984. This time he would see true muja-hedin training camps on the Afghan frontier—no more artificial training shows. Piekney met his Starlifter on the tarmac. Shortly after dawn one morn-ing they boarded Pakistani military helicopters and flew toward Afghanistan. It was the first time any helicopter had ever landed at an ISI camp. Casey wore a round, flat Afghan cap and a zippered green nylon coat with cloth trim. He looked like an unlikely rebel. Akhtar, his chief escort, wore sunglasses. At the first camp ISI trainers showed Casey scores of mujahedin in the midst of a ten-day guerrilla course. They learned basic assault rifle tactics, how to ap-proach and withdraw, rocket-propelled grenades, and a few mortar systems. American taxpayer dollars were hard at work here, Akhtar assured him. In his speeches to Afghan commanders and trainees, the ISI chief repeatedly em-phasized the need to put pressure on the Soviets and the Afghan communists in and around the capital. "Kabul must burn!" Akhtar declared. At the second camp they showed Casey the Chinese mine-clearing equipment that could blast a narrow furrow across a Soviet-laid minefield. ISI brigadiers lobbied Casey for better equipment: The tracks cleared by the Chinese system weren't wide enough for the mujahedin, and they were taking unnecessary casualties.[28]

Back at ISI headquarters in Rawalpindi, Casey raised the subject of the most sensitive operation then under way between the two intelligence ser-vices: pushing the Afghan jihad into the Soviet Union itself.

Beginning in the late 1970s, the CIA's covert action staff had produced proposals for secret publishing and propaganda efforts targeting Muslims liv-ing in Soviet Central Asia as well as Ukrainians. Carter's national security ad-viser, Zbigniew Brzezinski, was among the most passionate advocates for a covert American program to stir up nationalism in the Soviet Union's non-Russian border republics. But the State Department balked at the plans. Fo-menting rebellion inside the Soviet Union could provoke unpredictable retaliation by Moscow, even including attempts to launch attacks inside the United States. At Langley the idea stirred controversy.[29]

The CIA had strong contacts dating back decades among exiled national-ists from the Baltics and Ukraine. It knew far less about Soviet Central Asia, the vast and sparsely populated steppe and mountain region to Afghanistan's immediate north. Pushed by Casey, American scholars and CIA analysts had begun in the early 1980s to examine Soviet Central Asia for signs of restive-ness. There were reports that ethnic Uzbeks, Turkmen, Tajiks, and Kazakhs chafed under Russian ethnic domination. And there were also reports of ris-ing popular interest in Islam, fueled in part by the smuggling of underground

Korans, sermonizing cassette tapes, and Islamic texts by the Muslim Brotherhood and other proselytizing networks. The CIA reported on a May 1984 lecture in Moscow where the speaker told a public audience that Islam represented a serious internal problem. American diplomats operating out of the U.S. embassy in Moscow traveled regularly through Central Asia seeking evidence and fresh contacts, but they were closely shadowed by the KGB and could learn little.[30]

Drawing on his experiences running dissident Polish exiles as agents behind Nazi lines, Casey decided to revive the CIA's propaganda proposals targeting Central Asia. The CIA's specialists proposed to send in books about Central Asian culture and historical Soviet atrocities in the region. The ISI's generals said they would prefer to ship Korans in the local languages. Langley agreed. The CIA commissioned an Uzbek exile living in Germany to produce translations of the Koran in the Uzbek language. The CIA printed thousands of copies of the Muslim holy book and shipped them to Pakistan for distribution to the mujahedin. The ISI brigadier in charge recalled that the first Uzbek Korans arrived in December 1984, just as Casey's enthusiasm was waxing. ISI began pushing about five thousand books into northern Afghanistan and onward across the Soviet border by early 1985.[31]

At the same time, ISI's Afghan bureau selected small teams among the mujahedin who would be willing to mount violent sabotage attacks inside Soviet Central Asia. KGB-backed agents had killed hundreds of civilians in terrorist bombings inside Pakistan, and ISI wanted revenge. Mohammed Yousaf, the ISI brigadier who was the Afghan operations chief during this period, recalled that it was Casey who first urged these cross-border assaults during a meeting at ISI headquarters late in 1984, on the same visit that the CIA director traveled to the rebel training camps by helicopter.

As Yousaf recalled it, Casey said that there was a large Muslim population across the Amu Darya that could be stirred to action and could "do a lot of damage to the Soviet Union." The CIA director talked about the propaganda efforts but went further. Casey said, according to Yousaf, "We should take the books and try to raise the local population against them, and you can also think of sending arms and ammunition if possible." In Yousaf's recollection, Akhtar voiced agreement about the Koran smuggling efforts but remained silent about the sabotage operations. Robert Gates, Casey's executive assistant and later CIA director, has confirmed that Afghan rebels "began cross-border operations into the Soviet Union itself" during the spring of 1985. These operations included "raising cain on the Soviet side of the border." The attacks took place, according to Gates, "with Casey's encouragement."[32]

If Casey spoke the words Yousaf attributed to him, he was almost certainly breaking American law. No one but President Reagan possessed the authority to foment attacks inside the Soviet Union, and only then if the president notified senior members of the congressional intelligence committees. The risks of such operations in the nuclear age were so numerous that they hardly needed listing. Colleagues of Casey's at the CIA, the Pentagon, and the White House later expressed doubt that he had sanctioned cross-border attacks.[33] They suggested that Yousaf had probably conflated accurate recollections about Casey's support for the Koran and propaganda book smuggling with ISI's independent decision to begin secretly arming Afghan teams to penetrate Soviet Central Asia.

Perhaps. But Gates's account appears unambiguous, and Yousaf's recollections are precise. It would hardly have been unusual for Casey to pursue covert action outside the boundaries of presidential authority. ISI was the perfect cutout for operations on Soviet territory, providing the CIA with a layer of deniability. And as Gates reflected later, referring more generally to his sense of mission, Casey had not come to the CIA "with the purpose of making it better, managing it more effectively, reforming it, or improving the quality of intelligence. . . . Bill Casey came to the CIA primarily to wage war against the Soviet Union."[34]

In any event, the CIA's analysts and case officers knew what their Pakistani partners were doing across the Soviet border. Yousaf would pass along requests to the Islamabad station for such equipment as silent outboard motors, which he said he needed for river crossings on the Amu Darya. Piekney, the new station chief, lived in fear that one of these Afghan teams would be captured or killed in Soviet territory and that equipment in their possession would be traced to the CIA, creating an international incident on the scale of the 1960 U-2 shootdown.

Fear of such a public relations catastrophe, or worse, persuaded many analysts at Langley and at the State Department that ISI's guerrilla attacks on Soviet soil were reckless. Morton Abramowitz, then chief of intelligence at the State Department, saw classified reports about the mujahedin crossing over and urged that ISI be told such assaults were unacceptable. Piekney delivered the message in informal meetings with General Akhtar. The CIA station chief insisted that ISI "not authorize or encourage the Afghans to take the battle into Soviet territory," as Piekney recalled it. "We all understood, however, that the Afghans would exploit opportunities that arose and do pretty much what they wanted to do," Piekney remembered. Pakistani intelligence "privately felt it would not be a bad thing" if the Afghan rebels hit targets inside Soviet territory from time to time. "Our only real option was to withhold official U.S. endorsement of that kind of activity and discourage it, which we did." In any event, the less the CIA knew about the details, the better. Nobody could control armed Afghans determined to cross their northern border anyway, the CIA was prepared to argue if the operations became public.[35]

The north of Afghanistan lay separated from Pakistan by steep mountain ranges, snow-clogged passes, and large Soviet deployments, and was populated by Uzbeks, Tajiks, Turkmen, and adherents of Islam's minority Shia faith. The mujahedin commanders operating along the Soviet border had few connections to ISI's Pashto-speaking colonels and brigadiers who were handing out the big bags of money and guns in Peshawar. For the Soviets, too, the north of Afghanistan was exceptionally important. The region possessed natural gas resources, vital roads, and ethnic populations whose clans spilled into Soviet republics. As the war went badly, the Soviets considered at times just hunkering down in northern Afghanistan to protect the Soviet Union's southern rim.

But such a retreat was impractical. By the mid-1980s the Afghan rebels' most effective military and political leader operated in the northern provinces, right in the Soviet Union's mountainous backyard. Unlike the mujahedin commanders who would turn up for staged training camp demonstrations, this Afghan leader rarely traveled to Pakistan. He operated almost entirely from his own strategic blueprint. According to CIA reporting, his forces were responsible for some of the first attacks inside the Soviet Union in the spring of 1985. William Piekney wanted to arrange a meeting with him, but it was impossible to manage the logistics. He was too far away to visit.

Ahmed Shah Massoud seemed to prefer it that way.

"Who Is This Massoud?"

AHMED SHAH MASSOUD charged up the face of Ali Abad Mountain on the west side of Kabul, with a ragtag crew of a dozen soldiers in tow. Ali Abad was nothing more than a dusty, rock-strewn hill slouched in the middle of the 6,200-foot-high capital, but occupying its top would give Massoud a commanding position. He could gaze to the south at the pine-tree-laden campus of Kabul University, the country's premier institution of learning. To the north was Kabul Polytechnic Institute, a reputable science school dominated by the Soviets. To the east sprawled the city's downtown area. All around stood the jagged snowcapped peaks that walled the city in, cradling Kabul Valley in a cool embrace. Just before Massoud reached the hill's crest and faced his enemy—a rival faction of similar size—he sent a detachment of loyalists around the opposite side. The enemy never saw them coming. They surrendered immediately, and after briefly savoring his victory, Massoud paraded his captives back down the hill and into a ditch by the side of the road where he kept all of his prisoners of war. Then, with a wave of his hand, he dismissed his soldiers and freed his captives. From across the street his mother was calling him for dinner.

It was 1963, and he was eleven years old. His family had moved to Kabul only recently. Massoud did not consider the city home, but he had quickly mastered the heights of its bluffs and the depths of its ravines. There was no question among his peers as to who would play commander in neighborhood war games.[1]

His father was a colonel in the army of King Zahir Shah, a position of some prestige but little danger. From the 1930s until the early 1960s the entire span of the elder Massoud's military career, Afghanistan had remained at peace. Massoud led a transient life during his first decade. He had lived in Helmand in the south, Herat in the west, and then Kabul. But he and his family always considered home the Panjshir Valley town of Massoud's birth: Jangalak, in the district of Bazarak, several hours' drive north of the capital.

For seventy miles the Panjshir River cuts a harsh diagonal to the southwest through the Hindu Kush Mountains before spilling onto the Shomali Plains thirty miles above Kabul. On a map it looks like an arrow pointing the way directly toward Afghanistan's capital from the northeast. On the ground it is a chasm cut between bald, unforgiving cliffs that plunge steeply into the raging current. Only occasionally do the cliffs slope more gently, offering room for houses and crops on either side of the riverbed. There the valley erupts in lush, wavy green fields, and the river sits as placidly as a glacial lake, braided by grassy sandbars.

In front of the Massoud ancestral home in Jangalak, almost exactly halfway up the valley, the water is at its calmest. The Massoud family settled on this site on the western bank of the river around the beginning of the twentieth century. A relatively prosperous family, they initially built a low, mud-brick compound that, like countless other valley homes, appeared to rise organically from the rich brown soil. When Massoud's father inherited the place, he built an addition on the back that stretched farther up the mountainside. It was there that Massoud's mother gave birth to Ahmed Shah, her second son, in 1952.

The Panjshir of Massoud's birth had changed little in centuries. Along the valley's one true road—a rough, pockmarked dirt track that parallels the river's course—it was far more common to hear the high-pitched cry of a donkey weighted down by grain sacks than the muted purr of a motor engine. Food came from terraced fields of wheat, apple and almond trees that sprouted along the river banks, or the cattle, goats, and chickens that wandered freely, unable to range far since the valley is only about a mile at its widest.

Few in the Panjshir could read or write, but Massoud's parents were both exceptions. His father was formally educated. His mother was not, but she came from a family of lawyers who were prominent in Rokheh, the next town over from Jangalak. She taught herself to read and write, and urged her four sons and four daughters to improve themselves similarly. A stern woman who imposed rigid standards, Massoud's mother wanted her children to be educated, but she also wanted them to excel outside the classroom. Her oldest son, Yahya, once came home with grades putting him near the top of his class, a status the Massoud children often enjoyed. Massoud's father was thrilled and talked about rewarding his son with a motorbike. "I'm not happy with these things," his mother complained. She rebuked her husband: "I've told you many times: Teach your sons those things they need." She fired off examples: "Do your children ride horses? Can they use guns? Are they able to be in society and to be with people? These are the characteristics that make a man." Yahya did not get the motorbike.

Ahmed Shah Massoud's mother meted out family discipline, and because he was a child who seemed naturally inclined to mischief, his reprimands came often. She never struck her children physically, her sons recalled, but she could wither them with verbal lashings. Years later Massoud confided to siblings that perhaps the only person he had ever feared was his mother.

By the time Massoud reached high school in the late 1960s, his father had retired from the military and the family had settled in an upper-middle-class neighborhood of Kabul. They lived in a seven-bedroom stone and concrete house with panoramic views. It was the finest building on the block. Massoud attended the Lycée Istiqlal, an elite, French-sponsored high school. There he earned good grades, acquired French, and won a scholarship to attend college in France. The scholarship was his ticket out of Kabul's dusty, premodern alleys, but Massoud turned it down, to his family's surprise. He announced that he wanted to go to military school instead and to follow in his father's footsteps as an Afghan army officer. His father tried to use connections to get him into the country's premier military school, but failed. Massoud settled for Kabul Polytechnic Institute, the Soviet-sponsored school just down the hill from the family home.

In his first year of college, Massoud discovered he was a math whiz. He set up a tutoring service for classmates and talked hopefully about becoming an engineer or an architect. As it happened, he was destined to knock down many more buildings than he would ever build.

The Cold War had slipped into Afghanistan like a virus. By the late 1960s all of Kabul's universities were in the grip of fevered politics. Secret Marxist book clubs conspired against secret Islamist societies in damp concrete faculties and residences. The atmosphere was urgent: The country's weak, centuries-old monarchy was on its way out. Afghanistan was lurching toward a new politics. Would it be Marxist or Islamic, secular or religious, modern or traditional—or some blend of these? Every university professor seemed to have an opinion.

Massoud's parents had raised him as a devout Muslim and imbued in him an antipathy for communism. When he came home after his first year at the institute, he told his family about a mysterious new group he had joined called the Muslim Youth Organization. Ahmed Wali, his youngest full brother, noticed that Massoud was confidently explaining to not just family but shopkeepers and nearly anyone else who would listen that his group was going to wage war against the Marxists who were increasingly prominent on the capital's campuses, in government ministries, and in the army. Massoud's swagger was unmistakable: "He was giving that sort of impression, that tomorrow, he and four or five others are going to defeat the whole thing."[2]

THE ISLAMIC FAITH that Massoud acquired at Kabul Polytechnic Institute was not the faith of his father. It was a militant faith—conspiratorial and potentially violent. Its texts had arrived in Kabul in the satchels of Islamic law professors returning to their teaching posts in the Afghan capital after obtaining advanced degrees abroad, particularly from Islam's most prestigious citadel of learning, Al-Azhar University in Cairo. There a handful of Afghan doctoral candidates—including Abdurrab Rasul Sayyaf and Burhanuddin Rabbani—came under the influence of radical Egyptian Islamists exploring new forms of Islamic politics. Back in Kabul the Afghan junior professors began during the mid-1960s to teach Egyptian creeds in their classrooms, pressing radical ideas on bright, restless young Afghan students such as Massoud.[3]

For centuries religious faith in Afghanistan had reflected the country's political geography: It was diverse, decentralized, and rooted in local personalities. The territory that became Afghanistan had been crossed and occupied by ancient Buddhists, ancient Greeks (led by Alexander the Great), mystics, saints, Sikhs, and Islamic warriors, many of whom left monuments and decorated graves. Afghanistan's forbidding mountain ranges and isolated valleys ensured that no single dogmatic creed, spiritual or political, could take hold of all its people. As conquerors riding east from Persia and south from Central Asia's steppes gradually established Islam as the dominant faith, and as they returned from stints of occupation in Hindu India, they brought with them eclectic strains of mysticism and saint worship that blended comfortably with

Afghan tribalism and clan politics. The emphasis was on loyalty to the local Big Man. The Sufi strain of Islam became prominent in Afghanistan. Sufism taught personal contact with the divine through mystical devotions. Its leaders established orders of the initiated and were worshiped as saints and chieftains. Their elaborately decorated shrines dotted the country and spoke to a celebratory, personalized, ecstatic strain in traditional Afghan Islam.

Colonial and religious warfare during the nineteenth century infused the country's isolated valleys with more austere Islamic creeds. Muslim theologians based in Deoband, India, whose ideas echoed Saudi Arabia's Wahhabis, established *madrassas* and gained influence among Afghan Pashtun tribes. To galvanize popular support against invading Sikhs, an early-nineteenth-century Afghan king named Dost Mohammed appointed himself Amir-ul-Momineen, or commander of the faithful, and declared his cause a religious war. British imperialists seeking breathing space from an encroaching Russia later invaded Afghanistan twice, singing their Christian hymns and preaching of their superior civilization. Revolting Afghan tribesmen fired by Islamic zeal slaughtered them by the thousands, along with their trains of elephants, and forced an inglorious retreat. Abdur Rahman, the "Iron Emir" covertly supported in Kabul by the chastened British in the late nineteenth century, attempted to coerce the Afghans into "one grand community under one law and one rule." Across a hundred years all these events created new strains of xenophobia in Afghanistan and revived Islam as a national political and war-fighting doctrine. Still, even the country's most radical Islamists did not contemplate a war of civilizations or the proclamation of jihad in distant lands.

The country staggered into the twentieth century in peaceful but impoverished isolation, ruled by a succession of cautious kings in Kabul who increasingly relied on outside aid to govern, and whose writ in the provinces was weak. At the local level, by far the most important sphere, political and Islamic authorities accommodated one another.

It was during the 1960s, and then largely in the city of Kabul—on its tree-shaded university campuses and in its army barracks—that radical doctrines carried in from outside the country set the stage for cataclysm. As the KGB-sponsored Marxists formed their cabals and recruited followers, equally militant Afghan Islamists rose up to oppose them. Every university student now confronted a choice: communism or radical Islam. The contest was increasingly raucous. Each side's members staged demonstrations and counter-demonstrations, paraded flags, and carried bullhorns in case of a spontaneous roadside debate. In the space of just a few years during the late 1960s and early 1970s, what little there was of the center in Afghan politics melted away in Kabul under the friction of these confrontational, imported ideologies.[4]

The Egyptian texts carried to Kabul's universities were sharply focused on politics. The tracts sprang from the ideology of the Muslim Brotherhood, the transnational spiritual and political network founded during the 1920s by an Egyptian schoolteacher, Hassan al-Banna, as a protest movement against British colonial rule in Egypt. (Jamaat-e-Islami was, in effect, the Pakistani branch of the Muslim Brotherhood.) Muslim Brotherhood members believed that the only way to return the Islamic world to its rightful place of economic and political power was through a rigid adherence to core Islamic principles. Initiated brothers pledged to work secretly to create a pure Islamic society modeled on what they saw as the lost and triumphant Islamic civilizations founded in the seventh century. (One French scholar likened the brothers to the conservative, elite lay Catholic organizations in the West such as Opus Dei.[5] Throughout his life CIA director William Casey was attracted to these secretive lay Catholic groups.) As the movement's distinctive green flag with crossed white swords and a red Koran spread across Egypt, the Muslim Brotherhood's numbers swelled to half a million by 1949. British colonialists grew fed up and repressed the brothers violently. Some members, known as the Special Order Group, carried out guerrilla strikes, bombing British installations and murdering British soldiers and civilians.[6]

When Egyptian military leaders known as the Free Officers seized power during the 1950s under the leadership of Gamal Abdel Nasser, they continued the British pattern of trying to co-opt the Muslim Brotherhood and, when that failed, repressing them. In Egyptian prisons, "The brutal treadmill of torture broke bones, stripped out skins, shocked nerves, and killed souls," recalled Ayman al-Zawahiri, an Egyptian medical doctor who spent time in the jails and later became Osama bin Laden's chief lieutenant.[7] During one of the Egyptian government crackdowns, an imprisoned radical named Sayyed Qutb, who had tried unsuccessfully to assassinate Nasser, wrote from a jail cell a manifesto titled *Signposts,* which argued for a new Leninist approach to Islamic revolution. Qutb justified violence against nonbelievers and urged radical action to seize political power. His opinions had taken shape, at least in part, during a yearlong visit to the United States in 1948. The Egyptian government had sent him to Northern Colorado Teachers College in Greeley to learn about the American educational system, but he found the United States repugnant. America was materialistic, obsessed with sex, prejudiced against Arabs, and sympathetic to Israel. "Humanity today is living in a large brothel!

One has only to glance at its press, films, fashion shows, beauty contests, ball-rooms, wine bars, and broadcasting stations!" Qutb wrote upon his return.

Qutb argued that all impure governments must be overthrown. All true Muslims should join the "Party of God" (Hezbollah). Qutb linked a political revolution to coercive changes in social values, much as Lenin had done. *Signposts* attacked nominally Muslim leaders who governed through non-Islamic systems such as capitalism or communism. Those leaders, Qutb wrote, should be declared unbelievers and become the targets of revolutionary jihad.[8]

Qutb was executed in 1966, but his manifesto gradually emerged as a blue-print for Islamic radicals from Morocco to Indonesia. It was later taught at King Abdul Aziz University in Jedda in classes attended by Osama bin Laden. Qutb's ideas attracted excited adherents on the campus of Cairo's Al-Azhar University. (In 1971, Prince Turki's father, King Faisal, pledged $100 million to Al-Azhar's rector to aid the intellectual struggle of Islam against commu-nism.[9]) This was the context in which Sayyaf, Rabbani, and other junior pro-fessors carried Qutb's ideas to Kabul University's classrooms.

Rabbani translated *Signposts* into Dari, the Afghan language of learning. The returning Afghan professors adapted Qutb's Leninist model of a revolu-tionary party to the local tradition of Sufi brotherhoods. In 1973, at their first meeting as the leadership council of the Muslim Youth Organization, the group elected Rabbani its chairman and Sayyaf vice chairman.[10]

Gulbuddin Hekmatyar did not make it to the inaugural meeting of the Muslim Youth Organization that night in 1973. He was in jail for ordering the murder of a Maoist student. But the group selected him as its political direc-tor anyway because in his short time as a student in Kabul University's elite engineering school, Hekmatyar had already earned a reputation as a commit-ted radical. He was willing, it seemed, to protest anything. When the univer-sity tried to raise the passing grade from fifty to sixty, Hekmatyar cursed the school's administrators and stood on the front lines of mass demonstrations. He shook his fist at the government's un-Islamic ways and was rumored to spray acid in the faces of young women who dared set foot in public without donning a veil.[11]

Massoud kept his distance from Hekmatyar, but Rabbani's teachings ap-pealed to him. Just to hear Rabbani speak, he frequently hiked around the hill from the institute to Kabul University's Sharia faculty, a 1950s-era brick and flagstone building resembling an American middle school that nestled in a shaded vale near Ali Abad Mountain.

By the time King Zahir Shah's cousin, Mohammed Daoud, drawing on some communist support, seized national power in a coup on July 17, 1973, Massoud was a full-fledged member of the Muslim Youth Organization.

"Some of our brothers deem armed struggle necessary to topple this criminal government," Rabbani declared at one meeting at the Faculty of Islamic Law a few months later. They acquired weapons and built connections in the Afghan army, but they lacked a path to power. When Daoud cracked down on the Islamists a year later, Massoud, Hekmatyar, Rabbani, and the rest of the organization's members fled to Pakistan.

The Pakistani government embraced them. Daoud's nascent communist support had the Pakistani army worried. The exiled Islamists offered the army a way to pursue influence in Afghanistan. Massoud, Hekmatyar, and about five thousand other young exiles began secret military training under the direction of Prime Minister Zulfikar Ali Bhutto's Afghan affairs adviser, Brigadier General Naseerullah Babar.[12] Babar and Hekmatyar, both ethnic Pashtuns, soon became confidants, and together they hatched a plan for an uprising against Daoud in 1975. They drafted Massoud to sneak back into the Panjshir and start the revolt from there. He did so reluctantly, and the episode ended badly. Massoud fled to Pakistan for the second time in two years.[13]

The failed uprising exacerbated a split among the Afghan exiles, with bad blood all around. Hekmatyar created his own organization, Hezb-e-Islami (Islamic Party), composed primarily of ethnic Pashtuns, and he forged close relations with ISI. Massoud stuck by Rabbani in Jamaat-e-Islami (Islamic Society), which was made up mostly of ethnic Tajiks. When Massoud secretly returned to the Panjshir Valley once again in 1978, however, he did so on his own. He no longer trusted the other Afghan leaders, and he had no faith in Pakistan. He simply showed up in the Panjshir with thirty supporters, seventeen rifles, the equivalent of $130 in cash, and a letter asking the local people to declare jihad against their Soviet-backed government.[14]

BY HIS THIRTIETH BIRTHDAY Massoud had fended off six direct assaults by the world's largest conventional army.

The Politburo and the high command of the Soviet Fortieth Army had initially hoped that Soviet troops might play a supporting role in Afghanistan, backing up the communist-led Afghan army. Kremlin officials repeatedly assured themselves that the rebels were nothing more than *basmachi,* or bandits, the term used to describe Muslim rebels in Central Asia who unsuccessfully resisted Soviet authority following the Bolshevik Revolution of 1917. But desertions from Afghan army ranks only increased. Massive forcible conscription drives inflated the Afghan army's reported size but did little to improve its effectiveness. Gradually Soviet units took the war on for themselves.[15]

Massoud and his Panjshiri rebels stood near the top of their target list. The Panjshir Valley contained only about eighty thousand residents in a country of 15 million, but for the Soviets the valley proved vital. Just to the east of the Panjshir, through a forbidding mountain range, the Salang Highway cut a path between Kabul and Termez, the Soviet transit city on the Afghan border beside the Amu Darya River. For the Soviets to retain their grip on Afghanistan, the Salang Highway had to remain open. There was no other reliable overland

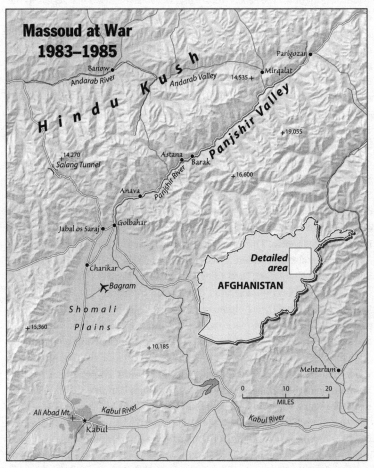

Credit: Richard Furno

supply route between the USSR and Kabul. Food, uniforms, fuel, weapons, ammunition—everything the Red Army and the Afghan army required rumbled down the Salang's treacherous, pitted, zigzag blacktop.

The Salang kept Massoud's forces fed, clothed, and armed as well. When a Soviet convoy tried to pass along the highway, Massoud's fighters streamed down from the mountains, unleashed a fusillade of gunfire, raided the convoy, and disappeared back into the shadows. They would then take apart whatever they had pilfered from the Soviets, be it an antitank missile or pieces of a tank, pack it onto the backs of horses, and trek to the Panjshir where mechanics reassembled them for the rebels' future use. Because Massoud had access to the Salang from the Panjshir, Red Army soldiers were dying at the hands of Red Army weapons fired by mujahedin clothed in Red Army uniforms. "We do not regard an attack against a convoy successful, even if we destroy many trucks or tanks, unless we bring back supplies," Massoud told a visiting journalist in 1981.[16] Massoud, the Soviets decided, was one bandit they had to stop quickly.

In each of the first six Soviet assaults on the Panjshir between the spring of 1980 and the fall of 1982, Massoud hardly seemed to stand a chance. At the time of the first campaign he had barely one thousand fighters. Two years later, that number had doubled, but he was still grossly outgunned. With each invasion the Soviets brought more men and more firepower. For the fall 1982 offensive, the Soviets sent ten thousand of their own troops, four thousand Afghan army soldiers, and scores of tanks, attack helicopters, and fighter jets from Kabul. Not only aimed at securing the Salang, the assaults were part of a wider, unannounced military plan. The Soviets had decided that to hold Afghanistan for the long run they should "achieve a decisive victory in the northern zones bordering the Soviet Union first," according to the KGB's archives.[17]

Massoud had become a serious, deeply read student of Mao Zedong, Che Guevara, and French revolutionary strategist Regis Debray. Following their precepts he did not try to face the Soviets and stop them. From the earliest days of the rebellion he maintained well-placed intelligence agents in the Afghan army and typically would find out days, weeks, or even months in advance that the Soviets were planning an attack. Just before the first aerial bombing runs began, Massoud's forces would melt away into the intricate network of side valleys that spread out from the Panjshir like veins on a leaf.

After the bombs had fallen, the Soviet and Afghan army ground forces would enter the valley and find it populated by women, children, old men, and a smattering of farm animals. But they would not find any mujahedin—at least not initially. Massoud might allow a column of Soviet tanks to advance well into the valley before ordering his men to attack. When they did, they would never stand and fight head-on. Instead, they might send a few particularly courageous soldiers to streak in with rocket-propelled grenades and take out the first and last tanks in the column. Larger rebel contingents, well hidden behind rocks and trees, would then spray the paralyzed column with gunfire before sprinting back to the safety of a side valley. In the narrow Panjshir, with only one road in and out, the Red Army soldiers often had no choice but to abandon their tanks. The crippled vehicles, with a little tinkering by Massoud's mechanics, sometimes became part of the mujahedin arsenal within a week.[18]

Massoud played the Afghan government soldiers off against their Soviet allies. A staggeringly large percentage of the army felt more allegiance to rebel leaders such as Massoud than they did to their Soviet handlers. In some cases Massoud even had to persuade sympathizers within the Afghan army *not* to defect because they were more valuable to him as informers than they were as fighters. During Panjshir invasions the Soviets often sent Afghan units just ahead of Red Army units on the theory that their Afghan comrades would then bear the brunt of the mujahedin's surprises. In time, Massoud picked up on this tactic and began to exploit it. When his lookouts spotted an enemy column advancing with Afghan forces in the lead, Massoud's men would try to isolate the units by blasting gigantic rocks out of the cliffs and hurtling them toward the road, in between where the Afghan units ended and the Soviet units began. More often than not, rather than put up a fight, the Afghan army soldiers defected immediately, bringing to the mujahedin side whatever weapons and munitions they happened to be carrying.[19]

The Soviets did not have the luxury of surrendering. Asked why there were no Red Army soldiers in his prisons, Massoud replied, "Hatred for the Russians is just too great. Many mujahedin have lost their families or homes through communist terror. Their first reaction when coming across a Russian is to kill him."[20]

By the time he repelled his sixth Soviet offensive, in 1982, Massoud had made a name for himself nationwide. He was the "Lion of the Panjshir." The word *Panjshir* itself had become a rallying cry across Afghanistan and abroad, a symbol of hope for the anticommunist resistance. Within the narrow valley Massoud was a hero, popular enough to have his own cult of personality and exert dictatorial control. Instead, he operated his rebellion through councils that provided Panjshiri elders and civilians, as well as subordinate rebel commanders, a voice in his affairs. As a result he was more constrained by local public opinion than rebel leaders who operated out of ISI-funded offices in

Pakistani exile. The Pakistan-based commanders took advantage of the refugee camps spreading around Peshawar and Quetta. Food rations were controlled by Hekmatyar, Sayyaf, Rabbani, and other ISI-supported mujahedin leaders. Hekmatyar, especially, used the camps as a blend of civilian refuge, military encampment, and political operations center. Massoud, on the other hand, ran his guerrilla army entirely inside Afghan territory and relied on the forbearance of Afghan civilians living under repeated vicious Soviet attacks. Massoud ran local police and civil affairs committees in the Panjshir and levied taxes on emerald and lapis miners. His militias depended directly on popular support. There were many other examples of indigenous revolutionary leadership emerging across Afghanistan, but Massoud was becoming the most prominent leader of what the French scholar Olivier Roy called "the only contemporary revivalist Muslim movement to take root among peasants." In Massoud's movement, "The fighting group is the civil society, with the same leadership and no professionalization of fighters."[21]

Soviet scorched earth tactics began to lay the land and its people to waste. Relentless Soviet bombing claimed thousands of civilian lives. By the end of 1982 more than 80 percent of the Panjshir's buildings had been damaged or destroyed. In an attempt to starve the valley out, the Soviets even resorted to that most infamous of Iron Curtain tactics: They built a wall. The six-foot-high concrete barrier at the southern mouth of the valley was intended to keep food and clothing from getting to the Panjshiris. It didn't work. The mujahedin managed to smuggle in everything from biscuits to chewing gum to transistor radios. But with their crops in ruins, their livestock slaughtered, and no end to the fighting in sight, it was unclear how much more hardship the valley's population could bear.

Massoud decided to cut a deal. In the spring of 1983 he announced an unprecedented truce. Under its terms the Soviets would stop attacking in the Panjshir if Massoud allowed the Afghan army to operate a base at the southern end of the valley. The truce followed three years of secret negotiations. For as long as Massoud had been fighting the Soviets, most Afghans outside the Panjshir Valley were shocked to learn, he also had been talking with them. The conversation started as letters exchanged with Soviet commanders across the front lines. In these Massoud and his enemy counterparts conversed like colleagues. Later they held face-to-face meetings. In the final two sessions Massoud brokered the terms personally. Writing from Moscow, Yuri Andropov, the former KGB chief and now Brezhnev's successor as general secretary of the Communist Party, formally endorsed the agreement for the Soviets.[22]

Many in Afghanistan and abroad saw the truce as a craven capitulation.

Massoud's deal was a blow to the mujahedin just "as Benedict Arnold was a blow to the Americans," one American pundit declared.[23] Leaders of Jamaat, Massoud's own party, felt particularly betrayed since Massoud had not bothered to consult them beforehand.

The shock of Massoud's truce helped strengthen his rival Hekmatyar. Pakistani intelligence, for years disdainful of non-Pashtun clients in northern Afghanistan, cited the deal when explaining to CIA counterparts why Massoud had to be cut off completely. "He set a policy of local cease-fire," recalled Brigadier General Syed Raza Ali, who worked in ISI's Afghan bureau throughout the 1980s. "So a man who's working against the Afghan war, why should we deal with him?"[24]

ALREADY STRONG, Hekmatyar emerged as the most powerful of ISI's Pakistan-based mujahedin clients just as Charlie Wilson and Bill Casey, along with Prince Turki, suddenly poured hundreds of millions of dollars' worth of new and more lethal supplies into ISI warehouses.

Hekmatyar had matured into a cold, ruthless, effective leader who tolerated no dissent and readily ordered the deaths of his opponents. He enhanced his power by running the tightest, most militaristic organization in Peshawar and in the refugee camps. "One could rely on them blindly," recalled the ISI brigadier Yousaf, who worked closely with Hekmatyar. "By giving them the weapons you were sure that weapons will not be sold in Pakistan because he was strict to the extent of being ruthless." Chuckling morbidly, Yousaf added: "Once you join his party it was difficult to leave." Hekmatyar "followed the totalitarian model of integrating all powers into the party," as the American scholar Barnett Rubin put it.[25]

Hekmatyar's Pashtun family came from a lesser tribal federation forcibly removed during the nineteenth century from the Pakistani border areas to a northern province of Afghanistan, Kunduz, not far from the Panjshir. That his family's tribal roots were of minority status within the Pashtun community made Hekmatyar attractive to Pakistani intelligence, which wanted to build up Pashtun clients outside of Afghanistan's traditional royal tribes. Hekmatyar attended high school in Kunduz and military school in Kabul before enrolling in the prestigious Faculty of Engineering at Kabul University. Once in Pakistani exile he gathered around him the most radical, anti-Western, transnational Islamists fighting in the jihad—including bin Laden and other Arabs who arrived as volunteers.

The older Muslim Brotherhood–influenced leaders such as Rabbani and

Sayyaf regarded Hekmatyar's group as a rash offshoot. The more professor-ial Afghan Islamists spoke of broad, global Islamic communities and gradual moral evolution. Not Hekmatyar: He was focused on power. His Islamic Party organization became the closest thing to an exiled army in the otherwise diverse, dispersed jihad. He adhered to Qutb's views about the need to van-quish corrupt Muslim leaders in order to establish true Islamic government. He took it upon himself to decide who was a true believer and who was an apostate. Over the centuries Afghan warfare had aimed at "restoring the bal-ance of power, not at destroying the enemy," as the scholar Olivier Roy put it. Hekmatyar, on the other hand, wanted to destroy his enemies. These included not only communist and Soviet occupation forces but mujahedin competitors.

He recognized Massoud as his most formidable military rival and began early on to attack him in the field and through maneuverings in Pakistan and Saudi Arabia. "We have a saying in Pashto," Hekmatyar told an Arab sup-porter who worried about the growing intensity of his rivalry with Massoud. "'There is a rooster who is so conceited it walks on the ceiling on his toes, be-cause he's afraid that the roof would fall.' That rooster is Massoud."[26] In his drive for power during the mid-1980s, Hekmatyar so often attacked Massoud and other mujahedin that intelligence analysts in Washington feared he might be a secret KGB plant whose mission was to sow disruption within the anti-communist resistance.[27]

Yet both at headquarters and in the field, CIA officers in the Near East Di-vision who were running the Afghan program also embraced Hekmatyar as their most dependable and effective ally. ISI officers urged Hekmatyar upon the CIA, and the agency concluded independently that he was the most effi-cient at killing Soviets. They believed this because as they reviewed battlefield damage reports, tracked the movements of weapons shipments, and toured the refugee camps to check on organizational strength among mujahedin par-ties, "analytically, the best fighters—the best organized fighters—were the fun-damentalists," led by Hekmatyar, as one officer then at headquarters put it.[28]

William Piekney, the CIA station chief, would drive down from Islamabad with ISI officers or visiting congressmen to meet with Hekmatyar in the rock-strewn border training camps. He admired Hekmatyar's fighting ability, but among the mujahedin leaders it was also Hekmatyar who gave him the deep-est chills. "I would put my arms around Gulbuddin and we'd hug, you know, like brothers in combat and stuff, and his coal black eyes would look back at you, and you just knew that there was only one thing holding this team to-gether and that was the Soviet Union."[29]

AT LEAST HEKMATYAR KNEW who the enemy was, the CIA's officers and analysts assured themselves. Massoud's truce with the Soviets, on the other hand, was his first public demonstration that in addition to being a military genius, he was also willing to cut a deal with anyone at any time and in any direction if he thought it would advance his goals.

Massoud felt the truce would raise his stature by placing him on equal footing with a superpower. "The Russians have negotiated with a valley," his aide Massoud Khalili crowed. The deal also bought Massoud time to regroup for what he had determined would be a long, long fight ahead. He sought not only to resist the Soviets but to compete for power in Kabul and on a national stage, as the revolutionaries he admired from his reading had done. Despite the uncertainties of the war, he planned early for a conventional army that could occupy Kabul after the Soviets left.[30] He used the period during the ceasefire—more than a year, as it turned out—to stockpile weapons and food for his critically malnourished and poorly armed troops. Panjshiri farmers, who hadn't enjoyed a peaceful growing season in several years, harvested crops unmolested. And many of his troops ranged to other parts of the country, building alliances on Massoud's behalf with mujahedin commanders who had never been to the Panjshir.

Massoud also capitalized on the calm to attack Hekmatyar's forces. Before the truce, a group aligned with Hekmatyar's party had been using an adjacent valley, the Andarab, to stage assaults on Massoud's flank and cut off his supply lines. With one swift commando raid, Massoud drove these fighters out of the valley and, for the time being, off his back. It was an opening action in an emerging war within the Afghan war.

By the time the truce began to unravel in the spring of 1984, Massoud was breezing through the Panjshir in a distinguished new black Volga sedan. The car had been intended as a gift from the Soviets for the Afghan defense minister, but Massoud's guerrillas picked it off on its way down the Salang Highway and hauled it back to the Panjshir in hundreds of pieces as a gift for their commander.[31]

The Soviets signaled their displeasure by sending an undercover Afghan agent into the Panjshir. The agent took a shot at Massoud from thirty feet away but missed. The assassination attempt exposed two other Afghan communist agents in the rebels' midst, including a Massoud cousin who had also been one of his commanders.

Massoud's own spy network remained a step ahead. In the spring of 1984 he learned that the Soviets intended to launch a twenty-thousand-man assault on the valley. Not only would the invasion be larger than anything seen before, but, according to Massoud's sources, the tactics would be far more ruthless. The Soviets planned to subject the valley to a week's worth of high-altitude aerial assaults and then sow the bomb-tilled soil with land mines to make it uninhabitable for years to come.

Massoud ordered the entire Panjshir Valley to evacuate in late April. Three days before Soviet bombers soared above its gorges, he led more than forty thousand Panjshiris out of the valley and into hiding. When Soviet ground troops—including numerous special forces units known as Spetsnaz—moved in a week later, they found the Panjshir Valley utterly ruined and almost completely deserted.

From the concealed caves surrounding the Panjshir where Massoud reestablished his organization, he cautiously plotted his return. His men launched operations from the ridgelines, shooting down at the helicopters that canvassed the valley floor. They ambushed the enemy, created diversions, and fought at night when the Soviets were most vulnerable.

But the introduction of the elite Spetsnaz, along with their advanced Mi-24D Hind attack helicopters and communications gear, gradually shifted war-fighting tactics in the Soviets' favor. As many as two thousand Spetsnaz were deployed in Afghanistan during 1984, and the Mi-24's armor-coated belly repulsed nearly all the antiaircraft guns available to the mujahedin. Massoud's men found themselves pursued on foot by heavily armed Spetsnaz troops who could scramble up the valley's rugged cliffs almost as fast as the locals. Kabul Radio reported that Massoud had been killed in action. When an interviewer late that spring asked Afghan President Babrak Karmal whether Massoud was alive or dead, Karmal dismissed the question. "Who is this Massoud that you speak of?" he asked contemptuously. "U.S. propaganda creates artificial personalities and false gods. . . . As an actor, Reagan knows well how to create puppets on the international stage. . . . These creations are clay idols that disintegrate just as fast. Massoud was an instrument of the imperialists. I don't know if he is alive or dead and I don't care. The Panjshir issue has been resolved."[32]

It had not been, but Massoud was reeling. "It has become a very hard war, far harder than before," the commander acknowledged to a visitor in between sips of tea while ensconced deep within one of his innumerable caves. "Their commandos have learned a great deal about mountain guerrilla warfare and are fighting much better than before."[33]

CIA analysts said the same in reports they circulated from Langley. The Soviet campaign in the Panjshir that spring featured "increased use of heliborne assaults," one such report said, along with "an unprecedented high-altitude bombing" campaign. Yet Massoud's advance warning of the assault and his covert evacuation of civilians made the difference because "Soviet intelligence apparently failed to discover that most guerrillas and their civilian supporters had left the valley." At the same time the CIA knew that the civil war now gathering momentum between Massoud and Hekmatyar was undermining the jihad. Intramural battles between the two groups "have hampered operations and resupply efforts of Massoud's Panjshir Valley insurgents," the CIA's classified report said.[34]

Until late 1984 and early 1985, Massoud had received relatively little outside assistance. The British intelligence service, MI6, which operated out of a small windowless office in Britain's Islamabad embassy, made contact with Massoud early in the war and provided him with money, a few weapons, and some communications equipment. British intelligence officers taught English to some of Massoud's trusted aides, such as his foreign policy liaison, Abdullah. The French, too, reached out to Massoud. Unburdened by the CIA's rules, which prohibited travel in Afghanistan, both intelligence services sent officers overland into the Panjshir posing as journalists. The CIA relied on British intelligence for reports about Massoud. At Langley "there was probably a little penis envy" of these border-hopping European spies, "you know, they were going in," as one officer involved put it. The French especially grated: "trying to find some liberator character" in the person of Massoud, making him out as an Afghan "Simon Bolivar, George Washington."[35]

Massoud charmed his British and French visitors. He dressed more stylishly than other Afghans. He spoke some French. His manner was calm and confident, never blustery. "He was never emotional or subjective," as his aide Khalili put it. "Always he was objective."[36] He horsed around lightly with his trusted senior commanders, pushing them in the water when they went swimming or teasing them as they went off together on dangerous missions. And while he prayed five times a day and fought unyieldingly in Allah's name, drawing on the radical texts he had learned at Kabul Polytechnic Institute, he seemed to outsiders more tolerant, more humane, and more rooted in the land than many other Afghan resistance commanders.

The CIA, honoring its agreement with Zia to work solely through ISI, had no direct contacts with Massoud during the early 1980s. ISI officers in the Afghan bureau saw the British "playing their own game" with Massoud, which provided yet another reason to withhold support from him. But the

CIA did begin in late 1984 to secretly pass money and light supplies to Massoud without telling Pakistan.[37]

"He was never a problem in any sense that he was the enemy or that we were trying to cut him off," according to one CIA officer involved. But neither was the CIA "ready to spend a lot of time and energy trying to push" Massoud forward. Massoud swore fealty to Rabbani, but relations between them were badly strained. Rabbani received ample supplies from ISI at his Peshawar offices but often did not pass much along to Massoud. "Rabbani was not a fool, he's a politician," the ISI's Yousaf recalled. "He cannot make a man stronger than him."[38] Rabbani wanted to build up his own influence across Afghanistan by recruiting Pashtun, Uzbek, and Shiite commanders, securing their loyalty with weapons. In doing so he sought to limit Massoud's relative power.

As a result almost everything Massoud's forces owned they scavenged from the enemy, including Massoud's own clothes: Red Army fatigues and Afghan army boots. Occasionally, Rabbani might send him a care package, originating with ISI or the Saudis, in the form of all the supplies that a dozen horses can carry. But Western journalists who spent months with Massoud's fighters in the early 1980s returned from the Panjshir with reports that U.S.-funded assistance to the mujahedin was nowhere to be found.

As the fighting grew more difficult, Massoud had to admit he needed outside help. He refused to leave Afghanistan, but he began to send his brothers out of the country, to Peshawar, London, and Washington, to make contact with the CIA officers and Pakistani generals who controlled the covert supply lines.

Among the items on his wish list were portable rations and vitamins to help his troops stay nourished; an X-ray machine to diagnose the wounded; infrared goggles and aiming devices for nighttime fighting; radios to improve coordination among commanders; and, above all, shoulder-fired antiaircraft rockets to defend against helicopters and planes. With that kind of support Massoud thought he could force the Soviets back to the negotiating table within six months. Without it, the war "could last 40 years."[39]

Massoud didn't know it, but in Washington that spring of 1985 some of his American admirers had reached similar conclusions.

"The Terrorists
Will Own the World"

I N HIS RISING ENTHUSIASM for the Afghan war and in his determination to punish the Soviets to the greatest possible degree, William Casey
found that he needed allies outside of CIA headquarters. Time did little to
shake his belief that the CIA's career clandestine officers were too timid. But
there were influential conservatives in the executive branch who could aid his
push for a more potent covert war. The Reagan administration had attracted
to Washington "an awful lot of *Soldier of Fortune* readers," recalled Frank Anderson, a clandestine service officer involved in the Afghan program. These
mercenary voyeurs included blunt paramilitary types such as Casey's friend
Oliver North and more cerebral anticommunist hawks who came from right-
wing think tanks.[1]

Casey connected with these allies as they developed a new plan for the
Afghan jihad. Known as National Security Decision Directive 166, with an
annex classified Top Secret/Codeword, the blueprint they produced became
the legal basis for a massive escalation of the CIA's role in Afghanistan, starting in 1985.

The new policy document provided a retroactive rationale for the huge increases in covert funds forced into the Afghan program late in 1984 by Char-

lie Wilson. It also looked forward to a new era of direct infusions of advanced U.S. military technology into Afghanistan, intensified training of Islamist guerrillas in explosives and sabotage techniques, and targeted attacks
on Soviet military officers designed to demoralize the Soviet high command.
Among other consequences these changes pushed the CIA, along with its
clients in the Afghan resistance and in Pakistani intelligence, closer to the gray
fields of assassination and terrorism.

The meetings that produced NSDD-166 changed the way the United
States directed its covert Afghan program. For the first time the CIA lost its
near-total control. The peculiar Washington institution known as "the interagency process" became dominant. This was typical of national security policy
making by the 1980s. Representatives from various agencies and Cabinet departments, selected for their relevance to the foreign policy issue at hand,
would form under supervision from the White House's National Security
Council. The committee often selected a vague name with a tongue-twisting
acronym that could be bandied about as a secret membership code. During
the Reagan administration the CIA worked continuously with one such
group, the Planning and Coordination Group, or PCG, the president's unpublicized body for the oversight of all secret covert actions. With Casey's cooperation the sweeping review of Afghan covert action was taken on early in
1985 by a PCG subset, the Policy Review Group, which began to meet in a
high-ceilinged warren of the Old Executive Office Building, next door to the
West Wing of the White House.

A striking gray gabled building imitating the styles of the French Renaissance, with capped peaks and sloping bays that spoke elaborately to 17th
Street's bland marble office boxes, the Old Executive Office Building housed
many of the national security personnel who couldn't fit inside the cramped
West Wing. Casey kept an office there. Behind most of its tall doors lay regional
National Security Council directorates. Here delegates from Langley, the Pentagon, and the State Department's headquarters building in the nearby Washington neighborhood known as Foggy Bottom would all tramp in to review
operations, debate policy, and prepare documents for presidential signature.

The new interagency group on Afghanistan, meeting in Room 208, forced
the CIA to share a table with civilians and uniformed officers from the Pentagon. In early 1985 the most influential new figure was Fred Iklé, a former
director of the Arms Control and Disarmament Agency and an elegant anticommunist hardliner. With him came Michael Pillsbury, an eager former congressional aide.

With Iklé's support, Pillsbury pushed a draft of NSDD-166 for Reagan's signature. For a midlevel aide with little authority on paper beyond his high-level security clearances, he defined his mission ambitiously. To help Afghan rebels overcome rising Soviet military pressure, he wanted to provide them with the best guerrilla weapons and satellite intelligence. To do this Pillsbury needed new legal authority for CIA covert action that went beyond the Carter-era policy goal of "harassing" Soviet occupation forces. He sought to expand dramatically the stated aims and the military means of the CIA's Afghan jihad.

The agency's career officers at the Near East Division saw Pillsbury as a reckless amateur. Pillsbury saw himself as a principled conservative who re-fused to be cowed by cautious agency bureaucrats. He wanted to define the purpose of the CIA's efforts in Afghanistan as "victory" over the Soviet forces. That language seemed too stark to CIA officers and State diplomats. Falling back, Pillsbury suggested they define the jihad's goal as "to drive the Soviets out." This, too, seemed provocative to other committee members. In the end they settled on language that directed the CIA to use "all available means" to support the mujahedin's drive for a free Afghanistan.

Pillsbury attracted support by offering budgetary blank checks to every agency remotely involved in Afghanistan—State, the Agency for Interna-tional Development, the United States Information Agency, and the Penta-gon. Casey's CIA would remain in the lead, working mainly through Pakistan's ISI. But the CIA would also be given new authority to operate on its own out-side of Pakistani eyesight. Other departments were encouraged to submit ambitious plans that could be integrated with the CIA's work. The new policy was that "everybody gets to do what everybody wants to" in support of the mujahedin, Pillsbury recalled. "Everybody got what they wanted into this document and, in return for all this harmony, the goal got changed."[2]

President Reagan signed the classified NSDD-166, titled "Expanded U.S. Aid to Afghan Guerrillas," in March 1985, formally anointing its confronta-tional language as covert U.S. policy in Afghanistan. His national security ad-viser, Robert McFarlane, signed the highly classified sixteen-page annex, which laid out specific new steps to be taken by the CIA.

For the first time the agency could use satellite photographs of the Afghan battlefield to help the mujahedin plan attacks on Soviet targets. The agency would soon send in secure "burst communications" sets that would allow the rebels to use advanced American technology to thwart Soviet interception of their radio traffic. The CIA would begin for the first time to recruit substantial numbers of "unilateral" agents in Afghanistan—agents who would be undeclared and unknown to Pakistani intelligence. Also for the first time, by at least one account, the document explicitly endorsed direct attacks on individual Soviet military officers.[3]

Rapidly ebbing now were the romanticized neocolonial days of Howard Hart's tour in the Islamabad station, a hands-off era of antique rifles, tea-sipping liaisons, and ink-splotched secret shipping manifests. Some of the agency's career officers in the Near East Division were not enthusiastic about the changes, especially the ones that contemplated attacks on Soviet officers. They saw Pillsbury and his cowboy civilian ilk as dragging the CIA out of its respectable core business of espionage and into the murky, treacherous realm of an escalating dirty war.

At one interagency committee meeting in the spring of 1985, Fred Ikle proposed skipping over Pakistani intelligence altogether by flying American C-130s over Afghanistan and dropping weapons caches to Afghan commanders by parachute. Someone asked: What if the Russians begin shooting down the U.S. planes and ignite World War III? "Hmmm," Iklé answered, according to Thomas Twetten, a senior officer in the CIA's clandestine service. "World War III. That's not such a bad idea." If he said such a thing, Iklé said later, he must have been kidding. But Twetten remembered "a roomful of dumb-struck people."[4]

Shooting Soviet officers was equally troubling to some at the agency. The CIA and KGB had settled during the 1980s into a shaky, unwritten gentlemen's agreement that sought to discourage targeting each other's salaried professional officers for kidnapping or murder. If that agreement broke down, there could be chaos in CIA stations worldwide. CIA officers in Pakistan made a point of treating gently the rare Soviet prisoners taken on the Afghan battlefield. The agency's officers figured this would help American military officers and spies captured by Soviet forces on other Cold War proxy battle-fields.[5]

But the congressmen writing the CIA's budgetary checks now wanted to start killing Soviet officers serving in Afghanistan. Senator Gordon Humphrey traveled to Kabul at one point and came home crowing about how you could see Soviet generals in the windows of their tattered concrete apartment blocks; all the mujahedin needed were some long-range sniper rifles, and they could start picking them off one at a time.[6]

Increasingly, too, under ISI direction, the mujahedin received training and malleable explosives to mount car bomb and even camel bomb attacks in

Soviet-occupied cities, usually designed to kill Soviet soldiers and command-ers. Casey endorsed these techniques despite the qualms of some CIA career officers.

Casey never argued for attacks on purely civilian targets, but he was in-clined toward aggressive force. In the worldwide antiterror campaign Casey began to envision during 1985, Afghanistan offered one way to attack the So-viet aggressors.

"We're arming the Afghans, right?" Casey asked during one of the debates of this period. He wanted authority to strike at Middle Eastern terrorists pre-emptively. "Every time a mujahedin rebel kills a Soviet rifleman, are we en-gaged in assassination? This is a rough business. If we're afraid to hit the terrorists because somebody's going to yell 'assassination,' it'll never stop. The terrorists will own the world."[7]

AT THE CIA STATION in Islamabad the new era arrived in the form of visiting delegations from Washington: Pentagon officers carrying satellite maps, special forces commandos offering a course in advanced explosives, and suitcase-carrying congressional visitors who wanted Disney-quality tours of mujahedin camps and plenty of time to buy handwoven carpets. William Piekney tried to move them all cheerfully through the turnstiles. With senior delegations he might drive them to ISI's unmarked headquarters for tea and talk with General Akhtar.

Iklé and Pillsbury touched down in Islamabad on April 30, 1985. They could not legally disclose the existence of NSDD-166, but they wanted Akhtar to understand its expansive goals. During a two-hour private conver-sation at the ISI chief's residence, Iklé was able "to convey the thrust of the President's new decision directive," as Pillsbury put it.[8]

The visitors wanted to pump up Akhtar's ambitions when he submitted quarterly lists of weapons needed by the mujahedin. The CIA's Afghan sup-ply system depended on these formal requests. Soon the classified lists cabled in from Islamabad included antiaircraft missiles, long-range sniper rifles, night-vision goggles, delayed timing devices for plastic explosives, and elec-tronic intercept equipment. The new requests made it harder than ever to maintain plausible deniability about the CIA's role in the jihad. This made the agency's professional secret-keepers uncomfortable. But even the most re-flexively clandestine among them recognized that by 1985 the Soviet leader-ship had already learned the outlines of the CIA's Afghan program from press reports, captured fighters, intercepted communications, and KGB-supervised espionage operations carried out among the rebels. Even the American public knew the outlines of Langley's work from newspaper stories and television documentaries. Increasingly, as the CIA and its gung-ho adversaries argued over the introduction of more sophisticated weapons, the issue was not whether the existence of an American covert supply line could be kept secret but whether the supply of precision American arms would provoke the Soviets into raiding Pakistan or retaliating against Americans.

Piekney's station began to run more and more unilateral intelligence agents across the Afghan border. The swelling volume of weapons shipments, the rising number of questions from visiting congressmen about ISI ripoffs, and the worsening violence on the Afghan battlefield all argued for deeper and more independent CIA reporting. To some extent it was a matter of protecting the CIA from intensifying congressional oversight: The agency needed to be able to demonstrate that it was independently auditing the large new flows of weaponry. It could not do so credibly if it relied only on Pakistani intelligence for its reporting.

Some of the CIA's unilateral reporting agents were Afghans; Hart's relationship with Abdul Haq was passed along to Piekney, for instance. But most of the new agents who traveled in Afghanistan on the CIA's behalf during the mid-1980s were European adventurers. These included European journalists, photographers, and ex–foreign legion members. Piekney's connections from his previous tour in Paris helped with the recruitments. Warren Marik, an undeclared CIA case officer operating out of the American consulate in Karachi, away from ISI surveillance in Islamabad, handled many of the Europeans. After they flew in to Karachi from France or Belgium, Marik would hook them up with trusted Afghan guides and sometimes provide false papers and cover identities. A few of the European agents were given secure communications gear so they could send in timely reports from the Afghan battlefield, but most went across the border carrying only notebooks and cameras. When they came out, Marik would fly them quickly to Europe for debriefings. The photographs these agents took provided the CIA with its own archive of close-up pictures of battlefield damage, Soviet weapons systems, and troop deployments. The agents' firsthand reports about Afghan commanders also provided a check on ISI claims about weapons handouts. And the Europeans came cheap, usually taking in the range of only $1,000 a month. They weren't in it for the money; they sought adventure.[9]

For their part, politically savvy Afghan commanders began to understand by 1985 that one way to lobby for weapons and power—and to outflank ISI's controlling brigadiers—was to build their own independent relationships in Washington or Riyadh. The Islamist radicals tended to cultivate wealthy patrons in Saudi Arabia. Sayyaf lectured there so often that he was awarded the kingdom's King Faisal Intellectual Prize during 1985. The self-described "moderate" Afghan rebel leaders with ties to the old royal family or the country's mystical Sufi brotherhoods relied more on support from Europe and Washington, particularly from Capitol Hill. A parade of well-tailored "Gucci muj," as the CIA Near East officers derisively called them, began to fly in from Pakistan and march from office to office in Washington.

Those Afghans who felt neglected by Pakistani intelligence tended to be the most active in Washington. These included the royalist Pashtuns from the Durrani tribal federation, whose political ancestry made them unattractive to the Pakistan army. They swore allegiance to former king Zahir Shah, who lived in exile in a villa outside Rome. They denounced Pakistani intelligence for its aid to Hekmatyar, from the rival Ghilzai tribal federation, whom they regarded as a dangerous megalomaniac.

Gradually, too, Ahmed Shah Massoud's brothers and Panjshiri aides began to make the rounds in Washington. Massoud's now widely publicized record as a war hero in the harsh Panjshir gave him more clout and credibility than the Durrani Pashtuns, who tended to be dismissed, especially at Langley, as political self-promoters with weak battlefield records.

The CIA's Near East Division found itself under rising pressure to direct more of the money and weapons flowing from NSDD-166's escalation toward Massoud. Yet the agency still had only the most tenuous connections to Massoud. The CIA tended to view all the Washington lobbying as evidence of innate Afghan factionalism, not as an expression of dissent about Pakistani intelligence policy. "It was quite a spectacle as the bearded and robed mujahedin political leaders went from office to office, building to building, making their personal and parochial cases for support," Directorate of Intelligence chief Robert Gates wrote later. "No one should have had any illusions about these people coming together politically—before or after a Soviet defeat."[10]

The CIA's leadership continued to regard Pakistani intelligence as the jihad's main implementing agency, even as more and more American trainers arrived in Pakistan to teach new weapons and techniques. All this ensured that ISI's Muslim Brotherhood–inspired clients—mainly Hekmatyar but also Sayyaf, Rabbani, and radical commanders who operated along the Pakistan border, such as Jallaladin Haqqanni—won the greatest share of support.

From its earliest days the Afghan war had been brutal, characterized by indiscriminate aerial bombing and the widespread slaughter of civilians. After six years the CIA, ISI, KGB, and Soviet special forces had all refined their tactics. Now, as the new American policy blueprint put it, each side sought to demoralize, sabotage, frighten, and confuse its enemy by whatever means necessary.

AS THE AFGHAN operations director for Pakistani intelligence between 1983 and 1987, Brigadier Mohammed Yousaf was Akhtar's "barbarian handler," as one CIA colleague put it, quoting an old Chinese moniker. Yousaf ran the clandestine training camps, kept the books on weapons handouts, received the new satellite maps, and occasionally accompanied mujahedin groups on commando missions. His strategy was "death by a thousand cuts." He emphasized attacks on Soviet command targets in Kabul. He saw the capital as a center of gravity for the Soviets. If the city became a secure sanctuary, Soviet generals might never leave.[11]

ISI-supplied Afghan guerrillas detonated a briefcase bomb under a dining room table at Kabul University in 1983, killing nine Soviets, including a female professor. Yousaf and the Afghan car bombing squads he trained regarded Kabul University professors as fair game since they were poisoning young minds with Marxist anti-Islamic dogma. Mujahedin commandos later assassinated the university's rector. Seven Soviet military officers were reported shot dead by Kabul assassins in a single year. By Yousaf's estimation, car bombing squads trained by Pakistan and supplied with CIA-funded explosives and detonators made "numerous" attempts to kill the chief of the Afghan secret police, the notorious torturer Najibullah, but they repeatedly failed to get him.[12]

Fear of poisoning, surprise attacks, and assassination became rife among Russian officers and soldiers in Kabul. The rebels fashioned booby-trapped bombs from gooey black contact explosives, supplied to Pakistani intelligence by the CIA, that could be molded into ordinary shapes or poured into innocent utensils. Russian soldiers began to find bombs made from pens, watches, cigarette lighters, and tape recorders. "Hidden death has been camouflaged so masterfully that only someone with a practiced eye can see it," the independent Russian writer Artyom Borovik reported during his travels. Kabul shopkeepers poisoned food eaten by Russian soldiers. Assassins lurked in the city's mud-rock alleys. A rhyme invented by Russian conscripts went:

Afghanistan
A wonderland
Just drop into a store
And you'll be seen no more[13]

Across the Pakistan border Yousaf saw himself treading a careful line between guerrilla war and terrorism. "We are as good or bad [a] civilized nation as anyone living in the West," he said later, "because when you carry out this sort of operation it has a double edge." His squads bombed Kabul cinemas and cultural shows, but the attacking Afghan guerrillas knew that most of their victims "would be the Soviet soldiers." Otherwise, Yousaf said, "You will not find any case of poisoning the water or any use of chemical or biological." Car bombs were supposed to be targeted only at military leaders, he said later. By all accounts there were few car bombings aimed at civilians during this period. However, once the uncontrolled mortaring of Kabul began in 1985, after the CIA shipped in Egyptian and Chinese rockets that could be remotely fired from long range, random civilian casualties in the city began to mount steadily.

The CIA officers that Yousaf worked with closely impressed upon him one rule: Never use the terms *sabotage* or *assassination* when speaking with visiting congressmen.[14]

The KGB had no such worries. By 1985, Soviet and Afghan intelligence operatives played a greater role in the counterinsurgency campaign than ever before. Najibullah, the secret police chief, was elevated to the Afghan Politburo in November 1985. By the following spring Moscow had sacked Babrak Karmal and appointed Najibullah as Afghanistan's president. His ruling councils were filled with ruthless intelligence operatives. The KGB-trained Afghan intelligence service swelled to about 30,000 professionals and 100,000 paid informers. Its domestic directorates, lacking cooperative sources among the population, routinely detained and tortured civilians in search of insight about mujahedin operations. The Afghan service also ran foreign operations in Iran and Pakistan. It maintained secret residencies in Quetta, Peshawar, Islamabad, New Delhi, Karachi, and elsewhere, communicating to Kabul through Soviet embassies and consulates. By planting agents in refugee camps Afghan intelligence gradually penetrated the mujahedin.[15]

Frustrated by the copious new supplies pouring into Afghanistan, the Soviet Fortieth Army deployed intelligence teams and helicopter-borne Spetsnaz special forces to try to seal the Pakistan border during 1985. They failed, but they wreaked havoc in the effort. Spetsnaz units dispatched high-tech communications intercept vehicles called "Omsk vans" to track mujahedin movements from Peshawar or Quetta. When they located a convoy, they sent the new, fearsome Mi-24D helicopters on intercept missions across the barren Pakistani hills. The helicopters would fly five or ten miles inside Pakistan, then swing around and move up behind the mujahedin as they slouched along canyon paths or desert culverts. Spetsnaz commandos poured out and ambushed the rebels. Increasingly Russian special forces captured mujahedin equipment, such as their ubiquitous Japanese-made pickup trucks, which were shipped in by the CIA. The Russian special forces began to operate in disguise, dressed as Islamic rebels. The KGB also ran "false bands" of mujahedin across Afghanistan, paying them to attack genuine rebel groups in an attempt to sow dissension.[16]

Mujahedin operating along the Pakistan border took heavy casualties in these Spetsnaz helicopter raids. They also had a few rare successes. Pakistani intelligence captured from Soviet defectors and handed over to Piekney the first intact Mi-24D ever taken in by the CIA. Langley ordered a team to Islamabad to load the dismantled prize on to a transport jet and fly it back to the United States; its exploitation saved the Pentagon millions of dollars in research and development costs, the Pentagon later reported.[17]

Encouraged by the CIA, Pakistani intelligence also focused on sabotage operations that would cut Soviet supply lines. But the missions often proved difficult because even the most ardent Afghan Islamists refused to mount suicide operations.

In his Wile E. Coyote–style efforts to blow up the Salang Tunnel north of Kabul, Yousaf tried to concoct truck bomb missions in which ISI would help load fuel tankers with explosives. Soviet soldiers moved quickly to intercept any truck that stalled inside the strategic tunnel, so there seemed no practical way to complete such a mission unless the truck driver was willing to die in the cause. The Afghans whom Yousaf trained uniformly denounced suicide attack proposals as against their religion. It was only the Arab volunteers— from Saudi Arabia, Jordan, Algeria, and other countries, who had been raised in an entirely different culture, spoke their own language, and preached their own interpretations of Islam while fighting far from their homes and families—who later advocated suicide attacks. Afghan jihadists, tightly woven into family, clan, and regional social networks, never embraced suicide tactics in significant numbers.[18]

Afghan fighters also often refused to attack bridges or trade routes if they were important to civilian traders or farmers. The Afghan tolerance of civilian commerce in the midst of dire conflict frustrated visiting Americans. A congressman on tour would fly over Afghanistan, see a bridge standing unmolested, and complain loudly on his return to Washington that it ought to be blown up. But when the satellite-mapped attack plan was passed down through ISI to a particular Afghan commando team, the Afghans would often shrug off the order or use the supplied weapons to hit a different target of their own choosing. They took tolls from bridges. The livelihood of their clan often depended on open roads.

Still, the CIA shipped to Pakistani intelligence many tons of C-4 plastic explosives for sabotage operations during this period. Britain's MI6 provided magnetic depth charges to attack bridge pylons, particularly the bridge near Termez that spanned the Amu Darya. After 1985 the CIA also supplied electronic timing and detonation devices that made it easier to set off explosions from a remote location. The most basic delay detonator was the "time pencil," a chemical device that wore down gradually and set off a bomb or rocket after a predictable period. It had been developed by the CIA's Office of Technical Services. Guerrillas could use these devices to set an explosive charge at night, retreat, and then watch it blow up at first light. After 1985 the CIA also shipped in "E cell" delay detonators, which used sophisticated electronics to achieve similar effects. Thousands of the delay timers were distributed on the frontier.

Speaking in an interview in July 1992, seven months before the first Islamist terrorist attack on the World Trade Center, a U.S. official closely involved in the CIA supply program was asked by the author to estimate the amount of plastic explosives that had been transferred by Pakistani intelligence to the mujahedin with CIA and Saudi support. The official spontaneously chose these words: "We could have probably blown up half of New York with the explosives that the Paks supplied."

CIA lawyers and operators at Langley were more sensitive than ever about second-guessing from Congress and the press. Casey's Nicaragua operations were going sour just as the covert Afghan war began to escalate. The agency was criticized sharply for placing mines in Nicaragua's harbors. There was a feeling taking hold in the Directorate of Operations by late 1985 that perhaps Casey had gone too far, that the agency was headed for another political crash.

In the Afghan program the CIA was now supplying many "dual use" weapons systems, meaning weapons that could be used against legitimate military targets but also could be employed in terrorism or assassination. These included the new electronic detonators, the malleable plastic explosives, and sniper rifle packages. The rough rule at Langley was that the CIA would not supply any weapon where "its most likely use would be for assassination or criminal enterprise," as one official involved put it. Since the CIA was not running the commando operations itself but was relying on Pakistani intelligence, "most likely use" could only be approximated. Langley's Afghan task force chief, the rough and aggressive anticommunist Gust Avrakatos, tried to evade CIA lawyers. "These aren't terrorist devices or assassination techniques," Avrakatos told his colleagues when weapons such as sniper rifles had to be described in cables and memos. "Henceforth these are individual defensive devices." He discouraged officers from putting too much in writing. When the Islamabad station sent a cable describing a borderline guerrilla tactic, he wrote back that the message had been garbled and that the station should not send "anything more on that subject ever again." He shopped in Egypt for sabotage devices such as wheelbarrows rigged as bombs that could be used to target Soviet officers in Kabul. "Do I want to order bicycle bombs to park in front of an officers' headquarters?" Avrakatos recalled asking. "Yes. That's what spreads fear." He endorsed a system run by Pakistani intelligence that rewarded Afghan commanders for the number of individual Soviet belt buckles they brought in.[19]

American law about assassination and terrorism was entering another of its periods of flux. The executive order banning assassination, enacted by President Ford in response to the exposure of CIA plots from the 1960s, had been sitting unexamined on the books for a decade. Not even the hardliners in the Reagan Cabinet wanted the ban removed, but they had begun to question its ambiguities. When did targeting a general or head of state in war or in response to a terrorist attack drift across the line and become assassination? Was the decision to target that general or head of state the issue, or was it the means employed to kill him? What if a preemptive assassination was undertaken to stop a terrorist from attacking the United States? The questions being debated were both strategic and pragmatic. For American national security, what policy was morally defensible and militarily effective? What, technically, did the Ford-era assassination ban cover? This had to be spelled out, CIA officers argued, or else agents and even civilian policy makers might inadvertently expose themselves to criminal prosecution.

Reagan's lawyers at the White House and the Justice Department believed that preemptive attacks on individuals carried out in self-defense—such as against a terrorist about to launch a strike—were clearly legal. But there were many questions about how such a standard should be defined and implemented.

In the Afghan program sniper rifles created the greatest unease. They were known as "buffalo guns" and could accurately fire large, potent bullets from distances of one or two kilometers. The idea to supply them to the Afghan rebels had originated with a Special Forces enthusiast in Washington named

Vaughan Forrest, who wrote a long report for the CIA and the National Security Council about how the mujahedin might counter Soviet Spetsnaz tactics by hitting Soviet commanders directly. "It doesn't take a genius to figure out that you need to hit them hard, you need to hit them deep, and you need to hit his heart and brains," Forrest said. His enthusiasm extended to a broader campaign of urban sabotage that some on the NSC interagency committee regarded as outright terrorism. But the idea of targeting Soviet commanders with the sniper rifles found support. "The phrase 'shooting ducks in a barrel' was used," one participant recalled. The sniper program's advocates wanted to "off Russian generals in series."[20]

Through the CIA station in Islamabad, Pakistani intelligence endorsed a formal written request for the buffalo guns, plus supporting equipment such as night-vision goggles and high-powered scopes that would allow a shooter to hit his target from a mile away under cover of darkness. The incoming cable set off alarms in the general counsel's office at the CIA. The night-vision equipment and scopes were clearly intended for missions that, if not outright assassination under the law, seemed uncomfortably close. Should the operation go sour, the Islamabad station chief might end up in handcuffs.

After several rounds of debate and teeth-gnashing, a compromise was reached: The guns could be shipped to Pakistan, but they would be stripped of the night-vision goggles and scopes that seemed to tilt their "most likely use" toward assassination. Also, the CIA would not provide ISI with target intelligence from satellites concerning where Soviet officers lived or how their apartment buildings might be approached stealthily. CIA officers tried to emphasize to ISI the guns' value as "antimaterial" weapons, meaning that they could be used to shoot out the tires in a convoy of trucks from a distant mountaintop or to drill holes in a fuel tanker. American specialists traveled to Pakistan to train ISI officers on the rifles so that they, in turn, could train rebel commando teams. In the end, dozens of the sniper rifles were shipped to Afghanistan.[21]

THE TERRORIST ATTACKS came one after another during 1985, all broadcast live on network television to tens of millions of Americans. In June two Lebanese terrorists hijacked TWA Flight 847, murdered a Navy diver on board, and negotiated while mugging for cameras on a Beirut runway. In October the Palestinian terrorist Abu Abbas hijacked the cruise ship *Achille Lauro* in Italy, murdered a sixty-nine-year-old Jewish-American tourist, Leon

Klinghoffer, dumped his body overboard, and ultimately escaped to Baghdad with Egyptian and Italian collaboration. Just after Christmas, Palestinian gunmen with the Abu Nidal Organization opened fire on passengers lined up at El Al ticket counters in Vienna and Rome, killing nineteen people, among them five Americans. One of the American victims was an eleven-year-old girl named Natasha Simpson who died in her father's arms after a gunman unloaded an extra round in her head just to make sure. The attackers, boyish products of Palestinian refugee camps, had been pumped full of amphetamines by their handlers just before the holiday attacks.

The shock of these events followed the 1983 bombing of the U.S. embassy in Lebanon, which claimed the lives of some of the CIA's brightest minds on the Middle East, and the bombing of the U.S. Marine barracks in Beirut, in which 241 Marines died. The Shiite terrorist organization Hezbollah had seized American hostages in Lebanon. Casey and Reagan had been galvanized by this violence in Lebanon against official Americans and journalists. Now they confronted a new, wider wave of attacks targeting American civilians and tourists.

During 1985 about 6.5 million Americans traveled overseas, of whom about 6,000 died for various reasons, mainly from illnesses. Seventeen were killed by terrorists. Yet by the end of the year millions of Americans were canceling travel plans and demanding action from their government. Palestinian and Lebanese Shiite terrorists had captured America's attention just as they had hoped to do.

"When we hijack a plane, it has more effect than if we killed a hundred Israelis in battle," the Palestinian Marxist leader George Habash once said. "At least the world is talking about us now." By the mid-1980s the American analyst Brian Jenkins's observation had become famous: "Terrorists want a lot of people watching and a lot of people listening and not a lot of people dead." He coined another oft-repeated phrase: "Terrorism is theater."[22]

In its modern form it was a theater invented largely by a stateless Palestinian diaspora whose leftist leaders sought dramatic means to attract attention to their national claims. In the new academic specialty of terrorist studies it was common to date the first modern terrorist event as the Habash-led hijacking of an El Al flight from Rome to Tel Aviv on July 22, 1968. Thereafter inventive Palestinian terrorists attacked the vulnerabilities of aviation and exploited the new global reach of television, creating a succession of made-for-TV terrorist events that emphasized the spectacular. At the same time, because a purpose of their movement was to negotiate for statehood, they often sought to limit and calibrate their violence to create the greatest impact without alienating important political allies. As at the Munich Olympics in 1972 and at the Rome and Vienna airports in late 1985, these efforts to control public relations sometimes failed. In Washington especially the politics of antiterrorism were becoming angrier and angrier.

Shortly after the airport attacks Casey summoned the chief of the CIA's European Division, Duane R. "Dewey" Clarridge, to his office on Langley's seventh floor. A New Hampshire Yankee educated at Brown University, Clarridge was a cigar-chomping career officer who craved action and bridled at supervision. He had served in Nepal and India during the early Cold War, running anti-Soviet operations on obscure frontiers. He had impressed Casey as a hearty risk-taker, and the director rewarded him with full control over his secret war in Nicaragua. There Clarridge pushed the operation to the limits, running speedy Q-boats to smuggle guns and plant mines. When his harbormining operations created a congressional uproar, Casey moved Clarridge to the European Division in the Directorate of Operations. Now the director wanted his help again.

Reagan was putting intense pressure on the CIA to show more initiative in the fight against terrorism, Casey told Clarridge. The director wanted to reply by forming action teams that could put the CIA on the offensive in a global campaign against terrorist groups. Clarridge told Casey what the director already believed: To succeed, the CIA had to attack the terrorist cells preemptively. If not, "The incidents would become bolder, bloodier, and more numerous."[23]

Casey erupted in a "sudden burst of animation" and told Clarridge to interview terrorism specialists around Washington and write up a proposal for a new covert CIA counterterrorist strategy. Clarridge found an office down the hall and started work just after New Year's Day 1986. By late January Clarridge had drafted his blueprint, an eight- or nine-page double-spaced memo addressed to Casey.

The CIA had several problems in confronting the global terrorist threat, Clarridge wrote. The biggest was its "defensive mentality." Terrorists operated worldwide "knowing there was little chance of retribution or of their being brought to justice." Clarridge wanted a new legal operating system for the CIA that would allow offensive strikes against terrorists. He proposed the formation of two super-secret "action teams" that would be funded and equipped to track, attack, and snatch terrorists globally. The action teams would be authorized to kill terrorists if doing so would preempt a terrorist event, or arrest them and bring them to justice if possible. One action team would be made up of foreign nationals who could blend more easily into landscapes overseas. The other action team would be Americans.

Clarridge wrote that the CIA's regional directorates, with their strict geographical borders, were a poor match for the international mobility of terrorist groups, especially the stateless Palestinians. Terrorism, Clarridge thought, "never fits one particular piece of real estate. It is effective precisely because it spreads all over the map." Not only the CIA but "the government is not organized as a whole to really deal with transnational problems."

He proposed a new interdisciplinary center at the CIA, global in reach, to be called the Counterterrorist Center, a "fusion center" that would combine resources from different directorates and break down the agency's walls. The new center would be located within the Directorate of Operations but would include analysts from the Directorate of Intelligence and tinkerers from the Directorate of Science and Technology. This would be a sharp break from traditional agency organization where action-oriented spies in the Directorate of Operations were separated physically—by bars in some parts of the Langley compound—from the agency's analysts in the Directorate of Intelligence, who wrote reports and forecasts. The separation helped protect the identities of espionage sources, clandestine service officers believed. But over the years the division had become calcified and unexamined.

The memo stirred sharp opposition from the Directorate of Operations. Among other things its officers feared the new center would poach resources and talent. Some spies in the D.O. sniffed at counterterrorism operations as "police work" best left to cops or the Federal Bureau of Investigation. But Robert Gates, then running the Directorate of Intelligence, weighed in to support Clarridge's ideas, and Casey lined up, too. The CIA's Counterterrorist Center was born on February 1, 1986. Clarridge was named its first director.

Clarridge helped draft a new highly classified presidential finding on terrorism, authorizing covert action by the CIA against terrorist groups worldwide. It was signed by Reagan at the time of the center's birth, along with a broader policy document, National Security Decision Directive 207, "The National Program for Combatting Terrorism," classified Top Secret.[24]

The covert action finding was developed through an interagency committee on terrorism formed at the National Security Council. The new NSC committee, under various names, would become the main locus for presidential decision-making about terrorism for years to come. Its founding directive highlighted counterterrorism questions that would surface repeatedly in the years ahead. Was terrorism a law enforcement problem or a national security issue? Should the CIA try to capture terrorists alive in order to try them on criminal charges in open courts, or should the goal be to bring them back in body bags? The policies set out in NSDD-207 came down on both sides of these questions. Yes, in some cases terrorism was a law enforcement problem, but in others it should be handled as a military matter. Terrorists should be captured for trial when possible, but that would not always be a requirement.

The initial draft finding authorized the new action teams Clarridge and Casey sought, and it permitted the CIA to undertake secret operations to defeat terrorism, both on its own and in liaison with foreign governments. The purpose of such covert action would be to detect, disrupt, and preempt terrorist strikes. This could include capturing terrorists for trial or striking militarily if the enemy were on the verge of launching a terrorist operation.

Clarridge interpreted the new finding as authority "to do pretty much anything he wanted against the terrorists," recalled Robert Baer, one of the center's early recruits from the Directorate of Operations. But the proposed action teams, particularly the one to be composed of foreigners, stirred nervous reaction on Capitol Hill. Some privately labeled them "hit teams."[25]

The CIA and the NSC had to brief the Senate Select Committee on Intelligence about the new presidential finding. Robert Gates recalled going to a secure Hill hearing room for one such session, "and we got to the question of when you could kill a terrorist, and we had this almost theological argument. 'Well, if the guy is driving toward the barracks with a truck full of explosives, can you kill him?' 'Yeah.' 'Well, what if he's in his apartment putting the explosives together?' 'Well, I don't know.'"[26]

It was a debate that would continue, more or less in that form and largely unresolved, for the next fifteen years, until the morning of September 11, 2001.

The Counterterrorist Center took life on Langley's sixth floor in a burst of "pure frenetic energy," Baer recalled. "Everyone worked in one huge, open bay. With the telephones ringing nonstop, printers clattering, files stacked all over the place, CNN playing on TV monitors bolted to the ceiling, hundreds of people in motion and at their computers, it gave the impression of a war room." But as the political and legal scandals surrounding Casey's adventures in Nicaragua and Iran swelled across Washington during 1986, the original "war room" vision for action teams and an offensive posture yielded to a more cautious, analytical, report-writing culture than Casey and Clarridge had originally imagined.

"Casey had envisaged it as something different than what it eventually became," recalled Vincent Cannistraro, who arrived as an operations officer soon after the center's founding. The Iran-Contra scandal had involved disclosures of illegal support by Oliver North, Casey, and other policy makers for Nicaraguan rebels as well as illegal shipments of missiles to Iran in an effort to free the American hostages in Lebanon. In the aftermath, "Casey, of course, was looked on as an adventurer and Dewey as kind of a cowboy," Cannistraro said. The appetite for risk-taking within the center and on the Hill oversight committees waned rapidly.[27]

Still, Clarridge remained in charge, and he began to push his colleagues.

Secular leftist groups carried out the most visible terrorist strikes in 1985 and 1986. Some of these groups advocated a nationalist cause—the Palestinian terrorists, the Irish Republican Army, the Basque separatists. Others chased more abstract Marxist revolutionary goals, such as Germany's Baader Meinhof Gang and Italy's Red Brigades. Most case officers and analysts at the CIA saw fewer direct links between the Soviet Union and these secular leftist terrorists than Casey did. Still, all these terrorists openly described themselves as vanguards in the left-right ideological struggle of the Cold War. Clarridge opened terrorism-focused liaisons with security services across Europe, providing technological help where possible, such as beacons that he inserted into planted weapons to help track the locations of Basque separatist cells in Spain.[28] The CIA's officers and their counterparts in Europe had long experience with these kinds of groups. They understood their mind-sets. In some cases they had attended the same universities as the radicals. They knew how to talk to them, how to recruit them, how to corrupt them.

At its start the Counterterrorist Center concentrated heavily on these leftist terrorists. The center was organized into subunits that targeted particular groups. One of the largest units focused on the Abu Nidal Organization, which had claimed hundreds of civilian lives in multiple strikes during the 1980s. Clarridge and his colleagues decided to sow dissent by exposing the group's financial operations and trying to raise suspicions among members. Abu Nidal had become a paranoid, self-immolating group on its own accord, but the agency helped accelerate its breakup through penetrations and disinformation. Abu Nidal faded as an effective terrorist organization within three years. There were other successes, especially in Germany and Italy, where the terrorists began to consume themselves, sometimes helped along by covert operations.

Hezbollah, on the other hand, proved a very hard target. It was the new center's first attempt to penetrate a committed Islamist terrorist organization that targeted American citizens. The experience offered ill omens for the future. A radical Islamic Shiite faction in Lebanon's civil war that began to serve as a proxy force for the Iranian Revolutionary Guard, Hezbollah had become a terrorist branch of the still-churning Iranian Revolution.

The CIA had no sources in Hezbollah's leadership. Hezbollah's pious members did not hang out in the hotels and salons that made Abu Nidal members such accessible targets. The CIA's unilateral resources in the Middle East were spread thin. Baer was one of only two Arabic speakers in the Counterterrorist Center at the time it was launched. For a full year after Hezbollah kidnapped and tortured the CIA's Beirut station chief, William Buckley, beginning in 1984, the agency "had absolutely no idea" who had taken him or the other American hostages in Lebanon, Baer recalled. Meanwhile, the Counterterrorist Center had to deal with hoax after hoax—some mounted by Hezbollah as disinformation—about where the hostages were located.[29]

Clarridge wanted to attack. He sought to enlist U.S. Special Forces to launch an elaborate hostage rescue operation in Beirut. He rigged up special refrigerator trucks in Europe, disguised to look as if they belonged to Lebanese merchants; he hoped they could be shipped in and used to run Delta Force commandos into West Beirut. But the Pentagon's generals, citing weak intelligence about where the hostages were actually being held, said they would not launch such an operation unless there were American "eyes on the target," confirming the presence of hostages, twenty-four hours before the operation began. They would not trust a Lebanese or other Arab spotter; they wanted an American in place.[30]

Clarridge had no obvious way to infiltrate an American agent into West Beirut. The Counterterrorist Center trained a Filipino-born Delta Force soldier for insertion in disguise into Beirut, in the hope that he might be able to provide the required American eyes on the target. But that high-risk operation foundered. The center was "totally incapable of collecting real-time intelligence on Hezbollah because, one, we didn't understand it," recalled Cannistraro. "We understood secular terrorism, radical terrorism; these were people we were comfortable with."

Clarridge wondered if technology might not solve the problem that human intelligence seemed unable to crack. He loved the Counterterrorist Center's engineers on the science and technology side; they took what Clarridge liked to call a "Radio Shack approach" to problem-solving. Clarridge commissioned them to work on a highly classified pilotless drone equipped with intercept equipment, an infrared camera, and low-noise wooden propellers. It might fly overhead at about 2,500 feet and locate the American hostages. He spent $7 million on five prototypes in what he dubbed the Eagle Program.

Another use for the drones might be sabotage operations in Libya. Clarridge wanted to load one drone with two hundred pounds of C-4 plastic explosives and one hundred pounds of ball bearings. His plan was to fly it onto Tripoli's air field at night, blow it up, and destroy "a whole bunch" of commercial airliners sitting unoccupied on the ground. He also tried to load small rockets onto the drones that could be used to fire at predesignated targets.[31] But all of the technology was in its infancy. And Clarridge made some of his colleagues very nervous, especially in the era of Iran-Contra.

Clarridge wanted to kill the terrorists outright. He found the American government's position against assassination of leaders who sponsored terrorism to be "hypocritical." The president would authorize the military "to carry out air attacks that may or may not hit and kill the real target" but would not authorize the Counterterrorist Center to stealthily assassinate the same man. He asked, "Why is an expensive military raid with heavy collateral damage to our allies and to innocent children okay—more morally acceptable than a bullet to the head?"[32]

BY EARLY 1986, Brigadier Yousaf had constructed a large and sophisticated secret infrastructure for guerrilla training along the Afghan frontier. Between sixteen thousand and eighteen thousand fresh recruits passed through his camps and training courses each year. He also began to facilitate independent guerrilla and sabotage training by Afghan rebel parties, outside of ISI control. From six thousand to seven thousand jihadists trained this way each year, Yousaf later estimated. Some of these were Arab volunteers.[33]

The syllabus offered by Pakistani intelligence became more specialized. New mujahedin recruits entered a two- to three-week basic training course where they learned how to maneuver and fire an assault rifle. The best were then selected for graduate courses in more complex weapons and tactics. Yousaf established specialized training camps for explosives work, urban sabotage and car bombing, antiaircraft weapons, sniper rifles, and land mines. Thousands of new graduates—the great majority Afghans, but also now some Algerians, Palestinians, Tunisians, Saudi Arabians, and Egyptians— fanned out across Afghanistan as mountain snows melted in the spring of 1986 and a new fighting season began. Across the Afghan border they established new camps in rock valleys and captured government garrisons; this allowed them to continue training on their own, to recruit new fighters, and to refine the sabotage and guerrilla techniques taught by Pakistani intelligence.

"Terrorism is often confused or equated with . . . guerrilla warfare," the terrorism theorist Bruce Hoffman once wrote. "This is not surprising, since guerrillas often employ the same tactics (assassination, kidnapping, bombings of public gathering-places, hostage-taking, etc.) for the same purposes (to intimidate or coerce, thereby affecting behavior through the arousal of fear) as terrorists."[34]

Ten years later the vast training infrastructure that Yousaf and his colleagues built with the enormous budgets endorsed by NSDD-166—the specialized camps, the sabotage training manuals, the electronic bomb detonators, and so on—would be referred to routinely in America as "terrorist infrastructure." At the time of its construction, however, it served a jihadist army that operated openly on the battlefield, attempted to seize and hold territory, and exercised sovereignty over civilian populations. They pursued a transparent national cause. By 1986, however, that Afghan cause entangled increasingly with the international Islamist networks whose leaders had a more ambitious goal: the toppling of corrupt and antireligious governments across the Islamic world.

In its first years the CIA's new Counterterrorist Center placed virtually no emphasis on the Muslim Brotherhood–inspired networks. After Abu Nidal and Hezbollah, the center's next largest branches all focused on secular leftist terrorist groups. These included multiple Palestinian groups, Marxist-Leninist terrorists in Europe, the Shining Path in Peru, and the Japanese Red Army.[35]

Continued ferment in Tehran generated fears among CIA analysts that other weak Middle Eastern regimes might succumb to Islamic revolt. But now more than six years had passed since the Iranian Revolution, and no other similar insurgency had yet erupted. There were stirrings of religious dissent in places such as Algeria and a few Islamist bombings in France. Britain's MI6, concerned about rising Islamic radicalism, commissioned a retired Arabist spy to travel for months through the Muslim world, from Morocco to Indonesia, to write a detailed report about contemporary Islamism on the street and in the mosques.[36] But these were minor efforts that attracted little attention within the CIA or outside it.

There was one other small blip on the Counterterrorist Center's screen. From Pakistan arrived reports of a new group called the Islamic Salvation Foundation that had been formed in Peshawar to recruit and support Arab volunteers for the Afghan jihad, outside the control of any of the ISI-backed rebel parties. The network was operating offices and guesthouses along the Afghan frontier. Osama bin Laden, a wealthy young Saudi, was spreading large sums of money around Peshawar to help the new center expand. He was tapping into ISI's guerrilla training camps on behalf of newly arrived Arab jihadists. The early reports of his activity that were passed along to the CIA's Counterterrorist Center in this period suggested that bin Laden "certainly was not engaged in any fighting. He was not a warrior," recalled Stanley Bedington, a senior analyst at the center from its beginning. Still, "When a man starts throwing around money like that, he comes to your notice."[37]

When they first learned of efforts by bin Laden and allied Islamic proselytizers to increase the number of Arab volunteers fighting the Soviets, some of the most ardent cold warriors at Langley thought this program should be formally endorsed and expanded. The more committed anti-Soviet fighters, the better, they argued. As more and more Arabs arrived in Pakistan during 1985 and 1986, the CIA "examined ways to increase their participation, perhaps in the form of some sort of 'international brigade,' but nothing came of it," Robert Gates recalled.[38]

At CIA headquarters Osama bin Laden was little more than a name in a file for now. But in tumultuous Peshawar he had begun to organize his own escalation of the Afghan war.

8

"Inshallah, You Will Know My Plans"

MILTON BEARDEN REPLACED William Piekney as CIA station chief in Islamabad in July 1986. A large-boned, heavyset, boyish-faced, slang-slinging Texan who aspired to novel writing and seemed to conduct himself as if his life were a Hollywood casting call, Bearden had drawn close to Casey a few years earlier when he was station chief in Khartoum, Sudan. There he had smuggled besieged Israeli intelligence officers out of the country in crates labeled as diplomatic mail, just the sort of dashing operation Casey loved. When Casey traveled in Africa in his blackened Starlifter, Bearden was his escort to late-night meetings with murderous intelligence chiefs. They were both romantics who reveled in the spy's life. The CIA director needed someone who could manage the massive escalation he had helped set in motion in Afghanistan. He called Bearden into his seventh-floor office at Langley and told him the new policy: "I want you to go out there and win."[1]

Bearden understood that Casey "had a giant vision" of global struggle against the Soviet Union through covert action and that "Afghanistan was a little part of it." Yet Casey made clear that he saw this last push along the Pakistan-Afghanistan border as an urgent moral mission. As Bearden saw it, Casey believed that sacrificing Afghan lives without pursuing total victory over the communists was a strategy for "small minds." Casey was "the best and worst director" the CIA had ever known, Bearden thought.

Inside the Directorate of Operations, Bearden was a popular figure— "Uncle Milty," an indulgent boss, an operator's operator, full of humor and bluster. He landed in hot, shapeless Islamabad charged by Casey's ambition. The station on the embassy's rebuilt third floor was still modest in size compared to the amount of money and paperwork it now handled. Bearden tore through the antiseptic office suites like a bull rider. "He carried a swagger stick, and he was on a high," a colleague remembered. He talked to everyone— including the stiff peacock, General Akhtar, the Pakistani intelligence chief— as if they were his personal guests at a Texas keg party. He buttonholed Soviet diplomats at polite receptions and quoted Shakespeare as Afghan policy: "Speak not of the manner of your leaving but leave at once." At regional conferences for CIA chiefs of station, Bearden would brag, "All of you guys out there, you try to recruit Soviets. Me, I just kill them." If he got angry at Pakistani intelligence over some problem in the weapons pipeline, he would refuse to take General Akhtar's calls for a week, just to let him stew. Still, he became a favorite of some Pakistani officers. When his family was snowed in on vacation, the Pakistani air force flew in a C-130 to get them out. Bearden cultivated an impression that the conspiracy-minded Pakistani elite were inclined toward anyway: that the CIA was the real power in the American government. Inside the walled U.S. embassy compound, Bearden's colleagues noted the small touches: The diplomatic license plate on his official car ended with "01," the number usually reserved for the ambassador.[2]

Bearden tried to tame the huge flow of material and money coming to Pakistan. Along the northern border between Pakistan and China, Bearden helped arrange the truck transport of hundreds of mules being sold to the CIA by the Chinese communists for use in smuggling guns that would be fired against Soviet communists. Because there weren't enough mules, Bearden ordered animals by ship from as far away as Texas and Djibouti. When a freighter from Djibouti went missing on the high seas, Bearden papered the world for several weeks with urgent classified cables headlined "SHIP OF MULES."[3]

The Islamabad station had warned in a broad July assessment cable that the pace of mujahedin attacks appeared to be slowing under the relentless helicopter assaults mounted by Soviet special forces, especially along the Pakistani border.[4] Langley analysts and Pakistani generals shared a fear in the summer of 1986 that the new Soviet assault tactics might be tipping the war's balance against the CIA-backed rebels. On September 26, 1986, about two months after Bearden's arrival, the balance began to tip back. Crouching in scrub rocks on a barren plain near the Jalalabad airport in eastern Afghanistan, just two hours' drive from Peshawar, a commander named Engineer Ghaffar ("the forgiver") and two bearded colleagues lifted onto their shoulders the first of a new type of antiaircraft weapon supplied to the rebels by the CIA. Powered by batteries and guided by the most effective portable heat-seeking system yet invented, the Stinger weapon was an American-made marvel of modern frontline arsenals. Its infrared tracking system made it impervious to countermeasures normally taken by Soviet pilots.

A military engineer trained in the Soviet Union, Ghaffar had been selected by Pakistani intelligence to attempt the first Stinger mission, and he had trained in secret in an ISI compound near Rawalpindi. Eight Soviet army Mi-24D helicopter gunships approached the Jalalabad runway. Ghaffar sighted his missile, pushed its black rubber "uncage" button on the grip stock, and pulled the trigger. His first shot pinged, misfired, and rattled in the rocks a few hundred yards away, but another flashed across the plain and smashed into a helicopter, destroying it in a fireball. More missiles flew in rapid succession, and two other helicopters fell, killing their Russian crews.

Akhtar called Bearden as soon as he received the radio report. The station chief sent a cable to Langley describing the strikes but warned there was no confirmation. A day later the Islamabad embassy's communications vault rattled with a startling reply: By sheer coincidence a U.S. KH-11 spy satellite had been passing overhead, taking routine pictures of the Afghan battlefield. The satellite had transmitted a clear photo of the Jalalabad airport showing three charred balls of steel scrap, formerly helicopters, lying side by side across an active runway. The incoming cable from Langley was triumphant:

> SATELLITE IMAGERY CONFIRMS THREE KILLS
> AT JALALABAD AS REPORTED. PLEASE PASS OUR
> CONGRATULATIONS FOR A JOB WELL DONE.

The CIA had learned years before that Ronald Reagan was not much of a reader. Dense, detailed briefings about global affairs rarely reached his desk. But Reagan loved movies. Casey encouraged his colleagues to distill important intelligence so the president could watch it on a movie screen. Before Reagan met visiting heads of state, he would sometimes screen a short CIA-produced classified bio movie about his visitor. Thinking partly of its most important customer, the CIA had equipped Engineer Ghaffar's team with a Sony video camera to record the Stinger's debut.

"Allahu Akhbar! Allahu Akhbar!" the shooters cried as they fired the Afghan war's first Stingers. By the time Ghaffar had hit the third helicopter, the videotape looked "like some kid at a football game," as Bearden later described it. "Everybody is jumping up and down—all you're getting is people jumping up and down—and seeing the earth kind of go back and forth." The tape's last sequence showed Ghaffar's crew unloading Kalashnikov rounds into the crumpled corpses of the Soviet crew as they lay sprawled on the Jalalabad tarmac. Within weeks the highly classified video had been ferried from Islamabad. President Reagan screened it at the White House. As the tape and the KH-11 satellite pictures were passed around the Old Executive Office Building and shared with a few members of Congress, a triumphal buzz of excitement spread in Washington.

The decision to supply Stingers had been made against the CIA's initial advice. Not long after National Security Decision Directive 166 took force, members of the interagency group on Afghanistan had begun to push for the missiles, arguing that they could repulse the Spetsnaz's helicopter assault tactics. Introducing a made-in-the-U.S.A. weapon on the Afghan battlefield would hand the Soviets a propaganda victory, the CIA's Near East Division feared. But Morton Abramowitz, the State Department's intelligence director, backed the idea. After a long and emotional debate, the CIA capitulated. Even then, months of secret negotiations were required with the Chinese and with Pakistani president Zia before all were satisfied that the risks of Soviet retaliation were worth bearing.[5]

Soon after Ghaffar's video trailer was screened at the White House, dozens of mujahedin commanders in eastern Afghanistan began to launch Stingers at Soviet helicopters and lumbering transport planes, with devastating results. Apprehensive Russian and Afghan crews ascended as often as possible above the Stinger's effective ceiling of about 12,500 feet, severely diminishing their ability to carry out low-flying attack raids. Soviet forces stopped evacuating the wounded by helicopter, demoralizing frontline officers. Within months Bearden had cabled Langley to declare that Stingers had become the war's "most significant battlefield development."[6]

If diverted from Afghanistan, a Stinger could easily be used as a terrorist weapon against passenger aircraft, the agency warned. Their spread in Afghanistan added urgency to the CIA's need for agents to monitor rebel commanders and Pakistani intelligence. What if Hekmatyar sold Stingers to terrorist groups? What if the missiles were stolen? How would the CIA even know? The agency needed more of its own reporting sources.

Even by its own rich standards, the jihad was now swimming in money. Congress secretly allocated about $470 million in U.S. funding for Afghan covert action in fiscal year 1986, and then upped that to about $630 million in fiscal 1987, not counting the matching funds from Saudi Arabia. With support from headquarters, Bearden expanded the CIA's unilateral recruitment of independent Afghan agents and commanders without the involvement of Pakistani intelligence. The money needed for such a payroll amounted to crumbs in comparison to the new budgets. The recruited commanders were asked to help the CIA keep track of weapons handouts, Pakistani corruption, and battlefield developments. The payroll had several tiers. A regional commander might draw an agency retainer of $20,000 or $25,000 a month in cash. A somewhat more influential leader might draw $50,000 a month. A commander with influence over one or more provinces might receive $100,000 monthly, sometimes more. An effective commander used these retainers not solely to enrich himself but to hold together clan or volunteer militias that required salaries, travel expenses, and support for families that often lived in squalid refugee camps.

Abdul Haq remained on the CIA's unilateral payroll. The CIA also continued to deliver payments and supplies directly to Ahmed Shah Massoud. (Unilateral CIA assistance had first been delivered to Massoud in 1984.) The CIA later sent in secure communications sets, allowing Massoud to interact with dispersed commanders and allies in Peshawar without fear of Soviet interception.

Bearden's Islamabad station expressed skepticism about Massoud. Some people involved thought it might be in part because of the testosterone-fed jockeying between the CIA and the British: Massoud was a British favorite, therefore the CIA didn't like him much.[7] Then, too, there was a residue of distrust dating to the truce deals that Massoud had cut with Soviet forces in 1983. Bearden told colleagues that he respected Massoud's track record as a fighter but saw Massoud already positioning himself to take power in postwar Kabul, hoarding supplies and limiting operations. "Ahmed, I know what you're doing, and I don't blame you, but don't do it on my nickel" was the thrust of Bearden's message. A CIA officer at Langley told a French counterpart, referring to the agency's support for Hekmatyar, "Gulbuddin is not as bad as you fear, and Massoud is not as good as you hope."[8]

The CIA's network of Afghan unilaterals swelled to about four dozen paid commanders and agents. That was a large number of running contacts to keep hidden for long from Pakistani intelligence, given that CIA case officers had to meet regularly with their clients. ISI routinely surveilled known CIA case officers even in the midst of a nominally friendly liaison. Practicing standard tradecraft, the Islamabad station organized its Afghan network so that no one CIA officer, not even Bearden, knew the real names of every agent in the system. Commanders on retainer were given cryptonyms for cabling purposes. Massoud was too well known to be hidden behind code names, but even so, knowledge of that liaison within the U.S. embassy was limited very tightly.

Because of the large sums of dollars now arriving, the Islamabad station tried to streamline its cash distributions to minimize the number of times when American officers had to travel on Pakistani roads carrying fortunes worthy of robbery and murder. The agency began to use electronic transfers for its subsidies to Pakistani intelligence, routing money through the Pakistan Ministry of Finance. To deliver cash to commanders, the CIA also began to use the *hawala* system, an informal banking network in the Middle East and South Asia that permits an individual to send money to a small trading stall in, say, Karachi, for instant delivery to a named recipient hundreds or thousands of miles away. Especially after the Iran-Contra scandal erupted in Washington late in 1986, the Islamabad station took great pains to document every transfer. Given the amounts now involved, it was as easy to misplace $3 million or $4 million as it was to leave your keys on your desk.[9]

Most of the reporting that began to flow from the unilateral agents focused on the impact of Stingers, weapons deliveries, and propaganda campaigns. But for the first time came complaints from some Afghan fighters to the CIA about a rising force in their jihad: Arab volunteers. Thousands of them were arriving in Afghanistan.

Afghan commanders would send out notes to the Islamabad station, sometimes with pictures showing a truckload of Arab jihad fighters driving through their territory. The Afghans called them "Wahhabis" because of their adherence to rigid Saudi Islamic doctrine banning adornment and the worship of shrines. Early on, some Afghan fighters clashed with Arab jihadists over the issue of decorated graves. Most Afghan mujahedin buried their dead in rough dirt and stone graves marked by green flags and modest adornments, following Sufi-influenced traditions. Echoing the methods of the Saudi Ikhwan near Jedda more than half a century earlier, the Wahhabis swept through and tore down these markers, proclaiming that they encouraged the worship of false idols. In at least a few cases the Afghans attacked and killed these Arab graveyard raiders. Bearden recalled the thrust of the very early reports arriving from Afghan commanders in the field: "They say we are dumb, and we do not know the Koran, and they are more trouble than they are ever going to be worth."[10]

OSAMA BIN LADEN moved his household (he had married and fathered his first children) from Saudi Arabia to Peshawar around the same time that Milton Bearden arrived in Islamabad as CIA station chief. He rented a two-story compound in a quiet, relatively prosperous, pine-tree-cooled section of the city called University Town, where charities, Western aid groups, diplomats, Arab preachers, and wealthy Afghan exiles all lived as uneasy neighbors in walled-off villas.[11]

From his regular visits, his work with Ahmed Badeeb and Saudi intelligence, his patronage of Arab charities, and his importation of bulldozers and other construction equipment, bin Laden was already a well-known figure among Muslim Brotherhood–connected Afghan rebels. He was closest to Hekmatyar and Sayyaf. His acquaintances in Peshawar viewed bin Laden as a young, sweet-tempered, soft-mannered, and above all fabulously wealthy patron of worthy jihad causes. He was a rising young sheikh, not much of an orator but a smiling visitor to the hospitals and orphanages, and, increasingly, an important discussion group member in Peshawar's radical Arab circles.

Bin Laden rode horses for pleasure, sometimes in the eastern tribal frontier, but for the most part his was a tea-pouring, meeting-oriented life in damp concrete houses where cushion-ringed reception rooms would fill with visiting Kuwaiti merchants and Syrian professors of Islamic law. Days would drift by in loose debates, *fatwa* (religious edict) drafting, humanitarian project development—a shifting mix of engineering, philanthropy, and theology.

"He speaks like a university professor," remembered an Arab journalist who met with bin Laden frequently in Peshawar. "'We will do this, we will do that,' like he is at the head of the table of the political committee." His quiet style was unusual: "He is not your typical Arabic popular speaker."

Peshawar by late 1986 was a city of makeshift warehouses and charities swelling and bursting from the money, food, trucks, mules, and medicine being shipped to the Afghan frontier in quantities double and triple those of six months before. The humanitarian aspects of the jihad were expanding as rapidly as the military campaign. In part this was a result of National Security Decision Directive 166, but in addition United Nations agencies, European charities such as Oxfam, proselytizing Christian missionaries, and government relief agencies such as U.S. AID had all come swarming into Peshawar after 1985 to build hospitals, schools, feeding stations, clinics, and cross-border ambulance services, much of it paid for by the American government. These projects operated on an unprecedented scale: One University of Nebraska–run school program worked at 1,300 sites inside Afghanistan. In one dusty University Town compound, profane, hard-traveled U.N. food specialists might be tossing sacks of seed onto blue-flagged trucks while neighboring American Baptist missionaries sat on wooden benches reading to Afghan children in English from the New Testament, while over the next wall bearded young volunteers from the Persian Gulf bent toward Mecca in chanted prayer.

Operating in self-imposed isolation, major Saudi Arabian charities and such organizations as the Saudi Red Crescent, the World Muslim League, the Kuwaiti Red Crescent, and the International Islamic Relief Organization set up their own offices in Peshawar. Funded in ever-rising amounts by Saudi intelligence and annual *zakat* contributions from mosques and wealthy individuals, they, too, built hospitals, clinics, schools, feeding stations, and battlefield medic services. European charities such as Médicins sans Frontières recruited volunteer surgeons from Brussels and Paris for short rotations to treat mujahedin victims in Peshawar, and the Islamic charities begin to recruit doctors from Cairo, Amman, Tunis, and Algiers for volunteer tours. Since the Muslim Brotherhood had a strong presence in the Arab professional classes—especially among Egyptian doctors and lawyers—the recruitment network for humanitarian volunteer work became intertwined with the political-religious networks that raised money and guns for the Islamist Afghan leaders such as Hekmatyar and Sayyaf.

Typical of the Brotherhood-recruited volunteers was Ayman al-Zawahiri, a young doctor, scion of a wealthy Egyptian family long active in the Islamist movement. Al-Zawahiri had been imprisoned in Cairo during the early 1980s for activity on the edges of the plot to assassinate Anwar Sadat. After his release he found his way via the Brotherhood's Islamic Medical Society to Peshawar, volunteering as a doctor at the Kuwaiti-funded Al Hilal Hospital on the Afghan frontier. "I saw this as an opportunity to get to know one of the arenas of jihad that might be a tributary and a base for jihad in Egypt and the Arab region," al-Zawahiri recalled. An Arab snob of sorts, he saw Egypt as "the heart of the Islamic world, where the basic battle of Islam was being fought." But to prevail back home, "a jihadist movement needs an arena that would act like an incubator, where its seeds would grow and where it can acquire practical experience in combat, politics and organizational matters." Peshawar seemed to him such a place. Al-Zawahiri settled there in 1986.[12]

Abdullah Azzam was by far the best known Arab Islamist in Peshawar at the time bin Laden and al-Zawahiri took up residence. He helped run a council of Peshawar's Arab and Islamic charities. Born in a village near the West Bank city of Jenin, Azzam earned a doctorate in Islamic law from Al-Azhar University in Cairo during the 1970s. He became close to the Egyptian exile Mohammed Qutb and began to preach and adapt the radical jihadist doctrines of Qutb's deceased brother. After teaching in Jedda during the late 1970s, he transferred as a lecturer to the new Islamic University in Islamabad, down the hill from Quaid-I-Azam's campus. In 1984 he moved down the Grand Trunk Road to Peshawar.

The title of the new humanitarian organization Azzam founded that year, the Office of Services, signaled his own thinking about the Afghan jihad: He wanted mainly to aid the Afghans. He traveled the Persian Gulf and lectured at Friday prayers in wealthy mosques from Jedda to Kuwait City, and as the charitable funds flowed, he used them to provide medical and relief services as well as military support.

Bin Laden, his former pupil in Jedda, became an important source of money and then an operations partner beginning in 1984. Together they recruited other volunteers from across the Arab world. Azzam announced that bin Laden would pay the expenses—about $300 per month—of any Arab who wanted to fight on Afghanistan's battlefields. In 1986 they opened their first office in the United States amid the large Arab community in Tucson, Arizona.[13]

Overall, the U.S. government looked favorably on the Arab recruitment drives. An international brigade of volunteers—modeled on the international socialist volunteers who had joined the Spanish civil war against Franco during the 1930s—would provide a way to broaden the formal coalition of nations involved in the anti-Soviet jihad, this argument went. As more and more Arabs arrived in Pakistan during 1985 and 1986, "the CIA examined ways to increase their participation," then-deputy CIA director Robert Gates recalled. An Afghan specialist in the State Department's intelligence bureau argued that "we should try and coordinate with them." The idea was "not to see them as the enemy." But the proposals never moved beyond the talking stage. At the Islamabad station Milt Bearden felt that bin Laden himself "actually did some very good things," as Bearden recalled it. "He put a lot of money in a lot of the right places in Afghanistan." Bin Laden was not regarded as "someone who was anti-American." The CIA did receive negative reports about the Arab volunteers from its Afghan agent network and from Western and Christian aid organizations. Their complaints coursed through the CIA and State

Department cabling system, but the issue was only an occasional subject for reporting and analysis. No policy or action plan was ever developed.[14]

Abdullah Azzam preached stridently against the United States. He would soon help found Hamas. Prince Turki al-Faisal and Saudi intelligence became important supporters. Azzam circulated in a world apart from the official Americans in Pakistan. Even relatively neutral European aid workers living in Peshawar had only sporadic contact with him.

By the summer of 1986 small signs of a split between bin Laden and Azzam had become visible to those involved in the closed circles of the Arab jihadists. Azzam was such a commanding figure, and bin Laden such a relatively minor pupil (however copious his wealth), that there was no question of an open challenge from the protégé, especially in a culture where seniority and scholarship were so respected. Yet bin Laden seemed to be heading in a new direction. The change arose partly from his swelling ego and partly from the political debates now developing in University Town's Arab parlors: Who was the true enemy of the jihad? The communists? The Americans? Israel? The impious government of Egypt? What was the relationship between the Afghan war and the global goals of the Muslim Brotherhood?[15]

Saudi and Pakistani intelligence had begun to collaborate on expensive road building and depot building projects along the Afghan frontier, hoping to create physical infrastructure that could withstand the Soviet Spetsnaz assaults. ISI created a sizable cell within its Afghan bureau devoted solely to humanitarian and building projects. When Soviets first attacked supply routes on the Pakistan border in 1984, Afghan rebels often fled. Their retreats disrupted supply flows to commanders inside Afghanistan—just as the Soviets intended. The new border infrastructure—roads, caves, warehouses, and military training camps—was designed to be defended against Soviet attacks. This would allow ISI to create forward supply dumps and more mechanized transport to push weapons into Afghanistan.

Prince Turki and his chief of staff, Ahmed Badeeb, flew to Pakistan as the projects got under way, traveling on the General Intelligence Department's Gulfstream jets. At ISI headquarters they were feted with elaborate meals and briefed on the war's developments with charts and maps drawn with the help of American satellites. In the evenings the Saudi embassy would usually host a reception in Turki's honor, inviting Arab diplomats, local Islamic scholars, and sometimes Osama bin Laden. Turki traveled occasionally to the Afghan border to inspect the new depots and roads. Badeeb stayed for longer periods at the safehouses he had established in Peshawar through the official Saudi charities.

Bin Laden's imported bulldozers were used for these civil-military projects between 1984 and 1986. Two regions received the most attention: a border area called Parrot's Beak, almost directly west of Peshawar where a cone of Pakistani territory protruded into Afghanistan, and an area farther south, near Miram Shah, a mountainous region across the border from the Afghan town of Khost. Bin Laden worked mainly in the latter area.

"It was largely Arab money that saved the system," the Pakistani intelligence brigadier Mohammed Yousaf recalled. The extra sums were spent on transport as well as border infrastructure, largely in support of the Muslim Brotherhood–linked Afghan parties and commanders. Jallaladin Haqqani attracted and organized the Arab volunteers. He fought in a border region populated by cantankerous, socially conservative Pashtun tribes, a place "steeped in cussedness," as an American who traveled there put it. An unshaven, thin man who draped himself in bandoliers of assault rifle ammunition, Haqqani emerged in the late 1980s as the ISI's main anticommunist battering ram around Khost. Celebrated as a kind of noble savage by slack-bellied preachers in Saudi Arabia's wealthy urban mosques, Haqqani became a militant folk hero to Wahhabi activists. He operated fund-raising offices in the Persian Gulf and hosted young Arab jihad volunteers in his tribal territory. In part because of Haqqani's patronage, the border regions nearest Pakistan became increasingly the province of interlocking networks of Pakistani intelligence officers, Arab volunteers, and Wahhabi *madrassas.*

Abdullah Azzam thought some of the cave building and road construction was a waste of money. Bin Laden wanted to spend great sums on a hospital clinic in a remote Afghan border village in Paktia province called Jaji. The crude clinic would be built in a defensible cave, in the same region where bin Laden had been helping to build roads. "Abdullah felt there were twenty-nine or thirty provinces in Afghanistan—why spend so much on one elaborate place right on the border, practically in Pakistan?" recalled one Arab volunteer involved.

But bin Laden's ambitions were widening: He wanted the Jaji complex so that he could have his own camp for Arab volunteers, a camp where he would be a leader. He opened his first training facility in 1986, modeled on those just over the barren hills run by Pakistani intelligence. Young Arab jihadists would learn how to use assault rifles, explosives, and detonators, and they would listen to lectures about why they had been called to fight. Bin Laden called his first training camp "the Lion's Den," by some accounts, "al Ansar" (a name of the earliest followers of the Prophet Mohammed) by others. And despite Abdullah Azzam's questions, he declared that he was going ahead with his other projects at Jaji.

"*Inshallah* [if it is God's will], you will know my plans," bin Laden told his mentor.[16]

THE ANTI-SOVIET AFGHAN JIHAD was coming to an end, but hardly anyone knew it or understood why. Not bin Laden. Not the CIA.

On November 13, 1986, behind the Kremlin's ramparts, the Soviet Politburo's inner circle met in secret at the behest of Mikhail Gorbachev, the opaque, windy, and ambitious reformer who had taken power twenty months before.

Marshal Sergei Akhromeyev, the Soviet armed forces chief of staff, explained that the Fortieth Army had so far deployed fifty thousand Soviet soldiers to seal the border between Pakistan and Afghanistan, "but they are unable to close all channels through which arms are being smuggled." The pack mules kept coming. Blacktopped roads were now being constructed. There was no sign of a realistic military solution.

"People ask: 'What are we doing there?'" Gorbachev observed. "Will we be there endlessly? Or should we end this war?"

If the Soviet Union did not get out of Afghanistan, "we'll disgrace ourselves in all our relations," Gorbachev answered himself. In the presence of the Politburo's inner circle and his closest advisers on reform, he had been thinking aloud about the Afghan problem since he first took office. He publicly referred to the war as a "bleeding wound" early in 1986. As the Fortieth Army failed to make progress on the ground, Gorbachev became bolder about an alternative: leaving Afghanistan altogether. By November the issue seemed to be mainly one of timing. "The strategic goal is to finish the war in one, maximum two years, and withdraw the troops," Gorbachev told his colleagues that day. "We have set a clear goal: Help speed up the process so we have a friendly neutral country, and get out of there."[17]

It was one of the most significant Politburo discussions of the late Cold War, but the CIA knew nothing about it. The Americans would not learn of Gorbachev's decision for another year. Analysts at the agency and elsewhere in the American intelligence community understood some of the intense pressures then facing Gorbachev and the Soviet leadership. The Soviet Union's economy was failing. Its technological achievements lagged badly behind the computerized West. Its people yearned for a more normal, open politics. Some analysts captured some of these pressures in their classified reporting, but on the whole the CIA's analysts understated the Soviet Union's internal problems. Policy makers in Reagan's Cabinet were also slow to grasp the determination of Gorbachev and his reformers to implement meaningful changes. Afghanistan was one litmus test for both sides.

During the earlier debates in Washington about the Afghan jihad, the National Security Council had obtained sensitive intelligence about discussions within the Politburo on Afghanistan. According to this reporting, which was classified at the highest possible level, known then as VEIL, Gorbachev had decided when he first took power in the spring of 1985 that he would give the Soviet Union's hard-line generals one or two years to win the war outright. This assessment seemed to justify an American escalation in reply. But as it turned out, the VEIL intelligence was just an isolated, even misleading fragment. It may have been accurate when it first surfaced, but by the autumn of 1986 the Politburo policy it described had been overtaken by Gorbachev's gathering plans to leave Afghanistan.[18]

The CIA's analysts understood the pressures buffeting Soviet society better than they understood decision-making at the top. The agency would not learn what was really happening inside the Politburo until after the Soviet Union had dissolved. "Our day-to-day reporting was accurate but limited by our lack of inside information on politics at the top level," Robert Gates, one of the CIA's leading Soviet analysts, would concede years later. "We monitored specific events but too often did not draw back to get a broader perspective."[19]

This included the basic insight that the Soviet Union was so decayed as to be near collapse. Some of the agency's analysts were relentlessly skeptical of Gorbachev's sincerity as a reformer, as were Reagan, his vice president, George Bush, Casey, Defense Secretary Caspar Weinberger, and other key presidential advisers. All evidence that Soviet power might be weakening seemed to be systematically discounted in Washington and at Langley even as the data mounted in plain view. The CIA's Soviet analysts continued to write reports suggesting that Moscow was a monolithic power advancing from strength to strength, and during Casey's reign there seemed little penalty for tacking too far to the ideological right. CIA analysis had been at least partially politicized by Casey, in the view of some career officers. Besides, in the CIA's Directorate of Intelligence, especially in the Soviet/East Europe Division, all the analysts' working lives, all their programs, budgets, and plans for the future were premised on the existence of a powerful and enduring communist enemy in Moscow. The Reagan administration was bound by a belief in Soviet power and skepticism about Gorbachev's reforms.

At the same time that Gorbachev was deciding secretly to initiate a withdrawal of his battered forces from Afghanistan, the CIA's Directorate of Intelligence circulated a report that the Afghan war "has not been a substantial drain on the Soviet economy" and that Moscow "shows continued willingness to incur whatever burden is necessary." At the CIA station in Islamabad "it still looked as though the war might just go on indefinitely or that the Soviets might even be on the verge of winning it."[20]

Gorbachev summoned his Afghan client, President Najibullah, to Moscow on a Friday in early December 1986. A medical student at Kabul University in the same years that Hekmatyar studied engineering there, Najibullah was a more plausible Afghan nationalist than some of the KGB's previous selections. He was a Ghilzai Pashtun with roots in eastern Afghanistan, and his wife hailed from tribal families with royal connections. Najibullah exuded confidence and spoke effectively. His main liability as a national leader was that the great majority of his countrymen considered him a mass murderer.

Gorbachev privately told Najibullah to try to strengthen his political position in Afghanistan in anticipation of a total withdrawal of Soviet forces within eighteen months to two years.[21]

As he tried to initiate quiet diplomatic talks to create ground for a withdrawal, Gorbachev seemed genuinely stunned to discover that the Americans didn't seem to want to negotiate about Afghanistan or the future of Central Asia at all. They remained devoted to their militaristic jihad, and they did not appear to take the possibility of a Soviet withdrawal at all seriously. At times it made Gorbachev furious. "The U.S. has set for itself the goal of disrupting a settlement in Afghanistan by any means," he told his inner circle. What were his options? Gorbachev wanted to end Soviet involvement. He doubted the Afghans could handle the war on their own, but in any settlement he wanted to preserve Soviet power and prestige. "A million of our soldiers went through Afghanistan," he observed. "And we will not be able to explain to our people why we did not complete it. We suffered such heavy losses! And what for?"[22]

ON DECEMBER 15, 1986, the Monday following Gorbachev's secret meeting with Najibullah, Bill Casey arrived at CIA headquarters to prepare for the upcoming Senate testimony about the Iran-Contra scandal. Just after ten o'clock, as the CIA physician took his blood pressure in his office, Casey's right arm and leg began to jerk violently. The doctor held him in his chair.

"What's happening to me?" Casey asked helplessly.

"I'm not sure," the doctor said. An ambulance rushed him to Georgetown Hospital. The seizures continued. A CAT scan showed a mass on the left side of the brain.

Casey never recovered. His deputy Robert Gates visited him in his hospital room a month later. "Time for me to get out of the way," the CIA director said. The next morning Gates returned with Attorney General Edwin Meese and White House Chief of Staff Donald T. Regan, a silver-haired former Wall Street executive.

Casey had tears in his eyes and could barely speak. Regan tried to ask him about the future of the CIA. "All I got was more 'argh, argh, argh,'" Regan recalled. Casey's wife, Sophia, interpreted: "Bill, what you mean is 'Get the best man you can,' right?"

Regan jumped in. "Bill, what you're saying is you want us to replace you, right?" Casey made more noises. "That's very generous and probably in everybody's best interest," Regan said. Then Casey's tears flowed again. "I gripped his hand. It was done," Regan recalled. "But there had been no real communication."[23]

Casey had served as CIA director for six years and one day. Four months later, at his estate on Long Island, he died at age seventy-four.

AS THE YEAR TURNED, Brigadier Mohammed Yousaf, the ISI Afghan operations chief who had been one of Casey's most enthusiastic admirers, planned for new cross-border attacks inside Soviet territory—missions that Yousaf said he had heard Casey endorse.

In April 1987 as the snows melted, three ISI-equipped teams secretly crossed the Amu Darya into Soviet Central Asia. The first team launched a rocket strike against an airfield near Termez in Uzbekistan. The second, a band of about twenty rebels equipped with rocket-propelled grenades and antitank mines, had been instructed by ISI to set up violent ambushes along a border road. They destroyed several Soviet vehicles. A third team hit a factory site more than ten miles inside the Soviet Union with a barrage of about thirty 107-millimeter high-explosive and incendiary rockets. The attacks took place at a time when the CIA was circulating satellite photographs in Washington showing riots on the streets of Alma-Ata, a Soviet Central Asian capital.[24]

A few days later Bearden's secure phone rang in the Islamabad station. Clair George, then chief of the CIA's Directorate of Operations, was on the line, and his voice was formal, measured.

"I want you to think very carefully before you answer the question I am about to ask," he said. "Were you in any way involved in an attack on an industrial site deep inside the Soviet Union . . . in Uzbekistan . . . anytime in the last month?"

 "If anything like that is going on, we're not involved here," Bearden said, equally careful.

He knew that American law prohibited his involvement in such operations; they went far beyond the scope of the CIA's authority. Iran-Contra and its related inquiries were now in full tilt. The agency was under political fire as it had not been since the 1970s. There were lawyers crawling all over the Directorate of Operations. Bearden and Clair, confronting similar dilemmas in the past, had long taken the view that once the CIA supplied weapons to Pakistani intelligence, it lost all title of ownership and therefore all legal responsibility for the weapons' use. "We stand by our position that once the stuff is delivered to the Paks, we lose all control over it," Bearden said.

The Soviets were fed up with the attacks on their own soil. As they counted their dead in Central Asia that April, they dispatched messengers with stark warnings to Islamabad and Washington. They threatened "the security and integrity of Pakistan," a euphemism for an invasion. The Americans assured Moscow that they had never sanctioned any military attacks by the mujahedin on Soviet soil. From army headquarters in Islamabad, Zia sent word to Yousaf that he had to pull back his teams. Yousaf pointed out that this might be difficult because none of his Afghan commandos had radios. But his superiors in ISI called every day to badger him: Stop the attacks.

Bearden called Yousaf for good measure. "Please don't start a third world war," he told him.[25]

The attacks ended. They were Casey's last hurrah.

THAT SAME MONTH, freed from the winter snows, Soviet forces in Afghanistan moved east again, attacking the mountain passes near Khost. On April 17, 1987, Soviet helicopters and bomber jets hit Osama bin Laden's new fortified compound at Jaji, an assemblage of small crevices and caves dug into rocky hills above the border village.

The battle lasted for about a week. Bin Laden and fifty Arab volunteers faced two hundred Russian troops, including elite Spetsnaz. The Arab volunteers took casualties but held out under intense fire for several days. More than a dozen of bin Laden's comrades were killed, and bin Laden himself apparently suffered a foot wound. He also reportedly required insulin injections and had to lie down periodically during the fighting. Eventually he and the other survivors concluded that they could not defend their position any longer, and they withdrew.[26]

Chronicled daily at the time by several Arab journalists who observed the fighting from a mile or two away, the battle of Jaji marked the birth of Osama bin Laden's public reputation as a warrior among Arab jihadists. When Winston Churchill recounted an 1897 battle he fought with the British army not far from the Khyber Pass, he remarked that there was no more thrilling sensation than being shot at and missed. Bin Laden apparently had a similar experience. After Jaji he began a media campaign designed to publicize the brave fight waged by Arab volunteers who stood their ground against a superpower. In interviews and speeches around Peshawar and back home in Saudi Arabia, bin Laden sought to recruit new fighters to his cause and to chronicle his own role as a military leader. He also began to expound on expansive new goals for the jihad.

Ayman al-Zawahiri, the Egyptian doctor who saw the Afghan war merely as "an incubator" and who wrote about the Afghan people with barely disguised condescension, apparently met bin Laden for the first time during this 1987 media campaign. Bin Laden visited the Kuwaiti hospital where he worked, al-Zawahiri recalled, "and talked to us about those lectures of his." Bin Laden had spoken openly about the need for a global jihad against not only the Soviet Union but the corrupt secular governments of the Middle East, the United States, and Israel. Al-Zawahiri listened and recalled telling bin Laden, "As of now, you should change the way in which you are guarded. You should alter your entire security system because your head is now wanted by the Americans and the Jews, not only by the communists and the Russians, because you are hitting the snake on the head."[27]

Bin Laden commissioned a fifty-minute video that showed him riding horses, talking to Arab volunteers, broadcasting on the radio, firing weapons—the same things many commanders without video cameras did routinely. He sought out Arab journalists and gave lengthy interviews designed "to use the media for attracting more Arabs, recruiting more Arabs to come to Afghanistan," as one of the journalists recalled. It was the birth of bin Laden's media strategy, aimed primarily at the Arabic-speaking world; in part he drew on some of the media tactics pioneered by secular Palestinian terrorists and nationalists during the 1970s and early 1980s.

In private, Abdullah Azzam resented bin Laden's campaign. "You see what

Osama is doing—he is collecting and training young people," a colleague then in Peshawar quoted Azzam as saying. "This is not our policy, our plan. We came to *serve* these people, that's why it's called the Office of Services. . . . He is collecting and organizing young people who don't like to participate with the Afghan people." Bin Laden, this participant recalled, "was just sitting in Peshawar and issuing *fatwas* against this leader and that government, playing politics."[28]

Bin Laden had been initiated in combat. In the months afterward he showed little interest in returning to the battlefield, but he had stumbled on a communications strategy far more expansive than his weeklong stand at Jaji.

CASEY'S DEATH foreshadowed changes in the CIA-Pakistani partnership. Under pressure from the United States, Zia had begun to relax martial law in Pakistan. He installed a civilian prime minister who quickly challenged the army's Afghan policies. After years as Zia's intelligence chief, Akhtar wanted a promotion, and Zia rewarded him with a ceremonial but prestigious title. Zia named as the new ISI chief a smooth chameleon who spoke English fluently, Lieutenant General Hamid Gul. Denied his own promotion to major general, Mohammed Yousaf retired as chief of operations for ISI's covert Afghan bureau that same spring. His successor, Brigadier Janjua, inherited an operation that had never been more richly funded but whose direction was beginning to drift.

The personal connections that had bound the CIA and ISI together during the jihad's early years were now broken. Back in Washington, the CIA was on the political defensive. Casey's postmortem reputation was plummeting under the weight of Iran-Contra indictments. Everything he had touched now appeared tainted. More Pentagon officers, more members of Congress, more think tank scholars, more journalists, and more diplomats became involved with the Afghan war. A jihad supply line that had been invented and managed for several years by four or five men had become by 1987 an operation with hundreds of participants.

For the first time pointed questions were being raised in Washington about the emphasis given by Pakistani intelligence and the CIA to Afghan leaders with radical Islamic outlooks. The questions came at first mainly from scholars, journalists, and skeptical members of Congress. They did not ask about the Arab jihadist volunteers—hardly anyone outside of Langley and the State Department's regional and intelligence bureaus were aware of them. Instead, they challenged the reliability of Hekmatyar. He had received several hundred million dollars in aid from American taxpayers, yet he had refused to travel to New York to shake hands with the infidel Ronald Reagan. Why was the CIA supporting him? The questioners were egged on by Hekmatyar's rivals in the resistance, such as those from the Afghan royalist factions and the champions of Massoud's cause.

At closed Capitol Hill hearings and in interagency discussions, officers from the CIA's Near East Division responded by adopting a defensive crouch. They adamantly defended ISI's support of Hekmatyar because he fielded the most effective anti-Soviet fighters. They derided the relatively pro-American Afghan royalists and their ilk as milquetoast politicians who couldn't find the business end of an assault rifle. They also rejected the charge that ISI was allocating "disproportionate" resources to Hekmatyar. Under congressional pressure, a series of heated and murky classified audits ensued, with congressional staff flying into Islamabad to examine the books kept by the CIA station and ISI to determine which Afghan commanders got which weapons.

Bearden and the Afghan task force chief at the CIA, Frank Anderson, resented all this criticism; they felt they had devoted long and tedious hours to ensuring that Hekmatyar received only between a fifth and a quarter of the total supplies filtered through ISI warehouses. Massoud's Peshawar-based leader, the former professor Burhanuddin Rabbani, received just as much from the official pipeline as Hekmatyar, although he passed relatively little of it through to the Panjshir Valley. It was true that Afghan royalist parties received relatively little, but the CIA officers insisted that this was not because the Pakistanis were trying to manipulate Afghan politics by backing the Islamists but, rather, because the royalists were weak fighters prone to corruption.

The CIA's statistical defenses were accurate as far as they went, but among other things they did not account for the massive weight of private Saudi and Arab funding that tilted the field toward the Islamists—up to $25 million a month by Bearden's own estimate. Nor did they account for the intimate tactical and strategic partnerships between Pakistani intelligence and the Afghan Islamists, especially along the Pakistan-Afghanistan border.[29] By the late 1980s ISI had effectively eliminated all the secular, leftist, and royalist political parties that had first formed when Afghan refugees fled communist rule. Still, Bearden defended ISI's strategy adamantly before every visiting congressional delegation, during briefings in the embassy bubble, and over touristic lunches in the mountains above Peshawar. The mission was to kill Soviets, Bearden kept repeating. Gulbuddin Hekmatyar killed Soviets. The king of Afghanistan, twirling pasta on his spoon outside Rome, had not killed a single one. The CIA was not going to have its jihad run "by some liberal arts jerkoff."[30]

Pakistani attitudes were in flux as well. The ISI's Afghan bureau had become one of the richest and most powerful units in the entire Pakistan army, and it, too, jealously guarded its prerogatives. Janjua, the new operations chief, was an ardent Islamist, much more religious than the typical Pakistani army officer, his CIA colleagues believed. In Peshawar the local Afghan bureau office was run by a formidable Pathan officer who took the nom de guerre Colonel Imam. He was very close personally to Hekmatyar, and over the years he began to make plain his Muslim Brotherhood views in private conversations with CIA counterparts. On ISI's front lines the Afghan cause was increasingly a matter of true belief by the Pakistani officers involved, an inflated mission that blended statecraft and religious fervor.[31]

Implementing Zia's vision, Pakistani intelligence was determined to install a friendly regime in Kabul and, by doing so, create breathing space on Pakistan's historically unstable western frontier. Islamism was their ideology—a personal creed, at least in some cases—and Hekmatyar was their primary client. Beyond Afghanistan, ISI's colonels and brigadiers envisioned Pakistani influence pushing north and west toward Soviet Central Asia. Key Pathan officers such as Imam simply did not rotate out of the Afghan bureau. They stayed and stayed. They could not get away with raking off millions in cash and stuffing it in Swiss bank accounts—the ISI and CIA controls were generally too tight for that sort of thing. Still, if an officer was inclined, there was plenty of opportunity to sell off one of the new CIA-imported Toyota trucks or take a small cash commission for facilitating local smugglers and heroin manufacturers. There was no remotely comparable revenue stream to tap if that same ISI major or colonel rotated to Karachi or worse, to some artillery unit facing India in the forsaken desert area of Rajasthan.

Among those now raising noisy doubts about Pakistani intelligence was the Afghan commander Abdul Haq, who had become a popular figure with American journalists covering the war from Peshawar. Since Haq had lost one foot to a land mine on a mission near Kabul, his travel inside was more limited than before. He collaborated with a CBS cameraman to film rocket attacks around Kabul, escorted journalists over the border, and flew off to Washington to lobby for support. He was the most credible, accessible commander to denounce ISI manipulation of Afghan politics. The questions he raised were pointed: Why should the last phase of the Afghan jihad be designed to serve Pakistani interests? A million Afghan lives had been lost; hundreds of thousands of intellectuals, businessmen, and tribal leaders had been forced into exile. Why was ISI determined to prevent the country's national leaders from beginning to construct a postwar Afghan political system that belonged to Afghans? Bearden grew furious because Haq seemed focused on public relations. The CIA station chief denounced him privately and cut him out of the CIA's unilateral network. At Langley, Frank Anderson saw Haq as "a pretty good commander who was also particularly effective at P.R." and who did not have "as many scalps" as less publicized CIA favorites, such as Jallaladin Haqqanni, the ardent Islamist close to bin Laden. Bearden felt that Abdul Haq was spending "much, much more time in Peshawar, possibly dealing with the media, than he was inside Afghanistan. I think he heard that I had, unfortunately, begun to call him 'Hollywood Haq,' and this got to him, and he became very, very angry with me."

Bearden met three times with Hekmatyar in Peshawar. Hekmatyar's English was excellent. In private meetings he was often ingratiating. As the debate about his anti-Americanism became more visible, he began to fear that the CIA might want to kill him.

"Why would I want to kill you?" Bearden asked him.

Hekmatyar answered: "The United States can no longer feel safe with me alive."

"I think the engineer flatters himself," Bearden said.[32]

SOVIET FOREIGN MINISTER Eduard Shevardnadze briefed the inner Politburo group in May about Najibullah's early efforts to pursue a new policy of "national reconciliation" that might outflank the CIA-backed rebels. The program was producing "a certain result, but very modest."

They were all frustrated with Afghanistan. How could you have a policy of national reconciliation without a nation? There was no sense of homeland in Afghanistan, they complained, nothing like the feeling they had for Russia.

"This needs to be remembered: There can be no Afghanistan without Islam," Gorbachev said. "There's nothing to replace it with now. But if the name of the party is kept, then the word 'Islamic' needs to be included in it. Afghanistan needs to be returned to a condition which is natural for it. The mujahedin need to be more aggressively invited into power at the grassroots."

The Americans were a large obstacle, they agreed. Surely they would align themselves with a Soviet decision to withdraw—if they knew it was serious.

And the superpowers would have certain goals in common: a desire for stability in the Central Asian region and a desire to contain Islamic fundamentalism.

"We have not approached the United States of America in a real way," Gorbachev said. "They need to be associated with the political solution, to be invited. This is the correct policy. There's an opportunity here."[33]

In Washington the following September, Shevardnadze used the personal trust that had developed between him and Secretary of State George Shultz to disclose for the first time the decision taken in the Politburo the previous autumn. Their staffs were in a working session on regional disputes when Shevardnadze called Shultz aside privately. The Georgian opened with a quiet directness, Shultz recalled. "We will leave Afghanistan," Shevardnadze said. "It may be in five months or a year, but it is not a question of it happening in the remote future." He chose his words so that Shultz would understand their gravity. "I say with all responsibility that a political decision to leave has been made."[34]

Shultz was so struck by the significance of the news that it half-panicked him. He feared that if he told the right-wingers in Reagan's Cabinet what Shevardnadze had said, and endorsed the disclosure as sincere, he would be accused of going soft on Moscow. He kept the conversation to himself for weeks.

Shevardnadze had asked for American cooperation in limiting the spread of "Islamic fundamentalism." Shultz was sympathetic, but no high-level Reagan administration officials ever gave much thought to the issue. They never considered pressing Pakistani intelligence to begin shifting support away from the Muslim Brotherhood–connected factions and toward more friendly Afghan leadership, whether for the Soviets' sake or America's. The CIA and others in Washington discounted warnings from Soviet leadership about Islamic radicalism. The warnings were just a way to deflect attention from Soviet failings, American hard-liners decided.[35]

Yet even in private the Soviets worried about Islamic radicalism encroaching on their southern rim, and they knew that once they withdrew from Afghanistan, their own border would mark the next frontier for the more ambitious jihadists. Still, their public denunciations of Hekmatyar and other Islamists remained wooden, awkward, hyperbolic, and easy to dismiss.

Gorbachev was moving faster now than the CIA could fully absorb.

On December 4, 1987, in a fancy Washington, D.C., bistro called Maison Blanche, Robert Gates, now the acting CIA director, sat down for dinner with his KGB counterpart, Vladimir Kryuchkov, chief of the Soviet spy agency. It was an unprecedented session. They talked about the entire gamut of U.S.-

Soviet relations. Kryuchkov was running a productive agent inside the CIA at the time, Aldrich Ames, which may have contributed to a certain smugness perceived by Gates.

On Afghanistan, Kryuchkov assured Gates that the Soviet Union now wanted to get out but needed CIA cooperation to find a political solution. He and other Soviet leaders were fearful about the rise to power in Afghanistan of another fundamentalist Islamic government, a Sunni complement to Shiite Iran. "You seem fully occupied in trying to deal with just one fundamentalist Islamic state," Kryuchkov told Gates.[36]

Gorbachev hoped that in exchange for a Soviet withdrawal he could persuade the CIA to cut off aid to its Afghan rebels. Reagan told him in a summit meeting five days later that this was impossible. The next day Gorbachev tried his luck with Vice President George Bush. "If we were to begin to withdraw troops while American aid continued, then this would lead to a bloody war in the country," Gorbachev pleaded.

Bush consoled him: "We are not in favor of installing an exclusively pro-American regime in Afghanistan. This is not U.S. policy."[37]

There was no American policy on Afghan politics at the time, only the de facto promotion of Pakistani goals as carried out by Pakistani intelligence. The CIA forecasted repeatedly during this period that postwar Afghanistan was going to be an awful mess; nobody could prevent that. Let the Pakistanis sort out the regional politics. This was their neighborhood.

Gates joined Shultz, Michael Armacost, Morton Abramowitz, and Deputy Secretary of State John Whitehead for a lighthearted luncheon on New Year's Eve. They joked their way through a serious debate about whether Shevardnadze meant what he said when he had told Shultz in September that they were getting out. At the table only Gates—reflecting the views of many of his colleagues at the CIA—argued that it would not happen, that no Soviet withdrawal was likely, that Moscow was engaged in a political deception.

The CIA director bet Armacost $25 that the Soviets would not be out of Afghanistan before the end of the Reagan administration. A few months later he paid Armacost the money.[38]

"We Won"

EDMUND MCWILLIAMS was a wiry, dark-haired American foreign service officer, intense, earnest, precise, and serious. He had a reputation as a tough anticommunist, hardworking, and skilled at languages. He had come of age in Rhode Island during the 1960s. His father was a mill worker, and his mother earned modest wages as an aide in a cafeteria. At the height of America's upheavals over Vietnam he was enrolled at the University of Rhode Island, concentrating in Southeast Asian studies and becoming increasingly involved in conservative causes. Even late in the war he was so certain that his country's involvement in Vietnam was just that he volunteered for the army, studied Vietnamese for forty-seven weeks, and rotated to Saigon in 1972 as a U.S. Army intelligence officer. He specialized in interrogations of Vietcong and North Vietnamese prisoners, moving between detention centers and extracting and analyzing details about communist battlefield operations, supplies, and strategic plans. When his tour was finished, he joined the diplomatic service. He added Russian to his language portfolio and moved to the U.S. embassy in Moscow in 1983; as a political officer he would concentrate on Soviet human rights violations. He traveled extensively in Central Asia, reporting on Soviet repression of nationalism and Islam. He became used to living under continuous KGB surveillance. He studied Dari, moved to Kabul in 1986 at the height of the Afghan war, and was number two in the small and pressured U.S. embassy. With a handful of case officers in the CIA station he drove the wide streets of the Afghan capital, a small camera often placed discreetly on the seat, photographing Soviet military equipment, deployments, troop movements—anything that might be helpful back in Washington. His cables from the embassy provided details about Soviet atrocities, battlefield failures, and political abuses. McWilliams and his embassy colleagues—who were surveilled by KGB and Afghan intelligence officers, prohibited from traveling outside the city, and limited largely to interactions with other diplomats and spies—had become "very much cold warriors," and "many of us felt it in a very sadistic way. . . . What we were being paid to do was to write, really, propaganda pieces against the Soviets."[1]

Early in 1988 there were two big questions at the U.S. embassy in Kabul: Were the Soviets really going to leave? And if they did, what would happen to the Afghan communist government they left behind, presided over by the former secret police chief Najibullah?

Circulating to policy makers in Washington and by diplomatic cable, the CIA's classified analysis in those weeks made two main points. Gates and the Soviet Division of the Directorate of Intelligence remained doubtful that Gorbachev would actually follow through with a troop withdrawal. And if the Soviet Fortieth Army did leave Afghanistan, Najibullah's communist government would collapse very quickly. In multiple reports the CIA's analysts asserted confidently in January and February that the Afghan communists could not possibly hold on to power after the Soviet troops left. Najibullah's generals, seeking survival, would defect with their equipment to the mujahedin one after another.

McWilliams debated these speculations with European diplomats at receptions and dinners that winter in the grim, snowy capital. McWilliams shared the CIA's belief that Najibullah was a puppet of Soviet military power and that he could not stand in Afghanistan on his own. But the British and French diplomats he talked with questioned the CIA's assumptions. There was a great deal of anxiety within the Afghan military and the city's civilian population about the prospect of a Pakistani-backed Islamic radical government coming to power, especially one led by Hekmatyar. However deprived and battered they were, Afghan civilians in Kabul enjoyed certain privileges they did not wish to surrender. There were ample if unproductive government jobs. Tens of thousands of women worked in offices, arriving each day in rough-cut East European–style skirts and high heels. What would their lives be like under the Islamists? The Afghan people hated Najibullah, but they feared Hekmatyar. What if Najibullah began to negotiate cease-fires with ambitious rebel commanders—perhaps even Massoud? If he preached Afghan nationalism, might not he be able to hang on? What if the Soviets poured billions of dollars of economic aid into Kabul even after their troops evacuated, providing Najibullah with a way to buy off warlords from the mujahedin's ranks?

That January, McWilliams sat down in his office and tapped out a confidential cable to Washington and Langley about this "nightmare scenario," emphasizing that it was not the Kabul embassy's viewpoint but rather a possibility "that some of the old hands in Kabul are beginning to fear could enable the current regime to survive largely intact." After describing in detail how Najibullah might construct his survival, McWilliams concluded, on behalf of the embassy, "We find this scenario troublingly plausible. It would achieve peace and the withdrawal of Soviet forces at the cost of [Afghan] self-determination."[2]

Gates joined Shultz and his top aides at Foggy Bottom on February 19. The CIA's analysts were united in the belief that post-Soviet Afghanistan "would be messy, with a struggle for power among different mujahedin groups, and that the outcome would most likely be a weak central government and powerful tribal leaders in the countryside." But as to Najibullah, most of the CIA's analysts simply did not believe his government could survive without active military support by Soviet forces.

John Whitehead and Morton Abramowitz said they thought the CIA was wrong. Najibullah would start cutting deals with rebel commanders, they predicted, allowing him to stay in power much longer than Langley assumed.

Colin Powell, recently appointed as Reagan's national security adviser, asked Gates directly: Could Najibullah last, and how long? How good is the Afghan army? Powell worried that the CIA had "very strong assumptions" about these "two givens," and he wanted them to rethink.[3]

Under Gates's supervision the entire American intelligence community reviewed the issues and produced a special National Intelligence Estimate, "USSR: Withdrawal from Afghanistan," classified Secret. "We judge that the Najibullah regime will not long survive the completion of Soviet withdrawal even with continued Soviet assistance," the estimate declared. "The regime may fall before withdrawal is complete."

The replacement government the CIA expected "will be Islamic—possibly strongly fundamentalist, but not as extreme as Iran. . . . We cannot be confident of the new government's orientation toward the West; at best it will be ambivalent, and at worst it may be actively hostile, especially toward the United States."[4]

If Kabul's next government might be "actively hostile" toward Washington, why didn't the United States push quickly for political negotiations that could produce a more friendly and stable Afghan regime, as they were being urged to do by Afghan intellectuals and royalists? If Najibullah's quick collapse was inevitable, as the CIA believed, wasn't the need for such political mediation more urgent than ever, to help contain Hekmatyar and his international Islamist allies?

But the councils of the American government were by now deeply divided on the most basic questions. Gorbachev's initiative on Afghanistan had neither been anticipated nor carefully reviewed. Individuals and departments pulled in different directions all at once. The CIA and the State Department were much more focused on Gorbachev and the Soviet Union than on Afghanistan. The entire nuclear and political balance of the Cold War seemed suddenly at stake as 1988 passed. Central Asia's future did not rank high on the priority list by comparison.

Gates continued to doubt Gorbachev's intentions. Shultz, isolated in his own cabinet and running out of time, wanted to find a formula for Soviet withdrawal from Afghanistan that would ensure the fastest, least complicated Soviet pullout possible, without restricting the ability of the mujahedin to fight their way into Kabul when the Soviets were gone. Trying to negotiate some sort of transitional government in Afghanistan seemed out of the question: It would make the pace of Soviet withdrawal dependent on American success in Afghan politics—a very poor bet.

For its part, the CIA's Near East Division, led by the Afghan task force director Frank Anderson, began to argue that the CIA's work in Afghanistan was finished. The agency should just get out of the country when the Soviets did. The covert action had been all about challenging Soviet power and aggression; it would be an error to try to convert the program now into some sort of reconstruction project. There was no way to succeed with such a project, the CIA's Near East officers argued.

As Bearden put it years later, "Did we really give a shit about the long-term future of Nangarhar? Maybe not. As it turned out, guess what? We didn't."[5]

The CIA's Near East hands were increasingly annoyed at the State Department diplomats who were now wheedling onto the CIA's turf at the moment of victory, continually questioning the agency's assumptions, harping on the Pakistani support for Hekmatyar and the Islamists, and wringing their hands about peace settlements. Where had these pin-striped assholes been when it counted, the grumbling at Langley went, when the CIA had been slogging away amid skepticism that they could ever succeed? What naïve earnestness led State's diplomats and their allies in Congress to believe that they could unscramble the Afghan war, hold a few conferences in Europe, and welcome the exiled Afghan king back to his Kabul palace, with a brass band playing on the lawn? The Afghans would have to figure things out themselves. The Americans couldn't help, and it was not in the interests of the United States to try. How much of this thinking within CIA's Near East Division was carefully considered and how much of it was an emotional rebellion against second-guessing from State and Congress was difficult to measure. They felt they had taken more than ample guff about the most successful covert action program in CIA history. The Soviets were leaving. Enough.

As to Afghan politics, the CIA was content to let Pakistani intelligence take the lead even if it did mean they installed their client Hekmatyar in Kabul. So what? Pakistani hegemony over Afghanistan, whether or not it was achieved through the ideology of political Islam, did not seem to pose any significant threat to American interests, the Near East Division's officers felt. Besides, if they had qualms about Hekmatyar—and most of them did—they did not see what they could do at this stage to block ISI's plans. So they moved to help ISI succeed. After consulting with Prince Turki, the CIA and Saudi intelligence both accelerated shipments of weapons to Pakistan, hoping to beat any diplomatic deadlines that might constrict supplies.

The new Pakistani intelligence chief, Hamid Gul, had taken over with fresh plans to push the rebels toward more formal military operations that could put pressure on major Afghan cities. Gul felt his job was "to get the Russians out. I'm not concerned about anything else." He was not as close personally to Hekmatyar as some of the colonels and brigadiers who had become fixtures in ISI's Afghan bureau, a bureau where Gul had little experience. Based on military liaison contacts with Gul in Islamabad, the Defense Intelligence Agency produced a biography of the new ISI chief that emphasized his pro-Western attitudes. The sketch of Gul's character turned out to be almost entirely wrong. A full-faced, fast-talking general who rolled easily through American idioms, Gul could change stripes quickly. From 1987 onward he worked very closely with Prince Turki, Turki's chief of staff Ahmed Badeeb, and other officers in Saudi intelligence. The Saudis knew Gul as a pious, committed Muslim and provided him with multiple gifts from the Saudi kingdom, including souvenirs from the holy Kaaba in Mecca. Yet his American partners in 1988 believed that Gul was their man. Gul described himself to Bearden as a "moderate Islamist."[6]

Gul was going to give money and guns to Hekmatyar and other Islamists mainly because they were willing to fight, he said. He was going to operate on a professional military basis. He certainly was not going to help out exiled Afghan intellectuals, technocrats, royalists, or other such politicians. Gul was determined to shut out those Afghans "who live a very good life [abroad] in the capitals of the world." In this he had the full support of the CIA station chief. Bearden regarded the Westernized Afghan rebel leaders such as Sibghat-ullah Mojaddedi as corrupt and ineffective. The "only real strength" of Mo-jaddedi's party "was its gift for public relations," as Bearden saw it. Pir Sayed Ahmad Gailani attended meetings with Bearden in "a silk-and-cashmere suit," and he "rarely, if ever, strayed into Afghanistan," earning Bearden's disdain. Bearden encouraged ISI to provide the most potent high-technology weapons, such as Stingers and Milan antitank missiles, to Islamist Pashtun commanders who fought along the Pakistan-Afghan border, especially in Paktia and Nangarhar provinces. These were the regions where "the Soviets were still mounting major assaults," as Bearden saw it.[7]

President Zia had wanted some sort of interim Afghan government to be agreed on before the Soviets left, to help ensure stability on Pakistan's western border. When it became clear that the Americans weren't interested, Zia said openly that Pakistan's army and intelligence service would work to install a friendly government in Kabul, one that would protect Pakistan's interests in its rivalry with India and prevent any stirrings of Pashtun nationalism on Pakistani territory. Zia felt this was only Pakistan's due: "We have earned the right to have [in Kabul] a power which is very friendly toward us. We have taken risks as a front-line state, and we will not permit a return to the prewar situation, marked by a large Indian and Soviet influence and Afghan claims on our own territory. The new power will be really Islamic, a part of the Islamic renaissance which, you will see, will someday extend itself to the Soviet Muslims."[8]

In Washington that winter, much more than the liberals it was the still-vigorous network of conservative anticommunist ideologues in the Reagan administration and on Capitol Hill who began to challenge the CIA-ISI combine. These young policy makers, many of whom had traveled at one point or another to the Khyber Pass and stared across the ridges for a few hours with mujahedin commanders, feared that a CIA pullback from Afghanistan would sell out the Afghan rebel cause. America could not give up now; its goal should be "Afghan self-determination," a government chosen by the "freedom fighters," and if Najibullah's thuggish neocommunist regime hung on in Kabul, the mujahedins' brave campaign would be betrayed. Opinion about Hekmatyar and the Islamists in these conservative American circles was divided; some admired him as a stalwart anticommunist, while others feared his anti-Americanism. But there was a growing belief that some counterforce to CIA analysis and decision-making was now required inside the American government. Senator Gordon Humphrey, among others, agitated in the spring of 1988 for the appointment of a special U.S. envoy on Afghanistan, someone who could work with the rebel leaders outside of ISI earshot, assess their needs, and make recommendations about U.S. policy. America needed an expert, someone who spoke the language and knew the region but who also had proven credentials as a hard-line anticommunist.

The State Department recommended Edmund McWilliams. He was nominated as U.S. special envoy to the Afghan rebels and dispatched to the U.S. embassy in Islamabad in the late spring of 1988. McWilliams was energized by his assignment. He would be able to report independently about the late stages of the Afghan jihad, circulate his cables to the CIA, State Department, and Congress, and provide a fresh, independent voice on the main controversies in U.S. policy at a critical moment.

It took only a few weeks after his arrival in the redbrick Islamabad embassy compound for CIA chief Milt Bearden to bestow upon McWilliams one of his pet nicknames. "That Evil Little Person," Bearden began to call him.[9]

SIGNED BY RANKING DIPLOMATS on April 14, 1988, the Geneva Accords ratified by treaty the formal terms of the Soviet withdrawal. It was an agreement among governments—Afghanistan's communist-led regime, Pakistan, the United States, and the Soviet Union. The Afghan rebels had no part in the negotiations, and some of them denounced the accord as a conspiracy against their cause. In fact, it assured that the rebels would remain militarily potent for years ahead. Gorbachev had hoped his willingness to get out of Afghanistan would persuade the Americans to end CIA aid to the mujahedin. But it was Ronald Reagan personally, apparently unscripted, who told a television interviewer early in 1988 that he just didn't think it would be fair if the Soviets continued to provide military and economic aid to Najibullah while the United States was forced to stop helping the Afghan rebels. Reagan's diplomatic negotiators had been preparing to accept an end to CIA assistance. Now they scrambled to change course. They negotiated a new formula called "positive symmetry," which permitted the CIA to supply guns and money to the mujahedin for as long as Moscow provided assistance to its allies in Kabul's government.

The first Soviet troops rolled out of Jalalabad a month later, some twelve thousand men and their equipment. Along with ISI's brigadiers, Bearden and his case officers spent many hours that spring of 1988 trying to persuade rebel commanders not to slaughter the Soviets during their retreat, as Afghan militia had done to retreating British imperial soldiers a century earlier. For the most part, rebel commanders allowed the Soviets to pass.

As the troops withdrew, Andrei Sakharov, the physicist and human rights activist whose freedom to speak signaled a new era of openness in Moscow, addressed the Congress of Peoples' Deputies. "The war in Afghanistan was in itself criminal, a criminal adventure," he told them. "This crime cost the lives of about a million Afghans, a war of destruction was waged against an entire people. . . . This is what lies on us as a terrible sin, a terrible reproach. We must cleanse ourselves of this shame that lies on our leadership."[10]

EARLY IN AUGUST, Bearden took a call at the Islamabad station from an excited ISI officer. A Soviet SU-25, an advanced military aircraft, had been hit by antiaircraft fire near Parrot's Beak on the Pakistani border. The Soviet pilot had bailed out, but the plane came down softly, grinding to a stop with little damage.

How much would you be willing to pay? the ISI officer asked.

Bearden inquired if the plane's nose cone, which carried its instrumentation, was in good condition and whether its weapons had survived. They had, he was assured. He began negotiating. In the end, ISI sold the plane to the CIA for about half a dozen Toyota double-cab pickup trucks and some BM-12 rockets. Bearden arranged to inspect it, and he summoned a joint CIA–Air Force team out from Washington to help load the prize onto a transport plane.

The next morning ISI called back. The pilot had survived and had been captured by Afghan rebels. "Jesus, tell them not to put him in the cook pot," Bearden said. The last thing they needed was a Soviet officer tortured or murdered in the middle of the troop withdrawal. Bearden offered some pickup trucks for the pilot, and ISI accepted. Pakistani intelligence interrogated the captive for four or five days. Bearden passed through the usual CIA offer to captured pilots: "The big-chested homecoming queen blonde, the bass boat, and the pickup truck with Arizona plates." But ISI reported the Soviet officer declined to defect. Bearden contacted the Soviets and arranged for a hand-over. The pilot's name was Alexander Rutskoi. Several years later he would lead a violent uprising against Russian president Boris Yeltsin.[11]

BEARDEN'S PHONE RANG again at home just a few days after he pur-chased the SU-25. It was August 17, 1988. The embassy officer said they had a very garbled report that President Zia's plane had gone down near Bhawal-pur where Zia, General Akhtar, Arnold Raphel (the American ambassador to Pakistan), and other Pakistani and American military officers had been watch-ing the demonstration of a new tank that the Americans wanted to sell.

Bearden sent a "critic" cable to Langley, the most urgent. If Zia was dead, the entire American government would have to mobilize quickly to assess the crisis. By the next morning it was confirmed. After the tank demonstration Zia had invited Akhtar, Raphel, an American brigadier general, and most of his own senior brass into the VIP compartment of his American-made C-130 for the short flight back to Islamabad. Minutes after takeoff the plane plum-meted to the ground, its propellered engines churning at full force. All the bodies and much of the plane burned to char.

Langley sent a cable to Bearden suggesting that he dispatch the Air Force team in Pakistan for the SU-25 to investigate the Zia plane crash. The team was qualified to examine the wreckage. Bearden sent a reply cable that said, as he recalled it, "It would be a mistake to use the visiting technicians. Whatever good they might be able to do would be outweighed by the fact that the CIA had people poking around in the rubble of Zia's plane a day after it went down. Questions would linger as to what we were doing at the crash site and what we'd added or removed to cover up our hand in the crash." There was no sense aggravating the suspicions and questions about how Zia died by getting the CIA involved in the investigation. He could already imagine ISI's conspiracy-obsessed minds thinking: Why wasn't Bearden sahib on that plane? How did he know to stay away?[12]

In Washington, Powell convened a meeting in the White House Situation Room. Thomas Twetten, then running the Near East Division of the CIA's Directorate of Operations, attended for the agency. Robert Oakley, the Na-tional Security Council's director for the region, backed up Powell. Richard

Armitage was there from the Pentagon and Michael Armacost from State. The Pakistanis were fearful that this might be a deliberate attack, perhaps the first in a series of strikes aimed at the country's very existence. The interagency group decided to send a senior team from Washington to Islamabad immediately, "to let the Paks know that we were solidly in support of them, whatever the threat might be, to mount the maximum intelligence search for what might have happened to this plane and what else might be coming," as Oakley later described it.[13]

The Americans weren't sure themselves what to think. Had the Russians done this, a final KGB act of revenge for Afghanistan? Was it the Iranians? The Indians? They began cabling warnings all over the world, saying, in Oakley's paraphrase, "Don't mess with the Paks, or the United States is going to be on your ass." They ordered every available intelligence asset to focus on intercepts, satellite pictures, anything that might turn up evidence of a conspiracy to kill Zia. They found nothing, but they were still unsure.

That night most of those in the Situation Room found their way to the Palm restaurant on 19th Street for a booze-soaked wake in remembrance of Ambassador Raphel, a well-known and well-liked foreign service officer. Shultz, in New Orleans for the Republican convention, called Oakley at the restaurant. He told him to get out to Andrews Air Force Base outside Washington to accompany him to Pakistan for Zia's funeral—and to pack heavy because Oakley was going to stay in Islamabad as the new U.S. ambassador, succeeding Raphel.

Charlie Wilson flew out on the plane with Shultz, as did Armitage and Armacost. They huddled together across the aisles, talking about contingencies, and they scratched out a new American policy toward Pakistan, literally on the fly. The United States would deepen ties to the Pakistani military, including Pakistani intelligence. They would need this intimate alliance more than ever now to get through the post-Zia transition. They would also support democratic elections for a new civilian government. Zia had been moving in this direction anyway; a date for national voting had been set. And they would help defend Pakistan from any external threats.[14]

It took weeks for the jitters to settle down. A joint U.S.-Pakistani air force investigation turned up circumstantial evidence of mechanical failure in the crash, although the exact cause remained a guess at best. The intelligence sweep turned up no chatter or other evidence about a murder conspiracy. Zia's successor as army chief of staff—a mild and bookish general, Mirza Aslam Beg—announced that the army would go forward with the scheduled elections and withdraw from politics. And the Soviets showed no sign of wavering from their planned withdrawal from Afghanistan. By October it appeared that the transition from Zia's long dictatorial reign would be smoother than anyone had had reason to expect at the time of his death.

The Afghan jihad had lost its founding father. General Akhtar, too, the architect of modern Pakistani intelligence, was dead. But Zia and Akhtar had left expansive, enduring legacies. In 1971 there had been only nine hundred *madrassas* in all of Pakistan. By the summer of 1988 there were about eight thousand official religious schools and an estimated twenty-five thousand unregistered ones, many of them clustered along the Pakistan-Afghanistan frontier and funded by wealthy patrons from Saudi Arabia and other Gulf states.[15] When Akhtar had taken over ISI almost a decade earlier, it was a small and demoralized unit within the Pakistan military, focused mainly on regime security and never-ending espionage games with India. Now ISI was an army within the army, boasting multiple deep-pocketed patrons, including the supremely deep-pocketed Prince Turki and his Saudi General Intelligence Department. ISI enjoyed an ongoing operational partnership with the CIA as well, with periodic access to the world's most sophisticated technology and intelligence collection systems. The service had welcomed to Pakistan legions of volunteers from across the Islamic world, fighters who were willing to pursue Pakistan's foreign policy agenda not only in Afghanistan but, increasingly, across its eastern borders in Kashmir, where jihadists trained in Afghanistan were just starting to bleed Indian troops. And as the leading domestic political bureau of the Pakistan army, ISI could tap telephones, bribe legislators, and control voting boxes across the country when it decided a cause was ripe. Outside the Pakistan army itself, less than ten years after the Soviet invasion of Afghanistan, ISI had been transformed by CIA and Saudi subsidies into Pakistan's most powerful institution. Whatever unfolded now would require ISI's consent.

ED MCWILLIAMS STRUCK OUT by jeep for the Afghan frontier soon after he arrived in Islamabad that summer. After the deaths of Zia and Ambassador Raphel, the U.S. embassy was in chaos. The new regime led by Robert Oakley was only just settling in. It seemed an ideal time for McWilliams to disappear into the field, to use his prestigious-sounding title of special envoy and his language skills to talk with as many Afghan commanders, intellectuals, and refugees as he could. He traveled on weekends to avoid escorts and official meetings set up by the embassy. He wanted to know what problems Afghan mujahedin were facing as the Soviets left, what American interests were in post-Soviet Afghanistan, and what was really happening on the ground.

For two months he traveled through Pakistan's tribal areas. In Peshawar he spent long hours with Abdul Haq and senior mujahedin leaders such as Pir Sayed Ahmad Gailani and Younis Khalis. Ahmed Shah Massoud's brother Yahya had moved to Peshawar and set up an office for the Panjshiri militia. McWilliams drove up into the hills and talked with merchants, travelers on the roads, and rebel recruits in training camps. He flew down to Quetta and met with the Afghan exiles from the country's royalist clans, including the Karzai family. He talked to commanders who operated in the west of Afghanistan, in the central Hazara region, and also some who fought near Kandahar, the southern city that was Afghanistan's historical royal capital. He drove up to Chaman on the Afghan border and talked with carpet merchants shuttling back and forth into Afghanistan. It had been a long time since an American in a po-sition to shape government policy had sat cross-legged on quite so many Afghan rugs or sipped so many cups of sugared green tea, asking Afghans themselves open-ended questions about their jihad. The accounts McWilliams heard began to disturb and anger him.

Nearly every Afghan he met impressed upon him the same message: As the Soviets withdrew, Gulbuddin Hekmatyar—backed by officers in ISI's Afghan bureau, operatives from the Muslim Brotherhood's Jamaat-e-Islami, officers from Saudi intelligence, and Arab volunteers from a dozen countries—was moving systematically to wipe out his rivals in the Afghan resistance. The scenes described by McWilliams's informants made Hekmatyar sound like a Mafia don taking over the territory of his rivals. Hekmatyar and his kingpin commanders were serially kidnapping and murdering mujahedin royalists, in-tellectuals, rival party commanders—anyone who threatened strong alterna-tive leadership. Pakistani intelligence was at the same time using its recently constructed network of border infrastructure—checkpoints, training camps, and the newly built roads and caves and depots around Parrot's Beak and Pak-tia province—to block the progress of mujahedin commanders who opposed Hekmatyar and to force independent commanders to join Hekmatyar's party. Added up, the circumstantial evidence seemed chilling: As the Soviet Union soldiers pulled out, Hekmatyar and ISI had embarked on a concerted, clan-destine plan to eliminate his rivals and establish his Muslim Brotherhood–dominated Islamic Party as the most powerful national force in Afghanistan.[16]

In University Town, Peshawar, gunmen on motorcycles killed the Afghan poet and philosopher Sayd Bahudin Majrooh, publisher of the most influential bulletin promoting traditional Afghan royalist and tribal leadership. Majrooh's independent Afghan Information Center had reported in a survey that 70 percent of Afghan refugees supported exiled King Zahir Shah rather than any of the Peshawar-based mujahedin leaders such as Hekmatyar.[17] There were no arrests in Majrooh's killing. The hit was interpreted among Afghans and at the CIA's Islamabad station as an early and intimidating strike by Hekmatyar against the Zahir Shah option for post-Soviet Afghanistan.[18]

The Ahmed Shah Massoud option came in for similar treatment: Around the same time that Majrooh was killed, Massoud's older half-brother Dean Mohammed was kidnapped and killed by mysterious assailants hours after he visited the American consulate in Peshawar to apply for a visa. Massoud's brothers believed for years afterward that ISI's Afghan cell had carried out the operation, although they could not be sure.[19]

In Quetta, McWilliams heard detailed accounts of how Pakistani intelligence had allied with Hekmatyar to isolate and defeat rival commanders around Kandahar. ISI's local office regulated food and cash handouts so that those who now agreed to join Hekmatyar would have ample supplies for fighters and civilians in areas they controlled. Those who didn't agree to join, however, would be starved, unable to pay their men or supply grain to their villages. ISI used a road permit system to ensure that only authorized commanders had permission to take humanitarian supplies across the Afghan border, McWilliams was told. At the same time, Pakistani intelligence and the Arab volunteers operating around Paktia used their access to newly built roads, clinics, and training camps to persuade local commanders that only by joining forces with them could they ensure that their wounded were evacuated quickly and treated by qualified doctors. Afghan witnesses reported seeing ISI officers with Hekmatyar commanders as they moved in force against rival mujahedin around Kandahar. They complained to McWilliams that Hekmatyar's people received preferential access to local training camps and weapons depots. Secular-minded royalist Afghans from the country's thin, exiled tribal leadership and commercial classes said they had long warned both the Americans and the Saudis, as one put it, "For God's sake, you're financing your own assassins." But the Americans had been convinced by Pakistani intelligence, they complained, that only the most radical Islamists could fight with determination.

A lifelong and passionate cold warrior, Ed McWilliams shared the conviction of conservative intellectuals in Washington that the CIA's long struggle for Afghan "self-determination" was morally just, even righteous. It appalled him to discover, as he believed he had, that American authority and billions of dollars in taxpayer funding had been hijacked at the war's end by a ruthless anti-American cabal of Islamists and Pakistani intelligence officers determined to impose their will on Afghanistan.

In the middle of October 1988, McWilliams sat down in the diplomatic section of the U.S. embassy in Islamabad and tapped out on its crude, secure telex system a twenty-eight-paragraph cable, classified Secret and titled "ISI, Gulbuddin and Afghan Self-Determination."[20] It was at that stage almost certainly the most detailed internal dissent about U.S. support for Pakistani intelligence, Saudi Arabian intelligence, and the Islamist Afghan rebels ever expressed in official U.S. government channels. The cable was distributed to the State Department, the CIA, the National Security Council, and a few members of Congress.

THERE IS A GROWING FRUSTRATION, BORDERING ON HOSTILITY, AMONG AFGHANS ACROSS THE IDEOLOGICAL SPECTRUM AND FROM A BROAD RANGE OF BACKGROUNDS, TOWARD THE GOVERNMENT OF PAKISTAN AND TOWARD THE U.S. . . . THE EXTENT OF THIS SENTIMENT APPEARS UNPRECEDENTED AND INTENSIFYING. . . . MOST OF THESE OBSERVERS CLAIM THAT THIS EFFORT [BY HEKMATYAR AND ISI] HAS THE SUPPORT OF THE RADICAL PAKISTANI POLITICAL PARTY JAMAAT ISLAMI AND OF RADICAL ARABS. . . . WHILE THESE CHARGES MAY BE EXAGGERATED, THE PERCEPTION THEY GIVE RISE TO IS DEEP AND BROAD—AND OMINOUS. . . .

In the course of his reporting, McWilliams had spoken with a number of American diplomats and analysts "who were not in a position to speak out, because indeed it was a rather intimidating atmosphere." He felt that he was describing their views of the ISI-CIA-Hekmatyar-Arab problem as well as his own.[21]

Within the U.S. embassy in Islamabad his cable detonated like a stink bomb. Normally a diplomatic officer had to clear his cabled analyses through the ambassador, but McWilliams had semi-independent status. Bearden was furious at "that little shit." McWilliams was misinformed, the CIA's officers felt. He didn't have access to all their classified information documenting how the CIA managed its unilateral Afghan reporting network, including its support for Massoud and Abdul Haq, or how the agency played its hand with ISI, seeking to ensure that Hekmatyar did not dominate the weapons pipeline. Besides, Bearden discounted some of the criticism of Hekmatyar as KGB pro-

paganda. He saw Hekmatyar "as an enemy," he said later, but he did not regard Massoud as an adequate instrument for the CIA's prosecution of the
war. Bearden accepted the view, shared by Pakistani intelligence, that Massoud "appeared to have established an undeclared cease-fire" with the Soviets
in the north. Massoud was "shoring up his position politically," not fighting as
hard as ISI's main Islamist clients, Bearden believed.

On a more personal, visceral level, the CIA officers found McWilliams uncompromising, humorless, not a team player. At the Kabul embassy McWilliams
had been involved in an administrative controversy involving accusations of
improper contacts with Afghans by a CIA case officer, and the reports reaching the Islamabad station suggested that McWilliams had squealed on the
CIA officer involved. Bearden thought McWilliams had endangered the CIA
officer by his conduct. His cable challenging CIA assumptions about the jihad
sent Bearden and Oakley into a cold fury.[22]

McWilliams found Oakley, his deputy Beth Jones, and Bearden unques-
tioning in their endorsement of current U.S. policy toward Pakistani intelligence. Oakley was a hardworking, intelligent diplomat, but he was also
intimidating and rude, McWilliams thought. Oakley and Bearden were both
Texans: double trouble when they were together, boisterous, and confident to
the point of arrogance. "Everybody is saying that you're a dumb asshole,"
Bearden teased Oakley once before a group of embassy colleagues. "But I
correct them. 'Oakley is not dumb,' I say."

For his part, McWilliams felt that he was only initiating a healthy debate
about the assumptions underlying the U.S. alliance with ISI. Why should that
anger his colleagues so intensely? But it did. McWilliams's underground allies
in the U.S. embassy and consulates in Pakistan opened a back channel to keep
him informed about just how thoroughly he had alienated Oakley and Bearden, McWilliams recalled. In the aftermath of his cable about Hekmatyar and
ISI, the U.S. embassy in Islamabad had quietly opened an internal investigation into McWilliams's integrity, the envoy's informants confided. The CIA
had raised serious questions about his handling of classified materials. The
embassy was watching his behavior and posing questions to those who knew
him. Was McWilliams a homosexual? He seemed to be a drinker. Did he have
some sort of problem with alcohol?

THE RUSSIAN WRITER Artyom Borovik traveled with the Soviet Fortieth
Army's last brigades as they prepared to rumble out of Kabul and up the
snowy Salang Highway in January and February 1989. It was an extraordinary

time in Soviet journalism and military culture, a newly permissive moment of dissent and uncensored speech. "It's been a strange war," a lieutenant colonel named Ushakov told Borovik. "We went in when stagnation was at its peak and now leave when truth is raging."

At the iron-gated, heavy-concrete Soviet embassy compound in Kabul, just down the road from the city zoo, fallen eucalyptus leaves swirled in the bottom of the empty swimming pool. The embassy's KGB chief insisted on his regular Friday tennis game. His forty-minute sets "seemed quite fantastic to me," Borovik wrote, "especially when the camouflaged helicopters that provided covering fire for the airborne troopers would fly above his gray-haired head." The Cold War's ending now seemed to echo far beyond Afghanistan. "Who knows where a person can feel safer these days—here or in Poland?" the Polish ambassador asked grimly. The old Soviet guard watched bitterly as the last tank convoys pulled out. A general read to Borovik from a dog-eared copy of a book about why Russia had been defeated in its war with Japan in 1904: "In the last few years, our government itself has headed the antiwar movement."

Boris Gromov was the Fortieth Army's last commander. He was short and stout, and his face was draped by bangs. He feared the Panjshir Valley. "There's Massoud with his four thousand troops, so there's still plenty to worry about," he told Borovik. The last Russian fatality, a soldier named Lashenenkov, was shot through the neck on the Salang Highway by a rebel sniper. He rode out of Afghanistan on a stretcher lashed to the top of an armored vehicle, his corpse draped in snow.[23]

On February 15, the day appointed by the Geneva Accords for the departure of the last Soviet troops, Gromov staged a ceremony for the international media on the Termez Bridge, still standing despite the multiple attempts by ISI to persuade Afghan commanders to knock it down. Gromov stopped his tank halfway across the bridge, climbed out of the hatch, and walked toward Uzbekistan as one of his sons approached him with a bouquet of carnations.[24]

At CIA headquarters in Langley the newly appointed director, William Webster, hosted a champagne party.

At the U.S. embassy in Islamabad, too, they threw a celebration. Bearden sent a cable to Langley: "WE WON." He decided on his own last act of private theater. His third-floor office in the CIA station lay in the direct line of sight of the KGB office in the Soviet embassy across barren scrub land. Bearden had made a point of always leaving the light on in his office, and at diplomatic receptions he would joke with his KGB counterparts about how hard he was working to bring them down. That night he switched off the light.[25]

Shevardnadze flew into snow-cradled Kabul that same night with Kryuch-kov, the Soviet KGB chief. Najibullah and his wife hosted them for dinner. All autumn and winter the Afghan president had been working to win defections to his cause, hoping to forestall a mujahedin onslaught and the collapse of his government, still being forecast confidently by the CIA. Najibullah had of-fered Massoud his defense ministry, and when Massoud sent a message re-fusing the job, the president had decided to leave the seat open, signaling that it could be Massoud's whenever he felt ready. Najibullah pushed through pay raises to special guard forces trained to defend Kabul. He organized militias to defend the northern gas fields that provided his government's only reliable income. He was doing what he could, he told his Soviet sponsors.

But by now the KGB shared the CIA's assumption that Najibullah was doomed without Soviet troops to protect him. That night over dinner Shev-ardnadze offered Najibullah and his wife a new home in Moscow if they wanted to leave Kabul. Shevardnadze worried about their safety. Najibullah's wife answered: "We would prefer to be killed on the doorsteps of this house rather than die in the eyes of our people by choosing the path of flight from their bitter misfortune. We will all stay with them here to the end, whether it be happy or bitter."[26]

It would be bitter.

PART TWO

THE ONE-EYED MAN
WAS KING

March 1989 to December 1997

"Serious Risks"

THERE WERE TWO CIA STATIONS crammed inside the U.S. embassy in Islamabad in the late winter of 1989 as the last Soviet soldiers withdrew across the Amu Darya River, out of Afghanistan.

Gary Schroen, newly appointed as Kabul station chief, arrived in Pakistan in temporary exile. Schroen had been away from Islamabad since student rioters sacked the embassy a decade earlier. He had been working in the Persian Gulf and on the CIA's Iranian operations. He was appointed to Kabul in the late summer of 1988, but he had been forced to wait in Langley as the White House debated whether to close the U.S. embassy in the Afghan capital. When the mission was ordered shut, mainly for security reasons, Schroen flew to Islamabad to wait a little longer. He and several Kabul-bound case officers squeezed themselves into Milton Bearden's office suite. As soon as Najibullah fell to the mujahedin that winter—in just a matter of weeks, CIA analysts at headquarters felt certain—Schroen and his team would drive up to Kabul from Pakistan, help reopen the embassy, and set up operations in a liberated country.

Weeks passed and then more weeks. Najibullah, his cabinet, and his army held firm. Amid heavy snows the Afghan military pushed out a new defensive

ring around the capital, holding the mujahedin farther at bay. Najibullah put
twenty thousand mullahs on his payroll to counter the rebels' religious messages. As March approached, the Afghan regime showed no fissures.

In Islamabad, Schroen told his colleagues that not for the first or last time
the CIA's predictions were proving wrong. He moved out of a cramped dormitory in the walled embassy compound, fixed up a room in an anonymous
guest house, requisitioned four-wheel-drive vehicles for his case officers, and
told them to settle in for the long haul. They might as well make themselves
useful by working from Islamabad.

Bearden agreed that Schroen's Kabul group should take the lead in running the Afghan rebel commanders on the CIA's payroll. These numbered
about forty by the first months of 1989. There were minor commanders receiving $5,000 monthly stipends, others receiving $50,000. Several of them
worked for Hekmatyar. The CIA had also increased its payments to Hekmatyar's rival, Massoud, who was by now secretly receiving $200,000 a month in
cash. Massoud's stipend had ballooned partly because the CIA knew that Pakistani intelligence shortchanged him routinely. Under pressure from Massoud's supporters in Congress, and hoping that the Panjshiri leader would
pressure the Afghan government's northern supply lines, the agency had sent
through a big raise. The CIA tried to keep all these payments hidden from
Pakistani intelligence.[1]

Massoud and other Afghan commanders in the CIA's unilateral network
had by now received secure radio sets with messaging software that allowed
them to transmit coded reports directly to the Islamabad embassy. The message traffic required time and attention from embassy case officers. And there
was a steady stream of face-to-face contact meetings to be managed in Peshawar and Quetta. Each contact had to be handled carefully so that neither
Pakistani intelligence nor rival mujahedin caught on. The plan was that once
Schroen's group of case officers made it to their new station in Kabul, they
would take many of their Afghan agent relationships with them.

All this depended on wresting the Afghan capital from Najibullah's control, however. For this, too, the CIA had a plan. Bearden and his group collaborated closely with Pakistani intelligence that winter, even as they tried to
shield their unilateral agent network from detection.

Hamid Gul, the Pakistani intelligence chief, proposed to rattle Najibullah
by launching an ambitious rebel attack against the eastern Afghan city of
Jalalabad, just a few hours' drive across the Khyber Pass from Peshawar. Once
the mujahedin captured Jalalabad, Gul said, they could install a new govern-

ment on Afghan soil and begin to move on Kabul. The short distance and open roads between Jalalabad and Peshawar would make it easy for ISI and the CIA to truck in supplies.[2]

Pakistani intelligence had put together a new Islamist-dominated Afghan government that could move to Jalalabad as soon as the city was captured. In February 1989, at a hotel in Rawalpindi, Afghan delegates were summoned to a consultative *shura* to elect new political leaders. Flush with about $25 million in cash provided by Prince Turki al-Faisal's Saudi intelligence department, Hamid Gul and colleagues from ISI's Afghan bureau twisted arms and spread money around until the delegates agreed on a cabinet for a self-declared Afghan interim government. To prevent either Hekmatyar or Massoud from seizing power, the delegates chose weak figurehead leaders and agreed to rotate offices. There was a lot of squabbling, and Hekmatyar, among others, went away angry. But at least a rebel government now existed on paper, Hamid Gul argued to his American counterparts. He felt that military pressure had to be directed quickly at Afghan cities "to make the transfer of power possible" to the rebels. Otherwise, "in the vacuum, there would be a lot of chaos in Afghanistan."[3]

For the CIA, Pakistan was becoming a far different place to carry out covert action than it had been during the anti-Soviet jihad. The agency had to reckon now with more than just the views of ISI. Civilians and the army shared power, opportunistic politicians debated every issue, and a free press clamored with dissent. Pakistan's newly elected prime minister was Benazir Bhutto, at thirty-six a beautiful, charismatic, and self-absorbed politician with no government experience. She was her country's first democratically elected leader in more than a decade. She had taken office with American support, and she cultivated American connections. Raised in a gilded world of feudal aristocratic entitlements, Bhutto had attended Radcliffe College at Harvard University as an undergraduate and retained many friends in Washington. She saw her American allies as a counterweight to her enemies in the Pakistani army command—an officer corps that had sent her father to the gallows a decade earlier.

She was especially distrustful of Pakistani intelligence. She knew that Hamid Gul's ISI was already tapping her telephones and fomenting opposition against her in the country's newly elected parliament. Stunned by Zia's death, the Pakistani army leadership had endorsed a restoration of democracy in the autumn of 1988, but the generals expected to retain control over national security policy. The chief of army staff, Mirza Aslam Beg, tolerated

Bhutto's role, but others in the army officer corps—especially some of the Islamists who had been close to Zia—saw her as a secularist, a socialist, and an enemy of Islam. This was especially true inside ISI's Afghan bureau. "I wonder if these people would ever have held elections if they knew that we were going to win," Bhutto remarked to her foreign policy adviser Iqbal Akhund on a flight to China in 1989. Akhund, cynical about ISI's competence, told her: "You owe your prime ministership to the intelligence agencies who, as always, gave the government a wishful assessment of how the elections would—or could be made to—turn out."

The U.S. ambassador Robert Oakley told embassy colleagues to tiptoe delicately. The CIA should continue to collaborate closely with ISI to defeat Najibullah in Afghanistan. At the same time Oakley hoped to shore up Bhutto as best he could against subterranean efforts by Pakistani intelligence to bring her down.[4]

The unfinished Afghan jihad loomed as Benazir Bhutto's first foreign policy challenge, her first attempt to establish authority over ISI on a major national security question. On March 6 she called a meeting in Islamabad of the interagency "Afghan cell" to discuss Hamid Gul's proposal to attack Jalalabad. There were no Afghans in the room. Bhutto was so anxious about ISI that she invited Oakley to attend the meeting. Oakley had no guidance from Washington about how to conduct himself before Pakistan's national security cabinet, but he went anyway.

They debated several questions. Should Pakistan and perhaps the United States immediately recognize the ISI-arranged Afghan interim government or wait until it captured territory inside Afghanistan? Yaqub Khan, Bhutto's foreign minister, thought the rebels needed to demonstrate they were "not just some Johnnies riding around Peshawar in Mercedes." Should they encourage Afghan fighters to hurl themselves at heavily defended Jalalabad or go more slowly? Pakistani intelligence and the CIA had already developed a detailed military plan for attacking Jalalabad, and they wanted to move fast. ISI had assembled five thousand to seven thousand Afghan rebels near the city. They were being equipped for a conventional frontal military assault on its garrisons. This approach was much different from the hit-and-run guerrilla tactics of the anti-Soviet campaign. Yet Hamid Gul promised Bhutto that Jalalabad would fall to the rebels within a week if she was "prepared to allow for a certain degree of bloodshed." The ISI chief's eyes were "blazing with passion," as Bhutto remembered it, and Gul spoke so forcefully that she thought Jalalabad would "fall in twenty-four hours, let alone in one week."

"There can be no cease-fire in a jihad against the Marxist unbeliever," Gul declared. "War must go on until *Darul Harb* [house of war] is cleansed and becomes *Darul Amn* [house of peace]!" Oakley, too, was optimistic.[5]

The CIA plunged in to help. Bearden's case officers, Schroen's case officers, and military officers from ISI's Afghan bureau—often led by the committed Islamists Brigadier Janjua and Colonel Imam—met frequently in Rawalpindi and Peshawar. CIA officers unveiled a covert plan to cut off the main supply line between Kabul and Jalalabad. There was only one motor route between the two cities, the Sarobi Road, which ran for miles through a narrow chasm, crisscrossing flimsy bridges. The CIA had imported specially shaped conical explosive charges, designed like very large household flower pots, that could blow huge craters in the road.

Pakistani intelligence summoned about a dozen commanders from the Sarobi area to a meeting at a safehouse in Peshawar. CIA officers spread out satellite photographs of the Sarobi Road on the floor. They all kneeled around the satellite images—bearded Afghans in draping turbans, CIA case officers in blue jeans, Pakistani intelligence officers in civilian *salwars*. They planned where to place the explosives and where to install machine gun nests for ambush attacks on Najibullah's convoys.

The Afghans could sense that the CIA's bank window was open, and suddenly it seemed that every commander within a hundred miles of Jalalabad needed new Toyota double-cab trucks to accomplish his part of the attack. The CIA purchased several hundred trucks in Japan that winter, shipped them to Karachi, and rolled them up to Peshawar to support the Jalalabad assault.[6]

The rebels had to run through Soviet-laid minefields as they approached fixed positions around Jalalabad. The Afghans were trained to send mules ahead of their soldiers to clear the fields. They would tie long wooden logs on ropes behind the mules and drive them into a minefield to set off the buried charges.

"I know you don't like this," an Afghan commander explained to Gary Schroen as the Jalalabad battle began, "but it's better than using people."

"Yes, but just don't take any pictures," Schroen advised. Nobody back in Washington "wants to see pictures of little donkeys blown up."[7]

The pictures they did see were worse. As the spring sun melted the snowy eastern passes, hundreds of Afghan boys and young men recruited from refugee camps for the glorious Jalalabad campaign poured off the rock ridges and fell before fusillades of machine gun fire from terrified government conscripts. Soviet-made bombers flown by the Afghan air force out of Kabul

struck the attackers in open plains from high altitude. Dozens of Scud missiles fired by Soviet advisers, who had clandestinely stayed behind after the official Soviet withdrawal, rained in deafening fury onto mujahedin positions.
The rebels pushed toward Jalalabad's outskirts but stalled. Commanders
squabbled over whose forces were supposed to be where. ISI officers participated in the assault but failed to unify and organize their Afghan attacking
force. A week passed, and Jalalabad did not fall. Then two weeks, then three.
"Fall it will," Hamid Gul assured Bhutto's civilian aides. Casualties mounted
among the mujahedin. Ambulances from the Arab and international charities
raced back and forth from Peshawar. By May their hand-scrawled lists of the
dead and maimed numbered in the thousands. Still Jalalabad and its airport remained in Najibullah's hands. Despite all the explosives and trucks shipped in,
the CIA plan to shut off the Sarobi Road fizzled.

In Kabul, Najibullah appeared before the international press, defiant and
emboldened. His generals and his Soviet sponsors began to take heart: Perhaps a rebel triumph in Kabul was not inevitable after all. Gorbachev authorized massive subsidies to Najibullah that spring. From air bases in Uzbekistan
the dying Soviet government ferried as much as $300 million per month in
food and ammunition to Kabul on giant transport planes, at least twice the
amount of aid being supplied by the CIA and Saudi intelligence to the mujahedin.[8] One after another, enormous white Soviet Ilyushin-76 cargo jets, expelling starburst flares to distract heat-seeking Stinger missiles, circled like
lumbering pterodactyls above the Kabul Valley, descending to the international airport or Bagram air base to its north. The flour, mortar shells, and
Scud missiles they disgorged each day gradually buoyed the morale of Kabul's
conscripts and bolstered the staying power of Najibullah's new tribal and ethnic militias.

Frustrated, the CIA officers working from Peshawar recruited an Afghan
Shiite commander in western Kabul, known for vicious urban guerrilla
bombings, to step up sabotage operations in the capital. They supplied his
Shiite commandos with Stingers to try to shoot down one of the Ilyushin
cargo planes, hoping to send a message to the Soviets that they would pay a
price for such extravagant aid to Najibullah. The team infiltrated a Stinger on
the outskirts of the Kabul airport and fired at an Ilyushin as it took off, but
one of the plane's hot defensive flares caught the missile's tracking system,
and the shot missed. The rebels sent out a videotape of the failed attack. The
CIA also recruited agents to drop boron carbide sludge into the gas tanks or
oil casings of transport vehicles to disable them.[9] But none of these opera-

tions put much of a dent in Najibullah's supply lines. And still the garrisons at Jalalabad stood.

The ISI bureaus in Peshawar and Quetta expanded propaganda operations against Najibullah. With CIA help they inserted anti-Najibullah commercials into bootleg videotapes of one of the Rambo movies, then greatly popular in Afghanistan, and they shipped the tapes across the border.[10] Najibullah stepped up his own propaganda campaign. He filled radio and television airwaves with programs that demonized Hekmatyar and his fellow Islamists as devilish Neanderthals and Pakistani stooges who would tear Afghanistan away from its cultural moorings.

What ordinary Afghans made of all the fear-mongering was difficult to say. Refugees poured out of Nangarhar province to escape the terrible fighting at Jalalabad, but as the stalemate continued that spring, most Afghan civilians and refugees sat still, many of them enduring a long and persistent misery. They waited for one side or the other to prevail so that they might go home.

THE BLOODY DISASTER at Jalalabad only deepened Ed McWilliams's conviction that the CIA and ISI were careening in the wrong direction. He could not understand why Oakley tolerated Bearden's collaborations with Pakistani intelligence and its anti-American clients, especially Hekmatyar and Sayyaf. It appalled him that the United States was staking its policy that spring on the Afghan interim government, a feckless fiction, as McWilliams saw it, bought and paid for by Pakistani and Saudi intelligence agents.

In February the incoming Bush administration had renewed the legal authority for CIA covert action in Afghanistan. (Each new president had to reaffirm ongoing covert action programs under a fresh signature.) President Bush adjusted the official goals of U.S. policy. The Reagan-era objective of Soviet withdrawal had been achieved. Under the revised finding, the most important purpose of continuing CIA covert action was to promote "self-determination" by the Afghan people. With its echoes from the American revolution, the phrase had been promoted by congressional conservatives who championed the mujahedin cause.[11]

McWilliams concluded that achieving true Afghan "self-determination" would now require the CIA to break with Pakistani intelligence. Increasingly, he believed, it was ISI and its Islamist agenda—rather than communism—that posed the greatest obstacle to Afghan independence.

Inside the Islamabad embassy, tensions deepened. The investigations of

McWilliams's drinking and sexual habits stalled—they turned up nothing—but a new inquiry opened about whether he had compromised classified data. With Oakley's support, Bearden insisted that McWilliams be accompanied by CIA case officers on his diplomatic reporting trips to Peshawar and Quetta. McWilliams chafed; he was insulted, angry, and more determined than before to put his views across.

Each cable to Washington now became a cause for gaming and intrigue in the embassy's communications suite. Oakley would scribble dissenting comments on McWilliams's drafts, and McWilliams would erase or ignore them and cable ahead on his own authority. McWilliams believed that Oakley had repressed a memo he wrote reporting the capture of Stinger missiles by Iran. On another occasion when he wandered by the cabling machine, he saw an outgoing high-level message from Oakley to Washington arguing that it was in America's interest to accept a Pakistani sphere of influence in Afghanistan. Appalled, McWilliams quietly photocopied the cable and slipped it into his private files—more ammunition.[12]

McWilliams's criticisms of the CIA now extended beyond his earlier view that Pakistani intelligence and Hekmatyar were dangerous American allies. By endorsing ISI's puppet Afghan interim government, the United States had become involved in Afghan politics for the first time, and in doing so it had betrayed American principles and self-interest, McWilliams argued.

Earlier, as Soviet troops prepared to leave Afghanistan, the United States had decided not to help Afghans negotiate a peaceful political transition because the CIA believed Najibullah would fall quickly. The CIA also feared that political talks would slow down the Soviet departure. McWilliams believed those arguments had now been overtaken by events. To prevent Pakistan from installing its anti-American clients in Kabul, to prevent further suffering by Afghan civilians, and to rebuild a stable and centrist politics in Afghanistan, the United States now had to ease off on its covert military strategy and begin to sponsor a broader political settlement, he argued.

The Afghan interim government, a paper cabinet formed to occupy cities captured by ISI's Islamists, "is the wrong vehicle to advance the entirely correct U.S. policy objective of achieving a genuinely representative Afghan government through Afghan self-determination," McWilliams wrote that spring in a confidential cable sent through the State Department's dissent channel. (The dissent channel was a special cable routing that permitted diplomats to express their personal views without having them edited by an embassy's ambassador.) Many Afghans had now "called for an early political settlement to the war," McWilliams wrote. Only a "relatively stable government will be able to address the massive problems of rehabilitation and refugee return in post-war Afghanistan." A large pool of Afghan intellectuals living abroad "would be prepared to give their talent and credibility to a neutral administration which could serve as a bridge rising above the current stalemated military situation and the sterile dialogue of propaganda exchanges." But the United States apparently intended to wait out the summer "fighting season" before considering such political talks. This decision "entails serious risks . . . [and] is not justifiable on either political or humanitarian grounds. We should press ahead now for a political settlement."[13]

As McWilliams's cables circulated in Washington, and as gossip about his tense disagreements with Bearden and Oakley spread, his policy prescriptions attracted new converts. The State Department's intelligence bureau privately endorsed McWilliams, citing in part the detailed evidence in his cables. British intelligence officers in Islamabad and London also weighed in on his behalf. After earlier backing the anti-Soviet jihad, they now wanted the CIA to move away from Hekmatyar and an ISI-led military solution. Military supplies to the mujahedin should continue, the British argued, and battlefield pressure on Najibullah's government forces should be maintained, but the time had also come to work with the United Nations to develop a political compromise for Afghanistan. This might involve a neutral transitional government of Afghan intellectuals living in Europe and the United States, Kabul technocrats, Kandahar royalists, and politically astute rebel commanders such as Massoud.[14]

The CIA remained adamant about its support for Pakistani intelligence, however. Bearden regarded McWilliams as little more than a nuisance. He took himself and his office much too seriously, Bearden felt. The State Department's real policy on Afghanistan was made by Michael Armacost and others on the seventh floor at headquarters, where the most senior officials worked. Anyway, McWilliams, his midlevel supporters at State, and the British (who had lost two wars in Afghanistan, Bearden noted pointedly) made the mistake of believing that there *was* such a thing as a political Afghanistan, separate from Pakistan, "just because a few white guys drew a line in the sand" in northwestern British India a century earlier, as Bearden saw it. Still, the more State Department officials mouthed the McWilliams line, the more Langley argued the contrary. Interagency debates grew caustic as the CIA's forecasts of a lightning rebel victory over Najibullah yielded to a grinding stalemate.[15]

The agency's operatives felt they had adjusted their approach in Afghanistan in many ways since the Soviets began to withdraw. They had responded to outside criticism by bypassing ISI and opening secret, direct lines with important Afghan commanders such as Massoud. They had directed CIA funding and logistical support toward massive humanitarian efforts on the Afghan border, to accompany the policy of military pressure. The problem with McWilliams, they told those with the proper clearances, was that he was cut out of the highly classified information channels that showed the full breadth of CIA covert policy. For instance, in May 1989, just as McWilliams was composing his most heated dissents, Gary Schroen had personally delivered a $900,000 lump sum payment to Massoud's brother, Ahmed Zia, over and above Massoud's $200,000 monthly stipend, to help fund a humanitarian reconstruction program in northern Afghanistan. Massoud passed through to the CIA photographs of road repair and irrigation projects under way, although the agency's officers doubted that the projects shown had been directly stimulated by their funding. In any event, the CIA argued, their cash payment represented a fresh political initiative: Massoud would have the resources that summer to win civilian support for his militias and local councils, and to start rebuilding the Panjshir. McWilliams knew nothing of this secret money. Besides, McWilliams seemed reflexively anti-American in his analysis, some of the CIA officers said. They denounced as naïve the prescriptions for a political solution pushed by McWilliams, the British, and the State Department. No stable government could be constructed in Kabul without Pakistani support, they argued. None was likely in any case. Afghan rebels from all parties, whether Islamist or royalist, extremist or moderate, were determined to finish their military jihad. That was what "self-determination" meant to them. Hekmatyar and the Muslim Brotherhood networks could be managed and contained.[16]

Increasingly, Oakley felt caught in the middle. He tacked carefully between the two sides. The problem with McWilliams, Oakley believed, was that he was trying to reshape White House policy from the middle levels of the bureaucracy. This simply could not be done. The State Department and the CIA clearly disagreed now about Afghanistan, but this disagreement had to be resolved in Washington, by the president and his Cabinet, not inside the Islamabad embassy.

James Baker, the Texas lawyer who had served as White House chief of staff and then treasury secretary during the Reagan administration, was the new secretary of state. He displayed little personal interest in Afghanistan or Pakistan. Oakley could see that Baker was not willing to challenge the CIA over Afghanistan policy. Unless he was willing to do so, all the Islamabad embassy could do was work with the current guidance, which put the CIA in a commanding position and kept the United States locked in its embrace with Pakistani intelligence.[17]

McWilliams, meanwhile, had to go, Oakley felt. McWilliams had persistently angered the embassy's three most powerful figures: Oakley, his deputy

Beth Jones, and Bearden. An opportunity arrived that spring when members of Congress finally appointed a formal ambassadorial-level special envoy to the Afghan resistance, a pet project of Gordon Humphrey. McWilliams was too junior in the Foreign Service to be elevated to this new post, so the question arose as to whether he should become the new envoy's deputy. Oakley stepped in and arranged for McWilliams to be transferred abruptly out of the Islamabad embassy and back to Washington. The first McWilliams knew of his transfer was a cable telling him that his "request for curtailment" of his tour of duty in Islamabad had been accepted—a request that McWilliams did not know he had made. Leaving only a few fingerprints, Oakley and Bearden had effectively fired him.

"It is my intention to leave without formally calling on you," McWilliams wrote Oakley in a farewell letter. "I did not want you to mistake this as an insult, however. I simply do not want to end our relationship with one more quarrel." Their problems were not personal but substantive, he explained. "I believed and continue to believe that we were wrong to have been so close to some in the alliance; wrong to have given ISI such power and (now) wrong not to be actively seeking a political settlement." He knew that Oakley had worked hard to try to get the ISI-created Afghan interim government on its feet, but "I just don't believe that bunch was worthy of your efforts. Afghanistan surely is, but the AIG is incapable of unity or leading.

"I wish you success in a massively difficult posting," McWilliams concluded. "I am sorry I became for you a part of the problem rather than a part of the solution. Perhaps I was in error, but I don't think so."[18]

IN A RIVER VALLEY just eight or ten miles across the Afghan border from Parrot's Beak, not far from large encampments of Arab volunteer jihadists, CIA officers set up a radio facility for clandestine rebel communications. They also helped build bunkers and rudimentary caves for munitions storage. The "beak" of Pakistani territory that thrust into Afghanistan in this region of Paktia province pointed directly at Kabul, and throughout the war the mujahedin and ISI had found its high, ravine-laced mountains ideal for infiltration and ambushes. A series of heights known as Tora Bora provided commanding access to Jalalabad. From nearby valleys it was also a relatively short walk to the outskirts of Kabul. The region was thick with rebel encampments dominated by commanders loyal to Hekmatyar and Sayyaf. Bin Laden's training camp for Arab volunteers lay only about thirty miles to the south.[19]

Even though it was strictly prohibited by agency rules, CIA officers continued to travel into Afghanistan occasionally with their Pakistani counterparts and with selected Afghan rebel escorts. Gary Schroen and his team traveled across the border at Parrot's Beak, and so did Bearden. There was no compelling need for these trips; it was just something the officers wanted to do. If they moved in the company of senior ISI officers and Afghan fighters, there seemed little risk.

Frank Anderson, the director of the Afghan task force at Langley headquarters, flew out to Pakistan to meet with Bearden and survey logistical challenges along the border. Anderson had argued unsuccessfully as the Soviet withdrawal approached that the CIA should end its involvement in Afghanistan altogether. More recently he had spent hours in Washington meetings defending the CIA's liaison with Pakistani intelligence against attacks from Ed McWilliams's supporters at the State Department and from critics in Congress, many of them Massoud's backers. In these Afghan policy wars Anderson and Bearden were close allies. Together in the field, free from their pointy-headed bureaucratic tormentors, the two of them decided to take a joy ride to the site of the new CIA-built radio station, Ali Khel, escorted by several ISI officers. They were on the Afghan border to ensure that a visit by Congressman Charlie Wilson went off without incident. They were in a triumphal mood. They got their hands on an ISI propaganda poster that showed a growling, wounded Soviet bear being stung by a swarm of Stinger missiles. Anderson and Bearden decided that they should tack the poster on the door of the abandoned Soviet garrison at Ali Khel, a symbolic declaration of victory.

They rattled across the border without much incident, found their way to the old Ali Khel garrison, and nailed up their poster in a private ceremony. On the way back they had to cross territory that belonged to Sayyaf, a region rife with Arab jihadist volunteers. They hit a roadblock manned by Arab Islamist radicals.

From the back of the jeep Anderson and Bearden heard their Afghan escort erupt into a screaming match with a Saudi rebel wielding an assault rifle. They were yelling in a patois of Arabic and Pashto. Anderson got out, walked around, and saw immediately that the Arab was threatening to execute them. He spoke to one of the jihadists in Arabic; the man's accent suggested he was a volunteer from the Persian Gulf. The Arab pointed his gun directly at the two CIA officers. They were infidels and had no business in Afghanistan, he said. Instantly alert, Anderson and Bearden surveyed their environment for weapons and maneuvered themselves so that their jeep blocked the Arab's line of fire. From this position Anderson began to talk to the Arab through his Afghan escort. Eventually the Saudi decided, reluctantly, that he would not attempt to kill them. The Americans bundled quickly back into the jeep and drove on to Pakistan.[20]

It was a rare direct encounter between CIA officers and the Arab volunteers their jihad had attracted to the border. It signaled the beginning of a fateful turn in the covert war, but few inside the agency grasped the implications. The CIA did accumulate and transmit to Langley more and more facts about the Arab volunteers and their activities. By the summer of 1989 the agency's network of Afghan agents described the Arabs operating in Paktia and farther south as a rising force and a rising problem. Algerian fighters marauded Afghan supply convoys, they said. Wahhabi proselytizers continued to desecrate Afghan graves, provoking violent retaliation. Christian charity workers crossing the frontier reported threats and harassment from Arabs as well as from ardent Afghan Islamists working with Hekmatyar and Sayyaf. American and European journalists, too, had dangerous and occasionally fatal encounters with Wahhabi fighters in the region. The CIA's Islamabad station estimated in a 1989 cable to Langley that there were probably about four thousand Arab volunteers in Afghanistan, mainly organized under Sayyaf's leadership.[21] He was in turn heavily supported by Saudi intelligence and Gulf charities.

Within the Islamabad station there was a growing sense of discomfort about the Arabs, reinforced by Bearden and Anderson's close encounter. But there was no discussion about any change in U.S. policy, and no effort was made at first to talk directly to the Saudis about their funding of Arab volunteer networks. The CIA station knew that large sums of money flowed from Prince Turki's General Intelligence Department to Pakistani intelligence, and that some of this money then passed through to Muslim Brotherhood–inspired jihadists. But the transnational Islamist networks still served a larger and more important cause, Bearden and his CIA colleagues believed. The Arabs might be disagreeable, but their Afghan allies, Hekmatyar especially, commanded some of the rebel movement's most effective fighters, especially in the crucial regions around Kabul and Khost. Throughout 1989 the CIA pumped yet more arms, money, food, and humanitarian supplies into the Paktia border regions where the Arabs were building up their strength. They encouraged Prince Turki to do the same.

At the center of this border nexus stood Jallaladin Haqqanni, the long-bearded, fearless Afghan rebel commander with strong Islamist beliefs who had grown very close to Pakistani and Saudi intelligence during the last years of the anti-Soviet war. Haqqanni operated south of Parrot's Beak, near bin

Laden's territory. He was seen by CIA officers in Islamabad and others as perhaps the most impressive Pashtun battlefield commander in the war. He sponsored some of the first Arab fighters who faced Soviet forces in 1987. He had been wounded in battle, in one case holding out in a cave under heavy assault for weeks. He later recovered in Saudi Arabia's best hospitals, and he made many connections among the kingdom's wealthy sheikhs at the annual *hajj* pilgrimage, as well as through General Intelligence Department introductions. He was in frequent contact with bin Laden and with ISI's brigadiers. For their part, Pakistani intelligence and the CIA came to rely on Haqqani for testing and experimentation with new weapons systems and tactics. Haqqani was so favored with supplies that he was in a position to broker them and to help equip the Arab volunteers gathering in his region. The CIA officers working from Islamabad regarded him as a proven commander who could put a lot of men under arms at short notice. Haqqani had the CIA's full support.[22]

In Haqqani's crude Paktia training camps and inside the Arab jihadist salons in Peshawar, it was a summer of discontent, however. Disputes erupted continually among the Arab volunteers during mid-1989. The Soviets were gone. What would now unite the jihad? Tensions rose between bin Laden and his mentor, Abdullah Azzam, the charismatic Palestinian Muslim Brotherhood preacher.

The rising civil war between Hekmatyar and Massoud drew in the Arab volunteers and divided them. Because he was based in Peshawar, where most of the Arabs stayed, and because he had wide-ranging contacts in the Muslim Brotherhood networks, Hekmatyar was better positioned than Massoud to attract Arab followers. But Massoud also found support from Arab volunteers, including from Abdullah Azzam, whose Algerian son-in-law was Massoud's chief Arab organizer.

Abdullah Azzam and some of his followers tried to organize an Arab religious group numbering about two hundred whose mission was to travel around Afghanistan, using Islamic principles to mediate a peace between Hekmatyar and Massoud. But neither of them was in a mood for compromise. Hekmatyar continued his assassination and intimidation campaign against moderate and royalist rivals in Peshawar. Inside Afghanistan he attacked Massoud's forces. On July 9, 1989, Hekmatyar's men ambushed a party of Massoud's senior commanders in northern Afghanistan, killing thirty officers, including eight important leaders of Massoud's elite fighting force. Massoud launched a manhunt for the killers. Open battles erupted with Hekmatyar's fighters across the north, producing hundreds of casualties.[23]

From Peshawar, Abdullah Azzam embarked by land for Takhar that summer to meet with Massoud. Azzam flatteringly compared Massoud to Napoleon. He tried to broker a fresh truce. But Hekmatyar continually denounced Massoud in Peshawar before audiences of Arab volunteers, saying (truthfully) that Massoud received aid from French intelligence, and (falsely) that he frolicked with French nurses in swimming pools at luxury compounds in the Panjshir. Increasingly, Osama bin Laden sided with Hekmatyar, alienating his mentor Azzam.[24]

The Arabs in University Town's salons argued about theology, too. Hekmatyar and Massoud both agreed that communist and capitalist systems were both corrupt because they were rooted in *jahiliyya,* the state of primitive barbarism that prevailed before Islam lit the world with truth. In this sense the Soviet Union and the United States were equally evil. Hekmatyar and Massoud also accepted that Islam was not only a personal faith but a body of laws and systems—the proper basis for politics and government. The goal of jihad was to establish an Islamic government in Afghanistan in order to implement these laws and ideals. Hekmatyar and Massoud also both endorsed Qutb's concept of *takfir,* by which true believers could identify imposter Muslims who had strayed from true Islam, and then proclaim these false Muslims *kaffir,* or outside of the Islamic community. Such imposters should be overthrown no matter how hard they worked to drape themselves in Islamic trappings. Najibullah was one such false ruler, they agreed.

In the Peshawar salons that year, however, Hekmatyar's followers began to express extreme views about who was a *kaffir* and who should therefore be the target of jihad now that the Soviets had left Afghanistan. Exiled Egyptian radicals such as al-Zawahiri proclaimed that Egyptian president Hosni Mubarak was one such enemy. Benazir Bhutto was declared a *kaffir* by others. Still others denounced the King of Jordan and the secular thugs who ruled Syria and Iraq. Abdullah Azzam, still Peshawar's most influential Arab theologian, resisted this *fatwa*-by-fax-machine approach. He adhered to the more traditional, cautious, evolutionary approach of the old Egyptian Muslim Brotherhood. Its mainstream leaders were content to build gradually toward the ideal of Islamic government, to create change one convert at a time. Also, Azzam felt that Afghanistan should be the focus of the Arab volunteers' attention, not faraway countries across the Middle East. Why start issuing calls to war against Egypt or Pakistan when the cause that had attracted them all to Peshawar remained very much unfinished?[25]

Bin Laden was among those who called for a wider war against impious rulers. "I'm very upset about Osama," Azzam told his son-in-law. The Saudi was a generous, sweet-tempered benefactor of the jihad, but he was being influenced by Arab radicals who cared little for the Afghan cause. "This heaven-sent man, like an angel," Azzam said of bin Laden. "I am worried about his future if he stays with these people."[26]

But it was Azzam who should have been concerned about the future. At midday on November 24, 1989, as he arrived to lead regular Friday prayers at Peshawar's Saba-e-Leil mosque, a car bomb detonated near the entrance, killing the Palestinian preacher and two of his sons. The crime was never solved. There were far more suspects with plausible motivations than there were facts. As the founder of Hamas, Azzam was increasingly in the crosshairs of Israel. Afghanistan's still-active intelligence service had him high on its enemies list. Hekmatyar was in the midst of a killing spree directed at nearly every rival for power he could reach. Azzam's connections to the Panjshir, including his trip north that summer, may have been enough to activate Hekmatyar's hit squads. Even bin Laden came under some suspicion, although some Arabs who knew him then discounted that possibility. Bin Laden was not yet much of an operator. He was still more comfortable talking on cushions, having himself filmed and photographed, providing interviews to the Arabic language press, and riding horses in the outback. He had a militant following, but it was not remotely as hardened or violent in 1989 as Hekmatyar's.

Bin Laden did seize the opportunity created by Azzam's death, however. He defeated Azzam's son-in-law, Massoud's ally, in a bid to take control of Azzam's jihad recruiting and support network, the Office of Services. Bin Laden and his extremist allies, close to Hekmatyar, folded the office into bin Laden's nascent al Qaeda, which he had formally established the year before, evoking images of his one grand battle against the Soviets at Jaji.[27]

Bin Laden continued to look beyond Afghanistan. He decided that the time had come to wage jihad against other corrupt rulers. He flew home to Jedda and resettled his family in Saudi Arabia. He continued to fly back and forth to Pakistan, but he began to spend less time on the Afghan frontier. He had new enemies in mind.

"A Rogue Elephant"

P ETER TOMSEN TOOK OVER Ed McWilliams's role in U.S. policy toward Afghanistan late in 1989, but at a higher level of the Washington bureaucracy. He was America's new special envoy to the Afghan resistance, with a mandate from Congress and the privileges of an ambassador. Tomsen was a bright-eyed, gentle-mannered, silver-haired career diplomat serving as deputy chief of mission at the U.S. embassy in Beijing at the time of his appointment. A multilingual officer with experience in South Asia, although none directly in Afghanistan, Tomsen was well schooled in Washington's interagency policy wars. He was collegial, articulate, and quick with a smile, but also sharp-minded, ambitious, and determined to defend the prerogatives of his new office. Tomsen lobbied for and won broad authority from Robert Kimmitt, the undersecretary of state, who had been assigned to watch Afghan policy for Secretary of State James Baker. Kimmitt signed off on a formal, classified "terms of reference" for Tomsen that spelled out the envoy's powers and his access to policy meetings, a key measure of clout in Washington.[1]

Tomsen planned to live in Washington and travel frequently to Pakistan until the mujahedin finally took Kabul. Then, he was told, he would be appointed as U.S. ambassador to Afghanistan. He made his first trip to Islamabad just as McWilliams was being shown the embassy's door.

In Peshawar and Quetta he traveled the same reporting trail as McWilliams had a year earlier, meeting with dozens of independent Afghan commanders and political activists, many of them openly hostile toward Pakistani intelligence and the CIA. He met Yahya and Ahmed Zia Massoud, Ahmed Shah's brothers, and heard angry accounts of Hekmatyar's campaign to massacre Massoud's commanders in the north. He met with Abdul Haq, now openly critical of his former CIA partners. Haq leveled pointed complaints about how Pakistani intelligence favored Hekmatyar and other radical Islamists. From exiled Afghan intellectuals and moderate tribal leaders, including Hamid Karzai, then a young rebel political organizer, he heard impassioned pleadings for an American engagement with King Zahir Shah in Rome, still seen by many Pashtun refugees as a symbol of traditional Afghan unity. Tomsen cabled his first impressions back to Washington: The Afghans he met were bound by their hatred of Najibullah and other former communists clinging to power in Kabul, but they were equally wary of Islamist extremists such as Hekmatyar and were angry about interference in the war by Pakistani intelligence.[2]

When he returned to Washington, Tomsen's reports reinforced doubts within the U.S. government about the CIA's covert war. The catastrophe at Jalalabad had discredited ISI and its supporters in Langley somewhat, strengthening those at the State Department and in Congress who backed McWilliams's analysis. The CIA was also under pressure from the mujahedin's champions in Congress because of logistical problems that had crimped the weapons pipeline to Pakistan. In addition, the civil war now raging openly between Hekmatyar and Massoud raised questions about whether the rebels could ever unite to overthrow Najibullah. The mujahedin had not captured a single provincial capital since the withdrawal of Soviet troops. The fall of the Berlin Wall in early November 1989 changed the Afghan war's geopolitical context, making it plain that whatever danger Najibullah might represent in Kabul, he was not the vanguard of hegemonic global communism anymore. And McWilliams's arguments about the dangers of Islamic radicalism had resonated in Washington. Within the State Department, tongues wagged about McWilliams's involuntary transfer from the Islamabad embassy apparently because of his dissenting views. Was Afghan policy so sacrosanct that it had become a loyalty test? Or had the time come to reconsider the all-out drive for a military victory over Najibullah?

That autumn in Washington, meeting at the State Department, Tomsen led a new interagency Afghan working group through a secret review of U.S. policy. Thomas Twetten, then chief of the Near East Division in the CIA's Directorate of Operations, attended for Langley. Richard Haas, from the National Security Council, participated in the sessions, as did delegates from the Pentagon and several sections of the State Department.[3]

An all-source intelligence analysis, classified Secret, had been produced as a backdrop to the policy debate. The document assessed all the internal government reporting about U.S. policy toward Afghanistan from the summer of 1988 to the summer of 1989. It laid out the splits among American analysts about whether Pakistani intelligence—with its close ties to the Muslim Brotherhood–linked Islamists—supported or conflicted with U.S. interests.[4]

Influenced by the McWilliams critique, members of the Afghan working group looked for a new policy direction. They were not prepared to give up completely on the CIA-led military track. The great majority of Afghans still sought Najibullah's overthrow, by force if necessary, and U.S. policy still supported Afghan "self-determination." Military force would also keep pressure on Gorbachev's reforming government in Moscow, challenging Soviet hardliners in the military and the KGB who remained a threat to both Gorbachev and the United States, in the working group's view. But after days of debate the members agreed that the time had come to introduce diplomatic negotiations into the mix. Ultimately, Tomsen finalized a secret new two-track policy, the first major change in the American approach to the Afghan war since the withdrawal of Soviet troops. The new policy still sought Najibullah's ouster, but it also promoted a moderate, broad-based successor government.

On the first track of the new approach, the State Department would open political negotiations aimed at "sidelining the extremists," meaning not only Najibullah but anti-American Islamists such as Hekmatyar and Sayyaf as well. American diplomats would begin talks at the United Nations with the Soviet Union, with Benazir Bhutto's government, and with exiled King Zahir Shah about the possibility of a political settlement for Afghanistan. The State Department could now honestly argue that U.S. policy was no longer the captive of Hekmatyar or Pakistani intelligence.

At the same time the CIA would continue to press the covert war to increase rebel military pressure against Najibullah. The use of force might coerce Najibullah to leave office as part of a political settlement, or it might topple him directly. The CIA would continue its collaboration with Pakistani intelligence and would also bypass ISI channels by providing cash and weapons directly to Afghan commanders fighting in the field. Tomsen hoped to overtake the moribund, discredited Afghan interim government with a new commanders' *shura* to be organized with American help, made up of rebel military leaders such as Massoud, Abdul Haq, and Ismail Khan. By strengthening these field commanders, the Afghan working group believed, the United States could circumvent the Islamist theologians in Peshawar and their allies in ISI. The new policy pointed the United States away from the Islamist agendas of Pakistani and Saudi intelligence—at least on paper.[5]

TOMSEN FLEW TO Islamabad early in 1990 to announce the new approach to Pakistan's government. Oakley arranged a meeting at the Pakistan foreign ministry. Milton Bearden had rotated back to Langley the previous summer; his successor as Islamabad station chief, known to his colleagues as Harry, attended for the CIA. Harry, a case officer from the old school, had a pleasant but unexpressive face, and he was very difficult to read. He was seen by his State Department colleagues as closed off, unusually secretive, and protective of CIA turf. Pakistani intelligence also sent a brigadier and a colonel to take notes. Tomsen had invited ISI in the hope that they would accept and implement his initiative. He described the secret new American policy in a formal presentation that lasted more than an hour. The Pakistanis expressed enthusiasm—especially the diplomats from Pakistan's foreign ministry, led by Yaqub Khan, who had long advocated a round-table political settlement involving King Zahir Shah. Even the Pakistani intelligence officers said they were in favor.

Tomsen planned to fly on to Riyadh to make the same presentation in private to Prince Turki at the headquarters of Saudi intelligence, and from there he would go to Rome to open discussions with the aging exiled Afghan king. But it took only a few hours to learn that the chorus of support expressed at the foreign ministry had been misleading. After the presentation, Tomsen and Oakley were talking in the ambassador's suite on the Islamabad embassy's third floor when the CIA station chief walked in.

"Peter can't go to Rome," Harry announced. "It's going to upset the offensive we have planned with ISI." The chief explained that with another Afghan fighting season approaching, the CIA's Islamabad station had been working that winter with Pakistani intelligence on a new military plan to bring down Najibullah. Rebel commanders around Afghanistan planned to launch simultaneous attacks on key Afghan cities and supply lines. The new offensive was poised and ready, and supplies were on the move. If word leaked out now that the United States was opening talks with King Zahir Shah, it would anger many of the Islamist mujahedin leaders in Peshawar who saw the king as a threat. The CIA chief also argued that Islamist mujahedin would not fight if they believed the king was "coming back." Hekmatyar and other Islamist leaders would almost certainly block the carefully planned offensive. Tomsen was livid. This was exactly the point: The new political talks were *supposed* to isolate the Islamist leaders in Peshawar. But they discovered that Harry had already contacted the CIA's Near East Division in Langley and that Thomas Twetten, the division chief, had already complained to Kimmitt at State, arguing that the opening to Zahir Shah should be delayed. Bureaucratically, Tomsen had been outflanked. "Why are you so pro-Zahir Shah?" Twetten asked Tomsen later.

Tomsen flew to Riyadh and met with Prince Turki to explain the new American policy—or, at least, the new State Department policy—but Rome was out for now. It was the beginning of another phase of intense struggle between State and the CIA, in many ways a continuation of the fight begun by McWilliams.[6]

What did it matter? At stake was the character of postwar, postcommunist Afghanistan. As Tomsen contemplated Afghanistan's future, he sought a political model in the only peaceful, modernizing period in Afghan history: the decades between 1919 and 1973 when Zahir Shah's weak but benign royal family governed from Kabul and a decentralized politics prevailed in the countryside, infused with Islamic faith and dominated by tribal or clan hierarchies. Tomsen believed the king's rule had produced a slow movement toward modernization and democratic politics. It had delivered a national constitution in 1963 and parliamentary elections in 1965 and 1969. By appealing to Zahir Shah as a symbolic ruler, the State Department hoped to create space in Afghanistan for federal, traditional politics. After so many years of war, it obviously would not be possible to return to the old royalist order, but wartime commanders such as Massoud and Abdul Haq, whose families had roots in traditional political communities, might construct a relatively peaceful transition. The alternative—the international Islamism of the Muslim Brotherhood, enforced by Pakistani military power—promised only continuing war and instability, Tomsen and his allies at State believed. CIA analysts, on the other hand, tended to view Afghanistan pessimistically. They believed that peace was beyond reach anytime soon. Pakistani influence in Afghanistan looked inevitable to some CIA operatives—Islamabad was relatively strong, Kabul weak. There was no reason for the United States to oppose an expansion of Pakistani power into Afghanistan, they felt, notwithstanding the anti-American rhetoric of ISI's jihadist clients.

Tomsen might possess an interagency policy document that committed the CIA to a new approach to the Afghan jihad, but he had yet to persuade CIA officers to embrace the policy. Some of them found Tomsen irritating; he had a habit, perhaps unconscious, of coughing up light laughter in the midst of serious conversation, including during solemn, tense interactions with key Afghan commanders or Pakistani generals. Some of the Afghans seemed to recoil at this, CIA officers observed. Tomsen sought to strengthen his position inside the embassy by building a partnership with Oakley, but the ambassador was an elusive ally, embracing the envoy and his views at some points but denouncing him disrespectfully in private at other times. More broadly, the CIA operated in Pakistan largely in secret and with great auton-omy. The Islamabad station was connected to Langley with a separate com-munication system to which diplomats did not have access. In the station and at headquarters most CIA officers regarded Tomsen's new policy as a naïve enterprise that was unlikely to succeed. They also saw it as an unwelcome dis-traction from the main business of finishing the covert war. As for postwar Afghan politics, the CIA's Twetten felt that the Afghans "were going to have to sort it out themselves. . . . It might get really messy." The United States should not get involved in picking political winners in Afghanistan or in ne-gotiating a new government for the country. There was nobody capable of putting Afghanistan back together again, Twetten believed, including Mas-soud.[7] Still, the CIA had a mission backed by a presidential finding: to support Afghan "self-determination," however messy, through covert action and close collaboration with Pakistani and Saudi intelligence. The CIA's Near East Division officers said they had no special sympathy for Hekmatyar or Sayyaf, but they remained deeply committed to a military solution in Afghanistan. They were going to finish the job.

A Pakistani military team traveled secretly to Washington to lay out an "ac-tion plan" for an early 1990 offensive. The plan would include support for a new conventional rebel army built around Hekmatyar's Lashkar-I-Isar, or Army of Sacrifice. Pursuing its own agenda, Pakistani intelligence had built up this militia force, equipping it with artillery and transport, to compete with Massoud's irregular army in the north.[8] Hekmatyar's army was becoming the most potent military wing of the ISI-backed Muslim Brotherhood networks based in Pakistan—a force that could operate in Afghanistan but also, in-creasingly, in Kashmir.

The CIA station in Islamabad helped that winter to coordinate broad attacks against Afghanistan's major cities and roads. Some of the planning involved ISI, but the CIA also reached out through its secret unilateral network to build up key Afghan commanders, including Massoud. If dispersed rebel units—even some at war with one another, such as those loyal to Hekmatyar and Massoud—could be persuaded to hit Najibullah's supply lines and cities at the same time, they might provide the last push needed to take Kabul. The CIA and Pakistani intelligence remained focused on the fall of Kabul, not on who would take power once Najibullah was gone.

Harry, Gary Schroen, and their case officers met repeatedly during that winter of 1989–1990 with officers in ISI's Afghan bureau to plan the new offensive. Harry met face-to-face with Hekmatyar. The CIA organized supplies so that Hekmatyar's forces could rocket the Bagram airport, north of Kabul, as the offensive began.[9]

Massoud figured centrally in the CIA's plans that winter. Schroen traveled to Peshawar in January to talk to Massoud on a secure radio maintained by his brother, Yahya. Schroen asked Massoud to cut off the Salang Highway as it entered Kabul from the north. If Massoud's forces closed the highway while other ISI-backed rebel groups smashed into Khost and Kabul from the east, Najibullah might not be able to resist for long, the CIA's officers believed. Massoud negotiated for a $500,000 cash payment, and Schroen delivered the money to one of Massoud's brothers on January 31, 1990.

But Massoud's forces never moved, as far as the CIA could tell. Furious at "that little bastard," as he called him in frustration, Harry cut Massoud's monthly stipend from $200,000 to $50,000. The Islamabad station sent a message to the Panjshir emphasizing the CIA's anger and dismay.

All across Afghanistan the CIA's offensive stalled. The mujahedin seemed uncoordinated, unmotivated, and distracted by internal warfare. They did not capture any major cities; Najibullah remained in power in Kabul, unmolested.

AS SPRING APPROACHED, the CIA station began to pick up reports from its unilateral Afghan agents that Pakistani intelligence was now secretly moving forward with its own plan to install Hekmatyar in Kabul as Afghanistan's new ruler. The CIA's informants reported that a wealthy fundamentalist Saudi sheikh, Osama bin Laden, was providing millions of dollars to support ISI's new plan for Hekmatyar. The Islamabad station transmitted these reports about bin Laden to Langley.[10]

On March 7, 1990, in downtown Kabul the conspiracy erupted into plain view. Afghan air force officers loyal to Najibullah's hard-line communist defense minister, Shahnawaz Tanai, swooped over the presidential palace in government jets, releasing bombs onto the rooftop and into the courtyard, hoping (but failing) to kill President Najibullah at his desk. Defecting armored forces loyal to Tanai drove south from the city, trying to open a cordon for Hekmatyar's Army of Sacrifice, which hurried toward Kabul from the Pakistani border.

With help from Pakistani intelligence Tanai and Hekmatyar had been holding secret talks about a coup attempt for months. The talks united a radical communist with a radical Islamist anticommunist. The pair shared Ghilzai Pashtun tribal heritage and a record of ruthless bloodletting. Tanai led a faction of Afghanistan's Communist Party, known as the Khalqis, who were rivals of Najibullah's faction.[11]

According to the CIA's reporting at the time, the money needed to buy off Afghan army units and win the support of rebel commanders came at least in part from bin Laden. These reports, while fragmentary, were consistent with the agency's portrait of bin Laden at the time as a copious funder of local Islamist causes, a donor rather than an operator, a sheikh with loose ties to Saudi officialdom who was flattered and cultivated in Peshawar by the recipients of his largesse, especially the radicals gathered around Hekmatyar and Sayyaf.[12]

During the same period that the Tanai coup was being planned—around December 1989—Pakistani intelligence reached out to bin Laden for money to bribe legislators to throw Benazir Bhutto out of office, according to reports that later reached Bhutto. According to Bhutto, ISI officers telephoned bin Laden in Saudi Arabia and asked him to fly to Pakistan to help organize a no-confidence vote in parliament against Bhutto's government, the first step in a Pakistan army plan to remove her forcibly from office.[13]

That winter, then, bin Laden worked with Pakistani intelligence against both Najibullah and Bhutto, the perceived twin enemies of Islam they saw holding power in Kabul and Islamabad. If Bhutto fell in Islamabad and Hekmatyar seized power with Tanai's help in Kabul, the Islamists would have pulled off a double coup.

Did bin Laden work on the Tanai coup attempt on his own or as a semi-official liaison for Saudi intelligence? The evidence remains thin and inconclusive. Bin Laden was still in good graces with the Saudi government at the time of the Tanai coup attempt; his first explicit break with Prince Turki and the royal family lay months in the future. While the CIA's Afghan informants named bin Laden as a funder of the Hekmatyar-Tanai coup, other accounts named Saudi intelligence as a source of funds. Were these separate funding tracks or the same? None of the reports then or later were firm or definitive.[14]

It was the beginning of a pattern for American intelligence analysts: Whenever bin Laden interacted with his own Saudi government, he seemed to do so inside a shroud.

Hekmatyar announced that he and Tanai had formed a new Revolutionary Council. But within hours of the first bombing attacks in downtown Kabul it became obvious to wavering Afghan commanders that the coup would fail. Government troops loyal to Najibullah routed Tanai's defectors in Kabul. Tanai himself fled to Pakistan where he and his cabal were sheltered by Pakistani intelligence. Hekmatyar's Army of Sacrifice never penetrated the capital's outskirts.

It remains unclear exactly when the CIA's Islamabad station learned of the Hekmatyar-Tanai coup attempt and whether its officers offered any comment—supportive or discouraging—to Pakistani intelligence. Many CIA operatives felt that Pakistani intelligence officers "never were honest with us on Hekmatyar," as Thomas Twetten, then number two in the Directorate of Operations, recalled it.[15] At a minimum, ISI's officers knew when they planned their coup that the CIA was creating a helpful context by organizing attacks on Najibullah's supply lines. But the CIA also kept secret from Pakistani intelligence the extent and details of its unilateral contacts with Afghan commanders such as Massoud. The agency did not inform ISI, for instance, about the $500,000 payment it made to Massoud on January 31, just five weeks before the coup attempt. The coup's timing is also swathed in mystery. Tanai may have moved hurriedly, ahead of schedule, because of a military treason trial under way that winter in Kabul that threatened to expose his plotting.

In the aftermath Massoud stood his ground in the north. The CIA might be angry at him for failing to hit the Salang Highway that winter, but what was he supposed to make of Hekmatyar's plot to take Kabul preemptively, a conspiracy so transparently sponsored by Pakistani intelligence, the CIA's intimate partner in the war? Massoud had ample cause to wonder whether the CIA, in making its $500,000 payment that winter, had been trying to use his forces in the north to help install Hekmatyar in Kabul.

Massoud told Arab mediators that he still hoped to avoid an all-out war with Hekmatyar. He did not want a direct confrontation with ISI, either. Massoud made plain his ambition to assume a major role in any future government in Kabul. He expected autonomy for his councils in the north. He did not aspire to rule the Pashtun areas of Afghanistan directly, however; he knew that was impractical for any Tajik leader. How much Massoud would be willing to negotiate with Pashtun leaders remained open to question. Peter Tomsen hoped his National Commanders Shura would provide a vehicle for such compromise beyond the control of Pakistani intelligence. One thing was certain: Massoud would not stand idly by while Hekmatyar seized power in the capital.

Massoud husbanded his supplies that spring, built up his alliances across the north, and waited. The long anticommunist jihad's last act still lay ahead.

HEKMATYAR'S EAGERNESS to conspire with a hard-line communist general and the willingness of Pakistani intelligence to support the plot appalled many Afghans and bolstered support for Peter Tomsen's new policy approach in Washington. The coup attempt made plain that Afghanistan's Cold War divides were dissolving rapidly. Extremists from seemingly opposite poles in the post–Soviet-Afghan war had linked up. It was all the more crucial, Tomsen and his allies argued, for the United States to build up moderate centrists in the Afghan rebel movement and to search for stable postwar politics.

It was by now conventional wisdom within the State Department that Saudi intelligence had become the Afghan war's most important hidden hand and that no new approach could be constructed without Prince Turki al-Faisal's personal support. Peter Tomsen and his team traveled frequently to Riyadh.[16]

Prince Turki remained an elusive, ambiguous figure. In the decade since his first meetings with Pakistan's General Akhtar and his Afghan clients in 1980, the prince had evolved into one of Saudi Arabia's most important leaders, a high-level interlocutor between American officials and the Saudi royal family, and a frequent and mysterious traveler to Middle Eastern capitals. He maintained palatial residences in Jedda and Riyadh. He summered at luxurious resorts in Europe. Now forty-five and no longer the boyish foreign policy expert he had been at the start of his career, Turki had become an elegant professional, an attentive consumer of satellite television news, and a reader of serious policy journals. He had built personal relationships with senior officers in every intelligence service in Europe and the Arab world. In addition to Pakistan he poured subsidies into the intelligence services of moderate Saudi allies such as Morocco and Jordan, buying access to information and people.[17] He seemed most at home on the luxurious circuit of foreign policy and international security conferences held at Davos, Switzerland, or the Aspen Institute in Colorado, where diplomats and generals debated the challenges of the post–Cold War world while smoking Cuban cigars. Within the Saudi royal family, Turki's influence was constrained by his relative youth. In a political system based on family and seniority, he languished in the second tier, tied by blood and political outlook to the family's most liberal and modernizing branch but not old or well placed enough to be its leader. Still, as CIA and other American officials identified Turki as perhaps the most reliable individual in the Saudi cabinet and as his reputation for serious work grew, Turki established an authority within the Saudi government far greater than his years would otherwise permit. On Afghanistan he was without question the man to see.

Whisked to the General Intelligence Department's boxy Riyadh headquarters in a long stretch limousine, Tomsen and his team, usually including the CIA's Riyadh station chief, sat for long hours with Turki in the spring of 1990 to talk about the new American approach to the covert war. These were languid sessions on overstuffed Louis XIV furniture in air-conditioned offices laden with tea and sweets. Turki seemed to revel in such conversation. The meetings would begin at 10 or 11 P.M. and drift toward dawn. The prince was unfailingly polite and persistently curious about the details—even the minutia—of the Afghan war. He tracked individual commanders, intellectual figures, and the most complex nuances of tribal politics. He had questions, too, about American policy and domestic politics, and like many other Georgetown University alumni influenced by Jesuit rigor, he seemed to enjoy abstract, conceptual policy issues.

Tomsen and others at the State Department tried to persuade Prince Turki that Saudi interests as well as American interests now lay in moving away from the Islamists backed by his own operatives and by Pakistani intelligence. Tomsen wanted Saudi funding to help build up his alternative *shura* of independent Afghan rebel commanders, outside of ISI control but with a strong role in the new movement for Massoud. In Washington, Tomsen arranged for a meeting between one of Massoud's representatives and the influential Saudi ambassador Prince Bandar, in the hope that Bandar would cable back his support for the commanders' *shura* to Prince Turki and others. Turki handled the appeal that spring the way Saudi intelligence usually dealt with sticky conflicts: He opened his checkbook, and he played both sides. Turki handed over millions of dollars to support Tomsen's new commanders' initiative.[18] At the same time Turki increased his support to Pakistani intelligence, Tomsen's nemesis, outstripping the CIA's contributions for the first time.

For the period from October 1989 through October 1990, Congress cut its secret allocation for the CIA's covert Afghan program by about 60 percent, to $280 million. Saudi intelligence, meanwhile, provided $435 million from the kingdom's official treasury and another $100 million from the private resources of various Saudi and Kuwaiti princes. Saudi and Kuwaiti funding continued to increase during the first seven months of 1990, bettering the CIA's contribution. Saudi intelligence organized what it called the King Fahd Plan for the Reconstruction of Afghanistan, a $250 million civil project of repair and construction. This tsunami of Gulf money ensured that even if the CIA's operatives cooperated fully with the new U.S. policy designed to isolate extremists such as Hekmatyar, the agency's efforts would be dwarfed by the unregulated money flowing from Saudi Arabia and the Persian Gulf.[19]

What was Prince Turki's motivation in this double game? The Americans who interacted with him, who mainly admired him, could only speculate. They accepted that Turki—like Prince Bandar, the Saudi ambassador to Washington, or Saud al-Faisal, the foreign minister—belonged to the pro-Western, modernizing wing of the Saudi royal family. Compared to some other senior princes, Turki embraced American and European culture and sought to emulate the West's models of economic development. Clearly he imagined a Saudi Arabia in the future where the kingdom's economy interacted closely with the United States and Europe, and where economic prosperity gradually produced a more open, tolerant, international culture in Saudi Arabia, albeit one still dominated by Islamic values. Yet Turki's funding of radical Islamists in Pakistan, Afghanistan, and elsewhere empowered leaders and movements violently opposed to the very Western systems Turki professed to admire. Why? Like the CIA, the Saudi government was slow to recognize the scope and violent ambitions of the international Islamist threat. Also, Turki saw Saudi Arabia in continual competition with its powerful Shiite Islamic neighbor, Iran. He needed credible Sunni, pro-Saudi Islamist clients to compete with Iran's clients, especially in countries like Pakistan and Afghanistan, which had sizable Shiite populations. The Saudis inevitably saw Massoud and his northern coalition through the prism of language: Massoud's followers predominantly spoke Farsi, or Persian, the language of Iran, and while Massoud and his Panjshiri group were Sunnis, there were Shias in their northern territory. Within Saudi Arabia itself, Prince Turki's modernizing wing of the royal family was attacked continually by the kingdom's conservative *ulama* who privately and sometimes publicly accused the royals of selling out to the Christian West, betraying Saudi Arabia's role as steward of the holiest places in the Islamic world. The internal struggle between the austere Ikhwan militia and the royal House of Saud, less than a century old, was far from over. Prince Turki and other liberal princes found it easier to appease their domestic Islamist rivals by allowing them to proselytize and make mischief abroad than to confront and resolve these tensions at home.

American motivations during this period were easier to describe. Indifference was the largest factor. President Bush paid hardly any attention to Afghanistan. CIA officers who met the president reported that he seemed barely aware that the war there was continuing. His National Security Council had few high-level meetings on the subject. The Soviet Union was dissolving and Germany was reuniting: These were the issues of the day. With Soviet troops gone, Afghanistan had suddenly become a third-tier foreign policy issue, pushed out to the edges of the Washington bureaucracy. The covert action policy, while formally endorsed by the president, by 1990 moved to a great extent on automatic pilot. Still, American negotiators made clear in public that they *were* trying to chart a new policy direction, however far they might operate from the center of White House power. Undersecretary of State Robert Kimmitt announced that the United States would not object if Najibullah participated in elections organized to settle the Afghan war. After the initial delay caused by the CIA, Tomsen opened the first direct talks between the United States and exiled king Zahir Shah.

"The impression is being created that the Americans are actually concerned with the danger of the spread of Islamic fundamentalism," Gorbachev confided to Najibullah in private that August. "They think, and they frankly say this, that the establishment today of fundamentalism in Afghanistan, Pakistan, and Iran would mean that tomorrow this phenomenon would encompass the entire Islamic world. And there are already symptoms of this, if you take Algeria, for example. But the Americans will remain Americans. And it would be naïve if one permitted the thought that we see only this side of their policy, and do not notice the other aspects."[20]

In Islamabad the CIA-ISI partnership was under pressure. There was continual turnover at the top of both intelligence agencies. Benazir Bhutto fired Hamid Gul as ISI chief because she learned that Gul was conspiring to overthrow her government. She tried to bring in a Bhutto family loyalist, a retired general, to run ISI, but the new man could never control the Afghan bureau and resigned. The next ISI chief, Asad Durrani, quickly discovered the outlines of the CIA Islamabad station's unilateral network of paid Afghan command-ers, including the agency's extensive independent contacts with Massoud.[21] This discovery reinforced the rising suspicions of Pakistani intelligence offi-cers that the Americans, in bed with Bhutto, were now playing their own dou-ble game.

Peter Tomsen deepened these Pakistani doubts by flying in and out of Is-lamabad, convening meeting after meeting to push both the CIA and Pakistani intelligence to support his new "grassroots" National Commanders Shura. The assembly convened for the first time in Paktia, attracting about three hundred mostly Pashtun commanders. To aid the effort, to bolster Massoud, and to improve Massoud's supply lines, the U.S. Agency for International De-velopment built all-weather roads from Pakistan to northern Afghanistan. At first the CIA objected to the emphasis on Massoud. The station had just cut Massoud's stipend because of his failure to attack the Salang Highway. (Be-cause of the agency's secrecy rules, CIA officers could not tell most of their State counterparts about what had happened, which exacerbated tensions be-tween the two groups.) Still, under continual pressure the agency agreed to give Massoud another chance.

Pakistani intelligence continued to build up Hekmatyar's Army of Sacri-fice, integrating Tanai and other former Afghan army officers into its com-mand. In October 1990 the CIA station's unilateral Afghan network reported a new alarm: A massive convoy of seven hundred Pakistani trucks carrying forty thousand long-range rockets had crossed the border from Peshawar, headed to Kabul's outskirts. There Hekmatyar planned to batter the capital into final submission with a massive artillery attack, the largest of the war by far, a barrage that would surely claim many hundreds of civilian lives. On Oc-tober 6, Tomsen met in Peshawar with ten leading independent commanders, including Abdul Haq and Massoud's representatives. Hekmatyar's planned rain of death on Kabul would be "worse than Jalalabad," the commander Amin Wardak warned. As a Confidential cable to Washington describing Tomsen's meeting put it, "The commanders were keenly aware that an un-successful military attack with heavy civilian casualties would rebound against the mujahedin." They would be seen in the eyes of the world as complicit in mass killings. Also, if Kabul fell without a replacement government, there would be "political chaos," Abdul Haq warned. Massoud and other command-ers who could not accept Hekmatyar would wage war against him. Wardak estimated "further destruction, perhaps 200–300 thousand casualties," the October 10 cable reported. As it happened, this was a grimly accurate forecast of Kabul's future.[22]

Only after Oakley warned of the gravest consequences for American-Pakistani relations if Pakistani intelligence did not abandon the plan did Durrani, the ISI chief, agree to call off the attack and turn the trucks back. "Tanai Two," as the planned mass rocket attack came to be known in the Islamabad embassy, had been aborted in the nick of time, but it signaled the Pakistani army's deepening break with American priorities. Oakley, now more firmly opposed to Pakistani intelligence than he had been during McWilliams's tour, denounced ISI as "a rogue elephant" in a meeting with Pakistan's president. Had the CIA known about this Hekmatyar rocket assault plan all along? Had Harry endorsed or acquiesced in it despite the prospect of thousands of civilian deaths in Kabul? Tomsen and others at State believed he had. They saw this episode as an example of the independent CIA war being commanded in secret from the Islamabad station while State's diplomats followed their own policies. Tomsen and Harry met at the station chief's house in Islamabad, and over tuna sandwiches and soup the CIA chief recounted the history of the October rocket attack plan as he knew it. He described a meeting he had attended with ISI and Hekmatyar at which Hekmatyar, boasting of his ability to capture Kabul for the mujahedin, had exclaimed, "I can do it!" The station chief said he had insisted that Hekmatyar work with other Afghan commanders. Tomsen concluded that the Islamabad station had likely endorsed the operation and perhaps even authorized weapons and other supplies. Tomsen regarded the decision as "not only a horribly bad one" but symptomatic of a larger danger. "It reflected all of the ills of the CIA's own self-compartmentalization and inability to understand the Afghan political context," Tomsen wrote at the time.[23]

Days after the excitement over Hekmatyar's aborted attack, Tomsen drove to the northern Pakistani town of Chitral to prepare a second National Commanders Shura. Massoud attended, as did prominent commanders from around Afghanistan. The organizers, who included Abdul Haq, banned Hekmatyar's commanders. Sayyaf ordered his commanders to boycott. But hundreds of other Afghan rebel leaders gathered for days of political and military discussions. It was the largest gathering of wartime Afghan field commanders in years. ISI's Durrani insisted on attending. He stayed in a tent nearby but was excluded from the meetings. Still, the ISI chief managed to get a message through to Massoud, and he invited him to Islamabad for a meeting.[24]

Massoud's representatives met with Prince Turki in Riyadh for the first time. Turki agreed to facilitate a new rapprochement with ISI. Massoud, who had been stung by the cutback of his CIA subsidy, agreed to travel to Pakistan for the first time in a decade. He was prepared to compete with Hekmatyar for support from Pakistani intelligence as the war's endgame approached. In Islamabad he met with Durrani and with Harry, the CIA station chief.[25]

Durrani, who sought to build trust with Massoud and enlist him in a unified rebel push against Najibullah, promised to resume military supplies to Massoud. Harry agreed to restore some of Massoud's retainer, increasing his stipend from $50,000 to $100,000 per month. The CIA instructed Pakistani intelligence to send more weapons convoys across the now half-built American road to the north. Some of these ISI shipments to Massoud, convoys as large as 250 trucks, did get through. On direct orders from the American embassy in Islamabad, Massoud received his first, albeit small, batch of Stinger missiles. But in other cases, heavy convoys dispatched by Pakistani intelligence to Afghanistan's north mysteriously disappeared, never reaching the Panjshir. The Americans suspected that Pakistani intelligence was doing all it could to resist their pressure to aid Massoud.[26]

A pattern in the CIA-ISI liaison was emerging: Faced with ardent demands from the Americans, ISI officers in the Afghan bureau now nodded their heads agreeably—and then followed their own policy to the extent they could, sometimes with CIA collaboration, sometimes unilaterally.

The dominant view among Pakistani generals, whether they were Islamists or secularists, was that Hekmatyar offered the best hope for a pro-Pakistan government in Kabul. The strong feeling even among the most liberal Punjabi generals—whose sons cavorted in London and who spent their own afternoons on the army's Rawalpindi golf course—was "We should settle this business. It's a sore on our backside."[27]

The Islamabad CIA station spent much of its time worrying about Pakistan's nuclear weapons program. In 1990, just as the agency's partnership with ISI on the Afghan frontier was fraying, the CIA's sources began to report that Pakistan's generals had pushed their nuclear program to a new and dangerous level. After a visit to Washington, Robert Oakley returned to Islamabad carrying a private message for Pakistan's army. Pakistan was now just one or two metaphorical turns of a screw away from possessing nuclear bombs, and the CIA knew it. Under an American law known as the Pressler Amendment, the CIA's conclusion automatically triggered the end of American military and economic assistance to the government of Pakistan—$564 million in aid that year.[28] After a decade of intensive U.S.-Pakistan cooperation, the United States had decided, in effect, to file for divorce.

American fears of nuclear proliferation from Pakistan were well grounded. Mirza Aslam Beg, the army chief of staff, opened discussions in Tehran with the Iranian Revolutionary Guard about the possibility of Pakistani nuclear cooperation with Iran. Beg discussed a deal in which Pakistan would trade its bombmaking expertise for Iranian oil. Oakley met with the Pakistani general to explain "what a disaster this would be, certainly in terms of the relationship with the United States," and Beg agreed to abandon the Iranian talks.[29] But it seemed now that in their relations with the Pakistan army, American officials were racing from one fire to the next.

A popular rebellion had erupted late in 1989 across Pakistan's border in the disputed territory of Kashmir, a vale of mountain lakes with a largely Muslim population that had been the site of three wars in four decades between India and Pakistan. Inspired by their success against Soviet forces in Afghanistan, Pakistani intelligence officers announced to Bhutto that they were prepared to use the same methods of covert jihad to drive India out of Kashmir. They had begun to build up Muslim Brotherhood militant networks in the Kashmir valley, using religious schools and professional organizations. ISI organized training camps for Kashmiri guerrillas in Afghanistan's Paktia province where the Arab volunteers had earlier organized their own camps. According to the CIA's reporting that year, the Kashmiri volunteers trained side by side with the Arab jihadists. The Kashmir guerrillas began to surface in Indian-held territory wielding Chinese-made Kalashnikov rifles and other weapons siphoned from the Afghan pipeline. The CIA became worried that Pakistani intelligence might also divert to Kashmir high-technology weapons such as the buffalo gun sniper rifles originally shipped to Pakistan to kill Soviet military officers. The United States passed private warnings to India to protect politicians and government officials traveling in Kashmir from long-range sniper attacks.[30]

The Afghan jihad had crossed one more border. It was about to expand again.

BY LATE 1990, bin Laden had returned to his family's business in Jedda, Saudi Arabia. He remained in cordial contact with Ahmed Badeeb, the chief of staff to Saudi intelligence, who offered bin Laden "business advice when he asked for it."[31]

Badeeb learned that bin Laden had begun to organize former Saudi and Yemeni volunteers from his days in Afghanistan to undertake a new jihad in South Yemen, then governed by Soviet-backed Marxists. Working from apartment buildings in Jedda, he had funded and equipped them to open a guerrilla war against the South Yemen government. Once bin Laden's mujahedin crossed the border, the Yemeni government picked up some of them and complained to Riyadh, denouncing bin Laden by name.[32]

By the autumn of 1990, bin Laden was agitated, too, about the threat facing Saudi Arabia from the Iraqi army forces that had invaded and occupied Kuwait in August. Bin Laden wanted to lead a new jihad against the Iraqis. He spoke out at schools and small gatherings in Jedda about how it would be possible to defeat Saddam Hussein by organizing battalions of righteous Islamic volunteers. Bin Laden objected violently to the decision of the Saudi royal family to invite American troops to defend the kingdom. He demanded an audience with senior princes in the Saudi royal family—and King Fahd himself—to present his plans for a new jihad.

Uncertain what to make of bin Laden's rantings and concerned about the violence he was stirring up in Yemen, a senior Saudi prince, along with a pro-government Islamic theologian named Khalil A. Khalil, traveled to Jedda to hear bin Laden out and assess his state of mind. Bin Laden brought bodyguards to the private meeting. He carried a proposal of about sixty pages, typed in Arabic, outlining his ideas.

Khalil found bin Laden "very formal, very tense." Bin Laden demanded to meet with King Fahd. He declared, "I want to fight against Saddam, an infidel. I want to establish a guerrilla war against Iraq." Khalil asked how many troops bin Laden had. "Sixty thousand," bin Laden boasted, "and twenty thousand Saudis." Khalil and the prince knew this was foolishness, but bin Laden boasted, "I don't need any weapons. I have plenty."

Finally, the senior prince at the meeting told bin Laden that the Saudi king would not meet with him. The king only met with *ulama,* religious scholars, he said. But since bin Laden was making a military proposal and since he was a respected scion of an important Saudi family, the prince agreed to arrange a meeting between bin Laden and Prince Sultan, Saudi Arabia's defense minister.

"I am the commander of an Islamic army. I am not afraid of being put in jail or being in prison. I am only afraid of Allah," bin Laden announced as the meeting ended, as Khalil recalled it.

The senior prince told bin Laden that what he had just said "is against the law and against principles. But it is not our custom to arrest someone whom you have agreed to meet in good faith. My advice is to examine yourself very carefully. We are not afraid of you. We are not afraid of your army. We know what to do."

"You listen to America—your master," bin Laden answered.[33]

In Riyadh, bin Laden arrived at the Defense Ministry with military maps and diagrams. Abdullah al-Turki, secretary-general of the Muslim World League, the largest worldwide Saudi proselytizing organization, joined the meeting. He was there to explain to bin Laden that the American troops invited to the kingdom had religious sanction. Mohammed had intended for no religion but Islam to dominate the Saudi peninsula, al-Turki said. But the Prophet had never objected to Jews and Christians traveling in the region or helping to defend it.

The Saudi kingdom could avoid using an army of American infidels to fight its war, bin Laden argued, if it would support his army of battle-tested Afghan war veterans.

Prince Sultan treated bin Laden with warmth and respect but said that he doubted that bin Laden's plan would work. The Iraqi army had four thousand tanks. "There are no caves in Kuwait," Prince Sultan said. "You cannot fight them from the mountains and caves. What will you do when he lobs the missiles at you with chemical and biological weapons?"

"We will fight him with faith," bin Laden said.[34]

The meeting ended inconclusively, with respectful salutations. Even if his ideas seemed crazy, bin Laden belonged to one of the kingdom's most important families. He had worked closely with the Saudi government. In situations like this, Saudi mores encouraged the avoidance of direct conflict.

Prince Turki saw bin Laden's meeting at the Defense Ministry as a watershed. From that time on the Saudi intelligence chief saw "radical changes" in bin Laden's personality: "He changed from a calm, peaceful, and gentle man interested in helping Muslims into a person who believed that he would be able to amass and command an army to liberate Kuwait. It revealed his arrogance and his haughtiness."[35]

IT WAS NOT ONLY bin Laden who shocked Prince Turki that autumn by rejecting the kingdom's alliance with the United States against Iraq. So did Hekmatyar and Sayyaf, despite all the millions of dollars in aid they had accepted from Saudi intelligence. As the prime minister of the Afghan interim government, Sayyaf delivered public speeches in Peshawar denouncing the Saudi royal family as anti-Islamic. The Bush administration dispatched diplomats to urge Pakistan and the Saudi royal family to rein in their Afghan clients. "Whereas before, their anti-Americanism did not have more than slight impact beyond the Afghan context, during the current crisis they fan anti-U.S.

and anti-Saudi sentiment in Pakistan and Afghanistan, as well as beyond," noted a State Department action memorandum. Furious, Turki sent Ahmed Badeeb to Pakistan.

By the time he arrived in Peshawar, Badeeb could barely contain his rage. "When I am upset, I lose my mind," Badeeb explained later. He barged into a public meeting where Sayyaf was denouncing Saudi Arabia for its bargain with the American devils.

"Now you are coming to tell us what to do in our religion?" Badeeb demanded. "Even your own name—I changed it! To become a Muslim name!" If the Afghan interim government wanted to send a delegation of mujahedin to help defend Saudi Arabia against the Iraqis, that might be a way to help people "recognize that there is something in the world called an Afghan Islamic republic." But if Sayyaf refused, "I am going to make you really regret what you have said."

In case he had not made himself clear, the chief of staff of Saudi intelligence told Sayyaf directly: "Fuck you and your family and the Afghans." And he stormed out.[36]

The threads of the Cold War's jihad alliance were coming apart.

"We Are in Danger"

B Y EARLY 1991 the Afghan policies pursued by the State Department and the CIA were in open competition with one another. Both departments sought a change of government in Kabul, but they had different Afghan clients. Peter Tomsen and his supporters in State's Bureau of Intelligence and Research pursued what they saw as a bottom-up or grassroots strategy. They channeled guns and money to the new rebel commanders' *shura,* which attracted members from across Afghanistan, and they emphasized the importance of Massoud. They also continued to negotiate for a broad political settlement that would include popular national figures such as the exiled king. The CIA sometimes cooperated with these efforts, however grudgingly, but it also continued to collaborate with Pakistani intelligence on a separate military track that mainly promoted Hekmatyar and other Islamist commanders operating near the Pakistani border. That winter the ISI and the CIA returned to the strategy that had been tried unsuccessfully in the two previous years: a massed attack on an eastern Afghan city, with direct participation by covert Pakistani forces.

In the previous campaign the CIA had tried to support such an attack by paying Massoud to close the Salang Highway, and the agency had been greatly disappointed. This time officers in the Directorate of Operations' Near East Division came up with a new idea. Early in March 1991, overwhelmed and in retreat, Saddam Hussein's army abandoned scores of Soviet-made tanks and artillery pieces in Kuwait and southern Iraq. The discarded weaponry offered the potential for a classical covert action play: The CIA would secretly use spoils captured from one of America's enemies to attack another enemy.

The CIA station in Riyadh, working with Saudi intelligence, assigned a team of covert logistics officers to round up abandoned T-55 and T-72 Iraqi tanks, armored personnel carriers, and artillery pieces. The CIA team worked with the U.S. military in southern Iraq to loot abandoned Iraqi armories and ammunition stores. They refurbished the captured equipment and rolled it to Kuwaiti ports for shipment to Karachi. From there Pakistani intelligence brought the armor and artillery to the Afghan border. Officers from ISI's Afghan bureau used the equipment to support massive new conventional attacks on the eastern city of Gardez, in Paktia province, the ISI-supplied stronghold of Jallaladin Haqqanni, Hekmatyar, and the Arab volunteers.[1]

Officers in the CIA's Near East Division had come to believe that the Afghan rebels needed more conventional assault equipment to match the firepower of Najibullah's Afghan army. There had been earlier talk of shipping in U.S.-made 155-millimeter howitzers, but now the Iraqi gambit seemed a better idea; it was cheaper, and the equipment could not be traced directly to Washington. Soviet-made Iraqi armor was of the same type that the mujahedin sometimes captured from Afghan government troops, so if a rebel force suddenly emerged on the outskirts of Khost or Gardez with a new tank brigade, it would not be obvious where their armor came from.

Peter Tomsen and others at the State Department agreed to support the secret transfers of Iraqi weapons. They worried about declining morale among the rebels after months of military stalemate and thought the new equipment might provide a much needed jolt. At the same time they did not want the Iraqi tanks and artillery to strengthen the discredited anti-American Islamists around Hekmatyar.

After Hekmatyar and Sayyaf failed to support Saudi Arabia publicly in its confrontation with Iraq, both the United States and Saudi intelligence initially vowed to cut them off. Saudi Arabia's ambassador to Pakistan, meeting at ISI headquarters with American diplomats and the chief of Pakistani intelligence, announced that all Saudi funding to Hekmatyar and Sayyaf should stop. But within months it became clear to the Americans that the Saudis were still secretly allowing cash and weapons to reach Hekmatyar and Sayyaf.[2]

The CIA's Afghan budget continued to shrink. Total funding allocated by Congress for the mujahedin fell again during calendar year 1991. What little aid there was should be used to build up the rebel leaders who opposed Hekmatyar, the State Department's diplomats argued. But the CIA maintained that it had never been able to control how Pakistani intelligence distributed the weapons it received. The agreement had always been that title passed to ISI once the equipment reached Pakistani soil. Tomsen and others at State complained that the CIA surely was capable of controlling the destination of its weapons, but Langley's officers said they could not. Besides, CIA officers argued, Hekmatyar's coup attempt with Tanai demonstrated his tactical daring; most of the rebel commanders were just sitting on their haunches waiting for the war to end.[3] Saudi intelligence endorsed the Iraqi tank gambit and fully supported the covert plan, the CIA reported. They would try to keep the tanks away from Hekmatyar and encourage Pakistani intelligence to send them to the rebel commander Jallaladin Haqqanni. After false starts in the two previous fighting seasons, here was a chance at last to help tip the military balance in Afghanistan against Najibullah, the agency's operatives argued.

With ISI officers helping to direct the attack from nearby hilltops, a coalition of mujahedin forces lay siege to Khost as spring arrived. Its main garrison fell in late March 1991, the most significant rebel victory since the withdrawal of Soviet troops. But Peter Tomsen's hope that the victory would boost the power of his commanders' *shura* was thwarted. Pakistani intelligence ensured that Hekmatyar reached the city with the first conquerors. He promptly claimed the victory as his own in public speeches. ISI chief Durrani drove across the Afghan border and made a triumphal tour of Khost, as did the Pakistani leader of Jamaat-e-Islami, Qazi Hussain Ahmed. Their appearances made plain the direct role of the Pakistani military and Muslim Brotherhood networks in the assault.[4]

The rising presence of radical Arab, Indonesian, Malaysian, Uzbek, and other volunteer fighters in Paktia was documented in the agency's own reporting from the field. CIA cables from Pakistan during this period, drawing on reports from Afghan agents, provided Langley with detailed accounts of the jihadist training camps in Paktia. The CIA reported, for instance, that Saudi radical volunteers were training side by side with Kashmiri radicals and that the Kashmiris were being prepared by Pakistani intelligence for infiltration into Indian-held territory. The CIA also reported that substantial numbers of Algerian and other North African Islamist radicals were training in Paktia, some fighting with Hekmatyar's Afghan forces and others with Sayyaf.[5]

All this detailed intelligence reporting about international Islamic radical-ism and its sanctuary in Afghanistan gathered dust in the middle levels of the bureaucracy. The Gulf War, the reunification of Germany, the final death throes of the Soviet Union—these enormous, all-consuming crises contin-ued to command the attention of the Bush administration's cabinet. By 1991, Afghanistan was rarely if ever on the agenda.

Milt Bearden, the former Islamabad station chief, found himself talking in passing about the Afghan war with President Bush. The president seemed puzzled that the CIA's covert pipeline through Pakistan was still active, as Bearden recalled it. Bush seemed surprised, too, that the Afghans were still fighting. "Is that thing still going on?" the president asked.[6]

SAUDI ARABIA'S ROYAL FAMILY spent generously to appease the king-dom's Islamist radicals in the years following the uprising at the Grand Mosque in 1979. Billions of dollars poured into the coffers of the kingdom's official *ulama,* who issued their *fatwas* increasingly from air-conditioned, oak-furnished offices. Billions more supported mosque-building campaigns in provincial towns and oasis villages. Thousands of idle young Saudi men were recruited into the domestic religious police and dispatched to the kingdom's gleaming new sandstone-and-glass shopping malls. There they harassed women who allowed high-heeled shoes to show beneath their black robes, and used wooden batons to round up Saudi men for daily prayers. New Islamic universities rose in Riyadh and Jedda, and thousands of students were enrolled to study the Koran. At the same time the royal family stoked its massive mod-ernization drive, constructing intercity highways, vast new housing, industrial plants, and hospitals. Saudi women entered the workforce in record numbers, although they often worked in strict segregation from men. Secular princes and princesses summered in London, Cannes, Costa del Sol, and Switzerland. There were at least six thousand self-described princes in the Saudi royal fam-ily by 1990, and their numbers grew by the year. Many of these royals paid lit-tle heed to the Islamic clergy who governed official Saudi culture.

Osama bin Laden returned to Saudi Arabia from Pakistan just as new fis-sures opened between its austere, proselytizing religious establishment and its diverse, undisciplined royal family. For many Saudis the Iraqi invasion and the arrival of hundreds of thousands of American troops to defend the kingdom shattered the myth of Saudi independence and ignited open debate about Saudi identity. To both Islamists and modernizers the war seemed a turning point. Saudi women staged protests against the kingdom's ban on female drivers, defiantly taking the wheel on the streets of Riyadh and Dhahran. Liberal political activists petitioned for a representative assembly that might advise the royal family. Islamists denounced the arrival of Christian troops as a violation of Islamic law. Two fiery young preachers known as the "Awakening Sheikhs" recorded anti-American sermons on cassette tapes and circulated millions of copies around the kingdom in late 1990 and early 1991. "It is not the world against Iraq. It is the West against Islam," declared Sheikh Safar al-Hawali, a bin Laden ally. "If Iraq has occupied Kuwait, then America has occupied Saudi Arabia. The real enemy is not Iraq. It is the West." Al-Hawali's best-known book, *Kissinger's Promise,* argued that American-led "crusaders" intended to conquer the Arabian Peninsula to seize its oil reserves. He warned Saudi citizens: "It will not be long until your blood is shed with impunity or you declare your abandonment of your belief in God." These were themes bin Laden himself propounded in informal lectures at Jedda mosques. He adopted al-Hawali's politics and some of the preacher's terminology. He found himself part of a widening movement in the kingdom. Other antiroyal agitators saw his participation as an indication of how serious the rebellion had become, recalled Saudi journalist and author Saudi Aburish, because bin Laden was a "member of the establishment" who had suddenly announced himself as "a radical Islamist against the regime."[7]

In May 1991 an underground Saudi network of Islamist preachers and activists obtained scores of signatures on a petition called the "Letter of Demands" that was submitted to King Fahd. The petition blended calls for quasi-democratic political reform with radical Islamist ideology. It sought the unquestioned primacy of Islamic law, equal distribution of public wealth, more funding for Islamic institutions, religious control of the media, and a consultative assembly independent of the royal family. The letter's publication shocked the Saudi royal family, in part because it revealed an extensive organization in the kingdom rallying in secret around a subversive agenda. Cassette tapes circulated that summer by the underground Islamist preachers grew in number and vitriol. A popular tape titled "America as I Saw It" informed its listeners that the United States was a "nation of beasts who fornicate and eat rotten food," a land where men marry men and parents are abandoned as they age.[8]

Pushed to its limit, the Saudi royal family retaliated, making scores of arrests. But the government managed its repression gently. Senior princes did not want their crackdown to be seen as violent or arbitrary or to create new waves of dissidents, stoking unrest. The Awakening Sheikhs were placed under house arrest, but the government quickly opened negotiations to address some of their demands. Senior princes quietly sent messages to the official *ulama* acknowledging that, yes, the presence of American troops in the kingdom was undesirable, and their numbers and visibility would be reduced as soon as possible. Saudi princes stepped out in public to emphasize their devotion to Islamic causes—especially in places outside of Saudi Arabia, such as Afghanistan and Bosnia. The kingdom's Ministry of Pilgrimage and Religious Trusts announced that the government had spent about $850 million on mosque construction in recent years, employed fifty-three thousand religious leaders in mosques, and planned to hire another 7,300 prayer leaders. King Fahd announced his intention to ship millions of free Korans to the newly independent, predominantly Muslim countries of Central Asia. The proper and legal outlet for Islamic activism, the royal family made clear, lay not inside the kingdom but abroad, in aid of the global *umma,* or community of Muslim believers.[9]

The rise of the Awakening Sheikhs and the emergence of the Letter of Demands prompted CIA officers and State Department diplomats to open talks with the Saudi royal family about the dangers of Islamic radicalism. American analysts were determined to intervene early with the Saudi royals, to encourage the Saudis to be alert and responsive to signs of serious internal dissent.

For the first time the CIA began to see evidence that Arab jihadists trained in Afghanistan posed a threat in Saudi Arabia itself. Gary Schroen, now in the CIA's Riyadh station, discussed with Prince Turki the problem of Saudi radicals moving in and out of Afghanistan. "There are a lot of Saudi citizens there who are fighting," Schroen said, as he recalled it. "They're being trained. They're young men who are really dedicated, really religious, and a lot of them are coming back. They're here."

"We understand that," Turki assured him. "We're watching that. There is no problem. We'll take care of it." The Saudi royal family had begun to worry. In Islamabad the Saudi ambassador to Pakistan sat down with American officials to warn them about Islamist charity organizations on the Afghan frontier that were raising funds in the United States, then spending the money on radical and violent causes in Pakistan, Afghanistan, and beyond. "You should know about this," the Saudi envoy warned. The U.S. consulate in Peshawar composed a classified cable for Washington based on the Saudi envoy's information. The cable listed charity organizations in California and Texas that were sending cash and fighters to the Islamist networks swirling around Hekmatyar and Sayyaf. The cable was routed to the FBI and CIA, but the State Department officers who helped compile it never heard of any follow-up investigation.[10]

Peter Tomsen and other emissaries from Washington discussed the rising Islamist threat with Prince Turki in the summer of 1991. Turki listened to their concerns, made few commitments, but repeated that he was on top of the problem. As so often, Turki, the most accessible contact for American spies and diplomats on the subject of political Islam, seemed reassuring. Turki was one of the liberals under assault from the underground Islamists. His sister had taken part in some of the attempts by women in Riyadh to win greater rights and visibility. She had been singled out and denounced as a prostitute by a preacher during Friday services at a Riyadh mosque. The next Friday, Turki attended the mosque, rose from the audience, and asked to speak. He denounced the slander against the women of his family, making clear that the attacks against liberals had gone too far.[11] Impressed by his willingness to take a public stand, the Americans who met him were quick to believe that Turki was on their side and that he had the Islamist threat under control.

At some of the meetings between Turki and the CIA, Osama bin Laden's name came up explicitly. The CIA continued to pick up reporting that he was funding radicals such as Hekmatyar in Afghanistan. Hekmatyar, Sayyaf, and Haqqanni all had officers around Saudi Arabia who collected money from mosques and wealthy sheikhs; bin Laden was one part of this wider fund-raising system. "His family has disowned him," Turki assured the Americans about bin Laden. Every effort had been made to persuade bin Laden to stop protesting against the Saudi royal family. These efforts had failed, Turki conceded, and the kingdom was now prepared to take sterner measures.[12]

Bin Laden learned of this when Saudi police arrived at his cushion-strewn, modestly furnished compound in Jedda to announce that he would have to leave the kingdom. According to an account later provided to the CIA by a source in Saudi intelligence, the Saudi officer assigned to carry out the expulsion assured bin Laden that this was being done for his own good. The officer blamed the Americans. The U.S. government was planning to kill him, he told bin Laden, by this account, so the royal family would do him a favor and get him out of the kingdom for his own protection. Two associates of bin Laden later offered a different version while under interrogation: They said a dissident member of the royal family helped him leave the country by arranging for bin Laden to attend an Islamic conference in Pakistan during the spring of 1991. So far as is known, bin Laden never returned to the king-dom.[13]

VODKA-SOAKED SOVIET HARD-LINERS, including leaders at the KGB, tried and failed to overthrow Mikhail Gorbachev on August 19, 1991. Within weeks the Communist Party of the Soviet Union, nemesis of the United States for almost half a century, collapsed as an effective political organi-zation. Russian liberals, Russian nationalists, Baltic nationalists, Ukrainians, Kazakhs, and Uzbeks now ruled what remained of the Soviet Union. A na-tion constructed from Stalin's terror hurtled toward its final dissolution.

Gorbachev's weakening cabinet, in search of rapid compromises with Washington, decided to abandon its aid to Najibullah in Afghanistan. In turn, the Bush Cabinet felt free at last to drop all support to the mujahedin. On September 13, U.S. Secretary of State James Baker and Soviet Foreign Minis-ter Boris Pankin pledged a mutual cutoff of arms to Najibullah and the Afghan rebels as of January 1, 1992.[14]

Twelve years after the Politburo decided to commit military force to de-fend communism in Afghanistan—twelve years and two months after Zbig-niew Brzezinski had presented Jimmy Carter with a draft presidential finding for CIA covert action to support anticommunist rebels—both superpowers agreed to stop fueling the Afghan war. Yet the war continued.

The brigadiers and colonels in Pakistani intelligence had never trusted that the CIA would see the Afghan jihad through to the end. Some of them had never really trusted the Americans, period. Bitterly, Pakistan's military officers congratulated themselves on how right they had been.

In Kabul, Najibullah remained in power. The former Afghan king, Zahir Shah, remained at his villa in Rome. United Nations diplomats shuttled in their blue-stenciled airplanes between Kabul and Islamabad by the week, but the prospects for a peaceful political settlement appeared dim. Hekmatyar and other Islamists backed by Pakistani intelligence were creeping toward Kabul in their captured Iraqi tanks. Ahmed Shah Massoud had assembled a rival invasion force, including captured Soviet tanks, to Kabul's north, poised for a decisive drive on the capital.

"An extremist seizure of Kabul would plunge Afghanistan into a fresh round of warfare, which could affect areas adjoining Afghanistan," Peter Tomsen warned in a Secret cable to Washington that September 1991. "Should Hekmatyar or Sayyaf get to Kabul, extremists in the Arab world would support them in stoking Islamic radicalism in the region, including the Soviet Central Asian republics, but also in Saudi Arabia and elsewhere in the Arab world." In December, Tomsen repeated his warnings in another cable, classified Secret and distributed throughout the national security bureaucracy in Washington. He feared "a scramble for power" that would "further attenuate central authority in favor of local warlords. . . . A political settlement must be put into place as rapidly as possible to forestall scenarios of continued instability and civil war in Afghanistan."

But few at Foggy Bottom or Langley were focused on the future of Islamic politics or stability in Central Asia. In Afghanistan the stage was set not for a triumphal reconciliation on one of the Cold War's most destructive battlefields but for an ugly new phase of regional and civil war. The CIA's analysts and operatives had long argued that after the withdrawal of Soviet forces, the Afghans would have to sort things out for themselves. They would have little choice now but to try.[15]

THE CIA'S LEGAL AUTHORITY to conduct covert action in Afghanistan effectively ended on January 1, 1992. By then the Soviet Union had formally dissolved. Peter Tomsen suggested a new finding that would allow unilateral CIA clients to be used to bolster the U.N. negotiations seeking a moderate coalition government in Afghanistan, but the CIA and other diplomats in the State Department opposed the idea. The Islamabad station retained some of its Afghan agents for months into the new year, but these were now classified only as reporting relationships—traditional spying. Some of the CIA's Afghan commanders were converted to work on the secret Stinger buyback program, begun after the Soviet troop withdrawal and now the only covert action program authorized in Afghanistan. Others were directed to report on new post–Cold War priorities such as drug trafficking.

From fertile Helmand in the south to the gorge valleys of the northeast, Afghanistan flowered each spring with one of the world's largest crops of opium poppies. Untroubled by government, and funded by smugglers and organized crime networks rooted in Pakistan, Afghan poppy farmers supplied heroin labs nestled in cities and along the lawless Afghanistan-Pakistan border. By 1992 hundreds of tons of refined heroin flowed from these labs east through Karachi's port or north through the new overland routes of the Russian mafia, destined for European cities. By the early 1990s, Afghanistan rivaled Colombia and Burma as a fountainhead of global heroin supply. The

CIA opened a new Counter-Narcotics Center, modeled on the Counterterrorist Center, and President Bush allocated secret funds for espionage in Afghanistan aimed at combatting the heroin rackets. Even so, within six months of the January 1 formal cutoff, the CIA's Afghan operation had atrophied to a shadow of its former strength.

The Islamabad station's liaison with ISI deteriorated by the week. The CIA had little to offer anymore. At one point the agency found itself in the awkward, even perverse position of attempting to apply the legal rules of the Pressler Amendment to the secret shipments of captured Iraqi tanks and artillery that had reached Pakistan, bound for the Afghan rebels. Pressler required an end to all military equipment aid and sales by the United States to Pakistan. The CIA's lawyers concluded that the law might apply even to covert supplies such as the Iraqi tanks, especially if the armor had not yet crossed the Afghan border, as was the case with dozens of the tanks. The CIA station in Islamabad informed ISI that it would have to destroy any stored armor and artillery. The agency wanted the weapons taken to an army test range and blown up—with CIA officers present to confirm the destruction. Surely you are joking, Pakistani intelligence officers told their CIA counterparts. Locked in an existential struggle with India, Pakistan was not about to blow up perfectly good tanks or artillery just because some lawyer in Langley was worried about a congressional subpoena. In the end the CIA gave up. Pakistan held on to as many as three or four dozen Iraqi tanks, by one CIA estimate, despite the Pressler restrictions.[16]

EDMUND MCWILLIAMS had been assigned to the inaugural U.S. embassy in Dushanbe, Tajikistan, a newly independent, predominantly Muslim former Soviet republic bordering Afghanistan. In February 1992 travelers reaching the Tajik capital told McWilliams that one of Najibullah's most important allies in northern Afghanistan, a communist Uzbek militia commander named Aburrashid Dostum, had defected to Massoud's Supreme Council of the North. The word was out all across northern Afghanistan, the travelers said. Najibullah's days were at last numbered. The sudden alliance of Massoud's Tajik army with Dostum's Uzbek militia—forty thousand strong, in control of tanks, artillery, and even aircraft—tilted the military balance against Najibullah just as his supplies from Moscow had been cut off. McWilliams cabled Washington: The fall of Kabul, so long predicted and so long delayed, appeared now to be finally at hand.[17]

"We have a common task—Afghanistan, the U.S.A., and the civilized world—to launch a joint struggle against fundamentalism," Najibullah told reporters in his palace office as the mujahedin closed to within rocketing distance. "If fundamentalism comes to Afghanistan, war will continue for many years. Afghanistan will turn into a center of world smuggling for narcotic drugs. Afghanistan will be turned into a center for terrorism."[18]

Najibullah could see the future, but there was no one to listen. He had lost his Soviet patrons, and he was discredited, desperate. A United Nations mediator, Benon Sevan, spent long hours with Najibullah that month, urging him to resign and throw his support to a peaceful transitional government that might isolate violent Islamist radicals like Hekmatyar. Najibullah agreed and read a speech on national television written for him by Sevan, saying that he would quit the presidency as soon as a successor government was formed under U.N. auspices.

The United States stood to the side. Oakley had left Islamabad. The embassy's chargé d'affaires, Beth Jones, preferred to defer to Pakistan. Tomsen could not do much to influence America's outlook because Washington had just announced a new policy: hands off.

JUST SOUTH OF KABUL, in a wide valley tucked beneath soaring peaks, Gulbuddin Hekmatyar slipped his forces into a village called Charasyab and set up military operations. There were barracks, a radio room, training areas, and a mosque set in a pine grove. Pakistani helicopters flew in and out carrying ISI officers for consultations. Tanks, armored personnel carriers, multiple rocket launchers, and artillery rolled into the base, lined up for the final thrust toward Kabul. From his command center Hekmatyar worked the radio, reopening talks with Afghan communists from the faction that had earlier allied with him in a coup attempt. Dozens of Arab jihadist volunteers, allies of Hekmatyar from the days of revolution in Peshawar, poured into Charasyab, and with them came Arab journalists prepared to document the final chapter of the Islamic revolution in Afghanistan.[19]

Hekmatyar was determined to seize the capital. In Kabul the Afghan communist government was splitting rapidly. One faction of the old Communist Party prepared to surrender to Hekmatyar. Another faction planned to surrender to Massoud.

In Peshawar, talks about a transitional government continued behind closed doors, led by ISI's Durrani and Prince Turki. Saudi scholars flew in hurriedly to join the talks and provide them with religious sanction. Peter Tomsen and Benon Sevan tried to persuade Turki to support a broad political settlement, but they found Turki cool and remote. Prince Turki, they believed, was using his influence to stitch together an alternative compromise, one that would unite all of the Islamist leaders into a single government. To achieve this, Turki had to help prevent violence between Massoud and Hekmatyar.

Even Osama bin Laden flew to Peshawar and joined the effort to forge cooperation between Hekmatyar and Massoud. He contacted Hekmatyar by radio from Peshawar and urged him to consider a compromise with Massoud.[20]

Bin Laden and other Islamist mediators arranged a half-hour radio conversation directly between Massoud and Hekmatyar. The essential question was whether the two commanders would control Kabul peacefully as allies or fight it out. Hekmatyar kept making speeches to Massoud. "I must enter Kabul and let the green flags fly over the capital," Hekmatyar said. He kept announcing to Massoud that he would not allow communists to "pollute our victory," a pointed reference to Massoud's new partner, Dostum, a recent communist. Of course Hekmatyar had his own ex-communist allies.

An Arab journalist with Hekmatyar at Charasyab during the radio talk remembered Massoud as soothing, respectful. "Massoud would answer him and say, 'Engineer sahib, with all respect, Kabul has fallen. Kabul cannot be conquered twice. Kabul is in your reach, it is in your hand, Engineer sahib. Please. Come to Peshawar and come back to Kabul with the rest of our leaders. I will not enter Kabul until the rest of our leaders have arrived.'" But Hekmatyar had secretly prepared yet another coup attempt. Even as he talked by radio with Massoud, his forces moved toward the gates of Kabul. Green flags were attached to his tanks and his jeeps. The cars were washed so they would gleam triumphantly when Hekmatyar rolled into Kabul the next day. In Peshawar, Hekmatyar's spokesman admitted, "Hekmatyar can't agree to anything that includes Ahmed Shah Massoud."[21]

Bin Laden called Hekmatyar once more on the radio. "Go back with your brothers," bin Laden said. He asked Hekmatyar once again to consider a grand compromise, including Massoud. Hekmatyar ignored him, recalled the Arab journalist who was present. Hekmatyar had already negotiated the surrender of the Kabul headquarters of the Interior Ministry, a few blocks from the Afghan presidential palace. He dispatched his agents to Kabul that night. Hekmatyar went to bed believing that he would roll into the capital in triumph in the morning. He led prayers with the Arabs who had come to Charasyab. He recited verses from the Koran that had been recited by the Prophet after the conquering of Mecca.

"So we went to sleep that night, victorious," recalled the Arab journalist. "It was great. Hekmatyar was happy. Everybody at the camp was happy. And

I was dreaming that next morning, after prayer, my camera is ready, I will march with the victorious team into Kabul.

"Afghans are weird. They turn off the wireless when they go to sleep—as if war will stop. So they switched the wireless off, we all went to sleep, and we woke up early in the morning. Prayed the dawn prayer. Spirits were high. Hekmatyar also made a very long prayer. The sun comes up again, they turn on the wireless—and the bad news starts pouring in."

Convinced that Hekmatyar had no intention of compromising, Massoud had preempted him. The faction of the Afghan Communist Party that had agreed to surrender to him had seized the Kabul airport, a short march from the capital's main government buildings. Transport planes poured into Kabul carrying hundreds of Dostum's fierce Uzbek militiamen. They seized strategic buildings all across the Kabul valley. Hekmatyar's forces quickly grabbed a few buildings, but by the end of the first day's infiltration Massoud's positions in the city were far superior. He had formed a ring facing south toward Hekmatyar's main position. It was just like the games Massoud had played as a child on Ali Abad Mountain, above Kabul University: He divided his forces, encircled Hekmatyar's militia in the city, and squeezed.[22]

On the morning of Hekmatyar's imagined triumph, tank battles and street-to-street fighting erupted on Kabul's wide avenues. Fires burned on the grounds of the presidential palace. Najibullah sought shelter in a small, walled United Nations compound. He was now formally out of office and under house arrest. Hekmatyar never made it out of Charasyab.

Massoud entered Kabul triumphantly from the north on a tank strewn with flowers. That night hundreds of his mujahedin fired their assault rifles into the air in celebration, their tracer bullets lighting the sky like electric rain. By dawn the trajectory of the tracers had shifted from vertical to horizontal, however. The first Afghan war was over. The second had begun.

Massoud's Panjshiri forces and Dostum's hardened, youthful Uzbek militia pounded Hekmatyar's remnants from block to block until they fled south from Kabul after about a week. Angry and desperate, Hekmatyar began to lob rockets blindly at Kabul. It was the latest in a series of failures by Hekmatyar and Pakistani intelligence to win their coveted Afghan prize. Jalalabad, the Tanai coup attempt, the second Tanai coup attempt, and now this—Hekmatyar and ISI might have a reputation for ruthless ambition, but they had yet to prove themselves competent.

In Peshawar, Yahya Massoud met with his handler in British intelligence. "We were right," the British officer told him smugly. "Hekmatyar failed and Massoud succeeded."[23]

FOR ALL THE MONEY and time it had spent anticipating the day, the CIA played a small role in the fall of Kabul. In the two previous years the agency had facilitated massive arms transfers to Hekmatyar and some to Massoud. The CIA's deference to Pakistani intelligence ensured that Hekmatyar received far more cash and weaponry in the last phase than he would have otherwise. But the lobbying by Peter Tomsen and many others in Washington and Islamabad—including a few within the CIA—had resulted in substantial supplies being routed to Massoud as well. Just as he was preparing for Kabul's fall, Massoud had received heavy weapons in Panjshir over the road built by the U.S. Agency for International Development. His large stipends from the agency, even with their ups and downs during 1990, had provided Massoud with substantial cash at a time when Hekmatyar was reaping large donations from rich Saudi sheikhs and the Muslim Brotherhood. To that extent the CIA, pressed by Tomsen and members of Congress, had ultimately helped underwrite Massoud's final victory in Kabul.

It rapidly proved Pyrrhic. By 1992 there were more personal weapons in Afghanistan than in India and Pakistan combined. By some estimates more such weapons had been shipped into Afghanistan during the previous decade than to any other country in the world. The Soviet Union had sent between $36 billion and $48 billion worth of military equipment from the time of the Afghan communist revolution; the equivalent U.S., Saudi, and Chinese aid combined totaled between $6 billion and $12 billion. About five hundred thousand people in Kabul depended on coupons for food in 1992. In the countryside millions more lived with malnourishment, far from any reliable food source. Hekmatyar's frustration and his deep supply lines ensured that violence would continue.[24]

With the fall of Najibullah and the arrival of a rebel government in Kabul—albeit one immediately at war with itself—there was no need any longer for a U.S. ambassador to the resistance. Kabul was still much too dangerous to host an American ambassador to Afghanistan. The U.S. embassy building in the Afghan capital remained closed. Peter Tomsen was appointed to a new post managing U.S. policy in East Asia.

As he prepared to move on, Tomsen wrote two memos, classified Confidential. He was influenced by his old contacts in the Afghan resistance who now feared the future. Abdul Haq wrote to Tomsen during this period: "Afghanistan runs the risk of becoming 50 or more separate kingdoms. Foreign extremists may want to move in, buying houses and weapons. Afghanistan may become unique in becoming both a training ground and munitions dump for foreign terrorists and at the same time, the world's largest poppy field." Tomsen, too, worried that extremist governments would control Kabul in the future and that by withdrawing from the field, the United States was throwing away a chance to exercise a moderating influence. It was in Washington's interests to block "Islamic extremists' efforts to use Afghanistan as a training/staging base for terrorism in the region and beyond," he wrote on December 18, 1992. Why was America walking away from Afghanistan so quickly, with so little consideration given to the consequences? Tomsen wrote a few weeks later: "U.S. perseverance in maintaining our already established position in Afghanistan—at little cost—could significantly contribute to the favorable moderate outcome, which would: sideline the extremists, maintain a friendship with a strategically located friendly country, help us accomplish our other objectives in Afghanistan and the broader Central Asian region, e.g., narcotics, Stinger recovery, anti-terrorism. . . . We are in danger of throwing away the assets we have built up in Afghanistan over the last 10 years, at great expense. . . . Our stakes there are important, if limited, in today's geostrategic context. The danger is that we will lose interest and abandon our investment assets in Afghanistan, which straddles a region where we have precious few levers."[25]

Tomsen's memos marked a last gasp from the tiny handful of American diplomats and spies who argued for continued, serious engagement by the United States in Afghanistan.

There would not be an American ambassador or CIA station chief assigned directly to Afghanistan for nearly a decade, until late in the autumn of 2001.

13

"A Friend of Your Enemy"

DURING THE 1992 American presidential campaign, leaders of the Republican and Democratic parties made no mention of Afghanistan in their foreign policy platforms. As he sought reelection President George H. W. Bush spoke occasionally and vaguely about the continuing civil war between Hekmatyar and Massoud: "The heartbreak is on both sides, the tragedy is on both sides." Governor Bill Clinton of Arkansas, who focused his campaign on the weak American economy, was never quoted speaking about Afghanistan at all. Clinton devoted only 141 words to foreign affairs in his 4,200-word acceptance speech at the Democratic convention. Anthony Lake and the foreign policy team working for Clinton felt "very much apart from the center," as Lake put it. The center was domestic policy. Lake had written a book about post–Cold War battlefields and had authored passages on Afghanistan, but as the campaign unfolded, it "was a small blip" on his radar screen, as he recalled it.[1]

Clinton sometimes spoke articulately about the global challenges America faced now that the Soviet Union was gone. He and Bush both identified terrorism and drug trafficking as emblematic threats of a new, unstable era.

"The biggest nuclear threat of the 1990s will come from thugs and terrorists rather than the Soviets," Clinton said early in the campaign. He wanted "strong special operations forces to deal with terrorist threats." But these insights came in fleeting mentions.[2]

Clinton had never traveled to Central Asia or the Indian subcontinent. His knowledge of the region was based on impressions. He was intrigued by the recently deposed Pakistani prime minister, Benazir Bhutto, who had been at Oxford University when Clinton attended as a Rhodes Scholar. Clinton had seen her in passing and was riveted by her beauty, poise, and reputation as a formidable debater, he told colleagues. His friends knew that he was also fascinated by India. He had no similar connection with Afghanistan. During his first months in office Clinton did not think of Afghanistan as a major base for international terrorism, he told colleagues years later. He was more seriously concerned about state sponsors of terrorism, such as Iraq and Iran, and about Shiite groups such as Hezbollah and Islamic Jihad, which had killed dozens of Americans during the 1980s. Clinton knew nothing of bin Laden during the first few years of his presidency. As for Afghanistan's war, the issue languished mainly from inertia, Lake said later; it had not been a major issue in the late Bush administration, either.[3]

After his election victory Clinton set up transition offices in Little Rock, Arkansas. Robert Gates, now the CIA director, installed a temporary CIA station—replete with security guards and secure communications—in a Comfort Inn near the Little Rock airport. Gates had decided to leave the CIA, but he agreed to stay on to help familiarize Clinton with intelligence issues and to give the new administration time to choose a new director.

Gates flew in to meet the president-elect at the Governor's Mansion. He found Clinton exhausted, drinking copious amounts of coffee to stay awake, but engaged. Gates and Clinton were both natural analysts, sifters and synthesizers of complex data. Gates felt that Clinton did not have the anti-intelligence, anti-CIA biases of Jimmy Carter or Michael Dukakis, the 1988 Democratic presidential nominee. Clinton consumed CIA analyses voraciously during the transition months. Gates dispatched his deputy director for intelligence to the station at the Comfort Inn. They began to provide the President's Daily Brief to Clinton almost immediately and commissioned a series of special intelligence studies at Clinton's request. The CIA quickly became the only department in the federal government whose senior officers were seeing the president-elect face-to-face every day. Gates became optimistic that President Clinton and the CIA would get along exceptionally well.[4]

He was wrong. The problems began with the selection of a new director. The choice was postponed until late in the transition process. Conservative Democrats on Capitol Hill urged Clinton to appoint someone with a right-leaning reputation to balance the liberals in his Cabinet. The Clinton team telephoned James Woolsey, a fifty-one-year-old Oklahoman, and told him to fly immediately to Little Rock. Woolsey was a lean, dome-headed man with soft gray eyes and a sharp, insistent voice. He had met Clinton only once, at a campaign fund-raiser held at the home of Washington socialite Pamela Harriman. But Clinton and Woolsey had common roots. Like the president-elect, Woolsey had risen from the rural southwest to win a Rhodes scholarship and graduate from Yale Law School. As a young army reserve lieutenant Woolsey had campaigned against the Vietnam War. Later, he had drifted to the political right, aligning himself with hard-line anticommunist Democrats such as Senator Henry "Scoop" Jackson.[5]

Woolsey spent several hours with Clinton at the Governor's Mansion. They talked at length about University of Arkansas and University of Oklahoma football, good places to fish in the Ozarks, and, at less length, their visions for the future of the CIA. At one point Clinton said that he really did not think the CIA director should be a policy adviser to the president. Woolsey agreed that the director "ought to just call the intelligence straight."[6]

Their meeting ended with no mention of a job offer, but the next day Warren Christopher called Woolsey at his hotel and summoned him to a press conference.

"Does the president want me to be the director of the CIA?" Woolsey asked.

"Sure. Just come over to the press conference, and we'll get it sorted out." Woolsey asked Christopher to be certain about the job offer. Christopher stuck his head in Clinton's office, came back on the phone, and said, "Yeah, that's what he wants."

In a living room of the mansion Woolsey found the Clintons, the Gores, Secretary of Defense nominee Les Aspin, Secretary of State nominee Warren Christopher, Tony Lake, Samuel L. "Sandy" Berger, and several political aides trying to anticipate questions they would hear from the press when Clinton introduced his new national security team. The president-elect's media specialists worried that reporters would accuse Clinton of appointing a bunch of Carter administration retreads. Woolsey could understand why, since "we were, in fact, a bunch of Carter administration retreads." Trying to be helpful, Woolsey mentioned that he had served in the Bush administration, leading a team that negotiated a reduction of conventional armed forces in Europe.

Clinton's press aide looked at Woolsey. "Admiral, I didn't know you served in the Bush administration." Dumbfounded, Woolsey pointed out that he had never been an admiral, only an army captain.[7]

The scene signaled the pattern of Clinton's relationship with the CIA during his first term: distant, mutually ill-informed, and strangely nonchalant. At Langley the change arrived abruptly. Outgoing President Bush, who had served briefly as CIA director during the Ford administration, had been the agency's most attentive White House patron in decades. He invited senior clandestine service officers to Christmas parties and to weekends at Camp David. He drew agency analysts and operators into key decision-making meetings. Within months of Clinton's inauguration the CIA's senior officers understood that they had shifted from being on the inside of a presidency to being almost completely on the outside.

They became puzzled and then angry. They interpreted Clinton's indifference in varied ways. Thomas Twetten, who was running the Directorate of Operations, saw Clinton as "personally afraid of any connection with the CIA," partly from long-standing suspicions of the agency and partly because he wanted to avoid immersing himself in foreign policy problems.[8] The agency's case officer population had grown more Republican during the 1980s, and many of these officers saw Clinton through a partisan lens. There remained many Democrats at the agency and it was difficult to generalize, but a substantial number of CIA officers began to see Clinton as softheaded and hostile to the intelligence services. Some of the agency's more conservative case officers were Vietnam veterans who resented Clinton's decision to evade the draft and who noted that both his new CIA director, Woolsey, and his national security adviser, Lake, had noisily protested the Vietnam War.

For their part, Clinton, Lake, and others in the new national security cabinet radiated a self-conscious nervousness around the Pentagon and the CIA. They seemed to avoid direct interaction. Hardly anyone from the CIA was ever invited to the White House, and Clinton did not visit Langley, even for major events such as a memorial for CIA officers killed in the line of duty. American defense and intelligence spending contracted after the Soviet Union's demise, beginning in the Bush administration and continuing under Clinton. The CIA's budgetary position was aggravated by its weak relations with the White House.

Woolsey himself got off to a troubled start. In an agency as large and secretive as the CIA, with so many career officers, a new director could have only limited influence. Yet the director had three crucial jobs that no one else could perform. He had to cultivate a personal relationship with the president of the United States, who alone could authorize CIA covert action. He had to massage the two intelligence committees in Congress, which wrote the agency's budget and continually reviewed its operations. And he had to keep up morale among the Langley rank and file. Within months of his arrival Woolsey had pulled off a stunning triple play of failure, some of the agency's senior officers felt. Woolsey forged strong connections with some CIA officers at Langley, especially those involved with technical and satellite intelligence collection, Woolsey's main professional focus. But he alienated many others, especially those in the Directorate of Operations. While awaiting Senate confirmation, Woolsey consulted his acquaintance Duane Clarridge, founder of the CIA's Counterterrorist Center. Clarridge concluded from their talk that Woolsey was "paranoid" about being "co-opted" by the insiders at the CIA, especially the career espionage officers in the Directorate of Operations. Some officers there saw Woolsey as aloof and untrusting. Worse, in closed hearings on Capitol Hill, Woolsey picked early fights with key senators who controlled the CIA's funding. And worst of all, Woolsey alienated President Clinton, the CIA's most important client.[9]

Woolsey did not have a private meeting with the president during Clinton's first year in office. Typically, CIA directors have an opportunity to brief the president first thing each morning, presenting the latest intelligence about global crises. But Clinton was a voracious consumer of information with scant patience for briefers who sat before him to read out documents that he could more efficiently read on his own time. The president was a night owl, prowling the White House residence into the early morning hours, reading briefs and working the telephone, sometimes waking members of Congress or journalists with 2 A.M. phone calls. In the morning he was often rough and slow to reenergize. Many of the senior White House staff avoided him until he came fully awake. Clinton's national security team, led by Tony Lake, found Woolsey a grating character: arrogant, tin-eared, and brittle. They didn't want to sit and chat with him in the chilly dawn any more than Clinton did. Woolsey met weekly with Lake, his deputy Sandy Berger, and Secretary of State Warren Christopher, but the White House team concluded that Woolsey was too combative. They found him too quick to argue his opinions on an issue and unable to calmly analyze all the available intelligence. Woolsey was a bulldog for his own point of view, especially if the issue involved the merits of technical intelligence.[10]

Try as he might, Woolsey could not get a meeting with the president. When a pilot on an apparent suicide mission crashed a single-engine Cessna into the south lawn of the White House in September 1994, the joke quickly circulated that it was Woolsey trying to get an appointment with Clinton. The joke angered Woolsey when he first heard it, but in time he became so accustomed to his pariah status that he began to tell it on himself.

Woolsey saw the White House as totally uninterested in foreign affairs. There was no appetite for strategy, no disciplined process for thinking about the big issues, he concluded. The Cold War had been won, Boris Yeltsin in Russia was a friend of America, and the Clinton team had decided not to be too tough on China. The White House's one creative aspiration in foreign policy, Woolsey thought, was the global pursuit of free trade, as evidenced by the personal effort Clinton had put into passage of the North American Free Trade Agreement. Otherwise, Woolsey interpreted his inability to see the president as much more than a broken personal connection. Clinton and Lake, Woolsey believed, both saw the CIA as just one more instrument for shaping domestic politics. In their minds, as Woolsey saw it, the agency's job was to help manage crises such as Bosnia, Haiti, and Somalia with an eye toward minimizing their political fallout in the United States. As the months passed, Woolsey grew not only alienated by the Clinton White House but disgusted by what he saw as its crass emphasis on electoral politics.[11]

Unencumbered by presidential direction or oversight, Woolsey was free to push the CIA in whatever direction he chose. As he settled into the director's office he concentrated on a campaign to refurbish the nation's spy satellite system. During the 1980s, as an arms control negotiator who depended on covert satellite photography to monitor adversaries, Woolsey came to believe that America's spy satellite capability had decayed dangerously. He understood the issues well. At Langley he put together a classified slide show that demonstrated how urgent the problem had become and what investments were required to fix it. Woolsey presented the spy satellite briefing again and again at the White House, in Congress, and at the Pentagon, lobbying hard for new funding. He was persuasive.[12] By what he chose to emphasize he also signaled that the CIA's major challenges lay in technical programs, not in human spying. By leaving the CIA alone, the White House had limited means to evaluate whether Woolsey's emphasis on technical intelligence, as opposed to human intelligence, was the right one or not.

AS WOOLSEY SETTLED INTO OFFICE, two young men of Pakistani origin living separately in the United States worked through the last logistical problems of their terrorist conspiracies. One of them lived with a roommate in a garden apartment in suburban Virginia. The other bunked with acquaintances in suburban New Jersey. The two had never met, but they had much in common. Both grew up in large, relatively privileged families with roots in the impoverished Pakistani province of Baluchistan, along the Afghan frontier. They were the sons of ambitious and hardworking fathers who could afford schooling and travel abroad. Yet both had also endured precarious, disrupted lives. They moved abruptly between traditional Baluch households, with their strict codes of sexual and family honor, and secular, freewheeling cultures in Europe and the United States. Both had been exposed during these years to passionate preaching by radical Islamic clerics who denounced the United States as an oppressor of Muslims. Both drifted away from their families and became enraged by the violence they watched between Israelis and Palestinians on satellite television. Each had decided during 1992—without awareness of the other—to organize a violent attack on a prominent target in the United States. As they planned their strikes, both spent long hours thinking about the political and theological bases for their actions. They reached slightly different conclusions about the legitimacy of their violence against civilians, but their creeds were remarkably similar.

Mir Amal Kasi was then twenty-eight years old. He had arrived in the United States in 1991. His father owned hotels and expansive orchards in and around Quetta, the capital of Baluchistan, only a few hours' drive from Afghanistan. Kasi was the only child of his father's second wife, who died when Kasi was nineteen years old. He earned a master's degree in English literature at Baluchistan University in 1989. Like many in frontier Pakistan he carried a sidearm. After his father's death that year from a heart attack, he began to travel abroad, first to Germany, then to the United States, where he took a job at a suburban courier company. Alone in Virginia, orphaned, and half a world from home, he spent hours watching news from the Middle East on CNN: the Gulf War, the subsequent upheaval in Iraq, the conflict between Israelis and Palestinians. He told his roommate that he was going to do "something big," maybe at the White House, maybe at the Israeli embassy in Washington. Eventually Kasi concluded that a better target would be the CIA, whose secluded entrance he passed regularly along the dual carriageway of Virginia's Route 123. Kasi believed that the agency was directly responsible for the deaths of many Muslims. From a Virginia gun shop he acquired an AK-47 assault rifle. Kasi expected to confront police in a shootout during his attack, but just in case he escaped, he bought an airline ticket home to Pakistan. On the day before his scheduled flight, he awoke in his garden apartment, pulled on a tan overcoat, loaded his weapon and five hundred rounds of ammunition into his brown station wagon, and drove to the entrance of the CIA.[13]

It was clear and cold that early morning of January 25, 1993. Cars lined up at the headquarters gate, their warm exhaust smoke billowing in steamy clouds. Kasi pulled his car into a left-hand-turn lane, stopped, swung his door open, and stepped into the road. He saw a man driving a Volkswagen Golf and fired at him through the car's rear window, then walked around and shot him three more times. Frank Darling, twenty-eight, an officer in the clandestine service, died on the floor of his car, his wife seated beside him. Kasi walked down the line and fired at four other men, killing one, Lansing Bennett, sixty-six, a doctor who analyzed the health of world leaders for the Directorate of Intelligence. Kasi looked around. He could see no more men in the cars nearby. He had decided before his attack that he would not shoot at women. He jumped back into his station wagon, drove a few miles to a McLean park, and hid there for ninety minutes. When no one came looking for him, he returned to his apartment and stuffed his AK-47 under the living room couch. He drove to a Days Inn hotel and checked in.[14] The next day he flew to Pakistan and disappeared.

The man who would become known as Ramzi Yousef was younger, then only twenty-four years old. His family, too, had roots in the Pakistani province of Baluchistan. Like hundreds of thousands of other Pakistanis seeking opportunity in the oil boom era, Yousef's father, an engineer, had migrated to the Persian Gulf. The Bedouin Arabs in Saudi Arabia and Kuwait, enriched by the oil bonanza, were thin in number and poorly trained in the technical skills required to construct a modern economy. They recruited fellow Muslims—drivers, cooks, welders, bricklayers, engineers, doctors, pilots—from impoverished neighboring countries such as Pakistan. For Baluchis such as Yousef's father the Gulf's pay scales delivered a middle-class urban life. He could send his children to private school and even European universities.

The Baluchis had been travelers and migrants for centuries, staunchly independent. They were historical cousins of the Pashtuns, with whom they mixed freely, blurring ethnic and tribal lines. Their population spilled indifferently across the borders drawn by imperial mapmakers. In the early 1990s large numbers of Baluchis lived contiguously in three countries: southwest Pakistan, southeast Iran, and southeast Afghanistan. In Pakistan their tribal leaders dominated politics and provincial government in Baluchistan, a vast but sparsely populated desert and mountain territory that ran along the

Afghan and Iranian borders and south to the Arabian Sea. As with the Pashtuns, the Baluchis adhered to very conservative tribal honor codes that defined women as property and revenge as justice.

Ramzi Yousef was born in Kuwait on April 27, 1968, as Abdul Basit Mahmoud Abdul Karim. He grew up in the tiny oil-addled emirate in the great years of its petrodollar expansion. In the first twenty years of his life Yousef saw Kuwait City transformed from a trash-blown minor port into a neon-blinking sprawl of marble shopping malls and luxury car dealerships. Like Kasi, Yousef trafficked among worlds, belonging to none. He lived among the ramshackle colonies of Pakistani, Palestinian, Egyptian, and Bangladeshi guest workers, cauldrons of resentment about issues near and far. He spoke Arabic, Baluch, Urdu, and English. He was a teenager in Kuwait when Abdullah Azzam preached for alms in the emirate's wealthy mosques, delivering fiery sermons about the Afghan jihad. Azzam's message was everywhere—on underground cassette tapes, in newspapers, in pamphlets—and it echoed sermons delivered by members of Yousef's own family. His great-uncle was a leader at a suburban mosque attended by Pakistani guest workers. After attending primary and secondary school in Kuwait, Yousef was sent to a technical institute in Swansea, Wales, between 1986 and 1989, to obtain a degree in electrical engineering and computer-aided electronics. It was the sort of practical English education that many upwardly mobile Pakistani families living in the Gulf wanted for their sons, so that the rising generation could expand the family's income in the big Arab oil cities. What Yousef made of coeducational campus life in Wales isn't known. His uncle, Khalid Sheikh Mohammed, was active in the Muslim Brotherhood and worked with the Saudi-backed Afghan leader Sayyaf in Pakistan. When he returned to the Gulf from Britain, Yousef found a job as a communications engineer in the National Computer Center of Kuwait's Ministry of Planning, a government sinecure that could ensure a comfortable life.[15]

A year later his family's upward trajectory came to an abrupt halt. Saddam Hussein's army invaded Kuwait on August 2, 1990, sacked the city, and sent thousands of foreign guest workers into hurried exile. Yousef's family fled to Quetta. They were refugees, albeit relatively wealthy ones. At some point after their return Yousef's parents slipped across the border and set up residence in Iran's province of Baluchistan.[16]

Yousef was a tinkerer. As a young unattached man with an advanced degree from Britain, he was ripe for a marriage arranged by his extended family. But Yousef was not ready to settle down. He gravitated toward another respectable vocation: He volunteered for jihad. He was an admirer of the anti-communist mujahedin. Two of his uncles had been martyred in battle against the Soviets. Yousef had his own pedigree: He was an Arabic speaker from the Persian Gulf with access to the transnational networks of Arab Islamist volunteers.

One of his uncles offered a connection to the Peshawar Islamist world: He was regional manager for a Kuwait-based charity called the Committee for Islamic Appeal. Yousef crossed into Afghanistan in late 1990 for training at an entry-level jihadist camp called Khalden, run by and for Arab mujahedin, not Afghans. He trained for about six months. He learned weapons tactics, basic explosives, and military maneuvers. There were about four or five dozen other Arab Islamists at the camp who were training to return to their home countries in the Middle East. Yousef later moved to a graduate-level camp for bomb makers, where he could apply his skills in electronics to the art of remote-controlled explosives. He learned the bombing techniques originally developed in the border-straddling guerrilla sabotage camps of Pakistani intelligence, which had been supplied with timing devices and plastic explosives by the CIA. He carried out a few attacks in Afghanistan, not because he sought to participate in the Afghan civil war, he said later, but mainly to experiment.

Early in 1991 he shifted back to Pakistan and married. During eighteen months of ensuing domesticity, he was in regular touch with radical Islamists along the Afghan border. He may have been in Peshawar during the spring of 1992 when bin Laden returned briefly from Saudi Arabia to Pakistan to participate with Prince Turki in an effort to mediate the Afghan civil war. But Yousef and bin Laden could not have been very close: Yousef had little money, and in the two years he lived along the Afghan border, he does not appear to have acquired a wealthy patron.[17]

In September 1992, Yousef flew to New York on a false Iraqi passport he had purchased in Peshawar for $100. His partner, Ahmed Ajaj, packed bomb-making manuals and materials into checked luggage. Yousef said later that his plan initially was to see what the United States was like, acquire an American passport, select targets to bomb, and then return to Pakistan to raise funds for his operation. But once in New York he decided to go forward with an attack immediately, despite his limited means. He may have had the World Trade Center in mind all along, but he seems to have chosen it firmly as a target only after arriving in New York. He decided that he should construct his bomb so that its force would wreck the central beam of one of the center's 110-story twin towers. Yousef hoped that as the first tower fell it would topple the second building. He calculated this would cause about 250,000 deaths, which he believed was roughly the number of casualties caused by America's atomic bombings of Hiroshima and Nagasaki during World War II.

Although his father was a Baluchi, he had Palestinian heritage on his mother's side. He considered attacking Israeli targets but found them extremely difficult because of high security. If it was impossible to attack the enemy directly, then the next best thing was to "attack a friend of your enemy," as he put it later.[18]

Yousef connected with Islamists in the New York area, a loose network of radicals who followed Sheikh Omar Abdal Rahman, a blind Egyptian preacher who had known Abdullah Azzam and other Muslim Brotherhood–inspired Islamists in Peshawar during the 1980s. Members of Rahman's group were in telephone contact with al Qaeda–related safehouses in Peshawar, but none of them could afford the materials needed for a bomb powerful enough to fell the two towers of the World Trade Center, to Yousef's regret.

On February 26, 1993, just a month after Kasi's highly publicized attack at the CIA, Yousef led his confederates in a two-vehicle convoy from Brooklyn to the B-2 level of an underground garage at the World Trade Center. Yousef set an electronic timer on the bomb and jumped into a rented red Chevrolet Corsica. The materials needed to construct Yousef's bomb cost about $400. When it detonated at 12:18 P.M., it killed six people lunching in a cafeteria above it, injured one thousand more who worked several floors higher, and caused just over $500 million in estimated damage. That night Yousef boarded a Pakistan International Airlines flight to Karachi and disappeared.

He mailed letters claiming responsibility to New York newspapers. The letters claimed the attack for the "Liberation Army, Fifth Battalion" and issued three political demands: an end to all U.S. aid to Israel, an end to diplomatic relations with Israel, and a pledge to end interference "with any of the Middle East countries [*sic*] interior affairs." If these demands were not met, Yousef and his colleagues wrote, the group would "continue to execute our missions against military and civilians [*sic*] targets in and out of the United States. This will include some potential Nuclear targets." The Liberation Army had 150 "suicidal soldiers ready to go ahead," the letters claimed. "The terrorism that Israel practices (which is supported by America) must be faced with a similar one." The American people should know "that their civilians who got killed are not better than those who are getting killed by the American weapons and support."[19]

For a terrorist sermon composed by a graduate of Arab jihad training camps in Afghanistan, his letter struck remarkably secular political themes. It made no references to Islam at all. Its specific demands might have been issued by Palestinian Marxists. Its talk of retaliation and eye-for-an-eye revenge echoed Baluch and Pashtun tribal codes. It seemed to define America as an enemy solely because of its support for Israel. Yousef had never been a serious student of theology. His letter and his later statements exuded a technologist's arrogance, a murderous cool. His confederates in the World Trade Center attack had been involved in the conspiracy to murder Rabbi Meir Kahane, founder of the militant Jewish Defense League. These New York residents in Yousef's cabal focused largely on anti-Israeli causes; their outlook may have shaped some of the letter's themes. At the same time Yousef and his confederates allied themselves with Muslim Brotherhood–inspired Islamists such as Sheikh Rahman and bin Laden. Above all the bomb maker in him searched for the spectacular. His lazy list of political demands may have reflected an essential pyromania. He wanted a big bang; he wanted to watch one tall building knock down another.

An earlier, discarded draft of Yousef's demand letter, found by American investigators on a computer belonging to one of his co-conspirators, added a warning which captured Yousef's frustration that he could not afford a potent enough bomb. "Unfortunately, our calculations were not very accurate this time" read the deleted sentence. "However, we promise you that next time, it will be very precise and WTC will continue to be one of our targets unless our demands have been met."[20]

THE CIA'S COUNTERTERRORIST CENTER immediately established a seven-day, twenty-four-hour task force to collect intelligence about the World Trade Center bombing. It set up a similar task force to hunt for Mir Amal Kasi. For weeks the sixth-floor cubicles at Langley hummed with activity and urgency. Woolsey issued a worldwide call for all-source intelligence collection about the bombing. The National Security Agency ramped up its telephone intercept network and combed its databases for clues. The NSA's listeners searched the airwaves for suggestive fragments: a foreign intelligence agent talking about the case in celebratory tones, or a foreign head of government hinting at credit in a private meeting. CIA stations worldwide reached out to their paid agents for reports and rumors about who had organized the New York attack. Weeks passed, but nothing of substance came in. The NSA could not find credible suggestions of a hidden hand in the attack.[21]

There was a strong presumption within the CIA that a foreign government lay behind the bombing and perhaps the Langley assault as well. Yousef and Kasi had such murky personal histories, National Security Adviser Tony Lake recalled, that it took a long time for their biographies to come into focus. State-sponsored terrorism had been the pattern throughout the 1980s: Whatever their declared cause, successful terrorists usually sought money, passports, asylum, or technical support from radical governments such as Iran or Libya.

This time Iraq led the list of suspects. During the Gulf War, Saddam Hussein's Baath Party government had secretly dispatched professional two-man terrorist teams to strike American targets. It was a clumsy operation. The Iraqi agents were issued passports with sequential numbers. The CIA soon intercepted most of the agents before they could act and worked with local governments to have the Iraqis arrested or deported. But the operation had signaled Saddam's active interest in striking American targets through terrorist attacks. Later in 1993, Saddam's intelligence service tried to assassinate former president Bush during a visit to Kuwait, and evidence emerged that one of Yousef's confederates had flown to Baghdad after the World Trade Center bombing.

Iran and Libya also seemed possible suspects in the World Trade Center case. The Counterterrorist Center staffed a permanent branch targeting Hezbollah. It had files of evidence about Tehran's sponsorship of terrorist strikes by Hezbollah's Shiite cadres, who saw themselves at war with Israel. The CIA's analysts viewed Iran as the world's most active sponsor of terrorism. "It was *the* priority," Lake recalled. Sudan, where an Islamist government had recently taken power in a coup, also seemed a possibility. Working with early, fragmentary evidence from informers and from the World Trade Center crime scene that seemed to connect the plot to Sudan's government, the Federal Bureau of Investigation initially called its investigation "Sudafed," meaning "Sudan Federal."[22]

This scattered list of suspects reflected the fractured character of terrorism worldwide. There had been fifteen officially designated terrorist incidents on United States soil between 1990 and 1992. Many involved attacks by Puerto Rican nationalists; one involved an Iranian Marxist group; others were carried out by American extremists. Globally the most active terrorist groups included Maoists in Peru and Tamil separatists in Sri Lanka. The pattern seemed to be that there was no pattern.

The CIA's Counterterrorist Center had evolved into a different organization from the one Duane Clarridge and Bill Casey had envisioned amid the

hostage crises of 1986. In the years following the Iran-Contra scandal, with
CIA operators facing trial for perjury and other crimes, it was much harder to
win support in Washington for clandestine or preemptive strikes against terrorists. The Counterterrorist Center remained close to the CIA's clandestine
service, and it continued to run risky espionage operations to collect intelligence, but there was little appetite at the CIA or the White House for covert
paramilitary operations, either in the Bush administration or the early Clinton
administration. More and more the Counterterrorist Center moved from operations to analysis. It was also under heavy budgetary pressure. As they investigated the World Trade Center bombing and the Kasi murders, the center's
managers attended a succession of budget reduction meetings. There were no
layoffs, but the center's resources shrank steadily. When an analyst or operator quit or retired, he or she often could not be replaced because of budget
constraints.[23] No more than one hundred people worked at the CIA's Counterterrorist Center during this period. They were divided into about a dozen
branches. They still focused heavily on secular terrorist groups such as Abu
Nidal. One branch tracked Islamic extremism in the mainstream Sunni Muslim world, but until 1993 it concentrated primarily on the violent Islamic radicals who challenged Algeria's socialist government.[24]

Washington's broader counterterrorist bureaucracy in 1993 was dispersed,
plagued by interagency rivalries, and fraying under budgetary pressure. The
State Department's counterterrorism office, on paper a focal point for policy,
was in a state of near chaos, wracked by infighting, leadership turnover, and
budget cuts. The National Security Council had yet to issue any formal directive about which government agency should take the lead in a case like the
World Trade Center bombing or how different agencies should work together. Early draft proposals about those issues sat at the White House unresolved for nearly two years.[25] The Federal Bureau of Investigation, meanwhile,
led by Louis Freeh, pushed to expand its role in criminal cases with international connections, including terrorism cases. Freeh wanted to place FBI
agents in U.S. embassies worldwide. Some CIA officers resisted the FBI's
global expansion, seeing it as an incursion into the agency's turf. Even those
at Langley who believed the CIA could profit by partnering with the FBI were
uncertain how the new system was supposed to work in detail.

One basic unresolved question was whether to tackle terrorism as a national security problem—as a kind of war—or as a law enforcement problem,
with police and prosecutors in the lead. In some cases terrorists looked like
enemy soldiers. At other times they were easy to dismiss as common criminals. Their sometimes spectacular media-conscious attacks might generate

widespread fear and draw intense scrutiny, but the actual impact of terrorism on American society was minimal. Americans were still much more likely to die from bee stings than from terrorist strikes during the early 1990s. In that respect it made more sense to treat terrorism as a law enforcement problem. Prosecuting and jailing a terrorist as an ordinary murderer effectively dismissed his claims to political legitimacy. This seemed to many American national security thinkers a more rational reply to terrorists than waging a paramilitary war or treating some half-educated Marxist thug with the dignity accorded to enemy soldiers.

By the time the Clinton administration settled into office, this legalistic approach to terrorism was well established within the American bureaucracy. In 1995 when Clinton at last made a decision about his antiterrorism policy, he formally designated the FBI as the lead agency in terrorism cases where Americans were victims. Clinton's relationship with Louis Freeh and the FBI was perhaps even worse than his relationship with Woolsey and the CIA. Clinton seemed to regard Freeh as a self-righteous Boy Scout drone, and the White House political team resented the FBI's role in what they saw as trivial, politically motivated investigations. Still, Clinton was a Yale Law School graduate, a former law professor, and a deep believer in the principles of the American legal system. As a matter of policy Clinton sought to cloak American power with the legitimacy of international law wherever possible. Emphasizing police work and courtroom prosecutions against terrorists seemed both a practical and principled approach.

The CIA did not typically work inside the American legal system. The agency was chartered by an American law—the National Security Act of 1947—and its employees were subject to prosecution in the United States if they defied orders, carried out unauthorized operations, or lied under oath. But the CIA's espionage and paramilitary operations overseas were conducted in secret and were not subject to review by American courts. CIA operators routinely burglarized foreign embassies to obtain intelligence. They paid warlords and murderers for inside information about American adversaries. The intelligence they collected often could not withstand scrutiny in an American courtroom. Nor did Congress *want* the CIA to participate in prosecuting criminals inside the United States. The CIA was created to prevent another Pearl Harbor. But in the aftermath of a catastrophic war against Nazism, Congress also sought to protect the American people from the rise of anything like Hitler's Gestapo, a secret force that combined spying and police methods. The CIA was therefore prohibited from spying on Americans or using intelligence it collected abroad to support directly criminal prosecutions in the American court system.[26]

Prosecutors and police, including the FBI, were also discouraged from sharing with the CIA leads or evidence they collected in domestic criminal cases. In many cases if an FBI agent or federal prosecutor passed along to the CIA files or witness statements obtained during a terrorism investigation before a grand jury—no matter how important that evidence might be to American national security—he or she could go to jail.

The FBI's hermetic culture had become infamous by the early 1990s: FBI agents would not tell local police what they were doing, were deeply reluctant to work on interagency teams, and would withhold crucial evidence even from other FBI agents. There were FBI agents stationed inside the CIA's Counterterrorist Center to aid information exchange, and in some respects the FBI's relations with the CIA were better than its relations with many other government agencies. Even so, after the World Trade Center bombing, as the FBI began to communicate with the CIA about Islamist terrorism cases, its agents carefully followed the laws banning disclosure of grand jury evidence.[27]

All of this inhibited the CIA's reaction to the World Trade Center attack. Since 1989 the FBI had been running paid informants inside circles of Islamic radicals in New York and New Jersey. In 1990, FBI agents carted away forty-seven boxes of documents and training manuals from the home of El Sayyid Nosair, Rabbi Meir Kahane's assassin. The FBI did not translate the material from Arabic into English for two years, and even then it did not share with the CIA crucial evidence about the terrorists' international network. The documents provided rich details about Afghan training camps and the growth of al Qaeda along the Afghan border and throughout the Middle East. Osama bin Laden's name surfaced in this initial FBI investigation because a relative of Nosair traveled to Saudi Arabia and received money from bin Laden to pay for Nosair's defense lawyers. The CIA was not told.[28] The CIA's analysts only learned about the full richness of the FBI's files several years after the World Trade Center bombing. National Security Council files from 1993 record at least one meeting between Woolsey and Lake at which bin Laden was discussed as a terrorist financier worthy of attention, but he was not a focus of the World Trade Center investigation. A CIA paper circulated on April 2, 1993, described bin Laden as an "independent actor [who] sometimes works with other individuals or governments" to promote "militant Islamic causes." The agency also continued to report on the Afghan training camps where bin Laden sometimes appeared. An issue of the classified National Intelligence Daily reported on April 20 that hundreds of Islamist militants had passed through the camps during the previous twelve months. In September, Langley cabled CIA stations worldwide to assess the vulnerabilities of bin Laden's network and in November the agency identified a series of bin Laden–related targets for further intelligence collection. Still, there was no clear picture during 1993 of what role bin Laden played, if any, in violent operations.[29]

Like the CIA's analysts, FBI agents were slow to see the jihadists emerging as an independent transnational force. They were slow to allocate resources to study and combat Sunni Islamic radicalism in general. They saw Shiite Iran as the primary fountainhead of religiously motivated terrorism. "Did we screw up, in retrospect?" asked Clinton's national security adviser, Tony Lake, years later, speaking of this broad array of problems. "Of course." Poorly understood and lightly challenged, the Afghanistan-spawned Islamist cells began to spread.[30]

"Maintain a Prudent Distance"

P AUL PILLAR ARRIVED AS CHIEF of analysis at the CIA's Counterterrorist Center six weeks after the World Trade Center bombing. He
was a tall, lanky man with a nervous blink and the careful, articulate voice of
a university professor. A U.S. army officer in Vietnam, he had degrees from
Dartmouth and Oxford, and a doctorate from Princeton. Fast-tracked in
management and intelligence analysis after he joined the CIA, he served as
executive assistant to CIA director William Webster, a position often set aside
at Langley for rising stars. Pillar reflected the high-minded traditions of the
CIA's analytical wing, the Directorate of Intelligence. He was not an Arabist,
but he had studied political Islam and the Middle East. He was a manager and
an intellectual, an author of books and academic journal articles. From within
the Counterterrorist Center he would emerge during the next six years as one
of the CIA's most influential terrorism analysts.[1]

Initially, Pillar was as stumped as the FBI was by the World Trade Center
case. The first group of suspects arrested in the New York area were a diverse, bumbling crew. It was easier to imagine them as pawns of some hidden
foreign government plot than as an independent terrorist cell. Gradually, as
the FBI's evidence accumulated, a new theory of the case began to emerge.

Informants quickly identified the blind Egyptian preacher Sheikh Rahman as a source of inspiration for the World Trade Center attack and several thwarted bombings of New York landmarks. The CIA's analysts began to look more closely at cross-border Islamist radicalism emanating from Egypt and its neighbors.

An Islamic political revival had swept through the Arab countries of North Africa during the previous four years. A violent offshoot of the Muslim Brotherhood in Egypt, the Islamic Group, had opened an assassination and bombing campaign against the secular government of Hosni Mubarak. The Islamic Group's cadres hailed from the impoverished, long-radicalized Upper Nile region, and their campaign revived a decades-old tradition of Islamist violence in Egypt. But the group also seemed to be newly stimulated by returning veterans from the Afghan jihad. The same was true in Algeria. There the Muslim Brotherhood–linked Islamic Salvation Front captured the political imagination of Algeria's poor and, increasingly, its angry middle classes, who saw their secular, socialist leaders as corrupt and politically exhausted. After the government aborted a 1991 election because it appeared the Islamists would win, young militants, some of them veterans of the Afghan jihad, went underground and formed a new violent resistance called the Armed Islamic Group. They opened a terror campaign against the government. Hundreds of Algerian civilians died each month in bombings, massacres, and assassinations carried out by both sides.[2]

Pillar and other CIA analysts, along with station chiefs in Cairo, Algiers, and Tunis, studied and debated these insurgencies intently in the months after the World Trade Center attack. They asked: What was the connection between these violent, national Islamist groups and terrorists who might threaten the United States or its allies? What policy should the United States adopt toward the Egyptian and Algerian Islamists? Should it regard all Islamic fundamentalists as dangerous, or should Washington reach out to the peaceful wings of the Muslim Brotherhood, while attempting to isolate and repress its violent offshoots? Should the United States encourage democratic elections even in countries such as Algeria or Egypt where the Islamists might win? How could Washington be sure that Islamists would continue with a democratic system after they won power?

Pillar and his colleagues saw the fall of the Soviet Union in 1991 and the fall of the Shah of Iran in 1979 as models of political failure from which they hoped to learn. In both of those historical cases corrupt, failing governments with little credibility had faced popular rebellions, tried to reform themselves, and collapsed anyway. Pillar thought the lesson might be that you had to avoid half measures: A government under violent siege should either strike back ruthlessly or open up its political system completely. Still, he felt the Algerians had made a terrible mistake by canceling their election and driving the Islamists underground. They had strengthened the extremists and isolated the Muslim Brotherhood's peaceful politicians.

Senior intelligence analysts and policy makers at the State Department and the National Security Council were also torn. Algeria and Tunisia, although not close American allies, were secular bulwarks, increasingly pro-Western on security issues. Egypt, the most populous and historically influential country in the Arab world, was one of America's closest allies, the second largest recipient of American aid after Israel, and a crucial partner with Washington in the Israeli-Palestinian peace process. Pillar and other CIA analysts believed the United States should do everything possible to shore up Mubarak's government against the Islamists despite Mubarak's obvious failings.

Yet the agency's analysts remembered the experience of the Iranian revolution, where the CIA and the White House had clung to a failing despotic ally for too long and, by doing so, had deprived themselves of a chance to work constructively with Iran's new revolutionary Islamic government. Pillar saw the Muslim Brotherhood in Jordan as a peaceful Islamist movement that was ready to participate in mainstream politics even though it voiced a radical philosophy. Perhaps the Muslim Brotherhood in other countries could be coaxed toward peaceful democracy.

Participants in these intelligence and policy debates during the first Clinton term recall them as fractured, disorganized, and inconclusive. Tony Lake had announced that the expansion of democracy worldwide would be a preeminent American goal during the 1990s. But with Islamist violence now raging in Algeria and Egypt, neither Lake nor Clinton was prepared to make a priority of urging democratic elections in the Arab world. The American embassy in Cairo reached out cautiously to the less violent leaders of the Muslim Brotherhood, but the dialogue never went very far.[3]

The most detailed intelligence collected by the CIA about radical Islamic movements in the Middle East during this early period came from its stations in Egypt, Algeria, Tunisia, and Israel. The CIA maintained a daily liaison with Egyptian intelligence and internal security forces. The agency's Tunis station developed a similar liaison with Tunisian security forces as they cracked down against a Muslim Brotherhood–inspired Islamist movement. The CIA had sent its first declared station chief to Algiers in 1985 and maintained a working relationship with Algerian security forces even as they plunged into a bloody civil war. In all three countries the station chiefs recorded and cabled to Langley detailed alarmist accounts from Arab intelligence and police chiefs about the rising danger of Islamic radicalism. The North African officers complained repeatedly about the role of returning veterans of the Afghan ji-had, the flow of Saudi Arabian funds, and the sanctuary available to violent radicals along the Pakistan-Afghanistan frontier. They complained also about the willingness of Britain, France, Germany, Sweden, and Denmark to grant asylum to exiled Islamist leaders.[4]

There was a clear pattern of international cooperation among the Islamic radicals tracked by the CIA's North African stations. Tunisian security forces captured clandestine weapons moving by camel caravan from Sudan across the Sahara desert to Algeria. For the Tunisians during the months after the World Trade Center bombing "there was no other issue" to discuss with the CIA other than the threat of border-hopping Islamic radicals, recalled Whit-ley Bruner, then the Tunis station chief.[5]

Yasser Arafat and the leadership of the Palestinian Liberation Organiza-tion grew equally alarmed by the rise of these Muslim Brotherhood–inspired networks. As it embraced peace negotiations with Israel, the PLO faced a ris-ing challenge from Hamas, the Palestinian branch of the Muslim Brother-hood. The PLO collected intelligence about Hamas's fund-raising in Saudi Arabia, its religious schools in Yemen, and its gunrunning networks in Sudan. Terrorists with a violent Hamas offshoot, called the Palestinian Islamic Jihad, had clustered around an exiled Saudi financier named Osama bin Laden, the PLO informed the CIA's station in Tel Aviv. The PLO hoped the CIA would join them in battle against the Islamists, disrupting Hamas.[6]

This early CIA reporting was tarnished by the poor reputations of its sources. Mubarak in Egypt, the massacre-sponsoring secret police in Algeria, the police state technocrats in Tunisia, and the corrupt leaders of the PLO all had self-serving reasons to exaggerate the dangers of their Islamic radical opponents. North Africa's secular Arab governments were undemocratic and unpopular. The Islamists, some of them peaceful, had challenged their legiti-macy. It frustrated some of the CIA station chiefs and case officers who worked closely with security services in these countries that their reports about the Islamists tended to be discounted in Washington.

Frank Anderson, the former Afghan task force director during the anti-Soviet covert war, had been promoted to run the Near East Division of the CIA's Directorate of Operations, responsible for all espionage and covert ac-tion in South Asia and the Middle East. Anderson had been a strong advocate of the CIA's support for Hekmatyar during the anti-Soviet jihad. He now argued that the returning jihadist veterans from Afghanistan were not as important as the Egyptian, Algerian, and Tunisian governments believed. Anderson argued that many Islamist radicals who claimed they had fought in Afghanistan were exaggerating their jihadist credentials. Any careful reading of Egyptian and Algerian history showed, Anderson argued, that radical Islam did not need to be imported from Afghanistan to fire a violent insurgency.[7]

All these fragmentary pieces of intelligence and hypotheses about the Afghan veterans swirled and recirculated by cable between Langley and the field. There was no consensus about what it all meant or how to respond. Still, in the CIA's Counterterrorist Center and at the State Department's Bureau of Intelligence and Research, a new analytical theory about Islamist terrorism gradually took hold.

Paul Pillar coined the phrase "ad hoc terrorists" to describe Ramzi Yousef and the World Trade Center plotters. While it was still possible that a government had a hand in the bombing, this seemed unlikely as the months passed. Yousef and his gang did not appear to belong to any formal group, despite their claims about a "Liberation Army, Fifth Battalion." The Yousef plotters were clearly connected to international jihad support networks in Peshawar and the Middle East, but the extent and importance of these ties were unclear. Pillar later dropped the "ad hoc" term because he feared it seemed too casual, as if Yousef and his pals had been drinking coffee one afternoon and decided spontaneously to go bomb a building. But he and other senior analysts at the Counterterrorist Center persisted in their belief that the World Trade Center conspiracy marked a watershed in global terrorism, the debut of a new blend of unaffiliated mobile religious violence.

The CIA was slow to confront this new enemy, however, even after it had been identified. Agency analysts saw Iran's intelligence service and proxy forces as a much graver terrorist threat to the United States than the Afghan veterans. Iranian-trained Hezbollah operatives bombed the Israeli cultural center in Argentina. Bitterness lingered at the CIA over Hezbollah's 1984 torture and murder of Beirut station chief William Buckley.

To the extent they received government support, the new Islamists found money and guns not in Tehran but in Saudi Arabia. Yet the CIA and the White House were reluctant to confront the role of Saudi Arabian proselytizers, financiers, and government agencies. In Riyadh the CIA made little effort to recruit paid agents or collect intelligence about these threats. Diplomats at the State Department worried that because Saudi Arabia remained such a crucial security partner and oil supplier for the United States, the price of getting caught in an espionage operation in the kingdom might be unusually high. The CIA still ran intelligence collection operations in Saudi Arabia, but they tended to be cautious. They relied on technical intercepts more than penetration agents. They concentrated on traditional subjects such as succession and rivalry within the Saudi royal family.[8]

Saudi intelligence chief Prince Turki al-Faisal remained the CIA's key liaison in the kingdom. He had an odd relationship with President Clinton, rooted in their time at Georgetown University. As he planned his run for the presidency from Little Rock, Clinton had gathered the addresses of his former classmates. He wrote them letters to ask for support. In his office at the General Intelligence Department in Riyadh, Prince Turki was surprised and entertained to receive one of these solicitations. At first he ignored it. He couldn't remember Clinton from their university days, and he doubted the governor of a tiny state had much political future. As Clinton's campaign gathered steam, Turki reevaluated. It could be useful for Saudi Arabia's intelligence chief to have a personal connection with a prospective American president. He wrote to Clinton and opened a correspondence.

In the late spring of 1993, Georgetown University held a class reunion, and Prince Turki attended. Afterward the Saudi spy chief accompanied Frank Anderson from the CIA and Prince Bandar, the Saudi ambassador in Washington, to the White House. They sat down with Clinton and listened as he talked in meandering and general terms about globalization. The president's discourse turned to the Middle East and Central Asia, and he asked Prince Turki: What policies should the United States pursue in countries such as Uzbekistan and Kazakhstan?

It was a typical Clinton session, more seminar than formal meeting. He was with some smart and interesting new people, and he wanted to hear their ideas about where American foreign policy should go. But Bandar and Turki left the White House disconcerted, shaking their heads. Clinton's questions about how America should define its policies left the Saudis uneasy. They said to each other, He's asking *us*?[9]

Still, shortly after the White House meeting, they sent a check for $20 million to fund a Middle Eastern studies program at the University of Arkansas, for which Clinton had tried to raise money while he was governor.[10] It was a Saudi handshake, a small housewarming gift for a new friend.

KABUL PLUNGED INTO VIOLENCE and deprivation during 1993. Hekmatyar pounded the city indiscriminately with hundreds of rockets from his ample stores, killing and wounding thousands of civilians. The old mujahedin leaders realigned themselves in bizarre temporary partnerships. They fought artillery duels along Kabul's avenues, dividing the city into a dense barricaded checkerboard of ethnic and ideological factions. Shiite militia fought against Hekmatyar around Kabul's zoo, then switched sides and fought against Massoud. Sayyaf's forces allied with his old Islamic law colleague Rabbani and hit the Shiites with unrestrained fury, beheading old men, women, children, and dogs. Dostum's Uzbek militias carried out a campaign of rapes and executions on Kabul's outskirts. Massoud hunkered down in the tattered defense ministry, a decaying former royal palace, and moved his troops north and south in running battles. The electricity in Kabul failed. The few remaining diplomats husbanded petrol for generators and held conferences by candlelight. Roads closed, food supplies shrank, and disease spread. About ten thousand Afghan civilians died violently by the year's end.[11]

Prince Turki flew into Islamabad for meetings with the Afghan faction leaders, hired former Pakistani intelligence chief Hamid Gul as a mediation partner, and tried to talk the combatants into a settlement. They worked with the current ISI chief, Lieutenant General Javed Nasir, who wore a long beard and openly preached Islamist theology at mosques and public meetings. He was the most explicitly religious leader of Pakistani intelligence in a generation. Even some of Nasir's colleagues within ISI were alarmed by his open proselytizing. They considered it a breach of the army's professional traditions.[12]

Edmund McWilliams, the State Department diplomat who had campaigned from within the Islamabad embassy against the Islamist agendas of Pakistani and Saudi intelligence during the late 1980s, had recently been transferred to Central Asia. He watched the civil war with growing disgust. He sent a Confidential cable to Washington early in 1993 titled "Implications of Continued Stalemate in Afghanistan." McWilliams argued that the "principled U.S. posture of letting Afghans find solutions to 'their problems' fails to take into account a central reality: Intense and continuing foreign involvement in Afghan affairs—by friendly and unfriendly governments and a myriad of well-financed fundamentalist organizations—thus far has precluded Afghans from finding 'their own solutions.'" The hands-off policy of the United States "serves neither Afghan interests nor our own. . . . The absence of an effective Kabul government also has allowed Afghanistan to become a spawning ground for insurgency against legally constituted governments. Afghan-trained Islamic fundamentalist guerrillas directly threaten Tajikistan and are being dispatched to stir trouble in Middle Eastern, southwest Asian, and African states."[13]

The McWilliams cable landed in a void. The White House formulated no policy toward Afghanistan during Clinton's first term other than a vague endorsement of fitful, quixotic efforts by the United Nations to negotiate peace. This left American policy solely in the hands of the State Department, the agency that represented the United States in every country worldwide even when there was no policy to represent. Neither Warren Christopher nor any of his deputies had any interest in Afghanistan. Christopher said he intended to stand behind "the Americas desk," meaning that foreign policy under Clinton would be managed to support domestic policies. Clinton appointed an acquaintance from his days at Oxford University as his assistant secretary of state for South Asia, in charge of diplomacy for India, Pakistan, and Afghanistan. Robin Raphel was a career foreign service officer who had risen to the rank of political counselor in the U.S. embassy in New Delhi, but she was relatively junior for the job. Blue-eyed, blond, and statuesque, she was an elegant, bright woman with an upper-crust air, and she was a serious equestrian. Apart from her personal history with the president, she had few connections at the White House or with the new team that had taken power at the State Department.[14]

Raphel tried to argue for continued humanitarian aid to Afghanistan. But as Clinton attempted to balance the federal budget after years of deficit spending, his administration drastically cut funding for the Agency for International Development, the government's main overseas aid organization. Clinton directed available funds away from countries like Afghanistan and toward the neediest cases in Africa, a dying continent that Lake and the new AID director, Brian Atwood, felt had been neglected for too long by Republican administrations. "Nobody wanted to return to the hot spots of the Reagan-Bush years," such as Afghanistan, recalled one member of Clinton's team at the aid agency. "They just wanted them to go away." South Asia was "just one of those black holes out there." Atwood faced hostility from Republicans in Congress who argued that American development aid was being wasted in poor, chaotic countries. After heated arguments within AID and despite resistance from Raphel, the United States ended all bilateral development aid to Afghanistan less than two years after Clinton took office.[15]

CIA director James Woolsey saw Afghanistan in these months merely as "a place where there was a lot of warlord-ism." Its civil war and its jihad training camps did not seem to him a significant factor in the rise of Islamist politics in North Africa. In this analysis he was influenced by Frank Anderson, his Near East operations chief. Woolsey liked and admired Anderson and relied on him heavily for analysis about Afghanistan and the Arab world.[16]

The CIA was active in Central Asia. After the Soviet Union's collapse the CIA's Directorate of Operations moved into the newly independent, former Soviet republics. Among other objectives the CIA sought to thwart Iranian ambitions in Central Asia. Officers tracked Iranian agents and tried to secure the region's loose nuclear bombs and materials. Oil-rich republics along the Caspian Sea opened their vast energy reserves to foreign corporations. American firms sought a piece of the action. For all these reasons the CIA's officers "were all over Ukraine and Central Asia, going in just as fast as we could, finding new opportunities," recalled Thomas Twetten, then chief of the Directorate of Operations and Frank Anderson's supervisor.[17]

But the CIA ignored Afghanistan and its civil war. Twetten felt there was nothing the United States could do to mediate the Afghan conflict or put the country back together again. There were too many other challenges in a world so suddenly and vastly changed by communism's collapse. The Afghan war threatened to destabilize the new Central Asian countries, but even that danger seemed remote. Afghanistan was "just really background" at the Directorate of Operations only two years after it had been at the center of one of the CIA's most important and richly funded covert programs.[18]

Charles Cogan, the former Near East Division chief who had helped create the anti-Soviet jihad, spoke for many at the agency during this period when he described the CIA and the Islamist rebels built up by Pakistani intelligence as merely "partners in time." They had no enduring interests in common. The United States "was no more able to put together a polity in the ghost town that Kabul had become than it can in Dushanbe or, alas, in Mogadishu. Nor should it try." American intervention in civil wars unfolding in former Cold War client states would "lead to a dangerous overextension of American forces and resources [and] it will draw upon us more hatreds and jealousies. In most cases, we would be well advised to maintain a prudent distance, in the words of Douglas MacArthur, from the 'internal purification problems' of others."[19]

Afghanistan was indeed about to purify itself. It was about to disgorge a radical Islamic militia as pure and unbending in its belief system as any in the Muslim world since King Saud's antimodern Ikhwan had stormed across the Arabian peninsula seven decades before.

"A New Generation"

COFER BLACK TRANSFERRED from London to Khartoum, Sudan, arriving as the CIA's station chief during 1993. The United States had concluded that Sudan's government sponsored terrorism and had imposed economic sanctions. This was not a country where the CIA's station chief could trust the host government enough to provide official notification of his presence. Black and his case officers masqueraded as embassy-based diplomats. Khartoum was a rough station but also the kind of place where energetic young CIA case officers liked to operate. The city's streets teemed with life, violence, and professional opportunity. The station effectively had just one subject on its Operating Directive: terrorism. In Europe, case officers might spend most of their time in bars and cafes with moody bureaucrats, trying to turn a source. In Khartoum they worked the streets, putting into practice all of the Farm's tradecraft: surveillance, countersurveillance, electronics, and weapons.

In Cofer Black they had an ambitious chief. He was a tall man, balding, bespectacled, full-shouldered, forceful, and sometimes theatrical in manner and speech. His long career as a spy working in former British colonies in Africa had left vaguely British inflections in his voice. He had grown up in comfortable circumstances in Connecticut, attending an all-boys preparatory school called Canterbury. His father flew Boeing-747 jets as an international pilot for Pan American Airways. When he was a boy, his father would take him along during breaks in school. They would fly to Accra, Ghana, or Lagos, Nigeria, and Cofer would stay for a week or two with family friends, exploring the African countryside, while his father hopped airline routes. In college at the University of Southern California he studied international relations. He had earned a master's degree and had begun work on a doctorate when he joined the CIA in 1974. After training in clandestine operations he volunteered for service in Africa. He was dispatched as a case officer to Lusaka, Zambia, during the Rhodesian war next door. He transferred to Somalia for two years during a Cold War–inspired conflict between Ethiopians and Somalis in the sands of the Ogaden desert. He worked in South Africa during the racist apartheid regime's dirty war against guerrilla movements representing the black majority. While assigned to Kinshasa, Zaire, Black was involved in the Reagan administration's covert action program to arm anticommunist guerrillas in neighboring Angola. By the time he arrived in Khartoum, he was steeped in Africa's complexities.[1]

Khartoum had become a haven for exiled radicals and terrorists during the previous three years. It was a city in desperate shape. Perched on a dust-blown plain at the junction of the White Nile and Blue Nile, Khartoum had once been a British garrison town; its avenues were laid out in the form of the Union Jack. By the early 1990s the city plan had deteriorated, full of impassable craters, downed electrical lines, blinding sandstorms, and sprawling slums. Decades of civil war, runaway inflation, and violent coups had left its population prostrate. A Muslim Brotherhood–inspired political party called the National Islamic Front, led by the Sorbonne-educated theologian Hasan al-Turabi, had recently taken power. Turabi proclaimed solidarity with oppressed Muslims worldwide and advertised his country as a safe base for Hamas, Hezbollah, Egypt's Islamic Group, and Algeria's Islamic Salvation Front. Sudan also granted asylum to secular terrorists such as Carlos the Jackal. And Turabi's government had welcomed Osama bin Laden after his expulsion from Saudi Arabia in 1991.

Black's station operated against all these targets. Their Operating Directive limited them in bin Laden's case to intelligence collection. They had no White House mandate for covert action specifically to attack or disrupt the Saudi's loose organization, nor did the CIA develop such a plan.[2]

The World Trade Center bombing and ongoing Islamist violence in Egypt and Algeria provided an urgent, enlivening backdrop for their work. They staked out Khartoum safehouses and office buildings, mapped the habits and movements of group leaders and foot soldiers, followed them clandestinely when they attended meetings, and recorded license plate numbers. The station penetrated local banks to obtain account numbers and details about international financial transfers, including those of bin Laden. They planted listening devices, translated conversations, and tried to identify connections. Who was working with whom? Who in the Sudanese government was being paid off? (Just about everybody who had power, the Khartoum station concluded.) What was the role of Iranian government agents in this nexus? What was the role of Iraqi agents who turned up in Khartoum occasionally during this period? Black and his colleagues cabled Cairo, Jerusalem, Tunis, Algiers, and Riyadh, trying to match up names and leads.[3]

Bin Laden was a significant target, but one among half a dozen. His money attracted a diverse crowd to his Khartoum compound. Pakistan announced one of its periodic crackdowns on Arab radicals in the spring of 1993, and bin Laden sent money to fly 480 of these jihadists to Khartoum. They became part of bin Laden's local guard. In May of that year the CIA received an intelligence report from Egypt and Saudi Arabia showing that bin Laden's businesses had begun to ship cash to Egyptian Islamists for printing presses and weapons.[4]

From this evidence Black and his case officers described bin Laden as an emerging leader. They saw him as determined to become a significant player in the Islamist movement. He was a financier, however, not yet an operator. Bin Laden was ready to fund and encourage a wide variety of Islamist and terrorist groups, but neither the Khartoum station nor CIA headquarters had solid evidence that he had joined directly in terrorist attacks.[5]

Bin Laden seemed soft, scholarly, and more of a tycoon and a lecturer than a hardened terrorist tactician. He did not behave like a typical underground terrorist leader. He was accessible and visible in Khartoum during these years; he was certainly not trying to hide. He spent many hours openly tending to his businesses. He bought a farm north of Khartoum for $250,000 and a salt farm near Port Sudan for about $180,000. At first he worked at the air-conditioned McNimr Street headquarters of his business empire, centered on a construction company, Al-Hijrah for Construction and Development. His office suite had eight or nine rooms and a phalanx of secretaries and receptionists. Later he bought a building in an upscale neighborhood called Riyadh City. Salaries for his aides ranged from $300 a month for the Sudanese to $1,500 a month for some of the favored Egyptians and Iraqis. He cut import-export deals through other companies and in partnership with Sudanese generals and government officials, whom he paid off generously. He secured a virtual monopoly on Sudanese exports of corn, sunflowers, gum, and other farm products. His agricultural subsidiary bought up hundreds of acres near Khartoum and in eastern Sudan. He rode horses with Turabi's sons. He visited road and commercial projects that he developed in partnership with members of the Sudanese government. With some of these partners he invested an estimated $50 million in a Sudanese bank.[6]

It was clear to the Khartoum station that bin Laden was financing Islamist violence across North Africa through some of these businesses, but the details were difficult to nail down. At one point bin Laden wired $210,000 to a contact in Texas to purchase and import a private jet to shuttle cargo, including weapons, between Pakistan and Sudan. He bought camels to smuggle guns through the desert to Egypt.[7]

They watched him move around Khartoum like a prestigious sheikh, acolytes and gun-toting bodyguards at his heel. He prayed and lectured at local mosques. He lived in a walled three-story compound, continually surrounded by Arab Afghan veterans. Bin Laden liked to sit in the front yard "and talk about jihad and about Islam and about al Qaeda in general," as one of his aides from this period recalled it. He lectured about politics and jihad every Thursday after sunset prayers. He was wary of newcomers to his inner circle, and he told his aides to watch out for agents of Middle Eastern intelligence services posing as volunteers.[8]

He had reason to worry. Four Arab veterans of the Afghan war tried to kill bin Laden during 1994. They apparently believed that his interpretation of Islam was not pure or radical enough. The assassins opened fire inside a Khartoum mosque where bin Laden preached. They shot several worshipers dead before they realized that bin Laden was not there. They jumped in their vehicles, drove to Riyadh City, and confronted his security guards in a shootout. Some of the attackers died; another was taken prisoner and executed.[9]

The failed assassination attempt ratified bin Laden's growing stature. In Peshawar during the 1980s he had been overshadowed by Abdullah Azzam. In Saudi Arabia he was just one rich young sheikh among hundreds. But in Khartoum his wealth made him a rare and commanding figure. He was powerful enough to order men to their deaths. Yet he fashioned himself a lecturer-businessman, an activist theologian in the image of Azzam. Bin Laden was not especially harsh. Many terrorist leaders established power over their groups by routinely executing rivals or transgressors. When bin Laden caught one of his trusted aides embezzling tens of thousands of dollars, he demanded only that his aide pay the money back in installments. He talked with the man at length about improving his dedication to jihad.[10]

Bin Laden was emerging now as a politician, a rising force in the underground and exiled Saudi opposition. The Islamist backlash against the Saudi royals that erupted after the Gulf War continued to gather momentum in 1994. Bin Laden allied himself early that year with a Saudi opposition group based in London that used fax machines and computer lines to denounce the royal family's "insatiable carnal desires." Bin Laden set up his own group, the Advisory and Reformation Committee, which also published hundreds of anti-Saudi pamphlets, all filled with bin Laden's picture. His tracts proposed the breakup of the Saudi state. Saudi Arabia's borders marked the reign of a single and illegitimate family, the al-Sauds, bin Laden argued. He proposed two new countries, Greater Yemen and Greater Hijaz, which would divide the Arabian Peninsula between them.[11]

The British and American governments were reluctant to crack down on these exiled centers of opposition Saudi politics. Some of the exiles embraced the language of democracy. It was an article of faith in Washington and London during the early 1990s that a little outside pressure, even if it came from Islamists, might help open up the Saudi kingdom to new voices, creating healthier and more stable politics in the long run.[12]

The Saudi royal family tried to co-opt its opposition. They had banished bin Laden, but they were reluctant to break with him entirely. Prince Turki sent a parade of delegates to Khartoum to persuade bin Laden to come home, make peace, and reclaim his full share of his family's fortune. From 1970 to about 1994 bin Laden had received a $1 million annual allowance from his family, American investigators later reported, but now he was cut off. The emissaries included bin Laden's mother, his eighty-year-old uncle, and some of his half-brothers. Bin Laden later recalled "almost nine visits to Khartoum" during this period, with each relative "asking me to stop and return to Arabia to apologize to King Fahd."[13]

The Saudi royals were embarrassed by complaints about bin Laden and angry about his antiroyal agitation. Yet Prince Turki and other senior Saudi princes had trouble believing that bin Laden was much of a threat to anyone. They saw him as a misguided rich kid, the black sheep of a prestigious family, a self-important and immature man who would likely be persuaded as he aged to find some sort of peaceful accommodation with his homeland. But bin Laden was stubborn. Again and again he rebuffed his relatives during 1993 and 1994. At last the Saudi government revoked his citizenship. As part of a campaign to isolate bin Laden, his half-brother Bakr, now running the family business empire, publicly expressed "regret, denunciation, and condemnation" of Osama's antiroyal politics.[14]

CIA analysis began by late 1994 to run in a different direction. The insights Black and his case officers could obtain into bin Laden's inner circle were limited, but they knew that bin Laden was working closely with the Sudanese intelligence services. They knew that Sudanese intelligence, in turn, was running paramilitary and terrorist operations in Egypt and elsewhere. Bin Laden had access to Sudanese military radios, weapons, and about two hundred Sudanese passports. These passports supplemented the false documents that bin Laden acquired for his aides from the travel papers of Arab volunteers who had been killed in the Afghan jihad. Working with liaison intelligence services across North Africa, Black and his Khartoum case officers tracked bin Laden to three training camps in northern Sudan. They learned that bin Laden funded the camps and used them to house violent Egyptian, Algerian, Tunisian, and Palestinian jihadists. Increasingly the Khartoum station cabled evidence to Langley that bin Laden had developed the beginnings of a multinational private army. He was a threat.

For Cofer Black this assessment was grounded in personal experience. Toward the end of his tour in Khartoum, bin Laden's men tried to assassinate him. They had detected CIA surveillance and traced the watchers to Black. They had learned, probably through contacts in Sudanese intelligence, that Black had played a role in the arrest and transport to France of Carlos the Jackal. From this bin Laden's group may have deduced that Black was CIA. In any event they began to follow his routes to and from the embassy. Black and his case officers picked up this surveillance and started to watch those who were watching them.

The CIA officers saw that bin Laden's men were setting up a "kill zone" near the U.S. embassy. They couldn't tell whether the attack was going to be a kidnapping, a car bombing, or an ambush with assault rifles, but they were able to watch bin Laden's group practice the operation on a Khartoum street. As the weeks passed, the surveillance and countersurveillance grew more and more intense. On one occasion they found themselves in a high-speed chase. On another the CIA officers leveled loaded shotguns at the Arabs who were following them. Eventually Black dispatched the U.S. ambassador to complain to the Sudanese government. Exposed, the plotters retreated.[15]

At a White House briefing early in 1995, CIA analysts described bin

Laden's Khartoum headquarters as the Ford Foundation of Sunni Islamic terrorism, a grant-giving source of cash for violent operations. Egyptian, Algerian, Tunisian, and other Islamist radicals would make proposals to bin Laden
for operations, and if bin Laden approved, he would hand over the funds.[16]
By 1995 the CIA's Khartoum station had no doubt that bin Laden's own aides
included some hardcore, well-trained killers. Black and his case officers wondered when and how the United States would confront bin Laden directly.

BRIAN PARR STOOD in the darkness beside an American military transport jet on the tarmac of Islamabad's civil-military airport. Parr was a six-year
Secret Service veteran assigned to the FBI's Joint Terrorism Task Force in
New York. He was a specialist in transporting dangerous prisoners. Twenty-
four hours earlier he had been summoned to Washington and told to scramble
for a flight to Pakistan. His prize now approached in a vehicle driven by Pakistani army and intelligence officers. It was just after sunset, February 8, 1995.
From the back of the vehicle stepped Ramzi Yousef. He wore a mustard color
military jumpsuit and a blindfold. A belly chain manacled his hands and feet.[17]

With FBI agents Bradley Garrett and Charles Stern, Parr escorted Yousef
into the American plane. The day before, Pakistani intelligence officers and
commandos had burst into Room 16 of the Su Casa guest house in Islamabad, arresting Yousef as he prepared to leave the capital. Pakistan's government had agreed immediately to turn Yousef over to the United States to face
charges in the World Trade Center bombing. The Pakistanis waived formal
extradition proceedings. This "rendition" technique, in which a detained terrorist was shipped from one country to another without appearing in court,
had lately become a preferred CIA method. It allowed the agency to ship suspects to allied countries for interrogation or back to the United States for trial,
as it pleased. The practice, illegal within the United States but permitted overseas, drew on national security policy that dated to the Reagan administration,
reaffirmed and revitalized by President Clinton.[18]

Aboard the plane the FBI team stripped Yousef of his clothes, searched
him, and photographed him. A medical doctor examined Yousef and pronounced him fit. The agents reclothed Yousef, shackled him, and took him to
a compartment in the back of the plane. A makeshift interview room had
been shielded with blankets and fitted with airline seats.

Yousef had already begun to talk to several FBI agents. He spoke English
well, and he seemed relaxed. He was curious about the American legal process
and eager to be credited as a terrorist innovator. Asked by Garrett whether he

had committed the World Trade Center bombing, Yousef replied, "I master-minded the explosion."[19]

Aboard the plane they talked for six hours of the twenty-hour flight. Garrett and Parr plumbed Yousef about his motivations. For two years the FBI and the CIA had speculated and argued about Yousef's role in the World Trade Center plot. Was he a government agent? Part of a network of Islamic radicals? A lone wolf? Some blend of these? Finally they could hear from Yousef himself.

Their prisoner explained that some Muslim leaders had philosophies similar to his own, but he considered himself an independent operator. Muslim leaders provided inspiration, but none controlled his work. Garrett asked which leaders Yousef was talking about. He refused to answer.[20]

Yousef said he took no thrill from killing American citizens and felt guilty about the civilian deaths he had caused. But his conscience was overridden by the strength of his desire to stop the killing of Arabs by Israeli troops. "It's nothing personal," he said, but bombing American targets was the "only way to cause change." He had come to the conclusion that only extreme acts could change the minds of people and the policies of nations. He cited as one example the suicide bombing of the U.S. Marine barracks in Lebanon in 1984, which ultimately led to the withdrawal of American troops from that country. As another example he mentioned the U.S. atomic bombing of Hiroshima and Nagasaki, a shock tactic that forced Japan to surrender quickly. Yousef said he "would like it to be different," but only terrible violence could force this kind of abrupt political change. He said that he truly believed his actions had been rational and logical in pursuit of a change in U.S. policy toward Israel.[21] He mentioned no other motivation during the flight and no other issue in American foreign policy that concerned him.

He told them about his desire to topple one of the World Trade Center towers into the other, a feat he thought would take about 250,000 lives. But he lacked the money and the equipment to make a bomb that was strong enough to bring the first tower down, and he complained about the quality of his confederates. The FBI agents asked why one of Yousef's partners had returned a rental car to pick up a deposit after the bombing, a move that had led to his arrest. "Stupid," Yousef said with a weary grin.[22]

He mentioned that when he escaped to Pakistan, he bought a first-class ticket because he had discovered the first-class passengers received less scrutiny than those in coach.

He was cagey when he talked about those who had aided him. In a Manila apartment where Yousef had hidden as a fugitive, investigators found a business card belonging to Mohammad Khalifa, a relative by marriage of Osama bin Laden. Yousef said only that the card had been given to him by one of his colleagues as a contact in case he needed help.

The agents asked if Yousef was familiar with the name Osama bin Laden. He said he knew that bin Laden was a relative of Khalifa. He refused to say anything more.[23]

Pakistani investigators eventually learned that for many months after the World Trade Center bombing Yousef had lived in a Pakistani guest house funded by bin Laden. They passed this information to the FBI and the CIA.[24]

On the plane that night Yousef asked several times whether he would face a death sentence in the United States. He expected to be put to death, he said. His only worry was whether he would have enough time to write a book about his exploits.[25]

FROM THE START the plan was to try Yousef in open court. Mary Jo White, the United States attorney overseeing terrorism prosecutions in Manhattan, presented evidence against Yousef to a federal grand jury. As these and related investigations unfolded, the FBI and CIA gathered new facts about Yousef's multinational support network. Among other things they discovered that in the two years since the World Trade Center attack, Yousef and his coconspirators had focused heavily on airplanes and airports.

The evidence of these aerial plots surfaced first in the Philippines. Police responded to a fire at the Tiffany Mansion apartments in Manila on January 7, 1995. The apartment belonged to Khalid Sheikh Mohammed, the Baluchi Islamist who was Yousef's uncle.[26] Inside the apartment police found one of Yousef's cohorts, Abdul Hakim Murad. They also found residue from bomb-making chemicals and laptop computers with encrypted files. Murad confessed that he had been working with Yousef on multiple terrorist plots: to bomb up to a dozen American commercial airliners flying over the Pacific, to assassinate President Clinton during a visit to the Philippines, to assassinate the Pope when he visited Manila, and to hijack a commercial airliner and crash it into the headquarters of the CIA.

The plot to bomb American passenger planes over the Pacific was far along. Yousef had concocted a timing device fashioned from a Casio watch and a mix of explosives that could not be detected by airport security screeners. He planned to board an interlocking sequence of civilian flights. He would place the explosives on board, set the timers, and exit at layover stops before the bombs went off. He had already killed a Japanese businessman when he detonated a small bomb during a practice run, planting the device in an airplane seat and exiting the flight at a stopover before it exploded. If his larger plan had not been disrupted, as many as a thousand Americans might have died in the attacks during the first months of 1995.

The plot to crash a plane into CIA headquarters was described in a briefing report written by the Manila police and sent to American investigators. Murad said the idea arose in conversation between himself and Yousef. The Filipino police wrote that winter that Murad planned "to board any American commercial aircraft pretending to be an ordinary passenger. Then he will hijack said aircraft, control its cockpit, and dive it at the CIA headquarters. There will be no bomb or any explosive that he will use in its execution. It is simply a suicidal mission that he is very much willing to execute."[27]

THESE WERE NOT the only indications early in 1995 that the United States faced a newly potent terrorist threat in the Sunni Islamic world. Islamist violence connected to Arab veterans of the Afghan jihad surged worldwide.

The attacks were diverse and the perpetrators often mysterious. Suicidal attacks became a more common motif. Increasingly, the attacks came from insurgent groups in North Africa, Egypt, Sudan, and Pakistan. Increasingly, evidence surfaced that Islamist terrorists had experimented with weapons of mass destruction. Increasingly, Osama bin Laden loomed in the background of the attacks as a source of inspiration or financial support or both.

In August 1994 three hooded North Africans killed two Spanish tourists in a Marrakesh hotel. The attackers and their handlers had trained in Afghanistan. Bombings of the Paris Metro later that year were traced to Algerians trained in Afghan camps. In December 1994 four Algerian terrorists from the Armed Islamic Group hijacked an Air France jet. They planned to fly to Paris and slam the plane kamikaze-style into the Eiffel Tower. French authorities fooled the hijackers into believing that they did not have enough fuel to reach Paris, so they diverted to Marseilles where all four were shot dead by French commandos. In March 1995, Belgian investigators seized a terrorist training manual from Algerian militants. The document explained how to make a bomb using a wristwatch as a timer, and its preface was dedicated to bin Laden. In April, Filipino guerrillas swearing loyalty to the Afghan mujahedin leader Abdurrab Rasul Sayyaf sacked the Mindanao island town of Ipil. They killed sixty-three people, robbed four banks, and took fifty-three hostages, killing a dozen of them. On June 26, 1995, Egyptian guerrillas with the Islamic Group, equipped with Sudanese passports, unsuccessfully attempted to assassinate Egyptian president Hosni Mubarak in Ethiopia. A month later a member of the Egyptian extremist group al-Jihad said in a published interview that bin Laden sometimes knew about their specific terrorist operations against Egyptian targets. On November 13, 1995, a car bomb loaded with about 250 pounds of explosives blew up near the three-story headquarters of the office of the program manager of the Saudi Arabian national guard in Riyadh. Five Americans died, and thirty-four were wounded. Months later one of the perpetrators confessed in a Saudi television broadcast that he was influenced by bin Laden and the Egyptian Islamist groups, and that he had learned how to make the car bomb because of "my experiences in explosives which I had during my participation in the Afghan jihad operations." One week after the Riyadh bombing, Islamist terrorists drove a suicide truck bomb into the Egyptian embassy in Islamabad, killing fifteen people and injuring eighty.[28]

Imprinted in these events was an outline of the future. The CIA's Counterterrorist Center and the FBI's analytical units recognized essential parts of the new pattern, but they did not see it all.

Murad's confession about a plan to hijack a civilian airliner and crash it into the CIA received little attention at the FBI because that plot was not part of the evidentiary case the bureau was building for courtroom prosecution. The FBI was distracted. Domestic terrorism overshadowed Islamist attacks during 1995. In April, Timothy McVeigh detonated a truck bomb outside the federal building in Oklahoma City, killing 168 and wounding hundreds more. The bombing galvanized the Clinton administration to focus on terrorism, but the long investigation drained FBI resources. The bureau never followed up with a detailed investigation of the airplane kamikaze plan.[29]

The CIA remained focused on Iranian and Shiite terrorist threats. Late in 1994 the CIA station in Riyadh reported on surveillance of American targets in the kingdom by Iranian agents and their radical Saudi Shiite allies. Woolsey visited the kingdom in December and huddled with Prince Turki. They discussed joint plans to monitor and disrupt the Iranian threat in the months ahead. CIA reporting about Iranian-sponsored terrorist threats inside Saudi Arabia continued at a high tempo throughout 1995. In October the White House received intelligence that the Iranian-backed, Shiite-dominated Hezbollah terrorist organization had dispatched a hit squad to assassinate National Security Adviser Tony Lake. He moved out of his home temporarily and into safehouses in Washington. Because the Saudi intelligence service was so heavily focused on the Shiites, Prince Turki recalled, the Riyadh bombing in November by bin Laden–inspired Afghan veterans came "out of nowhere." Even after that attack, Iran remained a major threat, drawing attention and resources away from bin Laden and his followers.[30]

The CIA's Near East Division of the Directorate of Operations, responsible for much of the Sunni Muslim world, also was distracted by Iraq. Its ambitious covert operations to overthrow Saddam Hussein from bases in northern Iraq were collapsing that spring.

All of this turmoil swirled in the weeks and months after Yousef's arrest, presenting investigators with a rich cache of evidence. The essential analytical questions remained the same as they had been for several years. Were terrorists like Ramzi Yousef best seen as solo entrepreneurs or as operatives of a larger movement? Where were the key nodes of leadership and resource support? Was CIA analyst Paul Pillar's notion of ad hoc terrorism adequate anymore, or did the United States now confront a more organized and potent circle of Sunni Muslim jihadists bent on spectacular attacks?

Hardly anyone in Washington or at Langley yet saw the full significance of bin Laden and al Qaeda. When President Clinton signed Executive Order 12947 on January 23, 1995, imposing sanctions on twelve terrorist groups because of their role in disrupting the Middle East peace process, neither al Qaeda nor bin Laden made the list.[31]

These blind spots among American intelligence analysts partly reflected the fragmentary, contradictory evidence they had to work with. Cofer Black's cables from Khartoum showed the diversity of bin Laden's multinational allies. Clearly bin Laden's network did not operate as a conventional hierarchical group.

Many American analysts clung to preconceived ideas about who in the Middle East was an ally and who was an enemy. American strategy in 1995, ratified by Clinton's National Security Council, was to contain and frustrate Iran and Iraq. In this mission Saudi Arabia was an elusive but essential ally. It was an embedded assumption of American foreign policy that Iraq and Iran could not be managed without Saudi cooperation. Then, too, there was the crucial importance of Saudi Arabia in the global oil markets. There was strong reluctance in Washington to challenge the Saudi royal family over its funding of Islamist radicals, its appeasement of anti-American preachers, or its ardent worldwide proselytizing. There was little impetus to step back and ask big, uncomfortable questions about whether Saudi charities represented a fundamental threat to American national security. The Saudis worked assiduously to maintain diverse contacts within the CIA, outside of official channels. Several retired Riyadh station chiefs and senior Near East Division managers went on the Saudi payroll as consultants during the mid-1990s.[32]

American Arabists had studied the Middle East for decades through a Cold War lens, their vision narrowed by continuous intimate contact with secular Arab elites. American spies and strategists rarely entered the lower-middle-class mosques of Algiers, Tunis, Cairo, Karachi, or Jedda, where anti-American cassette tape sermons were for sale on folding tables at the door.

Despite all these limitations, American intelligence analysts developed by mid-1995 a clearer picture of the new terrorist enemy. For the first time the image of a global network began to emerge. The FBI and the CIA each produced ambitious classified intelligence reports during the second half of 1995 that sifted the evidence in the Yousef case and pushed strong new forecasts.

As part of a long review of global terrorism circulated by the FBI, classi-fied Secret, the bureau's analysts assessed the emerging threat under the heading "Ramzi Ahmed Yousef: A New Generation of Sunni Islamic Terrorists."[33] The Yousef case "has led us to conclude that a new generation of terrorists has appeared on the world stage over the past few years," the FBI's analysts wrote. Yousef and his associates "have access to a worldwide network of sup-port for funding, training and safe haven." Increasingly, "Islamic extremists are working together to further their cause." It was "no coincidence" that their terrorism increased as the anti-Soviet Afghan war ended. Afghanistan's training camps were crucial to Yousef. The camps provided technical re-sources and allowed him to meet and recruit like-minded radicals. Pakistan and Bosnia had also become important bases for the jihadists.

The FBI's report noted the vulnerability of the American homeland to at-tacks. It specifically cited Murad's confessed plot to hijack a plane and fly it into CIA headquarters as an example.

"Unlike traditional forms of terrorism, such as state-sponsored or the Iran/Hezbollah model, Sunni extremists are neither surrogates of nor strongly influenced by one nation," the FBI's analysts wrote. "They are au-tonomous and indigenous." There was now reason to "suspect Yousef and his associates receive support from Osama bin Laden and may be able to tap into bin Laden's mujahedin support network." In addition, they may also have been able to draw on Islamic charities for support. The FBI analysis listed the huge semiofficial Saudi Arabian charity, the International Islamic Relief Organization, and the largest government-sponsored Saudi religious proselytizing organization, the Muslim World League, as important resources for the new terrorists. The cable concluded: "Yousef's group fits the mold for this new generation of Sunni Islamic terrorists. . . . The WTC bombing, the Manila plot, and the recent [Islamic Group] attack against Mubarak demonstrate that Islamic extremists can operate anywhere in the world. We believe the threat is not over."[34]

The CIA also saw Yousef's gang as independent from any hierarchy. "As far as we know," reported a classified agency cable in 1995, "Yousef and his confederates . . . are not allied with an organized terrorist group and cannot readily call upon such an organized unit to execute retaliatory strikes against the U.S. or countries that have cooperated with the U.S. in the extradition of Yousef and his associates." That same year, working through the National Intelligence Council, the CIA circulated to Clinton's Cabinet an annual National Intelligence Estimate on terrorism classified Secret. The estimate was titled "The Foreign Terrorist Threat in the United States" and drew on cables and analyses from across the American intelligence community. Echoing the FBI's language, the estimate called Yousef's gang a "new breed" of radical Sunni Islamic terrorist. This "new terrorist phenomenon" involved fluid, transient, multinational groupings of Islamic extremists who saw the United States as their enemy, the estimate warned. It then speculated about future attacks inside the United States. "Several targets are especially at risk: national symbols such as the White House and the Capitol, and symbols of U.S. capitalism such as Wall Street," the estimate predicted. "We assess that civil aviation will figure prominently among possible terrorist targets in the United States. This stems from the increasing domestic threat posed by foreign terrorists, the continuing appeal of civil aviation as a target, and a domestic aviation security system [whose weaknesses have] been the focus of media attention."[35]

It was now clear that Yousef and his colleagues had developed their terrorist plans by studying American airline security procedures. "If terrorists operating in this country are similarly methodical, they will identify serious vulnerabilities in the security system for domestic flights." The National Intelligence Estimate made no mention of Osama bin Laden.[36]

"Slowly, Slowly
Sucked into It"

T HE MAN WHO BECAME KNOWN as Ahmed Shah Durrani, a celebrated king of Afghanistan, began his career as an unsuccessful bodyguard. His liege, the Persian emperor Nadir Shah, had conquered lands and
treasure as far east as India, but he grew murderous and arbitrary even by the
standards of a tyrannical age. Angry courtiers attacked him in his royal desert
tent in 1747. Durrani found his ruler's headless torso in a bloody pool. Sens-
ing they were now on the wrong side of Persian court politics, Durrani and
his fellow guards mounted horses and rode east for Kandahar, homeland of
their tribes, known to the British as Pashtuns.[1]

Kandahar lay uncomfortably exposed in a semiarid plain between the two
great Islamic empires of the day: Persia, to the west, and the Mughal Empire,
ruled from Kabul to the north. In the Pashtun homeland luscious orchards
and farms dotted the banks of the snaking Helmand River. Mud-walled villages unmolested by outside authority nestled in fertile valleys. Swift snow-
melt rivers in the surrounding hills seemed to invigorate the strong-boned,
strong-willed pathwalkers who drank from them. The desert highways crossing
Kandahar carried great caravans between India and Persia, providing road taxes

for local governors and loot for tribal highwaymen. Yet Kandahar's fractious
tribes lacked the administrative and military depth of Persia's throne or the
natural defenses of Kabul's rock-mountain gorges. The region's two great tribal confederations were the Ghilzais, whose dispersed members lived to the
north, toward Jalalabad, and the Abdalis, centered in Kandahar. They marauded
against neighbors and passing armies. Chieftains of lineage clans consulted
in circle-shaped egalitarian *jirgas,* where they forged alliances and authorized
tribal risings as cyclical and devastating as monsoons. But they had yet to win
an empire of their own.

Ahmed Shah Durrani changed their fortune. His story recounts an inextri-
cable weave of historical fact and received myth. In the standard version,
when Durrani reached Kandahar from the scene of Nadir Shah's murder, he
joined a council of Abdali tribal leaders who had been summoned to a shrine
at Sher Surkh to choose a new king. In the first round many of the chiefs
boasted about their own qualifications. Ahmed, only twenty-four and from a
relatively weak subtribe of the Popalzai, remained silent. To break the dead-
lock a respected holy man placed a strand of wheat on his head and declared
that Ahmed should be king because he had given no cause for anger to the
others. The tribal chiefs soon put blades of grass in their mouths and hung
cloth yokes around their necks to show they agreed to be Ahmed's cattle. Presumably the spiritual symbols cloaked a practical decision: The most powerful Abdali chiefs had elected the weakest among them as leader, giving them
flexibility to rebel whenever they wished. This was a pattern of Pashtun
decision-making about kings and presidents that would persist into the twenty-
first century.[2]

Durrani proved a visionary leader. He crowned himself king in central
Kandahar, a flat dust-caked city constructed from sloping mud-brown brick.
Its mosques and shrines were decorated by tiles and jewels imported from
Persia and India. He called himself the Durr-I-Durrani, or Pearl of Pearls, because of his fondness for pearl earrings. From this the Abdalis became
known as the Durranis. His empire was launched with an act of highway robbery near Kandahar. A caravan from India moved toward Persia with a treasure trove. Ahmed seized the load and used it as an instant defense budget.
He hired a vast army of Pashtun warriors and subsidized the peace around
Kandahar. He struck out for India, occupied Delhi, and eventually controlled
lands as far away as Tibet. The Ghilzai Pashtun tribes submitted to his rule,
and he united the territory that would be known during the twentieth century
as Afghanistan. He summered in Kabul, but Kandahar was his capital. When

he died in 1773 after twenty-six years on the throne, the region's proud and grateful Durranis erected a decorated tomb with a soaring turquoise dome in the town center. Signaling the unity their king forged between Islam and a royal house, they built his memorial adjacent to Kandahar's most holy site, a three-story white mosque inlaid with mosaics. The mosque housed a sacred cloak reputedly worn by the Prophet Mohammed.

For two centuries Ahmed Shah Durrani's legacy shaped Afghan politics. His reign located the center of Pashtun tribal and spiritual power in Kandahar, creating an uneasy balance between that city and Kabul. His vast empire quickly disappeared, but its legend inspired expansive visions of Pashtun rule. His unification of Pashtun tribes in a grand royal house laid the foundation for future claims to royal legitimacy in Afghanistan. Many of the kings who followed him came from a different tribal branch, but they saw themselves as his political heirs. King Zahir Shah, overthrown in 1973, exactly two hundred years after Durrani's death, was the last ruler to claim the heritage of the *jirga* at Sher Surkh.[3]

By 1994 the Kandahar Durranis had fallen into disarray. Many prominent leaders lived in scattered exile in Pakistan, Europe, or the United States. Pakistan's army and intelligence service, fearing Pashtun royal power, squeezed out Durrani leaders who might revive claims to the Afghan throne. The mujahedin leaders most favored by Pakistani intelligence—Hekmatyar, Rabbani, Sayyaf, and Khalis—did not include any Durrani Pashtuns. Also, the geography of the anti-Soviet war sidelined Kandahar and its clans. The conflict's key supply lines flowed north from Kabul to the Soviet Union or east toward Pakistan. None of this was Durrani territory. Kandahar knew heavy fighting during the Soviet occupation, but in the war's strategic geography, it was often a cul-de-sac.

After the Soviet withdrawal the Kandahar region dissolved into a violent checkerboard—less awful than hellish Kabul, but awful still. Hekmatyar's well-armed, antiroyal forces, backed by Pakistani intelligence, lingered like a storm cloud on the city's outskirts. Trucking mafias that reaped huge profits from the heroin trade and other smuggling rackets propped up local warlords. Any group of young Pashtun fighters with a few Kalashnikovs and rocket-propelled grenade launchers could set up a checkpoint and extort payments on the highways. By 1994 the main road from Quetta in Pakistan through Kandahar and on toward Herat and Iran was choked by hundreds of extralegal roadblocks. So was the road from Kandahar to Kabul. Shopkeepers in the ramshackle markets clustered around Ahmed Shah Durrani's still magnificent tomb in central Kandahar—now a fume-choked city of perhaps 750,000—battled ruthless extortion and robbery gangs. Reports of unchecked rape and abduction, including child rape, fueled a local atmosphere of fear and smoldering anger. One of the most powerful Durrani warlords in Kandahar, Mullah Naqibullah, had fallen into a state of madness later diagnosed as a medical condition that required antipsychotic drugs. "I was crazy," Naqibullah admitted years later. "The doctors told me that I had a heavy workload, and it had damaged some of my brain cells."[4]

The birth and rise of the Taliban during 1994 and the emergence of the movement's supreme leader, Mullah Mohammed Omar, were often described in the United States and Europe as the triumph of a naïve, pious, determined band of religious students swept into power on a wave of popular revulsion over Kandahar's criminal warlords. The Taliban themselves emphasized this theme after they acquired power. As they constructed their founding narrative, they weaved in stories of Mullah Omar's visionary dreams for a new Islamic order for Afghanistan. They described his heroic rescue of abducted girls from warlord rapists. They publicized his yen for popular justice, as illustrated by the public hanging of depraved kidnappers. "It was like a myth," recalled the Pashtun broadcaster Spozhmai Maiwandi, who spoke frequently with Taliban leaders. "They were taking the Koran and the gun and going from village to village saying, 'For the Koran's sake, put down your weapons.'" If the warlords refused, the Taliban would kill them. "For us it was not strange," Maiwandi recalled. Religious students had meted out justice in rural Kandahar for ages. "We knew these people still existed."[5]

Much of this Taliban narrative was undoubtedly rooted in fact even if credible eyewitnesses to the most mythologized events of 1994, such as the hanging of notorious rapists from a tank barrel, proved stubbornly elusive. In the end, however, the facts may have mattered less than the narrative's claims on the past. The Taliban assembled their story so that Pashtuns could recognize it as a revival of old glory. The Taliban connected popular, rural Islamic values with a grassroots Durrani Pashtun tribal rising. They emerged at a moment when important wealthy Pashtun tribal leaders around Kandahar hungered for a unifying cause. The Taliban hinted that their militia would become a vehicle for the return to Afghanistan of King Zahir Shah from his exile in Rome. They preached for a reborn alliance of Islamic piety and Pashtun might.

Taliban, which can be translated as "students of Islam" or "seekers of knowledge," had been part of traditional village life in Kandahar's conservative "Koran belt" since even before the time of Ahmed Shah Durrani. Taliban were as familiar to southern Pashtun villagers as frocked Catholic priests were in the Irish countryside, and they played a similar role. They taught schoolchildren, led prayers, comforted the dying, and mediated local disputes. They studied in hundreds of small *madrassas*, memorizing the Koran, and they lived modestly on the charity of villagers. As a young adult a Talib might migrate to a larger *madrassa* in an Afghan city or across the border in Pakistan to complete his Koranic studies. Afterward he might return to a village school and mosque as a full-fledged *mullah*, a "giver" of knowledge now rather than a seeker. In a region unfamiliar with formal government, these religious travelers provided a loose Islamic civil service. The Taliban were memorialized in traditional Afghan folk songs, which sometimes made teasing, skeptical reference to their purity; the students were traditionally regarded as so chaste that Pashtun women might not bother to cover themselves when they came around for meals.[6]

After the communist revolution in Kabul in 1978, Islamic students and mullahs fervently took up arms in rural Pashtun regions. At the village level, far removed from the manipulations of foreign intelligence services, they fortified the anti-Soviet jihad with volunteers and religious sanction. But the war altered the context and curriculum of Islamic studies in the Pashtun belt. This was especially true just across the border in Pakistan. Saudi Arabia's World Muslim League, General Zia's partners at Jamaat-e-Islami, Saudi intelligence, and Pakistani intelligence built scores of new *madrassas* in Peshawar, Quetta, Karachi, and in between. Scholars introduced new texts based on austere Saudi theology and related creeds. One of the most influential and richly endowed of these wartime *madrassas*, Haqqannia, located along the Grand Trunk Road just east of Peshawar, attracted tens of thousands of Afghan and Pakistani Talibs with free education and boarding. The students included many exiled Pashtuns from Kandahar.[7]

Haqqannia's curriculum blended transnational Islamist politics with a theology known as Deobandism, named for a town in India that houses a centuries-old *madrassa*. During the nineteenth century the Deobandis led a conservative reform movement among Indian Muslims. Many Muslim scholars updated Islam's tenets to adapt to changing societies. The Deobandis rejected this approach. They argued that Muslims were obliged to live exactly as the earliest followers of the Prophet Mohammed had done. Deobandi scholars drew up long lists of minute rules designed to eliminate all modern intrusions from a pious Muslim life. They combined this approach with a Wahhabi-like disdain for decoration, adornment, and music.[8]

Nearly all of the Taliban's initial circle of Kandahar Durrani leaders had attended Haqqannia during the 1980s and early 1990s. They knew one another as theology classmates as well as veteran fighters in the anti-Soviet jihad.[9]

The Taliban leadership had no special tribal or royal status. They first surfaced as a small militia force operating near Kandahar city during the spring and summer of 1994, carrying out vigilante attacks against minor warlords, backed by a security fund of about $250,000 raised by local small businessmen. But as the months passed and their legend grew, they began to meet and appeal for backing from powerful Durrani Pashtun traders and chieftains. As these alliances developed, their movement was transformed.

Hashmat Ghani Ahmadzai ran lucrative transportation and manufacturing businesses from Pakistan to Central Asia. He was also a leader of the huge Ahmadzai tribe. He had known some of the Taliban's leaders as strong fighters around Kandahar during the anti-Soviet jihad. When he met them in late 1994, "the sell was very practical, and it made sense. They were saying, 'Look, all these commanders have looted the country. They're selling it piece by piece. They've got checkpoints. They're raping women.' And they wanted to bring in the king. They wanted to bring in national unity and have the *loya jirga* process," a grand assembly that would ratify national Afghan leadership. "It was not something you could turn down." Ahmadzai threw the Taliban his support.[10]

So did the Karzai family, the respected and influential Kandahar-born leaders of the Popalzai, the tribe of Ahmed Shah Durrani himself. Their decision to back the Taliban during 1994 signaled to Afghans that this student militia stood at the forefront of a broad movement—an uprising aimed at the enemies of Islam and also at the enemies of Pashtuns.

ABDUL AHAD KARZAI was the family patriarch. He and his son Hamid, then thirty-six years old, had been moderately important figures in the anti-Soviet resistance. As a boy Hamid Karzai had grown up in bucolic comfort on prewar Kandahar's outskirts. He and his brothers played in dusty lanes they shared with chickens and goats. Their family owned rich farmland; by local standards, they were wealthy. After the Soviet invasion they fled to Quetta.[11]

A lively, thin, bald, elflike man with bright eyes and an irrepressible voice, Hamid Karzai worked during the 1980s as a press, logistics, and humanitarian aid coordinator for the royalist mujahedin faction of Sibghatullah Mojaddedi. He spoke English fluently and maintained many American contacts, including diplomats such as Ed McWilliams and Peter Tomsen. They and other State Department emissaries saw Karzai as an attractive, reasonable royalist, a wily talker and politician. Two of his brothers operated Afghan restaurants in the United States. His royal Pashtun heritage and ease with foreigners allowed him to mediate across Afghan political and ethnic lines after the Soviet withdrawal. He was a born diplomat, rarely confrontational and always willing to gather in a circle and talk. He was appointed deputy foreign minister in the fractured, Massoud-dominated Kabul government during 1993.

Karzai tried to stitch his own fratricidal government back together. For months he shuttled between besieged Kabul and Gulbuddin Hekmatyar's hostile encampment at Charasyab. Karzai sought to mediate between the Kabul cabinet and its estranged prime minister even as they fired rockets at each other.

Early in 1994, Massoud's security chief, the gnome-faced Mohammed Fahim, received a report that Hamid Karzai was working with Pakistani intelligence. Fahim set in motion a bizarre chain of events that led the Karzais to offer their prestige and support to the Taliban.

Like all of Massoud's most trusted commanders, Fahim was an ethnic Tajik from the northeastern Panjshir Valley. By 1994 the Panjshiris were seen by many Pashtuns in Kabul as a kind of battle-fighting mafia. United by a decade of continuous war under Massoud's charismatic leadership, the Panjshiris were close-knit, tough, secretive, and a government within the government. The Kabul cabinet remained multiethnic on paper, but as the civil war deepened, the power of Massoud's Panjshiri-run defense and intelligence ministries grew. Relations with Pashtun leaders deteriorated.

An important cause was the unfinished war with Hekmatyar. Massoud saw Hekmatyar as an unreformed creature of Pakistani intelligence. He and his aides felt they could never be sure where the next ISI-backed conspiracy, fronted by Pashtun leaders, might be coming from. They were bathed in wartime rumors and had few reliable ways to sort fact from fiction. They were under continual bombardment in their candlelit Kabul offices. The war's chronic violence and deceit shaped their judgments about friend and foe.

Acting on a tip that he was plotting against the government, Fahim sent intelligence officers to Hamid Karzai's Kabul home. They arrested the deputy foreign minister and drove him to an interrogation center downtown, not far from the presidential palace. For several hours Fahim's operatives worked on Karzai, accusing him of collusion with Pakistan. Karzai has never provided a direct account of what happened inside the interrogation cell. Several people

he talked to afterward said that he was beaten up and that his face was bloodied and bruised. Some accounts place Fahim himself in the cell during parts
of the interrogation. It is not clear whether Massoud knew about the interrogation or authorized it, although his lieutenants denied that he did.

The session ended with a bang. A rocket lobbed routinely by Hekmatyar
into Kabul's center slammed into the intelligence compound where Karzai
was being interrogated. In the ensuing chaos Karzai slipped out of the building and walked dazed into Kabul's streets. He made his way to the city bus station and quietly slipped onto a bus headed for Jalalabad. There a friend from
the United Nations recognized Karzai walking on the street, his patrician face
banged up and bruised, and helped him to a relative's house. The next day
Hamid Karzai crossed the Khyber Pass into exile in Pakistan. He would not
return to Kabul for more than seven years.[12]

He joined his father in Quetta during the spring of 1994. Within months
he heard about the Taliban's rising. He knew many of the Taliban's leaders
from the days of the anti-Soviet jihad. "They were my buddies," he explained
later. "They were good people."[13]

They were also a way to challenge a Kabul government whose officers
had just beaten him into exile. Karzai was not especially wealthy by Western
standards—his hard currency accounts were often precariously low—but he
contributed $50,000 of his own funds to the Taliban as they began to orga-
nize around Kandahar. He also handed them a large cache of weapons he had
hidden away and introduced them to prominent Pashtun tribal leaders. Separately, the Taliban met with an enthusiastic Abdul Haq and with many Durranis who maintained close ties with the exiled king Zahir Shah. The Durrani
Pashtuns hoped now to achieve what the United Nations and American envoys such as Peter Tomsen had earlier failed to deliver. Urging their new
white-bannered, Koran-waving rural militia forward, they plotted a return of
the Afghan king.[14]

MOHAMMED OMAR was an unlikely heir to Pashtun glory. He reflected the
past through a mirror cracked and distorted by two decades of war. For a man
destined to make such an impact on global affairs, remarkably little is known
about his biography. He was born around 1950 in Nodeh Village in Kandahar
province. His small and undistinguished family clan occupied a single house
in the district, according to a biographical account given to U.S. diplomats by
the Taliban early in 1995. His was an impoverished, isolated boyhood domi-

nated by long hours in dim religious schools memorizing the Koran. From religious texts he learned to read and write in Arabic and Pashto only shakily. He never roamed far from Kandahar province. If he ever flew on an airplane, slept in a hotel, or watched a satellite movie, he gave no indication of it. In later years he had many opportunities to travel abroad but refused even a religious pilgrimage to holy Muslim shrines in Saudi Arabia. He declined to travel as far as Kabul except on very rare occasions. Kandahar was his world.[15]

During the anti-Soviet jihad, Omar served as a local subcommander with the Younis Khalis faction. He followed a prominent trader, Haji Bashar, who also funded a religious school in the area. He showed special ability with rocket-propelled grenade launchers and reportedly knocked out a number of Soviet tanks. By one account, he eventually became Khalis's deputy commander for Kandahar province, a relatively senior position, despite his being neither "charismatic nor articulate," as a Taliban colleague later put it.[16]

Exploding shrapnel struck Omar in the face during an attack near Kandahar. One piece badly damaged his right eye. Taliban legend holds that Omar cut his own eye out of the socket with a knife. More prosaic versions report his treatment at a Red Cross hospital in Pakistan where his eye was surgically removed. In any event, his right eyelid was stitched permanently shut.[17]

By the early 1990s, Omar had returned to religious studies. He served as a teacher and prayer leader in a tiny, poor village of about twenty-five families called Singesar, twenty miles outside of Kandahar in a wide, fertile valley of wheat fields and vineyards. In exchange for religious instruction, villagers provided him with food. He apparently had no other reliable source of income, although he retained ties to the relatively wealthy trader Bashar. He shuttled between the village's small mud-brick religious school and its small mud-brick mosque. He lived in a modest house about two hundred yards from the village *madrassa*.[18]

The only known photographs of Omar depict him as a relatively tall, well-built, thin-faced man with a light complexion and a bushy black beard. He spoke Pashto in a peasant's provincial accent. In meetings he would often sit silently for long periods. When he spoke, his voice was often no louder than a whisper. He modestly declined to call himself a *mullah* because he had not finished all of his Islamic studies. He sometimes talked about himself in the third person, as if he were a character in someone else's story.

He believed in the prophecy of dreams and spoke about them in political and military meetings, drawing on them to explain important decisions. During 1994, as the Taliban gathered influence around Kandahar, Omar repeatedly said he had been called into action by a dream in which Allah appeared before him in the form of a man and told him to lead the believers.

As he began to meet with Pashtun delegations around Kandahar, he would often receive visitors outside, seated on the ground. By one account, in an early Taliban organizational meeting, he was selected as leader of the movement's supreme council because unlike some of the more seasoned candidates, Omar did not seem to be interested in personal power.[19] The story was another plank in the Taliban's myth of Pashtun revival: The humble, quiet Mullah Omar echoed the silence of young Ahmed Shah Durrani at the Sher Surkh *jirga*.

He spoke rarely about his ambitions, but when he did, his language was direct. The Taliban was "a simple band of dedicated youths determined to establish the laws of God on Earth and prepared to sacrifice everything in pursuit of that goal," he said. "The Taliban will fight until there is no blood in Afghanistan left to be shed and Islam becomes a way of life for our people."[20]

When they sprang from Kandahar in 1994, the Taliban were a tabula rasa on which others could project their ambitions. The trouble was, as the French scholar Olivier Roy noted, the Taliban were different from other opportunistic Afghan factions: They meant what they said.[21]

BENAZIR BHUTTO also charted the future from the past. Pakistan's sputtering democracy had shuddered through another minor miracle—a semilegitimate national election—and voters had returned Bhutto to office as prime minister. Before her swearing-in she took long walks in Islamabad parks with old political allies. She wanted to talk candidly about her plans where Pakistani intelligence could not listen. She told her colleagues that she wanted to learn from the errors of her first term. She was determined to stay close to the Americans. She wanted to keep the Pakistani army happy as best she could—she would not pick unnecessary fights. She would have to keep watch on ISI, but she would try to listen to their demands and accommodate them. In this way she hoped to survive in office long enough to revive Pakistan's economy. Only if she created wealth for Pakistan's middle classes could Bhutto ensure her party's long-term strength, she and her advisers believed.[22]

Pakistan suffered from widespread poverty, low literacy rates, and a weak natural resource base. Yet it also had a strong business class, international ports, and thriving export industries. How could the country create sudden new wealth through external trade the way other Asian countries had managed to do during the 1980s? To the east lay India, the Pakistan army's reason for being and a foreign policy problem Bhutto could not hope to solve on her own. But to the west and north lay new possibilities for commerce and influence. Bhutto wanted, as she said later, to "market Pakistan internationally as . . . the crossroads to the old silk roads of trade between Europe and Asia." Like every young student on the subcontinent, she had grown up with history texts that chronicled invasions across the Khyber Pass. These ancient conquests had been inspired by lucrative trade routes that ran from Central Asia to Delhi. "So I thought, 'Okay, control of the trade routes is a way to get my country power and prestige.'" She imagined Pakistani exporters trucking televisions and washing machines to the newly independent Muslim republics of former Soviet Central Asia. She imagined cotton and oil flowing to Pakistan from Central Asia and Iran.[23]

But when she and her advisers looked at the map in 1994, they saw Afghanistan in the way, an impassable cauldron of warlords, a country engulfed by a civil war fueled by Pakistan's own intelligence service. Bhutto called in the ISI brigadiers, and, as she recalled it, they told her they wanted to keep pressure on Massoud because his government was "too pro-India." This seemed to her a dead-end policy, but she had pledged to go slowly with the army this time in office, to defer to them where she could. She wanted to create a discussion about an alternative Afghan policy that would include the views of the army and Pakistani intelligence.[24]

She organized an interagency group on Afghanistan. Beside her at the conference table sat a retired septuagenarian Pakistani general, Naseerullah Babar, who had agreed to serve as Bhutto's interior minister. A Pashtun notable, Babar had organized covert guerrilla training for Hekmatyar and Massoud when they first fled to Pakistan in the 1970s. He had been loyal to Bhutto's father, and Benazir trusted him. Babar had friendships inside the notoriously independent Afghan bureau of Pakistani intelligence. He brought some of the ISI brigadiers he knew to the early working sessions on Afghan policy. They argued about the risks of pulling support from Hekmatyar. Without his pressure on Massoud, the ISI's officers maintained, ethnic Tajiks and Uzbeks might lock up control of Kabul for many years. They would deepen ties with India and remain hostile to Pakistan and stir up trouble in its large Pashtun population. How could Bhutto pursue her dream of Central Asian trade in that case?

"Why do we need Kabul anyway?" Babar asked, as Bhutto recalled it. They could reach Central Asia by the southern route, through Kandahar and Herat. Bhutto thought this idea had promise. Her government could build roads, telephone lines, and other infrastructure right through Afghanistan's Pashtun country, all the way to Central Asia, bypassing Kabul and the ethnic gridlock to its north. Bhutto endorsed the new approach "if it could be done by paying local warlords" for free commercial passage via southern Afghanistan. Pakistani intelligence had no objection.[25]

Babar spearheaded the effort. In October 1994 he arranged a heavily publicized trial convoy carrying Pakistani textiles that he hoped to drive from Quetta to Turkmenistan, to demonstrate Pakistan's new ambitions. The convoy arrived on the Afghan border above Kandahar just as Mullah Omar and his Taliban *shura* opened their preaching campaign in the area.

Pakistani trucking interests had already begun to supply money and weapons to the Taliban, hoping they could unclog Kandahar's highways. It may have been these trucking overlords rather than Pakistan's government who aided the Taliban in their first military breakthrough. An Afghan commander in the border truck-stop town of Spin Boldak, loyal to Massoud on paper, handed the Taliban the keys to an enormous ISI-supplied weapons dump near the town, apparently in exchange for a large payment. The dump had been created in 1991 to receive weapons and ammunition rushed across the border by Pakistani and Saudi intelligence officers who were trying to comply with a deadline to end outside supplies to the Afghan war. The Spin Boldak dump's seventeen tunnels held enough weaponry for tens of thousands of soldiers.[26]

The Taliban broke it open in mid-October, issued public calls for volunteers from local *madrassas,* and handed out assault rifles still wrapped in plastic. Whether Babar or local ISI officers endorsed or aided this handover of weapons is not clear. Babar did capitalize quickly on the Taliban's new strength. When his demonstration convoy was blocked at rogue checkpoints twenty miles outside of Kandahar in early November, he waved the Taliban on to free his trucks.[27]

They did so with ease. Mullah Naqibullah and other long-feared Kandahar warlords who were allied with Massoud had terrorized the region without challenge for years. Suddenly, in just twenty-four hours, the Taliban moved into central Kandahar and captured the entire city. Mullah Omar took control of the provincial governor's arched sandstone headquarters, across from the tomb of Ahmed Shah Durrani. Naqibullah and his allies, unable or unwilling to resist their youthful and highly motivated attackers, simply melted away.[28]

By mid-November the Taliban's six-member *shura* ruled not only Kandahar but its airport, where they captured six MiG-21 fighter jets and four Mi-17 transport helicopters. They seized tanks and armored personnel carriers.[29] They announced that all highway roadblocks would be dismantled, all non-

Taliban militia disarmed, and all criminals subject to swift Islamic punishments. They lynched a few resisters to make their point.

Benazir Bhutto was suddenly the matron of a new Afghan faction. The Taliban might provide a battering ram to open trade routes to Central Asia, as she hoped, yet they also presented complications.

Pakistani intelligence already had one Pashtun client, Hekmatyar. The ISI Afghan bureau was in turmoil. The Rawalpindi army command had recently appointed a secular-minded, British-influenced general, Javed Ashraf Qazi, to take charge of ISI. Qazi's immediate predecessor, the bearded Islamist missionary Javed Nasir, had led the intelligence service toward overt religious preaching. The army brass now told Qazi to "put ISI right," as he recalled it, by purging the most open Islamists. Qazi systematically removed officers who had been promoted by Nasir. In doing so he shook up the Afghan bureau. Its relations with Hekmatyar were already a mess. Nasir's ardent personal beliefs had led him into obscure theological arguments with his putative client. ISI was supposed to be helping Hekmatyar pressure "the fox of Panjshir," as Qazi called Massoud. Instead, Javed Nasir picked fights over religion.[30]

ISI had even deeper interests at stake than Hekmatyar's fate. By 1994, Pakistani intelligence relied on the Islamist training camps in Hekmatyar-controlled Afghan territory to support its new covert jihad in Indian-held Kashmir. The political-religious networks around Hekmatyar trained and shipped foreign volunteers to Kashmir. Bhutto recalled that during this period, Pakistani intelligence officers repeatedly told her they could not fight the clandestine Kashmir war with Kashmiris alone; there just weren't enough effective native guerrillas to bleed Indian troops. They needed Afghan and Arab volunteers, and they needed the sanctuary of guerrilla training camps in Afghan territory.[31]

This complicated ISI's new relationship with the Taliban. Mullah Omar was determined to challenge Hekmatyar for supremacy among Pashtuns. If Pakistani intelligence suddenly shifted its support to Omar, it might put the covert Kashmir war at risk. Pakistani brigadiers working from Peshawar, close to Hekmatyar for years, wanted to stick with their longtime client. But ISI's Quetta and Kandahar offices, responsible for covert policy in southern Afghanistan, became intrigued by the Taliban, according to accounts later assembled by the CIA.

Qazi's "chap in Kandahar" urged that the ISI chief meet some of the new militia, as Qazi recalled it. He invited a Taliban delegation to ISI headquarters in Rawalpindi. Mullah Omar refused to travel, but a senior group arrived.

They picked up their dirty, sandled feet and sat cross-legged on top of the sofa cushions, as if they were sitting on the floor. Some of them were limbless. Others had been fitted with artificial legs or arms. "I was horrified to see they had emerged literally from the villages," recalled Qazi, a product of Pakistan's British-designed higher education system. "They had very little clue about international affairs or anything like that. They had their own peculiar set of ideas. The only thing I found was that they were well intentioned."

The Taliban delegation urged Qazi to withdraw ISI's support from other Afghan leaders, including Hekmatyar. Young and thick-bearded, their faces marked and wizened beyond their years, they declared that all other Afghan leaders had brought destruction to the country. They wanted "to hang all of them—*all of them.*" They also asked ISI for logistical help. The Taliban wanted to import gasoline from Pakistan and sought an exemption from trade rules. Qazi agreed, as he recalled it.[32]

Bhutto said that in the months that followed this first meeting between ISI and the Taliban, the requests from Pakistani intelligence for covert aid to their new clients grew gradually. "I became slowly, slowly sucked into it," Bhutto remembered. "It started out with a little fuel, then it became machinery" and spare parts for the Taliban's captured airplanes and tanks. Next ISI made requests for trade concessions that would enrich both the Taliban and the outside businessmen who supplied them. "Then it became money" direct from the Pakistani treasury, Bhutto recalled.

Each time Pakistani intelligence officers asked for more covert aid during 1995, they said they needed the funds to attain leverage over the Taliban. The ISI brigadiers complained to Bhutto that the Taliban's leaders were stubborn, that they would not follow the military and political advice Pakistan offered. By providing cash, military spare parts, and training, the Pakistani intelligence service told Bhutto, they could ensure that the Taliban stayed close to Pakistan as they began to challenge Massoud.

"I started sanctioning the money," Bhutto recalled. "Once I gave the go-ahead that they should get money, I don't know how much money they were ultimately given. . . . I know it was a lot. It was just carte blanche."[33]

By the spring of 1995 these covert supplies were visible across southern Afghanistan. ISI sent exiled Pashtun military officers and guerrilla leaders to the Taliban's cause. Former Afghan communist army officers loyal to Shahnawaz Tanai began to repair and operate Taliban tanks, aircraft, and helicopters. In eastern Afghanistan powerful local commanders such as Jallaladin Haqqanni declared for the Taliban. These political conversions were supported by money, weapons, pickup trucks, and supplies shipped across the Pakistan border. Volunteer fighters poured out of the border *madrassas*. When Herat fell to the Taliban in September, the die was cast. Omar and his Durrani militia now controlled all of southern Afghanistan. They announced their intention to march on Kabul.[34]

Benazir Bhutto felt that she was losing control of her new Afghan policy. She did not want Pakistani intelligence to back the Taliban in a military drive on Kabul. Bhutto argued that Pakistan should use the Taliban's rising strength as a new lever in negotiations for a coalition Afghan government. Some in the army and ISI agreed with her, but the Taliban did not care for these Pakistani diplomatic nuances. They still meant what they said: They did not want to negotiate with other Afghan leaders, they wanted to hang them.

Bhutto began to wonder if ISI was telling her everything about its covert aid to the Taliban. When Bhutto traveled to Tehran, Iranian president Ali Akbar Rafsanjani, who supported Massoud, lashed out at her in a private meeting, complaining angrily about covert Pakistani aid to the Taliban. Rafsanjani alleged that Pakistan's army sent disguised troops into Afghanistan to fight with the Taliban. Taken aback, Bhutto denied this, but later, when she heard that Massoud held Pakistani officers in his prisoner of war camps, she wondered about what she had not been told.[35]

Yet ISI's ambition was greater than its purse. Pakistan's army suffered from acute money problems during 1995. The army commanded the lion's share of Pakistan's budget, but with American aid cut over the nuclear issue, there was not much to go around. The country wallowed in debt. An arms race with India drained resources. As it had during the 1980s, ISI needed Saudi intelligence, and it needed wealthy Islamist patrons from the Persian Gulf.

EARLY IN 1995, Ahmed Badeeb, chief of staff to Prince Turki al-Faisal, the director of Saudi intelligence, descended toward Kandahar's airport in a Gulfstream-2 corporate jet. As the plane was about to touch down, Badeeb saw a cow in the middle of the runway. His pilot pulled up suddenly, flew around, and tried again. The Taliban's greeting party chased the cow away and crowded around Badeeb when he reached the tarmac.

"Don't you remember us?" some of the bearded young Taliban asked. Badeeb stared at them and confessed he did not.

"We were students in your school!"[36]

During the anti-Soviet jihad Ahmed Badeeb had funded a vocational school for Afghan boys along the Pakistani border. The school was personal charity, funded from his Islamic *zakat,* or tithe.

The Taliban explained that they had since moved Badeeb's entire school to Kandahar. One of the graduates was Mullah Mohammed Rabbani, a senior member of the founding Taliban ruling *shura* and a close associate of Mullah Omar. Rabbani (no relation to President Rabbani, Massoud's ally in Kabul) expressed deep gratitude to Badeeb. He led the Saudi to a waiting car. They drove to meet Mullah Omar in central Kandahar.

Afghan colleagues carried the Taliban leader into the meeting; he was having trouble with one of his legs. But Omar stood long enough to offer Badeeb a long, warm embrace. Over tea and plates of food Omar told the story of the Taliban's rise in Kandahar. As Badeeb recalled it, Omar told him the first weapons he received had come from Pakistan's Interior Ministry.

The Taliban leaders asked Badeeb for guidance and support. They needed to learn from Saudi Arabia about how to run a proper Islamic government, they said. Omar asked Badeeb to send in whatever texts Saudi Arabian schools used so they could be handed out in Taliban schools. He asked for food and assistance that would allow Afghan refugees to return home. Badeeb presented Omar with a copy of the Koran as a gift, and Omar said he would follow its teachings always.

"Whatever Saudi Arabia wants me to do, I will do," Omar told Badeeb, as Badeeb recalled it.[37]

Prince Turki had sent Badeeb on this mission to Kandahar. The Pakistanis were advertising the Taliban to the Saudis as an important new force on the Afghan scene. Babar referred to the Taliban as "my boys," and he gave both Badeeb and Prince Turki the impression that he had helped create them and was now building them up steadily.[38]

Prince Turki flew into Islamabad and met with Mullah Rabbani, Badeeb's former student. He wanted the Taliban to support an all-party peace proposal for Afghanistan. Turki remained personally involved in Afghan political negotiations. There was a sense among many Saudi officials when they looked at the Afghans that, but for the luck of Saudi oil, something like this might have been their fate. It bothered Turki greatly that the Americans had walked away from Afghanistan. A negotiated peace might deliver a modest success for Saudi foreign policy as well, checking rivals Iran and India, but Turki's interest in the issue often seemed as much personal as professional.

The Taliban's Rabbani was only in his twenties, but he seemed relatively sophisticated to Prince Turki, eager to learn about Saudi Arabia and international politics. Turki thought that Rabbani was someone the Saudi kingdom could and should help. "He told me that they are proud of having friendship with Saudi Arabia," as Turki recalled it, "and that they considered King Fahd as their *imam*," or spiritual leader.[39]

As the months passed, it became clear to both Turki and Badeeb that Pakistani intelligence had decided to back the Taliban at Hekmatyar's expense. Saudi intelligence had no objection to this betrayal: Hekmatyar had angered Turki by denouncing Saudi Arabia during the 1991 Gulf War.[40]

As the Taliban grew in military strength, so did the breadth and depth of its leaders' contacts with Saudi Arabia. Saudi intelligence maintained a close and direct relationship with ISI, allowing it to bypass the civilian government of Benazir Bhutto. Hamid Gul and other former ISI generals consulted with Prince Turki, traveled frequently to Saudi Arabia, and encouraged Saudi intelligence to support the Taliban. By one account Saudi intelligence paid annual cash bonuses to senior ISI officers designated by the Pakistani intelligence chief. Financial aid and discounted oil supplies from Riyadh buoyed the treasuries of Pakistan's army and intelligence service during these lean years of American economic sanctions. The Saudi liaison strengthened ISI as a shadow government within Pakistan and helped it to resist civilian political oversight.[41]

ISI offered regular "situation reports" to Prince Turki and his staff as the Taliban conquered new territory. The reports outlined the Taliban's plans and catalogued their problems and setbacks. Steadily the emphasis on peace talks faded and the emphasis on military victory rose.[42]

The scale of Saudi payments and subsidies to Pakistan's army and intelligence service during the mid-1990s has never been disclosed. Judging by the practices of the previous decade, direct transfers and oil price subsidies to Pakistan's military probably amounted in some years to at least several hundred million dollars. This bilateral support helped ISI build up its proxy jihad forces in both Kashmir and Afghanistan.[43]

Saudi charities and religious ministries also aided the Taliban's rise during 1995 and 1996. Prince Turki has acknowledged providing "humanitarian" support to the Taliban during this period via Saudi charities such as the International Islamic Relief Organization. Wealthy Saudi individuals also made contributions, Turki has acknowledged: "We didn't think we could control individuals who take their money and go and give it to them."[44] The *madrassas* along the Afghan border that had educated the Taliban's leaders and now supplied them with new recruits also received funding. Many of the Pakistani clerics who ran these *madrassas* had been trained in Saudi Arabia. The Saudi

Ministry for the Propagation of Virtue and the Prevention of Vice, the kingdom's religious police, tutored and supported the Taliban as they built up
their own Islamic police. The Taliban's virtue and vice ministry—which enforced punishments under Islamic law, policed female modesty, and forcibly
rounded up Afghan men for prayers—quickly grew richer than other arms of
Taliban government. This almost certainly was a result of direct subsidies and
training from Saudi Arabia's Islamic establishment.[45]

Saudi Arabia still feared Iranian influence in Afghanistan and Central Asia.
The Taliban were useful allies for the aims of Saudi statecraft, but they also
promoted Islamic values in accord with Saudi theology. Although there were
important differences between Saudi Islamic orthodoxy and the Taliban's
strange Deobandi rule making, there were also many similarities. There was a
naïve purity about the Taliban that attracted Saudi missionaries.

For his part Prince Turki believed the Taliban would grow and evolve into
a more normal, worldly, conservative Islamic political force. All revolutionary
movements started out in a radical vein and gradually moderated, and so
would the Taliban, Turki thought. In the meanwhile, the Taliban had much to
recommend them: They were not corrupt, they brought order to Afghan
cities, and they gratefully accepted Saudi and Pakistani patronage.

Saudi Arabia itself had been born seven decades earlier under the sword of
a radical Islamic militia, the Ikhwan. Gradually the kingdom had grown up,
stabilized, and partially modernized. More than any other previous Afghan
militia or political movement, the Taliban presented themselves in the Saudi
image. Surely, Prince Turki believed, they, too, would mature.[46]

AT THE U.S. EMBASSY in Islamabad the Taliban's rise was evaluated as
an isolated Afghan mystery. American diplomats in the Pakistani capital and
in Peshawar sifted contradictory rumors and reports, unable to discern the
Taliban's supply sources. "The Taliban have been characterized as simultaneously Pakistani tools and anti-Pakistan," the Peshawar consulate told Washington in a Confidential cable dispatched on November 3, 1994, as Mullah
Omar consolidated control. The consulate said it was "very possible" that the
Taliban had received aid from "a number of sources, including Pakistan," but
"their backers may find that they have created a tiger that is more than willing
to take independent action and not be anyone's tool." The consulate reported
ISI contacts with the Taliban but conceded that the movement's "origins,
goals and sponsors . . . remain unclear." A second November 1994 cable

from Peshawar to Washington, sardonically quoting the lyrics of the rock band the Who, asked about the Taliban: "Meet the New Boss. . . . Same as the Old Boss?" The movement's military equipment, some of it freshly unpacked from crates, seemed "too much of a coincidence," the Peshawar consulate initially reported, and probably suggested covert Pakistani involvement of the type that had previously strengthened Hekmatyar. Abdul Haq warned an American diplomat that same month, "It looks like Afghanistan was first destroyed by the communists, then by the fundamentalists, and now we might be destroyed by the mullahs." But the State Department was not ready to leap to such conclusions. Its cables that autumn and winter of the Taliban's rise described the militia as "an enigma" that was "certainly not acting to the exclusive benefit of any of the established vested interests," and enjoyed widespread popular support. As the Taliban swept west from Kandahar in sophisticated military formations, the U.S. embassy reported that their "use of tanks and helicopters strongly suggested Pakistani tutelage or direct control." Still, the extent and character of any Pakistani involvement remained "very much in doubt." Two American diplomats traveled to Kandahar on February 13, 1995, to meet with the Taliban mayor. The session began with a prayer calling for the conversion by unbelievers to Islam. The mayor refused to answer questions from the Americans about the Taliban's leadership or organization. The movement's leaders "appeared coached and the overall impression was one of disingenuity and a degree of deception," the American officials cabled afterward to Washington. It was the beginning of a long string of such lies and evasions—but the U.S. government had few resources in the region to dig beneath the surface. The CIA station and the Pentagon's defense attachés had other priorities. Afghanistan's civil war was no longer an important subject for intelligence collection.[47]

Benazir Bhutto, who was secretly authorizing the Taliban's covert aid, did not let the Americans know. She visited Washington in the spring of 1995, met with President Clinton, and promoted the Taliban as a pro-Pakistan force that could help stabilize Afghanistan. During her discussions with Clinton, "Afghanistan was not very high up in either person's agenda," Bhutto recalled. The country was "a dying issue." But she found a receptive audience among midlevel officials for her message about the Taliban's potential to bring peace. During her visit and for many months afterward Bhutto and her aides repeatedly lied to American government officials and members of Congress about the extent of Pakistani military and financial aid to the Taliban. At a meeting with then acting Secretary of State Strobe Talbott in Washington, Bhutto's foreign minister and ISI chief both "categorically denied that Pakistan provided military assistance to the Taliban," as a contemporaneous State Department cable put it. Talbott warned in reply that Pakistan's policies in Afghanistan were likely to produce "unintended consequences," because ultimately, groups like the Taliban "could not be controlled." Later Bhutto herself brazenly lied to Senator Hank Brown and Congressman Charlie Wilson over lunch in Islamabad, telling them that Pakistan's government "backed the U.N., not the Taliban, in Afghanistan." Bhutto had decided that it was more important to appease the Pakistani army and intelligence services than to level with her American friends.[48]

The relatively small number of American officials at the White House, the CIA, and the State Department who followed Afghanistan tended to accept the Taliban's own narrative: They were a cleansing, transitional force that would unite Pashtuns and create a new basis for peace. Regional specialists at State—influenced by such Westernized Taliban supporters as Hamid Karzai—welcomed the rise of a militia that might finally pull divided Pashtuns together. At the National Security Council the Taliban were seen in the early stages "as a force that could bring order to chaos," as one senior official there recalled it. At the CIA, analysts also concluded that the Taliban could stabilize Afghanistan. The Taliban might reduce factional bloodshed, curtail heroin trafficking, and create conditions for realistic peace talks, they believed. The speed at which the Taliban began to rack up military victories left some CIA analysts shaking their heads in amazement. But the Taliban seemed an idiosyncratic Afghan group with no larger significance. The dominant response to the Taliban by the American government was indifference. When Senator Brown, a Democrat from Colorado, tried to organize a new policy initiative, he hit a "wall of silence" at the State Department. "It wasn't that they favored the Taliban," he recalled. "It was simply that they didn't want to get engaged."[49]

Assistant Secretary of State Robin Raphel, the Clinton administration's most active Afghan policy maker, accepted many of Benazir Bhutto's claims and arguments about Afghanistan, and supported Bhutto's drive to open new trade routes between Pakistan and Central Asia. She defended Bhutto in public against charges that Pakistan was the secret force behind the Taliban's rise. She also wanted to lift U.S. economic sanctions against Pakistan. She thought the sanctions drove America and Pakistan apart without having any impact on Islamabad's nuclear ambitions. She and Clinton ultimately won new American aid for Bhutto's government. They hoped it would strengthen the prime min-

ister's hand in her struggles with the army and ISI. Since the Clinton administration was heavily invested in Bhutto and since she personally advocated U.S.
support for the Taliban, hardly anyone in Washington was inclined to raise
doubts as the militia swept north toward the outskirts of Kabul.

By then American policy in Central Asia had found another impetus: oil
and gas.

As Benazir Bhutto had done, executives at America's largest energy companies began late in 1995 to imagine the future by studying historical maps.
Across Afghanistan travelers along the Silk Road had created fortunes for
centuries by moving spice, jewels, and textiles to new markets. The profitable
game now—created by the Soviet Union's collapse—was oil and natural gas.
The key trade routes were the same as they had been for centuries. Many led
through Afghanistan.

Robin Raphel and others at the State Department and the White House
believed that for American oil companies, too, the Taliban could be an important part of a new Afghan solution.

"Dangling the Carrot"

MARTY MILLER'S LONG, strange journey into Afghanistan began during the summer of 1995. He was edging toward the end of his career, and he itched for a grand achievement. He had recently read The Prize, Daniel Yergin's epic history of global oil conquest and politics, and the book fired Miller's imagination. He had spent three decades in the oil business, all with one company, Unocal, America's twelfth largest energy corporation. He owned a comfortable house beside a golf course outside of Houston, Texas. His daughters had grown up and gone to college. He had worked over the years in faraway places—Indonesia, the North Sea, Thailand—and had risen to vice president in Unocal's Exploration and Production Division. Now he sought adventure. He could afford to take some risks.[1]

Unocal needed a gusher. After more than a century in the oil business, the company faced an identity crisis. It had lost $153 million during 1994, the result of sinking profits in its normally reliable refining and marketing division, and it continued to lag well behind the largest American oil firms.[2]

Miller's superiors thought they saw an opportunity to leapfrog ahead. Vast tracts of land and sea in former communist countries, previously closed to

American oil companies, had suddenly been thrown open for exploration. Instead of settling for life as "a midsized, integrated oil company," chief executive Roger C. Beach proclaimed that Unocal would bid to become "the world's largest energy resource company." The key was to go places where no one else dared. Afghanistan was such a place.[3]

Beach charged his deputy and designated successor, a charismatic yachtsman named John F. Imle Jr., to lead Unocal's gambit. Imle needed project managers who shared the company's budding appetite for risk. In Marty Miller, an avuncular, round man with combed-back white hair and a rosy face, Imle found a willing partner. As a boy Miller had worked in his grandfather's Colorado coal mine. He had barely been able to pay his way through college. When Unocal offered him a summer job on an oil rig, he switched his studies to petroleum engineering. After decades of international travel as an oil and gas executive, he remained a slangy, direct, casual, profane American businessman who called it as he saw it and who believed in capitalism, charity, and golf. He was a transparent Texan. He had sympathy for people everywhere but did not pretend to be a scholar about their cultures. Afghanistan, as Miller understood it, was "a friggin' mess." He had not really heard about the Taliban. He asked questions and learned that they did not like to have their pictures taken and that "they were very oppressive toward women and that kids couldn't fly kites and all this kind of stuff."

Unocal's Afghan strategy began in Turkmenistan, a newly independent republic carved from the corpse of the Soviet Union. The problem—and the opportunity—was referred to by oil men as "stranded gas." Turkmenistan's gas reserves ranked in the top dozen in the world, yet nobody bought them. The country had been independent for four years, but Russia still owned all the pipelines leading away from its gas fields. Russia and Turkmenistan fought bitterly over how the pipelines should be used. Their battles finally shut the fields down altogether. Until new pipelines were built, or the conflicts with Russia were resolved, Turkmenistan was stuck with 159 trillion cubic feet of gas, 32 billion barrels of oil, and no place to sell any of it.[4]

Benazir Bhutto's Pakistan faced an energy crisis. By 2010 the country would need nearly a trillion cubic feet of gas more than it could produce on its own.[5] Unocal saw a solution in the Central Asian trading routes that had captured Bhutto's imagination. John Imle authorized a development project in which Unocal would seek to build pipelines from Turkmenistan to Pakistan, across war-ravaged Afghanistan. The easiest way would be to pass through Kandahar along the same southern route favored by Bhutto for her trucking and transport schemes. This was now Taliban country.

Imle assigned the Afghan pipeline project to Marty Miller. It was "a moon-shot," Miller thought, but there was a romantic, grandiose scale to the plan. Miller's pipelines would cross ancient steppes traversed by Alexander the Great, Marco Polo, and Genghis Khan. He asked Daniel Yergin over dinner one night whether, if he pulled the project off for Unocal, he might even get a mention in *The Prize*'s next edition. "It would probably get a chapter," Yergin told him.[6]

MARTY MILLER stepped out of the climate-controlled interior of Unocal's Gulfstream jet and into a blistering Turkmenistan summer. It was August 1995, and the new $89 million airport in Ashkhabad, the country's capital, was still under construction. It would soon allow up to 4.5 million people to enter each year. The dreary city had never seen a tenth that many visitors, but Saparmurat Niyazov, Turkmenistan's autocratic leader, expected that with guests like Miller, the country's fortunes were about to change. Soon Turkmenistan would teem with European venture capitalists, Arab sheikhs, and American petroleum company executives. They would come to get rich on his oil and gas, or to entertain themselves at his planned Disneyland-style resort. Turkmenistan would become "the new Kuwait," Niyazov boasted. There had been a few glitches, however. In his zeal to construct a truly distinctive airport, Niyazov had built the control tower on the wrong side of the runway. Air traffic controllers looking to guide pilots into Ashkhabad had their views blocked by the gaudy new terminal.[7]

Miller's mission was to persuade Niyazov that Unocal was the right company to pipe his gas through neighboring Afghanistan. It was difficult to know how to construct a sales pitch for a president like Niyazov. He was a creature of the Soviet system, a Communist Party apparatchik trying to remake himself as a nationalist leader. Everywhere Miller looked in Ashkhabad, the plump, silver-haired face of Niyazov was there smiling back at him— from billboards, parade floats, and vodka bottle labels. *Turkmenbashi* (Father of All Turkmen), as he preferred to be called, had built a personality cult on Stalin's model. In the country of 4.5 million he brooked no opposition. Many trappings of the old Soviet system remained: a state-run press that spewed fawning doublespeak about their great leader, a rubber-stamp parliament that periodically extended the president's term, and an intelligence service that listened in on just about anything Niyazov wanted to hear. Yet he had been slow to introduce free market reforms, and the idea of negotiating multibillion-dollar international oil and gas deals with Western companies was new to him.

Niyazov had erected twenty-four brand-new, white marble, wedding cake–style hotels on the south side of Ashkhabad. Each hotel belonged to a government ministry, and Miller checked into the oil and gas ministry's favorite. The rooms had panoramic views of the Iranian mountains. They were as outsized as the airport and just as dysfunctional. Each day that summer Miller turned his little window air-conditioning unit on full blast, but to no avail. He roasted. Daily negotiations with his Turkmen counterparts did little to cool him down. Across the table there "was a lot of shouting, threats, intimidation, a very different approach to what we were used to," Miller recalled. "But at the end of the day you go and you drink some vodka and have some toasts—all this stuff, you know—and all's forgiven. Then the next day you put on the pads and away you go again."

To break out of this situation Miller called in John Imle. Niyazov invited Unocal's senior executives to his pink Italian-built summer mansion on the outskirts of Ashkhabad. They raised more vodka toasts. Imle and the Father of All Turkmen grew to be "real, real cozy," as Miller recalled it.

Miller turned to the U.S. embassy in Ashkhabad for more help. Tying a pipeline deal into the broader agenda of American foreign policy could provide Unocal with a competitive advantage. Some European or Middle Eastern companies seeking oil and gas deals in Central Asia arranged payoffs to local officials. Apart from Unocal, Niyazov dealt with an array of American consultants and middlemen, some of them thick with mysterious connections in Turkey and the Middle East. Unocal itself had a mysterious Saudi partner called Delta with little experience in the oil and gas field. If it was not on board to facilitate commissions to middlemen, its role was otherwise difficult to explain. But the Foreign Corrupt Practices Act in the United States made it very costly and risky for a large American company like Unocal to become directly involved with payoffs. What Unocal executives could offer instead was the credibility of a security alliance with the United States, grounded in big energy deals. As a salve for Russian pressure, Niyazov had long sought the attention of the U.S. government. By striking a major deal with Unocal he could insure himself against Russian intimidation. For its part the Clinton administration saw the promotion of American oil interests in the newly independent countries of Central Asia as sound foreign and economic policy. Trade between the United States and the newly independent states was soaring—up to $4.6 billion in the first half of 1995, a 35 percent increase over the previous year. Oil and gas interests led the way. In Turkmenistan, Kazakhstan, Azerbaijan, and Uzbekistan lay between 50 billion and 100 billion barrels of oil, plus nearly 250 trillion cubic feet of gas. The ex-Soviet governments in charge needed foreign companies to lift and export this energy.[8]

The Clinton administration's policy, said its leading National Security Council expert, was to "promote the independence of these oil-rich countries, to in essence break Russia's monopoly control over the transportation of oil in that region, and, frankly, to promote Western energy security through diversification of supply." The Clinton White House supported "multiple pipelines" from Central Asia along routes that did not benefit Russia or Iran. Clinton believed that these pipelines were crucial to an evolving American energy policy aimed at reducing dependence on Middle Eastern supplies. Blocking Iran from Central Asia's new oil riches was also a key goal of American policy, but there were only a few pipeline routes that could bypass Iran. Unocal's Afghan plan was a rare one that conformed exactly to Clinton's policy. Unocal proposed two pipelines, one for oil and one for gas; they would descend from the fields in southeastern Turkmenistan, snake through western and southern Afghanistan, and terminate in Pakistan. The U.S. ambassador in Ashkhabad and other American officials agreed to actively promote Unocal's cause with Niyazov.[9]

The Afghanistan pipeline project, Marty Miller believed, was "a no-brainer" if only "you set politics aside." As the weeks passed, however, the politics only thickened.

PRINCE TURKI AL-FAISAL had long seen Afghanistan as a kind of Central Asian fulcrum, a transit hub. It had been a wheelhouse for the Soviet Union's drive toward Middle Eastern oil, the Saudi intelligence chief believed. Now the country was emerging as a pivot point for trade and energy supplies in the post-Soviet era. Turki endorsed Benazir Bhutto's plans to enrich Pakistan by reviving the old Silk Road trading routes through Afghanistan. The Saudi prince admired anyone willing to take the leap of imagination necessary to pursue progress in Afghanistan and Muslim Central Asia. Lately Turki had met such a person: Carlos Bulgheroni, an elegant Argentinian oil man of Italian descent.

Bulgheroni, who spoke in a rich multinational accent, ran a family oil company, Bridas, based in Buenos Aires, that had embarked on quixotic efforts to strike a fortune in the new Central Asian republics. Seeking a partner, Bulgheroni contacted Prince Turki at the headquarters of Saudi intelligence in Riyadh. They met, and Turki was charmed by Bulgheroni's amazing ideas about doing business in difficult places. Bulgheroni had developed his own plans to rescue Turkmenistan's "stranded gas" and pipe it across Afghanistan to Pakistan—months before Unocal surfaced with a similar idea. Bulgheroni wanted Prince Turki to be his business partner; Saudi intelligence, after all, had great clout in all the countries where Bulgheroni hoped to develop his pipeline deal. Turki declined to become a direct partner, but he referred the Argentine to Saudi businessmen Turki knew.[10]

The Saudi intelligence chief also introduced Bulgheroni to his contacts in Pakistan. Javed Qazi, the general in charge of ISI, saw the pipeline as a terrific idea. Benazir Bhutto, impressed that such an important patron of Pakistan as Prince Turki had made the introduction, asked her petroleum and economics advisers to evaluate Bulgheroni's plan. They doubted it would work, but Bhutto told her colleagues there was no harm in signing a memorandum of understanding pledging Pakistan to buy Bulgheroni's gas if he ever managed to pipe it across Afghanistan.[11]

Miller met with Carlos Bulgheroni that summer in Turkmenistan. They talked about whether there was some way Unocal and Bridas could join forces, but they could not find common ground. Miller found Prince Turki's friend "a confusing guy" who talked "in riddles." As for the competitive tension, in Miller's experience there was nothing especially unusual about two multinational oil companies fighting over the same deal with similar plans. Unocal's pipeline would draw from different gas fields than Bridas. In any event, Miller found Niyazov willing to deal with Unocal. If Bulgheroni and Prince Turki were cut out, so be it. That was how the oil game was played.

After a few more shouting matches, Miller's breakthrough in Ashkhabad came in late September 1995. His Turkmen negotiators told him that Niyazov had decided once and for all to abandon Bulgheroni and go with Unocal. In its final form the Unocal contract spelled out an $8 billion project involving two pipelines that would each travel more than eight hundred miles across southern Afghanistan.

Niyazov insisted that Unocal stir up some publicity for their agreement. The Father of All Turkmen was traveling to New York for the fiftieth birthday celebration of the United Nations, and he wanted to throw a party to announce his new pipelines that would free him once and for all from Russia's grip. Unocal hired a venue planner, dressed an elegant Manhattan building in celebratory bunting, and hired Henry Kissinger to make a speech.

There were no Afghans invited to the Manhattan affair. John Imle promised that Unocal would open negotiations soon with "the appropriate parties."[12]

Kissinger noted the number of Afghan factions battling over the land where the Unocal pipeline might one day run and could not help but feel skeptical. Unocal's plan, Kissinger quipped, quoting Dr. Samuel Johnson, appeared to represent "the triumph of hope over experience."[13]

WITH TURKMENISTAN SEWED UP, Marty Miller now opened a Unocal lobbying campaign in two cities: Washington and Islamabad.

It was an easy time for an American oil executive to find an audience in the Clinton White House. Clinton had lost control of Congress to the Republican Party during the 1994 election, and his political team sought to raise massive campaign funds for a comeback attempt, plus Clinton's own reelection bid in 1996. Campaign finance rules had been greatly loosened. The White House wanted to assure corporate donors that the administration would listen to their concerns. Clinton's America-first policies emphasized the promotion of corporate interests abroad. American oil companies doing business in Central Asia also advanced the administration's efforts to contain Iran. For all these reasons, when Miller came knocking on doors in Washington, he found they opened quickly.

Miller flew to Washington from Houston every month or two. At the White House he met regularly with Sheila Heslin, the director of energy issues at the National Security Council, whose suite next to the West Wing coursed with visitors from American oil firms. Miller found Heslin responsive, full of information and ideas, and very supportive of Unocal's agenda in Afghanistan.

Across the river in Langley, some dissidents at the CIA saw Heslin's office that year as afloat on a "sea of self-absorption," as the Near East Division's Robert Baer put it. To him "the White House and the National Security Council became cathedrals of commerce where the interests of big business outweighed the interest of protecting American citizens at home and abroad." Because of what he described as sloppy oversight of his portfolio, Deputy National Security Adviser Sandy Berger held $90,000 worth of stock in Amoco at a time when he oversaw an interagency committee that worked with Heslin to devise U.S. policy toward the Caspian Sea, where Amoco had large contracts. Even Berger's political opponents did not argue that he had acted corruptly, but there was so much money in the air, so much talk of billion-dollar contracts and politically sensitive Central Asian negotiations, that it seemed to dictate American priorities.[14] An advocacy center at Clinton's Department of Commerce lobbied for American corporations in overseas contract competitions where there was only one U.S. company fighting against a foreign firm, as in Unocal's case.

For their part, Berger, Heslin, and their White House colleagues saw themselves engaged in a hardheaded synthesis of American commercial interests and national security goals. They wanted to use the profit-making motives of American oil companies to thwart one of the country's most determined enemies, Iran, and to contain the longer-term ambitions of a restless Russia. This was a traditional and creative form of American statecraft, they believed. The previous generation had produced America's crucial security and oil alliances with Saudi Arabia and other Persian Gulf emirates. Now big oil and gas deals could secure a new belt of American allies from Turkey to China.

Marty Miller found Robin Raphel, the Assistant Secretary of State for South Asia, who oversaw policy toward Afghanistan, "very helpful." He met with her whenever they were both in Washington. They compared notes about trips they each took to the region, the conversations they had, and the impressions they formed about Afghan and Pakistani politics.

Raphel believed the Unocal pipeline could help bring peace and jobs to Afghanistan. Pakistan and India needed the gas. The Afghans needed the revenue they would receive from transit fees if the pipeline were built. Here was a business deal that might literally tie Afghanistan together, she believed, creating new incentives for regional cooperation. In an administration where Raphel struggled to find any cause that would draw attention and resources toward Afghanistan, the Unocal pipeline offered a new and salable rationale for U.S. engagement in Afghanistan, which Raphel favored for many reasons, not only because of the pipeline.[15]

Moreover, the pipeline's economics seemed to promote the kind of all-party peace negotiations, including the Taliban, favored by Raphel and her State Department colleagues. Commercial banks were not likely to lend money to finance a project as risky as this one. If they did, their high interest rates would probably bust the deal. The most realistic way for Unocal to find the sums it needed, Miller said, would be to borrow from multilateral lenders such as the World Bank and the Asian Development Bank. These development banks were funded by rich governments to promote economic growth in poor countries. They would lend money only if Unocal's pipeline linked countries with recognized, stable governments. With the Taliban militia on the march from Kandahar and with the Kabul government's prime minister at war with its president, Afghanistan obviously was not such a place. Unocal could only achieve its goals, then, if it used the lure of its pipeline revenues to persuade Afghanistan's factions to unite around a single government blessed by the United Nations. This was also the stated goal of American policy toward Afghanistan, albeit a policy that was lightly examined, adrift, and poorly funded. As they examined the details of the pipeline project, Raphel and the Clinton White House persuaded themselves that what was good for Unocal might also be good for Afghanistan.

Marty Miller's second mission was to persuade Benazir Bhutto that what was good for Unocal might also be good for Pakistan. This was a more difficult sell. Prince Turki's friend Carlos Bulgheroni continued to fight for his own rival pipeline project. With the aid of Prince Turki's introduction, Bulgheroni had established close ties with officials in Bhutto's government.

Miller knew that until Pakistan agreed to buy the gas piped by Unocal across Afghanistan, there was no way he could finance the project. It was essential that Bhutto be convinced to drop Bulgheroni's pipeline and embrace Unocal's. Miller asked Robin Raphel, Sheila Heslin, and other Clinton administration officials for help in Islamabad. They agreed to pitch in.

THE AMERICAN AMBASSADOR to Pakistan early in 1996 was Tom Simons. He was a career foreign service officer and a specialist in East European and Soviet affairs. Like Miller, he was at the end of a long career. As a young boy he had spent a year in Karachi, from 1948 to 1949. Pakistan had just been born and was struggling to find its footing. Simons thought of himself as an honorary Pakistani and arrived at the U.S. embassy in Islamabad with few preconceptions. He had not followed South Asian affairs closely in decades. His last ambassadorial post had been in Poland, and he had seen the vast transformations in that country after it embraced capitalism. Surely Pakistan, with its established commercial classes, could find a way to break out of its old thinking and seize the opportunities of a post-Soviet world, Simons believed.[16]

As for neighboring Afghanistan, "There basically was no policy," he recalled.

When Simons settled in Islamabad, he quickly heard from Marty Miller and John Imle. Simons met with them or other Unocal executives at the embassy compound about every two to four weeks. They showed him computer-generated slides with "these wonderful graphics that, for a person of my age, it kind of wows you."

Persuading Bhutto's government to drop the Argentine pipeline and embrace Unocal was a policy to which nobody in Washington "ever objected,"

Simons recalled. "You did it in as quiet a way as possible. You didn't go beat the drums for it, and you tried to find practical ways." Simons educated himself about the deal and met with officials at Pakistan's petroleum ministry every few months to lobby on Unocal's behalf. Simons came to believe that construction of the pipelines could go a long way toward stabilizing Afghanistan. He even tried to persuade Unocal to incorporate small power stations along the route to allow Afghan regions more autonomy from Kabul.

But it wasn't clear how Unocal was going to persuade Bhutto to change her mind. At issue was not whether the pipeline was a good thing—Bhutto had already endorsed it in principle—but which oil company should benefit. Bhutto's government had a partner already.

Bhutto had entered into what many of her Westernized friends regarded as an unfortunate marriage. Her husband, Asif Zardari, was a Karachi businessman who seemed to style his ambitions on the godfather characters in Bollywood movies. Allegations about his corrupt business dealings had contributed to Bhutto's first sacking as prime minister in 1990. During Bhutto's second term Robin Raphel and other American officials gave her the benefit of the doubt. They assumed Zardari engaged in some corrupt dealings, but they had no firm evidence that he was stealing on a massive scale. For her part, Bhutto denounced the rumors about her husband as political trickery concocted by her sexist opponents to discredit her. She was emotional and unyielding in defense of her husband. She said her opponents were exploiting her unconventional marriage for political gain—a claim the Clintons, for two, could understand.[17]

Unocal's executives picked up rumors that Bhutto had decided to stick with her Argentinian pipeline deal because payoffs had been made to her husband. Unocal lobbyists began to drop hints to the Pakistani embassy in Washington that the company knew about the supposed payoffs. The message, as Bhutto and her allies understood it, seemed unmistakable: If Benazir Bhutto wanted to avoid trouble over the corruption issue, she should come clean and do business with Unocal.[18]

In Islamabad, Tom Simons also received indications that someone in Bhutto's government had been paid off on the Argentinian pipeline contract. Near the end of a spring day in 1996 he visited the prime minister in her office with an agenda three items long, each one having to do with an American corporation that wanted to do business in Pakistan. Bhutto arrived after long hours of boisterous political meetings. Her eyes were red, and she looked exhausted.

Simons said directly that Bhutto should cancel her memo of understanding with Bridas and sign with Unocal instead. Bhutto didn't like his tone. Members of her government had been under U.S. pressure over the Unocal pipeline for months. Simons seemed to be issuing a demand, not a request. "We could never do that because that's breaking the contract," she told him.

"But that's extortion!" Simons shot back forcefully. He did not elaborate, but it was clear that he was referring to Zardari, suggesting that her husband would only permit a Unocal deal if he was paid.

The word *extortion* sent Bhutto into a fury. "You cannot say that!" she exclaimed. "You cannot be speaking for your president!"

"Well, maybe it's not the right word, but . . ."

It was too late. Bhutto told Simons to leave. She ordered one of her advisers to draft a letter to the Clinton administration that night, complaining that the American ambassador had no right to treat Pakistan's prime minister this way. When Simons got back to the embassy, his phone began to ring from Washington. He drafted his own letter of apology.[19]

Simons explained sheepishly to Unocal's executives that he had not been a great help with Bhutto. Pakistan was not going to endorse Unocal's deal anytime soon. If Marty Miller was to secure the political agreements he needed, he would have to start finding friends elsewhere—inside Afghanistan.

MILLER FLEW THE UNOCAL JET into Quetta in the late spring of 1996. He and his colleagues checked into a comfortable hotel and began to organize a convoy to Kandahar. They hired a small caravan of Toyota double-cab pickup trucks, the Japanese sport utility vehicle favored by the CIA and its Afghan clients during the anti-Soviet jihad. To accompany himself and several other Unocal executives, Miller hired four drivers and about a dozen Afghan interpreters and guides. They called the Taliban to say they were coming.[20]

Miller did not mind admitting that he was scared. He did not know what to expect. The Taliban seemed to follow a lot of bizarre rules, and he had never been to a place like Kandahar. He had worked up a colorful slide show with maps and numbers that showed the benefits of Unocal's pipeline plans. He had paid to have the slides translated into Pashto and printed up as handouts for the Taliban. He threw the printouts and a few gifts into his truck and embarked on his way across the desert hills from Quetta.

They crossed at Spin Boldak, where the Taliban uprising had begun about eighteen months before. They rolled through the treeless mud-rock hills toward the vineyards east of Kandahar. Miller was shocked by what he saw. After all these years there was still rubble everywhere, the residue of the anti-Soviet

war. There was no wire between the telephone poles. In Kandahar there was
no running water. Everywhere he looked, it seemed, there was a sign saying
STAY AWAY—LANDMINES.

They were directed to a Taliban guest house with no furniture inside.
There were some rugs on the floor, and that was it, so Miller and his team
rolled out their sleeping bags.

As non-Muslims, they could not meet Mullah Omar, they were told. Other
Taliban officials tried to absorb the slide show printouts. Miller talked about
the millions of dollars that would flow into Afghanistan. "These are the good
things that can come," he told the Taliban, carefully listing the benefits. He felt
that selling these people was like "dangling the carrot in front of the donkey."

Miller went to a public park in Kandahar one afternoon and saw some
Afghan boys playing. He had thought the Taliban had banned ball games, but
now it looked as if maybe some games were okay. As possible gifts Miller had
stashed in his truck dozens of neon orange soccer balls and Frisbees. They
were leftovers from a Unocal marketing campaign in the United States. All the
balls and Frisbees were emblazoned with the Unocal logo. He went back to
ask his Taliban hosts if it would be okay to hand out his gifts. They said it
would be fine, so he returned to the park and distributed them. Soon the dirt
park looked like a neon orange pinball machine with dozens of balls in play
and Frisbees sailing through the air.

A little later, as he tried to schedule a meeting with the Taliban's assistant
foreign minister, Miller shrugged when the minister wondered aloud about
when afternoon prayers would be held. A Taliban member at the back of the
room, a Caucasian with a long beard and turban, called out in a pungent New
York accent: "I think prayer time is at five o'clock." Miller looked up, startled.

"Are you an American?"

He was. His adopted Muslim name was Salman. He had grown up in New
Jersey with his mother and sister. As a teenager he had struck out for Pakistan
to fight with Kashmiri separatists. He ended up in a training camp in Afghanistan, he said, run by a colonel from Pakistani intelligence.

"They found out I was an American, and the ISI colonel flipped out!"
Salman later told Charlie Santos, Miller's business partner on the pipeline
deal. Salman said he had been ordered to leave the training camp. He enlisted
with the Taliban, who did not seem to mind having an American in their
midst. "These guys are so pure, and they're such good guys," Salman said.

He asked how the Knicks were doing. Santos felt sorry that he did not have
much of a standings update.

Miller had brought along a three-page, nonbinding agreement letter that he wanted the Taliban to sign. It would confirm the Taliban's willingness to work with Unocal on the pipeline project. The leter outlined only a "preliminary basis for further discussions," and it said that the pipelines could only go forward with "the establishment of a single, internationally recognized entity" running Afghanistan, a government "authorized to act on behalf of all Afghan parties."[21]

Miller and Santos explained that Unocal wanted to work with all Afghan factions. "But we want to dominate," one of the Taliban's negotiators replied.

The Unocal group began to think that maybe the Taliban weren't the village idiots everyone thought they were. They wanted the pipeline contract, but only on their terms and only if it could be had without any involvement of Ahmed Shah Massoud's faction in Kabul, or any other Afghan rivals. Time, the Taliban's negotiators seemed to believe, was on their side.

Marty Miller gave up and drove west to meet with Taliban leaders in Herat. The long road from Kandahar was a potholed rut. Upon arrival the Taliban's local governor welcomed Miller by looking him in the eye and asking menacingly, "Why don't you convert to Islam?"

On the long, grinding drive back, Taliban militia forced Miller's convoy to stay overnight in a tiny mud hut along the highway. There was trouble on the road, and it was too dangerous to go farther in the dark. Other Afghan villagers had gathered at the checkpoint as well. They pressed around Miller, curious. Miller didn't like the attention, so he climbed back into his truck, lay down on the seat, and strapped his Walkman to his ears, trying to escape into his music. After a few minutes he looked up and saw dozens of Afghan eyes pressed against the truck window, staring at him. He stayed inside his truck cab all night.

The caravan stopped again briefly in Kandahar. The Taliban's leaders still would not sign Unocal's cooperation letter. Miller and his team climbed back in their pickups and left for Quetta.[22] When they crossed into Pakistan, Miller climbed out of his truck, kissed the ground, and did a little dance of celebration. There were some places even a Texas wildcatter did not belong.

"We Couldn't Indict Him"

A CIA CASE OFFICER visited Marty Miller regularly at Unocal's Sugarland, Texas, offices, usually after Miller had returned from a long overseas trip. Miller was not a CIA agent and did not take assignments, money, or instructions from the agency. But like some other American oil executives with access to the Middle East and Central Asia, he voluntarily provided briefings to the CIA's Houston station. William Casey had revitalized the CIA's contacts with American businessmen during the 1980s. He thought the agency overvalued its paid sources and missed out on the inside details that international businessmen picked up. Miller told the Houston officer about his negotiations in Turkmenistan and Pakistan, the gossip he overheard about corruption cases, and what he saw and heard when he traveled inside Afghanistan. The briefing sessions were dominated by Miller's reports, but occasionally the CIA officer would provide some useful detail in exchange. At one stage the CIA became worried about threats to Unocal executives in Central Asia from Iranian intelligence operatives. The agency invited Miller to Langley for a briefing on how to manage his movements to reduce risk. Miller's impression from his meetings was that the CIA was curious about

Unocal's Afghan pipeline plans but had no special interest in either the project or Afghanistan. In his efforts to win support for Unocal's pipeline plan within the U.S. government, Miller maintained more active lobbying contacts at the White House and the State Department than at the CIA.[1]

By early 1996 the agency was more estranged from its former Afghan and Pakistani contacts than at any time since the Soviet invasion in 1979. The U.S. ambassador in Islamabad, Tom Simons, was startled to find the CIA "had nothing" in Afghanistan. "They had taken out all their assets. They were basically past it."[2] Stinger missile recovery remained the only well-funded covert action program in the region. The Islamabad station did continue to collect intelligence on regional terrorism. Its officers tracked and mapped Afghan guerrilla training camps that supplied Islamist fighters in Kashmir. They continued to look for Mir Amal Kasi in the tribal territories along the Afghan border. But the liaison between the CIA's Islamabad station and Pakistani intelligence—the spine of American covert action and intelligence collection in the region for fifteen years—had cracked. Javed Qazi had been replaced as ISI chief by another mainstream general, Naseem Rana, a Punjabi officer with a background in the signals corps. Some of the Americans who dealt with him found Rana a dull-minded time server who was unwilling to go out of his way to help the United States. Pakistani intelligence offered little cooperation in the search for Karachi terrorists who murdered two Americans in 1995. After a raid on the Kasi family home in Quetta turned up nothing because of faulty intelligence supplied by the Americans, ISI essentially shut down its operations on that case. If the CIA developed hard, convincing evidence about Kasi's location—evidence that Pakistan could confirm—then ISI would assist in his capture, Rana said. But that was about it. Commission payments to ISI for recovered Stingers provided a thin basis for cooperation, but meetings between the CIA and Pakistani intelligence in Rawalpindi were infrequent and desultory compared to the past.[3]

Gary Schroen, the longtime CIA Afghan hand who had served two previous tours in Islamabad, arrived as station chief in January 1996. He told colleagues that the Unocal pipeline project was a fool's errand and that he was not going to pay any attention to it. The pipeline would never be built, Schroen predicted. Besides, the Islamabad station no longer had Afghanistan on its Operating Directive. This bureaucratic designation meant that Schroen and his case officers had no authority to collect intelligence on the Taliban's strengths, sources of supply, or military prospects. Nor could they develop similar intelligence about Hekmatyar's militia or Massoud's Kabul government. The Islamabad station could recruit Afghan agents if they were reporting on terrorism, drugs, or Stinger missiles. But the default assignment of the Afghan account to Langley created occasional confusion within the CIA about how to track the spillover effects of Afghanistan's civil war.[4]

CIA headquarters was distracted by scandal, shrinking budgets, a wave of early retirements, controversies in Congress, and leadership turmoil in the director's office. Not since the late 1970s had so many career agency officers felt so miserable about the place.

Clinton fired James Woolsey in early 1995, after the Aldrich Ames spy case broke. Ames had worked for Russia inside Langley headquarters for years, and his betrayal had gone undetected. The president struggled to find a successor and finally turned to John Deutch, then deputy secretary of defense, who told Clinton adamantly that he did not want the CIA job. Clinton insisted; there was no one else available who could win confirmation, he said. An MIT-educated chemist who had first come to Washington during the 1960s as a "whiz kid" analyst in Robert McNamara's Pentagon, Deutch was a large, bearish man with an ample belly. He had the independent, inquiring, self-certain mind of an accomplished scientist. He could be warm, sloppy, and professorial but also caustic, dismissive, and arrogant. He was happy at the Pentagon, where he worked with a friend and mathematician, William Perry. He had watched James Woolsey, whom he regarded as a very able man, fail spectacularly at Langley, and he had no desire to follow him. Yet once persuaded by the president, Deutch decided to hit the CIA with all of the force he could muster. Congress and the press were outraged over the Ames case. Senator Daniel Patrick Moynihan, a longtime CIA skeptic, had introduced legislation to abolish the agency and fold its role into other departments. Even the CIA's supporters could not understand how the clues about Ames's treachery—his outlandish personal spending, for instance—had been missed. Deutch joined the reformers: He pledged at his confirmation hearing to change the CIA "all the way down to the bare bones."[5]

Deutch openly described himself as "a technical guy, a satellite guy, a SIGINT guy," referring to "signals intelligence," or the art of communications intercepts. He used his early budget requests at Langley to direct more money proportionately to other agencies in the intelligence community, such as the National Reconnaissance Office at the Pentagon and the National Security Agency. He thought the CIA's historical strength was scientific and technical intelligence collection, and he wanted to concentrate on that. He was not impressed with the agency's human spying operations. He believed that the leadership of the Directorate of Operations had to be reformed. His sense was that the CIA's spies were just not very good anymore at their core job of agent recruitment and intelligence collection. They had forgotten the basics of espionage. They were not living up to their own professional standards, and he was not afraid to tell them so. "From what I know, the junior officers are waiting for some new direction," Deutch said publicly. "Now, I may be unhappily surprised."[6]

He was. Many of the CIA's career officers revolted against Deutch's change message. They saw his management reform campaign as just the latest wave in a series of attacks against the agency's core mission and culture. To them President Clinton seemed indifferent about the CIA's health. The agency's budget continued to shrink. In mid-1995 there were only a dozen new case officers being trained at the Farm as career spies. The Directorate of Operations now had fewer than eight hundred case officers worldwide, about a 25 percent decline from the peak years of the Cold War. Stations had closed not only in Afghanistan but across the Third World. There was a strong sense in the Directorate of Operations that the CIA was getting rolled in the budget process by the Pentagon and the FBI. After the Ames case, internal investigations into other possible spies operating at Langley placed dozens of case officers under suspicion, contributing to an atmosphere of distrust and uncertainty. When Deutch's new managers arrived, they emphasized gender and racial diversity as a prime CIA hiring goal, a mission that angered and dismayed the many white males among the agency's veterans. New management techniques promoted open criticism of supervisors, discussions about the CIA's purpose, focus groups, more interaction with the media—"California hot tub stuff," as one unhappy veteran called it. To achieve personnel reductions without firing anyone, CIA managers had to look for experienced officers who were vested enough in their pensions to be able to retire early without hardship. They sought out such veterans and encouraged them to leave. The retirements became wrenching and disruptive.[7]

On the day he accepted early departure, longtime Soviet analyst Fritz Ermarth filled out paperwork with his retirement counselor, an old acquaintance he had known since the days of CIA directors Stansfield Turner and William Casey. Ermarth posed the kind of question that he used to ask about the Soviet bureaucracies he analyzed: "Look, you process four hundred to five hundred people a year through this little cubicle, right? What's your portrait of the place?"

The counselor's eyes filled with tears. "I've never seen it so bad," she said, as Ermarth recalled it. He asked what she meant.

"Everybody says it's hard to put your finger on it," she replied, "but it's the growth in the importance of stuff that shouldn't matter relative to stuff that should."[8]

THE CIA'S COUNTERTERRORIST CENTER began to emerge as a modest exception to the agency's downward trend. For the first two years of the Clinton presidency, budgeting and policy making about terrorism had been dispersed and confused. The shock of the Oklahoma City bombing in the spring of 1995 created a new sense of urgency at the National Security Council, however. The bombers turned out to be a domestic cell of antigovernment militia. But their audacious strike coincided with a shocking chemical weapons attack by a Japanese-based cult in Tokyo. White House terrorism analysts believed the Japanese case showed that the United States was vulnerable to terrorists using weapons of mass destruction. Spurred by Clinton, the National Security Council organized its first terrorism policy review during the early months of 1995.

In June, Clinton signed Presidential Decision Directive-39, classified Secret, titled "U.S. Policy on Counterterrorism." The document echoed the presidential directive that President Reagan had signed during the last great wave of anti-American terrorism during the mid-1980s. It was also the first official recognition by any American president of the danger posed to the United States by terrorists who acquired nuclear, chemical, or biological weapons.[9]

The CIA was instructed to undertake "an aggressive program of foreign intelligence collection, analysis, counterintelligence, and covert action." If necessary, CIA operations would seek to return terrorist suspects "by force . . . without the cooperation of the host government" so that the accused could face justice in American courts.

"The acquisition of weapons of mass destruction by a terrorist group, through theft or manufacture, is unacceptable," the directive continued. "There is no higher priority than preventing the acquisition of this capability or removing this capability from terrorist groups potentially opposed to the U.S."[10]

On paper, at least, American policy was now more forceful and clearly stated than it had been in years. The document also centralized authority on counterterrorism policy at the White House for the first time. The challenge now was to put the words into practice.

IN JANUARY 1996 the CIA's Counterterrorist Center opened a new office to track Osama bin Laden. The agency had never before dedicated a unit of this kind to a single terrorist. Formally known as the "bin Laden Issue Station" and code-named "Alec," the group leased space in a suburban Virginia office park just a few miles from CIA headquarters. Employing about twelve staff members, it was designated a "virtual station." This meant that within the CIA's budgeting and cable routing systems, the unit would have the administrative status, privileges, and autonomy enjoyed by more traditional stations abroad. The idea was born from discussions in the Counterterrorist Center's senior management group. Bin Laden was still seen by CIA analysts primarily as a money man, but he was an emerging symbol of the new mobility of international terrorism. National Security Adviser Tony Lake, who approved the bin Laden unit at the CIA, recalled that he realized the Saudi had become an important terrorist when classified memos started referring to him by the acronym "UBL" (which referred to a spelling of bin Laden's transliterated first name as Usama). In Washington having an acronym was the ultimate sign of importance, Lake recalled sardonically. Because he operated across borders, bin Laden presented challenges to the CIA's old system of country-based intelligence collection. The CIA's managers wanted to experiment with a new kind of unit, a prototype that might be used against other transnational targets. They would fuse intelligence disciplines into one office—operations, analysis, signals intercepts, overhead photography, and so on. The National Security Agency had tapped into bin Laden's satellite telephone and kept track of his international conversations. These intercepts could be used by the new station to track his payments and connections in multiple countries.[11]

They chose bin Laden because by early 1996 there was a rising recognition of his importance, both at the CIA's Counterterrorist Center and at the White House. The unit's first project was to develop a strategic picture of bin Laden's activity. Some of the new focus on bin Laden came from Richard Clarke, a forceful career civil servant who in the summer of 1995 had been appointed Clinton's counterterrorism director, working from the National Security Council under the authorities spelled out in PDD-39. In addition, classified evidence about bin Laden was piling up, circulating in cables throughout the intelligence community. The reporting from the CIA's Khartoum station was by now voluminous. Bin Laden's name surfaced continually in reports from Egypt, Algeria, Tunisia, Israel, and elsewhere. As one regular reader of these cables recalled, it seemed as if every other cable about terrorism from North Africa contained the phrase "Osama bin Laden, financier of terrorists." The CIA now viewed bin Laden as "one of the most significant financial sponsors of Islamic extremist activities in the world," as a rare public statement put it. There was some new money available for the CIA's counterterrorism budget by fiscal 1996. Tony Lake chaired an interagency meeting that approved spending it on the CIA's virtual bin Laden station. Richard Clarke said later that he asked the CIA and the Pentagon to develop plans for "operating against" al Qaeda in Sudan, instead of merely collecting intelligence, but that neither department "was able successfully to develop a plan." Operators inside the virtual station began drafting plans to capture bin Laden early on, but none of these ideas was approved or carried forward by superiors or the White House. The agency's plan offered a way to try something new: "Let's yank on this bin Laden chain and see what happens," as one participant recalled.[12]

But before they could get a grip on him, bin Laden slipped beyond their reach into Afghanistan.

THE CIA STATION in the U.S. embassy in Khartoum, Sudan, had been conditioned during Cofer Black's 1993–95 tour to threats of violence from bin Laden's followers. After the aborted plot to assassinate or kidnap Black, an informant who walked into the embassy volunteered details about supposed plots to kill Tony Lake in Washington. (A State Department official relayed to Lake an assurance from Sudan's foreign minister: "He says that he's not trying to kill you." Lake answered, "It's the darndest thing, but I'm not trying to kill him, either.") CIA officers and embassy diplomats regularly faced hostile surveillance by Sudanese and foreign Arab radicals on the streets of Khartoum. Two CIA contractors reported being threatened on a Khartoum street, although the seriousness of this incident was debated within the agency. Even when one of the station's walk-in sources proved to be a liar, there remained a thick file of threats against the U.S. embassy and its personnel. The chancery building faced a crowded street in central Khartoum, vulnerable to car bombs, but Sudan's government did not respond to requests for new protection measures. By the fall of 1995 the embassy's Emergency Action Committee—which included the CIA station chief, the State Department's security officer, and senior diplomats—had drafted a cable to Washington recommending that the Khartoum embassy be closed to protect

American employees. Under this plan the CIA station housed in the embassy would also close, ending the agency's up-close perch for intelligence collection against bin Laden.[13]

The newly arrived U.S. ambassador to Sudan, Timothy Carney, a feisty career diplomat, thought this was a terrible idea. Carney believed his colleagues overstated the dangers. Cofer Black agreed with him, but Black had transferred from Khartoum to another assignment in the summer of 1995, and his successor at the Khartoum station expressed a more cautious attitude. Carney questioned the integrity of some of the intelligence sources on which the Emergency Action Committee based its threat analysis. Moreover, he thought that closing the embassy would send exactly the wrong signal to Sudan. The United States sought to end Sudan's support for terrorists, among other goals. Carney believed this could only be achieved through direct engagement with the Khartoum government. If the United States shut its embassy and pulled out, it would leave Sudan all the more isolated and desperate. The United States could reduce the threat of Islamic radicalism if it learned to interact with Islamists in more sophisticated ways, distinguishing between peaceful movements of religious revival and those bent on violence. Instead it was clinging to alliances in the Middle East with corrupt, failing secular regimes such as Egypt's, which encouraged Washington to lump all Islamic political groups into one "terrorist" camp. With this myopia, Carney believed, the United States was inadvertently pushing governments such as Sudan's toward more radical postures.[14]

When Carney set up shop in Khartoum in November, he found a draft Emergency Action Committee cable recommending the embassy's closure. He was appalled at the tone of the cable and its conclusion. But he had been a diplomat in the Vietnam era and had vowed that he would never suppress a cable from an embassy where he served even if he disagreed with it. The lesson of Vietnam was that the American government worked best when decision makers had all the arguments, even the ones they did not want to hear, Carney believed. He let the cable recommending closure go through to Washington.[15]

Based on its arguments, CIA director John Deutch told the White House formally that he believed the Khartoum embassy should be shut. Clinton's national security cabinet met two or three times to discuss the issue. Past attempts to negotiate with Sudan had yielded no improvements in its record of coddling terrorists and waging a brutal civil war against Christian rebels in the south, the cabinet group concluded. If closing the embassy isolated Khartoum's government, perhaps that would be the right signal after all, some of the participants in the meetings said. For his part Deutch focused on the security question: The risks of staying in Khartoum outweighed the benefits, he said.[16]

Carney flew to Washington and argued passionately to Secretary of State Warren Christopher that closing the embassy would be a catastrophic error. "An embassy's a tool," he said. "You need to keep the tool in place." But Deutch persisted in his judgment that the Khartoum station was just too dangerous to operate. Late in January 1996, Christopher acceded to Deutch's request. Carney flew back to Khartoum and told Sudan's foreign minister that the United States was pulling out because of terrorist threats to American personnel.[17]

The Sudanese were outraged. The Khartoum government had lately moved to curtail the influence of Islamic radicals in the country. The American decision would say to the world that Sudan was unsafe for investment and travel, that it was an outlaw government.

Carney said there was nothing he could do; the decision had been made. On February 6, 1996, he attended a farewell dinner at the Khartoum home of Sudanese vice president Ali Osman Taha. That night he and Taha fell into their first serious conversation about Sudan's support for terrorists. Carney said that if the Sudanese ever expected Washington to reconsider its decision, they had to show they were serious. Osama Bin Laden was one of Sudan's biggest sources of grief in Washington, Carney said. Sudan should expel him and provide information to the United States about his finances and his support for North African terrorists.[18]

With Carney's assistance Sudan arranged one month later to send a secret envoy, General Elfatih Erwa, to Washington for more talks. Erwa met with Carney and two CIA officers from the Africa Division in the Hyatt Hotel in Rosslyn, Virginia. On March 8, 1996, meeting alone with Erwa, the CIA officers handed him a list of demands that had been developed and endorsed by a working group at the White House. The CIA, the National Security Council, the Pentagon, and the State Department had all helped formulate this list. The two-page proposal was titled "Measures Sudan Can Take to Improve Relations with the United States." The second item on the list asked for intelligence about bin Laden's Khartoum followers: "Provide us with names, dates of arrival, departure and destination and passport data on mujaheddin that Usama Bin Laden has brought into Sudan." The memo also demanded details about the owners of specific cars and trucks that had been surveilling CIA personnel in Khartoum.[19]

The document did not specifically request bin Laden's expulsion from Sudan, but that idea surfaced in the discussions with Erwa and others. Bin Laden seemed to pick up on the talks. For the first time he granted an interview to an American journalist at his compound in Khartoum. "People are supposed to be innocent until proved guilty," bin Laden pleaded. "Well, not the Afghan fighters. They are the 'terrorists of the world.' But pushing them against the wall will do nothing except increase the terrorism."[20]

Years later the question of whether Sudan formally offered to turn bin Laden over to the United States became a subject of dispute. Sudan's government has said it did make such an offer. American officials say it did not. "We told the Americans we would be willing to hand him over if they had a legal case," according to a Sudanese official. "We said, 'If you have a legal case, you can take him.'" But several of the most senior American officials involved said they had never received such a message. Investigators with the National Commission on Terrorist Attacks later concluded there was no "reliable evidence" to support Sudanese claims of such an offer.[21]

At the White House, counterterrorism aides held a hypothetical discussion about whether the United States had a legal basis to take bin Laden into custody. Would the Justice Department indict him? Was there evidence to support a trial? At the meeting, a Justice representative said there was no way to hold bin Laden in the United States because there was no indictment, according to Sandy Berger, then deputy national security adviser. Berger, for his part, knew of no intelligence at the time showing that bin Laden had committed any crime against Americans.[22]

That was all the insight the White House and the CIA could obtain from Justice. Privately, federal prosecutors were considering a grand jury investigation of bin Laden's support for terrorism, a probe that could eventually produce an indictment. American law prohibited Justice prosecutors or the FBI agents who worked with them from telling anyone else in government about this investigation, however. They kept their evidence strictly secret.[23]

Saudi Arabia seemed the most logical place to send bin Laden if it was possible to detain him. Bin Laden had been expelled from the kingdom for antigovernment agitation. There was also a chance that another Arab country, under assault from violent Islamists who took money from bin Laden, might be willing to accept him for trial. Through CIA channels the United States separately asked Saudi Arabia, Egypt, and Jordan whether they would accept bin Laden into custody. Nothing came of it. Overall the White House strategy about bin Laden at the time was "to keep him moving," Lake remembered. American officials told Sudan that Saudi Arabia would not accept bin Laden for trial. The Saudis did not explain themselves, but it seemed clear to

Clinton's national security team that the royal family feared that if they executed or imprisoned bin Laden, they would provoke a backlash against the government. The Saudis "were afraid it was too much of a hot potato, and I understand where they were," Clinton recalled. "We couldn't indict him then because he hadn't killed anybody in America. He hadn't done anything to us." As for Egypt and Jordan, if Saudi intelligence and the Saudi royal family were unwilling to accept the political risks of incarcerating bin Laden, why should they?[24]

Nonetheless, Sudan's government opened discussions with Saudi Arabia about expelling bin Laden back to the kingdom, according to senior officials on both sides. Around the time of General Erwa's secret visit to Washington, the president of Sudan, Omar al-Bashir, traveled to Saudi Arabia for the annual *hajj* pilgrimage to the holy sites at Mecca. He met there with Saudi Arabia's de facto ruler, Crown Prince Abdullah. Accounts of this meeting differ. According to Saudi intelligence chief Prince Turki al-Faisal, Abdullah told Bashir that Saudi Arabia would be "happy" to take bin Laden into custody. But he quoted Bashir as insisting that bin Laden "must not face prosecution" in Saudi Arabia. "Nobody is above the law in the kingdom," Abdullah replied, according to Turki. By his account Saudi Arabia refused to accept bin Laden only because of the conditional terms proposed by Sudan.[25]

A Sudanese official recalled the discussion differently. By his account Abdullah and Prince Turki both announced that Saudi Arabia was not interested in accepting bin Laden for trial. Bashir did ask Abdullah during the Mecca meeting to pardon bin Laden for his provocative political writings. But Sudan never insisted on a Saudi promise to forgo prosecution, according to this account. Bashir recalled that in multiple conversations with Saudi officials about bin Laden, the Saudis "never mentioned that they accused Osama bin Laden of anything. The only thing they asked us was to just send him away." The Saudi attitude at Mecca, according to the Sudanese official, was "He is no more a Saudi citizen. We don't care where he goes, but if he stays [in Sudan], he may be a nuisance in our relations."[26] The Saudis did make clear that bin Laden's "presence in Sudan was considered an obstacle to the development of relations," said the Sudan cabinet minister Sharaf al-Din Banaqa, who was involved in the talks.[27]

It is difficult to know which account to credit. Either way, the long personal ties between bin Laden and Saudi intelligence may also have been a factor in the Saudi decision. Ahmed Badeeb, Prince Turki's chief of staff, recalled being torn over bin Laden's fate when the possibility of his expulsion from Sudan first arose. One of bin Laden's brothers told Badeeb, "Osama is no longer the Osama that you knew." This pained Badeeb: "I loved Osama and considered him a good citizen of Saudi Arabia."[28]

For their part White House counterterrorism officials regarded Sudan's offer to turn bin Laden over to Saudi Arabia as disingenuous. Sudan knew Saudi Arabia was unlikely to accept bin Laden for trial, the White House officials believed. They interpreted Sudan's offer as a safe way to curry favor in Washington since Khartoum knew it would never be called upon to act.[29]

By all accounts, Saudi Arabia had a serious chance early in 1996 to explore taking bin Laden into custody. Crown Prince Abdullah declined to press. The Saudi royal family regarded bin Laden as an irritation, but it would not confront him.

Sudan did not act promptly on the list of demands presented in March by the CIA. President Bashir concluded that he could never win back Washington's confidence—or American investment dollars—as long as bin Laden maintained his headquarters in Khartoum. Through an intermediary, Bashir told bin Laden to move out. Bin Laden replied, according to a Sudanese official involved in the exchange, "If you think it will be good for you, I will leave. But let me tell you one thing: If I stay or if I go, the Americans will not leave you alone."[30] Osama bin Laden now had every reason to believe that the United States was his primary persecutor. His political theology identified many enemies, but it was America that forced him into flight.

Whether bin Laden explored alternatives to exile in Afghanistan is not known. Mohammed al-Massari, a prominent Saudi dissident, recalled that he had often warned bin Laden that "Sudan is not a good place to stay. One day they will sell you to the Saudis." He urged bin Laden to find an alternative base. At some stage that spring bin Laden did contact Afghans in Jalalabad whom he had known during the anti-Soviet jihad. "They said, 'You are most welcome,'" according to a Sudanese official. "He was like a holy man to them." Sudan's government leased an Ariana Afghan jet and arranged to aid bin Laden's departure. It required two flights back and forth to move bin Laden, his three wives, his children, his furniture, and his followers to Jalalabad, according to the Sudanese official.[31]

According to Prince Turki and his chief of staff, Ahmed Badeeb, bin Laden arranged with the small Persian Gulf state of Qatar to land for refueling. Qatar, a tiny country on Saudi Arabia's flank that was perennially at odds with its larger neighbor, was in the midst of a succession crisis in its royal family. Radical Islamists held office in its ministry for religious affairs. Bin Laden chose Qatar because it "had good relations with both Sudan and Yemen," according to Badeeb, and because it was "safer than any other country" between Sudan and Afghanistan. American investigators later reported that according to Khalid Sheikh Mohammed, bin Laden refueled not in Qatar, but in nearby United Arab Emirates. In any event, his tank replenished, bin Laden lifted off a few hours later for Afghanistan.[32]

Sudan's government informed Carney and the White House of bin Laden's departure only after he was gone. The CIA station in Islamabad did not monitor bin Laden's arrival at Jalalabad's airport because it had no active sources in the area.[33]

The Americans were the "main enemy" of Muslims worldwide, an angry bin Laden told a British journalist who visited him in an eastern Afghan mountain camp weeks after his arrival in Jalalabad. Saudi Arabian authorities were only "secondary enemies," he declared. As bin Laden saw it, the world had now reached "the beginning of war between Muslims and the United States."[34]

THE UNCHALLENGED FLIGHT from Sudan was an inauspicious beginning of the CIA's experimental bin Laden station and the White House's beefed-up counterterrorism office. In those first months of 1996 it got worse.

Ever since Ramzi Yousef's arrest early in 1995 and the discovery of evidence about his plot to blow up American planes over the Pacific Ocean, the CIA and the FBI had been on the lookout for Khalid Sheikh Mohammed. After Yousef's arrest investigators discovered a $660 financial wire transfer sent by Mohammed from Qatar to New York to aid the World Trade Center bombers. When the CIA received the wire record and looked into it, officers determined that Mohammed was Yousef's uncle and had married a sister of Yousef's wife. Working from clues discovered among Yousef's possessions, investigators traced his movements. The CIA received evidence that Mohammed was hiding in Qatar. The agency eventually tracked him to Qatar's water department where he was employed as a mechanical engineer. The White House asked the CIA if it could quickly arrest Mohammed and fly him to the United States. The CIA reported that it did not have the officers or agents in Qatar to carry out such an operation. The Qatari minister of religious endowments, Sheikh Abdullah bin Khalid al-Tahni, was known to harbor Islamists loyal to bin Laden. If they asked the Qatar government for help in seizing bin Laden, it was likely that Mohammed would be alerted. The White House then turned to the Pentagon to plan a Special Forces raid to take Mohammed. The Pentagon came back with a large-scale plan that involved flying aircraft first into Bahrain and then launched a smaller attack force via helicopters for Qatar. Deputy National Security Adviser Sandy Berger chaired a White House meeting to consider this option. One problem with the Pentagon plan was that Bahrain and Qatar had been feuding recently over disputed islands in the Persian Gulf. What if Qatar interpreted the helicopters as an attack force arriving from Bahrain? While seeking to arrest a single terrorist clandestinely, the United States might inadvertently start a war. The Justice Department cited legal problems with the Pentagon plan. The White House noted that it was negotiating an important air force basing agreement with Qatar. In the end the plan was discarded. Investigators awaited a sealed indictment against Mohammed. It was handed down in January 1996. The FBI moved to arrest him through regular diplomatic channels. Qatar's government waffled; Mohammed escaped. "I have received disturbing information suggesting that Mohammed has again escaped the surveillance of your Security Services and that he appears to be aware of FBI interest in him," an angry Louis Freeh, the FBI director, wrote to Qatar's foreign minister. Nor did the CIA have a clear understanding of Mohammed's growing affinity for bin Laden's global war: The CIA's Counterterrorist Center did not assign his case to its new bin Laden unit, but chased him separately as a freelance extremist.[35]

It was the start of a pattern that would persist for several years as the Clinton administration's secret war against bin Laden and his Islamist network deepened. They had few reliable allies in the Middle East and Central Asia. The CIA's paramilitary forces were small and sometimes less than nimble. The Pentagon's planners thought in terms of large attack operations. Tactical intelligence about the enemy was patchy, fleeting.

If their campaign against bin Laden was to be waged this way, they would have to learn to thread a very small needle.

AT THE TIME OF bin Laden's arrival, Jalalabad was controlled, if not governed, by a regional *shura* of eastern Pashtun tribal leaders and former anti-Soviet guerrilla commanders. Many of them were involved in lucrative smuggling and trade rackets across the Pakistan border. They had resisted overtures to join the Taliban but had also kept their distance from Hekmatyar and Massoud. Their most prominent leader was Haji Qadir, sometimes referred to as the mayor of Jalalabad. Their most prominent patron from the anti-Soviet era was Younis Khalis, now an octogenarian who took teenage wives. Khalis and other Jalalabad *shura* leaders maintained contacts with Pakistani intelligence.[36]

Bin Laden certainly knew some of the Jalalabad group from the 1980s and early 1990s, and he had kept in touch during his years in Sudan. He may also have remained in touch with ISI. It is notable that bin Laden did not fly into Afghan territory controlled by the Taliban. Some American analysts later reported that bin Laden had sent money to the Taliban even prior to his return to Afghanistan.[37] Yet bin Laden apparently did not have a comfortable enough relationship with the Taliban's isolated, severe, mysterious leadership group to place himself and his family under their control.

The Taliban were entering a new phase of power and ambition just as bin Laden arrived. They were no longer the humble, consultative Pashtun country folk of late 1994 and early 1995. They had evolved into a political-military movement with national goals. Some of their leaders, such as Prince Turki's favorite, Mullah Rabbani, continued to hint to foreign visitors and United Nations diplomats that the Taliban were just a transition force. He and other "moderate" Taliban leaders, as they were now being called by American diplomats, said the Taliban would cleanse Afghanistan of its criminal warlords and create a fresh political start, perhaps including a return of the exiled king. But increasingly such claims had to be reconciled with menacing scenes of the Taliban's appetite for power. Its leaders openly denounced the Massoud-defended government in Kabul as "the root cause of all evils in Afghanistan."[38]

Omar summoned more than one thousand Pashtun religious scholars and tribal leaders to Kandahar for a two-week grand assembly in the early weeks of spring 1996. It was the most overt political meeting of Pashtuns under Taliban leadership since the movement's birth. Omar chose his ground and his symbols carefully. At the meeting's climax he called the delegates to the great stone-and-tile square across from the Kandahar governor's house. Within the square's gates stood the tomb of the eighteenth-century king Ahmed Shah Durrani and the tile-inlaid Mosque of the Cloak of the Holy Prophet.

Omar climbed to the mosque's roof and unveiled the holy cloak. As the crowd roared approval, he wrapped himself dramatically in the relic. The assembled delegates formally ratified him as Amir-ul-Momineen, "Commander of the Faithful." They created and sanctified a new name for the expanding territory under Taliban control: The Islamic Emirate of Afghanistan. They called for jihad against Massoud. Some denounced Zahir Shah as a criminal. Surrounded by the symbolic remnants of a lost Durrani empire, they had proclaimed their own one-eyed king.[39]

VIRTUALLY BY HERSELF in the Clinton administration, Robin Raphel tried to drum up a climate of urgency about all-party Afghan peace talks then being sponsored by the United Nations. Raphel had support from a few members of Congress but hardly any backing from the White House. The State Department's South Asia bureau, which Raphel ran, saw the Taliban as a distasteful but well-established faction on the Afghan checkerboard. The United States now endorsed Pakistan's view that peace talks must include the movement's leaders. By its secret support for the Taliban and its continual public lies, Pakistan had made the Taliban a fact of international diplomacy—and the Americans accepted their legitimacy. At the same time Raphel's public statements made clear that State opposed all efforts to solve the Afghan war by military victory, whether by the Taliban or Massoud.

Raphel traveled to Kabul, Kandahar, and Islamabad on April 19 and 20, 1996. "Tell President Clinton and the West that we are not bad people," a Taliban leader told her in the Pashtun capital. Raphel and U.S. ambassador Tom Simons concluded that the Taliban's humble, simplistic messages might reflect "a growing awareness, previously absent, of their own limitations," as Simons wrote in a cable to Washington. Raphel and the ambassador believed—wrongly—that "a consensus has emerged" in the Pakistan government's civilian and military leadership about the need to broaden their policies toward Afghanistan. As she had done before, Bhutto lied to Raphel in meetings and "emphasized that Pakistan was not providing military support to the Taliban and insisted that only minimal, nonlethal aid was being delivered." Raphel absorbed Pakistan's hostility toward Massoud and carried it into her meetings with the commander in Kabul. "Massoud outlined a vision for a bottom-up democracy" in Afghanistan, but Raphel and Simons dismissed this "rosy scenario" in a Confidential cable to Washington and denounced the "self-righteousness" of Massoud's besieged government. For their part, Massoud and his aides were put off by what they saw as Raphel's lecturing. Raphel seemed to treat Afghanistan "as a wilderness threatening the stability of Pakistan," as one of Massoud's intelligence officers put it. Massoud and his intelligence advisers worried that the CIA had covertly joined with ISI to engineer a Taliban takeover of Kabul to create favorable conditions for the Unocal pipeline. Massoud's government had signed an agreement with Unocal's Argentine rival, banking a $1 million payment in a New York account belonging to one of Massoud's advisers. They feared they had been branded as Unocal's—and therefore America's—enemy.[40]

In truth, nobody in Washington cared enough to conspire about Afghan politics. Still, Raphel and her State Department colleagues heard accusations about a CIA-led, Unocal-driven plot in Afghanistan over and over that spring.

A decade of covert action in the 1980s had conditioned many Afghans and Pakistanis to see the CIA as a powerful force in their affairs. Raphel and her colleagues heard the CIA-Unocal-Taliban conspiracy stories so often and in such credible detail that they privately asked Langley a few times for confirmation that there was no fire beneath all this smoke. They were assured that the CIA was clean.

More than any other American official at the time, Raphel outlined publicly the dangers an unstable Afghanistan posed to the world. The country "has become a conduit for drugs, crime, and terrorism that can undermine Pakistan [and] the neighboring Central Asian states and have an impact beyond Europe and Russia," she predicted. She warned that terrorist incidents in the Middle East had been traced back to Afghan training camps. She argued that the Taliban's severe interpretations of Islam defied Afghan traditions and that ultimately the balance of power would shift toward a more tolerant theology. Yet her policy prescriptions were all vague or narrowly drawn around commercial interests. The United States was "concerned that economic opportunities here will be missed," Raphel said publicly during her visit to Kabul that spring. She told a Russian counterpart in a private meeting, "The United States government now hopes that peace in the region will facilitate U.S. business interests." In Islamabad she declared that Unocal's pipeline "will be very good for Turkmenistan, for Pakistan and for Afghanistan as it will not only offer job opportunities but also energy in Afghanistan."[41]

It was a tawdry season in American diplomacy. After years of withdrawal and disengagement American policy had been captured by the language of corporate dealmaking. In the absence of alternatives the State Department had taken up Unocal's agenda as its own. Whatever the merits of the project, the sheer prominence it received by 1996 distorted the message and meaning of American power. American tolerance of the Taliban was publicly and inextricably linked to the financial goals of an oil corporation. There were by now about 1.5 million Afghan war dead, dating back to the Soviet invasion. The land was desolate, laced with mines. The average life expectancy for an Afghan was about forty-six years. The country ranked 173 out of 175 countries on the United Nations human development index.[42] Yet the few American officials who paid attention to Afghanistan at all talked as if it was a tax-free zone ripe for industrial revival, a place where vocational education in metallurgy could lead to a political breakthrough.

For Afghans themselves the central question in the spring of bin Laden's return was the military potential of the Taliban. For more than a decade the key to internal power in Afghanistan had been access to outside military supplies and cash—especially from Pakistan. Here, too, the ground was now shifting.

In Islamabad, in the secret councils of her national security cabinet, Benazir Bhutto had entered into a new phase of debate with Pakistani intelligence about the Taliban. By the spring of 1996 she had capitulated, she said later, to ISI's persistent requests for unlimited covert aid to the Islamic militia. But as the Taliban gathered strength and territory, Bhutto and her civilian allies clung to the hope that they could use the Taliban to force a negotiated, all-party political deal under the auspices of the United Nations. As Bhutto recalled it, ISI Director-General Naseem Rana and several of his key brigadiers asked her for permission to arm, equip, and train the Taliban for a final drive on Kabul. If the Taliban took control of the Afghan capital, ISI's officers argued, Pakistan would have at last achieved General Zia's dream: a loyal, Pashtun-led Islamist government in Kabul.

Bhutto resisted. She feared that a Taliban government would press its Islamic militancy on toward Central Asia, damaging the trade-driven relationships she sought to build there. It would be much more profitable to use the Taliban's clout to negotiate for a peace deal in Afghanistan that would include Massoud and other northern ethnic militias that had strong ties to Central Asia.

Bhutto turned for support to her secular-minded chief of army staff, General Jehangir Karamat, Pakistan's supreme military commander. "When the pressure would get too much," she recalled, "I would have a meeting with the army chief and with my defense cabinet and all of the military brass—the air force chief and the navy chief—and they would support my idea that, no, you must work with the U.N."[43] But Pakistani intelligence was more and more insistent, she recalled. It seemed evident that they intended to push the Taliban into Kabul without telling Bhutto. Whether ISI also evaded orders from Karamat or privately received a supportive nod from the army high command was never clear to Bhutto. All the while the prime minister and her aides continued to lie to American officials about the nature and extent of Pakistan's covert support to the Taliban.

The American ambassador to Pakistan, Tom Simons, talked repeatedly with Karamat and other senior generals as the Taliban approached Kabul's gates in the late spring and early summer of 1996. It seemed to Simons that the Pakistani army felt trapped by the momentum of its own policies in Afghanistan. The Punjabi secularists in their senior ranks viewed the Taliban cynically and worried that they had cooked up "a recipe for endless war" and that "Pakistan was going to be drained, and it was going to weaken Pakistan." Yet the generals told Simons "they also felt that there was no alternative, no realistic alternative for the country."[44]

KABUL'S FALL CAME SWIFTLY. Osama bin Laden, now Afghanistan's wealthiest sheikh, hurried it along.

Taliban forces launched a surprise attack against the Jalalabad *shura* in August. Haji Qadir and the rest of bin Laden's original greeting party fled across the border to Pakistan. The Taliban took control of the area, and bin Laden was now in their midst. The Saudi may have provided about $3 million from his personal treasury to pay off the remaining commanders who stood between the Taliban and Kabul, although bin Laden was under some financial pressure at the time. The Taliban may also have collected funds for these crucial bribes from other Saudi and Gulf patrons, the local trucking mafia, heroin traders, Pakistani intelligence, and other sources.[45]

Bin Laden spent his first summer back in Afghanistan writing a lengthy *fatwa* about the alliance of enemies that had delivered him to this exile. His "Declaration of Jihad on the Americans Occupying the Two Sacred Places" laid out his belief that the Saudi royal family had become "the agent" of an alliance between imperialist Jews and Christians. He protested that he had been "pursued in Pakistan, Sudan and Afghanistan." He referred to his new haven as Khorasan, a reference to a lost Islamic empire that had once encompassed Central Asia. He faxed his proclamation to London newspapers as the Taliban turned their speedy pickup trucks toward Kabul.[46]

Massoud lost the Afghan capital after forging one last ill-advised alliance with his old enemy, Gulbuddin Hekmatyar. Fearing (correctly) that ISI had abandoned him for the Taliban, Hekmatyar reached out to Massoud for help. Massoud had little choice. Hekmatyar's militia, however untrustworthy, extended his defensive perimeter east and south and held the Taliban farther out from Kabul. But Hekmatyar kept asking Massoud to bring his troops out from the capital to attack the Taliban. "Every day Hekmatyar was worried [saying], 'They're working to a plan. They've taken Paktia. . . . And you've done nothing, you're not cooperating, you're not fighting,'" Massoud said later. President Rabbani told Massoud, "Well, maybe Hekmatyar's right." But Massoud was now leading his troops into eastern and southern territory that he had never held during the long anti-Soviet war. He was not familiar with the terrain. He and his aides moved to meet the Taliban while studying their maps. "We came out," Massoud said, but "we didn't pay attention to the defensive line."[47]

The trap sprang shut on September 25 at Sarobi, Kabul's eastern gateway. Hekmatyar's local commanders sold out to the Taliban and stood aside. The Taliban had perfected mobile fighting with a cavalry of Japanese pickup trucks armed with powerful machine guns in their beds. They darted and swooped up the gorges from Sarobi and across Kabul's open southern plains. Massoud's helicopter and fighter-bomber strikes could not ward off these potent swarms. On September 26, Massoud told a council of generals that they had to withdraw. Overnight they rolled as many tanks and armored vehicles as they could organize north from the capital toward the Panjshir Valley, Massoud's fortified rock-gorge homeland.[48]

THE TALIBAN POURED INTO KABUL the next day. They wore black turbans and smeared their eyes with decorative kohl. They walked unopposed into pockmarked ministry buildings and unfurled their blankets on the floors. Within a day every major government building, palace, and military base in the city had been occupied by bands of Pashtun fighters.

After Kabul fell to the mujahedin in April 1992, the former Afghan president Najibullah lived under house arrest at a United Nations compound in the city. Rabbani and Massoud never brought the former communist and secret police chief to trial, nor were they willing to release him into exile. Najibullah spent his years of incarceration watching satellite television, lifting free weights, and translating a history of British-era Afghanistan called *The Great Game* from English into Pashto. "Afghans keep making the same mistake," he told one visitor, reflecting on his translation.[49]

The Taliban burst into Najibullah's house on September 27 while his brother was visiting. Judging by the conditions of their bodies when they were strung up above a traffic circle hours later, the brothers died slowly and painfully under blows from fists, stones, and sticks. The former president of Afghanistan—whose career began in the torture chambers of the secret police and ended at roundtables with international diplomats—probably expired before the wire tied around his neck pulled him up the ten-foot gallows pole selected by the Taliban for its visible location in central Kabul. "We killed him because he was the murderer of our people," Mullah Omar declared.[50]

The capital's new laws were announced as edicts on Kabul Radio, quickly renamed the Voice of the Sharia, or Islamic law. Toothpaste should be abandoned in favor of the natural root favored by the Prophet, the radio announcers declared. Their lists of banned items and activities unfurled as a roll call of life's small pleasures: marbles, cigarettes, dancing, music, singing, homing pigeons, kite-flying, television-watching. Businessmen and traders were warned that they should no longer wrap their goods in paper in case they inadvertently used pages from the Holy Koran. The Saudi-inspired Ministry for the Propagation of Virtue and the Prevention of Vice announced a ban on both sorcery and American-style haircuts.

Taliban leaders ordered women to disappear. "All of those sisters who are working in government offices are hereby informed to stay at home until further notice," the radio announced on the first day. Also: "Since *satar* [Islamic dress] is of great importance in Islam, all sisters are seriously asked . . . to cover their faces and the whole of their body when going out." Eight thousand female undergraduate students at Kabul University lost their places at the school. A similar number of schoolteachers lost their jobs. Thousands of women who worked as civil servants in bloated government ministries, contributing meager but steady salaries to their extended families, were banned from their offices.[51]

Six weeks later the Taliban announced a numbered list of regulations that would be enforced by their religious police. Number one said that to prevent "sedition and uncovered females," taxi drivers could not stop for any woman who did not wear a full Iranian-style *burqa*. Number twelve announced that all women found washing clothes in any river would be picked up by the religious police in a "respectful and Islamic manner" and returned to their homes, where their husbands would be severely punished. Number fifteen listed jail terms for tailors who took female body measurements or displayed fashion magazines.[52]

The State Department greeted these announcements with little protest. Its diplomats hoped to appease Kabul's new rulers. "We wish to engage the new Taliban 'interim government' at an early stage," declared a classified instructions cable sent from Washington to embassies abroad on September 28. In official meetings with the Taliban, American diplomats should strive to "demonstrate [American] willingness to deal with them as the new authorities in Kabul; seek information about their plans, programs, and policies; and express [U.S. government] views on areas of key concern to us—stability, human rights, narcotics, and terrorism." Bin Laden ranked last on the cable's more detailed list of issues for discussion. Washington's confidential talking points suggested two very gentle questions for Taliban leaders. One was: "We welcomed your assurances that you were closing the terrorist and militant training camps formerly run by Hekmatyar, Sayyaf, or Arab groups. Can you tell us the current status of those camps?" The second: "Do you know the location of ex-Saudi financier and radical Islamist Osama bin Laden? We had heard previously that he was in the eastern provinces. His continued presence here would not, we believe, serve Afghanistan's interests." Taliban leaders telephoned American diplomats in Islamabad and said they had no idea where bin Laden was.[53]

Ambassador Tom Simons met at the shaded Islamabad embassy compound on November 8 with Mullah Ghaus, the Taliban's acting foreign minister, who like Omar had only one eye. "I wish to say some things about America," Simons announced, according to notes taken by an American diplomat at the meeting. "The Americans are the most religious people in the Western world. They have great respect for Islam, which is now the fastest growing religious community in America. There are, in fact, now more American Muslims than American Jews," he added, as if this might assuage Taliban attitudes toward the United States. Yet Americans, Simons continued, "have learned that it is very difficult to discern the will of God. Their experience has taught them that it is dangerous for one group to try to impose its interpretation of the will of God on others, and especially dangerous to try to do so by force." Ghaus listened politely. He said the Taliban hoped for peace—but they would never yield to their enemies, especially not to Massoud and his allies to the north. On December 6 Simons' deputy relayed a letter to the Taliban from Secretary of State Warren Christopher offering engagement, but adding: "We wish to work with you to expel all terrorists and those who support terrorism" from Afghanistan. Robin Raphel handed the original to the man the Taliban hoped would agree to represent them at the United Nations: Hamid Karzai.[54]

Raphel outlined American policy to a closed meeting of the U.N. Security Council in New York. For the sake of peace, she argued, all nations should engage with the Taliban. "The Taliban control more than two-thirds of the country; they are Afghan, they are indigenous, they have demonstrated their staying power," Raphel said. "The real source of their success has been the willingness of many Afghans, particularly Pashtuns, to tacitly trade unending fighting and chaos for a measure of peace and security, even with severe social restrictions."

The Taliban were now a fact of international life, Raphel argued: "It is not in the interests of Afghanistan or any of us here that the Taliban be isolated."[55]

19

"We're Keeping
These Stingers"

ISLAMABAD STATION CHIEF Gary Schroen's secret flight into Kabul in September 1996 and his midnight discussion with Ahmed Shah Massoud about Stingers and bin Laden marked the rebirth of unilateral CIA engagements in Afghanistan after a four-year hiatus.[1]

The agency managed three secret programs that provided resources for Schroen and his Islamabad case officers. The National Security Council's decision early in 1996 to fund and approve the Counterterrorist Center's new "virtual" station to track Osama bin Laden meant there were now funds, analysts, and case officers dedicated to collecting intelligence on the Saudi and his operations. A walk-in defector from al Qaeda, Jamal al-Fadl, revealed to the bin Laden unit late in 1996 that they had been underestimating their target—bin Laden, the CIA now learned, had planned multiple terrorist operations and aspired to more. The virtual station needed help from Islamabad. Schroen's group maintained the agency's liaison with ISI, which had multiple connections to bin Laden's world. Schroen had also opened a dialogue with Massoud. Cables flowed steadily between the bin Laden station in Virginia and the Islamabad station even after Massoud retreated from Kabul.

In addition, from inside Langley headquarters the Counterterrorist Center maintained a full branch dedicated to finding Mir Amal Kasi, the fugitive Baluchi who had attacked CIA headquarters in 1993. The Kasi branch authorized funds for the Islamabad station to recruit paid unilateral agents—some of them Afghans—to look for Kasi. Most richly funded of all was the program Langley operated that had been the main impetus for Schroen's clandestine September visit to Massoud in Kabul: Stinger missile recovery.[2]

By the time the Taliban took Kabul, an estimated 600 of the approximately 2,300 Stinger missiles distributed by the CIA during the anti-Soviet war remained missing. There was an active market for the missiles across Central Asia and the Middle East. The Iranians were buying as many as they could. CIA officers estimated very roughly that Tehran had acquired about 100 Stingers. Most of the remaining inventory was believed to be in Afghanistan. Some Afghan warlords correctly saw possession of a batch of Stingers as a better financial investment than many of the local paper currencies. Through its intermediaries the CIA offered to buy not just the warheads for hard cash but also the tubes from which they were fired. A secondary market grew up in Afghanistan for empty tubes. Con artists tried to imitate the missile's design and sell fakes to middlemen. Prices for complete missiles soared from $70,000 to $150,000 as sellers hoarded their wares. The agency turned to allies across the Middle East for help. Prince Turki's chief of staff, Ahmed Badeeb, flew as far as Somalia to pick up Stingers that had been smuggled into Africa. But much of the program was run out of the Islamabad station where the Stingers had first been distributed. Until 1996 the CIA maintained a B-200 Cessna twin-engine turboprop airplane in Islamabad dedicated to Stinger recovery. CIA pilots flew it around the region to pick up missiles. They were then stored in Islamabad until a larger transport plane could ferry them to the United States, where they were turned over to the U.S. Army for destruction. Occasionally, if CIA officers bought missiles in some place where transport was impossible, they would dig a pit and blow them up with plastic explosives, taking photographs to document their destruction.[3]

After the Taliban took Kabul, the CIA decided to make a direct offer to the militia's leaders to buy back Stingers from them. The agency had been informed that Mullah Omar possessed fifty-three Stinger missiles that had been collected from various Pashtun warlords loyal to the Taliban. Early in 1997, Gary Schroen sought permission from headquarters to fly into Kandahar and make a cash buyback offer to senior Taliban mullahs. Langley agreed. With help from diplomats in the Islamabad embassy, Schroen contacted the Taliban *shura* in Kandahar. They sent back word that they would welcome an American delegation.[4]

At going rates a CIA repurchase of all the Taliban's Stingers would provide the militia force with an instant cash infusion of between $5 million and $8 million, about double the amount later reported to have been provided to the Taliban by bin Laden to aid the conquest of Kabul. (At the time of Schroen's request to travel to Kandahar, the United States had little evidence that bin Laden had connected with the Taliban.) While not a large amount by U.S. aid program standards, such a payment would still be a sizable infusion of unrestricted cash for a militia whose leaders daily announced new codes of medieval conduct. Yet a presidentially authorized covert action policy at the time encouraged the CIA to buy Stingers wherever they could be found.

It was unclear during the fall of 1996 whether the United States regarded the Taliban as friend or foe. In the weeks after the fall of Kabul, midlevel American officials issued a cacophony of statements—some skeptical, some apparently supportive—from which it was impossible to deduce a clear position. American diplomats in Islamabad told reporters that the Taliban could play a useful role in restoring a strong, central government to Afghanistan. The Taliban themselves, worried about rumors that they received support from the CIA and were a pro-American force, refused to receive a low-level State Department visitor to Kabul. "The U.S. does not support the Taliban, has not supported the Taliban, and will not support the Taliban," the spurned envoy, Lee Coldren, announced in reply. Within days then-U.S. ambassador to the United Nations Madeleine Albright denounced the Taliban decrees in Kabul as "impossible to justify or defend." But just three weeks after that Robin Raphel outlined the Taliban's claims to legitimacy before the U.N. Security Council and pleaded that they not be isolated. It was difficult to tell which of these State Department officials spoke for themselves and which spoke for the United States.[5]

Raphel's call for engagement with the Taliban attracted support outside the Clinton administration, especially from Unocal. Marty Miller and his colleagues hoped the Taliban takeover of Kabul would speed their pipeline negotiations. Within weeks of the capital's capture, Unocal formed a new financial partnership to build the pipeline, announced the creation of an advisory board made up of prestigious American experts on South and Central Asia, and opened a new office in the Taliban heartland, Kandahar. Marty Miller insisted publicly that Unocal remained "fanatically neutral" about Afghan politics, but it was clear that the Taliban's military victory would be helpful in reducing the number of parties to the Unocal pipeline talks.[6]

Republican and congressional experts also declared that America should give the Taliban a chance. "It is time for the United States to reengage," wrote Zalmay Khalilzad, one of the American government's leading Afghan specialists, soon after the Taliban takeover of Kabul. "The Taliban does not practice the anti-U.S. style of fundamentalism practiced by Iran. It is closer to the Saudi model."[7] This remained a common prism of American thinking about Islamist political movements: Saudi Arabia was conservative, pious, and nonthreatening, while Iran was active, violent, and revolutionary. As doctrinaire Sunni Muslims, the Taliban vehemently opposed Iran and its Shiite creed, and in that sense they were allied with American interests. Khalilzad was soon invited to join Unocal's advisory board, along with Robert Oakley, the former U.S. ambassador to Pakistan.

In this atmosphere of drift and desultory debate about the Taliban's meaning, Gary Schroen and a team of embassy diplomats flew into Kandahar in February 1997, on a scheduled United Nations charter. They circled down to a vast mud-baked plain laced by eroded riverbeds. The American team rolled from the airport through a dry, flat, treeless expanse where sagebrush hopped and tumbled in the desert wind. Shadowed rock hills rose to the west. On the buckled highway to town they passed state-owned farming cooperatives, green orchards, and walled farming villages. Amid smoky bustle, horse carts, and scooters they entered Kandahar city through a painted arch called "Chicken Post," protected by armed Taliban guards. Pedestrians crowded into the roadway—almost all of them tall, bearded Pashtun men in colorful turbans and loose, cool cotton robes. The city itself was a flat expanse of market stalls and mud-walled compounds. Mullah Omar's modest house lay behind a wall on the Herat Bazaar Road in the center of town, near Kandahar's university, which the Taliban had converted into a religious *madrassa*. In the city's central square the militia occasionally staged mock executions of radios and televisions, bashing them to pieces and hanging them by their cords. Schroen and his colleagues bunked overnight in a United Nations guest house, a small enclave of foreigners, fluorescent lights, and canned Coca-Cola. They contacted the Taliban foreign ministry to arrange their appointment. Omar declined to see them since they were not Muslims, but they were granted an audience with the local governor and Omar's chief aide, Mullah Wakil Ahmed.[8]

They drove the next day to the Governor's House, a striking, crumbling, arched sandstone building set in a garden of spruce trees and rosebushes. The Taliban did not give the impression that they cared much for its carved ceilings or Persian-influenced mosaics. They laced the building with mines and bombs, and kept their Stingers in a locked storage area off the inner courtyard.

Schroen joined a meeting that was to include diplomatic discussions about refugee and aid issues. Several local leaders sat on the Taliban side. None of the Taliban wore shoes or sandals. They picked continually at their feet, the Americans could not help but notice.

The Taliban governor of Kandahar was Mohammed Hassan, a former Quetta *madrassa* student who had fought against the Soviets in Uruzgan province. He had lost a fingertip and a leg in battle during the anti-Soviet jihad. He had been fitted with an artificial limb that had a spring and release mechanism. During the meeting he fooled with his leg, and it snapped out of position occasionally with a loud *ca-crack!* Then Hassan would grab it and slowly push it back into its locked set.

Afterward Schroen met privately with Hassan and Wakil. He outlined, through a translator, how the CIA's Stinger recovery program worked. The United States would be grateful if the Taliban would sell back the Stingers they had, and the Taliban would be well paid if they agreed. Schroen mentioned that one goal was to keep the missiles out of Iran's hands.

Hassan and Wakil said that they had no desire to sell their missiles. They were going to need them in the future. "We're keeping these Stingers because we're going to use them on the Iranians," they explained. Their first task was to finish off Ahmed Shah Massoud and his coalition in northern Afghanistan. After that they fully expected to end up in a war with Iran, they said. They needed the missiles to shoot down helicopters and jets from the Iranian air force. Surely, they said, the Americans could appreciate the Iranian threat.[9]

Schroen flew back to Islamabad empty-handed.

OSAMA BIN LADEN began to move his operations south, toward Kandahar, the center of Taliban power. In November 1996 the Palestinian newspaper editor Abdel Bari Atwan met him in a cave outside of Kandahar. Bin Laden had a personal computer in his bunker and a library of bound volumes. He told Atwan that he felt "back home, because the whole Islamic world is a homeland for Muslims." He made it clear that he regarded the United States as his enemy. Recent terrorist bombings against American targets in Saudi Arabia, at Riyadh and Dhahran, were "a laudable kind of terrorism, because it was against thieves." He boasted of his endurance: "Having borne arms against the Russians for ten years, we think our battle with the Americans will be easy by comparison, and we are now more determined to carry on until we see the face of God."[10]

That winter bin Laden worked to build his global reputation through the international media. He seemed determined to convince his audience in the Arab world that exile in Afghanistan had not marginalized him. To Palestinians he denounced American support for Israel, although he placed less emphasis on this issue than many other Arabs did. To his Saudi countrymen he repeated his attacks on the royal family for corruption, weak enforcement of Islamic laws, and most of all for allowing American troops on Saudi soil. For the first time he also began to reach out aggressively to American and English-language media to deliver warnings and sermons. Sometimes he shaped his message to his audience; other times he uncorked long theological speeches without apparent concern for his listeners. He spoke of Islam's wrath and his determination to evict Christian "Crusader" military forces from Muslim lands, especially Saudi Arabia. "The concentration at this point of jihad is against the American occupiers," he told a CNN interviewer.[11]

As he raised his media profile, bin Laden also insinuated himself into Mullah Omar's realm. He arrived in the desert warmth of Kandahar that winter with praise for Omar's wisdom and grand ideas about construction projects that could transform the Pashtun spiritual capital, filling it with enduring symbols of Taliban faith and power.

Pakistani intelligence may have facilitated bin Laden's introductions to the Taliban. To train militants for Kashmir, ISI used and subsidized guerrilla training camps that were now falling under bin Laden's sway. According to one former CIA case officer, ISI wired bin Laden's new house in Kandahar for security. Pakistani intelligence also allowed cross-border travel by journalists summoned by the Saudi.

For both the Taliban and ISI, bin Laden was in one sense an uncomfortable new ally and benefactor. His repeated denunciations of Saudi Arabia's royal family angered a wealthy and powerful patron of Pakistani intelligence and its Afghan clients. But Saudi intelligence chief Prince Turki al-Faisal made it clear to the Taliban after they took Kabul that he would not confront them over their hospitality to bin Laden.

After the fall of the Afghan capital, Prince Turki recalled, the Taliban sent a message to the kingdom: "We have this fellow here. Do you want us to hand him to you, or shall we keep him here? We offered him refuge." The Saudis had just turned away from a possible chance to take custody of bin Laden from Sudan the previous spring. The royal family still apparently believed it was better to have bin Laden at large in Afghanistan than at home in detention or in jail where he might become a magnet for antiroyal dissent. The

Saudis had ample evidence to charge bin Laden with serious crimes—they had already executed four of his followers for carrying out the Riyadh bombing of an American facility in November 1995—but they were still not prepared to endure the political risks of bin Laden's trial or martyrdom.

Prince Turki recalled that his government told the Taliban in reply, "Well, if you have already offered him refuge, make sure that he does not operate against the kingdom or say anything against the kingdom." Turki felt that the Taliban had agreed to take charge of "keeping his mouth shut."[12]

Bin Laden had his own plan: He would convert the Taliban to his cause.

UNOCAL RENTED A HOUSE in central Kandahar directly across the street from one of bin Laden's new compounds. They did not choose this location deliberately. Most of the decent houses in town straddled the Herat Bazaar Road. Also nearby was the Pakistani consulate, which housed officers from ISI. Charlie Santos, a former United Nations diplomat in Afghanistan, had been hired by Unocal's small Saudi partner, Delta, to provide analysis and consulting services on Afghan affairs as the American oil company tried to negotiate its contract.

Unocal visitors and consultants had an up-close view of bin Laden's rising impact on the city during the early months of 1997. The Saudi sheikh swept through Kandahar in convoys of pickup trucks and luxury Toyota sport utility vehicles with tinted windows. Moving with a formidable bodyguard of Arabs and Afghans, he came and went from downtown unannounced, a spectral presence in flowing white robes. As his convoy passed, Pashtun men in the fume-choked bazaars would point and whisper discreetly, "Osama, Osama." On some Fridays he delivered sermons at Kandahar's largest mosque. Afghans reported to Santos that Mullah Omar called bin Laden out of the audience at one sermon and praised him before the crowd as one of Islam's most important spiritual leaders. With the public rituals of mutual flattery came word of expensive construction projects designed to provide Kandahar with a new face. Ground was broken near the Governor's House on an elaborate new mosque to be financed by bin Laden and his supporters. There was also planning for a grand new Eid Mosque to celebrate breaking the fast at the end of Ramadan, to be constructed on the southern outskirts of Kandahar. It would be a true people's mosque, used only once each year. Wealthy Arabs from Saudi Arabia and elsewhere in the Persian Gulf flew into Kandahar for bustard-hunting in the nearby deserts. The Arabs arrived on chartered jets and brought mind-boggling luxuries for their weeks-long hunts. Bin Laden sometimes participated. These were potential donors to his operations.[13]

In addition to his urban Kandahar compound bin Laden installed his family and dozens of his Arab followers on the flat desert plains a dozen miles outside of town, near the Kandahar airport. During the early Cold War period when American contractors built the airport, they also constructed apartment buildings so that their expatriate workforce would have decent quarters. The apartments were some four decades old now, but they still compared favorably to local accommodations. The Taliban allowed bin Laden's Arab entourage to move in. They also gave him the keys to Tarnak Farm, a walled government-run agricultural cooperative complex on the outskirts of the airport. The farm had several dozen buildings and was isolated and secure in a stretch of empty desert. At least one of bin Laden's wives and a number of his children moved in during the first months of 1997.[14] Local Afghans also reported to Santos and the United Nations that bin Laden had announced plans to construct a training complex for Arab mujahedin in Uruzgan province where Mullah Omar had roots. Bin Laden planned to train foreign volunteers who would aid the Taliban in their continuing military campaign against Massoud.

The United States still had no legal indictment or covert action plan to target bin Laden. The virtual bin Laden station in Virginia tracked his financial dealings and analyzed his public statements but had yet to direct lethal operations against him. The CIA met with Unocal executives to debrief them on Central Asian pipeline politics, but they never asked for help in watching, capturing, or attacking bin Laden in Kandahar that winter. The U.S. embassy in Islamabad informed Senator Hank Brown late in 1996 that bin Laden had appeared at a meeting in Afghanistan and announced a $1 million reward for Brown's assassination. Brown was told that he should not travel to the region anymore. Yet this threat still did not galvanize a plan to attack bin Laden, whose paramilitary and terrorist ambitions remained something of a mystery to both the CIA and the White House counterterrorism office. In fact, bin Laden had already dispatched operatives to Africa and elsewhere to prepare for terrorist strikes against American targets, but the United States was unaware of these plans. The White House did not begin to push for covert operations against bin Laden beyond intelligence collection until the end of 1997, a year after he established himself openly in Mullah Omar's Kandahar.[15]

American and Saudi officials met regularly and cordially with Taliban representatives during these months. Unocal sponsored visits for Taliban leaders to the United States so they could see the company's oil operations, and its lobbyists helped to arrange meetings at the State Department.

These contacts encouraged the belief in Washington that there were Taliban moderates, sincere young Pashtuns in the leadership *shuras* interested in international dialogue who would lead their movement toward political responsibility. Mullah Ghaus was often credited with such potential, as was Mullah Rabbani, Saudi Arabia's protégé. Rabbani traveled that spring to Riyadh and declared after a meeting with the ailing King Fahd, "Since Saudi Arabia is the center of the Muslim world, we would like to have Saudi assistance. King Fahd expressed happiness at the good measures taken by the Taliban and over the imposition of Sharia in our country."[16] The Taliban also retained support during these months from important Durrani Pashtuns such as members of the Karzai family. The triumph of Taliban power in Kabul meant trade and economic opportunity for Durrani Pashtuns across the south. Relative to the recent past, Kandahar was now an Arab-funded boomtown.

Mullah Omar, who continued to demonstrate that he meant what he said, openly outlined his future plans. "War is a tricky game," he told a Pakistani visitor in March 1997. "We feel a military solution has better prospects now after numerous failed attempts to reach a peaceful, negotiated settlement."[17]

A few weeks later a Taliban spokesman formally acknowledged that Osama bin Laden had moved to Kandahar. Now bin Laden could "go and see the leader directly." The world had nothing to fear, he said. "We will not allow Afghanistan to be used to launch terrorist attacks."[18]

AHMED SHAH MASSOUD and his tattered army retreated from Kabul to a cold Panjshir winter. They had known this sort of hardship before, and worse, during the anti-Soviet campaigns of the 1980s. But to lose control of the capital was a deep blow. Massoud blamed his longtime political mentor, President Burhanuddin Rabbani, for failing to make coalition politics in Kabul work while Massoud concentrated on security and war. "Massoud felt cheated because he had never been able to focus full-time on politics," recalled his aide Haroun Amin. After Kabul's loss, "He thought that Rabbani and the other political leaders were incompetent—couldn't be trusted."[19] Massoud's men recovered steadily because they knew they faced a long war with an extremist Pashtun militia in which surrender would lead to annihilation. Massoud held open the possibility of a negotiated compromise with the Taliban, but his main emphasis that winter was on recovering the battlefield. "He never thought for a second that he would lose Afghanistan," recalled his brother Ahmed Wali. Within weeks he had assembled a meeting of defeated northern ethnic militias and announced a new alliance, initially called the Supreme Council for the Defense of the Motherland and later recast as the United Front.[20]

Massoud had grown isolated during his last years in Kabul. More than ever, he and his closest aides knew, they needed international support. Russia, Tajikistan, and Uzbekistan were all threatened by the Taliban's announced plans to liberate Central Asian Muslims. Massoud dispatched some of his longest-serving intelligence and foreign policy aides abroad to open talks with potential backers. Massoud offered himself as a bulwark against Islamist radicalism. He opened negotiations with Russia about arms supplies and airfield access as Moscow dispatched twenty-eight thousand soldiers to Central Asia, partly to defend against Taliban-sponsored incursions. Iran weighed in with offers of money, weapons, and humanitarian aid. India, ever ready to support an enemy of Pakistan or its proxies, would become another source of funding.

Massoud had to scratch together money and arms. There was cash available in his Panjshir redoubts from gem mining and drug smuggling. Massoud's militia ran heroin through Central Asia to Russia. They sold lapis and emeralds at gem shows as far away as Las Vegas. From his base in Taloqan, a ragged town to the west of the Panjshir Valley, Massoud appointed new commanders and intelligence chiefs to begin rebuilding his forces and his information networks across Afghanistan. He told his men that the Taliban would grow vulnerable with time. When Pashtuns discovered that the Taliban were bent on an Islamist totalitarian state, Massoud predicted, dissent would rise. "Day by day," recalled Mohammed Neem, Massoud's intelligence chief during this period, his loyal Panjshiri soldiers "gradually saw we could stand against the Taliban."[21]

Massoud and his men were very suspicious of the United States. It was difficult to believe that the Pakistani support for the Taliban they had witnessed as Kabul fell could have occurred without at least tacit American backing. Massoud had captured Pakistani citizens in the fighting around Kabul. Then there was the confusing, conspiracy-shrouded question of the Unocal pipeline project. Where did the Americans stand? Massoud's inner circle discussed the question at length, but they lacked confidence about the answer.

Had they known the truth they might not have believed it. Even at this late stage the American government and its intelligence services lacked a complete understanding of covert Pakistani support for the Taliban—an ignorance born mainly from lack of interest and effort. A December 1996 State Department cable reported that Pakistani intelligence was secretly supplying cash, equipment, and military advisers to the Taliban, and that high-level Pakistani officers from ISI were fighting inside Afghanistan along with uneducated recruits from Pakistan. "We recently have received more credible information about the extent and origin of Pakistani assistance and support to the Taliban," the Islamabad embassy reported. But the question was uncertain enough within confidential American government channels that ambassador Tom Simons could report to Washington just a few weeks later that Pakistani aid to the Taliban was "probably less malign than most imagine" and probably amounted to much less than rumored. "Military advice to the Taliban may be there, but is probably not all that significant," Simons concluded. Long practiced at covert programs in Afghanistan, the Pakistanis had deceived Washington about the Taliban for two solid years.

Massoud sought to attract American attention. In a general atmosphere of estrangement, especially from the State Department, there was one opening he could exploit: the offer made by Gary Schroen and the CIA to reopen a direct channel of cooperation. Massoud's first reaction to the Stinger-recovery proposal, recalled his Washington representative Daoud Mir, was "No way—I want to discuss with them the policy of Afghanistan, the future of Afghanistan." But with the loss of Kabul he had a new motivation: If he energetically brokered missile sales, "he could have an understanding and good relations between the United States and the United Front," as his aide Mohiden Mehdi put it. Massoud told his men to start making inquiries about Stingers with commanders across the north. He wanted something to show the Americans.[22]

Many of the warlords they approached had previously pledged allegiance to Hekmatyar. When Kabul fell, the Taliban had expelled Hekmatyar from Afghanistan, to exile in Iran. Many in Hekmatyar's old network switched allegiance to the Taliban, but some commanders in the north who were cut off needed money. Massoud's network even managed to buy a few Stingers from behind Taliban lines. For Massoud the reward was "to draw attention" from the CIA, as one of his intelligence aides put it. "We wanted to use it as a means of getting our message—the message of resistance and the message of the cause—back to Washington."[23]

Gary Schroen flew to Taloqan in the early spring of 1997 to renew talks with Massoud. He and Alan Eastham, then deputy chief of mission at the embassy in Islamabad, caught a scheduled United Nations charter. The Taliban were pushing north. As Schroen and Eastham prepared to meet with Massoud, a Taliban plane flew over and dropped a bomb. Gunfire echoed on Taloqan's outskirts.[24]

Schroen and his colleagues in the CIA's Near East Division were skeptical about whether Massoud could be a worthwhile ally against bin Laden. Massoud was candid about the problems: He had to worry about the Taliban, and the Arab training camps that concerned the CIA were a long distance off. He said he was happy to cooperate as best he could, but he didn't want the CIA to have inflated expectations. For his part, Schroen argued that Massoud could assist not only the United States but his own military cause if he helped eliminate bin Laden from the Afghan battlefield. The agency's Counterterrorist Center hoped to provide initial supplies of secure communications gear that would permit Massoud's intelligence aides to send messages and talk to Langley. The Center's bin Laden unit informed a congressional committee in closed session on April 10, 1997, that it was now running operations designed to collect target intelligence in Afghanistan for use in the future, should the United States decide to capture bin Laden or attack his organization. The communications gear would also permit Massoud's agents behind Taliban lines to report back about bin Laden's safe houses and movements. But there was no cash or firm planning yet available.

Schroen told Massoud that for follow-up contacts it would probably be best to use CIA stations in Central Asia. With Massoud now pushed so far north, it would be easier for officers to meet with him from Tashkent or Dushanbe than from Islamabad. Massoud's side, too, preferred to interact with the CIA in Central Asia. It had long bothered them that their contacts with the agency were centered on the Islamabad station, which maintained such close ties with Massoud's enemies at ISI. In Taloqan that March they talked about using CIA storage and transit facilities in Central Asia to move recovered Stingers out of the north.

Massoud and his advisers remained frustrated by the Americans. The United States was missing the real danger, they felt: the Taliban, Pakistani intelligence, and their Arab volunteers. Massoud and his men interpreted the CIA's agenda as Stingers, first and foremost. They respected Schroen and saw him as a tough, devoted operative, but their talks with him were fitful and sporadic. The political and military discussions, including those about bin Laden and terrorism, were as yet no deeper than those Massoud and his aides had routinely at foreign embassies. They felt they needed much more.[25]

On his own, Massoud rebuilt his intelligence networks and sabotage operations. There were many sympathetic Tajiks behind Taliban lines, especially around Kabul. Traders moved freely between the two zones. Massoud's special forces, some living as undercover cells in the capital, blew up Taliban equipment at the Kabul airport. His intelligence group established a special unit that year focused on Arab and Pakistani forces that fought alongside the Taliban.

Through their sources they picked up word about assassination plots against Massoud. They received one report that an assassin had been dispatched to kill Massoud by placing in his shoes a mysterious powder—possibly anthrax. Recalled Neem, the intelligence chief during 1997: "We appointed one person for one year to guard Ahmed Shah Massoud's shoes."[26]

THE TALIBAN SWEPT into Mazar-i-Sharif that May. The bearded, turbaned Pashtun and Pakistani *madrassa* graduates who poured into the city center in pickup trucks were as foreign an invasion force as the blue-eyed Russian conscripts who'd rumbled through on Soviet tanks eighteen years before. The largest and most important city in northern Afghanistan, Mazar was a secular, urbane, relatively prosperous city with sixteen channels of satellite television and billboards festooned with the clean-shaven, mustached face of its longtime overlord Aburrashid Dostum, a former communist general who wore his religion lightly. Mazar's dominant turquoise-domed mosque legendarily entombs a son-in-law of the Prophet Mohammed, a central figure in the Shia faith, anathema to the Taliban. The Taliban's shock troops were a long way from Kandahar now. They did not speak the local language. But Mullah Omar continued to believe his movement was destined to conquer all of Afghanistan by military force. His new consultant, Osama bin Laden, increasingly urged the revival of ancient Central Asian Islamic empires that would reach all the way to contemporary Russia. And Pakistani intelligence concluded that the Taliban had to seize Mazar if they were to make a plausible claim for international recognition as Afghanistan's government. ISI calculated in the spring of 1997 "that a recognized Taliban government which controlled the entire country would be easier to deal with than a Taliban movement," as the Pakistani writer Ahmed Rashid put it later. Neighboring countries would have to accept the Taliban as a reality, and they would turn to Pakistan for help, increasing Islamabad's leverage.[27]

Pakistan's army and president had ejected Benazir Bhutto from office shortly after the Taliban took Kabul. Her plans to buy time in the prime minister's chair by capitulating to the army's agenda had failed. She had managed to keep an uneasy peace with the military and ISI on Afghanistan and Kashmir, but she had been unable to control corruption in her family, her cabinet, and her party. She continued to suffer under the delusions of her family's aristocratic, landed political inheritance, the sense that she had been called to preside over "the people," or "the masses," who would buoy her in a struggle against her enemies. Instead she was on her way to London exile once more, a wandering daughter in an updated Greek myth of greed and family tragedy. The army endorsed new elections and arranged for the nomination of its longtime Punjabi businessman client Nawaz Sharif at the head of a military-friendly coalition. Sharif was a dull, agreeable, pasty man from a family of Lahore industrialists. He had managed an improbable career in politics by practicing the chameleon arts of the figurehead. Like Bhutto, he pledged to his advisers as he accepted Pakistan's prime ministership early in 1997 that he would leave the army and ISI alone.

As the Taliban neared Mazar, Pakistani intelligence signaled to Sharif that when the city fell, it would be time to formally recognize the Taliban as Afghanistan's legitimate government. The announcement was made by Pakistan's foreign ministry on May 26. Sharif first learned about it when the news flashed across his television. "He was furious," recalled his aide Mushahid Hussain. "He said, 'Who made that decision?'"[28]

Prince Turki's chief of staff at Saudi intelligence, Ahmed Badeeb, met with ISI in Rawalpindi as Mazar fell, and "they asked that we recognize [the] Taliban." Badeeb felt that the Taliban leaders "had no clue how to run a country," but he could see that Pakistani intelligence was deeply invested in them. Badeeb flew back to Riyadh and told the Saudi royal family, "They are very religious people. . . . I think we have to give them a chance." Prince Turki argued that if the Saudis granted the Taliban recognition, the kingdom would have a strong channel for engagement. "Due to Pakistani insistence and to the lack of any other options," Badeeb recalled, the kingdom decided to grant recognition "so as to fill the obvious vacuum" in Afghanistan. The United Arab Emirates, whose senior princes regularly embarked on luxurious falcon-hunting trips in Taliban country, joined in.[29]

But they had moved too fast. Mazar became a Taliban death trap. Within days of the three recognition announcements, the city's Uzbek and Shia populations revolted against their Pashtun occupiers. They massacred three hundred Taliban soldiers. They took another thousand prisoner and sent the militia reeling back down the Salang Highway toward Kabul. Suddenly the Taliban no longer possessed any meaningful piece of northern Afghanistan. But for Pakistan, Saudi Arabia, and the U.A.E., the deed was done: All three anointed the Taliban as Afghanistan's legitimate government.

To win the full privileges of recognition, the Taliban needed the United States to go along. As Mazar smoldered, a small coup attempt erupted half a world away, inside the decaying embassy of Afghanistan in Washington, D.C., a stately brick mansion on Wyoming Avenue that had earlier been the home of a U.S. Supreme Court justice. Like Afghanistan's distant war the embassy coup unfolded for the Americans at first as a nuisance, until it reached a stage where the threat of violence could no longer be ignored.

The Clinton administration declined to recognize the Taliban government. The Afghan embassy in Washington spoke for President Rabbani and Ahmed Shah Massoud even after their expulsion from Kabul by the Taliban. Since late 1994, Afghanistan had been represented in the United States by Yar Mohabbat, a Pashtun architect and longtime resident of Germany who was close to Rabbani. Mohabbat had lobbied in Congress, at the State Department, and at the CIA, even as the Taliban rose up from Kandahar. At the State Department, Mohabbat was shunted off to meetings with the lowest-ranking desk officers. "They were always looking at Afghanistan through Pakistan's eyes," he recalled. The CIA was more sympathetic. He opened up a channel at Langley when Massoud started buying back Stingers. The agency gave Mohabbat the telephone number of a third party in Washington he could call when he wanted to talk to a CIA officer. His main Langley contact knew Massoud well and obviously had spent a lot of time in Afghanistan. When Mohabbat complained that the United States underestimated the dangers of the Taliban and failed to recognize Massoud's potential as an ally, the CIA man "was shaking his head. 'I tell the State Department the same things that you're saying. They don't listen to me, either. They all think that Massoud is the problem.'" A woman from the FBI once dropped by to interview Mohabbat about Arab extremists training in Afghanistan. Otherwise, hardly anyone from the American government ever visited his embassy.[30]

Mohabbat was away for Memorial Day weekend in 1997 as the Taliban stormed Mazar. His deputy, Seraj Jamal, gave an interview to Voice of America's Pashto service and suddenly declared that he had switched sides to the Taliban. He proclaimed that under his leadership the Washington embassy now took orders from Mullah Omar.

Mohabbat feared a Taliban coup at the embassy would create momentum for official American recognition. He rushed to the building and saw the Taliban's white flag fluttering on the pole outside. Stunned, he announced to Seraj—who had given no hint of his budding conversion in their months working together—that he was going to pull the Taliban banner down the next day and raise again the Rabbani government's black, white, and green flag.

That night a Pashto-speaking Afghan called Mohabbat at home and threatened to kill him. "Death must come from God," Mohabbat told the caller, as he remembered it. "This is not Afghanistan. This is not Pakistan. This is America. You can't do that here."

"It's easier to do here," the caller said, "because all I need to do is give money to someone, and they'll kill you for me."[31]

Officers from the FBI and State's Bureau of Diplomatic Security swarmed over the embassy's grounds the next morning with bomb-sniffing dogs. They sent police to Mohabbat's house and provided protection for his wife. Mohabbat moved back into an office on the embassy's ground floor while Seraj claimed the second floor for the Taliban and turned it into living quarters. For weeks Seraj tried to harass Mohabbat into leaving the embassy. Each day was a new battle: Seraj would plaster photographs of Mullah Omar on the walls, and Mohabbat would promote Rabbani and Massoud. When Mohabbat toured the Taliban-occupied floor of the embassy, he saw computers, fax machines, and printers, each affixed with a label: PROPERTY OF THE EMBASSY OF SAUDI ARABIA, WASHINGTON, D.C.[32]

The State Department's South Asia bureau wanted nothing to do with this battle. They declined to choose a winner. They sponsored a few mediation sessions, but these produced no progress. Finally, in August, State's Afghan desk officer called Mohabbat and Seraj in for a meeting. He told them that the United States had decided to close the Afghan embassy altogether. As far as the United States was concerned, Afghanistan's existence as a government in the international system had been suspended.[33]

Mohabbat moved to St. Louis, hoping to avoid Taliban reprisals. Seraj moved to the Taliban's unofficial delegation at the United Nations.

It was another tawdry season of American diplomacy. The United Nations estimated that Taliban-ruled Kabul now held fifty thousand widows unable to work or walk in the streets without the risk of beatings from religious police. Those widows were the mothers of some 400,000 children. The U.N. appealed for $133 million in humanitarian aid for Afghanistan during 1997 but received only $56 million.[34] The United States was in the midst of an economic boom, but Congress, the State Department, and the White House were all convinced that nothing more could be done, that more aid to Afghanistan would only be wasted on warlords. Even the threat of terrorism emanating from Afghanistan did not attract much attention. The State Department, adhering to a new economic sanctions regime, announced its first list of officially designated Foreign Terrorist Organizations that autumn of 1997. Bin Laden and al Qaeda were not on the list.

There were small changes stirring in American policy as Clinton entered his second term. Hillary Clinton had visited India in 1995 and became determined to push her husband toward greater involvement in the region. Madeleine Albright, who arrived as secretary of state, was more sharply attuned to human rights violators such as the Taliban than Warren Christopher had been. An anti-Taliban petition drive organized by the Feminist Majority and Mavis Leno, the wife of late-night comedian Jay Leno, captured Albright's attention. Her new deputy, Thomas Pickering, a former ambassador to India, was also determined to reexamine American policy in South Asia. The former Special Envoy to the Afghan resistance, Peter Tomsen, now the U.S. ambassador to Armenia, wrote a pleading Secret cable to State principals: "We have long underestimated the geo-political threat of Afghan instability to U.S. interests. . . . We should conduct a major Afghan policy review and implement a more resolute Afghan policy. A passive U.S. approach will continue to leave the field to the Pakistani and Arab groups supporting the Islamic extremists."[35]

The National Security Council led a South Asia policy review during the first months of 1997, culminating in a memorandum to the president in August, just as the White House authorized the shutdown of the Afghan embassy in Washington. The policy memo concentrated mainly on India and Pakistan, urging more sustained American contacts with both Islamabad and New Delhi.

On Afghanistan, however, the NSC memo merely reiterated American support for the U.N. peace process. It was essentially the same policy that the United States had pursued on Afghanistan since the CIA covert pipeline shut down on December 31, 1991.

As it would turn out, a more significant transformation was beginning across the Potomac River that summer at CIA headquarters. John Deutch had quit after only nineteen months as director. He was the fifth director in ten years; the turnover and instability in the agency's leadership seemed to be getting worse. When Deutch left, the president tried to nominate Tony Lake to run the CIA, but the Republican-controlled Senate made it clear that the confirmation process would be a political bloodbath. That left George J. Tenet, Deutch's deputy, a former congressional aide with limited experience. Tenet might not have the burnished credentials of past CIA directors, but he had two qualities that appealed strongly to a Clinton White House with weak ties to Langley: He was well liked, and he could be easily confirmed by Congress.

None of those who supported his candidacy in that summer of 1997 predicted that George Tenet would become one of the longest-serving directors in the CIA's history, its most important leader since William Casey, or an architect of the agency's covert return to Afghanistan.

"Does America Need
the CIA?"

PRESIDENT CLINTON DID NOT attend George J. Tenet's swearing-in ceremony at the White House on July 31, 1997. He sent Vice President Al Gore in his stead. In Deutch and now Tenet, Clinton had placed leaders at Langley whom he liked and trusted. Yet the president remained skeptical of the CIA as an institution. His exceptionally smart friend John Deutch had impressed upon him a belief that the Directorate of Operations just wasn't very good at spying. A failed covert action program targeting Saddam Hussein in the summer of 1996 had embarrassed and frustrated the White House. Clinton was innately skeptical of covert action as a substitute for overt foreign policy, and the Iraq episode had only reinforced his instincts. Some of the agency's career operatives had then revolted against Clinton's nomination of Tony Lake as director. Tenet's relationship with the new national security adviser, Sandy Berger, was excellent, and he could count on Clinton's personal attention when he needed it. But he was being appointed that summer to run an agency whose most important client, the president, remained aloof and unimpressed.

Tenet, just forty-four years old, was in many ways an unlikely candidate to repair the breach. He had never run for political office, managed a large organization, served in the military, worked as an intelligence officer, shaped American foreign policy, or authored a book or significant journal article. He had risen to the position of America's chief spy partly by political accident but also because he was exceptionally gifted with people and with the Washington bureaucratic art typically called "process." He was gregarious, direct, funny, unpretentious, hardworking, a natural coalition builder, and "the ultimate staff guy," as his colleague Nick Burns put it. He was an insider, a creature of permanent Washington. He had arrived in the capital two decades before to study international relations at Georgetown University. His first job in the city, as a lobbyist, was a tongue-twisting classic of the enduring Washington: director of photovoltaics and international programs at the Solar Energy Industries Association. On Capitol Hill he worked for a decade as a staff professional for Republicans and Democrats alike. Some of his closest friends did not know his political affiliation (he was a registered Democrat) because he rarely spoke about partisan issues.[1]

He had been appointed as Deutch's deputy at the CIA in early 1995 for the same reason that Clinton appointed him as director in the summer of 1997: His personal connections on both sides of the Senate aisle made him very easy to confirm. Tenet was very loyal to Deutch, but he understood when he took charge in the summer of 1997 that the CIA was near rock bottom. Constant turnover in the director's office had set the agency far adrift. Recruitment had stalled: Only 25 trainees became clandestine officers in 1995. Attrition and early retirement continued to drain off talent and spirit. This was true in every division. The Directorate of Operations was probably the worst, but the Directorate of Intelligence and even the Directorate of Science and Technology were suffering as well. The agency's budget was overstretched, despite the new funds for counterterrorism. The morale problems caused by the Aldrich Ames case remained, exacerbated by minor arguments with Congress over agent recruitment in Central America, episodes which reinforced a sense at Langley that everything the agency touched was bound to turn to scandal, at least in the eyes of Congress and the press.

In his two years as Deutch's deputy, as liaison to the Directorate of Operations, Tenet had absorbed these problems the way a Geiger counter absorbs radiation signals. He was a student of people and institutions. He had uncanny intuition about their moods and sufferings, and he often seemed to know just the right thing to say. By far his strongest instincts about the CIA involved its internal health. He did not move into the director's suite on the seventh floor that summer with grand, compelling ideas about global politics.

Virtually all of his views about national security threats and foreign policy reflected the capital's centrist consensus. Bill Casey had come to the CIA to wage war against the Soviet Union. George Tenet measured his ambitions at first largely by the CIA's institutional needs: a more clearly defined mission, higher morale, better execution of core espionage and analysis, more recruits, better training, and more resources. "This is all about focusing on basics," he told CIA staff at a meeting called to announce his priorities. He was going to break the pattern of the last decade. "It is truly unfortunate" that the agency had endured three directors in just five years, he said. "This one is staying." His approach, he told them, would put "a premium on hard work for commonsense goals."[2]

This was the way he had been raised. His father was Greek by ancestry but Albanian by birth. John Tenet left Albania when he was thirteen and spent the next seven years working in French coal mines. With little money and few possessions, he came through Ellis Island on the eve of the Great Depression. George Tenet's mother escaped communism by fleeing her native Epirus (a region on the border between Greece and Albania) in the hull of a British submarine at the end of World War II. She never saw her parents again. She met John Tenet in New York, married, and on January 5, 1953, gave birth to a son, William, and six minutes later to his fraternal twin, George.[3]

They lived in a two-story row house on Marathon Parkway in Little Neck, Queens. The house faced a quiet, tree-lined residential road where the boys played stickball. George Tenet was renowned for his hitting power, capable of knocking a spaldeen two sewers from home. He also played guard on the St. Nicholas Greek Orthodox Church basketball team. His father opened the 20th Century Diner around the block from the family home. George and Bill worked as busboys throughout their teens. They were little alike. Bill was reserved, precise, and studious; he would become a cardiologist. George was loud, sloppy, and boisterous. At the diner he was called "The Mouthpiece." Sol Winder, a family friend, recalled that he "was always talking, that kid. He was the type of guy who could never keep a secret." He was also a news junkie. At age eight he wrote a series of letters to the host of a local current affairs show, who sent back an autograph: "To the future editorial page editor of *The New York Times*." His parents drove home the immigrant creed: hard work, education, family, faith, ambition. His father worked sixteen-hour days so the twins could make it in America. Both apparently took internal vows to do so or die trying.[4]

In 1982, at twenty-nine, George Tenet landed his first job on Capitol Hill, as legislative assistant to Senator John Heinz, a Republican from Pennsylvania. Tenet was a "guy's guy, a sports nut," as a colleague recalled. He had season tickets to Georgetown University basketball. He was so devoted to the Hoyas that he wrote an outraged, sardonic letter to *Sports Illustrated* after the magazine published a critical article about the team's recruitment practices. But Tenet had no fixed political ideology, his colleagues remembered, other than wanting to ensure that the United States maintained its advantage over the rest of the world. He stood out because he could connect at a personal level with senators and staff. Heinz was a demanding, detail-oriented boss who consumed data and pushed his staff hard. He tested new arrivals early on to see if they could meet his standards; if not, he froze them out until they left. Tenet failed the initial test; he was new to the Hill, did not know the role of staff members, and was not an especially strong writer. But he fought his way back into Heinz's good graces. "He was the only person I ever saw there that slid downhill and then pulled himself back up," recalled his colleague Bill Reinsch. Tenet did it by "force of personality and hard work."[5]

Hill staffers often went out in the evening, but Tenet never finished his first beer, much less ordered a second round. He was already married, to Stephanie Glakas, the outgoing daughter of a career foreign service officer. She worked as a dorm mother at the all-female Marymount College on Foxhall Road, near Georgetown, and when they settled in Washington together, Tenet moved into the dorm—it was cheap housing. Later they bought the Maryland house Glakas had grown up in. Tenet organized his life around Capitol Hill, his suburban home, his newborn son, Georgetown basketball, and occasional rounds of golf on cheap public courses. He was profane and comical, not sanctimonious or naïve, but also a very straight arrow, his colleagues felt. At the office or passing on a street corner he was quick with "typical New York, in-your-face" banter, but it was "friendly, not hostile," and he managed not to bruise people, a colleague remembered. He worked Senate hearing rooms the way he had worked the Queens diner counter, vamping for attention. He was a bulky man, overweight, and a chronic poacher of office junk food. His friends worried about his health, but he seemed to be completely comfortable in his own skin. "George has a powerful personality," recalled his Senate staff colleague Gary Sojka. "He could have been a longshoreman."[6]

He deferred to senators and did not attempt to usurp their power or prerogatives. "He was very, very careful in dealing with members, irrespective of party," recalled Senator Warren Rudman. He was direct and won the trust of his superiors by delivering bad news in a way that did not upset them. Recalled his colleague Eric Newsom, "George sort of proved something I saw happen over and over in the Senate, which was that experience mattered less than the ability to interact effectively with people." He had a "very unbureaucratic way of talking," crisp and colorful. To some seasoned colleagues Tenet's style of speech appeared to oversimplify complex issues, but it was effective and allowed him to stand out from the crowd.[7]

Tenet left Heinz to join the Senate Select Committee on Intelligence as an aide to Senator Patrick Leahy, a liberal Democrat, in the summer of 1985. He was a junior staffer who worked on oversight of Cold War arms control negotiations. When Leahy left the committee because of regular rotations, Tenet almost lost his job, but the incoming chairman, David Boren, a conservative Democrat from Oklahoma, agreed to keep him on the payroll for a few months. Tenet ingratiated himself with Boren and within a year had been named staff director of the elite, secretive Senate committee charged with keeping track of the CIA's budget, regulations, and covert action programs.

"The thing that I found most valuable is, he would march right in and say, 'You don't want to hear this, but you need to know such and such.' Or 'You're out on a limb on this,'" Boren recalled. "He's very blunt, straightforward. And then totally loyal."[8] Tenet had never worked in intelligence and had rarely traveled, and what he knew about the agency he had learned only from hearings, conversations, and briefing books. But aside from the elected members themselves, he was now the CIA's most important overseer in the United States Senate.

He could be tough on the agency. Tenet helped draft and pass laws that tightened congressional oversight of CIA operations. He had a budget-cutting streak and felt taxpayer money was sometimes wasted by the intelligence community. "He was always giving the third degree to the agency," Boren recalled. On one occasion, involving disputes over an internal audit, "it got so heated that they were accusing Tenet of witch-hunting." William Webster, then CIA director, turned up at the next closed Senate oversight meeting in a bulletproof vest, trying to slough off Tenet with humor. Yet as Tenet began to make contact with the CIA's career spies, he also gradually became loyal and helpful to them, just as he was to the senators. Veteran officers such as Thomas Twetten spent long hours cultivating Tenet and educating him about the details of espionage tradecraft. When longtime CIA analyst and manager Robert Gates was nominated as the agency's director, Tenet carefully shepherded him through the confirmation hearings, protecting him from partisan attack. He began to build a network of relationships at Langley.[9]

Tenet rarely revealed his political and foreign policy views. A colleague remembers him denouncing Dan Quayle and speaking up for the Texas Democrat Lloyd Bentsen during the 1988 vice presidential debates, but this colleague also remembers Tenet as skeptical about a fellow Greek, the liberal Democrat Michael Dukakis. Tenet was conservative on arms control verification, progressive on women's rights, and elusively neutral or centrist on much else. "He had an ambidextrous quality that was something Boren particularly valued," recalled John Despres, a colleague on the intelligence committee. Tenet has "never been a great intellect. He's an operator." His role was to synthesize and organize the views of others so that elected officials could make decisions. There were hundreds and hundreds of people in Washington with strong opinions and ideologies. There were thousands of pointy-headed foreign policy experts and technical specialists. Much rarer was the staff man who knew how to traffic among them all, picking pockets and getting things done.[10]

On one occasion where he provided strong advice, it did not go very well. When a closely divided Congress faced an emotional vote over whether to authorize President Bush to launch war against Iraq to expel Saddam Hussein's army from Kuwait, Tenet recommended to Boren that he vote against the war. "I think Senator Boren relied on him to a large degree," recalled a colleague. Classified briefings from the Defense Intelligence Agency had emphasized the potential for bloody disaster. "There was a concern there would be a lot of casualties. It was a cautious vote." Boren, who had been seen as presidential material, was hurt politically by his decision, as were other congressional Democrats who opposed what turned out to be a swift and popular war that took thousands of Iraqi lives but produced few American casualties.[11]

This would become a Tenet pattern until 2001: He did not often offer direct, forceful policy advice, preferring to assemble options and analysis for others to act upon. But when he did make policy recommendations, he could at times be cautious, especially if there was a risk of casualties or unknowable consequences.

Clinton had few experts in intelligence to draw upon after his election in 1992. The Democrats had been out of the executive branch for twelve years. The main place where the party had loyal members with deep, recent experience in foreign affairs was Congress. Tenet's resume might have been thin by historical standards, but he was a natural to serve as a transition director for intelligence issues after Clinton's election. The transition job "was where you showed whether you were capable of being a member of the administration," recalled Newsom, Tenet's colleague on the intelligence committee. "It was a cattle show to see if you were going to pass muster."[12] Tenet did, and he followed Lake and Berger to the National Security Council as senior director for intelligence. This was a sensitive staff job run out of the Old Executive Office Building, beside the West Wing of the White House. Tenet's office was the bureaucratic junction between the CIA, the White House, and Congress on intelligence operations and policy. His daily work involved not only continuous negotiations over budgets and oversight issues but legal reviews of proposed covert actions. He worked so hard at the job in 1993 and 1994 that he suffered a heart attack, an event that caused him to give up cigar smoking but had little apparent impact on his schedule.

Memos about covert action plans, international criminal cases, and intelligence policy flowed continually between Tenet's desk and the CIA's Office of General Counsel, the NSC, the Justice Department, and the Pentagon. As the chief supervisor of this paper flow, helping to organize it for presidential decision-making, Tenet became steeped in the politics and regulation of espionage, the use and impact of intelligence analysis at the White House, and the legal and budgetary architecture of American spy agencies. By osmosis and participation he also began to learn the major foreign policy issues in even greater detail. He watched presidential decision-making about espionage and covert action from up close.

This insider's track shaped Tenet's agenda when he arrived at Langley. When he was promoted to the CIA director's office in the summer of 1997, Tenet conceived his reform program by looking at the CIA's original blueprint. He was attracted to the agency's "streak of eccentric genius," as Tenet put it. He also had a large sentimental streak, and he saw his own success against the backdrop of the American myth: "Nowhere in the world could the son of an immigrant stand before you as the Director of Central Intelligence," he said as he was sworn in. "This is simply the greatest country on the face of the earth."[13]

In his early weeks as director he was invited by former president Gerald Ford to appear on a panel titled "Does America Need the CIA?" The mere existence of such an event signaled how low the agency had fallen. As he prepared his speech, Tenet returned to the CIA's founding by Harry Truman. The agency's purpose was to prevent another Pearl Harbor. The CIA was "an insurance policy" against that sort of strategic surprise. "It is clear to me that the potential for dangerous surprise is as great as ever," he told Ford's panel. "That is true whether I look at terrorist groups whose sole purpose is to harm American interests, the biological weapons that Saddam Hussein is still trying to build and to hide in Iraq, or the programs Iran has for building intermediate range missiles and nuclear weapons."[14]

Tenet vowed to improve the agency's core ability to warn presidents about unexpected danger. This in turn meant refocusing on collecting intelligence, especially from human sources, against "hard targets," the states and groups most likely to deliver a nasty surprise. Some of the CIA's critics argued that in an age of global, digital media, where policy makers had instant access to multiple sources of news and information worldwide, the CIA was becoming just another news organization. Tenet thought that was a stupid assertion, even absurd, but to refute the critics the CIA had to deliver what no other information source in Washington could. To do this it had to steal secrets and recruit paid agents with exclusive access to hard targets.

Tenet also argued that the CIA had to improve analysis work so that it did not miss future threats by failing to track them as they percolated in the early stages. Such all-source analysis was the agency's "core function," Tenet said. The CIA's first job was to "protect the lives of Americans." To concentrate on the basics, the CIA needed to move away from "soft targets" like economic issues and human migration. Whatever their importance, those kinds of crises would not likely produce another Pearl Harbor. The agency had to focus on the most pointed lethal threats.[15]

The lessons of the two previous Langley regimes, and of failed CIA directors dating back to Stansfield Turner, seemed clear enough: Do not attempt to impose change by bringing in outsiders to clean house. Work from within. Find the career employees who have respect, win them to your cause, put them in charge, and let them do the work for you. Tenet reached out for help that first summer to former directors such as Richard Helms. He appointed the influential veteran spy Jack Downing as chief of the Directorate of Operations. He refused to criticize the agency or its employees in public even when there was cause. He walked around the building in his swaggering, bantering, tactile way, throwing arms around people, plopping down at cafeteria tables, and adopting the bluff macho style common at the agency.

At the same time Tenet sought to build bridges with the White House and Congress. His career had been shaped by the oversight process; Tenet's CIA was not going to elude regulations or the law even when that constrained operations. "We are more transparent than we used to be to policymakers within the executive branch, and more integrated into their decision-making," Tenet said approvingly in an early speech. "I dare say the CIA receives more oversight from the Congress than any other agency in the federal government. This is not a complaint. In fact, this oversight is our most vital and direct link to the American people—a source of strength that separates us from all other countries of the world."[16]

There was an all-things-to-all-people quality about Tenet's reform program. The CIA's sharpest critics in Congress feared that he would be too forgiving of the agency's incompetents. Some of his former mid-level colleagues
in the bureaucracy, stunned at his rocket-speed ascension to the CIA directorship, grumbled that Tenet was more salesman than substantive leader.
Tenet did have the accomplished Washington staffer's ability to create a clear
list of priorities without offending any important constituents. He said early
on that he wanted to create "a program based on common sense which ac-
celerates and deepens what we have already begun to do in all-source analysis
and clandestine collection." The agency was not broken, in other words, but
he would fix it.[17]

Tenet deemphasized lethal covert action and paramilitary programs, which
placed the CIA at the greatest political risk. He pointed out that of the CIA's
major functions, "covert action is by far the smallest," yet it was "also the
most controversial." At the same time Tenet assured the agency's paramilitary
operatives that he was determined to "sustain the infrastructure we need
when the President directs us to act." He defended the CIA's small paramilitary department, modeled on some of the Pentagon's Special Forces units, on
the grounds that every president since Truman had found a need at times for
this capability. Covert action was "a critical instrument of U.S. foreign policy,"
but it "should never be the last resort of failed policy," Tenet said, carefully arguing both sides.[18] Tenet could get away with all this because he was so forceful and convincing personally. His eclectic, inclusive outlook did not seem to
be a dodge; it seemed to reflect authentically who he was.[19]

His views about the global threats America faced in the summer of 1997
stood squarely in the center of CIA and Clinton administration analysis. He
saw five "critical challenges" to the United States. These were the "transformation of Russia and China"; the threat of rogue states such as North Korea,
Iran, and Iraq; the "transnational issues" such as terrorism, nuclear proliferation, drugs, and organized crime; regional crises; and failing states in places
such as Africa and the former Yugoslavia. There was nothing remotely controversial about Tenet's list; it covered such a wide range of potential foreign
policy problems as to be almost immune from criticism. To the extent it made
choices, it was a list of hard targets, and it focused on the potential for strategic surprise. It was also the list of a synthesizer, a collator of other people's
analyses, including, crucially, the president's. Clinton had provided the intelligence community with a list of priorities in a classified 1995 presidential decision directive. First on the list was intelligence support to the Pentagon during
military operations. Second was "political, economic and military intelligence

about countries hostile to the United States." Third was "intelligence about specific trans-national threats to our security, such as weapons proliferation, terrorism, drug trafficking, organized crime, illicit trade practices and environmental issues of great gravity." It was a long, sprawling mandate.[20]

Tenet was sharpest when he reflected on the CIA's core mission of strategic warning against surprise attack. "It's easy to become complacent," he said. With the Soviet Union gone and American economic and military strength unchallenged, "the world is different, but it is not safe."[21] The CIA's job was to tell presidents about dangerous surprises, it was that simple. This led Tenet quickly to the threat of terrorism, missiles, and weapons of mass destruction. Through discussions at the White House he absorbed and then recapitulated Clinton's own emerging obsessions with terrorism and especially biological weapons.

At Tenet's confirmation hearing, Senator Bob Kerrey asked the nominee if he thought the threat of terrorism "may be overstated." The question reflected a broader skepticism on Capitol Hill and in the press that summer. The CIA and the FBI, according to an oft-repeated argument, were hyping terrorism to win budget increases. But Tenet told Kerrey that the terrorist threat was real and that it was growing. "The sophistication of the groups capable of launching terrorism against U.S. interests now is worldwide. They have a capability to move money and people and explosives, and the level of activity continues to be enormously worrisome to U.S. intelligence. They're fanatical. They have every reason to continue doing what they're doing. . . . The activity worldwide at this moment in time is unprecedented and the threat to U.S. interests is enormously high."[22]

It was the terrorists, far more than the governments of Russia or China, or even Iraq or Iran, who would most likely deliver a devastating shock to the United States. "What are the forces at play that we must contend with?" Tenet asked the CIA staff early on. He answered his own question: "First, the threat environment is growing more diverse, complex, and dangerous— biological agents, terrorism, information warfare. It's easier and easier for smaller and smaller groups to do serious damage, with less visibility and warning. The potential for surprise has increased enormously."[23]

BY THE AUTUMN OF 1997 persistent lobbying against the Taliban by the Feminist Majority had influenced the two most important women in the Clinton administration, Madeleine Albright and Hillary Clinton. When Albright visited a refugee camp in Peshawar that November, she departed from her prepared script and denounced the Taliban's policies toward women as "despicable." It was the first time a Clinton Cabinet member had made such a forceful statement about Taliban human rights violations. A few weeks later Hillary Clinton used a major speech about human rights at the United Nations to single out the Taliban. "Even now the Taliban in Afghanistan are blocking girls from attending schools," Clinton said. The Taliban were harassing those "who would speak out against this injustice." It was the first time that either of the Clintons had seriously criticized the Taliban in public.[24]

The impetus had come from old friends of Albright and Hillary Clinton in the feminist policy networks of the Democratic Party. These were accomplished, professional women of the baby boomer generation now stepping into powerful positions that women had not held in Washington before, at least not in these numbers. They kept in touch with one another and worked each other's issues. The Taliban had now slipped onto the agenda of this fax machine network. Sitting cross-legged in their barren ministries thousands of miles away in Kandahar, the Taliban's leaders had no idea where this turn in American attitudes had come from. They made little effort to find out. When pressed on the issue of education for girls by the occasional visiting American delegation, they said, "This is God's law," recalled the State Department's Leonard Scensny. "This is the way it's supposed to be. Leave us alone."[25]

Despite the loss of their embassy in Washington, Massoud's closest aides pressed their worldwide lobbying campaign to rally support for their war against the Taliban. In Washington that fall, Abdullah, now officially deputy foreign minister in Massoud's rump government, told State Department officials that bin Laden was financing the Taliban. He tried to persuade the handful of Afghan experts he met at Foggy Bottom that the Taliban should be seen as part of a regional network of Islamist radicalism funded by bin Laden and other wealthy Persian Gulf sheikhs.

In comments such as Albright's, Abdullah could see "signs of some change" in American attitudes, but at the working level of the State Department, all he heard about was the need for Massoud to negotiate with the Taliban. There seemed little belief that the Taliban posed a serious threat. Most of all, "what was lacking there was a policy," Abdullah recalled. The path of least resistance at the State Department was "to accept the presence of the Taliban as a reality" in Afghanistan and try to negotiate solutions "through Pakistan," as Abdullah recalled it. On the American side, "We wanted to see if there was a way to bring about a peaceful settlement of the continuing civil war," remembered Karl F. "Rick" Inderfurth, then assistant secretary of state for South Asian affairs. The State Department's analysts believed late in 1997 that "the Taliban had to be dealt with, it couldn't be wished away."[26]

UNOCAL CONTINUED TO FLOOD Foggy Bottom and the National Security Council with the same advice: The Taliban were a reality, and they could also be part of a new Afghan solution. Marty Miller searched energetically during 1997 for a way to convert the Taliban's triumph in Kabul into a final pipeline deal. He met regularly with Sheila Heslin at the White House. He announced that the Taliban might earn as much as $100 million annually from transit fees if they would only allow the pipeline to be built.

Miller had decided early in 1997 that Unocal needed better contacts in Afghanistan and Pakistan. He began to rely more on Robert Oakley, the former U.S. ambassador to Pakistan and a member of the Unocal advisory board. Oakley's wife, Phyllis, was at this time the chief of the State Department's intelligence wing, the Bureau of Intelligence and Research. She had access to virtually all of the U.S. government's most sensitive intelligence reporting.[27]

Robert Oakley advised Miller to reach the Taliban by working through Pakistan's government. He also suggested that Unocal hire Thomas Gouttierre, an Afghan specialist at the University of Nebraska at Omaha, to develop a job training program in Kandahar that would teach Pashtuns the technical skills needed to build a pipeline. Gouttierre had worked on U.S.-funded humanitarian aid inside Afghanistan during the late years of the anti-Soviet jihad when Oakley was ambassador in Islamabad. Now Unocal agreed to pay $900,000 via the University of Nebraska to set up a Unocal training facility on a fifty-six-acre site in Kandahar, not far from bin Laden's compounds. Gouttierre traveled in and out of Afghanistan and met with Taliban leaders. Oakley lobbied Nawaz Sharif's government in Islamabad on the oil company's behalf. In December 1997, Gouttierre worked with Miller to arrange for another Taliban delegation to visit the United States, this time led by Mullah Wakil Ahmed, Omar's chief aide.[28]

By now it was reasonable for the Taliban to believe that Unocal was effectively an arm of the United States government. The Taliban had more intimate, more focused, and more attentive contact with Unocal executives and their paid consultants than with any American officials. The Unocal executives did not just talk about oil pipelines, they talked about a path to negotiated peace in Afghanistan.

Miller's team provided escorts and transportation for the Taliban that December and helped arrange a meeting for three Taliban ministers at the State Department. Assistant Secretary of State Inderfurth expressed his strongest concerns to the visitors about the condition of Afghan women. He also admonished the Taliban about their tolerance of drug trafficking. He talked about demining, the peace process, and other subjects, never even raising the topics of terrorism or bin Laden. Only after Inderfurth left for another meeting did the subject come up. One of the Taliban ministers explained that his movement had inherited the bin Laden problem, as he was already in Afghanistan "as a guest of the previous regime." The Taliban, this minister said, had stopped allowing bin Laden "to give public interviews and had frustrated Iranian and Iraqi attempts to get in contact with him," according to a Confidential State Department account of the meeting prepared at the time. As for the Unocal pipeline, one of Inderfurth's deputies told the delegation that it was "unlikely to be financed unless there was peace in Afghanistan."[29]

Miller also rented a meeting room for the Taliban delegation at the Watergate Hotel. The itinerary included a visit to NASA headquarters and Mount Rushmore. The idea was to stir the Taliban with images of American ambition and tradition, to build a connection with Mullah Omar's closest aides that went beyond money and jobs. Marty Miller had been aggravated by Albright's public denunciations of Taliban human rights violations. He needed to convince the Taliban that they could do business with the United States.

Pakistan's government, nervous about where these independent contacts between the Taliban and the United States might lead, sent an ISI officer with the Taliban delegation to keep watch on them.[30]

Marty Miller arranged for Zalmay Khalilzad, the leading Republican expert on Afghanistan, to meet with the Taliban at the luxury Four Seasons Hotel in Houston. Over dinner Khalilzad opened a debate with the Taliban's information minister, Amir Khan Mutaqqi, over the Taliban's treatment of women. They argued over exactly what the Koran said about this issue.

Marty Miller invited the Taliban for dinner at his suburban home overlooking a golf course. He was nervous that some of the decorations in his house might offend the Taliban. Before they arrived for dinner, he invited one of Unocal's consultants, an Afghan named Dr. Izimi, to walk through the house looking for potential causes of offense. He had pictures on the walls and all sorts of knickknacks, and he worried that "what is innocuous to us might be offensive to them." Izimi found some statues near Miller's swimming pool that had been bought in Indonesia. The statues were originally grave markers made for indigenous tribes, and they depicted nude people. The statues made it very obvious "who the guy and who the gal are," as Miller put it.

Izimi gave them a good look and said, "Hmm, I don't think these are going to cut it."

"Do you want me to take them down?" Miller asked.

"No, I'll tell you what we'll do," Izimi said. "Why don't we just put a *burqa* on them?"

They went into Miller's kitchen and found some trash bags, returned to the pool, and tied the bags over the statues.

Miller's wife was involved in a group that raised funds for court-appointed advocates for children. This year the Miller house was part of a fundraising tour of seven or eight suburban houses fixed up with Christmas decorations. As a result, Miller had seven Christmas trees in his house, each elaborately decorated with tinsel, gleaming balls, and blinking lights, plus many other Christmas decorations in every room.

The Taliban "were just stunned to see all these Christmas trees," Miller recalled. They kept asking Miller what the Christmas tree meant in the larger story of Jesus and the Christmas holiday. Miller actually had no idea how the Christmas tree had become a symbol of Jesus's birthday, but he talked about it as best he could.[31]

The Taliban leaders asked Miller if they could have their photographs taken standing in front of a Christmas tree. One or two members of the visiting delegation declined to participate, adhering even in Houston to the Taliban's ban on representative images of the human form. But Mullah Wakil and the rest of the long-bearded Taliban leaders stood before one of the blinking Christmas trees, scrunched shoulder to shoulder and grinning.

GEORGE TENET WAS AWARE of Osama bin Laden. He supported the small bin Laden tracking unit in the Counterterrorist Center. But by the end of 1997, neither the new CIA director nor the agency placed bin Laden very high on their priority lists. The agency's view of bin Laden remained similar to Prince Turki's: He was a blowhard, a dangerous and wealthy egomaniac, and a financier of other radicals, but he was also isolated in Afghanistan.

Tenet was "most concerned," he told a Senate panel, about the spread of nuclear, chemical, and biological weapons around the world, "because of the direct threat this poses to the lives of Americans." Statistically, the threat of terrorism remained steady, although the number of attacks against American targets was rising slightly. But in comparison to the potential devastation of a nuclear-armed missile launched against an American city, the threat posed by independent terrorists such as bin Laden appeared modest. As Tenet scanned the horizon in search of potential Pearl Harbors, he saw unstable countries such as Russia and China that already had the capacity to launch such a surprise attack, and he saw governments such as Iran, North Korea, and Iraq that might have the motivation to do so if they could acquire the means. Stacked up against these challenges, bin Laden looked to many officers and analysts at the CIA like a dangerous criminal but not an existential threat.[32]

The CIA did periodically obtain evidence that terrorist groups were interested in weapons of mass destruction. Tenet did not talk about it in public, but bin Laden now figured in this alarming, if fragmentary, CIA reporting. Late in 1996 a former bin Laden aide and courier, Jamal al-Fadl, entered an American witness protection program and provided detailed accounts of bin Laden's earlier operations in Sudan. The CIA was involved in al-Fadl's secret debriefings. Al-Fadl said that bin Laden had authorized attempts to buy uranium that might be used to fashion a nuclear bomb. This effort had failed as far as al-Fadl knew, but if he was telling the truth—and al-Fadl passed the polygraph tests he was given—his testimony suggested the scale of bin Laden's ambitions. The CIA also had reports of contacts between bin Laden and Iraqi intelligence agents dating back to bin Laden's years in Sudan, and there were some fragmentary indications that these Iraqi contacts had involved training in the development and use of chemical weapons.[33] Still, neither the White House nor the CIA as yet had any covert action program targeting bin Laden that went beyond intelligence collection and analysis. The CIA's Counterterrorist Center was trying to watch bin Laden. Its leaders had not yet seriously attempted to arrest or kill him.

That planning was about to begin.

PART THREE

THE DISTANT ENEMY

January 1998 to September 10, 2001

"You Are to
Capture Him Alive"

THE FIRST FORMAL CIA PLAN to capture or kill Osama bin Laden began as a blueprint to arrest Mir Amal Kasi, the Baluchi migrant who had shot up the entrance to the agency's headquarters in 1993.

Kasi remained a fugitive in the Afghanistan-Pakistan-Iran borderlands. The CIA's Counterterrorist Center at Langley asked the Islamabad station for help recruiting agents who might be able to track him down. The station identified and contacted a family-based group of Afghan tribal fighters whose leadership had formal military training and who had worked for the CIA during the anti-Soviet jihad. Case officers met with the group and won their agreement to come back on the agency payroll to hunt for Kasi. At Langley, officers in the Counterterrorist Center's Kasi cell secured budget approval for the recruitment. The headquarters unit shipped hundreds of thousands of dollars in cash, AK-47 assault rifles, land mines, motorcycles, trucks, secure communications equipment, and electronic listening devices to put its new Afghan agents into business. Langley also supplied mobile beacons that could be used to pinpoint the exact location of buildings by connecting to satellites hovering miles overhead. The technology would allow an American counterterrorism team to swarm an obscure location quickly once it was lit up by the

Afghan agents. The tribal team had been code-named GE/SENIOR during the anti-Soviet years. Now they were dubbed by a new cryptonym, FD/TRODPINT. The suddenly enriched and provisioned Afghans set up residences around Kandahar, traveled back and forth to Pakistan, and began to track leads that might eventually take them to Kasi. In effect they had signed up as lethal, exceptionally well paid CIA bounty hunters.[1]

There were clear authorities for the recruitment under U.S. law. Kasi had been indicted for murder in the United States. Under federal law such fugitives could be arrested abroad and returned to the United States for trial. By collecting intelligence overseas about a suspect's whereabouts, the CIA could aid such an arrest under standing legal authorities approved by the president. Under these federal rules, the role played by CIA case officers and paid Afghan agents in tracking Kasi down need never be known. If the tracking team found Kasi in Pakistan, they were to contact the CIA station in Islamabad. Case officers would then attempt to work with Pakistani intelligence and police to make an arrest without revealing the existence of their paid Afghan agents.

A trickier scenario would arise if the tribal agents found Kasi hiding in southern Afghanistan, however. The Taliban controlled most of the traditional Baluch territory where Kasi was presumed to be moving. Given the record of stilted, sometimes bizarre contacts between American officials and the Taliban's Kandahar leadership, it was impossible to conceive of a cooperative approach with them. Legally, the United States did not even recognize the Taliban. Yet the Rabbani-Massoud government, which did have tentative legal standing, had no practical authority in Taliban country. If the CIA was going to take Kasi into custody in that area, it was going to have to find a way to do so on its own.

Agency case officers in Islamabad met with their tribal team to develop a formal, specific plan to capture Kasi in southern Afghanistan and fly him to the United States for trial. The plan would require the Afghan agents to hold Kasi securely in place long enough for an American arrest team to fly in secretly, bundle the fugitive aboard an airplane or helicopter, and lift off safely for the United States.

Because of their military training, the tribal agents talked convincingly about their ability to mount such a capture operation. The Afghan team worked well with maps. They had a sense of time and military sequence. They could identify assembly points, rally points, escape routes. One question was how to insert an American squad into Afghanistan if the tracking team located and detained Kasi on its own. The CIA's case officers provided their Afghan recruits with specifications for a suitable landing strip that could be prepared in advance. The chosen desert ground had to be hard and stable enough to support an aircraft landing and takeoff. It had to be secure from Taliban forces, preferably in a lightly populated and isolated valley. It had to be adequate for pilot navigation. The Afghan agents struck out on their motorcycles around Kandahar. They carried satellite measuring devices to pinpoint coordinates for possible airstrip sites. When they found a candidate location, they transmitted the data to Islamabad, and the station then ordered satellite photography to examine the site's parameters from above. Eventually the CIA found a remote strip that looked suitable, at least from the vantage of satellites.

The CIA and the Pentagon did not typically send American officers into harm's way based solely on satellite pictures and the investigations of paid Afghan recruits. What if the dirt at the landing site proved too soft despite the agents' assurances, and the American team's plane got stuck in the sand?

At Langley the Counterterrorist Center proposed and won approval for what CIA officers call a "black op," a secret operation classified at the highest possible level. The mission would both confirm the desert landing site's suitability and rehearse for the day when Kasi was actually in agent custody. A special operations team flew secretly into Afghanistan. Without Pakistan's knowledge, they mounted a nighttime low-level flight, tested the chosen landing zone marked by the tribal agents, found it satisfactory, double-checked its satellite coordinates, and withdrew. The CIA's Afghan capture plan for Mir Amal Kasi was now as ready as it could be for launch.

But month after month passed during 1996 and early 1997, and Kasi could not be found. The CIA's deteriorating relationship with Pakistani intelligence was one factor; the agency received little access to Pakistani police resources in the borderlands. The sprawling, centuries-rooted web of clan and tribal protection available to any Baluch in trouble in the territory of his birth was perhaps a greater problem. The CIA's case officers sought to combat Kasi's call on clan loyalty with appeals to greed. They offered multimillion-dollar rewards both openly and privately to anyone willing to reveal Kasi's whereabouts. But for months there were no takers. Under traditional Baluch revenge codes, anyone exposed as Kasi's betrayer risked not only his own life but his family's as well. For a while the CIA picked up rumors that Kasi was staying in a massive fortress compound near the Afghan border, but the agency could not persuade Pakistani police to move against the place. The operation would have been unusually difficult because the compound was heavily defended. CIA officers tried a technical solution: They rigged a special television with a roving camera that looked out from behind the TV screen. They arranged to deliver the set inside the compound, hoping to catch a picture of Kasi on film. The operation turned up nothing, however. It was never clear whether Kasi had ever been inside the place.

Finally their luck turned. In late May 1997 a Baluch man walked into the U.S. consulate in Karachi and told a clerk he had information about Kasi. He was taken to a young female CIA officer who was chief of base in Karachi (an agency "base" is a subunit of a countrywide station). She interviewed the informant and concluded he was credible. The CIA officer and the FBI's attaché in Pakistan, Scott Jessie, arranged more interviews. The source claimed that about two years earlier Kasi had been placed under the protection of a prominent Baluch tribal leader; the pair had become confidants and business partners, and traveled together frequently. Now, the source explained, the tribal leader had decided to sell out Kasi to the U.S. government in exchange for the reward money. The source handed over an application for a Pakistani driver's license filled out by Kasi under an alias; it contained a photo and a thumbprint that confirmed they had their man. The tribal leader who had befriended Kasi flew to Karachi and worked out an arrest plan with the CIA and the FBI. The tribal chief would be visiting a central Pakistani town called Dera Ghazi Khan on business in mid-June. He promised to lure Kasi to the Shalimar Hotel where the FBI could arrest him.

Naseem Rana, the director of Pakistani intelligence, had repeatedly told CIA station chief Gary Schroen that if he could locate Kasi, Pakistani police would help arrest him. Now Schroen and Jessie met with ISI officers and laid out their specific plan. They asked the Pakistanis to fly teams of CIA officers and FBI agents on a military plane to Multan, the largest Pakistani city near Dera Ghazi Khan. ISI would then provide ground transportation to the Shalimar and secure the perimeter while the FBI went in. Then they would all fly back to Islamabad where ISI would allow Kasi to be flown immediately to the United States. Rana agreed to the plan in its entirety.

The CIA's Karachi base chief and the tribal leader flew into Multan for the big day. Just before dawn on June 15, 1997, Kasi's betrayer knocked on the hotel room door and shouted that it was time to get up for dawn prayers. FBI agents stood at his shoulder. Schroen and two CIA colleagues waited outside, holding a secure satellite radio linked to Langley headquarters. FBI Special Agent Brad Garrett kicked through the door, straddled Kasi on the floor, pressed the suspect's left thumb onto an ink pad, studied the result with a magnifying glass, and declared exultantly, "It's a match!" They raced to the Multan airport in six sport utility vehicles, with gunmen from Pakistani intelligence hanging from the windows. On the tarmac next to a CIA helicopter an agency officer connected Schroen's secure radio to Langley where Tenet and other senior officials had gathered to monitor the operation. "This is Red Light Zulu," Schroen announced, declaring his call sign. "The package was successfully picked up and is safely bundled and being loaded onto an aircraft for movement to Islamabad. All personnel on the team are safe. This was a totally successful mission."[2]

A case that ranked first at CIA headquarters had finally been closed. George Tenet summoned five hundred employees to the Langley auditorium and arranged a closed-circuit television broadcast throughout headquarters. He played a recording of Schroen's "Red Light Zulu" message for the entire CIA staff. "No terrorist should sleep soundly as long as this agency exists," Tenet announced triumphantly. He urged his colleagues to give one another high-fives and hugs, and to "have a cocktail before noon."[3]

In the heady weeks that followed a question arose inside the CIA's Counterterrorist Center about what would now become of their elaborately equipped and financed TRODPINT tracking team assets. It seemed a shame to just cut them loose. A few flimsy U.S. government partitions away from the Kasi tracking team stood the small cluster of analysts and operators who made up the bin Laden issue unit. (After a relatively brief life in a Virginia office park, the station had been reincorporated into the headquarters of the Counterterrorist Center.) By the summer of 1997 the unit was reporting regularly to policy makers in classified channels about threats issued by bin Laden against American targets, especially American military forces stationed in Saudi Arabia. The CIA continued to describe bin Laden as an active, dangerous financier of Islamist extremism in Egypt, Sudan, Algeria, and Kashmir.

Yet the CIA had few ways to keep track of bin Laden on its own. Now the tribal team beckoned. The paid, well-organized Afghan agents could monitor or harass bin Laden up close, under direct CIA control.

Paul Pillar, the Princeton-educated analyst who had helped shape the CIA's thinking about the terrorist threat in the Middle East during the early 1990s, was now the center's deputy director. His superior, the Counterterrorist Center's director in the summer of 1997, Jeff O'Connell, was a veteran from the Directorate of Operations who had experience in Yemen, knew Egypt well, and had long studied the threat of Islamist extremism then rising in the Arab world.[4] He approved a plan that summer to transfer the Afghan agent team from the Kasi cell to the bin Laden unit, which had been developing draft plans to attack bin Laden's facilities and financial assets since 1996.

The agents' new CIA controllers modified the Kasi capture plan so it could be used to seize bin Laden and bring him to justice. At the CIA's Islamabad station this initiative arrived that summer of 1997 in the form of cables from Langley authorizing meetings with the tribal team leadership to explain that if they wanted to remain on the agency payroll, they now had to go after bin Laden. The Afghan TRODPINT team agreed.

As a target for capture, bin Laden was an easier mark than Kasi. At least they knew for certain where bin Laden lived some of the time: in the compounds provided by Mullah Omar in and around Kandahar. As Unocal's executives and liaisons had discovered early in 1997, bin Laden moved freely through the Taliban capital. His bodyguard and some of his wives and children lived openly near the Kandahar airport.

Working with the Afghan agents, the CIA began to use satellites and other technology to map in detail Osama bin Laden's Kandahar world. An anchor of the planning remained the southern Afghan desert airstrip confirmed by the American special operations team. The plan's premise was that the tribal team would take bin Laden into custody near Kandahar, hold him under their own authority, and then summon the Americans.

By the time the Americans took physical custody of bin Laden, they would have arranged for their captive's legal disposition. The plan presumed that a federal grand jury would deliver an indictment against bin Laden or that Egypt or Saudi Arabia would agree to accept him for trial. The Islamabad station was a little confused about these uncertain and seemingly provisional legal arrangements. As their plans progressed, station chief Gary Schroen kept asking the Counterterrorist Center at Langley, "Do we have an indictment?" The answers were cryptic: Bin Laden was "indictable," the Islamabad station was assured. In Washington, Clinton's aides approved the concept of the capture plan by the spring of 1998.[5]

A federal grand jury in New York had opened a secret investigation of bin Laden's terrorist financing activity months before. The grand jury investigation was moving toward criminal charges, but none had yet been delivered.[6] Under American law no one outside the Justice Department was supposed to know about the grand jury's work or whether it was likely to produce criminal charges. Unofficially, however, the status of the investigation began to leak to people involved with the CIA's planning.

Even if an indictment did not come through, Egypt was a serious possibility. The CIA worked closely during 1997 with Egyptian intelligence and security services in a large-scale, multinational campaign to break the back of its violent Islamist movement. CIA officers seized a number of Egyptian fugitives in foreign countries such as Azerbaijan and Albania and secretly shipped them to Cairo for trial.[7] It seemed conceivable that if the CIA captured bin Laden, the Egyptians might be willing this time to accept him for trial even though they had turned down that idea when bin Laden was leaving Sudan. Then, too, it was possible that the American government, working harder than it had in 1996, might persuade Saudi Arabia to take bin Laden for trial if the Afghan agent team had him in physical custody.

The tribal team developed a detailed plan for the CIA in which it would hold bin Laden in a cave in southern Afghanistan for thirty days before the Americans flew in clandestinely to take him away. The tribal team located a cave where they could hide out comfortably. They assured the CIA that they had acquired and stored at the cave enough food and water to keep bin Laden healthy during his stay. The main purpose of the cave detention was to allow some time to pass after bin Laden's initial capture so that al Qaeda's agitated lieutenants would be less alert when the Americans moved in to bundle bin Laden off. Also, the thirty-day detention would allow time to arrange for legal authorities. Under the plan, as soon as the Afghan agents had bin Laden on his way to the provisioned cave, the team would notify the Islamabad station, which in turn would signal Langley and Washington that they needed an indictment or a nod from an Arab government in a hurry. Once this indictment or rendition was arranged, an American special operations team would fly to the prearranged rural Kandahar airstrip, and the tribal team would hand over their Saudi captive.

Under American law and policy, this kidnapping plan looked acceptable because there was no Afghan government or law to offend. Freelance Afghans would be detaining bin Laden for an indefinite time on Afghan territory that was effectively ungoverned. CIA authority to transfer suspects offshore from one place to another—as in the case of rendition to Egypt or Saudi Arabia—was carefully documented in a succession of classified White House executive orders and national security memoranda, all of them briefed repeatedly to Congress. These included a Presidential Decision Directive, signed by President Clinton in 1995, which explicitly instructed the CIA to undertake covert "rendition" programs if they would enhance American national security. As for the scenario where CIA officers might fly in to receive bin Laden for an American trial, they would then be operating under the authority of Executive Order 12333, signed by President Ronald Reagan in 1981 and renewed by successive presidents. This order stated that while the CIA may not participate directly in law enforcement, the agency and its employees could "provide specialized equipment, technical knowledge or assistance, or expert personnel for use by any department or agency" and could "render any other assistance and cooperation to law enforcement authorities not precluded by applicable law." A thick archive of Justice Department memoranda and court cases upheld the right of American agents to abduct fugitives overseas and return them to U.S. courts in most instances.[8]

The CIA plan to capture bin Laden also had to accommodate another layer of American law governing covert action: the presidential ban on assassination by the CIA or its agents, a ban initiated by President Gerald R. Ford in 1976 and renewed by Reagan in the same Executive Order 12333. To comply with this part of the law, when they met with their agents to develop their plan, the CIA officers had to make clear that the effort to capture bin Laden could not turn into an assassination hit. The Afghans had to try to take bin Laden alive. CIA officers were assigned to sit down with the team leaders to make it as clear as possible. "I want to reinforce this with you," station chief Gary Schroen told the Afghans, as he later described the meeting in cables to Langley and Washington. "You are to capture him alive."[9]

Bin Laden always traveled with armed bodyguards who were certain to defend him fiercely. These Arab jihadists guarded the entrances to his several residences and packed into bin Laden's Land Cruiser with assault rifles and rocket-propelled grenade launchers. Everyone involved in the CIA planning understood that a firefight was likely if the Afghan agents attempted a kidnapping. But as long as the agents made a reasonable effort to capture bin Laden alive—as long as they used their weapons in the course of a legitimate attempt to take bin Laden into custody—this would not pose a legal problem. The Islamabad case officers tried to ram this point home in their meetings with the tribal team, but they could never be sure how their pleadings actually registered, unconditioned as the Afghans were by any culture of nitpicking lawyers. As a backup, Langley and the Islamabad station created a careful paper trail to document their meetings and instructions.

Both at the CIA and the White House, almost everyone involved in the closely held planning knew what was likely: The tribal agents would say that they were going to try to take bin Laden captive, but in fact they would launch what CIA officers referred to as "the Afghan ambush," in which you "open up with everything you have, shoot everybody that's out there, and then let

God sort 'em out," as Gary Schroen put it. Schroen figured that the agents would return to them and say, "We killed the big guy. I'm sorry." That would be all right as far as nearly everyone at the CIA and the White House was concerned—if the instructions had been clear and sincere, the paper trail was in place, and nothing too awful went wrong during the operation. As soon as the Afghans began to move on such an operation, they were supposed to communicate with the Islamabad station and describe their circumstances, but they were granted autonomy to initiate a strike.

The team reported one unsuccessful ambush during 1997, on a road near Kandahar, against what the agents described as bin Laden's convoy. The ambush site had been favored by the agents during the anti-Soviet war. In this case, however, they failed to properly seal off bin Laden's convoy by forming an L-shape at the ambush site. In an L-shaped ambush, attackers rake a convoy first from the side and then seal the vehicles off from the front. The Afghan agents lined up only along the side of the road and opened fire. By the agents' account, several Arabs traveling with bin Laden were killed, but bin Laden himself managed to escape by driving through the crossfire. The CIA had no way to confirm this account. Its officers concluded that bin Laden had probably been in the reported convoy and that he had probably been shot at, but it was impossible to know for certain. White House officials who reviewed the reports were skeptical. They wondered if the Afghan agents, like the spy protagonist of Graham Greene's *Our Man in Havana,* were making up stories of derring-do for the home office in order to hold on to their retainers.

By early 1998 the CIA had studied the compound where bin Laden frequently stayed outside of Kandahar. The Saudi made only limited efforts to disguise his visits. He talked openly on a satellite telephone that the Americans could tap. The question arose: Could the tribal agents be equipped to raid Osama bin Laden's house and take him from his bed?

AS THE CIA PLOTTED, bin Laden expanded his ambitions. He had settled comfortably into Afghanistan. His increasingly intimate relationship with the Taliban leadership in Kandahar, girded by bin Laden's lavish construction projects and generous donations, was plain for anyone in the Pashtun capital to see. He also moved freely through the Taliban-controlled eastern Afghan territory around Khost where his legend as an anti-Soviet jihadist had been born almost a dozen years before. His sponsorship of training camps for Pakistani and other volunteer fighters bound for Kashmir and Chechnya provided a way for bin Laden to organize his own private international fighting force outside of Taliban control—a force far more potent than the loose collection of hardened bodyguards he had retained in Sudan. His continued openness to print and television media, and his ability to fund technology-laden promotional offices in London and elsewhere, ensured that his voice remained prominent in worldwide radical Islamist politics.

Nearing middle age, bin Laden clearly saw himself as a man of destiny, an exiled sheikh battling in the name of Islam to liberate occupied lands from Jerusalem to Central Asia. His emotion about American military occupation of his native Saudi Arabia was undimmed. He raged publicly at everything about American policy in the Middle East: its support of Israel, its alliance with the Saudi royal family, and its killing of Iraqi soldiers and civilians during the Gulf War. Increasingly bin Laden's political vision and the secret operations he funded had global reach.

On February 23, 1998, bin Laden unveiled a coalition that reflected his spreading ambition and rising international charisma. He announced a new enterprise: the International Islamic Front for Jihad Against Jews and Crusaders. Bin Laden had worked for hours on the front's manifesto. Its contents were dictated over his satellite telephone to editors at a prominent London-based Arabic-language newspaper.[10] An angry litany of anti-American threats and grievances, the manifesto was signed by militant leaders from Egypt, Pakistan, Bangladesh, and Kashmir. Its publication represented bin Laden's first explicit attempt to lead an international coalition of Islamic radicals in violent attacks against the United States.

At the center of bin Laden's reasoning lay the cause of his own personal humiliation in late 1990. Then he had sought to persuade the Saudi royal family to let him lead a jihad against Saddam Hussein's Iraq, to expel Iraqi forces from Kuwait. Instead the royal family had invited the American military to wage the war and had banished bin Laden from the kingdom for protesting. Since the Gulf War in 1991, bin Laden now declared, the United States "has been occupying the most sacred lands of Islam: the Arabian Peninsula. It has been stealing its resources, dictating to its leaders, humiliating its people, and frightening its neighbors. It is using its rule in the Peninsula as a weapon to fight the neighboring peoples of Islam." The Americans had declared war "on Allah, His Prophet, and Muslims." In reply, the signatories of the manifesto "hereby give all Muslims the following judgment: The judgment to kill and fight Americans and their allies, whether civilians or military, is an obligation for every Muslim who is able to do so in any country."[11]

Among the signatures at the bottom of the declaration was that of Ayman al-Zawahiri, the Egyptian physician and Islamist who had first encountered bin Laden in 1987 at a charity hospital for anti-Soviet mujahedin in Peshawar. They had remained in contact over the ensuing decade as each became forcibly exiled from his native country. In Sudan, bin Laden provided support for al-Zawahiri's faction of the Egyptian Islamist movement, an exceptionally violent splinter group known as the Egyptian Islamic Jihad. At a personal level, bin Laden and al-Zawahiri had much in common, compared to the teenage drifters from Tunis or Algiers or Karachi who made up the infantry troops of the international jihadist movement. They both had university educations. They both came from privileged, modern families. Al-Zawahiri was the son of a university professor and the great nephew of a Grand Imam of Al-Azhar University in Cairo, Islam's theological citadel. His brother was a dermatologist and his cousins were chemists, pharmacists, judges, and politicians. But like bin Laden in Saudi Arabia, al-Zawahiri had grown up near the Egyptian elite but never had belonged to it. Like bin Laden he had embraced Islam as a teenager while many others in his family lived secular, multinational lives. Al-Zawahiri struck his relatives as shy and insular, and they interpreted his religiosity as a kind of escape, an insistent choice of tradition as a refuge from the confusions of modernity. This was also the way some of bin Laden's relatives saw Osama.[12]

Among Western intelligence analysts it became common to view al-Zawahiri as dominant over bin Laden. He was often described as a mentor, a successor to Abdullah Azzam as an intellectual father figure in bin Laden's life. The Egyptian had grown from a lean, awkward youth whose face was framed by oversized eyeglasses into a fleshy, squat man with a round head and a long gray-flecked beard. He still wore square, plastic eyeglass frames, but the effect now was owlish. Al-Zawahiri was eight years older than bin Laden; he came from a more sophisticated Cairo world, and he had traveled more widely. He was a practicing physician who had been tortured while in prison, and he had emerged as a more hardened terrorist operator, a veteran of long prison debates about Islam and politics. He had the sharp convictions that bin Laden sometimes seemed to lack.

Certainly al-Zawahiri was by 1997 a more experienced killer than the still soft-mannered, long-winded, project-oriented, media-conscious bin Laden. He had supervised terrorist operations from Cairo to Islamabad for nearly two decades. Some aspects of their personalities and careers might suggest that it was bin Laden who was the real leader between them. Accounts of al-Zawahiri's life from family friends and prison cellmates paint him as an awkward, withdrawn, disputatious man of little grace and much violence. Between them it was bin Laden who had developed a greater sense of entitlement, presence, and public ambition. Al-Zawahiri and his Egyptian colleagues entered into endless internal battles over ideology, power, and leadership, struggles in which al-Zawahiri became increasingly isolated and reviled even among hard-core Egyptian radicals.[13] This was not bin Laden's style. Through his wealth and his personal charisma he managed over many years to ingratiate himself with a wide range of fellow Islamists, even those whose outlooks and interests differed markedly from his own. It is difficult to know, then, how bin Laden and al-Zawahiri interacted in private—where the power in their relationship lay, how much tension was present and when.

In Sudan they began to work together on at least some terrorist operations against Egyptian and American targets, including an effort to train Somali militiamen to kill U.S. soldiers there. But when bin Laden migrated to Afghanistan in the spring of 1996, al-Zawahiri did not follow. He tried initially to travel to Chechnya to restart his own independent branch of the Islamic Jihad. He was arrested by Russian authorities in Dagestan and jailed for months, but because he was traveling on a false passport, the Russians never learned who he was and eventually released him.[14] Hunted by Egyptian authorities, he slipped into Afghanistan and reunited with bin Laden. The manifesto they jointly published on February 23, 1998, marked the public rebirth of their partnership.

Al-Zawahiri had spent most of his life in determined personal warfare against the government of Egypt, but by early 1998, exiled to Afghanistan and repudiated by many of his Egyptian colleagues, he had no plausible way to carry that battle on. Like bin Laden, al-Zawahiri decided to redirect his effort and his anger from "the near enemy" in Cairo toward the United States, which he called "the distant enemy."[15]

Bin Laden often spoke about the imperative for Islamist violence in frightening but general terms. Al-Zawahiri, on the other hand, spoke like a bloodthirsty staff sergeant just back from the trenches. "Tracking down the Americans and the Jews is not impossible," he wrote. "Killing them with a single bullet, a stab, or a device made up of a popular mix of explosives, or hitting them with an iron rod is not impossible. . . . With the available means, small groups could prove to be a frightening horror for the Americans and the Jews."[16]

Like bin Laden, al-Zawahiri believed that it was time for jihadists to carry the war to "the distant enemy" because, once provoked, the Americans would probably reply with revenge attacks and "personally wage the battle against the Muslims," which would make them ripe for a "clear-cut jihad against infidels."

A key war-fighting principle, al-Zawahiri believed, was "the need to inflict the maximum casualties against the opponent, for this is the language understood by the West, no matter how much time and effort such operations take."[17]

THE BIN LADEN UNIT at the CIA's Counterterrorist Center issued an alert memo within days of this manifesto's issuance. The unit's professional analysts, specialists in political Islam—the majority of them women, as it happened—had become nuanced students of bin Laden's threats, media appearances, and self-styled *fatwas*. They recognized an escalation in the February 23 attack on "Crusaders and Jews." The statements were "the first from these groups that explicitly justify attacks on American civilians anywhere in the world. . . . This is the first religious ruling sanctifying such attacks," the CIA's analysts wrote.[18] Within weeks the State Department issued a worldwide alert calling attention to bin Laden's threat.[19] The government travel warning could offer no specifics, however. This would become a familiar limitation in the months and years ahead.

At State's Foggy Bottom headquarters, across the Potomac River from the CIA, bin Laden did not loom as a special concern that winter even in the small South Asia bureau. There the focus remained on larger, seemingly more pressing regional issues: nuclear proliferation in India and Pakistan; the steady rise of Hindu nationalism in India; corruption and political opportunism in Pakistan. State's diplomats understood the poisonous alliance growing among the Taliban, al Qaeda, and Pakistani intelligence. When a U.S. diplomat formally protested to Pakistan about bin Laden's threats on March 9, he discussed Pakistan's arms shipments to the Taliban and its decision to let the Taliban "load up their planes" with fuel at Pakistani air bases. But bin Laden figured mainly as a subset of an already low-ranked issue. He was a talking point in routine *démarches* (from the French term for formal diplomatic communications). He could not be described as a priority.[20]

When Madeleine Albright became secretary of state, she left the post of U.S. ambassador to the United Nations. President Clinton appointed as her successor Bill Richardson, a lively, candid, and pudgy Hispanic former congressman from New Mexico with an adventurous spirit and a keen instinct for publicity. Richardson seemed to be a student of the Jesse Jackson school of international diplomacy: He was a self-promoting troubleshooter who loved to make lightning strikes behind enemy lines in search of dramatic negotiating breakthroughs, especially if they might deliver soundbite opportunities on the national network news programs. The post of ambassador to the United Nations was an ideal platform for such forays. It offered a ticket to the world and few political constraints. During Albright's tour at the U.N., one of her key deputies had been Rick Inderfurth, the former ABC News correspondent who in 1997 had followed her to Foggy Bottom as assistant secretary of state for South Asian affairs. During a brief overlap at the U.N., Inderfurth had suggested that Richardson consider Afghanistan as a destination for one of his signature foreign tours. Nobody had claimed Afghanistan as a policy priority at the State Department, Richardson recalled, and as a result "our policy seemed a little rudderless." He saw opportunity.[21]

In the winter of 1998, Richardson scheduled a South Asian trip. He invited the NBC News correspondent Andrea Mitchell to accompany him. Richardson planned to travel to India and Pakistan to talk about nuclear proliferation, to Sri Lanka to discuss the civil war, and to Afghanistan to see if he could jump-start peace negotiations with the Taliban. Mitchell could follow along and file exclusive reports to NBC *Nightly News.*

Bin Laden and al-Zawahiri issued their anti-American manifesto just as Richardson was preparing to leave. The CIA caught wind of his schedule and set up an intelligence briefing before he departed. Bin Laden had been "a secondary issue," as Richardson recalled, but the manifesto against Crusaders and Jews demonstrated the Saudi's "growing strength" and presented a fresh opportunity to lobby the Taliban for bin Laden's extradition. To whom bin Laden might be extradited was not clear since no American grand jury had yet handed down an indictment. Still, Richardson developed talking points that urged the Taliban "to extradite him . . . [that] we have evidence that he is a terrorist that is conspiring to hurt the American people."[22]

Richardson discussed his plans in a brief sidebar chat with President Clinton after a White House Cabinet meeting. Clinton half-joked with Richardson, as the latter recalled it: "Hey, geez, I'm really jealous. You're going to Afghanistan. . . . That should be a lot of fun." He added, turning serious, "God, if we can get some stability there . . . that would be terrific."

Clinton pointed at Richardson and told him, "Make sure you get briefed by Langley." As Richardson understood it, the president was referring to bin Laden's recent threats.[23]

Bruce Riedel, a CIA officer assigned to the National Security Council, walked Richardson through the Afghanistan issue set, including bin Laden, but he did not inform him about the Counterterrorist Center's ongoing plans to use Afghan agents to kidnap the Saudi and render him to justice. To protect the integrity of such operations and the identity of paid agents, the CIA compartmented such material at a level of Top Secret classification so high that hardly anyone at the State Department knew of its existence.

The CIA's main worry about Richardson's trip was that bin Laden would seize the presence of an American Cabinet member in Kabul to make good on the threats in his February declaration. The agency urged Richardson to consider canceling the Afghan leg of his travel. But Pakistan's ambassador to the U.N., seeing an opportunity to legitimize the Taliban in international eyes, promised to make Richardson's visit a success. Any harm to Richardson would rebound disastrously on Pakistan, now widely seen as the Taliban's sponsors. Richardson figured that he could count on Pakistan's self-interested influence with Mullah Omar to keep his travel party safe.

Just in case, American fighter jets tailed Richardson's U.N. plane as it banked across the barren Hindu Kush Mountains toward the Afghan capital. "God, the mountains," Richardson exclaimed as he deplaned in the same lucky blue blazer he wore on all his troubleshooting journeys.[24]

His bearded, robed Taliban hosts proudly drove him, Inderfurth, and Andrea Mitchell to the Kabul traffic circle where they had strung up the former Afghan president Najibullah and his brother eighteen months before. Their tour continued at the shuttered U.S. embassy. Afghan employees who swept the compound's empty walkways greeted Richardson in celebration, hoping vainly that his visit marked an American return. On a Kabul parade ground the Taliban mustered an honor guard bearing swords.

Mullah Rabbani, chairman of the Kabul *shura,* swept into a meeting room with bearded colleagues who carried Kalishnikov rifles and immediately began to pray. They were cordial but never looked at Richardson directly. The ambassador declared that he hoped to begin political negotiations that would lead to a cease-fire between the Taliban and Massoud's Northern Alliance. To his amazement Mullah Rabbani said that he would be willing to participate in such talks. They adjourned to a nearby hall. Richardson and Rabbani talked privately about bin Laden over lunch, a heaping banquet of Afghan rice, meats, and fruits spread across a long table.

"Look, bin Laden is in your territory," Richardson told Rabbani. "He's a bad guy. We have evidence that he has a terrorist network, that he's conducted terrorist acts, that he's using your country as a base, and we want you to turn him over to us. We would then legally find a way for this to happen."[25]

The conversation about bin Laden lasted for about forty-five minutes, as

Richardson remembered it, with himself, Rabbani, Inderfurth, U.S. ambassador to Islamabad Tom Simons, and two CIA officers listening intently. Inderfurth noticed that in a bookshelf behind them lay tattered leather-bound volumes of the *Complete Works of George Washington,* apparently left behind by some long-forgotten cultural exchange program of the United States Information Agency.[26]

The Taliban offered no concrete concessions. They denied that bin Laden was under their direct control or that he represented a significant threat to the United States.

"He's with you," Simons told the Taliban official next to him. "He is not obeying you, whatever you told him, not to be politically active. There's this *fatwa* in February which says that it's an individual obligation to kill Americans." The Taliban leaders listened, seemingly puzzled. Bin Laden was not a qualified Islamic scholar, they assured the Americans.[27]

And with that, it was over. Richardson was back at Kabul's airport in the afternoon, boarding his U.N. jet for another leg of his tight itinerary. The Taliban and their political sponsors in Pakistan had achieved their objective: a highly publicized visit with a Clinton Cabinet officer that showed the Taliban as accommodating, reasonable, and open to negotiations.

The all-Afghan political talks initially agreed to by Rabbani collapsed within weeks. The Taliban's war with Massoud resumed as if there had been no pause. In June, Richardson left his post at the United Nations for a new job as secretary of energy.

At the U.S. embassy in Islamabad, Ambassador Tom Simons watched the empty aftermath of Richardson's flying tour with cynical bemusement. Richardson was a "good guy," hard to dislike, an able troubleshooter, but the visit seemed typical of the Clinton administration's approach to Afghanistan. "I won't call it fey," Simons said later, "but you know the Clinton administration: 'Hey, let's try something!' "[28]

IN RANK Richard Clarke labored one or two rungs down the Washington ladder from Bill Richardson. In political character he represented the other end of the capital's spectrum. Richardson was an elected politician, a campaigner, a gifted popularizer, a master of media and public mood. Richard Clarke was a shadowy member of Washington's permanent intelligence and bureaucratic classes, a self-styled "national security manager" who seemed to wield enormous power precisely because hardly anyone knew who he was or what exactly he did for a living.[29]

As Richardson jetted with a camera crew around South Asia that spring, Clarke secluded himself for long hours in his high-ceilinged third-floor suite in a corner of the Old Executive Office Building, next door to the White House. He was working on three classified presidential decision directives that would transform the Clinton administration's management of terrorism threats, catastrophic attacks, budgets, and decision-making. In doing so, the directives would elevate Clarke's own power, confirming him formally as a de facto member of Clinton's Cabinet on terrorism issues. Yet only a handful of other bureaucrats in Washington understood what Clarke was up to that spring. The memoranda he worked with were all classified, and the organizational issues were so obscured by jargon and the complex flowcharts of the Washington interagency process that they could not be easily understood even if they were accessed. Clarke's plans seemed at once obscure and ambitious. THINK GLOBALLY—ACT GLOBALLY read a small sign near his desk.[30]

Clarke's tall office windows looked south across the Ellipse to the Potomac River and National Airport. His suite had been occupied during the mid-1980s by Colonel Oliver North, and it was possible to believe that Clarke had chosen it for just this reason, so palpably did he thrive on an air of sinister mystery. His preferred method of communication was the short, blunt intra–White House email delivered down classified channels in a signature red font. The son of a Boston chocolate factory worker, Clarke was a pale, stout man whose cropped red hair had turned steadily gray under the pressures of his work. He had ascended through education and restless work, winning entrance by competitive exam to the Boston Latin School, a centuries-old six-year high school whose Revolutionary War–era alumni included John Hancock, Paul Revere, and Benjamin Franklin, and which more recently had launched Joseph Kennedy, the political family's patriarch. Clarke enrolled at age eleven, just as John F. Kennedy became president. Kennedy's message about the importance of government service was drummed into Clarke and his classmates "to the extent of brainwashing," as he recalled it.

Clarke moved on to the University of Pennsylvania and then the Massachusetts Institute of Technology. At college he was active in student government and was selected to join The Sphinx, an elite club for Penn seniors. It became only the first in a series of hidden, self-selected social networks in which Clarke thrived. After working as an intelligence analyst at the Pentagon he was appointed in 1985, at age thirty-four, as the deputy chief of intelligence and research at the State Department. There he authored a plan to spook Libyan leader Muammar Qaddafy by detonating sonic booms over Tripoli, floating rubber rafts mysteriously to the Libyan shore, and spreading false rumors of American military action. The scheme fell apart when the Reagan administration was exposed for planting false stories in an American newspaper. Later Clarke became embroiled in a bitter struggle over accusations that he had turned a blind eye to transfers of military equipment from Israel to China. The State Department's inspector general concluded that Clarke had usurped his superiors, turning himself into a one-man foreign policy czar and arms-trafficking shop. But Clarke battled back, survived, and transferred to the National Security Council at the White House. His reputation for deft bureaucratic maneuvering grew. Even his friends conceded that he was a blunt instrument, a bully, and occasionally abusive. His enemies regarded him as not only mean but dangerous. Either way, the Israel affair would not be the last time Clarke was accused of running a unilateral American foreign policy.[31]

During the first Clinton term Clarke popped up as an indispensable figure in some of the administration's most interesting foreign policy episodes. He managed the American withdrawal from Somalia, the campaign to replace Boutros Boutros-Ghali as U.N. secretary general, the refugee crisis in east Africa after the Rwandan genocide, and dozens of other complex issues that required White House coordination of vast, divided federal departments. Officially a member of the Senior Executive Service, the highest class of permanent civil servant in the U.S. government, Clarke honed the art of the interagency maneuver in national security affairs. It was not only that he worked hard and bullied opponents until they did his bidding, but he understood in a precise, disciplined way how to use his seat at the White House to manipulate money in the federal budget to reinforce policy priorities that he personally championed. Clarke had also learned how to manage a formal, seemingly inclusive interagency decision-making process—one that involved regular meetings at which minutes were kept—while privately priming the process through an informal, back-channel network of personal connections. Rivals attributed to Clarke the unseen powers of a Rasputin, and even where these fears were exaggerated, Clarke did little to disabuse the believers. He shook his head modestly and said he was just trying to bring people together.

One of Clarke's talents was to sense where national security issues were going before most other people did, and to position himself as a player on the rising questions of the day. By 1997 he gravitated toward counterterrorism. In the aftermath of the Oklahoma City bombing and the downing of TWA Flight 800 (mistakenly believed at first to be a terrorist incident), the White House requested and Congress wrote enormous new appropriations for counterterrorist programs in a dozen federal departments. In an era of tight federal budgets, terrorism was a rare bureaucratic growth industry. From his National Security Council suite Clarke shaped these financial decisions. He also took control over interagency reviews of terrorist threats and counterterrorist policy. Backed by National Security Adviser Sandy Berger, Clarke reorganized day-to-day policy making on terrorism and what later would become known as homeland defense.[32]

Clarke declared that America faced a new era of terrorist threats for which it was woefully unprepared. He proposed a newly muscled Counterterrorism Security Group to be chaired by a new national security official, the National Coordinator for Infrastructure Protection and Counterterrorism. Naturally, his colleagues noted as memoranda and position papers flew back and forth to define this new job, it emerged that no one was better qualified to take it on than Richard Clarke himself.

In this elevated role, he would chair a new working group whose core members would be the heads of the counterterrorist departments of the CIA, FBI, Joint Chiefs of Staff, and Departments of Defense, Justice, and State. At the Pentagon and the FBI, officials who had been running counterterrorist programs without any White House oversight balked at Clarke's power grabs. They protested that he was setting himself up to become another Oliver North, that the National Security Council would "go operational" by running secret counterterrorist programs. Clarke said his critics were "paranoid." He was just trying to "facilitate" decision-making. In the end Clarke's opponents did force President Clinton to insert language in his final, classified decision directive to make clear that Clarke had no operational power. But the rest of Presidential Decision Directive-62, as it was called, signed by Clinton on May 22, 1998, anointed Clarke as the White House's new counterterrorism czar, with unprecedented authority. Over time he acquired a seat at Clinton's Cabinet table as a "principal," equal in rank to the secretary of defense or the secretary of state, whenever the Cabinet met to discuss terrorism. No national security staffer of Clarke's rank had ever enjoyed such Cabinet status in White House history. PDD-62, formally titled "Protection Against Unconventional Threat to the Homeland and Americans Overseas," laid out a counterterrorism mission on ten related tracks, with a lead federal agency assigned to each one. The CIA's track was "disruption" of terrorist groups.[33]

Clarke's ascension meant the CIA's Counterterrorist Center managers had a new man to please at the White House. CIA director Tenet enjoyed a close working relationship with Sandy Berger and others at the National Security Council because of Tenet's years on the White House staff. But the CIA managers who worked two rungs down now had to build an equally effective relationship with Richard Clarke, no easy task given his forceful personality. On policy issues the CIA managers mainly regarded Clarke as an ally. He "got" the seriousness of the bin Laden threat, it was commonly said in the agency's Counterterrorist Center, and Clarke generally supported the CIA's nascent programs to capture or disrupt bin Laden in Afghanistan. Indeed, Clarke sometimes pushed harder for action on bin Laden than the CIA's own officers recommended. The trouble was, Clarke could be such a bully that when the CIA managers felt he was wrong, they had no way to go around him. On the whole, this suited a White House wary of Langley's unwieldy bureaucracy. As Berger said later: "I wanted a pile driver."

Bin Laden was by no means Richard Clarke's only counterterrorist priority. Reflecting President Clinton's private fears, he repeatedly sounded alarms about the danger of a biological weapons attack against the United States. He pushed for new vaccination stocks against smallpox and other threats, and he lashed departments such as the Federal Emergency Management Agency to prepare for unexpected terrorist-spawned epidemics. Clarke spent equally long hours on new policies to guard government and business against the threat of cyberterrorism—"an electronic Pearl Harbor," as he called it.[34]

To galvanize action he repeatedly issued frightening statements about the new terrorist danger facing the United States. American military superiority "forces potential future opponents to look for ways to attack us other than traditional, direct military attacks. How do you do that? Through truck bombs. Through nerve gas attacks on populated areas. Through biological attacks on populated areas." Clarke compared his crusade to Winston Churchill's lonely, isolated campaign during the 1930s to call attention to rising Nazi power before it was too late. If Churchill had prevailed when he first called for action, Clarke said, he would have gone down in history "as a hawk, as someone who exaggerated the threat, who saber-rattled and did needless things."[35] Increasingly, this was the charge Clarke himself faced. National security analysts and members of Congress accused him of hyping the terrorist threat to scare Congress into allocating ever greater sums of federal funds so that Clarke's own influence and authority would grow.

"I would be delighted three or four years from now to say we've wasted money," Clarke said in reply. "I'd much rather have that happen than have to explain to the Congress and the American people why we weren't ready, and why we let so many Americans die."[36]

A S T H E Y R E F I N E D their snatch plans in the spring of 1998, the bin Laden unit at the CIA's Counterterrorist Center looked with rising interest at Tarnak Farm. This was a compound of perhaps a hundred acres that lay isolated on a stretch of desert about three miles from the American-built terminal building at Kandahar airport. On many nights, the CIA learned, bin Laden slept at Tarnak with one of his wives.

Tarnak presented a raiding party with no challenges of terrain or urban maneuver. It had been constructed by the Afghan government years before as an agricultural cooperative. The farm itself was encircled by a mud-brick wall perhaps ten feet high. Inside were about eighty modest one-story and two-story structures made from concrete or mud-brick. These included dormitory-style housing, storage facilities, a tiny mosque, and a building that bin Laden converted into a small medical clinic for his family and his followers. On the edge of the compound stood a crumbling, water-streaked, six-story office building originally erected for bureaucrats from the government's agricultural departments. Immediately outside the compound walls were a few irrigated plots, canals, and drainage ditches. But the most remarkable feature of Tarnak Farm was its stark physical isolation. Flat plains of sand and sagebrush extended for miles. Vineyards and irrigated fields dotted the landscape in checkerboard patches, but there were virtually no trees in any direction. The nearest buildings, haphazard extensions of the airport complex, were more than a mile away. Kandahar's crowded bazaars lay half an hour's drive beyond.[37]

Case officers in Islamabad spent long hours with the tribal team's leaders devising a plan to attack Tarnak in the middle of the night. The Afghans would seize and hold bin Laden prisoner until the Americans figured out what to do with him. They ran two rehearsals in the United States late in 1997. Tenet briefed Berger in February. A third rehearsal took place in March. Still, Clarke wrote Berger that he felt the CIA seemed "months away from doing anything."

The raid plan was meticulously detailed. The Afghans had scouted and mapped Tarnak up close, and the CIA had photographed it from satellites. The agents had organized an attack party of about thirty fighters. They identified a staging point where they would assemble all of their CIA-supplied vehicles—motorcycles, trucks, and Land Cruisers. They would drive from there to a secondary rallying point a few miles away from Tarnak. The main raiding party, armed with assault rifles, secure communications, and other

To Kandahar

Airport

AIRPORT ROAD

*Enlarged
below*

AIRPORT ROAD

Irrigated plots

Bin Laden's Tarnak Farm

Attackers would have approached
the compound in a drainage ditch
and entered under the wall.

ROAD

ROAD

ROAD

To airport

Ten-foot wall
surrounds
the farm

ROAD

ROAD

About 80 living
structures are
within the walls

Six-story office building
(bombed out in 2001)

Photo taken after Tarnak Farm had been bombed in the 2001 Afghan war.

Photo modifications: Richard Furno

PHOTOS: SPACE IMAGING

equipment, planned to walk across the flat plain toward Tarnak in blackened night, arriving at its walls around 2 A.M. They had scouted a path to avoid minefields and use deep gulleys to mask their approach. On the airport side of the compound a drainage ditch ran underneath Tarnak's outer wall. The attackers intended to enter by crawling through the ditch. As they did, a second group would roll quietly and slowly toward the front gate in two jeeps. They would carry silenced pistols to take out the two guards stationed at the entrance. Meanwhile the walk-in party would have burst into each of the several small huts where bin Laden's wives slept. When they found the tall, bearded Saudi, they would cuff him, drag him toward the gate, and load him in a Land Cruiser. A second group of vehicles at the rally point would approach in sequence, and they would all drive together to the cave complex thirty miles away that had been stocked with food and water. Recalled station chief Gary Schroen, "It was as well conceived as a group of amateur soldiers with some training could do." He wrote Langley on May 6 that the tribals were now "almost as professional" as U.S. commandos.[38]

As they finalized the plan, the CIA officers found themselves pulled into emotional debates about legal authorities and the potential for civilian casualties if a shoot-out erupted at Tarnak. Satellite photography and reports from the ground indicated that there were dozens of women and children living at Tarnak. Langley headquarters asked for detailed explanations from the tribal team about how they planned to minimize harm to women and children during their assault. Case officers sat down with the team leaders and walked through a series of questions: "Okay, you identify that building. What if he's not in that building? What if he's next door? And what are you going to do about collateral damage?" It was a frustrating discussion on both sides. The Americans thought their agents were serious, semiprofessional fighters who were trying to cooperate with the CIA as best they could. Yet "if you understood the Afghan mind-set and the context," Schroen put it later, you understood that in any raid on Tarnak, realistically, the Afghans were probably going to have to fire indiscriminately to get the job done.[39]

During these talks the tribal agents would say, in effect, as Schroen recalled it, "Well, we're going to do our best. We're going to be selective about who we'll shoot." But by the time the cables describing these assurances and conversations circulated at Langley, where the plan awaited approval from senior managers, there were some at CIA headquarters who began to attack the proposed Tarnak raid as reckless. Schroen urged his superiors to "step back and keep our fingers crossed" and hope the tribals "prove as good (and as lucky) as they think they will be." But the deputy chief of the CIA's clandestine ser-

vice, James Pavitt, worried aloud about casualties and financial costs. A classified memo to approve the raid reached the White House in May. The CIA ran
a final rehearsal late that month and awaited a decision.[40]

BIN LADEN CONTINUED to call public attention to himself. When India
unexpectedly tested a nuclear weapon that May, bin Laden called on "the
Muslim nation and Pakistan" to "prepare for the jihad," which should "include a nuclear force." In an interview with ABC News, broadcast to the network's sizable national audience, bin Laden declared that his coalition's "battle
against the Americans is far greater than our battle was against the Russians.
We anticipate a black future for America. Instead of remaining the United
States, it shall end up separated states and shall have to carry the bodies of its
sons back to America." Americans would withdraw from Saudi Arabia "when
the bodies of American soldiers and civilians are sent in the wooden boxes
and coffins," he declared.[41]

As these threats echoed, Richard Clarke pulled meetings together at the
White House to consider options. The CIA Counterterrorist Center was represented at these sessions, but the CIA officer present was cautious about discussing the center's tribal assets. Very few people in or out of the agency
knew of the draft plan to snatch bin Laden at Tarnak Farm.

There was a natural tension between Richard Clarke's counterterrorism
shop at the White House and the CIA's Counterterrorist Center. Clarke personified presidential authority and control over CIA prerogatives. He could
influence budgets and help write legal guidance. There was a suspicion at the
CIA that Clarke wanted direct control over agency operations. For their part,
Clarke and his team saw Langley as self-protectively secretive and sometimes
defensive about their plans. The White House team suspected that the CIA
used its classification rules not only to protect its agents but also to deflect
outside scrutiny of its covert operations. In one sense Clarke and the CIA's
counterterrorist officers were allies: They all strongly believed by the spring of
1998 that bin Laden was a serious threat and that action was warranted to
bring him into custody. In other respects, however, they mistrusted each
other's motives and worried about who would be blamed if something went
wrong in a risky operation. The CIA, in particular, had been conditioned by
history to recoil from gung-ho "allies" at the National Security Council. Too
often in the past, as in the case of Oliver North, CIA managers felt the agency
had been goaded into risky or illegal operations by politically motivated White

House cowboys, only to be left twisting after the operations went bad. White House officials came and went in the rhythm of electoral seasons; the CIA had permanent institutional interests to protect.

Clarke and his counterterrorism group were interested in a snatch operation against bin Laden that could succeed. But they were skeptical about the Tarnak raid. Their sense was that the agents were old anti-Soviet mujahedin who had long since passed their peak fighting years and that they were probably milking the CIA for money while minimizing the risks they took on the ground. Some in the White House felt that the agents seemed unlikely to mount a serious attack on Tarnak. Worse, if they did go through with it, they would probably not be able to distinguish between a seven-year-old girl on a tricycle and a man who looked like Osama bin Laden holding an assault rifle. Women and children would die, and bin Laden would probably escape. Such a massacre would undermine U.S. national interests in the Muslim world and elsewhere.[42]

The CIA's leadership reviewed the proposed raid in late May. The discussion surfaced doubts among senior officers in the Directorate of Operations about the raid's chances for success. In the end, as Tenet described it to colleagues years later, all of the CIA's relevant chain of command—Jack Downing, then chief of the D.O., his deputy Jim Pavitt, Counterterrorist Center Chief O'Connell, and his deputy Paul Pillar—told Tenet the Tarnak raid was a bad idea. There was also no enthusiasm for it at the White House. Recalled one senior Clinton administration official involved: "From our perspective, and from George's, it was a stupid plan. It was an open plain. . . . I couldn't believe this was their great plan—it was a frontal assault." Richard Clarke, by this official's account, did little to disguise his disdain. He asked his White House colleagues and the CIA's Counterterrorist Center team sarcastically, "Am I missing something? Aren't these people going to be mowed down on their way to the wall?"

Tenet never formally presented the Tarnak Farm raid plan for President Clinton's approval. Tenet's antennae about political risk had been well calibrated during his years as a congressional and White House staffer. He was unlikely to endorse any operation that posed high risks of civilian casualties. He also was in the midst of a new, secret diplomatic initiative against bin Laden involving Saudi Arabia; a failed attack on Tarnak might end that effort.

The decision was cabled to Islamabad: There would be no raid. Mike Scheuer, the chief of the bin Laden unit, wrote to colleagues that he had been told that Clinton's cabinet feared "collateral damage" and accusations of assassination. Decision-makers feared that "the purpose and nature of the operation would be subject to unavoidable misinterpretation ... in the event that bin Laden, despite our best intentions and efforts, did not survive."[43] The tribal team's plans should be set aside, perhaps to be revived later. Meanwhile the agents were encouraged to continue to look for opportunities to catch bin Laden away from Tarnak, traveling only with his bodyguard.

Some of the field-level CIA officers involved in the Tarnak planning reacted bitterly to the decision. They had put a great deal of effort into their work. They believed the raid could succeed. If bin Laden was not stopped now, the challenge he presented would only deepen.

As it happened, this was only the beginning of their frustration.

"The Kingdom's Interests"

P RINCE TURKI AL-FAISAL, the Saudi intelligence chief, saw the
threat posed by Osama bin Laden through a lens colored by Saudi Arabian politics. Bin Laden and al-Zawahiri preached against the kingdom in its
own language: They denounced the royal family's claim to be the true and legitimate guardians of Sunni Islam's two most important holy places, Mecca
and Medina. They appealed to the Koran as inspiration for violent revolt
against the ruling al-Sauds. Bin Laden continued to use his wealth and the
global channels of digital technology to link up with other Saudi Islamist dissidents inside the kingdom and in exile. For years the Saudis had tried to hold
bin Laden at a distance, hoping to isolate and outlast him. "There are no permanent enemies here in Saudi Arabia," a leading prince once remarked, describing the kingdom's swirling webs of family-rooted alliances and enmities.[1]
With his shrill cries for jihad against the royal family, however, bin Laden was
starting to make himself an exception.

By the late spring of 1998, Turki and other senior princes, including the
kingdom's de facto ruler, Crown Prince Abdullah, had become alarmed. Saudi
security forces arrested militant bin Laden followers who had smuggled

surface-to-air missiles into the kingdom. In March the Saudis secured the defection of bin Laden's Afghanistan-based treasurer, Mohammed bin Moisalih.
He revealed the names of prominent Saudis who had been secretly sending
funds to bin Laden. All the while bin Laden kept holding press conferences
and television interviews to denounce the Saudi royals in menacing, unyielding terms. The interviews were beamed by satellite across the Arab world and
to the ubiquitous reception dishes sprouting on Saudi rooftops. Aware of this
turmoil, Clinton sent Tenet secretly to Riyadh to urge Saudi cooperation. Abdullah authorized Turki to undertake a secret visit to Kandahar. As Turki later
described it, he was instructed to meet with Mullah Omar and discuss options
for putting bin Laden out of action.[2]

The mission was constrained by the complexities of Saudi royal power.
Then seventy-four, Crown Prince Abdullah had emerged as a newly confident
force. His flaccid older brother, King Fahd, remained incapacitated by a
stroke suffered several years earlier. With the passage of time royal power had
gradually consolidated around Abdullah. A goateed, bulky man with attentive
black eyes and Asiatic cheeks, Abdullah had won praise within the kingdom
for his straight talk, his hard-headed Saudi nationalism, his ease with ordinary
Saudi soldiers and citizens, and his relatively austere lifestyle. He did not summer in Cannes casinos, indulge undisciplined sexual appetites, or recklessly pilot stunt planes, and in the context of the Saudi royal family, this made him
a ramrod figure. In Saudi tradition he continued to marry younger wives and
father children as he aged. By 1998 he lived in a series of manicured palace
complexes that resembled midsized American colleges, with pathways and
driveways weaving through watered lawns and stately rows of desert arbor.
He kept an idiosyncratic schedule, sleeping in two four-hour shifts, once between 9 P.M. and 1 A.M., and then again between 8 A.M. and noon. In the wee
hours he swam in his royal pool and busied himself with paperwork. Each
Saturday he flew to Jedda with several of his brothers, boarded his yacht, mo-
tored into the Red Sea for a few hours, ate lunch, and retired for a nap, rock-
ing on the waves. Each Wednesday he went via bus to a desert farm where he
bred Arabian horses. He was hardworking and serious about his political responsibilities, but he was austere only in the ways that a multibillionaire with
enormous palaces, yachts, and horse farms can be austere.[3]

Abdullah was skeptical about the eagerness of some Saudi princes to curry
favor at any price with the United States. The crown prince understood that
Saudi Arabia was not strong enough militarily to abandon its protective alliance with Washington, but he wanted to establish more independence in the
relationship. He thought Saudi Arabia should pursue a balanced foreign pol-

icy that included outreach to ambivalent American friends in Europe, especially France. He wanted a rapprochement between Saudi Arabia and Iran even though the United States was opposed. He wanted to help the United States achieve a lasting peace between Israel and the Palestinians but rejected American support for the Israeli government. Abdullah pursued what he saw as an independent brand of Saudi nationalism, and while he was not hostile to American interests, he was not as accommodating as some previous Saudi monarchs had been. Fear of communism no longer united Riyadh and Washington. Abdullah felt he could recast the alliance without undermining its basic solidity.[4]

Abdullah's ascension changed and complicated Prince Turki's position within the royal family. In Saudi political culture, which venerated seniority and family, Turki remained a relatively junior figure. Educated at Georgetown and Oxford, he was one of the royal cabinet's most obviously pro-American princes, not necessarily an asset in the Abdullah era. Turki's vast personal riches and the wealth accumulated by his aides, such as the Badeeb brothers, bothered some of his rivals in the royal family. They felt the Saudi intelligence department had become a financial black hole. In keeping with Abdullah's calls for increased professionalism in Saudi government, Turki's rivals clamored for accountability at the General Intelligence Department.

On the bin Laden question, Turki had to compete for influence with his uncle, the more senior Saudi interior minister Prince Naif, who was the Saudi equivalent of the attorney general and the FBI director combined. Naif and his powerful sons jealously guarded Saudi sovereignty against American interference. They often seemed to hold explicitly anti-American attitudes. They refused repeatedly to respond to requests for investigative assistance from the FBI, the White House counterterrorism office, and the CIA. They interpreted Saudi laws so as to minimize American access to their police files and interrogations. Naif made exceptions and occasionally cooperated with the FBI, but his general policy of stonewalling the Americans put Turki in an awkward position. Turki was the CIA's primary liaison to the Saudi government, and he tried to maintain open channels to Langley. He worked closely with George Tenet on the Middle East peace process and tried to establish a secret, joint working group to share intelligence about the threat posed by bin Laden. But Naif often scuttled his efforts at openness. On terrorism, at least, Turki was unable to deliver much for the CIA. On a desert camping trip, the prince suffered carbon monoxide poisoning after a heater failed inside his tent, and for a while his colleagues at Langley wondered if he had been permanently impaired. As Turki faded, physically and politically, the CIA watched its links to Saudi Arabia fray—a bond that had been an important part of the agency's worldwide clandestine operations for two decades.[5]

ON A MID-JUNE DAY IN 1998, Prince Turki's jet banked above Kandahar airport. He looked out the airplane window and spotted Tarnak Farm. He had been briefed about bin Laden's use of the compound and had been told to watch out for it as he landed. He could see it now on the barren plain—no better than a squatter's encampment by the standards of Saudi Arabia. Its primitive facilities were centuries removed from the luxuries Turki enjoyed in Jedda, Riyadh, Paris, and beyond. Turki often reflected on the tensions inherent in Saudi Arabia's oil-fed drive for modernization. The combustible interactions of wealth and Islamic faith, Bedouin tradition and global culture, had opened deep fault lines in the Saudi kingdom. Osama bin Laden had fallen through the cracks, and here he was, in a mud-walled compound on the outskirts of Kandahar, preaching revolution.

Beside the prince on the jet sat Sheikh Abdullah bin Turki, then the Saudi minister of religious endowments. The intelligence chief had invited the sheikh, an Islamic scholar, in the hope that he could convincingly quote Koranic scripture and Islamic philosophy to Mullah Omar to persuade the Taliban leader that it was time to do something about his troublemaking Saudi guest.[6] The Ministry of Religious Endowments also represented the part of the Saudi establishment that maintained the closest ties to the Taliban through charities and Wahhabi proselytizing groups. Prince Turki hoped to convince Mullah Omar that the Taliban would benefit in many ways if they broke with bin Laden. Saudi charities and religious groups could deliver on that promise.

Turki had never met Mullah Omar. The Taliban leaders he had met, such as Mullah Rabbani, had told him that Omar was very brave and deeply religious. Other Afghans had tried to convince Turki that Omar was reclusive, a religious extremist, intolerant, and unwilling to change his decisions once they were made no matter what the risks. Apart from these assessments from visiting Afghans, Turki had few other ways to evaluate Omar. Turki had only tentative, formal relations with the sectors of the Saudi religious establishment that were closest to the Taliban. Bin Laden's recent manifestos and *fatwas* had attracted Turki's attention, however, and his analysts had studied and catalogued the published texts. Turki's department estimated bin Laden's following of non-Afghans at about two thousand hard-core members. The Saudi intelligence chief regarded bin Laden himself as the movement's key decision maker. Much of the painstaking, sometimes nasty work of tracking down bin Laden sympathizers inside Saudi Arabia, interrogating them, and investigating leads was carried out by the Naif-led clan at the Interior Ministry, however. Turki was not directly involved in that work, although he often saw the intelligence it produced.[7]

A dozen senior Taliban mullahs, led by their one-eyed emir, met Turki's entourage at Taliban headquarters downtown. Omar offered warm embraces, elaborate courtesies, and steaming cups of green tea. They settled in for a long discussion. As far as Turki was concerned, bin Laden was the only subject.

Turki said later that he "briefed" the Taliban leaders on bin Laden's persistent speeches and interviews denouncing the Saudi kingdom. The prince highlighted what bin Laden "had done against the kingdom's interests." Bin Laden's offense was to seek the violent overthrow of Saudi Arabia's Islamic government, which had special responsibilities to all Muslims worldwide. Turki demanded, as he recalled it, that Mullah Omar either oust bin Laden from Afghan territory or turn him over to Saudi custody. "We made it plain that if they wanted to have good relations with Saudi Arabia, they have to get bin Laden out of Afghanistan," the prince said later. This could be accomplished through strict adherence to Islamic principles, Turki and his guest scholar assured Mullah Omar.[8]

The Taliban leader agreed to Turki's request in principle but suggested that Saudi Arabia and Taliban leaders establish a joint commission of religious scholars to work out how bin Laden would be brought to court in accordance with Islamic law. Turki said later that he regarded this commission idea as a way to help the Taliban save face. It would provide public justification for bin Laden's extradition. Turki interpreted Omar's words as a clear decision to force bin Laden out of Afghanistan. "I repeated to Sheikh Mullah Omar," Turki recalled: " 'Do you agree that you're going to hand over this fellow and that the only thing required is for us to sit down together and work out the modalities?' And he said, 'Assure the king and the crown prince that this is my view.' "[9]

No one present at the meeting has directly challenged Turki's account of it, but differences and suspicions about what really happened in Kandahar that day persisted for years. Published accounts of the meeting in Pakistan, for example, suggested that Turki had discussed military strategy with the Taliban, offering to fund a drive against Massoud and other holdouts in the Northern Alliance. Turki did not tell the Americans in advance about his visit, nor did he give them a detailed briefing afterward. Longtime Saudi watchers at the CIA and the White House came to believe that in addition to whatever issues of religious law were discussed, Prince Turki had pursued his usual method, opening his checkbook in front of Mullah Omar and offering enormous financial support if the Taliban solved the bin Laden problem to Turki's satisfaction. Some estimated Turki's offer in the hundreds of millions of dollars.[10]

The more suspicious American analysts, conditioned by past Saudi deceptions, wondered if Turki might have met with bin Laden himself in Kandahar and perhaps renewed the kingdom's efforts to negotiate his peaceful return. Some analysts at the CIA Counterterrorist Center doubted that Turki's visit had been in any way a sincere effort to incarcerate bin Laden. These analysts had no idea what Turki was up to, but they doubted it was good. Their skepticism reflected the gradual erosion of CIA faith in Saudi Arabia, especially inside the Counterterrorist Center, as the bin Laden threat grew. There was no hard evidence to support the suspicion that Turki met with bin Laden in Kandahar, however. As for the offer of financial support to the Taliban if they cooperated, Turki's own public accounts of the meeting hinted as much. Such an offer would have been consistent with the agenda Turki said he pursued in Kandahar: He wanted to use incentives, arguments, and threats to persuade the Taliban to break with bin Laden.

White House counterterrorism officials remained convinced that Saudi Arabia still had little desire to put bin Laden on trial. It would be much easier for the royal family if the Americans captured bin Laden and put him in the dock. That way, bin Laden would be out of the royal family's hair, but they would not have to accept any political risk. They could instead deflect popular Saudi anger about bin Laden's punishment toward the United States and away from themselves.

According to Prince Turki, the Taliban sent a delegation to the kingdom in July 1998 to begin the commission talks on how to expel bin Laden from Afghanistan. The delegates returned to Kandahar with more specific proposals, by this account.

Prince Turki did not hear back from the Taliban leader, however. July yielded to August, and still there was no word.

Osama bin Laden certainly knew as August began that the entire context of Prince Turki's negotiations with the Taliban was about to change. What, if anything, bin Laden told Mullah Omar about the plans he had in motion that summer is unknown. His alliance with al-Zawahiri and other hard-core Egyptian militants had delivered him to a new phase of ambition. Within days he would be the most famous Islamic radical in the world.

THE CONSPIRATORS all had been trained, inspired, or recruited in Afghanistan. Wadih el Hage was a Lebanese Christian raised amid the roiling Muslim exile populations of Kuwait. He had been born with a deformity, a withered and weak right arm. As a teenager he converted to Islam, and at twenty-three, at the height of the anti-Soviet jihad, he traveled to the Afghan frontier to work with refugees. Mohammed Odeh learned about the Afghan jihad while attending a university in southeast Asia; he was a college student one week and a volunteer on the Afghan battlefield the next. K. K. Mohammed traveled to Afghanistan from his native Tanzania after years of Islamic studies. In 1994, at an Afghan training camp for multinational volunteers, a friend asked him if he wanted to "get involved in a jihad job," and he eagerly said yes. Some of them swore direct fealty to Osama bin Laden and the war-fighting organization he now called al Qaeda. Others said they never met bin Laden, nor did they consider him their general. They only knew that they were part of a righteous Islamic army fighting on behalf of the *umma,* or the worldwide community of the faithful.[11]

Some of the conspirators lived quietly for years in Africa after their training in Afghanistan. They were the first in a new constellation of operational al Qaeda sleeper cells spread out around the world, directed by bin Laden and his Egyptian allies from Taliban-protected safehouses in Kandahar and Kabul or from barren camps in the eastern Afghan mountains.

Shortly before 10:30 A.M. on Friday, August 7, 1998, two teams of suicide bombers rolled through two sprawling African capital cities. In Nairobi a wobbling truck packed with homemade explosives turned into the exit lane of a parking lot behind the American embassy and approached a barrier of steel bollards. One of the attackers jumped out, tossed a flash grenade at the Kenyan guards, and fled. When the truck detonated, it sheared off the U.S. embassy's rear façade. Glass shards, jagged concrete, and splintered furniture flew through the interior offices, killing and wounding Americans and Africans at their desks. The adjacent Ufundi Building collapsed, killing scores of Africans inside, including students at a secretarial college. Pedestrians in the crowded streets beside the embassy died where they stood.

About nine minutes later, in Dar es Salaam, Tanzania, a second truck turned into the parking lot of the American embassy and exploded. By sheer luck a filled embassy water tanker stood between the truck bomb and the building; the water tanker flew three stories into the air and splashed beside the chancery, absorbing much of the explosive impact. In Nairobi, 213 people died in the suicide bombing, 12 of them Americans. Another 32 of the dead were Kenyans who worked in the U.S. embassy. About 4,000 people were wounded. In Dar es Salaam 11 Africans died and 85 people were wounded. It was the most devastating terrorist attack against American targets since the suicide bombing of a Marine barracks in Lebanon by Shiite Islamic radicals in 1983.[12]

There was no warning. The CIA's Counterterrorist Center issued an alert on July 29 about a possible chemical, biological, or radiological attack by bin Laden, but it knew nothing of his plans in Africa. Bin Laden's press conference threats earlier in the year had led the State Department's diplomatic security office to issue a series of terrorist alerts, publicly and through classified channels, but none of these was specific enough to be useful. Nairobi and Dares Salaam were each deemed medium threat posts, but security officers worried at least as much about muggings and carjackings as they did about terrorists.[13]

The CIA knew bin Laden had followers in Nairobi. The Counterterrorist Center and the Africa division, working with the FBI, had tracked Afghan-trained bin Laden followers, including el Hage, to a ramshackle Nairobi charity office in 1996 and 1997. Their investigation included liaison with the Kenyan police and unannounced visits by FBI agents during the summer of 1997 to the homes of suspected militants. El Hage felt so much pressure that he left for the United States. The FBI followed him, pulled him off an airplane in New York, and dragged him before a federal grand jury for interrogation. But the suspect lied about his relations with bin Laden and was released. He moved to Texas, seemingly out of action, and his departure from Nairobi persuaded American investigators that they had disrupted bin Laden's east African cell. But other Afghan-trained sleepers had stayed behind.

With aid from bin Laden operatives who flew in from Pakistan they managed to evade attention while they manufactured their truck bombs in the backyards of two impoverished rental houses. For seven months prior to the bombings neither the Nairobi nor the Dar es Salaam CIA station picked up credible threats of a coming attack. This was typical of terrorist violence. Over two decades the CIA had learned again and again that it could not hope to defend against terrorists by relying solely on its ability to detect specific attacks in advance. No matter how many warnings they picked up, no matter how many terrorist cells they disrupted, at least some attackers were going to get through. Officers in the Counterterrorist Center privately compared themselves to soccer goalies: They wanted to be the best in their league, they wanted to record as many shutouts as possible, but they knew they were going to give up scores to their opponents. Ultimately, many of them believed, the only way to defeat terrorists was to get out of the net and try to take the enemy off the field.[14]

In a broader sense the bin Laden tracking unit inside the Counterterrorist Center had seen this coming. The center's analysts and officers worked eight to twelve hours a day in government cubicles reading and analyzing translated text from bin Laden's press conferences, television interviews, and intercepted messages and telephone calls. It seemed obvious to the dozen of them that bin Laden meant what he said: He had decided to launch a new jihad against the United States, and he would attack American targets wherever he could reach them. Yet the bin Laden unit's officers had been unable to persuade their bosses to act on the plan to raid Tarnak Farm.

Some of them were devastated and angry as they watched the television images of death and rescue in Africa. One of the bin Laden unit's female analysts confronted CIA director Tenet: "You are responsible for those deaths because you didn't act on the information we had, when we could have gotten him," she told him, according to an American official familiar with the accusation. The woman was "crying and sobbing, and it was a very rough scene," the official recalled.[15]

Tenet stood there and took it. He was a boisterous, emotional man, and he did not shrink from honest confrontation, his colleagues felt. Whether spurred by this challenge or in spite of it, Tenet redoubled his commitment to the agency's covert campaign against bin Laden in the weeks ahead.

For those who had worked on the Tarnak raid plan, the questions lingered: Why had Tenet never recommended the idea to Sandy Berger and President Clinton? Why had they been unwilling to risk civilian casualties among bin Laden's followers at the camp when it was clear that civilians were going to die in terrorist strikes, as they now had in Africa? Had the Counterterrorist Center's leaders pitched it aggressively enough to Tenet? Down in the trenches of a bureaucracy enveloped in secrecy, it was impossible to know why or how decisions of this kind were made. The resentments festered, amplified by rumors and the intensity of the daily grind.

SIX YEARS INTO HIS PRESIDENCY, Clinton had ample experience in decision-making about responses to terrorist attacks. His national security cabinet had been through the drill in both international and domestic cases: the attempted Iraqi assassination of President Bush in 1993; Kasi's attack at the CIA; the World Trade Center bombing; and the bombing of the federal building in Oklahoma City. That Friday, August 7, the White House Situation Room became the frantic locus of immediate relief and rescue response. Upstairs in the Oval Office, Clinton began to talk informally with his most trusted senior national security advisers, an inner circle that soon became known as the Small Group: Sandy Berger, George Tenet, Madeleine Albright, Janet Reno, Defense Secretary William Cohen, and the chairman of the Joint Chiefs of Staff, General Hugh Shelton. Of these Clinton was closest by far to Berger, his longtime friend and confidant. He worked comfortably with Tenet. Clinton's relationships with the rest of the Small Group members were more formal and distant. Still, while there were some chronic disagreements and tensions—Berger felt that Reno was defensive and uncooperative; Albright and Cohen clashed about policy questions—they often worked together well. Clinton encouraged open, loquacious discussion. The Small Group usually took him up.[16]

The first phase of their meetings involved what was known in national security jargon as the "attribution" question. What terrorist group had carried out the bombings? Had it received help from a foreign government? These questions had both legal and political aspects. If Clinton decided to strike back against the terrorists, he would have to justify the targets he chose and the proportion of violence he unleashed to the American people, allied governments, and the United Nations. A lawyer and an advocate of international institutions, Clinton paid attention to evidence and to legal standards governing the use of military force, including the doctrines of customary international law. When presented with presidential "findings" for lethal covert action, for instance, Clinton sometimes rewrote the CIA's authorizing language in his own hand, like an attorney honing an important brief. In the Africa case the first and most important question was whether the United States had adequate evidence about who was responsible for the embassy attacks. In domestic terrorist cases the president relied on the FBI and the Justice Department to marshal evidence and prosecute the guilty. In an overseas attack it was the CIA that traditionally presented the evidence. If Clinton concluded that the evidence was strong, he could then decide whether to respond by military force, placing the Pentagon in the lead; by covert action, with the CIA in charge; or by traditional law enforcement methods, pursued and prosecuted by Justice.

For a week after the attacks George Tenet and his senior aides briefed Clinton daily on the evidence. From the start it seemed likely that bin Laden was behind the attacks. The earlier CIA-FBI efforts to break up bin Laden's

Nairobi cell provided one archive of clues. Interrogation of a detained participant in the attacks, evidence seized in Nairobi, fax and satellite phone calls between Africa and Afghanistan, and electronic intercepts left little doubt, as the CIA saw it, that bin Laden had planned, funded, and ordered the bombings. On Friday, August 14, a week after the attacks, Tenet delivered to the Small Group the CIA's formal judgment that bin Laden and his senior Egyptian aides were responsible. "Intelligence from a variety of human and technical sources, statements of arrested suspects, and public statements by bin Laden's organization left no doubt about its responsibilities," according to Paul Pillar, then deputy director of the CIA Counterterrorist Center. The evidence "spoke for itself pretty clearly," recalled one person who saw the file. "There was a high degree of confidence." Recounting this moment to a colleague years afterward, Clinton called it "the first compelling evidence" that bin Laden personally "had been responsible for the deaths of Americans."[17]

With attribution established, the question became how to react. Bin Laden was a dangerous but obscure Islamic militant living in isolated caves halfway around the world. He had become an inspirational leader for national, violent Islamist movements in Algeria and Egypt. He directly controlled scattered Islamist revolutionary cells elsewhere. He contracted with Pakistani intelligence to train Islamist fighters for Kashmir, he colluded with the Taliban to train fighters against the Northern Alliance, and he hosted volunteer militants from Chechnya, Uzbekistan, and China. He was, in other words, a complex and widely distributed enemy. Was bin Laden individually the enemy? His elusive, shadowy al Qaeda network? Where did the Taliban fit?

Clinton and his Small Group gave relatively little attention to the Afghan context from which the embassy bombings arose. They had a sophisticated grasp of terrorism and counterterrorist doctrine, but Afghanistan and its tribal and ethnic conflicts seemed a violent muddle, and there were no real Afghan experts among them. They saw the Taliban as an obscurantist, bizarre militia reigning in a primitive, vicious land whose fighters had recently bled the once-vaunted Soviet Red Army. They understood and discussed some of the links among the Taliban, bin Laden, Pakistani intelligence, and the multinational militants who trained in Afghanistan. But the full picture of these links was not clear. No American president since Ronald Reagan had given serious consideration to Afghanistan as a foreign policy problem. Now the place had abruptly forced itself to the top of the Oval Office agenda as the locus of a shocking terrorist crime.

There was no serious discussion among them that August about a broad U.S.-led military campaign against the Taliban. Congress and the American people would not sanction such a war as an answer to the embassy attacks, Sandy Berger said later; the idea was all out of proportion. Clinton told a colleague later that "as despicable as the embassy bombings were," he was certain that even "our closest allies would not support us" if he ordered a sustained ground attack in Afghanistan. Besides, as skeptical as Madeleine Albright was about the Taliban, many regional specialists at her State Department and elsewhere believed—as Prince Turki did—that Mullah Omar could be persuaded by threats and enticements to break with bin Laden eventually. These American analysts believed, as Prince Turki and Pakistani intelligence repeatedly argued, that the Taliban would eventually mature into a Saudi-like moderate Islamic government. The Small Group did review that first week Pentagon-drawn options for a Special Forces raid into Afghanistan. But the size of the force that Joint Chiefs chairman Shelton said would be required, the slow pace at which it could be assembled, and the lack of obvious targets to attack inside Afghanistan led the group to set aside this idea quickly.[18]

These were strange, strange days on Pennsylvania Avenue. In between urgent Oval Office review sessions with the Small Group, Clinton was bracing himself and his closest friends for a painful decision. After eight months of public and private lies, the president had concluded that he had no choice but to confess to his wife and to the American people about his sexual liaison with the former White House intern Monica Lewinsky. On August 17, Clinton testified at the White House, before video cameras and cross-examining prosecutors, about the history of his sordid affair. That same day George Tenet privately briefed the Small Group about possible targets for cruise missile strikes against bin Laden's "infrastructure" in Afghanistan and Sudan. That night the president appeared on national television to admit publicly that he had been lying about his relationship with Lewinsky for months. In the media storm that followed he flew to Martha's Vineyard to stay with friends. Two days later he turned fifty years old.[19]

Describing this period later, Clinton insisted to a colleague that that August's public spectacle and private anguish had "absolutely no impact" on his willingness to act against bin Laden. It was clear to every member of the national security team, Clinton believed, that he was willing to retaliate against the Saudi for the embassy bombings. His aides later described the president as stalwart and focused during these Afghanistan meetings, fully able to separate the serious national security questions from the political squalor of the Lewinsky matter. Clinton would not let political considerations deter him from acting against bin Laden, his aides remembered him saying. "If I have to take more criticism for this, I will," he reportedly said.[20] Even if these accounts are credited, Clinton's instantly weakened presidency was plain for all to see. That August and for six months to come, as he became only the second president in American history to face impeachment charges, Clinton had neither the credibility nor the political strength required to lead the United States into a sustained military conflict even if it was an unconventional or low-grade war fought by Special Forces. His realistic options were severely limited. And Clinton could be certain that he would be harshly criticized no matter what he did or did not do.

Cruise missile strikes seemed the most obvious instrument. There was precedent for such an attack dating back to President Reagan's 1986 bombing of Tripoli, Libya, after Reagan reviewed evidence of Libyan involvement in a terrorist attack on American soldiers in a Berlin disco. Clinton had sent cruise missiles into Iraq's intelligence service headquarters in Baghdad after receiving clear evidence of Saddam Hussein's involvement in the 1993 assassination attempt on former president Bush. International law did not recognize revenge or punishment as justification for a military attack, but the customary laws of self-defense did sanction such strikes if they were designed to disrupt or preempt an enemy's ability to carry out future attacks. This principle helped shape the Pentagon's target list: They would emphasize bin Laden's ongoing operations, the threat he posed to the United States in the future, and his ability to give orders. The Pentagon had been studying possible Afghan targets in the same spring that the CIA had been drawing up its secret plan to raid Tarnak Farm. Bin Laden's televised threats had stimulated these exercises.[21] The CIA's covert satellite mapping had helped build a new Afghan target archive. Afghanistan was not the world's richest "target set," as the Pentagon jargon put it (bin Laden's training camps, like Tarnak Farm, were mainly dirt-rock expanses filled with mud-brick shacks and a few rope sleeping cots), but at least the Pentagon and CIA knew where the camps were and had good overhead imagery to work with. In some cases they had been mapping these camps since the anti-Soviet jihad of the 1980s.

As Clinton coped with his family crisis, incoming intelligence from the CIA accelerated attack plans. The day after the embassy bombings the CIA received a report that senior leaders of Islamist militant and terrorist groups linked to bin Laden planned to meet on August 20 at the Zawhar Kili camp complex about seven miles south of Khost in eastern Afghanistan. The intelligence indicated that bin Laden himself might attend the meeting. Zawhar Kili was near the scene of bin Laden's myth-making glory, the place he legendarily battled

Soviet troops. It had been his February announcement of the forthcoming jihad against "Crusaders and Jews." It had been the site of his May press conference and one-on-one television interviews. By striking the complex, the Americans would be attacking the birthplace of bin Laden's war and a symbol of his power. The complex routinely served as a training ground for jihadist fighters who were supported by Pakistani intelligence. Some of these groups sent militant volunteers to Kashmir. Others waged violent sectarian campaigns in Pakistan's large cities against clerical and political leaders of the country's Shia Muslim minority. Arab, Chechen, and Central Asian jihadists also passed through. The facility had a base headquarters and five satellite training areas, all of them primitively equipped. Because it was so close to the Pakistani border, officers from Pakistan's Inter-Services Intelligence Directorate could make easy day trips for meetings, training, and inspections.

Participants later differed about the quality of the CIA's intelligence on the Zawhar Kili meeting. The report suggested a very large gathering, perhaps two hundred or three hundred militants and leaders. General Anthony Zinni, then the senior military officer for the Middle East and Afghanistan, recalled that "the intelligence wasn't that solid." He felt launching cruise missiles into the camp during the August 20 meeting would be "a long shot, very iffy." The CIA's Paul Pillar and two senior directors in Richard Clarke's White House counterterrorism office recalled that the intelligence predicted bin Laden's presence at the meeting. Other participants recalled the opposite, that the report offered no specific assurance bin Laden would attend. Whatever the uncertainties, there was no doubt from Clinton on down that an objective of the American attack was to kill bin Laden.[22]

The August 20 meeting was not much of a secret: It was known to Pakistani intelligence. Former ISI chief Hamid Gul later said that he provided the Taliban with advance warning of the American attack, according to reports that circulated inside the U.S. government. Mushahid Hussain, a cabinet minister in the civilian government of Pakistani prime minister Nawaz Sharif, was in Saudi Arabia on an official visit on August 19. He called the head of Pakistan's Intelligence Bureau on an open phone line to see how everything was going back home. "So I said, 'What's happening?' . . . [He said] 'Bin Laden is having a meeting tomorrow. . . . He's called a summit.' I said, 'Do the Americans know?' He said, 'Of course.'"[23]

"The attack will come this evening," Hussain told his Saudi hosts the next morning. If he could anticipate the strikes, he reflected later, "surely bin Laden with all of his resources would have known what was coming."[24]

In Islamabad, General Joseph Ralston, vice chairman of the Joint Chiefs of Staff, sat down to dinner on the evening of August 20 with General Jehangir Karamat, Sharif's army chief. The Americans had war-gamed the Afghanistan attack in Washington the previous week, and they feared that Pakistan might mistake the missiles for a nuclear strike by India. Ralston's role was to assure Karamat that the incoming missiles were American.[25]

Seventy-five Tomahawk cruise missiles, each costing about $750,000, slammed into Zawhar Kili's rock gorges at about 10 P.M. local time. At least twenty-one Pakistani jihadist volunteers died, and dozens more were wounded. Bin Laden was not among them.

The CIA later reported to Clinton that it had received information that bin Laden had been at Zawhar Kili but that he had left several hours before the strikes. There was no way to be certain.[26] They had made a symbolic reply to the embassy bombings and perhaps had killed a few Pakistani terrorists bound for Kashmir or Karachi's Shiite slums, but as to bin Laden and his hard-core leadership, they had missed.

Simultaneously with the Zawhar Kili attack, thirteen cruise missiles slammed into a chemical factory in Khartoum, Sudan, called the al Shifa plant. From the beginning there had been a strong push within the Small Group to identify at least some additional targets outside Afghanistan. There were several reasons. Richard Clarke's new Counterterrorism Security Group had begun the previous spring to target bin Laden's global finances. The Saudi's money was one of his distinguishing features as a terrorist. Bin Laden's network had been the focus of the multiyear federal grand jury investigation that finally produced a sealed indictment the previous June. It named bin Laden as the sole defendant in a "conspiracy to attack defense utilities of the United States." Any cruise missile attack intended to disrupt bin Laden's future operations ought to do more than kick up dirt in eastern Afghanistan. It should also hurt his financial network, Clarke and his aides argued. CIA reporting showed ownership links between bin Laden and the al Shifa plant. Moreover, an Egyptian agent working with the CIA had returned soil samples from al Shifa that showed precursor substances associated with chemical weapons. The CIA had reported on this finding to the White House in late July, just before the African bombings. Previous CIA reporting from bin Laden's days of exile in Sudan, including the credible account of defector Jamal al-Fadl, had produced evidence of bin Laden's interest in chemical and nuclear weapons. Moreover, Clinton had developed a personal and specific conviction that the United States faced a grave, even existential danger from terrorists seeking to acquire biological, chemical, or nuclear arms. Richard Clarke had led a secret, multihour exercise just weeks earlier at Blair House in which top Clinton administration officials rehearsed their reaction to an attack by terrorists using weapons of mass destruction. The CIA put al Shifa on the table as a legitimate target because of the evidence it had collected about ownership and chemical precursors. Clinton embraced the target, one of his aides recalled, in part because he talked about terrorists acquiring weapons of mass destruction "all the time, and it was very much on his mind."[27]

Clinton announced to the American public that bin Laden had launched "a terrorist war" against the United States and that he had decided to strike back. "I think it's very important for the American people to understand that we are involved here in a long-term struggle," Madeleine Albright said. But Clinton and his aides came under withering criticism in Washington in the weeks after the missile strikes. Republicans and media pundits accused them of launching cruise missiles in a vain effort to distract public attention from Clinton's confession about Lewinsky. A movie called *Wag the Dog,* in which a fictional American president launches a war in Albania to deflect political criticism, had just been released; the cruise missile strikes were denounced widely as life imitating art. Sudan's government launched a publicity campaign in an effort to prove that the CIA had acted on false information in singling out the al Shifa plant. Bin Laden's supporters in Pakistan poured into the streets to protest the American assault. Pakistani politicians blamed the United States for abandoning Afghanistan in the first place. "You left us with the baby," said Riaz Khokhar, the Pakistani ambassador to Washington. "In this game we have to take care of our own interests."[28]

At the CIA's Counterterrorist Center, Deputy Director Paul Pillar felt all the *Wag the Dog* talk "muddied the message that the missile strikes were intended to send." Also, "The physical impact of the missile strike . . . was limited by the primitive nature of the facilities." The attacks "might have resulted in plans for further terrorist attacks being postponed, although this outcome is uncertain."[29]

Bin Laden's reputation in the Islamic world had been enhanced. He had been shot at by a high-tech superpower and the superpower missed. Two instant celebratory biographies of bin Laden appeared in Pakistani stores. Without seeming to work very hard at it, bin Laden had crafted one of the era's most successful terrorist media strategies. The missile strikes were his biggest publicity payoff to date.

All of this criticism constrained Clinton's options as he pursued the "war" against al Qaeda that he had announced to the public. The president was so unsettled by the criticism over the strike on the al Shifa plant in Sudan that he ordered a detailed review of the evidence that had led the CIA to recommend it as a target. For a president conditioned by his friend John Deutch and by his own experience to be skeptical about CIA competence, here was another episode to feed his doubts. Tenet was stung by the outcry over al Shifa. He remained convinced that it was a legitimate target, but he and his staff now had to invest time and effort to prove they were right. At the Pentagon the Joint Chiefs of Staff planned for additional cruise missile strikes, working under the code name Operation Infinite Resolve. Clarke told senior national security officials that Clinton wanted to launch new strikes soon. But the Pentagon planners had doubts. Walter Slocombe, the number three civilian official in the Defense Department, wrote to Defense Secretary William Cohen about a lack of attractive targets in Afghanistan. Fallout from the initial cruise missile strikes "has only confirmed the importance of defining a clearly articulated rationale for military action" that would really make a difference, he wrote. At the same time, Clinton's burlesque public struggle in the Lewinsky case reached its humiliating nadir. Weeks after the missile strikes the special prosecutor's office released what became known as the "Starr Report," chronicling in near-pornographic detail the history of the president's conduct. In the climate of political conflict and hysteria that ensued, it was unlikely that Clinton would return readily to a new round of cruise missile strikes. He could not afford to miscalculate.

Under the circumstances CIA-led covert action in Afghanistan seemed a promising pathway. By their very stealth the agency's efforts to capture or kill bin Laden would help Clinton evade the political problems of waging a military campaign, even a limited one, during an impeachment crisis. Tenet told the Senate intelligence committee in a closed session on September 2 that "key elements" of the CIA's emerging secret strategy would include hitting bin Laden's infrastructure, working with liaison intelligence services to "break up cells and carry out arrests," a plan to "recruit or expose his operatives," as well as pressure on the Taliban and efforts to improve "unilateral capability to capture him."[30]

In some respects this was the kind of covert action campaign that Tenet had warned about. When he took over at Langley, Tenet had cautioned against using CIA covert action programs as an expedient substitute for failed overt policies. But he had also noted that time and again in American history presidents called on the CIA to solve foreign policy problems in secret. Just as Kennedy had decades earlier wished for the agency to solve his Fidel Castro problem with a silver bullet, Clinton now needed the CIA to take the lead against bin Laden. But the United States was not prepared to take on as a serious foreign policy challenge Afghanistan's broader regional war in which bin Laden was now a key participant. That war would have required choosing sides against the Taliban and confronting the movement's supporters in Pakistani intelligence, among many other complications. It would be much easier if the CIA could just quietly slip into Afghanistan and bundle up bin Laden in a burlap sack.

PRINCE TURKI FLEW BACK to Kandahar in mid-September. Naseem Rana, the chief of Pakistani intelligence, accompanied him. A Pashtun ISI officer came along to handle translations.[31] They landed again within sight of Tarnak Farm and drove across the desert into the center of town. Turki hoped that the shock of the Africa bombings and the hostility of the American response had jarred the Taliban and that Mullah Omar would now recalculate the costs of his hospitality to bin Laden. Clinton had enacted a first round of sanctions against the Taliban that summer, signing an executive order that froze the militia's assets in the United States. More than ever, it seemed to Prince Turki, the Taliban had reason to embrace the economic rewards that would follow if they broke with bin Laden.

As they sat with their tea, the Saudi prince opened by explaining that the Americans strongly believed they had evidence proving bin Laden was behind the Africa bombings. "We've been waiting for you," Prince Turki said. "You gave us your word that you were going to deliver Osama bin Laden to us."[32]

Mullah Omar wheeled on him. He was more agitated than Turki had ever seen him. By one account he doused his head with water, explaining that he was so angry, he needed to cool himself down. "Why are you doing this? Why are you persecuting and harassing this courageous, valiant Muslim?" Omar demanded, referring to bin Laden. He continued to rant, with the Pakistani intelligence officer uncomfortably translating his insults into English for the Saudi prince. "Instead of doing that," he suggested to Turki, "why don't you put your hands in ours and let us go together and liberate the Arabian peninsula from the infidel soldiers!"[33]

Furious, Turki stood up. "I'm not going to take any more of this," he announced. As he left, he told Mullah Omar, "What you are doing today is going to bring great harm, not just to you but to Afghanistan."[34]

Days later Saudi Arabia withdrew its ambassador from Kabul. Yet as with so many other episodes of Saudi Arabian intelligence and foreign policy,

Turki's split with Omar looked murky—even suspicious—at the White House and at Langley. It was typical of the staccato, mutually distrustful communications between the two governments that Turki provided no detailed briefing to the Americans after he returned from Kandahar. Abdullah did brief Clinton and Gore on his efforts when he visited Washington that month. Still, perpetually leery of American motives, the Saudis continued to see little benefit in transparent information sharing with Washington. The kingdom's ministry of religious endowments, its proselytizing religious charities, and its Islamist businessmen all ran what amounted to separate foreign policies, channeling large sums to favored causes abroad. Some of them regarded the Taliban and bin Laden as comrades and heroes now more than ever.

At the bin Laden unit of the Counterterrorist Center, cynicism about the Saudis only deepened. The bin Laden unit's leader, an analyst known to his colleagues as Mike, argued with rising emotion that the CIA and the White House had become prisoners of their alliances with Saudi Arabia and Pakistani intelligence. America was in a war against a dangerous terrorist network. As it waged that war, it was placing far too much faith in unreliable allies. The CIA needed to break out of its lazy dependence on liaisons with corrupt, Islamist-riddled intelligence services such as the ISI and the Saudi General Intelligence Department, he argued. If it did not, he insisted, the CIA and the United States would pay a price.

His arguments cut against the grain of prevailing CIA assumptions and long-standing practice. Some of his colleagues feared that he was campaigning so emotionally and vociferously against the Saudis and the Pakistanis that he was beginning to jeopardize his agency career.[35]

"We Are at War"

THE CIA'S MISSION was to prevent surprise attacks. In this it was joined by the eavesdropping National Security Agency and the intelligence arms of the Pentagon, State, FBI, and other departments. Many of the thousands of analysts, linguists, technicians, communicators, and operations officers employed in the intelligence bureaucracy spent their time on soft analytic subjects such as political and scientific trends. A sizable minority assessed and disseminated all credible evidence about active threats to American lives or facilities. This massive warning bureaucracy had been honed during the Cold War to protect the United States against a sudden nuclear strike. By 1998 it directed much of its attention to fragmentary evidence about terrorist threats. In physical form the system was a network of classified computer systems, fax machines, videoconference facilities, and other secure communications that linked American embassies and military bases worldwide with government offices in and around Washington. The network allowed for fast, secure distribution of classified warning reports between the CIA, the White House, the Federal Aviation Administration, and thousands of local U.S. law enforcement agencies. The rules for writing, categorizing, and distributing these daily warning reports were specific and routinized. What the specialists called "raw" or unedited intelligence—intercept transcripts and notes from interrogation reports—might be sent to one distribution list of professional analysts. "Finished" product, more carefully written and edited but also sometimes flat and homogenized, poured out by the ream to policy makers.

It was a vast, pulsing, self-perpetuating, highly sensitive network on continuous alert. Its listening posts were attuned to even the most isolated and dubious evidence of pending attacks. Its analysts were continually encouraged to share information as widely as possible among those with appropriate security clearances. History had taught the professionals who worked inside the warning network that even the most insignificant bits of evidence could occasionally provide a clue that stopped a catastrophic attack. Human nature led them to err heavily on the side of caution as they decided what information to pass along. No analyst wanted to be the one who mistakenly discounted an intercept that might have stopped a terrorist bombing. From George Tenet to the lowest-paid linguist in the Counterterrorist Center, the system was biased toward sounding the alarm.[1] It was an imperfect arrangement, many on the inside believed, but it was the only way to ensure that the intelligence community did all it could to detect surprises before they erupted.

The daily operations of this threat and warning network dominated the American government's reponse to the Africa embassy bombings. In effect, the government cranked up the volume on a warning system that was already sensitive. The CIA "surged," in its jargon, to collect fresh intelligence about bin Laden's network and strike plans. The Counterterrorist Center poured this threat reporting through classified electronic messaging channels, sometimes transmitting raw intercepts and cables at a rate of more than one dozen per hour. The White House encouraged these gushers of warning. Clinton's counterterrorist and national security aides had been rocked by the bombings and dreaded a new wave of attacks. If bin Laden pummeled American targets while Clinton struggled through his impeachment crisis, the Saudi radical and his followers might seriously weaken the power and prestige of the United States, White House officials feared. Their job was to protect Clinton's presidency from disaster; they felt isolated in their detailed, highly classified knowledge about just how vulnerable the country appeared to be, and how motivated the Islamist terrorists had become.[2]

In one respect the system reacted as it was programmed to do. The Africa bombings signaled a serious ongoing threat, and the government's warning system recalibrated itself at a higher state of alert. In another sense bin Laden unwittingly achieved a tactical victory. The immediate American emphasis on threat reporting, warning, and defense helped define the next phase of the conflict on terms favorable to bin Laden. Al Qaeda generated massive amounts of nonspecific threat information. As it did, time, money, and manpower poured into the American government's patchwork system of defensive shields. Yet there was a consensus among the professionals that no such system could ever be adequate to stop all terrorist attacks. "Focusing heavily on the stream of day-to-day threat reporting not only risks forgetting that the next real threat may go unreported," Counterterrorist Center deputy director Paul Pillar believed, "it also means diversion of attention and resources."[3]

The day-to-day work on terrorist threats was difficult, frustrating, and contentious. Soon after the Africa attacks Richard Clarke established a unit of the White House–led Counterterrorism Security Group to focus exclusively on incoming threat reports. Many of these reports were collected by CIA stations abroad and routed through Pillar's office at the CIA Counterterrorist Center. The center's policy was to "never sit on threat information that you can't dismiss out of hand," as one participant recalled it. CIA threat cables came to the White House with commentary that might cast doubt on the value or authenticity of a particular report. But the CIA's customers across the administration began to feel as if they were drowning in unedited threats. Clarke's aides grumbled that the CIA was giving Clinton too much unfiltered intelligence, especially in the President's Daily Brief, warnings included not for their relevance but to protect the CIA's reputation if a fresh attack came. For its part, the CIA Counterterrorist Center complained that the White House hectored and bullied them over reports that they had never intended to be taken so seriously. They were being pressured to share information, and then they got blamed for sharing too much.[4]

On both sides of the Potomac they tried not to let the friction interfere with their solemn duty to get the facts right. American lives were at stake. But the analytical work, one fragmentary telephone intercept at a time, could be elusive and unrewarding. Each time they gathered in the White House Situation Room or spoke by secure telephone or video conference, they had complex, practical decisions to make. Should they order CIA surveillance against an obscure Arab militant named by a suspect in detention in Egypt? Should they order the American embassy in Rome to close on the day of a specific, though vaguely worded threat? Should they instruct United Airlines to cancel a flight from Paris without explanation to its passengers because an intercepted phone call had made a passing reference to that air route? If they failed to cancel the flight and it was attacked, how could they justify their silence?

One of their rules was "no double standards." Those around the table with access to highly classified threat information—Pillar or his designees from the CIA, Steven Simon or Daniel Benjamin in Clarke's office at the White House, officers from the Pentagon and the FBI—should not be able to use threat reports to plan their own travel or activities if that intelligence could just as easily be used to warn the general population. They had to decide when a specific, credible threat warranted public announcement, and when it was enough to take narrower protective measures in secret. Inevitably their daily judgments about threat reports were partially subjective. There was no way for any of them to be certain whether an interrogated suspect was lying or whether an Islamist activist bragging about an attack on the telephone was just trying to impress a friend. The "no double standards" rule provided one intuitive check for any specific decision. If an incoming threat to blow up an unnamed public square in London next Saturday looked credible enough so that any one of them would avoid such areas if he happened to be in London, then their duty was to issue a public alert. If the threat was against the U.S. embassy, they might consider a more targeted, secret alert to employees there. They issued dozens of such warnings in public and private in the weeks after the Africa attacks.[5]

They were aware that bin Laden and his leadership group were probably planting disinformation to distract them. They assumed that the more they closed embassies and issued alerts, the more they encouraged this disinformation campaign. Yet they could see no alternative. They had to collect as much threat information as they could, they had to assess it, and they had to act defensively when the intelligence looked credible.

There was plenty that looked truly dangerous. The CIA pushed European security services, Pakistan, Egypt, Saudi Arabia, and other governments to crack down that autumn on known associates of bin Laden. Cooperation was mixed, but several dozen militants were arrested, including bin Laden's long-time spokesman in London. Computers and telephone records seized in these cases made plain that al Qaeda's global cells were metastasizing. The CIA saw a level of lethality, professionalism, and imagination among some of these detained Islamists—particularly among the well-educated Arabs who had settled in Europe—that was on a par with the more sophisticated secular Palestinian terrorist groups of the 1970s. Their connections with one another and with bin Laden often seemed loose. Yet increasingly the Islamist cells were united in determination to carry out the anti-American *fatwas* that had been issued by bin Laden and al-Zawahiri from Afghanistan.

Within the morass of intelligence lay ominous patterns. One was an interest by bin Laden's operatives in the use of aircraft. A classified September 1998 threat report warned that in bin Laden's next strike his operatives might fly an explosive-laden airplane into an American airport and blow it up. Another report that fall, unavailable to the public, highlighted a plot involving aircraft in New York and Washington. In a third case, in November, Turkish authorities broke up a plan by an Islamic extremist group to fly a plane loaded with explosives into the tomb of modern Turkey's founder, Ataturk, during a ceremony marking the anniversary of his death. Some of these threats against aviation targets were included in classified databases about bin Laden and his followers maintained by the FBI and the CIA.[6] There these strands joined the evidence about suicide airplane attacks and aircraft bombings dating back to the 1995 arrest of Ramzi Yousef. Yet at the Counterterrorism Security Group meetings and at the CIA's Counterterrorist Center there was no special emphasis placed on bin Laden's threat to civil aviation or on the several exposed plots where his followers had considered turning hijacked airplanes into cruise missiles. Aviation had been a terrorist target for three decades; hijacking threats and even suicide airplane plots had for years been part of the analytical landscape. The threat reports and the pattern of past bin Laden attacks emphasized other target categories more prominently, such as embassies and military bases. If they had any analytical bias, Clinton, Tenet, and Clarke tended to be most worried about weapons of mass destruction because of the casualties and economic damage such an attack might produce. Several classified reports that fall warned that bin Laden was considering a new attack using poisons in food, water, or the air shafts of American embassies. Aviation was an issue but not a priority.[7]

A second pattern in the threats that fall did galvanize attention: It seemed increasingly obvious that bin Laden planned to attack inside the United States. In September the CIA and the FBI prepared a classified memo for Clinton's national security cabinet outlining al Qaeda's American infrastructure, including charities and other groups that sometimes operated as fronts for terrorist activity. In October the intelligence community picked up reports that bin Laden sought to establish an operations cell in the United States by recruiting American Islamists or Arab expatriates. In November came another classified report that a bin Laden cell was seeking to recruit a group of five to seven young men from the United States to travel to the Middle East for training. When the FBI announced a $5 million reward for bin Laden's capture, the CIA picked up reports that bin Laden had authorized $9 million bounties for the assassination of each of four top CIA officers. Many of the intelligence reports were vague. Still, the pattern was unmistakable. "The intelligence community has strong indications," declared a December classified memo endorsed by the CIA and circulated at the highest levels of the U.S. government, "that bin Laden intends to conduct or sponsor attacks inside the United States."[8]

AFTER THE AFRICA EMBASSY BOMBINGS, National Security Adviser Sandy Berger ordered the Pentagon to station navy ships and two cruise-missile-bearing submarines beneath the Arabian Sea, off the coast of Pakistan. The secret deployment order was so closely held that even some senior directors at the CIA did not know the submarines were in place. Cruise missiles could twist and turn across hundreds of miles as they flew preprogrammed paths to their targets. Their software guided them to coordinates marked by satellites in fixed, stationary orbits. The White House hoped that CIA agents on the ground in Afghanistan—at this time mainly the tribal agents operating near Kandahar—would track bin Laden and relay the coordinates of one of his meeting places or overnight guest houses. Some of the coordinates of bin Laden's known camps, such as the buildings in the Tarnak Farm compound, had already been loaded into the submarines' missile computers. Other places could be marked by laser targeting equipment carried by the mobile tracking team, then quickly relayed as GPS coordinates to the submarines. Clinton made it clear to his senior White House aides that if they could produce strong intelligence about bin Laden's location, he would give the order to strike. Clarke's counterterrorism office initiated classified exercises with the Pentagon and discovered they could reduce the time from a presidential order to missile impact in Afghanistan to as little as four hours. Still, as they considered a launch, a vexing question remained: How certain did they need to be that bin Laden was really at the target? In a political-military plan he called "Delenda," from the Latin "to destroy," Clarke argued that they should move beyond trying to decapitate al Qaeda's leadership and should instead strike broadly at bin Laden's infrastructure. The Delenda Plan recommended diplomatic approaches, financial disruption, covert action inside Afghanistan, and sustained military strikes against Taliban and al Qaeda targets. Some of Clarke's ideas rolled into continuing discussions about how to pressure bin Laden, but none of Clinton's national security cabinet agreed with his approach to military targeting. Broad strikes in Afghanistan would provide "little benefit, lots of blowback against [a] bomb-happy U.S.," recalled Deputy National Security Adviser James Steinberg, who like Berger opposed Clarke's proposal for attacks against al Qaeda camps or Taliban infrastructure, such as it might be. Still, Clinton and his senior aides said they remained ready to fire missiles directly at bin Laden or his most senior leaders if they could be located precisely.[9]

Late in 1998 the CIA relayed a report to the White House from one of its agents that bin Laden had been tracked to Kandahar. The report was that bin Laden would sleep in the Haji Habash house, part of the governor's residence complex. The CIA had reported that there were fifty-two Stinger missiles hidden on the grounds. A bomb or cruise missile might kill bin Laden and Omar or other senior Taliban, plus destroy the missiles—a counterterrorism trifecta. "Hit him tonight," Gary Schroen cabled from Islamabad. "We may not get another chance." The Cabinet principals on terrorism issues, including Tenet and Richard Clarke, discussed the report.[10] Target maps showed that the building where they expected bin Laden to be was near a small mosque. Clinton knew from painful experience that for all the amazing accuracy of cruise missiles, they were far from perfect. When the president had launched missiles against the Iraqi intelligence headquarters in 1993, one missile had fallen a few hundred yards short and had killed one of the most prominent female artists in the Arab world. Clinton had never forgotten that. Now he and others around the table worried that if one of the missiles fell short again, it would destroy the mosque and whoever happened to be inside. Civilian casualties had not been an issue for Clinton during discussions about the August cruise missile strikes, he told a colleague years later, because Clinton felt they had a serious chance in that attack to get bin Laden. Now the prospect of success seemed less certain, Clinton believed. The president said that he would not allow minimizing civilian casualties to become a higher priority than killing or capturing bin Laden, but he wanted to achieve both objectives if possible. In a memo written at the time, Clarke said Clinton had been forced to weigh 50 percent confidence in the CIA's intelligence against the possibility of as many as three hundred casualties. The two issues—the likelihood of innocent deaths and the uncertainty about bin Laden's exact whereabouts—often were discussed together in the Small Group after mid-1998.

Tenet said the intelligence he had about bin Laden's location this time was "single-threaded," meaning that he lacked a second, independent source. The CIA was searching for confirmation of bin Laden's presence but didn't yet have it. As his Delenda memo reflected, Clarke believed that they should fire the missiles anyway. He felt that if they missed bin Laden, Clinton could just declare to the public that he had been targeting Taliban and al Qaeda "infrastructure" and "terrorist training camps" because of continuing threats. Clinton, however, was not enthusiastic about bombing Taliban and al Qaeda camps that Hugh Shelton derided as little more than "jungle gyms" if there was scant expectation that bin Laden or his top lieutenants would be killed. To strike at bin Laden and miss would hurt the United States, Clinton believed.[11]

Berger told his colleagues that the costs of failure might be very high. Every time the United States shot off one of its expensive missiles at bin Laden and failed to get him, it looked feckless, Berger argued, reinforcing Clinton's view. As Berger later recalled it: "The judgment was [that] to hit a camp and not get top bin Laden people would have made the United States look weak and bin Laden look strong."[12] Berger did not demand absolute certainty from Tenet or the CIA about bin Laden's location. The standard he laid down for a decision to strike was a "significant" or "substantial" probability of success. But could the CIA promise even that much?[13]

Tenet reported back to the group: He did not have a second source. He would not recommend a missile launch. In this judgment he was supported by several of his senior aides at the CIA and the Pentagon's commanders. The submarines returned to their patrols off Pakistan, still on alert. "I'm sure we'll regret not acting last night," wrote Mike Scheuer, the bin Laden unit chief, to Gary Schroen. "We should have done it last night," Schroen replied. Increasingly, the CIA was chasing a roving spectre.

IN ADDITION TO the submarine order Clinton signed a Top Secret "Memorandum of Notification" within days of the embassy bombings to authorize the CIA or its agents to use lethal force if necessary in an attempt to capture bin Laden, Ayman al-Zawahiri, and several other top lieutenants. Clinton had a specific understanding of bin Laden's leadership group. He understood al-Zawahiri as someone who was "as smart as bin Laden, not quite as charismatic, but equally ruthless." The squat Egyptian doctor remained fixed in Clinton's mind as a participant in the conspiracy that assassinated Anwar Sadat, whom Clinton saw as a rare progressive in the Middle East. His memo provided legal authority for CIA covert operations aimed at taking a specific list of al Qaeda leaders into custody for purposes of returning them to the United States for trial on federal charges of terrorism and murder.[14]

The MON, as it was called, added new specificity to a previously approved CIA covert action program. The agency already had legal authority to disrupt and arrest terrorists under the 1986 presidential finding that established its

Counterterrorist Center. A new finding would trigger all sorts of complex bureaucratic, budgetary, and legal steps. It seemed wiser to use a MON to amend the legal authority the center already possessed, to make it more specific.

By 1998 government lawyers had been intimately woven into the American system of spying and covert action. After the Iran-Contra scandal the White House established a new position of chief legal counsel to the president's national security adviser. This office, headed at the time of the Africa embassy bombings by Jamie Baker, occupied a suite on the third floor of the Old Executive Office Building, next to the chief White House adviser on intelligence policy. Baker ran a highly secret interagency committee of lawyers that drafted, debated, and approved presidential findings and MONs. They spent long hours on subtle legal issues that arose in America's lethal covert action programs: When is a targeted killing not an assassination? When is it permissible to shoot a suspect overseas in the course of an attempted arrest?[15]

Those and similar questions swirled around the CIA's secret program to track and capture Osama bin Laden in Afghanistan. From Tenet on down, the CIA's senior managers wanted the White House lawyers to be crystal clear about what was permissible and what was not. They wanted the rules of engagement spelled out in writing and signed by the president so that every CIA officer in the field who ever handed a gun or a map to an Afghan agent could be assured that he was operating legally.[16]

This was the role of the MON. It was typically about seven or eight pages long, written in the form of a presidential decision memo drafted for Clinton's signature. The August 1998 memo began with what the lawyers called a "predicate," or a statement about how bin Laden and his aides had attacked the United States. It also outlined and analyzed possible repercussions of the covert action being planned to arrest them. The MON made clear that the president was aware of the risks he was assuming as he sent the CIA into action. Any covert arrest operations in Afghanistan might go sour, and agents or civilians might be killed. Difficulties might be created for American diplomacy if the operations failed or were exposed. There was also language to address the issue of civilian casualties. Typically this was a boilerplate phrase which in effect urged that "every effort must be taken" by the CIA to avoid such casualties where possible.[17]

Some of the most sensitive language in the MON concerned the specific authorization to use deadly force. The lawyers had to make clear to the CIA in writing that it was okay to shoot and kill bin Laden's bodyguards or bin Laden himself as long as the force was employed in self-defense and in the course of a legitimate attempt to make an arrest. "We wanted to make clear to the people in the field that we preferred arrest, but we recognized that that probably wasn't going to be possible," Richard Clarke said later. After the Africa bombings the intent of the White House, Clinton's national security aides insisted later, was to encourage the CIA to carry out an operation, not to riddle the agency with constraints or doubts. Yet Clinton's aides did not want to write the authorization so that it could be interpreted as an unrestricted license to kill. For one thing, the Justice Department signaled that it would oppose such language if it was brought to Clinton for a signature. Their compromise language, in a succession of bin Laden–focused MONs, always expressed some ambiguity. Typical language might instruct the CIA to "apprehend with lethal force as authorized."[18] Those sorts of abstract phrases had wiggle room in them. Some CIA officers and supervisors read their MONs and worried that if an operation in Afghanistan went bad, they would be accused of having acted outside the memo's scope.

As time passed, private recriminations grew between the CIA and the White House. It was common among senior National Security Council aides to see the CIA as much too cautious, paralyzed by fears of legal and political risk. They were not alone in this view. Porter Goss, a former CIA officer who had entered Congress and now chaired the House intelligence committee, declared just six weeks after the Africa bombings that the Directorate of Operations had become too "gun-shy." The CIA's outgoing inspector general, Fred Hitz, wrote at the same time that the CIA "needs to recapture the esprit de corps it manifested during the height of the Cold War."[19] At Langley this criticism rankled. Midlevel officers noted that they were the ones who had developed the Tarnak snatch operation even before the Africa attacks, only to have it turned down. The CIA's senior managers felt that Clinton's White House aides, in particular, wanted to have it both ways. They liked to blame the CIA for its supposed lack of aggression, yet the White House lawyers wrote covert action authorities full of wiggle words. CIA managers had been conditioned by history to read their written findings and MONs literally. Where the words were not clear, they recommended caution to their officers in the field.

The classified legal memos reflected a wider ambiguity in Clinton's covert policy toward bin Laden that autumn. There was little question at either the National Security Council or the CIA that under American law it was entirely permissible to kill Osama bin Laden and his top aides, at least after evidence showed they were responsible for the Africa attacks. The ban on assassinations contained in Executive Order 12333 did not apply to military targets, the Office of Legal Counsel in Clinton's Justice Department had previously ruled in classified opinions.[20] Tarnak Farm or other terrorist encampments in

Afghanistan were legitimate military targets under this definition, the White House lawyers agreed. In addition, the assassination ban did not apply to attacks carried out in preemptive self-defense where it seemed likely that the target was planning to strike the United States. Clearly bin Laden qualified under this standard as well. Under American law, then, Clinton might have signed MONs that made no reference to seeking bin Laden's arrest, capture, or rendition for trial. He might have legally authorized the agency to carry out covert action for the sole purpose of killing bin Laden, al-Zawahiri, and other al Qaeda leaders.

But Clinton did not choose this path. Janet Reno, the attorney general, from whom Clinton was somewhat estranged, opposed MONs that would approve pure lethal operations against bin Laden by the CIA. Reno's position, expressed in Jamie Baker's top-secret council of lawyers and in other communications with Richard Clarke's counterterrorism group, was nuanced and complex, according to officials who interacted with the attorney general and her aides. She told the White House that she would approve lethal strikes against bin Laden if the Saudi threatened an imminent attack against the United States. But what was the definition of "imminent"? Clarke argued that the threat reporting about bin Laden made clear that al Qaeda had attacks in motion, but it was impossible to be sure about the timing or location of specific bin Laden operations. Reno accepted that they could not predict specific attacks, but when the strikes that Clarke warned about did not occur right away, Reno sometimes renewed her private objections to broad lethal authority for the CIA.

Reno's disapproval mattered because National Security Adviser Sandy Berger sought a consensus within the Cabinet about the exact wording of the CIA's instructions. Even though they felt they were on very solid legal ground, the language they were working with month after month, memo after memo, lived in uncomfortable proximity to the long-standing White House ban on assassinations. They did not want Reno to develop dissents to Clinton's decisions about bin Laden in this area. In the midst of the impeachment mess, none of them wanted to wake up to a newspaper headline that read: ATTORNEY GENERAL OBJECTS TO CLINTON'S TERRORIST ASSASSINATION PLANS. So Jamie Baker's group drafted and redrafted language to accommodate Reno's concerns. The resulting consensus formulations, conceded one White House senior official involved, were often convoluted and "Talmudic."

More broadly, the president's covert policy—as fashioned by Sandy Berger, his deputy James Steinberg, Richard Clarke, and the national security cabinet—

pursued two different goals at the same time. On the one hand, they ordered cruise missile–equipped submarines to patrol secretly under the Arabian Sea. They hoped to use the submarines to kill bin Laden if they could find him sitting still long enough to strike. On the other hand, they authorized the CIA to carry out operations designed at least on paper to take bin Laden alive. The Small Group debated "whether to consider this a law enforcement matter demanding a judicial response or a military matter in which the use of armed force was justified," Madeleine Albright recalled. "We decided it was both." William Cohen argued that debate over war versus law enforcement was a "false choice"; all instruments of American power were required at once.

The split policy reflected unresolved divisions inside the national security cabinet. Attorney General Janet Reno and FBI director Louis Freeh, along with others at Justice, had invested themselves deeply in the law enforcement approach to terrorism. American counterterrorist policy had since 1986 emphasized bringing terrorists to justice in courtrooms. Even though killing bin Laden would be legal under American law, some at Justice and the White House nonetheless felt uneasy at times about that approach. There might be unintended consequences. They had been willing to endorse the August cruise missile strikes in the immediate aftermath of the embassy bombings. There was a sense of proportion in those attacks. Now, as an ongoing matter, some of them preferred to seek bin Laden's arrest, not to launch a low-grade war.[21]

Clinton himself seemed to lean in both directions. If anything, by his actions and decisions the president seemed to favor lethal force against bin Laden and al-Zawahiri if he could find a way to make an immaculate strike. "Clinton's desire to kill them was very clear to us early on," recalled one of his senior aides. But he did not commit himself all the way. The first MON he signed in the summer of 1998 authorized covert action aimed at taking bin Laden and his aides into custody for trial. The ambiguous language might have been crafted to assure Janet Reno's support, but Clinton etched his own signature on the memo. Yet the president's second MON explicitly authorized bin Laden's death in one narrow set of hypothetical circumstances—without overriding the general order in the first memo.

At one of Richard Clarke's Counterterrorism Security Group meetings that autumn, they reviewed intelligence about how bin Laden moved around Afghanistan. Sometimes he traveled by road in heavily armed convoys of Land Cruisers. Occasionally, however, he flew in helicopters and aircraft maintained by al Qaeda in conjunction with the Taliban's small air force. The

CIA received occasional reports from its tribal tracking team and other sources about bin Laden's flights. They wanted to be certain their agents had legal permission to shoot at a helicopter or airplane if they knew that bin Laden was on board. The Pentagon also ordered planning late in 1998 for operations to intercept al Qaeda aircraft. Downing an airplane was not an operation likely to produce an arrest or capture, so it did not seem to be covered by the prevailing MON. Also, such an attack could violate international treaties banning air piracy. This was an area the National Security Council lawyers often worried about: A covert operation might be legal under domestic U.S. law, but it might at the same time violate American treaty commitments abroad. This could lead other countries to abandon *their* pledges under international treaties. Also, in some cases the United States had passed laws making any treaty violation a domestic crime. A MON might permit crimes abroad but nonetheless place an individual CIA officer in legal jeopardy inside the United States.[22]

Jamie Baker's office presented a new MON for Clinton's signature. It would authorize the CIA or the Pentagon to shoot down bin Laden's helicopters or airplanes under certain circumstances. There was no pretense in this MON that bin Laden would be captured for trial. Clinton signed it.

The president had now authorized the CIA to capture bin Laden for trial and, separately, to kill him. Pentagon planning was equally divided: A December 1998 order sought options for capturing al Qaeda leaders and transporting them from Kandahar, while other plans contemplated stand-off air strikes. Some CIA managers saw their instructions from the White House as legalistic, restrictive, and ambiguous. The drafts of more straightforward proposed instructions they sent over to the White House from Langley came back full of abstract phrases open to multiple interpretations. The CIA received no "written word nor verbal order to conduct a lethal action," one official involved recalled. "The objective was to render this guy to law enforcement." Under its written authorities from the White House the CIA had to recruit agents "to grab [bin Laden] and bring him to a secure place where we can turn him over to the FBI." Some CIA managers saw a big difference between the August 1998 MON language and a pure lethal action. "If they had said 'lethal action,' it would have been a whole different kettle of fish and much easier," the official recalled. Credible planning and supervision of an arrest operation inside Afghanistan, transfer to FBI agents, and extraction to the United States was far more complicated than planning for a lethal strike. The exact language Clinton sent to Langley in his bin Laden-related MONS zigzagged on the issue of lethal force. The first document after the embassy bombings said the CIA's tribal agents could use lethal force during a capture operation only in self-defense. The TRODPINTS were told they would only be paid if they captured bin Laden, not if they killed him. At the end of 1998 Clinton reversed course and approved paying the tribals either way, as long as they did not execute prisoners or otherwise grossly violate the rules. A new memo during this period also authorized the CIA's agents to kill bin Laden if capturing him did not look feasible. Yet Clinton later signed at least two other classified memos about operations against bin Laden that reverted to the earlier, less permissive language. The changes demoralized CIA field officers and encouraged them to believe that they and their Afghan allies would be held to account on issues of legal nuance.[23]

White House aides saw the same instructions as providing the clearest possible signal that the CIA should get after bin Laden and his leadership group and kill them if necessary. Capture for trial was the stated objective of the August MON, yes, but the White House aides believed they had written the document to provide the CIA with the maximum flexibility to kill bin Laden in the course of an arrest operation. All of them, including the CIA's managers and lawyers, knew that as a practical matter bin Laden and his bodyguards would resist capture. These were committed jihadists. They would likely martyr themselves long before they were handcuffed. Under the White House's authorities, as soon as bin Laden's men shot back, the CIA's several dozen armed Afghan agents could take them out. Also, as the months passed and new MONs were written, the CIA's authorizing language, while still ambiguous, was changed to make the use of lethal force more likely. At first the CIA was permitted to use lethal force only in the course of a legitimate attempt to make an arrest of bin Laden or his top aides. Later the key language allowed for a snatch operation _or_ a pure lethal attack if an arrest was not plausible.

Clinton's aides thought the CIA's managers were using the legal issues as a dodge. The agency sometimes seemed to believe that under the MON, "unless you find him walking alone, unarmed, with a sign that says 'I am Osama' on him, that we weren't going to attempt the operation," one White House official involved recalled. "I think we were concerned that there were too many people [at Langley] who will just see the downsides and not enough people motivated to get the job done." Yet CIA leaders and lawyers alike interpreted their instructions the same way—as orders to capture, not kill, except in certain circumstances.[24]

Sandy Berger later recalled his frustration about this hidden debate, confined at the time to only a few dozen officials and lawyers with the proper security clearances: "It was no question, the cruise missiles were not trying to capture him. They were not law enforcement techniques." Berger said that if "there was ever any confusion, it was never conveyed to me or the president by the DCI or anybody else."[25] What the White House needed most was "actionable intelligence" about bin Laden's precise location. They depended on the CIA to provide it. The agency had ample authority to put its Afghan agents into action, Berger believed.

The tension festered. It would not be resolved anytime soon.

IN THE SAME WEEK that bin Laden's operatives struck two U.S. embassies in Africa, Mullah Omar's turbaned Taliban soldiers, their ranks swollen with jihadist volunteers from Pakistan's *madrassas* and aided by officers from Pakistani intelligence, finally captured their last major prize in the north of Afghanistan: the sprawling city of Mazar-i-Sharif. "My boys and I are riding into Mazar-i-Sharif," the longtime ISI Afghan bureau officer Colonel Imam, once a close partner of the CIA, boasted in an intercepted telephone call at the height of the battle.[26]

Mazar's defenders, commanders allied with Ahmed Shah Massoud, succumbed to bribes paid by Pakistani officers, Massoud told his men at a military assembly. The leading local warlord, Abdul Malik, "delivered his city for a fistful of dollars," Massoud declared.[27] Massoud and his militias still controlled the northern town of Taloqan, but increasingly they were being painted into a corner.

Just weeks after the embassy bombings Massoud wrote a letter to the United States Senate urging that America help him in his war against the Taliban, Pakistani intelligence, and bin Laden. After the expulsion of Soviet troops, Massoud wrote, Afghanistan's people "were thrust into a whirlwind of foreign intrigue, deception, great-gamesmanship and internal strife.... We Afghans erred, too. Our shortcomings were a result of political innocence, inexperience, vulnerability, victimization, bickering and inflated egos. But by no means does this justify what some of our so-called Cold War allies did to undermine this just victory." Pakistan and its Arab Islamist allies had fielded twenty-eight thousand paramilitary and military forces in Afghanistan to aid the Taliban's drive for conquest, Massoud wrote. Afghanistan had been delivered to "fanatics, extremists, terrorists, mercenaries, drug mafias and professional murderers." America should help him turn them away. Washington should break its long debilitating dependence on Pakistan in shaping its Afghan policies, Massoud urged.[28]

But the Clinton administration, especially diplomats at the State Department, remained disdainful of Massoud and his pleas. With the fall of Mazar, the Taliban seemed more than ever an irreversible force inside Afghanistan. Madeleine Albright, Undersecretary Tom Pickering, and regional specialists in State's South Asia bureau all recommended that the administration continue its policy of diplomatic engagement with the Taliban. They would use pressure and promises of future aid to persuade Omar to break with bin Laden. The U.S. embassy in Islamabad promoted this argument in its cables to Washington. Most State diplomats saw Ahmed Shah Massoud as a spent force tainted by his recent deals to accept arms supplies from Iran and by his reliance on heroin trafficking for income. Some at State, including Inderfurth, said later that they thought it was useful for Massoud to remain viable as a military force in northern Afghanistan because he offered a check on the Taliban's cross-border Islamist ambitions in Central Asia. But from Albright on down, the State Department certainly was not prepared to join Massoud's military campaign against the Taliban.[29]

State diplomats sought to convince the Taliban's leaders that America did not see them as the enemy, that the United States was targeting only bin Laden and his Arab lieutenants. The August cruise missile attack "was not directed against Afghanistan or the Taliban," Assistant Secretary of State Rick Inderfurth explained in October 1998. The Taliban "need to understand that by harboring terrorists, they are becoming increasingly complicit in the acts those terrorists commit." But there was still time for the Taliban to change its stripes. "We urge the Taliban to respond," Inderfurth declared. "If it does not, we will have to respond accordingly and adjust our policies."[30]

The underlying premise of this outreach, rarely stated aloud so as to preserve America's bargaining position, was to trade U.S. diplomatic recognition of the Taliban as Afghanistan's legitimate government in exchange for custody of Osama bin Laden. Among other things, State's diplomats hoped Pakistan and its intelligence service would use their presumed leverage over the Taliban to help cut this deal. In effect this was the continuation of an American policy that had long been willing to accept Pakistani hegemony over Afghanistan in the name of regional stability.

AT THE HEART OF the matter lay an unresolved factual and policy question: Who was the enemy? There was a second question, also unresolved: How dangerous, really, was the threat?

By the late 1990s, presiding over a historic economic and stock market boom, Bill Clinton had concluded that terrorism—along with ethnic war, diseases such as AIDS, and regressive religious regimes like the Taliban—represented "the dark side" of the "breathtaking increase in global interdependence" witnessed since the collapse of communism. Satellites, air travel, and more recently the World Wide Web had collapsed time and space, suddenly forcing disparate nations and religions and cultures into roiling interaction. America had reaped enormous benefits from these changes. Its rapidly rising wealth flowed directly from "tearing down the walls, collapsing the distances, and spreading the information that we have across the world," as Clinton put it later. Yet at the same time "you cannot collapse walls, collapse differences, and spread information without making yourself more vulnerable to forces of destruction." Clinton believed that America's mission was to accelerate these trends, not resist them. He sought to lead the country and the world from a period of global "interdependence" to one of more complete worldwide "integration." Terrorist attacks were a "painful and powerful example of the fact that we live in an interdependent world that is not yet an integrated global community," he believed. Yet Clinton did not want to build walls. He saw the reactionary forces of terrorism, nationalism, and fundamentalism as inevitable; they were intricately connected to the sources of global progress. They were also doomed. In human history, he asserted with questionable accuracy, "no terrorist campaign has ever succeeded."[31]

More specifically, Clinton saw bin Laden and Islamic radicals like him as part of a long historical continuum of "fanatics" who "think they've got the truth, and if you share their truth, your life has value. And if you don't, you're a legitimate target." Clinton often described his own Christian faith—shaped in part by his exposure at Georgetown University to the Jesuit tradition—as rooted in a search for God that was constrained by human fallibility. "Most of us believe that no one has the absolute truth," Clinton said. "As children of God, we are by definition limited in this life, in this body, with our minds." Life could only be "a journey toward truth," never fully completed until salvation. The Taliban, bin Laden, and al Qaeda had "very different ideas [than] we have about the nature of truth, the value of life."[32]

Clinton was prepared to "take Mr. Bin Laden out of the picture" if he could, he said later. Yet he defined the broader purpose of his foreign policy as one that would "spread the benefits" of global integration and "reduce the risks" of terrorism by making "more partners and fewer terrorists in the future." He was inclined to see bin Laden as an isolated fanatic, flailing dangerously but quixotically against the forces of global progress.[33]

Most of the Clinton administration's debates about counterterrorism policy took place far from public view. Some of the most pointed occurred within the Counterterrorism Security Group where virtually every memo was highly classified. Here the CIA's main representative, Paul Pillar, joined tense, sometimes hostile debates with Richard Clarke and his principal counterterrorism aides, Steven Simon and Daniel Benjamin. Their day-to-day arguments involved some of the most critical strategic issues.

Their discussions were substantive, intellectual, and visceral. They involved basic questions about modern terrorism, bin Laden's network, its threats, and American policy. All four men were exceptionally intelligent and well spoken. They were bookish, intense, well read, nervous, and argumentative. Their disagreements had the hyperarticulate character and unyielding passion of ideological disputes among Ivy League faculty. The hours they worked together were long beyond count, and the pay was mediocre. Yet they were debating day to day the most important issues in their country's clandestine war against bin Laden. The pressure was almost unbearable. There was little reward for being right in these disputes. There was the continual potential of catastrophe for being wrong.

The four of them agreed about a great deal. Their differences were often subtle, yet they were also substantial. As the longtime deputy director of the Counterterrorist Center, Pillar wielded great influence over the CIA's terrorism analysis. Along with Clarke, Simon and Benjamin were instrumental in White House counterterrorism policy in the first year after the Africa embassy bombings.

Pillar saw terrorism fundamentally as "a challenge to be managed, not solved," as he put it later. Terrorist attacks seemed likely to become a permanent feature of American experience, he believed. He objected to the metaphor of waging "war" against terrorism because "it is a war that cannot be won" and also "unlike most wars, it has neither a fixed set of enemies nor the prospect of coming to closure." A better analogy than war might be "the effort by public health authorities to control communicable diseases." A lesson of American counterterrorism efforts since the 1980s was that the threat could not be defeated, only "reduced, attenuated, and to some degree controlled." Striving for zero terrorist attacks would be as unhealthy for American foreign policy as pushing for zero unemployment would be for the economy, Pillar believed. In a broad sense, Pillar's outlook accorded with Clinton's: Terrorism was an inevitable feature of global change.[34]

The White House aides felt Pillar did a solid job, although Clarke could be viciously critical of him in meetings. But they worried that CIA careerists like

Pillar did not feel a sense of urgency—and political vulnerability—about terrorism, as they did. It sometimes seemed to his White House colleagues that Pillar looked out on the terrorist threat from the CIA's wooded Langley campus in the weary way a veteran homicide detective might gaze out his office window at a darkened city, listening to the ambulance sirens wail in mournful repetition. The best way to attack the terrorists, Pillar argued, was through painstaking professional work, cell by cell, case by case, working closely with foreign intelligence and police services. This might not be glamorous or exciting, but it was effective, essential, pragmatic. "The U.S. hand can stay hidden, and the risk of terrorist reprisals is minimal" in this approach, Pillar argued. America should work the terrorist threat one interrogation room at a time, with foreign partners close at hand.[35]

The emphasis Clinton, Clarke, Simon, and Benjamin placed on the danger of terrorists acquiring weapons of mass destruction seemed overwrought to Pillar. It was a diversion, a kind of hysteria, he thought. It produced "often sensational public discussion of seemingly ever-expanding ways in which terrorists could use chemical, biological, radiological or nuclear terrorism to inflict mass casualties in the United States." The Clinton team seemed obsessed with the most unlikely scenarios. Clinton's personal interest had catalyzed these discussions and diverted resources from more sensible uses, Pillar wrote at the time, such as funding anemic CIA liaisons with foreign intelligence and police forces. The hype about weapons of mass destruction created "skewed priorities and misdirected resources." The White House would be better off spending more money and time on the basics of CIA-led intelligence collection and counterterrorist work.[36]

Also, those at the White House, Congress, and elsewhere who criticized the CIA for not being aggressive enough, for failing to station enough officers undercover overseas, just didn't understand the intelligence business. As Pillar put it sarcastically, "The image of the Ivy Leaguer who goes where it is dangerous to drink the water and, unencumbered by annoying instructions from headquarters, applies his brilliance and James Bond–like daring to the job of saving America from terrorism appeals to our imaginations but has little to do with the real business of intelligence and counterterrorism."[37]

Pillar worried that Osama bin Laden had become "a preoccupation" for the United States after the Africa embassy bombings. Capturing bin Laden had become "a grail" whose pursuit threatened to overshadow all else. "Certainly bin Laden is a significant foe," Pillar acknowledged, "whose call to kill Americans . . . is backed up by considerable ability to do just that." Religiously motivated terrorism such as that preached by bin Laden was on the rise, and this terrorism threatened greater casualties than past forms, Pillar acknowledged. Taking bin Laden out of action would be "a positive development," he believed, yet al Qaeda would likely survive, other leaders would emerge, and Sunni Islamist extremism in Afghanistan and across the Arab world would continue. Pillar worried that "fixating" on bin Laden personally only inflated the Saudi's global reputation and represented another "misallocation of attention and resources" by the Clinton White House. As Pillar summed it up: "Having counterterrorist managers and many of their officers concentrating on a single enemy may be an unaffordable luxury when the same people have to handle other current terrorist threats as well as staying ahead of the next bin Laden."[38]

It was this sort of commentary that fueled suspicions in Clinton's White House that the CIA was just not up to the job at hand. Clarke, Simon, and Benjamin had their "hair on fire" over their fear of bin Laden's next strike, they readily admitted to their colleagues. They endorsed much of Pillar's analysis and his painstaking cell-by-cell counterterrorism tactics, but it frustrated them that one of the CIA's most senior counterterrorism managers and thinkers did not, in their estimation, share their sense of urgency or alarm. After the Africa bombings Simon and Benjamin began to call attention to what they later called "a new, religiously motivated terrorism" whose most important feature was that it did not feel "constrained by the limits on violence that state sponsors have observed themselves or placed on their proxies." Where Pillar saw a permanent condition of chronic disease, Simon and Benjamin saw "unmistakable harbingers of a new and vastly more threatening terrorism, one that aims to produce casualties on a massive scale."[39]

Simon and Benjamin recast the terrorism analyst Brian Jenkins's 1970s-era observation that terrorists wanted a lot of people watching their attacks but not a lot of people dead. Osama bin Laden and his adherents, Simon and Benjamin warned, "want a lot of people watching *and* a lot of people dead."[40]

To an extent the major Cabinet departments involved in counterterrorism in the autumn of 1998 possessed institutional viewpoints on bin Laden. The White House, most sensitive to the political consequences of both terrorism and failed covert action, rang loud alarm bells about the threats but also proved cautious about operations that might go bad. The State Department emphasized diplomatic engagements and the value of enduring alliances with Saudi Arabia and Pakistan. The Justice Department promoted law enforcement approaches. Yet within each department there was debate among senior officials. Office mates in the South Asia bureau of the State Department disagreed vehemently about whether the Taliban would ever negotiate in good faith or whether Ahmed Shah Massoud deserved American aid. At the FBI some senior agents were alarmed and engaged by the al Qaeda threat, while others dismissed it as a distraction, one terrorism problem among many.

At the CIA, Pillar's articulate skepticism reflected in part the intellectual traditions of the Directorate of Intelligence. They would not be cowed by political fashion; they would take the long view. Spies and operators from the Directorate of Operations tended to have a more openly alarmist, aggressive view of the bin Laden threat. This was also true inside the bin Laden unit of the Counterterrorist Center, where analysts and operations officers became nearly obsessive about their mission after the Africa bombings. If anyone suffered from a "grail" complex about capturing bin Laden, it was Pillar's own colleagues in the CIA's bin Laden tracking group.

Increasingly George Tenet seemed to be with them, at least in spirit. The CIA director talked frequently with Berger and Clarke at the White House. He absorbed their anxieties, and he could read the threat reporting for himself; it was often scary stuff. Reading the cables every day, it did not take Pillar's Princeton Ph.D. to see that bin Laden could easily be the source of a sudden, terrible attack. Tenet would call Berger regularly and urge him to share particularly worrisome threat reports with President Clinton.[41]

Nor did Tenet share Pillar's wariness about the metaphor of waging "war" on bin Laden. In fact, Tenet's instinct was to think of the challenge in just those terms. As the weeks passed that autumn he worried that his colleagues were losing their momentum. On December 4, 1998, Tenet wrote a memo to his senior deputies at Langley headquarters.

"We must now enter a new phase in our efforts against bin Laden," Tenet declared. "Our work to date has been remarkable and in some instances heroic; yet each day we all acknowledge that retaliation is inevitable and that its scope may be far larger than we have previously experienced. . . .

"We are at war. I want no resources or people spared in this effort."[42]

It did not happen. Resources and people at the Counterterrorist Center remained tight. Tenet and other managers tried to shift budgets around to help the bin Laden unit but they did not have the money to fight anything more than a metaphorical war. Tenet was not prepared to tear down other bureaus of the CIA and pour every dollar into the campaign against al Qaeda. There were too many other active threats and important national priorities that demanded expensive intelligence collection, he believed. On paper, as Director of Central Intelligence, Tenet set priorities for all of the resources of the American intelligence community, including those at the behemoth Pentagon. In practical reality he could only control the CIA's relatively modest budget. In the classified bureaucratic system that tried to define priorities for all government intelligence collection, targets were ranked in tiers. Late in 1998 Tenet designated the bin Laden threat as "Tier 0," the very highest. Yet few elsewhere in the scattered and Balkanized intelligence bureaucracy took notice. The prioritization process was so broad and diffuse that it was worthless, some involved believed. The result was that an American government that spent hundreds of billions of dollars annually on defense and national security directed an infinitesimally tiny fraction of that money to disrupt and combat an enemy group identified by the CIA director as a mortal, even existential threat to the United States. Who, ultimately, was responsible? President Clinton had perhaps the greatest power to change these resource allocations; the Republican-controlled Congress was a close second. Tenet and other intelligence department heads had some discretionary power over the budgets they did possess. "In hindsight, I wish I had said, 'Let's take the whole enterprise down' and put five hundred more people there sooner," Tenet said later. But he did not. The practical result was that "we never had enough officers from the Directorate of Operations," recalled one former chief of the CIA's Counterterrorist Center. "The officers we had were greatly overworked. . . . We also received marginal analytic support from the Directorate of Intelligence." Tenet felt the CIA's budget needed an infusion of about $1 billion annually for at least five years, but when he advocated for these numbers at the White House and in classified hearings on Capitol Hill, he "never got to first base."[43]

To wage even a modest war it was usually necessary to fight with reliable allies. For nearly two decades the CIA had been running covert action in Afghanistan through its liaison with Pakistani intelligence. To disrupt bin Laden's embedded network in Afghanistan and capture al Qaeda's leaders, the agency would have to revive its partnership with Pakistan's ISI—or, if this failed, the CIA would soon have to find another intelligence service to work with in Afghanistan's rough neighborhood.

"Let's Just Blow
the Thing Up"

PAKISTANI PRIME MINISTER Nawaz Sharif lived in continual fear of his own army. Generals had invented the Sharifs as a political dynasty. They endorsed Nawaz as the civilian face of their favored alliance, a center-right artifice of industrialists, landlords, Muslim clerics, and freelance opportunists. Sharif was attentive to his self-interest if not always witting about how to secure it. He was presumed to be raking millions from Pakistan's treasury for his family's benefit. He also knew that any Pakistani politician, especially one handpicked by the army, risked overthrow if the generals felt threatened by the civilian's independence or popularity. Sharif sought to forestall this fate by manipulating appointments at the top of the army command. He stacked the senior ranks with generals he believed were loyal to him and his family. The two crucial jobs were the chief of army staff, traditionally the top military job in Pakistan, and the position of chief spy, the director-general of ISI.

Two months after the American cruise missile strikes in Afghanistan, Sharif fired his army chief. Jehangir Karamat was a secular thinker who supported civilian-led democracy. Yet Sharif interpreted speeches that Karamat had made about civil-military relations as portents of an army-led coup. Later it became clear that Sharif had badly misread the situation. Still, in typical style, the prime minister plunged ahead. He named Pervez Musharraf, a little-known general with a liberal reputation, to head the army. Although he had no intimate relationship with Musharraf, Sharif let it be known in the Pakistani press that Musharraf was his personally chosen general, his protégé. This was a public relations blunder that ensured Musharraf would distance himself from Sharif, at a minimum to preserve his credibility with other generals.[1]

At the same time Sharif appointed General Khwaja Ziauddin as the new chief of Pakistani intelligence. This, too, was an overtly political decision. Ziauddin had made his career in the engineering corps, a section of the military that rarely produced army leaders. But he had married into a wealthy, connected family in Lahore, and he was a frequent social visitor at the sprawling Model Town estate of Nawaz Sharif's influential father. It was a violation of army protocol for a rising general to allow himself to become visible socially, especially under the wing of a civilian political family like the Sharifs. Still, Sharif's father tapped Ziauddin as a favored brigadier, and he won an appointment to army headquarters, where he worked with the country's top-secret nuclear program. When Sharif sent him in the fall of 1998 to run ISI, Ziauddin was widely regarded as an emissary and protector of the prime minister.[2]

Sharif hoped to further defend himself from his army by drawing close to the Clinton administration. This was by now an old tactic of weak civilian prime ministers in Pakistan. Bill Clinton seemed to have a soft spot for Sharif. They had spent long hours on the telephone in the spring of 1998 when Clinton unsuccessfully sought to persuade the prime minister to forgo nuclear weapons tests in response to a surprise test by India. But many of Clinton's senior aides and diplomats, especially those who knew Pakistan well, regarded Sharif as an unusually dull, muddled politician. He seemed to offer a bovine, placid gaze in private meetings where he sometimes read awkwardly from note cards. Still, Sharif tried to make himself indispensable in continuing American-led talks over the region's nuclear crisis. Now there was suddenly another way for Sharif to make himself useful to the Americans: He could aid the secret effort to capture or kill Osama bin Laden.

The new U.S. ambassador to Pakistan was a lively career diplomat named William Milam, an ambassador previously in crisis-ridden Liberia and Bangladesh. A mustached, suspender-snapping man with a potbelly and an easy laugh, Milam was accustomed to security threats and unstable politics, and he got along well with his CIA station chief, Gary Schroen. The pair opened private talks about bin Laden and Afghanistan with Musharraf and Ziauddin.

The CIA hoped to persuade Ziauddin to betray bin Laden, to set him up for capture or ambush. The Islamabad station remained heavily invested in its tribal tracking force of former anti-Soviet mujahedin. Bin Laden was suddenly a much more difficult target, however. He moved frequently and unpredictably. After newspapers disclosed that the Americans had tapped his satellite telephone, bin Laden stopped using it, making it harder still to track him. Schroen and other CIA officers concluded that the best way to capture bin Laden was to enlist help from Pakistani intelligence officers who had his trust. They wanted ISI to lure him into a trap.[3]

Milam, Schroen, and their colleagues in the Islamabad embassy found Ziauddin a straightforward, accessible character. The new Pakistani intelligence chief was a stocky man, about five feet nine inches tall, and his face looked as if it had been boxed around in a few fights. He was not shy, as some generals were, about talking openly with the CIA about Pakistani politics. He also acknowledged that neither he nor Sharif could work their will down the ranks by just snapping their fingers. He wanted to cooperate closely with the CIA and the Americans where he could, Ziauddin said, but the CIA would have to understand what was politically feasible in Pakistan.[4]

By the fall of 1998, CIA and other American intelligence reporting had documented many links between ISI, the Taliban, bin Laden, and other Islamist militants operating from Afghanistan. Classified American reporting showed that Pakistani intelligence maintained about eight stations inside Afghanistan, staffed by active ISI officers or retired officers on contract. CIA reporting showed that Pakistani intelligence officers at about the colonel level met with bin Laden or his representatives to coordinate access to training camps for volunteer fighters headed for Kashmir. The CIA suspected that Pakistani intelligence might provide funds or equipment to bin Laden as part of the operating agreements at these camps. There was no evidence that ISI officers worked with bin Laden on his overseas terrorist strikes, such as the embassy bombings in Africa. The reported liaison involved Pakistan's regional agenda: bleeding Indian forces in Kashmir and helping the Taliban defeat Massoud's Northern Alliance.[5]

American intelligence analysts assumed that it was very difficult for ISI headquarters in Rawalpindi to control officers who worked inside Afghanistan. There seemed little reason to hope that Nawaz Sharif, nervous as a cat around anyone in his military, could easily issue orders to undercover colonels in Afghanistan. Nor was Ziauddin, with no background in intelligence and a reputation as Sharif's lackey, likely to exercise uncontested control.

Senior Clinton administration officials who consumed this classified reporting about Pakistan intelligence officers in Afghanistan "assumed," as one of them put it later, "that those ISI individuals were perhaps profiteering, engaged in the drug running, the arms running." Not only was Ziauddin probably unable to control them, but "headquarters, to some extent, probably didn't know what they were doing." At the same time these Pakistani intelligence officers clearly *were* following orders from Islamabad in a broad sense. In their use of jihad to extend Pakistan's influence east and west, they had full backing from their country's army and from sectors of the civilian political class. "The policy of the government, never declared, particularly in Kashmir, was to foster guerrilla warfare," recalled one American official who regularly read the CIA's reporting that autumn. Ziauddin and his senior colleagues, as well as their colonels on the ground, "thought they were carrying out the overall policy of their government." At the White House, Clinton's senior foreign policy team saw "an incredibly unholy alliance that was not only supporting all the terrorism that would be directed against us" but also threatened "to provoke a nuclear war in Kashmir."[6]

Still, it was possible that Ziauddin would cooperate on bin Laden, CIA officers believed. Perhaps he or his men would help sell bin Laden out for money. Perhaps they could be persuaded of the political benefits to Pakistan. If bin Laden were removed as an impediment, the United States might eventually recognize the Taliban as Afghanistan's rightful government. That, in turn, would crown a decade of covert Pakistani policy in the region and put India on the defensive. Although they were careful not to put it so bluntly, the Americans told Sharif's generals that the army could better achieve its regional military aims if it betrayed bin Laden than if it stuck with him.[7]

Schroen's main operations proposal was simple. Pakistani intelligence would schedule a meeting with bin Laden at Kandahar's airport. ISI officers would tell bin Laden that they had a message for his eyes only. The CIA would then put its tribal agents into position on the long, open desert road to the airport. There was only one way in and out, and it would be relatively easy to set up the ambush. A senior ISI officer might fly into Kandahar for the supposed meeting. When bin Laden failed to turn up, the Pakistani officer could just shrug his shoulders and fly back to Islamabad.

Ziauddin took in the CIA's proposal with apparent interest. He said that he would consult with Sharif and others in Pakistani intelligence to see if the trap could be arranged. Days later he reported back: Impossible. The politics were just too hot, he told the Americans. If the ambush failed and the plan was exposed, Pakistan would pay too high a price with the Taliban, with Islamist politicians and army officers in Pakistan.[8]

If Pakistani intelligence was going to cooperate with the CIA to capture bin Laden, they would have to come up with a different approach. Ziauddin had his own ideas about that.

NAWAZ SHARIF FLEW to Washington in early December 1998 to meet with President Clinton. Ziauddin came along as an undeclared senior member of the Pakistani delegation. The trip had been designed in part to boost Sharif's political standing at home by showing that he was close to Clinton and could obtain benefits for Pakistan from his friendship. Clinton had agreed to waive certain trade sanctions and to announce the release of about $500 million in Pakistani funds frozen by the United States in 1991 because of the nuclear issue.[9]

Clinton, Albright, and Berger met with Sharif, Ziauddin, and other Pakistani officials in the Oval Office for a scripted meeting at 1:30 P.M. on Wednesday, December 2, 1998. Clinton made clear that the issue he cared most about was Pakistan's nuclear weapons program. The president's college friend Strobe Talbott, now deputy secretary of state, ran the ongoing talks with Pakistan and India, trying to persuade them to freeze or dismantle their bomb programs. In the Oval Office that afternoon, as the Americans read out their formal talking points, "the number one issue on our agenda," as National Security Council staffer Bruce Riedel put it, was Pakistan's nuclear program. Second on the list was Pakistan's economy. Clinton hoped that free trade would help lift Pakistan out of poverty and debt, easing its chronic political and social crises. Third came terrorism and bin Laden.[10]

Clinton repeatedly signaled to Pakistan's highest leadership that bin Laden was a lesser priority than nuclear proliferation. Pakistan's army saw its confrontation with India as a matter of national life or death. Compromise on either the nuclear issue or the use of jihadist guerrillas to tie down India's large army would mark a sharp change in Pakistani strategy. With the stakes so high, "anything second on your list" was not likely to get the generals' attention, as a White House official recalled. American officials ranking in the second tier sometimes met with Pakistani counterparts to talk forcefully—and solely—about bin Laden. But when Clinton himself met with Pakistani leaders, his agenda list always had several items, and bin Laden never was at the top. Afghanistan's war fell even lower down.

The group meeting lasted that afternoon for thirty minutes. By prior arrangement, Sharif asked for time alone with Clinton. They met one-on-one for twenty minutes in the Oval Office.[11] It was here, participants in the group meetings were told afterward, that Sharif first raised a proposal that Pakistani intelligence might, with CIA assistance, train a secret commando team for the purpose of capturing Osama bin Laden and "bringing him to justice," as the American side put it.

The Pakistanis had not been told about the CIA's Afghan tracking team. They were proposing a larger, more formal commando unit drawn from recently retired members of the Special Services Group, Pakistan's elite special forces unit. As enlisted men, sergeants, and a few officers retired from the SSG, they could be placed on contract and sent directly to the new bin Laden strike force. Their skills and training would be fresh.[12]

Clinton made clear that he expected his aides to follow up on the offer, to put the plan into motion. "We tried to get the Pakistanis involved in this, realizing that it was a difficult thing for them," Clinton said later. "They had both the greatest opportunity, but the greatest political risk in getting him," Clinton believed.[13]

They discussed bin Laden again over lunch. Sharif joked that the Americans had wasted their money by launching so many expensive cruise missiles at the Saudi fugitive. They should just have sent a few men into Afghanistan with briefcases full of dollars, and they would have gotten the job done, Sharif said.

The Pakistanis offered an intelligence report: Bin Laden, they said, appeared to be seriously ill. Their information was that bin Laden suffered from kidney disease and that his illness might explain why he had recently disappeared from public view.[14] That day and afterward the Americans were never sure what to make of these reports and similar ones relayed by Saudi intelligence about bin Laden's supposed poor health. A few thought the reports might be plausible. Others dismissed them as deliberate misdirection.

Across the lunch table the two sides exchanged their familiar stalemated opinions about the Taliban and Afghanistan. Albright said the United States had very serious problems with the Taliban, including their treatment of women and children. Sharif repeated his usual formulation: Pakistan itself was a victim of Afghanistan's unfinished war, especially its spillover effects, such as refugees and drug trafficking. Pakistan, too, was a victim of terrorism, he said.

Berger and Albright both told Sharif that "of primary importance" to the U.S. government "is the expulsion of Osama bin Laden from Afghanistan so that he can be brought to justice."[15]

Sharif rounded out his American visit with a few speeches and flew home.

Later, many of the Americans involved said they were deeply cynical about Pakistan's proposal for joint covert action. They thought Sharif was just trying to cook up something that would distract the Americans and shut them up about bin Laden. They did not believe, they said later, that Pakistani intelligence would ever take the risk of ordering the commando team into action.

If Pakistani intelligence wanted to help the CIA capture bin Laden, they did not need an expensive commando team to get it done, many of the Americans involved believed. They could just tell the CIA reliably where bin Laden was, and the United States would strike either with cruise missiles or with a kidnap operation mounted by its Afghan agents. The Americans repeatedly asked ISI for this sort of intelligence on bin Laden, and they were repeatedly rebuffed. Pakistani intelligence officers sometimes complained to the CIA in private that bin Laden now distrusted them. As a result, the Pakistanis said, they did not have the ability to track bin Laden's movements or predict his whereabouts effectively. The Americans doubted this. Even if bin Laden was now more wary of ISI than in the past, Pakistani intelligence had so many allies in the Afghan-rooted Islamist networks that it could easily set up bin Laden if its officers had the will to do so, they believed.[16]

Pakistan's army and political class had calculated that the benefits they reaped from supporting Afghan-based jihadist guerrillas—including those trained and funded by bin Laden—outstripped the costs, some of Clinton's aides concluded. As one White House official put it bluntly, "Since just telling us to fuck off seemed to do the trick," why should the Pakistanis change their strategy?[17]

Sandy Berger, his deputy Jim Steinberg, Richard Clarke, and George Tenet discussed their options. The consensus among them was that the Pakistanis "had neither the ability nor the inclination" to carry the commando plan through, as one official put it. On the other hand, what was the downside? The CIA would be out a few hundred thousand dollars on salaries for some retired Pakistani soldiers plus the costs of training and equipment—small change. The commando project could provide a vehicle for deepening contacts and trust among CIA officers, Ziauddin, and other officers in Pakistani intelligence. This could be useful for intelligence collection and, potentially, unilateral recruitments by the CIA. And even if the chances that the com-

mando team would be deployed against bin Laden were very small—less than
1 percent, the most cynical of the Americans estimated—they had to try
every conceivable path.[18]

The White House approved the plan some months later. Through the Islamabad station, the CIA paid salaries and supplied communications and
other gear, as directed by Ziauddin. As it turned out, even the most cynical
Americans were perhaps not cynical enough about Ziauddin's motivations.
On paper the CIA-funded secret commando team was being trained for action against bin Laden in Afghanistan. But Ziauddin later demonstrated that
he saw another role for the unit: as a small, elite strike force loyal to Pakistan's
prime minister and his intelligence chief. If the army ever moved against
Sharif, the prime minister would have a secret bodyguard that might be called
in to help defend him.

Nor did ISI change its conduct on the Afghan frontier. Just weeks after the
Oval Office meeting, white Land Cruisers pulled up at the darkened Peshawar
compound of Abdul Haq, the anti-Soviet Afghan commander and estranged
former CIA client. Now a businessman in Dubai, Haq had begun to organize
anti-Taliban opposition among prominent Pashtun tribal families such as his
own. Pakistani intelligence had warned him to stop making trouble, but Haq
had persisted. Ever since his first meeting with CIA station chief Howard
Hart, he had seen himself as an independent leader, disdainful of the manipulations of ISI.[19]

That night, January 12, 1999, mysterious assailants smothered Haq's bodyguards, entered his home, and murdered his wife and children. Haq's aides
investigated the case and concluded that the attack had been organized with
help from Pakistani intelligence. Pakistani police made no arrests. The former
American ambassador to the mujahedin, Peter Tomsen, who remained close
to Haq, later reported that the killers had been trained at the Taliban intelligence school supported by bin Laden at Tarnak Farm.[20]

This was the war as many Afghans who challenged the Taliban knew it. It
was not a war in which ISI cooperation against bin Laden seemed remotely
plausible. By contrast, as far as these Afghans could tell, those who openly defied bin Laden or Pakistani intelligence risked everything they had.

WITHIN WEEKS of Sharif's visit to Washington, the CIA station in Islamabad received its most promising report on bin Laden's whereabouts since the
August cruise missile strikes. In early February 1999 agents in Afghanistan

reported that bin Laden had traveled to Helmand Province in southern Afghanistan to join an encamped desert hunting party organized by wealthy Bedouin sheikhs from the Persian Gulf.[21]

The CIA sent its tracking team on the road, equipped with sighting equipment, satellite beacons to determine GPS coordinates, secure communications, and other spy gear. They raced out on the nomad highways that snaked through the barren desert. By February 9 the team reported to the Islamabad station: They had found the hunting camp. It was an elaborately provisioned place far from any city but near an isolated airstrip big enough to handle C-130 cargo planes. The camp's tents billowed in the wind, cooled by generators and stocked with refrigerators. The tracking team reported that they strongly believed they had found bin Laden. He was a guest of the camp's Arab sheikhs, they reported, and it looked as if he would be staying for a while. There would be plenty of time to bomb the camp with precision weapons or to launch cruise missiles from ships or submarines in the Arabian Sea.

Bin Laden had grown up in Bedouin tradition. Falcon hunting, especially for the elusive houbara bustard, had been a passionate and romanticized sport in Saudi Arabia and neighboring kingdoms for generations. Each year Arab sheikhs with the money to do so chased the houbara across its winter migration route. Pakistan granted special permits to the visiting Arab sheikhs, dividing its northern hills and southwestern deserts into carefully marked zones where rival royals pitched their tents and sent their falcons aloft.[22]

One of the most passionate hunters was Sheikh Khalifa bin Zayed al-Nahayan, the billionaire crown prince of Abu Dhabi in the United Arab Emirates. Equally devoted was Sheikh Maktoum, the leader of Dubai, another emirate in the oil-rich confederation. Scores of other fabulously rich U.A.E. notables flew to Pakistan each season to hunt. So entrenched did the alliance with Pakistan around houbara hunts become that the Pakistani air force agreed secretly to lease one of its northern air bases to the United Arab Emirates so that the sheikhs could more conveniently stage the aircraft and supplies required for their hunts. Pakistani personnel maintained the air base, but the U.A.E. paid for its upkeep. They flew in and out on C-130s and on smaller planes that could reach remote hunting grounds.[23]

Some of the best winter houbara grounds were in Afghanistan. Pakistani politicians had hosted Arab hunting trips there since the mid-1990s. They had introduced wealthy sheikhs to the leadership of the Taliban, creating connections for future private finance of the Islamist militia. Bin Laden circulated in this Afghan hunting world after he arrived in the country in 1996.[24] So the

CIA report that he had joined a large, stationary camp in western Afghanistan that winter seemed consistent with previous reporting about bin Laden.

The CIA's tracking team marked the hunting camp with beacons and obtained its GPS coordinates. They began to watch on the ground from a safe distance. At Langley the Counterterrorist Center immediately ordered satellite coverage. Photographs of the billowing tents unspooled daily in the secure communications vault in the Islamabad embassy. The pictures confirmed what the agents had reported from the ground. Working closely with the Counterterrorist Center, the Islamabad station reported: "It's still a viable target."[25]

Richard Clarke, Sandy Berger, and a few White House aides with the highest security clearances reviewed the satellite pictures and the reporting from the TRODPINT tracking team. Along with senior managers at the CIA, they began to fire questions back to the Islamabad station: Which tent is he in? What time of day is he in the tent? Where does he go to pray? Bin Laden was reported to visit frequently a camp next to the main hunting camp. The CIA radioed the tracking team that was hovering near the camp, asking for answers. One person involved remembered that the CIA actually identified the specific tent where they believed bin Laden was sleeping. Still, Clarke worried that the sightings by the Afghan tracking team might not be reliable; they were roaming far from their home territory. Clarke told Deputy National Security Adviser Donald Kerrick on February 10 that the Pentagon might be able to launch cruise missiles the next morning, but that other options, possibly involving a Special Forces raid, would take longer.

The questions kept pouring into the Islamabad station. Langley and the White House wanted more precision. Days passed. Some of the CIA officers involved thought the evidence was very solid, good enough to shoot. As the questions seeking more targeting detail poured across their computer screens, Islamabad station chief Gary Schroen and his case officer colleagues began to ask sarcastically: "What is it going to come down to—when is he going to take a leak?"[26]

The feeling of some of the officers involved was, as Schroen put it, "Let's just blow the thing up. And if we kill bin Laden, and five sheikhs are killed, I'm sorry. What are they doing with bin Laden? He's a terrorist. You lie down with the dog, you get up with fleas."[27]

Support for a missile or bombing strike was especially passionate inside the bin Laden unit at the Counterterrorist Center in Langley. This was their life. They felt bin Laden had the United States in his sights. They came in every morning to new in-trays full of threat reports. They had been down this road of near misses too many times before. They wanted to shoot.

Years later, recollections differed about exactly when and how it first became apparent that the hunting camp had been organized by royalty from the United Arab Emirates. Several officials remembered that the satellite photography showed a C-130 on the ground near the camp and that the plane was painted in a camouflage pattern used by the U.A.E. air force. One participant recalled that the satellite photos also captured a tail number on the C-130 that was eventually traced to the U.A.E. government.

Richard Clarke knew the U.A.E. royal family very well. He had worked for years with the U.A.E.'s intelligence service as well as its royal family and military. He negotiated arms deals and basing agreements, and he exchanged occasional tips and favors with the U.A.E. security services. He had just returned from the country, where he had held talks on terrorism and arms purchases. The likelihood that U.A.E. royalty were on the ground raised the stakes mightily. The emirates were crucial suppliers of oil and gas to America and its allies. They cooperated with the American military on basing agreements. The port of Dubai received more port calls by the U.S. Navy than any port in the region; it was the only place in the Persian Gulf that could comfortably dock American aircraft carriers. The U.A.E. royal family had also been targeted by the Clinton administration's "buy American" campaign to win overseas contracts for weapons manufacturers and other corporations. And Sheikh Zayed had come through in a very big way: In May 1998, in a deal partially smoothed by Clarke, the U.A.E. had agreed to an $8 billion multiyear contract to buy 80 F-16 military jets. The contract would enrich American defense companies. The planes were to be manufactured in Texas, creating good jobs in a politically crucial state.[28] If the United States bombed the camp and killed a few princes, it could put all that in jeopardy—even if bin Laden were killed at the same time. Hardly anyone in the Persian Gulf saw bin Laden as a threat serious enough to warrant the deaths of their own royalty. They would react to such a strike angrily, with unknown consequences for the United States. And if it turned out that bin Laden was not in the hunting camp after all, the anti-American reaction would make the controversy over the cruise missile strike on the al Shifa plant in Sudan the previous summer seem mild by comparison.

All this was discussed at the White House just two days before President Clinton faced a final vote on impeachment charges in the U.S. Senate. It seemed clear that Clinton would win the trial and finish out his term, but his power had fallen to its nadir. This hardly seemed an ideal time for an all-or-nothing attack against a terrorist who made few Americans feel directly menaced.

Some of the CIA officers involved could not understand the White House's hesitation. The CIA's reporting—human agents, the tracking team outside the camp, the satellite photography, signals intelligence—left some officers involved with an unusually high feeling of certainty that bin Laden was really there. It was rare to see bin Laden sit still in one place for so long. Some in the U.S. embassy in Islamabad speculated that perhaps the recent Pakistani report about bin Laden's illness was truthful and bin Laden had traveled to the luxurious camp to recuperate.[29]

Neither the Islamabad station nor the Counterterrorist Center at Langley could offer a 100 percent guarantee that bin Laden was in the hunting camp, however. They did not have a picture of bin Laden standing outside his tent. The satellites could not take a photograph of that quality, and the tracking team could not get close enough. If they launched a strike, they would have to accept some doubt. George Tenet, for one, was not convinced that the reporting was completely solid.

The U.S. military relied heavily on its alliances with the wealthy Persian Gulf emirates despite their occasional support for Islamists. To even consider a strike against bin Laden they needed to be completely sure, some of those involved argued. In the American military, recalled Gary Schroen, "Nobody wanted to say, 'Well, you blew up a camp full of U.A.E. princes and half of the royal family of the U.A.E.'s dead—and you guys didn't get him.'"[30]

Clinton's national security cabinet had been tracking the camp for more than a week. They had learned what they could; they had to decide. Richard Clarke recommended against a cruise missile shot. George Tenet, too, recommended no. By February 12, the day of Clinton's acquittal on impeachment charges, bin Laden reportedly had left the camp.

Afterward, the U.S. embassy in Abu Dhabi, capital of the U.A.E., contacted Sheikh Zayed's government and asked for precise coordinates of the family's Afghan hunting camp. The aviation maps and other data supplied through the U.A.E. foreign ministry confirmed that it had been the royal family's camp. The U.A.E. later reported to the White House that no members of the royal family had been present at the hunt and that as far as they could determine, bin Laden had not been there, either. The Americans later concluded that high-level U.A.E. officials had, in fact, been at the camp, which was quickly torn down in March, after Clarke called U.A.E. officials. The call angered some CIA officers who had hoped to watch the camp quietly, hoping bin Laden would return. The U.S. embassy in Abu Dhabi began pressuring the royal family to cease its hunting trips altogether. The Americans argued that the trips violated United Nations sanctions meant to isolate the Taliban. Based on United Nations and other reporting, the Americans also suspected that the C-130s flying out of Dubai carried weapons to the Taliban. The U.A.E. government was one of three in the world that recognized the Taliban, yet its officials told the Americans that they "wanted to cooperate and wanted to know what they could do to help," recalled a State Department officer involved in relaying the map data about the Afghan hunting camps.

For its part the U.A.E. was anxious to make sure the data it handed over were properly entered into American targeting computers. The royal family "had its own concern, in the aftermath of al Shifa, about making sure their camps were properly understood," the State official recalled.[31]

For some of the ground-level officers involved in the bin Laden chase the decision to hold fire seemed almost unforgivable. It had been one thing before the Africa embassy bombings to have their plan to raid Tarnak Farm and kidnap bin Laden turned down. That plan contained a great deal of risk and uncertainty. But with the desert camp, recalled Schroen, reflecting the views of other officers as well, "We knew he was there. We had assets in place. There was little risk to life and limb to anybody—not our Afghan colleagues, nobody on the American side. And it would have been, we thought, definitive. We could take him out. Yeah, some of these other people would be killed, but we would really be able to take him out." Some of them blamed Clarke, speculating that he was so close to the U.A.E. royal family because of defense deals he had previously negotiated that he would never take the risk of offending them.[32]

The cycle of frustration repeated itself that May. A CIA source reported with unusual specificity about bin Laden's movements and sleeping patterns over five nights in Kandahar. A cruise missile attack was again prepared; the national security cabinet again discussed whether they had enough intelligence to fire, and whether the risk of civilian deaths was too great. As the White House hesitated, Mike Scheuer, the discouraged chief of the Counterterrorist Center's bin Laden unit, wrote to a colleague in the field that "having a chance to get UBL three times in 36 hours and foregoing the chance each time has made me a bit angry . . . the DCI finds himself alone at the table, with the other princip[als] basically saying 'we'll go along with your decision Mr. Director,' and implicitly saying that the Agency will hang alone if the attack doesn't get bin Laden." For his part, even when he "knew more or less" where bin Laden might spend the night, Clinton remembered how he had been told that bin Laden would attend a leadership meeting in eastern Afghanistan just after the Africa embassy bombings, and yet, "he left a couple of hours before" the missiles struck. As new single-threaded reports of bin Laden's whereabouts arrived, Clinton remembered, "So what did I have? A 40 percent chance of knowing we could have hit it."

Around this time Scheuer fired off more emails protesting the agency's heavy reliance on its liaison with untrustworthy allies in the Persian Gulf. The bin Laden unit leader personified the single-minded passion that prevailed inside the Counterterrorist Center's partitioned office suite. He was a disheveled, blunt, undiplomatic career officer who felt the United States ought to kill Osama bin Laden as a matter of the greatest urgency. The White House sometimes complained to Tenet that Scheuer was not well suited to manage the bin Laden group; he was too myopic in his approach. The email exchanges Scheuer generated after the hunting camp incident were angry, unusual, and widely circulated, according to one person who read them. During his three years in the bin Laden unit, Scheuer said later, he believed the CIA's Directorate of Operations "was the only component of the Intelligence Community that could be said to have been waging the war that bin Laden declared against the United States in August of 1996. The rest of the CIA and the Intelligence Community looked on our efforts as eccentric and, at times, fanatic." Afterward Scheuer transferred to another position at Langley headquarters. In the heavily compartmented CIA, where by careful design officers knew little about one another's work, his colleagues could not be sure exactly what had happened, but among at least a few of them a belief settled in that Scheuer had been exiled, in effect, for becoming too passionate about the bin Laden threat, too angry about the failure to attack at Tarnak Farm and at the desert hunting camp.[33]

Tenet did not widely explain his reasoning. He made clear years later that in every case where Clinton's Cabinet discussed cruise missile strikes, a decisive problem was the lack of absolute certainty that bin Laden was present. Tenet concluded that the CIA's strategy against bin Laden had to be reexamined. Early in 1999, Tenet ordered the Counterterrorist Center to begin a "baseline" review of the CIA's operational strategy against bin Laden. He wanted the entire operation turned upside down, looked at from fresh angles. From the White House, Clarke lobbied Tenet for change, arguing that neither Scheuer at the bin Laden unit nor senior managers such as Paul Pillar were the right leaders for a campaign against bin Laden.[34]

Within months Tenet had dispatched a fast-track executive assistant from

the seventh floor—a traditional breeding ground of CIA leadership—to replace Scheuer in the bin Laden unit. When the Counterterrorist Center's director, Jeff O'Connell, rotated out of his position (he soon became the CIA
station chief in Tel Aviv), Tenet had another opportunity to shake things up.
Who would know better how to get after Osama bin Laden—or be better
motivated to break the stalemate—than a CIA officer bin Laden had once
tried to kill?

25

"The Manson Family"

BY EARLY 1999, George Tenet believed that bin Laden could strike the United States again at any time. There was "not the slightest doubt" that bin Laden was planning new attacks, Tenet said. The CIA director issued this warning in public and in private. He saw evidence that bin Laden had contacts inside the United States. Tenet anticipated "bombing attempts with conventional explosives," he told Congress and the White House. Bin Laden's operatives were also "capable of kidnappings and assassinations." He worried that al Qaeda might acquire and use weapons of mass destruction. Tenet believed a chemical or biological attack by bin Laden or his allies was now a "serious prospect."[1]

Tenet grew frustrated by the on-and-off attention paid to the al Qaeda threat within Clinton's Cabinet. He spent weekends watching his son play soccer in the suburbs, and he complained to his CIA colleagues that the administration's bin Laden policy sometimes seemed "like two-year-olds playing soccer—they all go to the ball," then their interest would wane, and they would run to the other side of the field to chase something else.[2]

Yet for all his stark warnings, the CIA director did not describe bin Laden in 1999 as the gravest, most important threat faced by the United States. Like the president he served, Tenet worried most about the global spread of nuclear, chemical, and biological weapons and of the missiles that could deliver them to the American homeland. When he inventoried the threats faced by the United States, Tenet listed bin Laden second, after the proliferation of unconventional weapons. In a ninety-seven-paragraph unclassified statement he issued that winter about rising dangers in an unstable world, Tenet devoted four paragraphs to bin Laden. Also, the CIA director placed virtually no emphasis on Afghanistan as a cause or context of bin Laden's menace. Tenet never said publicly that bin Laden and al Qaeda were a powerful faction in Afghanistan's civil war, that they thrived on their links to Pakistani intelligence, or that they took succor from Saudi and Persian Gulf sheikhs and proselytizers. In the statement he issued that winter, for instance, Tenet only mentioned the Taliban in passing as a potential source of inspiration for Islamist extremists in Pakistan. He did not describe the Taliban as a threat to the United States or to stability in Central and South Asia, or as bin Laden's most important military allies.[3]

Years later Tenet rued that among the "daunting impediments" facing the CIA's campaign against al Qaeda during 1999 was that "U.S. policy stopped short of replacing the Taliban regime, limiting the ability of the U.S. government to exert pressure on bin Laden." But if Tenet felt frustrated by that policy at the time or conceived alternatives to it, he did not say so in public and did not press his views within the Cabinet.[4]

Tenet had matured at Langley and had succeeded in a job that had thwarted more experienced predecessors. By early 1999 he had proved himself an exceptional manager and leader of people, and he had won Clinton's personal confidence. Yet he remained to some extent the staff director he had been on Capitol Hill, a synthesizer and manager of other people's views. A profoundly visceral person, Tenet felt the bin Laden threat in his gut and responded actively with warnings and exhortations to his covert action team at the Counterterrorist Center. But Tenet seemed to accept the bin Laden problem on its received terms, as a traditional antiterrorism or policing issue best addressed by a lightning covert capture operation or a decapitating missile strike. As Tenet noted later, to confront bin Laden and the Taliban more broadly would have required a new foreign policy.

More than a decade earlier the passionate anticommunist William Casey had helped create and drive his president's global policies from Langley. That was not George Tenet's vision of himself or of the CIA.

In shuffling his lineup at the Counterterrorist Center that spring of 1999, Tenet demanded "a new, comprehensive operational plan of attack" against bin Laden and his allies. The plan's purpose would be "to capture and bring to justice bin Laden and his principal lieutenants." For this the CIA needed better intelligence about bin Laden's movements. Tenet wanted more human sources in Afghanistan, deeper liaison with regional intelligence services, and more effective technical collection, including communications intercepts and satellite photography.[5]

The sense in Tenet's seventh-floor suite—as well as in the counterterrorism office at the White House—was that the CIA's Counterterrorist Center had grown too dependent on the gang of tribal agents in southern Afghanistan. One of Tenet's aides referred to them derisively as "weekend warriors," middle-aged and now prosperous Afghan fighters with a few Kalishnikovs in their closets. The tribal agents were being asked to take on vicious, religiously motivated bin Laden bodyguards who would fight to the death; it was small wonder that the team was reluctant to attack. Their reporting about bin Laden's movements was very good although often a day or two behind. The agents communicated reliably. As in the episode at the desert hunting camp, they were willing to take risks as a tracking team, spying on bin Laden from a distance. But it was too much to expect them to act as a decisive paramilitary force against al Qaeda's hardened Arab killers, especially since the White House's rules of engagement cautioned them against indiscriminate attacks.[6]

Tenet's push for a new bin Laden plan emphasized operations: agent recruitment, risky insertion of technical collection equipment, paramilitary covert action. But the bin Laden tracking unit at the Counterterrorist Center was heavily staffed by analysts from the Directorate of Intelligence, not spies from the Directorate of Operations. That spring, 70 percent of the unit's professionals were women, and two-thirds had backgrounds as analysts. They could call on spies in the CIA's far-flung stations, but their own operating experience was limited. They were highly educated, worked unusually long hours, and had become fanatically motivated about the bin Laden threat. They studied bin Laden's *fatwas,* drew up elaborate charts of his international networks, scrutinized interrogation reports, and monitored the most obscure nuances in theological debates among Sunni Islamist extremists. They were a relatively junior group, with an average of three years' experience, as compared to the average of eight years in the mainline Directorate of Intelligence. They struggled at times to persuade case officers in the Directorate of Operations to work on their requests. CIA field officers abroad did not like to "take direction from the ladies" working back at Langley, one Counterterrorist Center manager recalled.[7]

The bin Laden unit's analysts were so intense about their work that they made some of their CIA colleagues uncomfortable. The unit had about twenty-five professionals in the summer of 1999. They called themselves "the Manson Family" because they had acquired a reputation for crazed alarmism about the rising al Qaeda threat. "Jonestown," said one person involved, asked to sum up the unit's atmosphere. "I outlawed Kool-Aid." Some of their colleagues thought they had lost their perspective. "It was a cult," recalled a second American official. "There was frustration: Why didn't everybody else share their view on things?"[8]

Tenet valued the bin Laden unit's intensity, but he needed a breakthrough. "We have seen numerous reports that bin Laden and his associates are planning terrorist attacks against U.S. officials and facilities in a variety of locations, including in the U.S.," he told a closed Senate hearing on June 24. That spring the director appointed one of his deputy's key executive assistants, known to his colleagues as Rich, to take charge of the bin Laden unit. The new chief had worked as a case officer in Algeria during the early 1990s, in the midst of a gruesome uprising waged by violent Islamist radicals, some of them veterans of Afghanistan. He knew the bin Laden issue, he knew the Third World, and he did not mind high-risk travel. Like his new colleagues Rich was intense and sometimes emotional and combative. Since he came directly from Tenet's leadership group, his arrival was seen as a signal of renewed high-level interest in the bin Laden case. The new chief's connections presumably would help attract resources to the cause and smooth decision-making.

Tenet quickly followed this appointment with another: He named Cofer Black as director of the entire Counterterrorist Center. It had been just four years earlier that Black had left Khartoum, Sudan. As station chief there he had supervised intensive undercover intelligence collection operations against bin Laden, chasing the Saudi and his men around in jeeps and cars. Black had disrupted rehearsals by bin Laden's lieutenants to ambush and kill him on a road near the U.S. embassy. He took the bin Laden case personally.

"This is bad business," Tenet told Black, as an official involved in the transition recalled. "These guys are getting stronger and stronger. We're going to get struck. We've got to engage this target. We've got to get more penetrations. We've got to go out after these guys."[9]

Black's bluff speech, vaguely British inflections, and love of warrior metaphors created a new table-thumping martial air at the Counterterrorist Center.

He and the new bin Laden unit chief knew each other well from their years in the Directorate of Operations. They wanted to shake up the unit's strategy.

Cofer Black was not a natural partner for Paul Pillar, the intellectual terrorism analyst who was the Counterterrorist Center's long-serving deputy director. Pillar's emphasis on managing permanent terrorist threats, and his skepticism about how the Clinton administration had personalized its campaign against bin Laden, stood in some contrast to Black's gung-ho ambitions. After years of exhausting, nerve-racking service, Pillar soon left the center for a fellowship at a Washington think tank.

Black and his new bin Laden unit wanted to "project" into Afghanistan, to "penetrate" bin Laden's Afghan sanctuaries. They described their plan as military officers might. They sought to surround Afghanistan with secure covert bases for CIA operations—as many bases as they could arrange. Then they would mount operations from each of these platforms, trying to move inside Afghanistan and as close to bin Laden as they could get to recruit agents and to attempt capture operations.

Sometimes they would work with regional intelligence services, Black announced. Other times they would work on their own. They would not try to pick and choose their partners fastidiously. Black declared that he wanted to develop liaison operations especially aimed at agent recruitment with every intelligence service in the Middle East and South Asia that might possibly offer a way to get at bin Laden and his lieutenants.

"Eight to eighty, blind, crippled or crazy, we don't care what you are, we want to be in contact," Black told his colleagues. "We are at war," declared a document presented to a closed Counterterrorist Center meeting on September 10. They had to continue to sow doubt in bin Laden's mind about the "security of his operations." And Black did not want to sit around in restaurants and exchange written reports, the traditional emphasis of intelligence liaison. He wanted recruitments, and he wanted to develop commando or paramilitary strike teams made up of officers and men who could "blend" into the region's Muslim populations.[10]

Even with Tenet's support they struggled for resources. In the same weeks that he began to talk at the White House, FBI, and Pentagon about what he called "The Plan" for revived global operations against bin Laden, Black was forced to implement a 30 percent cut in cash operating budgets at the Counterterrorist Center—including in the bin Laden unit. The CIA had started to reverse its decline in personnel, but by the end of 1999 it still had 25 percent fewer operations officers than it had fielded when the decade began. The annual cash crunch at the Counterterrorist Center could often be partly offset by budgetary scavenging at the end of a fiscal year, but these were distracting and uncertain efforts. As he developed briefing slides for Tenet and the White House that summer, Black boasted that "The Plan" was comprehensive, global, and newly ambitious. But his colorful slides masked a threadbare checking account. A study commissioned by Black and presented to a CIA conference on September 16, 1999, concluded that the Counterterrorist Center could not carry out its more ambitious plans against al Qaeda without more money and people.[11]

Worse, the geopolitical map that Black and the new bin Laden unit chief pored over did not look promising. Taliban-ruled Afghanistan was a "denied area" in CIA parlance, with no secure bases for permanent operations. Pakistan seemed a highly unreliable partner, Black and the new bin Laden unit chief agreed. Pakistani intelligence was so penetrated by Taliban and bin Laden sympathizers, they believed, that there was little basis to rely on joint operations such as the commando training the CIA was providing. Iran shared a long border with Afghanistan but was out of the question as a partner. Turkmenistan, another neighbor, wanted nothing to do with the CIA. A civil war engulfed Tajikistan to the northeast.

That left only Uzbekistan, which bordered Afghanistan to the north, far from the southern and eastern Taliban strongholds where bin Laden mainly operated. But at least Uzbekistan's government was not penetrated by Taliban sympathizers, Black and his colleagues calculated. A jowly, secular ex-communist autocrat named Islam Karimov ruled the country as if it were his estate. Karimov jailed and sometimes tortured democratic and Islamist opponents. He had no sympathy for bin Laden. Karimov's hold on power was threatened by a violent radical group called the Islamic Movement of Uzbekistan; its leaders had been inspired by Saudi proselytizing and later found exile with bin Laden in Afghanistan. By 1999, bin Laden and the Taliban leadership saw these Uzbek Islamists as important allies. The IMU fought as committed shock troops in the Taliban's war against Massoud's forces in northern Afghanistan. They were also a vanguard of bin Laden's grandiose plans to sponsor a thrust by Islamist forces into Central Asia to overthrow the region's secular leaders and establish new caliphates.

Bin Laden provided the Uzbek radicals with funding, weapons, and access to training camps. The Taliban provided them with bases and housing in Kabul and farther north. Uzbek terrorist units began to sneak across the border to mount operations against Karimov's government. On February 16,

1999, they announced themselves in the capital of Tashkent: As Karimov drove in a limousine to a cabinet meeting, the radicals detonated six car bombs in a downtown plaza. Karimov escaped, but sixteen people died. Within days Karimov arrested at least two thousand Islamic activists. Many of these arrests were indiscriminate, sweeping up peaceful democratic parties challenging Karimov's iron-fisted rule. But Karimov described the crackdown as war against bin Laden's allies.[12]

Cofer Black and his colleagues saw this turmoil as an opportunity. Through the CIA station in Tashkent they reached out to Karimov's government and proposed a new intelligence alliance focused on their mutual enemies in Afghanistan. Karimov wanted CIA assistance but was nervous about the political price he might pay if his contacts with Langley became known. He agreed to explore the CIA's proposals but insisted that all of his dealings be kept secret.

Black and the new bin Laden unit chief, Rich, flew discreetly into Tashkent, a Soviet-style city of broad avenues and monumental government buildings in the Central Asian steppe, to outline a new CIA liaison program. Black proposed CIA funding and training for a counterterrorism strike force to be commanded by the Uzbek military. The CIA hoped the force, once fully trained and equipped, might carry out covert snatch operations against bin Laden or his lieutenants.[13]

Karimov accepted the plan. He made Uzbek air bases available to the CIA for small-scale transit and helicopter operations. He allowed the CIA and the National Security Agency to install monitoring equipment designed to intercept Taliban and al Qaeda communications. He agreed to share what intelligence his government had about bin Laden's bases in Afghanistan. Karimov and his aides hinted that they might be willing to join the CIA in military operations once the new commando force was ready.

The CIA's officers were excited and optimistic. They admired Karimov's willingness to take political risks to go after bin Laden. Finally they had found a new partner less penetrated than Pakistan and less complicated than Saudi Arabia. Karimov and his intelligence aides agreed to just about every request the CIA put forward.[14]

At the White House, National Security Council aides drafted the highly classified legal approvals and budgetary papers for the new Uzbek liaison in a mood of jaundiced, sometimes acid skepticism. "Uzbek motivations were highly suspect to say the least," recalled one official. To these skeptics the CIA liaison did not seem like "a plan that fit into anything larger than 'Get something going with the Uzbeks.'" Tashkent was a long way from Kandahar, but it was "certainly closer than Langley," so at least it was something. There were fears at the White House about Uzbek corruption, human rights abuses, and scandal. Some of the White House aides saw the CIA itself as "passive-aggressive" about the Uzbek outreach in the sense that Langley pushed to get the liaison going and then worried aloud about rules and financial audits. One White House official remembered a CIA counterpart announcing wearily, "We're going to have to deploy hundreds of accountants to Uzbekistan to make sure every piece of equipment that we send to these people is accounted for."[15]

Formal CIA and Pentagon liaisons like the one in Uzbekistan had a natural bureaucratic shape and momentum that emphasized office meetings, long training sessions, equipment purchases, audits, and slide presentations. They often chewed up more time on process and planning than on covert operations.

On the ground in Afghanistan during that summer of 1999 there was only one leader waging war and collecting intelligence day in and day out against the Taliban, Osama bin Laden, and their international Islamist allies. His disputed government possessed no real capital, no international airport, and little credibility. His budget was cobbled together week to week, partly from heroin smuggling deals. He did not have much of an office and, for lack of electricity, could not rely much on slide projectors. He had acquired a few tanks, a good supply of mortars, many small arms, and a few tattered helicopters pasted together from incompatible spare parts and with rotors that continually threatened to detach and fly away.

Ahmed Shah Massoud remained a charismatic force among his own Tajik people, especially in the northeastern Panjshir Valley. He was by far the most formidable military commander in Afghanistan yet to be defeated by the Taliban. The CIA had continued to maintain regular contact with Massoud in the two years since Gary Schroen's visit to the commander in Taloqan in the spring of 1997. A series of clandestine CIA teams carrying electronic intercept equipment and relatively small amounts of cash—up to $250,000 per trip—had visited Massoud in the Panjshir Valley several times since then. Sometimes the teams were led by officers from the Near East Division of the Directorate of Operations, where Schroen was now deputy chief. Other times they were led by officers from the Counterterrorist Center. When Near East was in the lead, the missions were code-named NALT, for Northern Afghanistan Liaison Team. When the Counterterrorist Center was in charge, they were dubbed JAWBREAKER. The first group, NALT-1, flew on one of Massoud's helicopters from Dushanbe to the Panjshir late in 1997. Three other CIA teams had gone in by the summer of 1999. They typically stayed in

Barak village, near Massoud's headquarters, for a week or two and met with the commander several times. The intercept equipment they delivered allowed Massoud to monitor Taliban battlefield radio transmissions. In exchange the CIA officers asked Massoud to let them know immediately if his men ever heard accounts on the Taliban radios indicating that bin Laden or his lieutenants were on the move in a particular sector. The agency teams established secure communications links to Langley so that Massoud could pass along such bin Laden alerts.

Both the Near East Division and the Counterterrorist Center supported the liaison with Massoud, but they disagreed about its purpose and potential. Within Near East there were many, including Schroen, who remembered the commander's stubborn independence in years past even when he was handsomely paid to follow the CIA's lead. They wondered if Massoud could really be a reliable partner against bin Laden. In any event they wanted to support Massoud against the Taliban to keep his northern forces viable and to provide a foothold in Afghanistan for CIA intelligence collection and operations. The Near East officers did not doubt Massoud's contempt for bin Laden and his Arab volunteers, but Schroen argued that geography and logistics made operations against bin Laden nearly impossible for Massoud. Even the Near East Division's TRODPINT tracking team, operating on al Qaeda's home turf around Kandahar, had been unable to produce reliable forecasts of bin Laden's movements. Massoud was even more remote from the target.

But Black and especially Rich argued that they had to renew their effort to bring Massoud into the campaign against bin Laden. They saw Massoud as many of his admirers in Europe did, as an epochal figure, extraordinarily skillful and determined. They had no personal history with him, no legacy of disappointments or conflicts involving Pakistani intelligence. If the CIA really intended to reinvent its plan to disrupt and capture bin Laden, they asked that summer, how could the agency possibly succeed if it did not begin to do serious business with Massoud?

THE AFGHAN WAR was changing. The murder by Taliban agents of Abdul Haq's family in Peshawar early in 1999 presaged new opposition to Mullah Omar among Pashtuns. That spring the Karzai family, who had backed the Taliban's initial rise, began to explore armed opposition.

The Karzais' frustration with the Taliban had been rising for months. At Hamid Karzai's April wedding in Quetta, his father, Abdul Ahad Karzai, the family patriarch and a former Afghan senator, called his sons and several other

Pashtun leaders to a late-night meeting and declared, as Hamid's brother Qayam remembered it, that "our country is gone and it's somebody else's country now, and it would remain that way unless we resisted." The Karzai patriarch declared that "the only option left is that we have to start from within. We would have to be more diligent, we would have to be more stubborn. We would have to start talking to Massoud." They decided to seek American assistance but agreed this would be a long shot.[16]

Hamid Karzai worked with his father from the family compound in Quetta that spring and early summer to organize political resistance to the Taliban among prominent royalist Pashtuns. He coordinated meetings of tribal chiefs in Pakistan and in Rome. He promoted a formal *loya jirga* to reconsider Afghan politics, and his father agitated for the return of the Afghan king. Hamid Karzai wrote a letter to Mullah Omar, inviting him to attend some of these political meetings but also warning him that the Taliban had to change, "that they must remove the foreigners that were with them here killing and destroying our country, ruining our lives," as Karzai recalled it.[17]

The Taliban sent their reply on July 15. As the elderly Karzai patriarch walked home from a mosque through Quetta's mud-rock alleyways, Afghan assassins on motorcycles roared up and opened fire, killing him instantly.

Heir to his father's political position, Hamid Karzai sought to avenge his death. Within weeks of Abdul Ahad's grand Kandahar funeral—a mix of mourning and anti-Taliban politics—Hamid Karzai redoubled his efforts. He already had numerous American contacts and helped funnel humanitarian aid to Afghanistan from Quetta. Now he asked Bill Milam, the U.S. ambassador to Pakistan, for weapons. Milam told Karzai he was being reckless and unrealistic. The Taliban or their Arab allies would slaughter him if he attempted an uprising; the political ground had not been laid.[18]

Karzai was inclined to concede the point, but he pressed anyway. He felt rash, he said later. Officers in the CIA's Islamabad station believed that an armed uprising was unrealistic but urged continuing talks and cooperation. Karzai was a "small player," one U.S. official recalled, but his political and tribal allies were well wired in Kandahar and could provide helpful information about the Taliban and bin Laden. Arms supplies seemed implausible, however. "I would go every week to Islamabad," Karzai recalled of this period. "I would go to the Americans, I would go to the French, I would go to the English, I would go to the Germans, I would go to the Italians . . . [and] tell them about the readiness of the Afghan people to move against the Taliban. They wouldn't trust me. They wouldn't believe me. . . . They didn't see it. They didn't even see it in Washington."[19]

Some State Department officials and some analysts at the CIA still believed—despite little supporting evidence—that the Taliban might voluntarily turn bin Laden over for trial in exchange for diplomatic recognition and relief from economic sanctions. Pressure from Karzai and other dissident Pashtuns might encourage the Taliban to compromise, but otherwise it was not something the State Department sought to encourage. Albright, Tom Pickering, and Rick Inderfurth declared publicly again and again that the United States would not take sides in the Afghan war.

State Department intelligence analysts did report during the first half of 1999 that resistance to the Taliban was growing. Still, "We believe there is no military solution to this conflict," Inderfurth said. "The United States supports no individual Afghan faction but maintains contacts with all to further progress toward a peaceful settlement."[20]

At interagency meetings CIA officials had raised the possibility of a new American alliance with Massoud, possibly involving covert arms supplies. But outside of the CIA, the Clinton administration remained deeply skeptical about the commander and his northern warlord allies. At an ambassadors' meeting in Washington in May, Albright canvassed her envoys to Pakistan and Central Asia: What did they think about a new tilt toward Massoud? Milam was adamantly opposed. Arms supplies to Massoud would only deepen the war and kill more innocent Afghans, he and his colleagues at the Islamabad embassy firmly believed. Massoud could not defeat the Taliban on the battlefield. He was bottled up in the north and losing ground.[21]

The influential Pickering argued that no Afghan policy could succeed if it did not involve the Pashtuns in the south. If the U.S. tilted toward Massoud in the north, it would only exacerbate Afghanistan's ethnic divisions—and in a quixotic military cause.[22] Other State and White House officials recalled the horrible violence against civilians in Kabul during the mid-1990s while Massoud was defense minister and pointed to persistent reports that he relied on drug trafficking. He was not a worthy ally of the United States, they argued.

MASSOUD TOLD HIS AIDES he was confident that the Taliban would wither. They would overextend themselves, and opposition among Pashtuns would gradually rise.[23]

Twice Massoud spoke by satellite telephone to Mullah Omar. As his aides listened, Massoud told the Taliban leader that history clearly showed Afghanistan could never be ruled by one faction, that the country could only be governed by a coalition. But the only history Omar had ever read was in the Koran, and he refused to compromise.

Massoud persisted. He dispatched his intelligence aide, Amrullah Saleh, to Switzerland to meet secretly with Taliban representatives. They also held back-channel talks in Uzbekistan and Turkmenistan. But the Taliban were buoyed by their support from ISI, Saudi, and other Persian Gulf donors. "They were very arrogant," recalled one of Massoud's aides.

Still, Massoud counseled patience. His strategy in 1999, recalled his brother Ahmed Wali, was similar to what it had been a decade earlier, when Soviet troops withdrew: He planned to outlast and eventually outmaneuver Pakistani intelligence. Eventually, Massoud said, the United States would recognize that the Taliban was its enemy. When that happened, he would be ready to receive American help. Meanwhile, through the Stinger missile recovery program and occasional meetings with CIA officers at safehouses in Tajikistan and in the Panjshir, Massoud kept his lines to Langley open.

At the State Department, Pickering and Inderfurth evolved a more nuanced policy toward Massoud by the summer of 1999. They still strongly opposed American arms supplies, but they privately made clear to Russia and Iran that the United States had no objections to the covert arms *those* countries supplied Massoud. They defended this policy by saying they did not want to see the Northern Alliance completely overrun. If Massoud's forces were expelled from Afghanistan, that would leave the Taliban triumphantly unchallenged—and less willing than ever to negotiate.[24]

Inderfurth traveled to Tashkent that July for multiparty peace talks with Afghan leaders sponsored by the United Nations. Massoud also decided to attend. Inderfurth's opening statement offered olive branches to every group, including the Taliban. The conference's "Tashkent Declaration on Fundamental Principles for a Peaceful Settlement of the Conflict in Afghanistan" was a testament to muddled policy and dead-end negotiations. Its preamble expressed "profound concern" about the status of Afghan minorities and women and then declared that the signatories were "deeply distressed" about drug trafficking and, thirdly, were "also concerned" about terrorism. Pakistan and Iran pledged to end arms shipments to their favored Afghan militias, pledges they did not intend to keep, as the United States well understood.[25]

On the night the talks broke up, Inderfurth met with Massoud and his aides in a side room of the behemoth Soviet-era hall where the conference had been held. Massoud swept in wearing pressed khaki robes and a wool cap, radiating "charisma and presence," as Inderfurth recalled it. As the American envoy reviewed diplomatic issues, Massoud seemed bored, but when Inderfurth asked about the war, Massoud lit up and leaned forward to describe his defenses and plans.[26]

Inderfurth asked if Massoud needed military equipment to undertake his summer operations. Massoud demurred. His aides said later they did not request weapons because they knew the Clinton administration had ruled out such supplies. Also, Russia, Iran, and India "were finding themselves comfortable providing us means to counter the Taliban because there was no objection from the U.S. on shipment of arms," one of Massoud's aides recalled.

Massoud expressed disappointment about U.S. indifference to Afghanistan, as Inderfurth recalled it. Massoud's aides remember him as more than disappointed. He liked Inderfurth better than some other U.S. diplomats, they said, but Massoud saw American policy as profoundly misguided, and he could not understand why it was so slow to change. At the Tashkent sessions the Americans kept talking about the Taliban and the Northern Alliance as two equally culpable "warring factions." This seemed outrageous to Massoud. It showed expediency and a loss of perspective in American foreign policy, he thought. As the Taliban became more powerful, even the United States moved to appease them, Massoud believed.[27]

Massoud tried to inventory for Inderfurth the massacres of civilians carried out by Taliban and al Qaeda forces. Summoning an argument designed to resonate in Washington, he described the Taliban as among the world's most egregious human rights violators, a regime that systematically repressed women and Shiite minorities. "We said, 'The United States is the only major power in this world pursuing a policy basically oriented on human rights. Let us see the reality,'" recalled a senior Massoud aide who was present. Massoud sought to convince Inderfurth that the Taliban were beginning to weaken, his aide recalled. Now was the time for the United States to pressure Pakistan to cut off aid to the Taliban, Massoud argued.

Inderfurth and Pickering believed they were pushing Pakistan as hard as they could, yet they had limited leverage in Islamabad. Counterterrorism officials such as the State Department's Michael Sheehan argued in internal memos during this period that State could push harder by placing terrorism at the very top of the American agenda. But State's brain trust—Albright, Pickering, and Strobe Talbott—felt that the United States could not afford to take such a narrow approach. America had other compelling interests: nuclear weapons, Kashmir, and the stability of Pakistani society. The support flowing to the Taliban from the Pakistani army and ISI had to be challenged in this broader context of American concerns, State's leadership insisted. Clinton agreed. The United States had a full agenda with Pakistan—the threat of war with India, nuclear weapons, terrorism, democracy, Kashmir—and all of it was important, Clinton believed.[28]

A decade before, it had been the State Department's Peter Tomsen, among others, who pushed a reluctant CIA to move closer to Ahmed Shah Massoud and away from Pakistani intelligence. Now the bureaucratic chairs had been reversed. It was State Department diplomats, along with some officers at the CIA, who resisted calls for a closer alliance with Massoud during 1999. Sandy Berger, Clinton's national security adviser and political gatekeeper on foreign policy, endorsed their view. There were isolated, individual advocates for a new alliance with Massoud at State, the White House, and in Congress, but it was mainly at the CIA's Counterterrorist Center—especially in the bin Laden unit—that Massoud had the most ardent believers.

Whatever the doubts about his independent outlook, whatever the fears about his drug trafficking, the CIA's Manson Family knew one thing for certain: Ahmed Shah Massoud was the enemy of their enemy.

COFER BLACK INITIATED paperwork and approvals with Richard Clarke's White House counterterrorism office late that summer. Black said he wanted to send a CIA team, led by his new bin Laden unit chief, inside Afghanistan to meet with Massoud and his lieutenants, in order to reenergize Massoud's efforts against bin Laden. This would be the fifth CIA mission to the Panjshir since the autumn of 1997, code-named JAWBREAKER-5. The mission's goal was to establish a renewed counterterrorism liaison. The CIA would offer to train, equip, and expand Massoud's existing intelligence service based in the Panjshir Valley and help it operate as widely and securely as possible in Afghan cities and provinces. The agency would offer Massoud more cash, more secure communications, listening devices, and other nonlethal spy gear.[29]

Black and his bin Laden unit hoped to establish with Massoud a robust program of intelligence exchange, concentrating on the daily mystery of bin Laden's whereabouts. Tenet and his colleagues overseeing technical collection moved a satellite to obtain better coverage of Afghanistan, and the National Security Agency developed intercept equipment for use inside the country. The bin Laden unit hoped Massoud would enhance these technical approaches on the ground. In his war against the Taliban and its allies, Massoud often maneuvered in battle against bin Laden's Arab brigade, Pakistani volunteers, and Chechen irregulars. Ultimately the CIA hoped Massoud would order

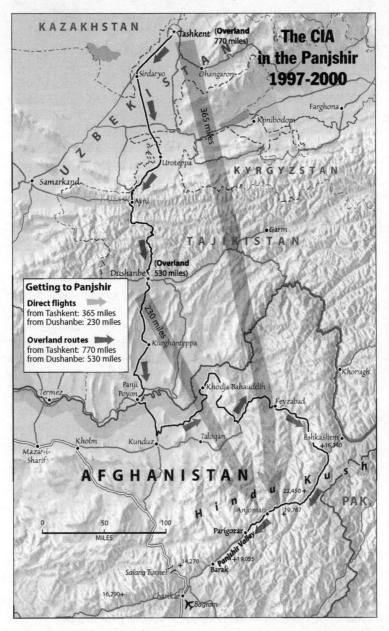

KAZAKHSTAN

★ Tashkent (Overland 770 miles)

Sirdaryo

Ohangaron

Farghona

The CIA
in the Panjshir
1997-2000

Konibodon

Uroteppa

KYRGYZSTAN

Samarkand

Ayni

Garm

TAJIKISTAN

Dushanbe ★ (Overland 530 miles)

Getting to Panjshir

Direct flights
from Tashkent: 365 miles
from Dushanbe: 230 miles

Overland routes
from Tashkent: 770 miles
from Dushanbe: 530 miles

Kurghonteppa

Khorugh

Panji
Poyon

Khodja Bahauddin

Feyzabad

Termez

Kholm

Kunduz

Taloqan

Eshkashem
+16,340

Mazar-i-
Sharif

AFGHANISTAN

Hindu Kush

PAK

22,450+

Anjoman

+19,767

0   50   100
MILES

Parigozar

Panjshir Valley

+19,055

+14,270

Salang Tunnel

Barak

16,290+

Charikar

Bagram

his militia to capture bin Laden during one of these engagements and either kill him or hand him over to the United States.

The new CIA program would eventually complement commando training in Uzbekistan and Pakistan as well as continuing work with the longer-established tribal tracking team in southern Afghanistan, Black explained. The Counterterrorist Center hoped to surround al Qaeda militias with trained, equipped forces drawn from local populations. Then it would seek to locate bin Laden or his lieutenants and maneuver them into a trap.

Given the doubts about Massoud inside the Clinton administration, the Panjshir missions faced close legal and policy review. "It was all CIA initiated," recalled a senior White House official. The Counterterrorist Center needed approval to make its small cash payments to Massoud on each trip. "Well, how small is small?" the White House official asked. A few hundred thousand dollars, the CIA replied. Clarke and Berger assented.[30]

The intelligence policy and legal offices at the National Security Council drafted formal, binding policy guidance for the JAWBREAKER-5 mission. Black got involved; he wanted everything written down clearly so there would be no recriminations later if CIA gear or cash was misused by Massoud. "Put it down in 'Special English' so people can understand," Black would say sardonically to his colleagues. He wanted his men to be able to hold copies of the White House legal authorities in their hands when they met with Massoud and his intelligence aides in the Panjshir. He wanted the CIA officers to be able to literally read out their White House guidance in clear terms that were easy to translate. There would be no improvisation, Black said. The Counterterrorist Center chief occasionally cited the English king Henry II's famous attempt in 1170 to commission the assassination of Thomas Becket, the archbishop of Canterbury, by asking an ambiguous question. Henry II had asked open-endedly: "Who will rid me of this meddlesome priest?" Black ranted sarcastically to his colleagues: The CIA is not in the "rid me of this priest" business anymore. He wanted presidential orders that were specific and exacting. "You've got to spell it out," he told the White House.[31]

Massoud was at war with the Taliban. The United States declared a policy of strict neutrality in that war. The White House also wanted to ensure that the CIA's counterterrorism mission to the Panjshir Valley did not become some kind of Trojan horse strategy for a rogue CIA effort to boost Massoud's strength and capability in his battles against the Taliban. Clinton said he was prepared to work with Massoud on intelligence operations, despite his record of brutality, but he was not ready to arm the Northern Alliance. The

Pentagon and intelligence community both provided analysis to Clinton, as he recalled it years later, arguing that Massoud was receiving all the weapons he could handle from other suppliers, and that in any event he would never be able to defeat the Taliban or govern Afghanistan from Kabul. This certainly was Shelton's consistent view from the Pentagon. At Langley, the CIA was divided on the question. After absorbing the briefs, Clinton made clear that he was not prepared to have the United States join the Afghan war on Massoud's side, against the Taliban and al Qaeda. Clinton hand-wrote changes to a February 1999 authorizing memo to emphasize that Massoud's men could only use lethal force against bin Laden in self-defense. The National Security Council approved written guidance to authorize intelligence cooperation with Massoud, while making clear that the CIA could provide no assistance that would "fundamentally alter the Afghan battlefield."[32]

Black underlined this point to the bin Laden unit as its chief prepared to fly to Central Asia. The CIA would be interpreting this White House policy rule at its peril. It would be up to the agency's colonel-level officers to decide, day in and day out, what kind of intelligence aid would "fundamentally alter" Massoud's military position against the Taliban and what would not. If they did not get this right, they could wind up in a federal courtroom, Black warned.

Rich, the Algiers veteran and bin Laden unit chief, led the JAWBREAKER team to the Panjshir in October 1999. They flew secretly to Dushanbe, the pockmarked capital of the former Soviet republic of Tajikistan, a desolate city recovering from postcommunist civil war. At an airfield where Massoud maintained a clandestine logistics base, they boarded an old Soviet-made Mi-17 transport helicopter and swooped toward Afghanistan's jagged, snow-draped northern peaks.

Beyond the Anjuman Pass, two miles high, they descended into the narrow, cragged river valley that was Massoud's fortress homeland. He had agreed to receive the CIA team at his principal residence, in a compound near where his family had lived for generations and where Massoud's own legend as an anti-Soviet guerrilla leader had been born. They stayed for seven days. Most of the time they worked with Massoud's intelligence officers on operations, equipment, and procedures for communication. The CIA set up secure lines between Massoud, his Dushanbe safehouses, and the Counterterrorist Center at Langley so that any fix on bin Laden's whereabouts could be instantly transmitted to CIA headquarters and from there to the White House.[33]

Rich and his team met with Massoud twice, once at the beginning of the visit and once at the end. The CIA officers admired Massoud greatly. They saw him as a Che Guevara figure, a great actor on history's stage. Massoud was a poet, a military genius, a religious man, and a leader of enormous courage who defied death and accepted its inevitability, they thought. Among Third World guerrilla leaders the CIA officers had met, there were few so well rounded. Massoud prayed five times a day during their visit. In his house there were thousands of books: Persian poetry, histories of the Afghan war in multiple languages, biographies of other military and guerrilla leaders. In their meetings Massoud wove sophisticated, measured references to Afghan history and global politics into his arguments. He was quiet, forceful, reserved, and full of dignity, but also light in spirit. The CIA team had gone into the Panjshir as unabashed admirers of Massoud. Now their convictions deepened even as they recognized that the agency's new partnership with the Northern Alliance would be awkward, limited, and perhaps unlikely to succeed.

The meetings with Massoud were formal and partially scripted. Each side spoke for about fifteen minutes, and then there was time for questions and answers.

"We have a common enemy," the CIA team leader said. "Let's work together."[34]

Massoud said he was willing, but he was explicit about his limitations. Bin Laden spent most of his time near Kandahar and in the eastern Afghan mountains, far from where Massoud's forces operated. Occasionally bin Laden visited Jalalabad or Kabul, closer to Massoud's lines. In these areas Massoud's intelligence service had active agents, and perhaps they could develop more sources.

Because he had a few helicopters and many battle-tested commanders, the CIA team also hoped to eventually set up a snatch operation in which Massoud would order an airborne assault to take bin Laden alive. But for now the Counterterrorist Center had no legal authority from the White House to promote lethal operations with Massoud. The initial visit was to set up a system for collection and sharing of intelligence about bin Laden, and to establish connections with Massoud for future operations.

The agency men recognized that in their focus on bin Laden they were promoting a narrow "American solution" to an American problem in the midst of Afghanistan's broader, complex war. Still, they hoped Massoud would calculate that if he went along with the CIA's capture operation, it might lead eventually to a deeper political and military alliance with the United States.[35]

Massoud told the CIA delegation that American policy toward bin Laden was myopic and doomed to fail. The Americans put all their effort against bin

Laden himself and a handful of his senior aides, but they failed to see the larger context in which al Qaeda thrived. What about the Taliban? What about Pakistani intelligence? What about Saudi Arabia and the United Arab Emirates?

Even if the CIA succeeded in capturing or killing bin Laden, Massoud argued to his CIA visitors, the United States would still have a huge problem in Afghanistan. Al Qaeda was now much bigger than bin Laden or al-Zawahiri alone. Protected by the Taliban, its hundreds and even thousands of international jihadists would carry on bin Laden's war against both the United States and secular Central Asian governments.

"Even if we succeed in what you are asking for," Massoud told the CIA delegation, as his aide and translator Abdullah recalled it, "that will not solve the bigger problem that is growing."[36] This part of the conversation was tricky for the Americans. The CIA team leader and his colleagues privately agreed with Massoud's criticisms of American policy. The CIA men saw little distinction between al Qaeda and the Taliban. They felt frustrated by the State Department diplomats who argued moderate Taliban leadership might eventually expel bin Laden bloodlessly.

The Americans told Massoud they agreed with his critique, but they had their orders. The policy of the United States government now focused on capturing bin Laden and his lieutenants for criminal trial. Yet this policy was not static. Already the CIA was lobbying for a new approach to Massoud in Washington—that was how they had won permission for this mission in the first place. If they worked together now, built up their cooperation on intelligence collection, the CIA—or at least the officers in the Counterterrorist Center—would continue to lobby for the United States to choose sides in the Afghan war and support Massoud. The CIA could not rewrite government policy, but it had influence, they explained. The more Massoud cooperated against bin Laden, the more credible the CIA's arguments in Washington would become.

Massoud and his aides agreed they had nothing to lose. "First of all it was an effort against a common enemy," recalled Abdullah. "Second, we had the hope that it would get the U.S. to know better about the situation in Afghanistan." As the counterterrorism and intelligence work grew, the United States might finally intervene in the Afghan war more forcefully, "perhaps in the later stages," Massoud calculated, as Abdullah recalled it.[37]

Meanwhile, if Massoud's men found themselves "in a position to kill Osama bin Laden, we wouldn't have waited for approval from the United States," Abdullah recalled. "We were not doing this just for the U.S. interests. We were doing it for our own interests."[38]

In the end Massoud's men did not object to the discussions about legal limitations as much as they did to what they saw as the selfish, single-minded focus of American policy. "What was irritating was that in this whole tragedy, in this whole chaotic situation, at times that a nation was suffering," recalled one of Massoud's intelligence aides who worked closely with the CIA during this period, "they were talking about this very small piece of it: bin Laden. And if you were on our side, it would have been difficult for you to accept that this was the problem. For us it was an element of the problem but not the problem."[39]

The CIA team pledged to push Massoud's arguments in Washington, but they sensed their own isolation in the American bureaucracy. They understood State's objections. They knew that backing Massoud's grinding war against the Taliban carried many risks and costs, not least the certainty of more Afghan civilian deaths. They had to make the case—unpopular and to many American officials still unproven—that the Taliban and al Qaeda posed such a grave risk to the United States that it required an extraordinary change.

"That Unit Disappeared"

THE JAWBREAKER TEAM choppered out to Dushanbe, leaving Afghanistan clandestinely across the Tajikistan border. Within a few weeks, several hundred miles to the south, four young middle-class Arab men who had sworn themselves to secrecy and jihad entered Afghanistan from Pakistan. The Taliban facilitated their travel and accommodation, first in Quetta and then in Kandahar.[1]

Mohammed Atta, thirty-one, was a wiry, severe, taciturn Egyptian of medium height, the only son of a frustrated Cairo lawyer who had pushed his children hard. He had just earned a degree in urban planning from the Technical University of Hamburg-Harburg, completing a 152-page thesis on development planning and historic preservation in ancient Aleppo, Syria. Ziad Jarrah was the only son of a Lebanese family that drove Mercedes cars, owned a Beirut apartment, and kept a vacation home in the country. He had emigrated to Germany to attend the University of Applied Sciences in Hamburg, where he studied aircraft construction. He initially caroused and smoked hashish, fell tumultuously in and out with his Turkish girlfriend, and then grew intensely religious and withdrawn. His girlfriend challenged his Islamic beliefs; at times he hit her in frustration. Marwan al-Shehhi had been raised amid the prosperity of the United Arab Emirates in the years of the OPEC oil boom. He served as a sergeant in the U.A.E. army. His parents, too, could afford a German university education for him. Of the four conspirators, only Ramzi Binalshibh, then twenty-five, could not rely on family money. Small, wiry, talkative, and charismatic, he excelled in school and won a scholarship to college in Bonn, but his widowed mother struggled at home in rural Yemen. The Binalshibhs came from Amad, a town in the mountains of Hadramaut province—the province from which, six decades earlier, Mohammed bin Laden struck out for Saudi Arabia to make his name and fortune.[2]

The arrival of the four in Afghanistan suggested the complexity of al Qaeda just as American intelligence began to grasp more firmly its shape and membership. In their classified reports and assessments, analysts in the CIA's Counterterrorist Center described al Qaeda by 1999 as an extraordinarily diverse and dispersed enemy. The mid-1990s courtroom trials in the World Trade Center bombing and related cases, and evidence from the Africa bombing investigations, had revealed the organization as a paradox: tightly supervised at the top but very loosely spread at the bottom. By 1999 it had become common at the CIA to describe al Qaeda as a constellation or a series of concentric circles. Around the core bin Laden leadership group in Afghanistan—the main target of the CIA's covert snatch operations—lay protective rings of militant regional allies. These included the Taliban, elements of Pakistani intelligence, Uzbek and Chechen exiles, extremist anti-Shia groups in Pakistan, and Kashmiri radicals. Beyond these lay softer circles of financial, recruiting, and political support: international charities, proselytizing groups, and radical Islamic mosques, education centers and political parties from Indonesia to Yemen, from Saudi Arabia to the Gaza strip, from Europe to the United States.[3]

Al Qaeda operated as an organization in more than sixty countries, the CIA's Counterterrorist Center calculated by late 1999. Its formal, sworn, hard-core membership might number in the hundreds.[4] Thousands more joined allied militias such as the Taliban or the Chechen rebel groups or Abu Sayyaf in the Philippines or the Islamic Movement of Uzbekistan. These volunteers could be recruited for covert terrorist missions elsewhere if they seemed qualified. New jihadists turned up each week at al Qaeda–linked mosques and recruitment centers worldwide. They were inspired by fire-breathing local imams, satellite television news, or Internet sites devoted to jihadist violence in Palestine, Chechnya, and Afghanistan. Many of the Arab volunteers from countries such as Algeria or Yemen were poor, eager, and undereducated; they had more daring than ability and could barely afford the airfare to Pakistan. Yet some were middle class and college-educated. A few—like the four men who arrived secretly in Kandahar in the autumn of 1999: Atta, Jarrah, al-Shehhi, and Binalshibh—carried passports and visas that facilitated travel to Europe and the United States. These relatively elite volunteers moved like self-propelled shooting stars through al Qaeda's global constellation. Their reasons to join were as diverse as their transnational biographies. In many ways they retraced the trails of radicalization followed in the early 1990s by Ramzi Yousef and Mir Amal Kasi. They were mainly intelligent, well-educated men from ambitious, prosperous families. They migrated to Europe, studied demanding technical subjects, and attempted—unsuccessfully—to establish themselves as modern professionals far from the family embrace and conservative Islamic culture they had known in their youths. As they joined a violent movement led by the alienated, itinerant son of a Saudi construction magnate and a disputatious, ostracized Egyptian doctor, they pledged their loyalty to men strikingly like themselves.

The Hamburg cell, as it came to be known, coalesced at a shabby mosque in the urban heart of Germany's gray, industrial, northern port city. A coffee shop and a gymnasium for bodybuilders squeezed the Al Quds Mosque where Arab men in exile gathered for prayers, sermons, and conspiracy. Prostitutes, heroin dealers, and underemployed immigrants shared the streets. A 330-pound Syrian car mechanic who was a veteran of Afghanistan's wars championed bin Laden's message at the mosque. Mohammed Haydar Zammar was one of perhaps hundreds of such self-appointed soapbox preachers for al Qaeda scattered in city mosques and Islamic centers around the world. Zammar was well known to CIA and FBI counterterrorist officers based in Germany. The CIA repeatedly produced reports on Zammar and asked German police to challenge him. But German laws enacted after the Holocaust elaborately protected religious freedom, and German police did not see al Qaeda as a grave threat. The young men who came to pray with Zammar gradually embraced his ideas and his politics; Zammar, in turn, saw their potential as operatives.[5]

Even in the dim cement block dormitories and rental apartments of polytechnic Hamburg, the Al Quds crew saw themselves as members of a global Islamist underground. They used cell phones, the Internet, and prepaid calling cards to communicate with other mosques, guest houses in Afghanistan, and dissident preachers in Saudi Arabia, including Safar al-Hawali and Saman al-Auda, the original "Awakening Sheikhs" whose vitriolic attacks on the Saudi royal family in 1991 had stimulated bin Laden's revolutionary ambitions.[6]

Atta was among the oldest in the Hamburg group. Born in the Egyptian countryside, he had moved at a young age with his parents and two sisters to a small apartment in a crowded, decaying neighborhood of colonial-era Cairo. They could afford seaside vacations, but they did not live extravagantly. His striving, austere father created "a house of study—no playing, no entertainment, just study," a family friend recalled. His father saw Atta, with some derision, as "a very sensitive man; he is soft and was extremely attached to his mother," as he put it years later. Atta sat affectionately on his mother's lap well into his twenties. His father used to chide his mother "that she is raising him as a girl, and that I have three girls, but she never stopped pampering him," as he recalled it. Atta's older sisters thrived under their father's pressure; one became a botanist, the other a doctor. Atta shut out all distraction to follow them into higher studies, to meet his father's expectations or his own. If a belly dancer came on the family television, he shaded his eyes and walked out of the room. Worried that his son would languish forever in Egypt, wallowing in his mother's pampering, Atta's father "almost tricked him," as he later put it, into continuing his education in Germany. Once there, his son grew steadily more angry and withdrawn. He worked four years as a draftsman, never questioning his assignments or offering ideas. His supervisor later said that Atta "embodied the idea of drawing. 'I am the drawer. I draw.'" His roommates found him intolerant, sullen, sloppy, and inconsiderate. While traveling in the Arab world Atta could be relaxed, even playful, but the Europeans who knew him in Germany found him alienated and closed. Increasingly he seemed to use Islam and its precepts—prayer, segregation from women, a calendar of ritual—as a shield between himself and Hamburg.[7]

By late 1999, Atta and others in the Al Quds group had committed themselves to martyrdom through jihad. Ramzi Binalshibh, who shared roots with bin Laden and seemed to know his people, helped make their contacts in Afghanistan. Binalshibh ranted at a wedding that October about the "danger" Jews posed to the Islamic world. Handwritten notes made by Ziad Jarrah just before the quartet's autumn trip to Kandahar describe their gathering zeal: "The morning will come. The victors will come. We swear to beat you." A week later he wrote: "I came to you with men who love the death just as you love life. . . . Oh, the smell of paradise is rising."[8]

Bin Laden and his senior planners had already seized on the idea of using airplanes to attack the United States when Jarrah, Atta, al-Shehhi, and Binalshibh turned up in Kandahar that autumn, according to admissions under interrogation later made by Binalshibh and Khalid Sheikh Mohammed, the plot's mastermind. A fugitive from an American indictment because of his earlier work with his nephew Ramzi Yousef, Mohammed found sanctuary in Afghanistan in mid-1996, just as bin Laden arrived from Sudan. He had known bin Laden during the 1980s anti-Soviet jihad and used that connection to win a meeting. Mohammed pitched bin Laden and his Egyptian military chief, Mohammed Atef, on several plans to attack American targets. One of his ideas, he told interrogators later, was an ambitious plot to hijack ten passenger jets with trained pilots and fly them kamikaze-style into the White House or the Capitol, the Pentagon, the headquarters of the CIA and the FBI, the two towers of the World Trade Center, the tallest buildings in California and Washington state, and perhaps a nuclear power plant. Mohammed said he proposed to hijack and pilot the tenth plane himself. Rather than crash it into a target, he planned to kill all the male adult passengers, land the plane at a U.S. airport, issue statements denouncing U.S. policies in the Middle East, and then release the surviving women and children.[9]

By Mohammed's account, bin Laden and his aide listened to his ideas but declined to commit their support. Bin Laden had barely settled in Afghanistan. The country was in turmoil, his finances were under pressure, and he lacked a stable headquarters. Only after the Africa embassy bombings in 1998 did Mohammed realize that bin Laden might be ready to renew their ambitious talks—and he was right. They met again in Kandahar in early 1999 and bin Laden declared that Mohammed's suicide hijacking plan now had al Qaeda's backing. Bin Laden wanted to scale back the attack to make it more manageable. He also said he preferred the White House to the Capitol as a target and that he favored hitting the Pentagon. Mohammed pushed for the World Trade Center. His nephew had bombed the towers six years before but had failed to bring them down, and now languished in an American high-security prison; Mohammed sought to finish the job.

Bin Laden provided two potential Saudi suicide pilots who were veterans of jihadist fighting in Bosnia, as well as two Yemeni volunteers who ultimately were unable to obtain visas to the United States. Mohammed taught several of them how to live and travel in the United States, drawing on his own experiences as a college student there. He showed them how to use the Internet, book plane flights, read telephone directories, and communicate with headquarters. They practiced with flight simulators on personal computers and began to puzzle out how to hijack multiple flights that would be in the air at the same time. As this training proceeded the four volunteers from Hamburg arrived in Kandahar, traveling separately. They pledged formal allegiance to bin Laden. Binalshibh, Atta, and Jarrah met with military chief Atef, who instructed them to go back to Germany and start training as pilots. After Atta was selected as the mission's leader he met with bin Laden personally to discuss targets. The Hamburg group already knew how to operate comfortably in Western society, but before returning to Europe some of them spent time with Mohammed in Karachi, studying airline schedules and discussing life in the United States.[10]

The four returned to Hamburg late that winter. Jarrah announced to his girlfriend that after years of drift he had at last discovered his life's ambition: He wanted to fly passenger jets. Atta used his Hotmail account to email American pilot schools. "We are a small group (2–3) of young men from different arab [*sic*] countries," he wrote. "Now we are living in Germany since a while for study purposes. We would like to start training for the career of airline professional pilots. In this field we haven't yet any knowledge, but we are ready to undergo an intensive training program."[11]

PERVEZ MUSHARRAF'S DAUGHTER married a documentary filmmaker. His son worked in Boston as a financial analyst. His father was a successful civil servant of secular mind. His mother did not hide behind a veil. She was a lively, talkative woman who orchestrated her family like the conductor of a chamber symphony. Doctors, diplomats, businessmen, and modernizers filled her family albums. Musharraf himself was typically called a liberal, which in Pakistan's political vernacular meant he did not blanch at whiskey, danced when the mood was upon him, and believed Pakistan should be a normal country—Islamic in some respects but also capitalistic and to some extent democratic. Yet Pervez Musharraf, chief of Pakistan's army staff, also believed firmly in the necessity of the Taliban in Afghanistan, for all of their medieval and illiberal practices. He believed, too, in the strategic value of their allied jihadists, especially those fighting in Kashmir.[12]

This was the aspect of the Pakistani officer corps that sometimes eluded American analysts, in the opinion of some Pakistani civilian liberals. *Every* Pakistani general, liberal or religious, believed in the jihadists by 1999, not from personal Islamic conviction, in most cases, but because the jihadists had proved themselves over many years as the one force able to frighten, flummox, and bog down the Hindu-dominated Indian army. About a dozen Indian divisions had been tied up in Kashmir during the late 1990s to suppress a few thousand well-trained, paradise-seeking Islamist guerrillas. What more could Pakistan ask? The jihadist guerrillas were a more practical day-to-day strategic defense against Indian hegemony than even a nuclear bomb. To the west, in Afghanistan, the Taliban provided geopolitical "strategic depth" against India and protection from rebellion by Pakistan's own restive Pashtun population. For Musharraf, as for many other liberal Pakistani generals, jihad was not a calling, it was a professional imperative. It was something he did at the office. At quitting time he packed up his briefcase, straightened the braid on his uniform, and went home to his normal life.

To the extent it was personal or emotional for him, it was about India. He was a small, compact man with round cheeks, a boyish face, a neat mustache, and graying hair parted in the middle. He exuded a certain puffed-up vanity, but he could also be disarmingly casual and relaxed in private. Born in New Delhi in 1943, the son of an imperial bureaucrat, he and his family migrated to Pakistan unscathed amid the bloodshed of partition. He attended elite Christian boys' schools in Karachi and Lahore, then won a place at Pakistan's leading military academy. As a young officer he fought artillery duels in the second of his country's three wars with India. In the catastrophic war of 1971, when Pakistan lost almost half its territory as Bangladesh won independence, Musharraf served as a gung-ho major in the elite commandos. When he heard of the final humiliating cease-fire with India, a friend remembered, "he took off his commando jacket and threw it on the floor. . . . He thought it a defeat. We all did." Like hundreds of his colleagues, Musharraf's commitment to revenge hardened. On sabbatical at a British military college in 1990, now a brigadier general, he argued in his thesis that Pakistan only wanted "down to earth, respectable survival" while India arrogantly sought "dominant power status" in South Asia. As army chief in 1999, it was his role, Musharraf believed, to craft and execute his country's survival strategy even if that meant defending the Taliban or tolerating bin Laden as the Saudi trained and inspired self-sacrificing fighters in Kashmir.[13]

That spring, in secret meetings with his senior commanders at Rawalpindi, Musharraf went further. Perhaps it was his commando background. Perhaps it was the success his army had recently enjoyed in Afghanistan when it inserted clandestine officers and volunteers to fight secretly with the Taliban against Ahmed Shah Massoud. Perhaps it was the unremitting popular pressure in Pakistan to score a breakthrough against Indian troops in Kashmir. In any case, as the U.S. embassy in Islamabad later pieced it together, Musharraf pulled off his shelf a years-old army plan for a secret strike against a fifteen-thousand-foot strategic height in Kashmir known as Kargil. The idea was to send Pakistani army officers and soldiers in civilian disguise to the area, seize it, and hold it against Indian counterattack. Then Pakistan would possess an impregnable firing position above a strategic road in Indian-held Kashmir, cutting off a section of the disputed territory called Ladakh. With one stiletto thrust, Musharraf calculated, his army could sever a piece of Kashmir from Indian control.[14]

He briefed this audacious plan to the prime minister, Nawaz Sharif, who approved. As one longtime analyst of the Pakistani army later observed, it was perhaps the greatest strategic error by an overmatched military since Pearl Harbor, yet neither Sharif nor Musharraf seemed able to imagine how India or the world would react.[15]

In early May, Pakistani commandos disguised as jihadist volunteers seized Kargil without a fight. The disaster unfolded quickly. Pakistani army officers summoned ambassadors to a meeting in Islamabad and admitted the Kargil attackers were regular Pakistani army troops in disguise—even as other government spokesmen publicly insisted the incursion was an independent guerrilla uprising. Stunned, Bill Milam, the U.S. ambassador, poured classified cables into Washington reporting that Pakistan had in effect started a war. India launched aerial bombardments and a worldwide campaign to whip up outrage about Pakistan's aggression. Its politicians threatened a wider conflict to finish off Pakistan's army once and for all. Fearing nuclear escalation, Clinton delivered a dozen secret letters to Sharif and Pakistani generals in as many weeks, each time imploring them to see their folly and withdraw. He also pressured Sharif on the Taliban and al Qaeda. "I urge you in the strongest way to get the Taliban to expel bin Laden," Clinton wrote Sharif on June 19. But the crisis only deepened. In early July the CIA picked up intelligence that Pakistan's army was preparing nuclear-tipped missiles for launch against India if necessary.[16]

An overwhelmed Sharif feared he had lost his shaky grip. He flew hurriedly to Washington to meet with Clinton on July 4. He brought his wife and children, as if he might be flying into exile.[17]

At Blair House on Pennsylvania Avenue, with only a National Security Council note taker present, Clinton ripped into Pakistan's prime minister. Clinton had "asked repeatedly for Pakistani help to bring Osama bin Laden to justice from Afghanistan," the president ranted. Sharif had "promised often to do so but had done nothing. Instead the ISI worked with bin Laden and the Taliban to foment terrorists." It was an outrage, Clinton said. He was going to release a statement calling worldwide attention to Pakistan's support for terrorists. Is that what Sharif wanted? Clinton demanded. Did Sharif order the Pakistani nuclear missile force to get ready for action? Did he realize how crazy that was?

"You've put me in the middle today, set the U.S. up to fail, and I won't let it happen," Clinton said. "Pakistan is messing with nuclear war."[18]

Doughy and evasive, Sharif gave in. He had already been working with Saudi Arabia, Europe, and by back channels with India to find a way to climb down. He announced a total withdrawal of Pakistani forces from Kargil. By doing so he ended the crisis, but he took heavy heat at home. Sharif blamed the army for getting him into this mess. The generals let it be known that it was all the prime minister's fault. An army-led coup attempt seemed possible, perhaps likely, the U.S. embassy reported.

But Musharraf hung back. In late summer he and the prime minister traveled to an army celebration near the Kashmir line of control. The general and Sharif ate, talked, and even danced, and they tried to patch things up. On a walk back to their hotel rooms, Sharif pulled an adviser aside and asked, referring to Musharraf, "What do you think?" In English, self-consciously quoting what Margaret Thatcher had once said of Mikhail Gorbachev, the minister replied: "I think he's a guy you can do business with."[19]

Sharif hoped that Pakistani intelligence might yet rescue him. The prime minister remained much closer to his intelligence chief, Khwaja Ziauddin, his family's friend and political protégé, than to Musharraf.

Clinton's rant at Blair House spurred Pakistan to deliver on a plan to train commandos who might be sent into Afghanistan to snatch bin Laden. Sharif tried to shore up his connection to the CIA. Nearly every politician in Pakistan believed, at least some of the time, that the CIA decided who served as prime minister in Islamabad. In September, Ziauddin flew to Washington to meet with Cofer Black, the new head of the Counterterrorist Center, and Gary Schroen. Ziauddin carried a message: "I want to help you. We want to get bin Laden. . . . If you find him, we'll help you." The Pakistani commando training accelerated, and the agency brought the snatch team to "a pretty good standard," as an American official recalled. The commandos moved up to the Afghanistan border. A staging camp was constructed. From Langley and the Islamabad station, the Counterterrorist Center was positioning its agents and collection assets and "getting ready to provide intelligence for action," the American official recalled.[20]

That same week Sharif sent his brother and confidential adviser, Shahbaz, to Washington. Ensconced at the Willard Hotel, all Shahbaz wanted to discuss was "what the U.S. could do to help his brother stay in power," as Bruce Riedel of the National Security Council recalled it. "He all but said that they knew a military coup was coming."[21] The State Department's Rick Inderfurth, speaking to reporters on background, warned against any "extraconstitutional" measures by Pakistan's army. In Rawalpindi, Musharraf and his officers fumed. Why did they need another lecture about democracy from the Americans? Who said they were about to launch a coup anyway? It was Sharif who was the greater danger to Pakistan. And what kind of game was his crony, General Ziauddin, cooking up at the CIA? In the parlors of Islamabad's and Rawalpindi's elite, where conspiracy talk is appetizer and aperitif, suspicion piled upon suspicion as September ended.

Ziauddin heard an earful at Foggy Bottom from Undersecretary of State Pickering, who urged the ISI chief to intervene personally with Mullah Omar about bin Laden. In desperate need of allies, Sharif and his intelligence chief wanted to do all they could to ingratiate themselves with the CIA. Ziauddin flew into Kandahar on October 7 and met with Omar to tell him how strongly the Americans felt about bin Laden. The Taliban leader, as he had so many times before, rebuffed him.[22]

Sharif tried again to ease the tension. He appointed Musharraf to the additional post of chairman of Pakistan's joint chiefs of staff. This was a largely symbolic job, but Sharif had left it open for a year, creating the impression that he might use it to kick Musharraf upstairs, out of direct army command. Now Sharif seemed to make clear that he did not want Musharraf to go. The general felt relaxed enough to take his wife on a working golf junket to Sri Lanka. Bill Milam forecast a temporary peace and left for vacation in California.

On October 12, 1999, as Musharraf flew back to Karachi on a Pakistan International Airlines jet, Nawaz Sharif announced that he was firing his army chief. Against all protocol, he elevated Ziauddin to take Musharraf's place. Ziauddin had few friends among the powerful army corps commanders. He had risen as an engineer on the army's margins, and his turn at ISI had won him more allies in Langley than in Rawalpindi. He had so few connections in General Headquarters that when Sharif told him of his promotion, Ziauddin had to shop for the proper epaulets in a commercial market in Rawalpindi, according to accounts that later reached the U.S. embassy.

The first hours after Sharif's stunning decision unfolded in confusion. It took time for word of Musharraf's dismissal to circulate among senior generals and for them to discuss a response. They intended to hold to military discipline. Musharraf was still in charge, but he was airborne and difficult to reach.

The CIA-funded secret anti–bin Laden commando force on the Afghan border now teetered in the balance. As the new army chief on paper, Ziauddin called the commandos to the capital to help defend his new office and

Nawaz Sharif. There were not many of them, but they could provide a lethal bodyguard.[23]

The commando team's leaders knew that in political terms they were Zia-uddin's men. If they moved now on his behalf, they might reap rewards. But if they tried to defend the general against a hostile army command, they could find themselves under arrest or worse. In the first hours several of the commando team's officers, dressed in plain clothes, moved quietly into Rawalpindi to assess how Ziauddin's faction was doing. They did not want to commit until they could estimate their chances of success.

According to accounts later circulated by the CIA, the commando team leaders quickly discovered the army's outrage about Musharraf's dismissal. The high command intended to move against Sharif and his allies. The army's Tenth Corps, the politically sensitive unit barracked nearest to Islamabad, soon rolled into the streets to detain Sharif and his political allies, including Ziauddin. Without calling attention to themselves, the commando leaders hurriedly communicated to their men: This is a losing cause.

"That unit disappeared" almost overnight, an American official recalled. "I mean, it just dissolved." By one Pakistani account, some of the commandos had become uneasy about their mission against bin Laden. Another U.S. official who was managing the coup crisis in Washington remembered: "The expression I did hear was that they were heading for the hills and haven't been heard from since."[24]

Desperate, Sharif ordered the Karachi airport to refuse permission for Musharraf's plane to land. The jet had only twenty minutes of fuel left, the pilot reported. Circling above the Arabian Sea, the airplane pitched and turned. "The hostess was white as a sheet," recalled Musharraf's wife, Sheba. "Two anti-hijacking guards had come forward. We were gaining and losing height. I could see the lights of Karachi receding."[25]

The army prevailed on the controllers and the plane landed. Musharraf barely had time to absorb that he was now Pakistan's supreme leader. Wearing mismatched civilian clothes hurriedly borrowed, he interrupted the bland folk dancing that had soothed viewers of state-run television during the crisis. Backed by tanks now spreading across Pakistan's major cities, Musharraf declared that a new political era in Pakistan had begun and that Sharif had been dismissed. A day later he issued an emergency decree and appointed himself chief executive.

The coup severely disrupted the Clinton administration's covert campaign against bin Laden. Musharraf immediately arrested Ziauddin. The ISI-supplied, CIA-trained commando team was lost. Richard Clarke and others at the National Security Council had invested little hope in the group, but some CIA officers thought there was at least a 25 percent chance it might have gone into action around Kandahar.

Pakistani intelligence was in for another leadership upheaval. Musharraf had personal cause for suspicion of his own intelligence service. ISI's internal security group had investigated the general's suitability for high office when Sharif was considering him for army chief, Musharraf complained angrily. Now he would have to clean house at ISI to make sure that it was under control, loyal to his new government, and not off running private errands for Clinton or the CIA.

Bill Milam flew back hurriedly to Islamabad and met Musharraf privately at 11 A.M. on Friday, October 15, at General Headquarters in Rawalpindi. Musharraf wore his uniform and surrounded himself with aides. He seemed uncomfortable. Milam had met with Musharraf monthly over the previous year. At first the discussions had been formal and constrained. Gradually they evolved into private, more candid talks. Now Milam handed Musharraf a letter from President Clinton. It chastised the general for taking power and urged him to establish a "roadmap" for restoring democracy. If they discussed any issue besides the army takeover, it was only in passing. Musharraf explained his reasons: Sharif had pulled Pakistan down to one of the lowest points in its history. The general unfurled a long account of his hours on the PIA jet, uncertain of his fate. "He was actually, clearly quite angry with Nawaz," recalled an American involved. "He thought Nawaz was trying to kill him."[26]

Milam knew from his previous meetings that Musharraf had traditional, uncompromising views about Afghanistan and Kashmir. By the time of the coup, Musharraf and his corps commanders felt that "the Americans had adopted a certain approach towards the Taliban without really understanding what the Taliban was all about," as one senior Pakistani official close to the general put it. Musharraf believed that "by marginalizing the Taliban" the Clinton administration had "made them more dependent on the Arabs," and therefore the United States "had ended up with a self-fulfilling prophecy" of rising terrorism. Musharraf wanted Clinton to engage with the Taliban, to seek their moderation, and "to win the hearts and minds of Afghans."[27]

Clinton's Cabinet split over how to react to Musharraf's takeover. Richard Clarke and his allies in the counterterrorism bureaucracy did not want to alienate Musharraf for fear that he would make a difficult bin Laden problem even worse. Albright and others argued that, given Clinton's emphasis on the promotion of democracy worldwide, it would be hypocritical to accept an army-led coup against an elected prime minister, however great Sharif's flaws. Musharraf was the architect of Kargil, she and other skeptics pointed out. He facilitated terrorism in Kashmir. The whole debate about how bad Musharraf might be "diverted the discussion" about counterterrorism in the Cabinet and at the White House, one participant recalled. The coup "introduced a whole new issue in our bilateral relationship; in addition to Kashmir, in addition to proliferation, now there was the issue about the return to democracy."[28]

With Pakistan, at least, bin Laden and al Qaeda were slipping yet further down the list.

AS CELEBRATIONS of the end of the millennium and the dawn of 2000 neared, George Tenet called his old mentor from his days on Capitol Hill, the former senator from Oklahoma, David Boren.

"Don't travel," Tenet told him. "Don't go anyplace where there are big crowds."

Boren was incredulous. "Oh, come on, George," he said dismissively.

"No, no, no," Tenet answered, serious. "You don't understand. You don't understand people like bin Laden." Boren thought Tenet sounded obsessive, but he paid attention.[29]

It had been a rough autumn for the threat-reporting managers at the CIA's Counterterrorist Center. Beginning in September they picked up multiple signs that bin Laden had set in motion major terrorist attacks timed to the turn of the year. Jordan's security services tapped telephones of suspected al Qaeda members and began to gather evidence about one apparent plot to hit American and Israeli targets. There were many other ominous fragments in the CIA's daily threat matrix.

Tenet went to the White House to deliver a forecast: He expected between five and fifteen terrorist attacks around the millennium. "Because the U.S. is [bin Laden's] ultimate goal," Tenet reported, "we must assume that several of these targets will be in the U.S."[30] He grabbed the National Security Council's attention with that prediction. Yet there was still an undercurrent of tension between Richard Clarke's office at the White House and the Counterterrorist Center at the CIA over how much threat reporting was too much. Clarke's two principal aides at the time, Steven Simon and Daniel Benjamin, wrote later that the CIA was still "overloading the President's Daily Brief" that autumn with alarming but inconclusive threat reports, "so great was the fear of failing to give timely notice." This sort of caustic skepticism about CIA motivations frustrated Langley's officers. They believed the White House—especially Clarke's office—would be the first to pounce on them if they failed to pass along a relevant warning.[31]

Two arrests—one made public at the time, the other kept secret initially—shocked them all into panicked cooperation. On November 30, Jordanian intelligence listened as one of bin Laden's top lieutenants, Abu Zubaydah, gave orders by international telephone to begin carrying out an attack he called "the day of the millennium." Jordanian police swooped down on the Amman houses they had under surveillance. In the early hours of December 5, a militant in custody led them to a house with a false floor covered by cinder blocks. Beneath an iron hatch and down a ladder they found seventy-one plastic containers of nitric acid and sulfuric acid. It was enough for explosives as powerful as sixteen tons of TNT, enough to destroy a hotel and the neighborhood around it. The Islamists arrested confessed they had already picked a target: a Radisson Hotel that expected to host American and Israeli tourists for a gala millennium party. The suspects admitted to another plan: They intended to release cyanide gas inside a crowded movie theater that was popular with foreigners.[32]

National Security Adviser Sandy Berger convened daily hour-long White House meetings to review every thread of intelligence, surveillance, and warning available. The interagency group issued streams of nationwide and international alerts. From Langley, Tenet and Cofer Black cabled stations worldwide. They ordered intensified collection and disruption campaigns against any known Islamist individuals or groups whose record suggested they might be involved in the millennium attacks. They sought to target "operations we knew were being planned for the millennium turnover," as one CIA officer at the Counterterrorist Center recalled, "and that we suspected would carry over to the end of the Muslim month of Ramadan in early January 2000."[33]

Nine days after the explosives cache was unearthed in Jordan, a watchful customs agent named Diane Dean saw a Middle Eastern man sweat profusely as he sat in the back of a line of cars exiting a ferry from Canada, through Port Angeles, Washington. She popped the trunk of the man's Chrysler and found enough explosives to level a section of the Los Angeles International Airport, which he later admitted was his target.

Ahmed Ressam, an Algerian, had migrated to Canada, fallen in with a cell of Montreal Islamists, and then traveled to Afghanistan to enroll in camps run by bin Laden. His proximity to America attracted bin Laden's recruiters, and he was enrolled in graduate-level training in explosives at Derunta, a camp near Jalalabad. In mid-January 1999, Ressam departed from Afghanistan with $12,000 in cash and extensive course notes about how to build a devastating bomb.[34]

After Ressam's arrest Clinton telephoned General Musharraf in Pakistan. He demanded that Musharraf find a way to disrupt or arrest bin Laden, according to notes of the conversation kept by the American side. Musharraf's coup offered a potential fresh start in U.S.-Pakistan relations, Clinton said, but the potential benefits of a renewal—economic aid and trade relief—depended on whether Pakistan's army helped remove bin Laden as a threat. Musharraf pledged to cooperate, but he was "unwilling to take the political heat at home," cabled U.S. ambassador William Milam.[35]

Clarke and the CIA's Counterterrorist Center spent New Year's Eve in restless watch for last-minute evidence of an attack. Midnight struck, but no terrorists did. As it happened, they had missed one bin Laden team on the verge of an assault. In Yemen a team of suicide bombers moved against the USS *The Sullivans,* an American destroyer, as it docked at Aden just after New Year's Day. But the plotters overloaded their suicide skiff with explosives and struggled helplessly as it sank in the harbor. They salvaged the boat, but it would be months before they could organize another attack. Nobody noticed them.[36]

At the CIA's Counterterrorist Center, "We were frantic," Cofer Black recalled. "Nobody was sleeping. We were going full tilt." They had launched "the largest collection and disruption activity in the history of mankind against terrorism," he recalled, with "hundreds" of operations under way simultaneously.[37]

In the midst of this surge a piece of intelligence originally turned up by the FBI during its investigations of the Africa embassy bombings "provided a kind of tuning fork that buzzed," as one CIA officer later put it. A phone tap in the Middle East indicated that two Arab men with links to al Qaeda planned a trip to Kuala Lumpur, Malaysia. A Counterterrorist Center officer noticed the connections and sought approval for surveillance operations to try to learn the men's names and, "ideally, what they were doing," as the CIA officer put it.[38]

By January 5, 2000, the CIA had obtained a copy of one of their target's passports. Khalid al-Mihdhar, a middle-class Saudi Arabian with no known links to terrorism, had been issued a U.S. B1/B2 multiple-entry visa in Jedda the previous spring, a visa that would not expire until April 6, 2000, the passport showed.[39]

Working with a Malaysian internal security unit that cooperated regularly with the CIA station in Kuala Lumpur, officers photographed the suspects in and around a golf course condominium owned by an Islamic radical named Yazid Sofaat. The group included a number of known or suspected al Qaeda terrorists. "We surveil them. We surveil the guy they're there to meet," Black recalled. "Not close enough to hear what they're actually saying, but we're covering, taking pictures, watching their behavior. They're acting kind of spooky. They're not using the phone in the apartment. They're going around, walking in circles, just like junior spies. Going up to phone booths, making a lot of calls. It's like, 'Who are these dudes?'"[40]

The Counterterrorist Center briefed Tenet and FBI Director Louis Freeh, but when al-Mihdhar and his companions flew out of Kuala Lumpur, the CIA lost their trail. "Thus far, a lot of suspicious activity has been observed, but nothing that would indicate evidence of an impending attack or criminal enterprise," one CIA officer wrote to another that week.[41]

The email's author had recently been posted to the Counterterrorist Center to help improve communication with the FBI. The officer reported that the FBI had been told "as soon as something concrete is developed leading us into the criminal arena or to known FBI cases, we will immediately bring FBI into the loop."[42]

None of the CIA officers at the Counterterrorist Center, who knew about al-Mihdhar's valid American visa, and none of the FBI officers who were briefed thought to place al-Mihdhar on official American terrorist watch lists. A Counterterrorist Center circular had reminded officers of proper watch-listing procedures only weeks earlier. These lists were designed to alert customs, law enforcement, and immigration officers to the names of those whose entry to the United States should be blocked or reviewed. The CIA at the time was adding several hundred names to the watch list every month.

The agency's "lapse" in al-Mihdhar's case, Tenet said later, "was caused by a combination of inadequate training of some of our officers, their intense focus on achieving the objectives of the operation itself, determining whether the Kuala Lumpur meeting was a prelude to a terrorist attack, and the extra-ordinary pace of operational activity at the time." The first error in January was compounded by another weeks later when the CIA discovered that the second Saudi identified in Malaysia, Nawaf al-Hazmi, had flown to Los Angeles on January 15, 2000, and entered the United States. A March 5 cable to Langley from a CIA station abroad reporting this fact did not trigger a review of either of the Saudis. Nor was either of them placed on the watch list at this second opportunity. As it happened, both men were al Qaeda veterans of wars in Afghanistan and Bosnia.[43]

Without the watch list there was little chance the suspects would face scrutiny. Under the State Department's consular policies, as one investigator later put it, "Saudi Arabia was one of the countries that did not fit the profile for terrorism or illegal immigration."[44] For all of its sour experiences with the Saudi government on terrorism issues and for all of the mutual frustration and suspicion dating back two decades, the United States was still loath to re-examine any of the core assumptions governing its alliance with Riyadh.

Beyond the names of the two mysterious Saudis and the inconclusive photography relayed from Kuala Lumpur, the CIA knew nothing at this stage about the multistranded plot that bin Laden had set in motion in Kandahar late in 1999 to attack American aviation.[45] What Tenet did know about al Qaeda that winter frightened him more than ever before. The cyanide plot in Jordan and the evidence of populous Algerian networks in Canada and Europe stunned the CIA director and his senior colleagues. Among other things, the new cases reinforced Tenet's fears about bin Laden's ambitions to use weapons of mass destruction. Taken together, the evidence "confirms our conviction," Tenet told the Senate Intelligence Committee on February 2, that bin Laden "wants to strike further blows against America" and is "placing increased emphasis on developing surrogates to carry out attacks in an effort to avoid detection." Al Qaeda had now emerged as "an intricate web of alliances among Sunni extremists worldwide, including North Africans, radical Palestinians, Pakistanis, and Central Asians," Tenet warned. The Taliban was an increasingly obvious part of the problem, he said. Illicit profits that the Taliban reaped from opium trafficking reached extremists such as bin Laden "to support their campaign of terrorism."[46]

Still, in this briefing and others to the intelligence committees that winter, as he delivered his warnings in rough order of priority, Tenet continued to place the proliferation of weapons of mass destruction just ahead of the danger of terrorism. "It is simply not enough to look at al Qaeda in isolation," Tenet explained later. The 1990s "saw a number of conflicting and competing trends." He felt he could not concentrate only on terrorism. The CIA had to provide intelligence for American military forces deployed worldwide. It had to watch nuclear proliferation, chemical and biological weapons, tensions in the Middle East, and other pressing issues—and do so with "far fewer intelligence dollars and manpower" than in the past.[47]

The senators, for their part, spent more time that February grilling Tenet about a controversy over the use of classified information by his predecessor at the CIA, John Deutch, than they did asking questions about bin Laden, Afghanistan, or the threat of spectacular terrorism.

For all of the CIA's global surge that winter, none of the wiretaps or inter-rogation reports picked up evidence of the four Arab men from Hamburg who had moved quietly in and out of Afghanistan that winter. The CIA and FBI pressed Germany's police continually for help in watching Islamists in that country, including in Hamburg, but the efforts were frustrated by Ger-man laws and attitudes. Only half a century removed from the Nazi Gestapo, German courts adamantly limited police spying. Many German politicians and intellectuals saw American fears of Islamic terrorism as overblown, even naïve. Nor did CIA cooperation with Pakistani intelligence yield day-to-day exchanges about Arab men entering and leaving the country on Taliban-sponsored visits to Afghanistan. In any event, the Hamburg four finalized their plans for pilot training in the United States without attracting attention from police or intelligence agencies.[48]

Marwan al-Shehhi fell into conversation that spring with a Hamburg li-brarian, Angela Duile, as he prepared to depart for America. "Something will happen and there will be thousands dead," he told her. He mentioned the World Trade Center, she recalled. She did not think he was serious.

"You Crazy White Guys"

A FEW WEEKS AFTER THE MILLENNIUM had passed, the CIA's Counterterrorist Center picked up intelligence that Osama bin Laden had arrived in Derunta Camp, in a jagged valley near Jalalabad.

The camp had become a focus of White House and CIA intelligence collection efforts. It was a typical bin Laden facility: crude, mainly dirt and rocks, with a few modest buildings protected by ridges. Massoud's intelligence sources reported that no Afghans were permitted in Derunta, only Arabs. Testimony from al Qaeda defectors and interrogation of Arab jihadists showed that Derunta was a graduate school for elite recruits. Ahmed Ressam had trained there. Richard Clarke's Counterterrorism Security Group had examined evidence that al Qaeda pursued experiments with poisons and chemical weapons at Derunta. The Defense Intelligence Agency had reported about a year before the millennium that bin Laden aides were developing chemical arms at the camp. The Pentagon routed satellites above Derunta and took pictures. The CIA recruited Afghan agents who traveled or lived in the Jalalabad region. It was an area of high mobility and weak Taliban control, and it did not take long for the agency to develop sources. Through its new liaison in the Panjshir, the Counterterrorist Center pushed technical intelligence collection equipment to Massoud's southern lines. These efforts produced intercepts of Taliban radio traffic in Kabul and Jalalabad. In addition, the CIA inserted an optical device, derived from technology used by offshore spy planes, that could produce photographic images from a distance of more than ten miles. Massoud's men, with help from CIA officers, set up an overlook above Derunta and tried to watch the place with the agency's high-tech spyglass. This intense collection effort did not produce conclusive evidence that bin Laden possessed chemical, biological, or nuclear weapons, but it showed that he wanted them. The Derunta reporting fed Tenet's fear that bin Laden's acquisition of weapons of mass destruction was a "serious prospect."[1]

The Counterterrorist Center relayed its report to Massoud that bin Laden had arrived in Derunta. Bin Laden frequently inspected training camps, where he met with lieutenants, made speeches, and shot a few guns. He moved continuously in unannounced, zigzag loops around Afghanistan. He lectured at mosques, received delegations, and graced banquets with his presence, always surrounded by dozens of Arab bodyguards. Derunta was a regular stop.

Massoud ordered a mission on the basis of the CIA's report. He rounded up "a bunch of mules," as an American official put it, and loaded them up with Soviet-designed Katyusha rockets. He dispatched a small commando team toward Derunta. Massoud's shifting southern lines often allowed his men to move within artillery distance of Kabul and Jalalabad. Fighters who knew the terrain could walk on footpaths through the mountains to secure elevated firing positions.

After the team was on its way, Massoud reported his plan to Langley. The CIA's lawyers convulsed in alarm. The White House legal authorities that provided guidance for the new liaison with Massoud had not authorized pure lethal operations against bin Laden. The Massoud partnership, for now, was supposed to be about intelligence collection. Now the CIA had, in effect, provided intelligence for a rocket attack on Derunta. The CIA was legally complicit in Massoud's operation, the lawyers feared, and the agency had no authority to be involved.

The bin Laden unit at Langley shot a message to the Panjshir: You've got to recall the mission. We have no legal standing to provide intelligence that will be used in rocket attacks against bin Laden, the CIA officers pleaded. Massoud's aides replied, in effect, as an American official put it, "What do you think this is, the Eighty-Second Airborne? We're on mules. They're gone." There was no way to reach the attack team. They did not carry satellite phones or portable radios. They were walking to their launch site, and then they would fire off their rockets, turn around, and walk back.[2]

Langley's officers waited nervously. Some of them muttered sarcastically about the absurd intersections of American law and a secret war they were expected to manage. The worst case would be if the rocket attack went badly and killed innocent civilians. The best case would be if Massoud's men killed bin Laden; they could take the heat if that happened. Days passed, and then weeks. Massoud's aides eventually reported that they had, in fact, shelled Derunta Camp. But the CIA could pick up no independent confirmation of the attack or its consequences. The lawyers relaxed, and the incident passed, unpublicized.[3]

For the bin Laden unit's officers the episode only underlined the issues Massoud had emphasized at their meetings in the Panjshir. Why was the United States unable to choose sides more firmly in Massoud's war against the Taliban? "What is our policy toward Afghanistan?" the bin Laden unit officers demanded in agency discussions. "Is it counterterrorism? Is it political?"[4]

Although Clarke was a relative hawk on bin Laden in the Clinton Cabinet, increasingly Cofer Black and his colleagues at the Counterterrorist Center resented the role played by the White House–run Counterterrorism Security Group. They were in broad agreement about the seriousness of the bin Laden threat, but the CIA's field operatives—"we who actually *did things*," as one of them put it—sought only two kinds of support from Clarke's White House team: funding and permissive policy guidance. By 1999 they felt increasingly that Clarke and Berger could not or would not deliver on either front. "We certainly were not better off by their intervention in ops matters in which they had no experience," recalled one officer involved. In the CIA's executive suites Tenet and clandestine service chief James Pavitt stressed that Langley would not make policy on its own—that was the lesson of the Iran-Contra debacle, they believed. For their part, Clarke and his White House colleagues repeatedly questioned the CIA's ability to act creatively and decisively against bin Laden. Clarke felt that the current generation of CIA officers had "over-learned" the lessons of the 1960s and 1980s that covert action "is risky and likely to blow up in your face." Clinton's Cabinet lacked confidence in its spy service. Explaining what she perceived to be CIA caution in the field, Secretary of State Madeleine Albright quipped to her Cabinet colleagues that because of the scandals and trials suffered during earlier decades, the CIA's active generation of field officers were still coping with the deep bruises of their "abused childhood."

Under the revised guidelines the CIA and Massoud's men could only develop plans for bin Laden's capture. They needed to have a way to bundle him up and fly him out of Afghanistan as part of the plan. Massoud's men could use lethal force if they encountered resistance from bin Laden's bodyguards—as they almost certainly would. The CIA also still had to avoid any action that would fundamentally alter Massoud's military position against the Taliban.

Albright and Berger continued to believe that providing covert military aid to Massoud would only lead to more Afghan civilian deaths while prolonging the country's military stalemate. Massoud's forces were too small and too discredited by their past atrocities to ever overthrow the Taliban or unite the country, they and many analysts inside the State Department believed. Increasingly the White House and even senior CIA managers such as Cofer Black worried as well about Pakistan's stability. If they angered Pakistan's army by embracing the Taliban's enemy, Massoud, this could destroy the Clinton administration's attempt to negotiate controls on Islamabad's nuclear weapons program. As so often before, Pakistan's Islamist-tinged elite managed to appear just dangerous and unpredictable enough to intimidate American officials. The Pentagon, especially General Anthony Zinni at CENTCOM, who remained close to Musharraf personally, emphasized engagement with Pakistan's generals. To covertly provide weapons or battlefield intelligence to Massoud would be to join India, among others, in a proxy war against Pakistan. Zinni also opposed more missile strikes in Afghanistan.

On the front lines of the Panjshir Valley, Massoud and his men took a jaundiced view of American priorities. Episodes like the Derunta attack confused and entertained them. "We were puzzled," remembered one of Massoud's senior aides. "What was 'unlethal' operations if you have an enemy that is armed to the teeth; they have everything. Then you are not allowed to have lethal operations against him?" Still, Massoud recognized that the CIA "represented a democracy, they represented an organized society where institutions function with restrictions," as the senior aide recalled. Massoud also believed that within the American bureaucracy, "intelligence people are always aggressive." Massoud and his advisers were "confident that the CIA wished to do a lot in Afghanistan, but their hands were tied. It was not intelligence failure. It was political failure." When they met with visiting CIA officers or exchanged messages about the new, detailed rules for operations against bin Laden, even after the Derunta attack, "we never heard the word 'kill' from any American we talked to," the senior Massoud aide remembered. "And I can tell you that most of the individuals who were reading these legal notes were also laughing. It was not their draft."[5]

For two decades Massoud had watched in frustration as the United States deferred to Pakistan in its policies toward Afghanistan. In that sense the Clinton administration's policy was not new. Massoud understood that Washington's "relationship with Pakistan was considered strategic," as his senior aide put it. "Pakistan's interference in Afghanistan was considered a minor issue," and so the United States ignored it. This continuing American deference to Islamabad fueled Massoud's cynicism about the CIA's campaign against bin Laden, however. About a dozen Americans had died in the Africa embassy bombings. Many hundreds of Afghan civilians, the kin of Massoud's commanders and guerrillas, had been slaughtered soon afterward by Taliban forces on the Shomali Plains north of Kabul. Yet American law did not indict the Taliban masterminds of the Shomali massacres. It did not permit military aid to attack the Taliban. American politicians rarely even spoke about these massacres. This seemed to some of Massoud's men a profound and even unforgivable kind of hypocrisy.[6]

GEORGE TENET'S EXHORTATIONS about bin Laden cascaded through the CIA. It was rare for the Director of Central Intelligence to personally invest himself in a single counterterrorist mission, as Tenet had done. The result during 1999 and early 2000 was a surge in recruitments of unilateral agents who could operate or travel in Afghanistan. It was the largest CIA drive for unilateral Afghan agents since the late years of the anti-Soviet war. Near East Division case officers and officers dispatched by the Counterterrorist Center sought contact with every potential Afghan source they could find. Some might be informal sources, helping the CIA because of their political opposition to the Taliban. Others were recruited secretly onto the CIA's unilateral payroll. Case officers began to turn some Taliban military leaders, including a brigade-level commander in eastern Afghanistan. One energetic young case officer operating from Islamabad single-handedly recruited six or seven Taliban commanders operating in eastern Afghan border regions. The Islamabad-based case officers also contacted every mujahedin veteran of the anti-Soviet period who was known to the CIA. These included old commanders with Abdurrab Rasul Sayyaf, who was now an ally of Massoud and opposed to the Taliban; Shiite commanders who had worked with the CIA around Kabul during the late 1980s; and Pashtun elders and political figures who spent most of their time in Pakistan but who had kin networks in eastern Afghanistan and sometimes traveled across the border. (An exception was Abdul Haq, still regarded as unreliable by his former CIA allies.) All of these recruitments and contacts were kept secret from Pakistani intelligence, just as the unilateral program had been in the late 1980s. None of the recruited agents was close to bin Laden. Despite several years of effort the CIA had been unable to recruit a single agent inside the core al Qaeda leadership. Black knew that the CIA was in trouble "without penetrations of [the] UBL organization," as a classified Counterterrorist Center briefing to Clinton's national security Small Group put it late in 1999. "While we need to disrupt operations . . . we need also to recruit sources," Black's briefing documents declared, even though "recruiting terrorist sources is difficult." Still, the growing size of the CIA's private agent network on the edges of the leadership, Tenet said later, could be measured in the agent reports that flowed through Langley headquarters: In 1999, for the first time, the CIA generated more unilateral reports about bin Laden from its own agents than reports from liaisons with other intelligence agencies. The Defense Intelligence Agency, working its own Pakistani and Afghan sources, produced scores of its own classified reports about bin Laden.[7]

One purpose of the recruitments was to collect detailed intelligence about bin Laden's movements, his training camps, the houses where he stayed, the houses where his wives stayed, and the houses where al-Zawahiri, Mohammed Atef, and other top lieutenants lived or worked. Gradually the CIA built up a detailed map of bin Laden's infrastructure in Afghanistan. Reports and photography from unilateral agents were matched against satellite imagery to fill in maps of camps and urban neighborhoods.

Bin Laden practiced intensive operational security. He was wary of telephones. He allowed no Afghans into his personal bodyguard, only Arabs he had known and trusted for many years. He varied his routes, did not stay in any one place for long, and never told anyone but his Arab inner circle about his plans. These practices limited the effectiveness of the CIA's recruitments because the agency's sources and paid agents were mainly Afghans who were kept at bay by bin Laden's core bodyguard and leadership group. The CIA was unable to penetrate the inner circle, but bin Laden did have one security weakness, as agency operatives saw it: his several wives. Even after it was obvious that the Americans knew about Tarnak Farm near Kandahar, for example, bin Laden kept one of his families there and visited regularly. As a pious Muslim he tried to follow the Islamic practice of treating all his wives equally. The women had nearly identical lodging. At one point the CIA believed bin Laden had two different wives in Kabul. He would visit their houses regularly. The Islamabad station, through its tribal agents in Kandahar, recruited an Afghan who worked as a security guard at one of the Kabul houses bin Laden used. But the agent was so far down the al Qaeda information chain that he never knew when bin Laden was going to turn up; he was summoned to guard duty just as the Saudi's Land Cruisers rolled in, and it was difficult to get a message out before bin Laden was gone again. "We occasionally learned where bin Laden had been or where he might be going or where someone who looked a little like him might be," Madeleine Albright recalled. "We heard of suspicious caravans or of someone tall with a beard moving about with bodyguards . . . it was maddening."[8]

The CIA's agent networks and operational problems were different in each of the cities where bin Laden stayed. The agency had the best coverage around Kandahar, where its core group of paid tribal assets had been operating for years. Their reporting was now supplemented by swelling networks of anti-Taliban Pashtun activists who could move in and out of the region from Pakistan with ease. "Anytime he went to Kandahar, we would know it," an American official recalled. "We had very good sources in Kandahar. The problem was . . . nobody could say where he was going to be the next day at noon." Kandahar also was the Taliban's military stronghold. Even if the CIA pinpointed bin Laden downtown, there was no easy way to organize a snatch operation; the attacking force would face strong opposition from Taliban units. There was also a likelihood of civilian casualties if the White House ordered missile strikes in the city. Besides, American counterterrorism policy did not identify Mullah Omar or the Taliban as the enemy. By Clinton's declared policy at the United Nations and elsewhere, the Taliban was not fair game for targeted strikes.[9]

It would be less complicated to catch bin Laden at a training camp, on a road in rural Kandahar, or in nearby Uruzgan province, Mullah Omar's home. In the summer of 1999 a truck bomb detonated outside Omar's downtown Kandahar house, killing and wounding some of his relatives. In the aftermath bin Laden used his wealth to construct new compounds for the Taliban leader. He built Omar an extravagant, unapproachable walled palace on Kandahar's outskirts. And bin Laden began a construction program in Uruzgan, including a new training complex for foreign al Qaeda volunteers. When the CIA learned about the Uruzgan project, it ordered satellite imagery and agent reports to document the camp. Its officers also hoped bin Laden might wander in for an inspection. Abdullah, Massoud's foreign policy adviser, recalled that the CIA supplied detailed maps of the Uruzgan camp, based on satellite photography, in the hope that Massoud's agents would mount an attack if bin

Laden visited. At one point a team of four or five Afghan CIA agents with the southern tribal group approached the camp at night to scout it firsthand. Al Qaeda guards opened fire and wounded one of the agents. Bin Laden opened a similar camp near the Helmand River, to the west of Kandahar, but the CIA had few recruits whose tribal and ethnic heritage allowed them to travel comfortably in that area.[10]

Kabul was an easier place to spy in than Kandahar. The Afghan capital was a sprawling and ethnically diverse city, a place of strangers and travelers, where any Afghan could claim to belong. At one stage the CIA's southern tribal team moved north to Kabul's outskirts and rented a farm as a base. They moved in and out of Kabul to scout homes where bin Laden stayed. They developed plans in which—if they had the right intelligence—they would strike a Kabul house where bin Laden slept, snatch the Saudi from his bed, and retreat from the city in jeeps. This was a variation on the 1998 plan to attack bin Laden at Tarnak Farm, which had been reviewed skeptically by White House aides and rejected by CIA managers. The tribal group even ordered explosives from the CIA because their plan called for them to blow up small bridges over culverts as they made their escape.

The group never acted. Their elaborate plans were not matched by any apparent desire to carry them out. The agents reported about half a dozen aborted attacks. In some cases they claimed bin Laden had changed routes unexpectedly. In one case they reported women and children were with bin Laden, and that they held off in compliance with CIA guidance. At the White House the few Clinton aides who knew about the group had long been cynical about their intentions. Between late 1998 and early 2000 the White House attitude toward the TRODPINT team had evolved from "hopeful skepticism to outright mockery," as one official recalled it. Now even the CIA, which still valued the group's reporting and defended them against critics, realized they were not likely to mount risky assaults. The CIA's assessment was that the tribal team knew it might succeed in killing bin Laden in a raid but was likely to suffer heavy losses in the effort. To try to kidnap bin Laden in a city as bustling as Kabul and move him to a safe location while being chased by his bodyguard, as U.S. policy officially required, looked like an implausible episode of *Mission: Impossible*. The group's rented farm, paid for by the CIA, was a working vineyard. Bill Milam, the U.S. ambassador in Islamabad, who was briefed on the operation, would ask his intelligence colleagues sarcastically, "So what are they waiting for—the wine to ferment?" Still, the agents did help map al Qaeda safehouses around the capital, including three different places where bin Laden stayed and houses frequented by his Egyptian lieutenant, Ayman al-Zawahiri.[11]

The CIA's tribal grape growers had been run mainly by case officers in the Near East Division. The new liaison with Massoud offered a chance for the Counterterrorist Center to attempt a fresh penetration of Kabul by working through the intelligence service of the Northern Alliance. About half of the capital's population was Tajik. Massoud had a rich network of intelligence sources among Tajik residents and even some Taliban government officials. But bin Laden himself was "extremely elusive" while in Kabul, recalled Zekrullah Jahed Khan, one of Massoud's intelligence aides. The Saudi might stay in Kabul for two straight months, but he would stay at one base for only two or three hours. He spent much more time in the eastern mountains and Kandahar than in the capital. Al-Zawahiri and Mohammed Atef were easier to track. The Egyptian doctor spent much of his time in Kabul. Atef traveled frequently to the military front lines around the capital. Recalled an American official: "We said, 'Okay, bin Laden's too hard. How about al-Zawahiri? And Atef?'"[12]

That effort became a focus of day-to-day work between Langley's Counterterrorist Center and Massoud's intelligence network. The CIA supplied collection equipment and used satellite photography to validate observations made by Massoud's agents on the ground. Together they developed "a pretty good idea of where the bad guys were," as one American official recalled. One visual signature they relied on was the clustering of luxury sport utility vehicles. Most Afghans did not own cars, much less SUVs. The CIA would put its satellites over Kabul, and its analysts would say, as an official remembered, "Well, eight Land Cruisers. Someone is bad in that house." But al-Zawahiri's entourage was not as large or as conspicuous as bin Laden's. He was not easy to track. Besides, when Massoud's men began to get a fix, they confronted the problem of legal authorities for lethal operations. The CIA was not permitted to fly into the Panjshir with a sniper rifle and a satellite map of al-Zawahiri's house even if it could develop one. Any joint operation had to be a plausible, well-planned attempt to capture the Egyptian. When they tried to discuss these kinds of plans with Massoud's men, the Americans found them evasive. As an American official recalled: "The Northern Alliance thought, 'Oh, okay, you want us to capture him. Right. You crazy white guys.'"[13s]

Reporting from Massoud's intelligence service and unilateral Afghan agents, however, raised some hope that bin Laden might one day step unwittingly into a Northern Alliance trap. Massoud's aides told the CIA that bin Laden sometimes inspected al Qaeda troops near Kabul or in northern Afghanistan. Once in a while bin Laden wandered into the wrong place. In a recent battle northeast of Kabul, Massoud's men reported, bin Laden had gone on an inspection tour and become trapped on the northern side of Massoud's position. He had escaped only by packing out over mountain paths. After the CIA obtained authorities for operations with Massoud, American officials began to hope that bin Laden would mistakenly stray behind Northern Alliance lines one more time.

CIA and White House officials also were encouraged to discover that bin Laden had, at least once, traveled all the way to the northern border between Afghanistan and Uzbekistan, to the port town of Hairaton on the Amu Darya River. According to Afghans who had seen him, bin Laden made speeches there about coming Islamist political and military triumphs in Central Asia; he had wanted to see the sites of his future conquests for himself. The northern border region was controlled by the Taliban, but local commanders often were not committed to the cause; many had switched their allegiance from Massoud's alliance only recently. The CIA harbored hopes that bin Laden would travel to the far north again. This was one reason they had invested so much effort training and equipping the Uzbekistan commando team: A strike just across the Amu Darya border into Uzbek areas of Afghanistan might be relatively easy to mount if they had the right intelligence. Mohammed Atef, too, traveled north to command military operations. He was not as conspicuous or famous a figure as bin Laden, but he might be a more accessible target.[14]

Bin Laden's journeys west and north followed a somewhat predictable path: He would ride west on the Ring Road from Kandahar, then loop north and east through Ghowr province where there was a valley he liked to visit. The CIA mapped houses in obscure Ghowr, one of Afghanistan's most isolated and impoverished regions. From there the Saudi usually moved east to Kabul and then sometimes on to Jalalabad before turning south again to Paktia and Kandahar. Americans who studied this track called it "the circuit." They tried to map reliable reports of bin Laden's movements in great detail. At Richard Clarke's Counterterrorism Security Group they even tried to develop logarithmic formulas that attempted to predict, based on past behavior, where bin Laden was likely to move next when he was at any given point on the circuit. Over time, even the most security-conscious people can repeat themselves out of habit or unconscious instinct.

The agency's working idea was to try to keep bin Laden out of "KKJ," an insider's acronym for the densely populated cities of Kabul, Kandahar, and

Jalalabad. It did not seem plausible after 1999 that a CIA proxy force could mount a successful snatch operation in a Taliban-ruled urban area, but during 2000, bin Laden traveled to rural northern areas less frequently. The CIA picked up reports that he and his men had been intimidated by banditry and robbery gangs on some of the more lawless northern roads where the Taliban's writ did not run. There were no more triumphal speeches on the border of Central Asia, and the Uzbek commandos languished.[15]

The CIA developed a specific visual signature for bin Laden's traveling convoy: several Land Cruisers and a bodyguard of twenty to one hundred Arab men. It was the daily work of officers at the Counterterrorist Center to develop and discuss specific operational plans for an armed snatch attempt against bin Laden. After the disappearance of the Pakistani commando team, they had three realistic options: the Uzbek commandos, Massoud's forces, or the grape-growing tribal tracking team around Kandahar. The tactical problem was obvious: The CIA's most plausible proxy forces operated in Afghanistan's north, while bin Laden spent most of his time in the south and east. The CIA struggled to find a convincing plan.[16]

SIX FEET FIVE INCHES TALL, chiseled and square-faced, General Hugh Shelton was a civilian's idea of what a general should look like. Defense Secretary William Cohen appointed him Chairman of the Joint Chiefs of Staff, the top position in the American military, shortly before the Africa embassy bombings. After bin Laden became a pressing national security priority in the autumn of 1998, Shelton seemed an ideal Pentagon partner. He had been a Special Forces team leader in Vietnam, a commander of elite airborne troops, and finally commander of all American Special Forces. Unlike many generals he had direct experience in unconventional tactics, counterinsurgency, and the use of small strike teams in the Third World. As a military leader he preferred to operate by consultation and consensus. He did not seem to his civilian colleagues an especially original or forceful general, but his record of battlefield valor and field command marked him as an authentic war fighter, not one of the Washington generals who made their careers as uniformed politicians.[17]

The White House first asked the Pentagon for detailed military plans to attack and arrest bin Laden in the autumn of 1998. When Shelton and his aides briefed Sandy Berger at the White House, they reported that a "boots on the ground" operation involving American Special Forces or Army Rangers would require large numbers of troops—thousands—plus aircraft carriers, transport planes, and refueling tankers. Even so, the chances of success were not great,

Shelton said. They lacked a foothold in the region, a secure base of operations. "We don't have Pakistan," Shelton observed, as Sandy Berger remembered it. "We don't have Uzbekistan, we don't have Tajikistan." Without
better intelligence than what they were seeing from the CIA, even a well-
supported mission was "likely to fail," the Pentagon's planners believed.[18]

Shelton, Cohen, and their senior aides saw the CIA's reporting from Afghanistan every day. Even as the size and scope of the agency's unilateral agent
network grew, the intelligence it produced looked unsound to them as a basis
for committing American soldiers to Afghanistan. The CIA's agents simply
could not keep track of bin Laden on a daily basis. "All we had was a brother
who had a brother of a man who was allegedly in his security detail, or the
cousin of somebody who had once been told, 'Get the feast ready, because
the sheikh is coming,'" remembered a Pentagon civilian who regularly reviewed
the CIA's reporting. Cohen recalled telling his colleagues: "We can do this. It's
high risk, but if you've got the information to tell us where he is, we will be
prepared to recommend that we use force." But Cohen was cautioned by his
recent experiences watching U.S. Special Forces hunt with limited success for
fugitive war criminals in the Balkans. He concluded that "someone who exercises good tradecraft is very difficult to locate and capture in enemy territory,"
and that bin Laden's tradecraft was "better than senior Serb war criminals."[19]

There was no way to be certain how Taliban troops would react to a U.S.
Special Forces raid; any sensible plan had to assume the Taliban would be
hostile. A raid in an urban area, therefore, looked highly dangerous. The CIA's
clandestine effort to track bin Laden outside of "KKJ" and snare him in less
heavily defended border areas made more sense in theory, but there was no
joint planning with the CIA about this possibility. In any event the Pentagon
saw huge tactical and political problems if the United States tried to operate
on its own anywhere near Pakistan.[20]

Clinton, Berger, the National Security Council staff, and Pickering at the
State Department all saw Shelton as too cautious, too mired in conventional
Pentagon doctrine about logistics and force protection. Pickering saw Shelton's slide shows about how many thousands of troops would be required to
snatch bin Laden as "a standard military position—give us forty-eight months
and five divisions. These were gold-plated arguments. . . . They thought, perhaps with some justification, that the NSC and State wanted to correct every
problem with them as cannon fodder." Clinton pleaded with Shelton after a
Cabinet meeting for even a symbolic raid: "You know," the president told the
general, "it would scare the shit out of al Qaeda if suddenly a bunch of black

ninjas rappelled out of helicopters into the middle of their camp. It would get us enormous deterrence and show these guys we're not afraid." But when Shelton returned with an options briefing, his plans all outlined large deployments and cautioned that there would be scant probability of success.[21]

Shelton felt the pressure from Richard Clarke especially. Clarke pressed the Pentagon relentlessly for smaller, stealthier plans to attack bin Laden. Shelton saw the White House counterterrorism chief as "a rabid dog." He conceded that "you need that in government—you need somebody who won't take no for an answer." Still, Shelton and the generals felt Clarke and other White House civilians had "some dumb-ass ideas, not militarily feasible. They read something in a Tom Clancy novel and thought you can ignore distances, you can ignore the time-distance factors."[22]

In Special Forces doctrine the quality of intelligence determines the size of the force required to conduct a raid. The more uncertain the intelligence, the larger the required force. The calculation is as much art as science, but it rests on common sense. If an American Delta Force commando, for instance, is able to watch a target with his own eyes and communicate by secure radio to attacking forces, then a commander can be highly certain about when to launch, and he might feel confident about sending a relatively small force. But if the tactical intelligence is being relayed by non-Americans of uncertain competence or loyalty, and if their intelligence is fragmentary or subject to sudden change—as was the case with the CIA's reporting about bin Laden in Afghanistan—then a commander should size the attacking force to cope with unpredictable resistance. Shelton felt he had a very hard time convincing the civilians in Clinton's White House of these plain ideas.[23]

Any raid by American forces into Afghanistan would have to launch from the sea and cross either Iranian or Pakistani airspace. The Pentagon had no land-basing arrangements close enough to Afghanistan for a helicopter to make a round-trip. Special Forces helicopters and some specially equipped C-130 support transports could evade Iranian or Pakistani radar, but seaborne helicopter carriers would have to circle in waters off the coast and could not hide. Pakistan and Iran both kept close watch on ships moving in international waters near their shores. Pentagon intelligence had monitored Pakistani communications well enough to know that Pakistan tracked American warships and reported on their positions when they neared Pakistan's shores. Only submarines could reliably evade such detection. The Pentagon had permanently stationed cruise missile–equipped subs rather than surface ships off Pakistan's coast in case the president ordered another missile strike against bin

Laden. The Pentagon assumed that Pakistan maintained spy networks in Oman and the Persian Gulf to watch American armadas come and go. Shelton also assumed that if Pakistan detected a U.S. raiding mission, it would alert the Taliban; the Taliban would then alert bin Laden, allowing him to escape or prepare an ambush for American forces. The list of catastrophic precedents rang in Shelton's ears: Desert One, the failed U.S. Special Forces raid in 1980 to rescue American hostages in Tehran; the 1993 disaster in Mogadishu, Somalia (which al Qaeda operatives had helped to carry out); the ambush losses suffered by Soviet special forces in Afghanistan during the late 1980s. Shelton repeatedly cited Desert One to Clinton's White House aides as a cautionary example. He made an impression. Some of Clinton's senior aides believed that that failed raid had effectively ended the presidency of the last Democrat in the White House, Jimmy Carter.[24]

A generation earlier the CIA had possessed its own sizable covert paramilitary forces—sea, land, and air—which it used to attack problems like this one. The CIA had run a small war in Guatemala, a failed raid at Cuba's Bay of Pigs, and a secret air war in Laos. The agency's Special Activities Division retained some paramilitary assets, but the unit was a fraction of its previous size. Its strengths were intelligence collection missions, covert operations with local militia forces, and very small strikes. Some American officials believed it did not possess the airplanes or support facilities to pull off a mission in Afghanistan without help from the Pentagon. Still, it bothered some of Clinton's aides that the CIA never even suggested using its own forces to go after bin Laden.[25]

For their part, officers at the Pentagon and the CIA believed that Clinton, as commander in chief, had failed to make—or to force his Cabinet to make—a firm tactical decision about how best to capture or kill bin Laden and his lieutenants. There were no good options, they all admitted. But the White House fostered dispersed, highly compartmented, isolated operations and planning at the CIA and the Pentagon. Clinton's policy seemed to involve the pursuit of many policies at once. He did not make clear, for instance, whether his priority was to kill bin Laden with cruise missiles or to mount a lethal capture operation. Clarke's Counterterrorism Security Group tried to fuse and share intelligence reporting and to seize opportunities for sudden strikes against al Qaeda, but Clinton himself hung back. He goaded Clarke's efforts with "need to do more"–style notations on the margins of National Security Council memos, but he never insisted on final plans or attack decisions. As a result the CIA Counterterrorist Center attempted to develop both the cruise missile track and a snatch operation using proxy forces, but its officers never collaborated with the Pentagon in a concentrated fashion on either one. Staggering through impeachment, it would have taken an exceptional act of will for the president to push through a decision to attack, given the difficulties of the target and the divisions in his Cabinet. At the White House, Clinton's National Security Council aides firmly believed that they were the aggressive ones on the al Qaeda case, pursuing every possible avenue to get at bin Laden over calcified resistance or incompetence within the CIA and Pentagon bureaucracies. From the other side of the Potomac, Clinton's White House often looked undisciplined, unfocused, and uncertain—and the bin Laden planning was no exception.[26]

Politics entwined these debates with more threads of doubt. In the context of impeachment and Clinton's uncomfortable relations with the military, some White House aides suspected that Shelton's reluctance to attack bin Laden was partially political, that neither he nor other generals were prepared to take risks for a weakened president they did not trust. For his part, Clinton worried about his "personal responsibility to the soldiers and their families," recalled one of his senior aides. "People underestimate what that's like." The worst case would be "a failed mission in which you insert a few hundred Special Forces and they get routed."[27]

They all kept returning to the same issues. Among the most important was the status of the Taliban. By 2000 there were still a few analysts at the State Department's intelligence bureau who argued for patient engagement with the Taliban. But most of Clinton's Cabinet now accepted that al Qaeda had hijacked Mullah Omar. Clinton squeezed the Taliban with economic sanctions, but he also continued to endorse negotiations with them, declared a policy of neutrality in Afghanistan's war, and resisted entreaties to aid Massoud.

This divided policy affected internal debates about the cruise missile option. Clarke said to Berger that if the White House openly recognized the Taliban as the enemy, it could take a more flexible approach to cruise missile strikes. Clinton then would no longer require precise, two-source intelligence about bin Laden's location. Clinton could pursue a bomb-and-pause approach against the Taliban, choosing his targets carefully based on the best available CIA intelligence about bin Laden, but defending the strikes in public as an attack against the Taliban and terrorist infrastructure. The strikes could be tied to the long-standing American demand that the Taliban turn bin Laden and his lieutenants over for trial. If the Taliban refused, the United States could just bomb again, especially when it had strong intelligence about bin Laden, al-Zawahiri, Atef, or other leaders. Shelton recalled that the idea of hitting Taliban infrastructure and leadership targets developed to the point where he was asked to examine the residences of Taliban leaders and places where they worked, and to develop target data "in the event that we wanted to make that decision," to bomb the Taliban directly.[28]

Sandy Berger rejected this proposal for a wider war. The August 1998 cruise missile strikes against al Qaeda had been a political disaster at home and abroad. The repeated firing of cruise missiles at impoverished, long-suffering Afghanistan—without strong intelligence about who would be killed and with the near-certainty of civilian deaths—would only raise bin Laden's standing in the Islamic world, foster new al Qaeda recruitments, and draw worldwide condemnation of the United States. Pickering agreed with Berger. "We had force in the region and were prepared to use it," Pickering recalled, if they had a precise fix on bin Laden's location. "But we were not prepared to fire Tomahawks on a daily basis or to try to use bombing aircraft, crossing Pakistani airspace when, in fact, we didn't have even the right intelligence or the right predicate to do it." Sixty-seven Americans had been killed by terrorists during the Clinton presidency, Berger noted pointedly. There was no political context for an American war in Afghanistan. Instead Berger worked on the issues he felt were realistic. After the Millennium near-miss Clarke wrote that it seemed clear that the U.S. campaign against al Qaeda had "not put too much of a dent" in bin Laden's organization and that "sleeper cells" had formed on American soil. Berger pulled the national security cabinet together on March 10 to endorse new efforts: More support for CIA operations abroad; more attention to foreign terrorist groups at home; and tighter border security. It was a campaign of budget allocations, law tightening, and foreign liaison programs—practical but limited.[29]

IT WOULD BE SO MUCH EASIER if Massoud or his allies would just take care of bin Laden themselves. But would he do so even if he had the chance? The White House and the CIA debated Massoud's motivations. The officers who met the commander in the Panjshir or who had known him previously understood that Massoud was a pious Muslim who saw himself as a global Islamic leader. If he struck out against bin Laden and killed him—or worse, if he bundled him off to the Americans—he would pay a heavy price in the Muslim world. Massoud might be able to defend a decision to kill bin Laden in battle—he was in a war—but to kidnap an Islamic sheikh on behalf of the

CIA and to deliver him to a humiliating trial in an American courtroom? That would not do much to burnish Massoud's reputation as an independent-minded guerrilla legend. What was his incentive to take that kind of chance even if such an operation were possible? The CIA could not offer him the prospect of American military or even political support against the Taliban. Shelton and others at the Pentagon were skeptical about even a covert military partnership with Massoud. The Northern Alliance "had its own baggage," Shelton recalled, "and when you attach the U.S. flag to their formation, and you become a partner with them, then you also become one who can be held accountable for their actions." Massoud was not a partner that Shelton wanted to embrace.[30]

Still, the CIA deepened its intelligence partnership with Massoud's men during 2000. Some of Clinton's White House aides figured Massoud would just tell the agency what it wanted to hear, pocket the relatively small amounts of money and equipment on offer, and go about his business as before. But even so, why not give it a try? They had few other plausible options.

There was an argument about which section of the agency would make additional secret trips into northern Afghanistan. Was Massoud now a Counterterrorist Center account, or did he belong to the Afghanistan section of Near East? The discussions produced a Solomonic decision: Future missions to the Panjshir would be alternated between the Counterterrorist Center's JAWBREAKER teams and the NALT teams drawn from the Near East Division.[31]

Cofer Black flew out to Tajikistan with a team from the bin Laden unit in the early summer of 2000. In tattered Dushanbe, Massoud's men picked him up in an old Mercedes-Benz which they proudly claimed had belonged once to Najibullah, Afghanistan's communist-era secret police chief and doomed president. They drove the American team to one of Massoud's safehouses. Inside, with aides and translators, Massoud laid out a battle map and reviewed the Taliban's positions. As always when he had an American audience, he talked about the broader threat that the Taliban posed to the Islamic world and to the West. He talked about the sufferings endured by the Afghan people under Taliban oppression.[32]

Black wanted to solidify their partnership and advance their efforts at shared intelligence collection. He asked if Massoud had any Arab prisoners who could be interrogated. Massoud said he had only a few, none of any value. They had trouble taking prisoners when they fought Brigade 55, bin Laden's Arab mercenary force. When Massoud's forces closed in, the Arab soldiers hurriedly gathered in a circle, pulled the pins on their grenades, and committed collective suicide. Massoud became very specific about "problems of the resistance," as one of his intelligence aides in the meeting recalled, including "the problems of purchasing weapons from Russia," and the kind of military equipment that the Americans could supply if they wanted to make a difference in the war.

Massoud "made it very clear to the American side that it was a good time, if they wanted, to somehow punish the Taliban," his aide remembered. The Taliban were weakening politically, but Massoud's forces were struggling. The CIA team reported to their colleagues that Massoud portrayed himself as the only anchor, the only force challenging the Taliban. Massoud had asked them for substantial support, they reported to Langley.

The CIA team said they were arguing on his behalf in interagency councils in Washington. "They were trying to show Mr. Massoud that he had succeeded in finding an audience in the United States," recalled Massoud's intelligence aide, "and that his mission and his cause was on the U.S. agenda. . . . They wanted to tell him that maybe in the future they will assist him."

Massoud's men knew it would be hard for the CIA to keep that promise. The agency's intelligence aid was helpful, but as a means to change American policy in Afghanistan, the CIA seemed like a limited partner. "Things were going well but very slowly—very slowly," recalled Abdullah, Massoud's foreign policy adviser. "I was never of the opinion that we could get big changes" even with the CIA's help in policy debates. "The system in the United States—it takes dramatic events for things to move."[33]

"Is There Any Policy?"

PERVEZ MUSHARRAF HOPED to position himself as a modern, even progressive military usurper. He called himself Pakistan's "chief executive," appeared publicly in business suits, and issued extravagant promises about reform and democratic restoration. He hired a Washington lobbyist, Lanny J. Davis, who had been Clinton's mouthpiece during impeachment, to convince the White House of his liberal outlook. But in Islamabad, within the councils of his own army, Musharraf had to establish a new order, and he could not pay a lobbyist to help. He was especially beholden to one general, Mahmoud Ahmed, who had been the frontline commander of the raid into Kargil, reporting directly to Musharraf, and who at the time of the coup had been the commander of the Tenth Corps, the army unit barracked in Rawalpindi and responsible for security in the capital. On that perilous October evening in 1999, as his superior circled uncertainly on a plane above Karachi, Mahmoud (as he was called by his colleagues) rolled a brigade into Islamabad to detain Nawaz Sharif and secure the government for the army. Then, honoring the chain of command, Mahmoud stood aside. All of the Pakistani political elite understood that Musharraf owed his power to Mahmoud's conduct, and they watched in the first weeks after the coup to see how this debt would be repaid. They did not have to wait long: Musharraf quickly announced that Mahmoud would become the new director-general of ISI. Mahmoud would clean up the mess left by Ziauddin, Sharif's lackey who now was under house arrest in Lahore.[1]

In Ziauddin's fall from power the CIA's South Asia branch had lost an ally. The general was dull-minded and his authority was weak, but at least he was cooperative, always ready to hold a meeting. Now the CIA had to establish a new relationship with Mahmoud. If Pakistani intelligence could be turned to the American agenda, it offered by far the fastest, easiest path to disrupt al Qaeda's Afghan sanctuary and capture or kill bin Laden.

The CIA began to research Mahmoud's biography, looking for a way to establish a connection with him. He was an artillery officer. He had served with Musharraf in the same unit earlier in their careers. Case officers discovered that when Mahmoud was a student at Pakistan's elite officers' college, he had written his thesis on the battle of Gettysburg. The new Islamabad station chief, known to his colleagues as Bob, talked with Mahmoud about visiting the United States to meet with counterparts at Langley, including George Tenet. The CIA promised to arrange an expert guided tour of Gettysburg. It would be a chance for intelligence officers on both sides to get to know each other better.[2]

The U.S. embassy in Islamabad already had a passing acquaintance with Mahmoud. Pakistan's army prohibited ambassadors or station chiefs from making official visits to corps commanders, but the Americans saw Mahmoud anyway. The general's duties with the Tenth Corps meant he sometimes received dignitaries at the Islamabad airport, and he occasionally socialized on the capital's diplomatic circuit. He seemed to be a general of a certain Pakistani type: British in comportment, spit and polish in appearance, disciplined and correct. He wore a waxed handlebar mustache in the colonial style. He obviously was an ardent nationalist, and his authorship of the Kargil raid suggested the depths of his animus toward India. Yet on the surface he did not seem to be an unusually religious general. He spoke openly with the Americans about the need to bring military discipline and chain-of-command authority to Pakistan's intelligence service. These private comments could be interpreted as a repudiation of how Ziauddin had tried to politicize ISI to protect Sharif and flank the army, but they also hinted at a desire to manage Pakistani intelligence more closely, to rein in rogue elements—or so some of the Americans who talked with Mahmoud that winter chose to believe.[3]

Clinton's national security advisers, still divided over how to react to Musharraf's coup, debated early in 2000 about whether the American president should visit Pakistan. Clinton had committed to visit India in March. The Secret Service maintained that a stopover in Pakistan would be too dangerous. Pakistani intelligence could not be trusted to protect details of Clinton's itinerary, they argued, and there were too many motivated, well-equipped terrorist groups in the region. Al Qaeda or Taliban squads might move Stingers from Kandahar and fire at the American president's plane. Musharraf's government, watching India lobby hard in Washington to persuade Clinton to shun Pakistan, pushed the White House for a reciprocal visit. Lanny Davis worked Capitol Hill. In Islamabad the government made gestures on terrorism. Mahmoud volunteered to help the CIA take custody of two Arab militants, one with an American passport, who had been secretly detained by Pakistani police. Musharraf announced that he was "actively considering" a trip to Kandahar to lobby Mullah Omar to hand bin Laden over to the Americans.[4] It was in many ways a cynical charm offensive, designed to compete with India's diplomacy. It did not mark a shift in Pakistan's jihad strategy. Pakistan's army had long ago learned that it could earn credits with the Americans, especially with the CIA and FBI, by cracking down on relatively small numbers of al Qaeda terrorists who were not important to Pakistan's policies in Kashmir or Afghanistan.

The tactic seemed to work again: Clinton decided in March on a one-day visit to Islamabad. Clinton's decision had many facets. He wanted to coax Pakistan away from nuclear dangers, promote American engagement, and cultivate regional stability. Partly because there were so many sensitive issues, Clinton's team did not want to push the Pakistani army too hard on terrorism. Reading the American agenda attentively, Musharraf quietly allowed Kashmiri radical groups with close ties to ISI and al Qaeda—including one whose leader signed bin Laden's original 1998 *fatwa* declaring war on the United States—to reorganize and dramatically expand their recruitments across Pakistan on the eve of Clinton's trip.[5]

Clinton's visit was one of the strangest in presidential history. He was the first American president to visit Pakistan since Richard Nixon in 1969.[6] By defying advice to stay away he forced the Secret Service into an elaborate, deception-laden security regime for the Islamabad stopover on the way back from India. "We're going to show them a new look," a Secret Service agent announced on the tarmac in Bombay, adapting the language of American football coaches to the challenge of counterterrorism. A Clinton lookalike wandered between two white executive jets and boarded one marked with the presidential seal. The real president slipped into an unmarked CIA G-5. His aides were already aboard; the window shades were drawn shut.

"Are we going to have these windows down the whole time?" Clinton asked. "I can't fly like that."

"Mr. President, as soon as we get up in the air . . ."[7]

Clinton seemed indifferent to the threat of Stingers. He napped, did a crossword puzzle, and then took a short briefing from his Pakistan specialists. On the ground in Islamabad his double walked conspicuously to the terminal, prepared to draw the fire of assassins. When all proved safe, Clinton slipped into an armored car for a ride down Islamabad's broad avenues to a meeting in Musharraf's modern boxy office complex. There were no waving crowds; the Secret Service had ordered that the roads be absolutely clear.[8]

On a balcony downtown Clinton looked out and remarked, "I don't see any people around."

"Mr. President, you can't because we were asked to make sure that there weren't any people around," one of his hosts from the Pakistan foreign ministry explained.

"Oh, really? I didn't know that."

"Didn't you notice that from the airport to this place there weren't any people around?"

"Yes, it did strike me." They joked about how it was now possible to visit a country without actually seeing anyone who lived there. Recalled the Pakistani official: "It was really quite humiliating, there's no question about it." Many elite Pakistanis felt that Clinton had treated their entire nation like the inmate population of a medium-security prison.[9]

Clinton and Musharraf talked for almost two hours, surrounded by aides for all but a few minutes. The Americans listed their talking points in the usual order of priority: nuclear proliferation, regional tensions, and economic issues, then terrorism and other problems. Clinton's counterterrorism aides said later that there were worries about whether Musharraf would survive long in office, and so they did not want to talk about bin Laden in front of Pakistanis of "uncertain loyalties."[10]

In a smaller session with Musharraf, recalled National Security Adviser Sandy Berger, Clinton pressed "very hard" and told the general "to use Pakistan's influence with the Taliban to get bin Laden." A Pakistani official present remembered Clinton worrying aloud that bin Laden would acquire weapons of mass destruction. Musharraf said he would do as much as he could. But he urged engagement with the Taliban to encourage good behavior. The next day Musharraf told Thomas Pickering that Pakistan had little leverage in any event.[11]

Clinton spoke live on Pakistani television for fifteen minutes. Through the relative safety of a broadcast camera lens he warned the people he had not seen against the "danger that Pakistan may grow even more isolated, draining even more resources away from the needs of the people, moving even closer to a conflict that no one can win."[12]

The CIA used the visit to secure Mahmoud's commitment to travel to the United States. The ISI chief flew to Washington in April. The agency arranged for a private tour of the Gettysburg battlefield, escorted by a teacher from the U.S. Army War College at Carlisle Barracks in Pennsylvania. Gary Schroen and other CIA officers came along as well. Their tour guide had spent many hours walking the battlefield park to retrace the 1863 command decisions of Robert E. Lee. Mahmoud came alive and talked animatedly about battle tactics, personalities, and the fateful turning points of the American Civil War. The Pakistani general was relaxed, talkative, seemingly engaged. The CIA men had made a personal connection with Mahmoud, a first step toward deeper cooperation or recruitment, it seemed.[13]

There were limits to their hopes. Officers in the bin Laden unit at the Counterterrorist Center remained deeply skeptical that Mahmoud or any other Pakistani general would ever do the right thing about the Taliban. Also, when Mahmoud talked with CIA officers at Langley and with officials at the White House, he often seemed to condescend and evade. One official who met with him recalled, speaking caustically, "His orientation toward the Americans was to attempt to educate us about the complexities of that area of the world. With very little prompting he would do me the kindness to bring out a map and show me how high the mountains are, how difficult it is to operate."[14]

These sorts of repetitious frustrations with ISI generals and brigadiers had built to the point where at least a few American officials suggested that Clinton present an ultimatum: Either Pakistan moved to cut off aid to the Taliban, or it would be placed on the official list of countries that supported terrorism. But Chairman of the Joint Chiefs Hugh Shelton and others at the Pentagon urged caution. Shelton remembered that he "vacillated a couple of times" during these months as he tried to decide whether America had crossed into appeasement of Pakistan or whether it just had to accept the obstacles and continue to engage. General Zinni of CENTCOM declared that Pakistan "may hold the key to stability in Afghanistan and Central Asia." America had to keep reaching out, he argued. The Clinton national security team forged an informal compromise: The CIA's Near East Division and Islamabad station would try to butter up Mahmoud and recruit him into partnership, while other American officials would try to pressure him hard.[15]

Thomas Pickering had become Clinton's diplomatic intimidator, a designated bad cop assigned to deliver tough messages that other officials in liaison roles felt they could not afford to send. A bald, bulky diplomat with several decades of experience in political and intelligence issues, Pickering often leaned into his guests as he spoke, and he could unfurl rapid-fire sentences with direct and solemn force. In his office above C Street on April 4, 2000, Pickering lit into Mahmoud about Pakistan's support for the Taliban. He warned that the Taliban were harboring terrorists who had killed Americans. "People who do that are our enemies, and people who support those people will also be treated as our enemies," Pickering intoned. Pakistan ought not to "put itself in that position." Of course, announced American policy still offered the Taliban hope of reward if it reformed, and American officials never called Mullah Omar an enemy in public. After earlier reports of sharp tensions between Taliban leaders and bin Laden, U.S. intelligence discovered that the Taliban's Council of Ministers had unanimously endorsed its alliance with al Qaeda at the end of 1999. Mullah Omar had even reportedly executed Taliban dissenters over the issue. Pickering warned Mahmoud that U.S. policy was on the verge of a turn: Washington might even sanction support for Ahmed Shah Massoud in the Afghan war if the Taliban did not do something about bin Laden soon.[16]

Mahmoud flew back to Pakistan and quickly arranged a trip to Kandahar to meet with Mullah Omar. Classified Pakistani papers later discovered in Kabul describe the talking points Mahmoud carried to the meeting. The Pakistani intelligence chief told Omar that the situation was becoming serious. Mahmoud listed America's demands: "Nothing short of the extradition of Osama bin Laden to a place where he could be brought to justice would satisfy the U.S." Also, "Washington wants immediate results." If the Taliban refused to comply, the Americans were demanding that Pakistan end all support.[17]

Even more dramatically, Mahmoud reported, the Americans might endorse "missile attacks targeting the Taliban's military assets. Osama—and even Omar himself—could be targeted." In addition, "Russia and its allies could be given the go ahead to embark on hot pursuit against terrorists" into Afghanistan. They could bomb strategic targets in northern Afghanistan, "thereby eliminating the military potential of the Taliban to the complete advantage of Ahmed Shah Massoud. . . . The U.S. and Russia could coordinate their actions in pursuance of the above measures."[18]

It was all a bluff. The Clinton administration was not prepared to follow through on these sorts of threats. Pickering had opened a few talks with Russian intelligence about possible cooperation on Afghanistan but nothing so advanced as what Mahmoud reported to Mullah Omar. Richard Clarke and others had urged missile strikes against Taliban targets, but Sandy Berger, among others, remained opposed. Still, the United States could always make threats. Perhaps the Taliban would capitulate.

Mahmoud asked Omar to "resolve the Osama bin Laden issue before it is too late. . . . The U.S. must be given a plan of action. The Osama issue also affects Pakistan because his aides are using Pakistan as a transit point."

The Taliban leader replied, according to Mahmoud's report, that he "wanted to get rid of Osama but did not know how."[19]

It was impossible for the Americans to tell how sincerely Mahmoud pressured the Taliban at this meeting. Was it all just for show, winks all around? Or did Mahmoud truly believe it would be better for Pakistan if bin Laden was gone? The Americans could see that Pakistan's army continued to play the Afghan issue both ways in the spring and summer of 2000. Mahmoud might relay American threats, but ISI was not prepared to cut off oil, money, or military supplies to the Taliban. When FBI Director Louis Freeh met Musharraf in Lahore on April 6 and pleaded for help on bin Laden, he found the general "polite but unhelpful." Musharraf explained that he had "personal assurances from Mullah Omar" that bin Laden was innocent of terrorism.

When Musharraf met with Omar's interior minister in May, he did not threaten any economic punishment, and he did not even demand that bin Laden be handed over. Musharraf said instead he might revive the idea of forming an Islamic court to try bin Laden, a proposal long ago rejected by the Clinton administration. George Tenet flew secretly to Islamabad and met with Musharraf on June 21. Musharraf accepted his proposal for a joint working group on terrorism. Tenet said he was not asking the Pakistanis to deliver bin Laden the next Tuesday—he was "ambitious but not crazy," he said. The Americans were lowering their expectations, accepting Musharraf's stall.[20]

Meanwhile, there was the war against Massoud: On the ground in Afghanistan that summer, Pakistani volunteers poured across the border to fight with the Taliban against the Northern Alliance.

It was around this time that the Pakistani intelligence chief began to talk openly with some of his colleagues about a new Islamic religiosity in his life. Explaining what he meant, speaking in English, Mahmoud said that he had become a "born-again Muslim."[21] In the gossip-obsessed parlors of elite Islamabad, a casual confession like that from the chief of ISI got around. Eventually the American embassy learned of it, too. Neither the embassy's diplomats nor the Pakistani officials who worked more closely with Mahmoud were quite sure what to make of his private declarations about Islam. The general did not grow a beard or proselytize openly or ask his wife to take the veil at home—a step so rare among the Pakistani elite that it would have signaled a powerful conversion. Still, in the roiling sea of ambiguity that was ISI and the Pakistan army, the notion that a born-again Muslim was now in charge of the intelligence agency and the jihad campaigns seemed foreboding.

Some of his colleagues saw Mahmoud as angry and hurt in part because of the dressing down he had taken from Pickering in Washington. Pakistan's generals and diplomats were proud but easily bruised. "He went back feeling very humiliated," one senior Pakistani official recalled. "And he told the CIA forces, 'You brought me here, and I don't need to listen to this. I thought you wanted to engage and hear from us.'"[22]

Whatever the cause, CIA officers could see that soon after Mahmoud returned from Washington that spring, he began to shut them off. The official CIA-ISI intelligence liaison in Islamabad went cold. CIA officers had been able to meet with Ziauddin once a week or more often if they wished. Now they could barely get in to visit Mahmoud once a month. The daily paper exchanges of intelligence continued, but the high-level partnership between the CIA and Pakistani intelligence turned icy. There was no prospect, for instance, that a secret Pakistani commando team to capture bin Laden could be revived. Musharraf delivered a speech that summer declaring that he had completed a review of Pakistan's policy toward Afghanistan, and he had decided to carry on as before. Mahmoud Ahmed had seen Gettysburg. Now he had his own wars to tend.[23]

SAUDI ARABIA COMPETED with Pakistan for the status of America's most frustrating counterterrorism ally. As on Pakistan, the Manson Family in the bin Laden unit of the CIA's Counterterrorist Center took one of the hardest lines. Time after time the CIA asked the Saudi interior ministry or its intelligence department for help investigating specific al Qaeda operatives and cells. The agency's frontline officers felt they got next to zero cooperation. They could only guess at Saudi motives. They knew that the kingdom's politically insecure royal family convulsed whenever news of their helping the Americans became public, out of fear that such publicity would aid their Islamist opposition. Even the most confidential terrorism investigations in the American system inevitably leaked to the press. That seemed to be one reason that the Saudis refused to get involved. Some among the Manson Family wondered, in addition, whether the Saudis had forged some kind of unofficial pact with bin Laden in which he agreed to concentrate his fire on the United States, away from Saudi Arabia. That certainly seemed to be the effect, if not the conscious intent, of Saudi interactions with bin Laden. Even if there was no such formal understanding, the Saudis seemed to regard American worries about bin Laden as alarmist, overwrought.[24]

By 2000 the Saudi royal family, like Pakistan's army, had developed multi-layered defenses against American pressure on terrorism issues. Like Pakistan's elite, the liberals in Saudi Arabia's royal family positioned themselves in Washington as America's lonely and besieged allies, doing all they could—thanklessly—to protect the United States from the Islamist hatred of their country's Muslim masses. The Saudis continued to prove their loyalty month after month by managing global oil prices with American interests firmly in mind. By cooperating on the fundamental questions of oil and military basing rights, the Saudis acquired the freedom to pursue their own agenda on secondary issues: the Palestinians, rapprochement with Iran, and the threat of Saudi-born Islamic extremism. They pushed forward a clean-shaven, well-dressed spokesman, Adel al-Jubeir, who defended Saudi policy in a fluent American idiom. From a kingdom where politics arose from family ties and power was bargained through personal contacts, the Saudi royals concentrated nearly all their effort on networks of friends at the highest levels of the American government. This approach insulated the Saudi elite from their country's harsh and sometimes fulminating critics at the working levels of the U.S. police and intelligence bureaucracies.

The Americans struggled to understand just how much support reached bin Laden in Afghanistan from Saudi sources. It appeared to be substantial, even into 2000. A Saudi government audit of the National Commercial Bank, the kingdom's largest, showed that at least $3 million had flowed from its accounts to bin Laden. One of Saudi Arabia's largest charities, the International Islamic Relief Organization, acknowledged that it had sent about $60 million to the Taliban.[25]

But when Michael Sheehan, the State Department's counterterrorism chief, tried to send a cable urging American embassies to push their host governments to crack down on Islamic charity groups, other State diplomats managed to suppress the cable and overturn its recommendations. They argued that Sheehan did not understand all the good works Islamic charities performed worldwide.[26]

The pattern was repeated elsewhere in the national security bureaucracy. When they attacked Saudi Arabia as uncooperative or dangerous, counterterrorism specialists were chided by their colleagues at State or the Pentagon as narrow-minded cops who were unable to fit their concerns into the larger context of the U.S.-Saudi alliance. Describing the global terrorist threat in 2000, the State Department's official annual report made no mention of Saudi Wahhabi proselytizing, and it referred only to "allegations" that Saudi Islamic charities might be aiding terrorists. The Saudi royal family had "reaffirmed its commitment to combating terrorism," the State Department reported, but it was "not clear," the department continued gently, whether all of the government's regulations "were enforced consistently." American investigators later reported that they could find "no evidence that the Saudi government as an institution or senior officials within the Saudi government funded al Qaeda. Still, al Qaeda found fertile fundraising ground in the kingdom" in part because of "very limited oversight" of private charitable donations.[27]

Prince Turki faded further. After his break with Mullah Omar in 1998, he tried to facilitate cooperation with the CIA on terrorism but was rarely able to deliver, at least in the view of mid-level American officers.

Turki's own fear about bin Laden's ability to strike at Saudi interests "kept rising" during 1999 and 2000, he recalled, because "the leadership of the Taliban had committed themselves 100 percent to bin Laden. And hence he would have even more leeway to act than he did before." Turki considered trying to plant an agent inside bin Laden's circle in Afghanistan "many, many times," but he could not come up with a plausible plan. He tried to turn captured Islamists back on al Qaeda as agents working for Saudi intelligence "without much success," as he recalled. But he would not send his own intelligence officers on such a mission to Afghanistan. "It was too dangerous, and I never did it. . . . I would not sacrifice one of our people." Congressional investigators later concluded that the CIA and other American intelligence agencies "did not effectively develop and use human sources to penetrate the al Qaeda inner circle" and that "in part, at least," this failure was "a product of an excessive reliance on foreign liaison services."[28]

MASSOUD BELIEVED by the summer of 2000 that he had regained some military and political momentum against the Taliban. He had repeated his great survival feat of the 1980s anti-Soviet war. By fierce personal will, by his refusal to leave Afghan soil, by his ability to lead and hold the loyalty of his Tajik followers, he had weathered the worst periods of hopelessness and isolation after the fall of Kabul to the Taliban. Now he had passable supply lines to Iran. He had commercial deals to buy ammunition from Russia. India chipped in about $10 million and built a hospital in his territory. He had modest intelligence aid from the CIA. His enemies remained formidable, especially the suicide platoons of al Qaeda and the seemingly inexhaustible waves of Pakistani volunteers bused from *madrassas* to the northern battlefields. Yet to many Afghans there were more and more signs that the Taliban were weakening. In February 2000 the famed leader of the original 1979 Afghan mutiny against Soviet occupiers in Herat, Ismail Khan, escaped from a Kandahar prison, fled to Iran, and stirred new revolts against the Taliban in western Afghanistan. Pashtun tribal leaders staged protests against Taliban conscription. Prominent Pashtun exiles—Abdul Haq, King Zahir Shah, Hamid Karzai—opened talks with Massoud's representatives about a grand anti-Taliban political alliance that would unite Afghanistan's north and south.[29]

Massoud encouraged these political discussions. He was skeptical of exiles who refused to risk their lives and their comfort by fighting from Afghan soil. He and Abdul Haq remained uncomfortable rivals. Massoud's aides had suspicions about Pashtuns like Karzai who lived in Pakistan and who had earlier supported the Taliban. But with the help of private intermediaries such as Peter Tomsen, the former American ambassador to the Afghan mujahedin, the Taliban's Pashtun opponents linked up with Massoud. Some of them wanted Massoud to participate in political talks that would create a unified Afghan government in exile, symbolically blessed by the king, to which disaffected Taliban commanders could defect. Others, like Hamid Karzai, wanted Massoud's help to mount armed rebellions against the Taliban in Pashtun areas of southern Afghanistan.

During 2000, Massoud envisioned a military campaign against the Taliban that would unfold in stages. His first goal was to rebuild the strength of the Northern Alliance. The Taliban remained weakest in the north because it lacked an ethnic and tribal base. Massoud hoped that Ismail Khan, Aburrashid Dostum, and other anti-Taliban commanders could seed small pockets of sustainable rebellion in isolated, defensible mountain areas. His strategy was to light little brush fires all around northern and western Afghanistan, wherever the Taliban were weak, and then fan the flames. As these rebel pockets emerged and stabilized, Massoud would drive toward them with his more formal armored militia, trying to link up on roadways, choking off Taliban-ruled cities and towns and gradually expanding the territory under his control.

Once he had more solid footing in the north, Massoud planned to pursue the same strategy in the Pashtun south, helping rebels like Karzai seed themselves first in defensible mountain areas, then moving gradually to attack towns and cities. "Commander Massoud's idea was that Karzai should send commanders to these areas where it was liberated so they could revolt," recalled Massoud's foreign policy adviser, Abdullah. Karzai could also establish bases in safer Northern Alliance territory such as the Panjshir "and then expand." Massoud dispatched Abdullah and other aides to meet with Karzai's people to develop these ideas. "He was thinking it would not be easy," Abdullah remembered. "It will not be overnight. It will be a long-term struggle." Massoud "was absolutely confident of liberating the north sooner or later," recalled one of his senior intelligence aides. "And he was projecting a force for the south for a longer struggle."[30]

To develop this plan in a serious way Massoud needed helicopters, jeeps, and trucks. He needed to resupply allied rebels separated by vast distances. The country's few passable roads were tightly controlled by the Taliban. Massoud wanted to leapfrog quickly around the north to avoid frontal battles, get behind Taliban and al Qaeda lines, and emerge from his defensive crouch in the Panjshir. But to do this effectively he would need greater mobility.

Organizers of this nascent anti-Taliban alliance traveled to Washington in the summer of 2000 to ask for American political support and practical aid. Senator Sam Brownback, a Kansas Republican who was one of the few members of Congress to take an interest in Afghanistan, held hearings. Hardly anyone paid attention. Danielle Pletka, who ran the Afghan issue at the Senate Foreign Relations Committee, cringed whenever she arranged meetings for Karzai and Massoud's aides because she feared that not a single member or congressional aide would bother to show up, and she would be left red-faced and alone at the conference table. "No one cared," she recalled. At typical meetings on Afghanistan "anywhere from none to two" members or staff would attend.[31]

The State Department offered modest support for the political track of the Massoud-Karzai alliance. Inderfurth traveled to Rome and met the exiled king, Zahir Shah. State contributed a few hundred thousand dollars to organize meetings, but that was as far as the department was willing to go. Pickering met the well-dressed Abdullah, Massoud's envoy, in Washington and told colleagues that he worried the Northern Alliance was another liberal insurgent movement like the Iraqi National Congress—professional rebels and exiles.[32]

American intelligence and diplomatic reporting documented the Taliban's weakening grip during 2000. The Taliban's "popularity and legitimacy now appear to be in decline," Inderfurth testified to Congress on July 20. "We believe the Taliban have reached their high-water mark." Yet American policy remained paralyzed over whether to confront the Taliban or engage. Inderfurth described the Clinton administration's evolving strategy as "two-pronged." One track put "firm pressure" on the Taliban with threats and economic sanctions; on the other track they sought "to engage the Taliban in a serious dialogue." Despite the new, promising links forged between Massoud and the moderate royalist Pashtuns, the United States refused to choose sides. "My strong criticism of the Taliban should not be read to imply U.S. recognition for the opposition Northern Alliance led by Ahmed Shah Massoud," Inderfurth emphasized.[33]

It was in many ways the same failure of political vision that had shaped American policy toward Afghanistan between 1988 and 1992, under two Republican administrations. Then, as in 2000, the United States refused to commit to an emerging fragile alliance between Massoud and centrist Pashtuns. The effect of this refusal, in both periods, was to cede the field to Pakistan's extremist clients: Hekmatyar earlier, and the Taliban later.

The CIA's Near East Division, responsible for Afghan politics, did not regard the emerging anti-Taliban movement among Pashtuns as a serious force. CIA officers dismissed Abdul Haq as an egomaniac and a blowhard. They respected Karzai but saw him as a very small player. As they recruited among anti-Taliban Pashtuns, they struggled to find anyone who could really deliver. Jallaladin Haqqanni, a CIA favorite during the 1980s, pledged firm allegiance to the Taliban. Old warlords like Gul Agha Sherzai did not seem especially motivated or capable. The agency's case officers revived many Pashtun contacts in search of recruitments but came away skeptical.

Conditioned by past experiences as well as their decades-old liaison with ISI, some Near East officers remained highly doubtful about Massoud even as the Counterterrorist Center–led contacts with him deepened. They did not see much potential, either, in a Massoud-royalist alliance as a basis for military rebellion. U.S. ambassador to Pakistan Bill Milam and the CIA's Islamabad station chief both "felt Massoud and the Northern Alliance could not govern Afghanistan and that, secondly, they probably couldn't beat the Taliban anyway," recalled one American official. The CIA also concluded, as Gary Schroen put it, that "there was no Pashtun opposition. The Pashtuns were totally disorganized, fragmented, disarmed by the Taliban."[34] But this was a view shaped and distorted by Pakistani intelligence. As in the past, by refusing to take a risk and partner more aggressively with Massoud, the United States passively allowed Pakistan's policy to become its own.

Richard Clarke's counterterrorism group at the White House, which usually pressed for the most aggressive tactics against bin Laden, opposed a deep military alliance with Massoud during the summer of 2000. Clarke argued that the Northern Alliance was "not a very good group of people to begin with," as one official involved put it. "They're drug runners. They're human rights abusers. They're an ethnic minority. It's just not something that you're going to build a national government around."[35]

Without full-fledged U.S. support, Karzai and Massoud took matters into their own hands. Karzai traveled that autumn to the Panjshir with a delegation of royalist Pashtuns. They hoped their meeting would send a signal to wavering Afghans that a new anti-Taliban alliance was in embryo.

In private talks Karzai told Massoud he was ready to slip inside Afghanistan and fight. "Don't move into Kandahar," Massoud told him, as Karzai recalled it. "You must go to a place where you can hold your base." There were too many Arabs around Kandahar. It might be too early to mount a southern rebellion, Massoud warned. Perhaps Karzai should consider operating out of the north until their joint revolt was further developed. Karzai said he would consider that.

"He was very wise," Karzai recalled. "I was sort of pushy and reckless."[36]

Karzai's friends warned him that if he became too vocal about his opposition to the Taliban, Pakistani intelligence would respond. Karzai still maintained a home in Quetta. His friends reminded him of his father's fate and of the unsolved murders of Abdul Haq's family members in Peshawar. Recalled Afrasiab Khattak, a Pashtun nationalist and Pakistani human rights activist who knew Karzai: "I pressed him to leave this country because he would be killed."[37]

THE CIA STRUGGLED to maintain its liaison with Massoud. It was difficult and risky for the agency's officers to reach the Panjshir. The only practical way in was through Dushanbe in Tajikistan. From there the CIA teams usually took one of the few rusting, patched-together Mi-17 transport helicopters the Northern Alliance managed to keep in the air. CIA officers alarmed Langley with the cables describing their travel. On one trip the Taliban scrambled MiG-21 jets in an effort to shoot down Massoud's helicopter. If they had succeeded, they would have discovered American corpses in the wreckage. Even on the best days the choppers would shake and rattle, and the cabin would fill with the smell of fuel. The overland routes to see Massoud were no better: miles and miles of bone-jarring Afghan mountain ruts snaking along sheer cliffsides. When a Near East Division team drove in from Dushanbe, one of its vehicles flipped and a veteran CIA officer, a former station chief in Cairo, dislocated his shoulder.[38]

These reports accumulated in Langley on the desk of Deputy Director of Operations James Pavitt, who had overall responsibility for the management of CIA espionage. Pavitt was a blue-eyed, white-haired former case officer and station chief who had served in Europe during the Cold War, including tours in East and West Berlin. He had written speeches for a Democratic congressman as a young man, then served in the White House as a CIA liaison during the first Bush administration. Like Tenet, who had appointed him, he was a spy manager with a feel for politics. Pavitt began to ask why CIA officers were taking such huge physical risks to work with Massoud. Were they getting enough from the liaison to justify the possibility of death or injury? If a CIA officer was killed on one of these trips, Pavitt was the one who would have to visit his widow and explain why it had all mattered so much. Was it likely that Massoud would help capture or kill bin Laden, or were they taking unnecessary chances?

Pavitt's questions provoked sometimes heated replies from working-level officers in the Counterterrorist Center. The bin Laden unit chief—who had flown in Massoud's helicopters himself—and the center's operations chief, known to his colleagues as Hank, passionately argued that the Panjshir liaison had to continue, that the risks were worth it. The liaison with the Northern Alliance was by now producing several hundred CIA intelligence reports each year. It would be cowardly to drop contact with Massoud because of safety concerns, they implied. This was typical uncompromising Manson Family ardor, thought some officials who heard the debates. "There was a lot of concern about engagement in Afghanistan because it was very, very, very risky," remembered one American official. Those opposed to the CIA's Panjshir missions argued, as this official recalled, "You're sending people to their deaths." Cofer Black, mediating with Pavitt, took a more sympathetic view of Pavitt's fears. He said he endorsed Pavitt's worries about the helicopters. Counterterrorist officers were the ones who would die if one of these ungainly machines went down.[39]

The agency sent out a team of mechanics knowledgeable about Russian helicopters to try to resolve the issue. Massoud's men took them to their Dushanbe airfield and opened up one of the Mi-17s. The CIA mechanics were stunned: Massoud had managed to patch an engine originally made for a Hind attack helicopter into the bay of the Mi-17 transport. It was a mismatched, gum-and-baling-wire machine, a flying miracle. The CIA mechanics were so appalled that they did not even want Massoud's pilots to fire up the helicopter's rotors. They were afraid the whole thing would come apart and send shrapnel flying.

At Langley the debates about risk and reward persisted. Cofer Black continued to worry aloud about the safety question but argued that the Counterterrorist Center had to maintain contact with Massoud to prepare for the day—a virtual certainty, he and the officers in the bin Laden unit said—when al Qaeda pulled off a major attack against the United States. Then the White House would change its policies toward the Taliban, and it would need Massoud. Black was not much for understatement. He told his colleagues that this aspect of the CIA's Panjshir mission was about "preparing the battlefield for World War Three."

Tenet signed off on a compromise: The CIA would secretly buy its own airworthy Mi-17 helicopter, maintain it properly in Tashkent, Uzbekistan, and use CIA pilots to fly clandestine teams into the Panjshir.

The helicopter issue was a symptom of a larger problem. By the late summer of 2000 the CIA's liaison with Massoud was fraying on both sides. On the American side, the most passionate believers in Massoud were in the Counterterrorist Center, especially in the bin Laden unit. Officers with the unit who worked out of the Islamabad station were seen by their colleagues as "slightly over the top," recalled one American official. Massoud's intelligence network cooperated on collection and planning, but it became increasingly clear that Massoud did not intend to launch a snatch raid against bin Laden.

The CIA's Counter-Narcotics Center reported that Massoud's men continued to smuggle large amounts of opium and heroin into Europe. The British reported the same. They could all readily imagine the headlines if their operation was exposed: CIA SUPPORTS AFGHAN DRUG LORD. The Counterterrorist Center's view of Massoud's strategic importance to the United States was "not embraced," recalled one American official involved. "There was much gnashing of teeth and angst and clucking and hand-wringing."

For their part, Massoud's aides had hoped their work with the CIA would lead to wider political support in Washington and perhaps military aid. They could see no evidence that this was developing. Instead they were badgered repeatedly about an attack on bin Laden. "We never thought of capturing bin Laden alive in that type of Hollywood operation," recalled one of Massoud's intelligence aides. "It was never a consideration for people who knew the real situation in Afghanistan." The Northern Alliance's few shaky helicopters could barely clear the mountain passes. They had no air cover. Their forces were not very mobile on the ground. Bin Laden usually was surrounded not only by his own bodyguard but by hundreds if not thousands of Taliban soldiers. One of Massoud's aides likened the mission urged on them by the CIA to a game of chess in which they would have to capture the king without touching any other piece on the board.[40]

Massoud and his men respected many of the individual CIA officers they dealt with but increasingly felt frustrated by the agency's policies and tactics. Massoud's men asked their CIA counterparts, as this intelligence aide recalled it: "Is there any policy in the government of the American states to help Afghanistan if the people of Afghanistan help you get rid of your most wanted man?" America's decision to abandon Afghanistan after the Soviet withdrawal was never far from their minds. But the CIA officers could make no such promise. The most they could say was that bin Laden's capture "would definitely influence policy in Washington," creating goodwill toward the Northern Alliance.

This was not enough. Massoud's men could easily imagine—and discussed among themselves many times—mounting a joint operation with the CIA to assassinate bin Laden by sniper fire, bombing, or a commando raid if this would result in a new American policy recognizing the Northern Alliance. But the CIA was not permitted to engage in that sort of military planning, and the agency had been unable to deliver any change in U.S. policy toward the Afghan war, either.[41]

"Daring Me
to Kill Them"

BY THE LATE SPRING OF 2000, Richard Clarke and his White House counterterrorism group had grown frustrated by the quality of intelligence reporting on Osama bin Laden's whereabouts. The CIA's unilateral human sources and its liaisons with Pakistan, Uzbekistan, and Massoud had generated volumes of fragmented hearsay but nothing solid enough to warrant missile strikes or a snatch operation. Clarke and his aides brainstormed for new ideas. Could they find a way to place a beacon on one of bin Laden's aircraft so they could track the plane with bin Laden aboard and shoot it down in flight? Could they erect an enormous phony television tower near the Afghan border and use long-range spy cameras to watch for bin Laden? Clarke and his aides observed Pentagon Special Forces train British and French teams that planned to capture fugitive Balkan war criminals. Could one of these teams be inserted into Afghanistan?

Clarke asked his longtime acquaintance in the national security bureaucracy, Charles Allen, who ran all of the CIA's intelligence collection efforts, to work with Admiral Scott Fry, head of operations at the Joint Chiefs of Staff, on fresh approaches to the bin Laden problem. Clarke and his aides continued to hope the Pentagon would come up with a plan to use American commandos in Afghanistan. Their detailed tracking maps of bin Laden's travels from Kandahar to Kabul to the eastern Afghan mountains seemed to offer a way forward. Clarke and the bin Laden unit at CIA felt they had established that it was highly probable, for instance, that bin Laden would return again and again to Tarnak Farm near the Kandahar airport. Wasn't there a way to put reliable American eyes on that compound, equipped with secure communications that could be linked to missile submarines? Could a Special Forces team be provisioned to lie buried in the sand flats near Tarnak for a few weeks, ready to call in a strike whenever bin Laden turned up? As he pushed for answers, Clarke summoned the direct authority of President Clinton. In February 2000, National Security Adviser Sandy Berger had submitted a long memo to Clinton describing all the ongoing efforts to capture or disrupt bin Laden. Clinton had scribbled his dissatisfaction about the results in the margin. A savvy bureaucrat, Clarke photocopied the president's scrawl and used it as a cudgel at interagency meetings.[1]

Several years later a number of people involved in these highly classified discussions claimed credit for the idea of sending Predator reconnaissance drones to Afghanistan to search for bin Laden. Despite the confusion of competing recollections, it seems clear, in a general sense, that Clarke, Fry, Berger, Allen, Black, and officers in the CIA's bin Laden unit jointly conspired, amid persistent squabbling among themselves, to launch the Predator experiment. Allen recalled that CIA senior management were at first reluctant, and that it was "a bloody struggle." They hoped to solve the primary problem that had dogged their hunt for bin Laden since the winter of 1999 when they had stared day after day at satellite pictures of the Arab hunting camp in western Afghanistan, unable to develop enough confidence to fire missiles. Satellite and U-2 reconnaissance photography could identify fixed targets such as buildings, homes, and training camps with high precision, but these systems could not single out mobile targets or individual faces. In the case of the hunting camp, Clinton's counterterrorism group had been forced to rely on identifications provided by the CIA's Afghan tracking team. They had not been able to look directly at live photographs or video of bin Laden to develop a consensus within the national security cabinet that the risks of a missile or bombing attack were justified. The Predator, they hoped, could bridge these intelligence gaps.[2]

The CIA and the Pentagon had each experimented with unmanned reconnaissance drones since the early 1980s. In the first years of the agency's Counterterrorist Center, Dewey Clarridge had sought drones to help search for American hostages in denied areas of Beirut and rural Lebanon. As early as

1987 the CIA secretly adapted kit airplanes manufactured in California to carry cameras in a highly classifed project called the Eagle program. Clarridge hoped to operate the drones out of a hotel room in Beirut. The agency bought special wooden propellers made in Germany to help the drones fly quietly. Clarridge also experimented with arming the drones with small rockets that could be fired by remote control, but the rockets selected proved wildly inaccurate.[3] In the same period, and sometimes in cooperation with the CIA, the Pentagon's laboratory for experimental security technology, the Defense Advanced Research Projects Agency, funded prototypes of a long-endurance, unmanned drone called Amber. This was an extraordinarily lightweight (815 pounds) wasplike drone invented by Abraham Karem, the former chief designer for the Israeli air force. A lively engineer with unbounded imagination, Karem immigrated to the United States in the late 1970s and started an experimental aircraft company in California. The Amber prototypes he produced flew longer and better than any drone to date. But Karem's company went bankrupt amid bureaucratic battles in Washington. The Pentagon tended to invest in large, fast, complex drones that resembled pilotless fighter jets. These were very expensive, technically sophisticated, and politically unpopular. The CIA preferred smaller, lighter, cheaper drones that could take pictures and intercept communications in situations where satellites or high-flying spy planes did not offer enough coverage. Its experiments were easier to fund, but many at the Pentagon and in Congress dismissed the smaller prototypes as clunky toys of marginal value.[4]

The Predator had gasped to programmatic life in the early 1990s as an awkward bastard child of the Amber. A large defense contractor bought up Karem's assets, including his designs, and the U.S. Navy pitched in funds for more prototypes. The CIA's director of espionage operations in the early Clinton administration, Thomas Twetten, held a review of the agency's own secret drone projects, all still in experimental stages. When he listed options for CIA director James Woolsey, the director's eyes lit up. Woolsey had met Abe Karem in Israel, and he also knew about Amber. "I know the guy" who can get this done, Woolsey told Twetten. The pair flew to California and tracked Karem down at the defense contractor who had bailed him out. They were selling prototypes to Turkey. Woolsey declared that he would take five on the spot for the CIA. The only problem was that the nascent Predator—long and ungainly—sounded like "a lawnmower in the sky," as Twetten recalled it. The CIA managers told Karem he had to silence the motor, and he agreed.[5]

From the CIA's first purchases Predator operations required close cooperation between the agency and the Pentagon. This was never easy. The Air

Force howled when it learned Woolsey had bought Predators in secret. The CIA chafed as it tried to sort out budgetary and operating rules with the Air Force. There were times when it seemed that the Predator's chief innovations lay in its ability to generate table-thumping, vein-pumping bureaucratic agitation inside secure Virginia conference rooms. Ultimately the CIA arranged for Air Force teams trained by the Eleventh Reconnaissance Squadron at Nellis Air Force Base, Nevada, to operate the agency's clandestine drones. First in Bosnia and then in Kosovo, CIA officers began to see the first practical returns on their decades-old fantasy of using aerial robots to collect intelligence.[6]

The Predators deployed secretly to Bosnia in 1995 were designed to loiter over targets for twenty-four hours and could fly as far as five hundred miles from their home base at an altitude of up to twenty-five thousand feet. They were extraordinarily slow—their average speed was just seventy miles per hour—and they were so light that they sometimes drifted backward in the teeth of headwinds. A Predator's "pilot" sat with several enlisted "payload specialists" inside a sealed, unmarked van near the runway of the drone's operating base. (In its Balkans operations, the CIA flew Predators secretly out of Hungary and Albania.) At first the Air Force recruited pilots for the drones who had been grounded from normal flight by medical disabilities. Generators and satellite dishes surrounded the flight van. Inside, the pilot toggled a joystick before a video screen that showed the view from the Predator's nose. Radio signals controlled the drone's runway takeoff and initial ascent. Then communications shifted to military satellite networks linked to the pilot's van. The Predator's nose carried a swiveling Sony camera similar to those used by TV station helicopters that report on freeway traffic. It also could carry radar imaging and electronic intercept equipment.[7]

In the first flights over Bosnia the CIA linked its Langley headquarters to the pilot's van. Woolsey emailed a pilot as he watched video images relayed to Virginia. "I'd say, 'What direction for Mostar? . . . Is that the river?'" Woolsey recalled. "And he'd say, 'Yeah. Do you want to look at the bridge? . . . Is that a guy walking across the bridge? . . . Let's zoom further, it looks like he has a big funny hat on.'"[8]

There were serious glitches. Pilots struggled to learn how to fly such a light, awkward plane from satellite-delayed television images. After tugging their joysticks, it would take several seconds for the plane to respond. There was no adequate system to control ice on the Predator's wings. The drone was not stealthy and could be targeted by antiaircraft fire. And after Bosnia there were debates about the Predator's ultimate mission.

One camp favored using the drone only for traditional intelligence collection: taking pictures and verifying reports from human agents on the ground. But others argued that the Predator could be a powerful weapon if it was integrated into what military officers sometimes called "the kill chain." The Air Force had long struggled to develop weapons systems that could accurately track and attack isolated mobile targets such as cars and trucks. Its new airborne sensor and command system, known as J-Stars, could follow moving vehicles on a battlefield and identify, for example, whether the vehicles had wheels or tank tracks. But the J-Stars system could not make a close-up identification of a human face or a license plate number. The Predator's cameras might provide this ability if the drone's roving eye could be connected in real time to the larger Air Force command network. In that case the Predator might hover over a moving vehicle, transmit a running image of its license plate to CIA officers or Pentagon commanders in Virginia, tag the truck with a laser beam, and hold the beam on the target while a bomber swooped in to drop computer-aided munitions directly onto the truck. Or possibly the Predator itself could be armed with a remotely fired air-to-ground weapon if the technical problems of weight and missile velocity could be solved. As early as 1995 the Navy fashioned tests to link the Predator's roving cameras to cruise missile submarines submerged offshore. In the Kosovo conflict of 1999 the Air Force secretly equipped Predators with laser target finders and satellite links that would make drone-guided bombing operations possible for the first time, although no such attacks were actually carried out.[9]

All of this history—all of these unresolved questions about the Predator's purpose and value—shaped debate among CIA officers, White House aides, and Pentagon brass as they considered how to use the drone in the hunt for bin Laden in the summer of 2000. The Predator was cheap by the lavish standards of Pentagon weapons programs, but at about $3 million per drone, each one lost would take a bite out of the CIA's pinched budgets. Influential skeptics such as Thomas Pickering worried about the intelligence community's built-in bias for "a near-term technical solution, rather than the long-term buildup" of reliable sources and recruits. Jim Pavitt feared that funds allocated to the Predator would inevitably come at the expense of money for human intelligence—HUMINT, in Washington's acronym vernacular. Richard Clarke replied with his usual bluntness: "Your valuable HUMINT program hasn't worked for years. I want to try something else." Cofer Black, at the Counterterrorist Center, sided with Clarke while trying not to offend Pavitt. Frustrated at the hand-wringing and endless argument, Clarke enlisted Sandy Berger to formally order the Predator to Afghanistan. Berger did.[10]

Then they argued more about the scope of the Predator's mission. Clarke was intrigued by the idea of linking the Predator's camera to the cruise missile submarines lurking secretly in the Arabian Sea. He pushed for a lethal operation in Afghanistan, not one that would solely take pictures. Berger was interested, but officers at the CIA were skeptical about the submarine proposal. There were too many unknowns. It would take too long to get munitions to the target even if the Predator saw bin Laden. "The Agency was very clear," remembered a White House official. "They wanted to do an initial period of testing. . . . They didn't want to hardwire it to the submarines" or to some other bombing plan. This official recalled "some skepticism" at the CIA "that you could get that kind of clarity" from the drone's cameras to justify a missile launch.[11]

Black advocated arming the Predator itself with an air-to-ground missile so it could fire instantly if it located bin Laden. But State Department lawyers objected, arguing that an armed drone might violate the Intermediate Nuclear Forces Treaty, which banned the United States from acquiring new long-range cruise missiles. Was an armed Predator the same as a cruise missile? While the lawyers debated, Black and the Counterterrorist Center, now officially in command of the nascent mission ordered by the White House, proposed a different kind of experiment.[12]

In the Balkans and in Iraq, Predator pilots and their support equipment (the pilot's van, satellite dishes, and generators) had been parked at air bases in friendly neighboring nations. The operations were sensitive and clandestine, but the host governments were not unduly frightened about exposure. Here the situation was different. As the planning developed in the early summer of 2000, Uzbekistan agreed to allow secret Predator flights from one of its air bases for a limited period of time, but Islam Karimov's government was adamant about secrecy. The agency's officers feared that even the small cluster of vans and satellite dishes necessary to pilot a Predator would attract unwanted attention among Uzbek soldiers and officers. The cooperation between the CIA and the Uzbeks was so secret that many people in Karimov's own government still did not know about it.[13]

To address this problem the CIA proposed to experiment with a new stage in Predator operations. Improvements in communications systems now made it possible, at least in theory, to fly the drone remotely from great distances. It was no longer necessary to use close-up radio signals during the Predator's takeoff and ascent. The entire flight could be controlled by satellite from any command center with the right equipment. The CIA proposed to attempt over Afghanistan the first fully remote Predator flight operations, piloted from Langley. The drone itself would be housed and recovered at hangars on a remote Uzbek airfield, but it would be flown with a joystick propped on a table inside a CIA operations center in Virginia.

President Clinton approved a limited "proof of concept" mission to launch Predators over Afghanistan in September. The concept to be proven, recalled Air Force Secretary Whit Peters, was the CIA's ability to fly the Predator "from barren and difficult airfields, controlled via satellites from a ground site many thousands of miles away." The CIA would complete the mission without its pilots or commanding officers ever leaving the Virginia suburbs.[14]

The bin Laden unit drew up maps and plans for fifteen Predator flights, each lasting just under twenty-four hours. They decided to fly over places they had previously identified as bin Laden's main haunts, especially in eastern and southern Afghanistan. They also lit up their agent network on the ground. They sought detailed reporting about bin Laden's movements, hoping to steer the Predator overhead and photograph him. Clarke urged the White House to be prepared to attack bin Laden if the Predator found him. Berger cautioned that they would need more than just bin Laden's location—they would also want a reliable forecast of his plans or movements during any cruise missile flight times.

Previous operations in the Balkans and Iraq had shown that the Predator was most effective in daylight hours. The drone could carry night vision equipment, but the images were much harder to decipher. Daylight hours in Afghanistan began in the dead of night in Virginia. A large video screen loomed in the middle of the CIA's makeshift flight operations center. Air Force drone pilots and CIA officers from the Counterterrorist Center and the bin Laden unit huddled in the darkened room on the wooded Langley campus from midnight to dawn, watching black-and-white aerials of Afghanistan unfurl eerily before them.

Richard Clarke would drive out after midnight, clear the CIA's security gates, park in the darkened parking lots, and wander through empty hallways to the flight center. Other curious visitors arrived at odd hours as well. They were like a secret society of video game junkies, role-players in a futuristic scenario, and they were well aware of their role in pioneering a kind of technical espionage that Hollywood might promote. They sipped coffee and talked to their pilot. "Oh, look at that truck! That truck looks like the one he uses! Follow that truck!" Remembered one participant: "It was very much the O.J. thing, with a helicopter following a car down the freeway." Clarke wrote Berger that the images were "truly astonishing." Berger replied with encouragement, but also cautioned: "Unfortunately, the light at the end of the tunnel is another tunnel."[15]

The Taliban's air defense units monitored flights across the Uzbek border. One night the CIA's drone flew above a Taliban airfield where a MiG fighter jet prepared to take off on an intercept mission. In the Langley operations room they could see the fireball light up the MiG's tail as it thundered down the runway. The Predator's eavesdropping equipment captured chatter between the MiG pilot and the control tower. "I can't find it! There's nothing here!" the Taliban pilot complained to his commander. Suddenly the Predator's camera picked up the MiG flying right toward the drone at jet speed. "As the MiG flew by, half the people in the room ducked," recalled an American official who was watching from Langley. The MiG pilot never spotted the drone and returned to base. At Langley the audience slumped in its chairs, relieved and amazed.[16]

While hovering over Tarnak Farm outside of Kandahar, the Predator photographed a man who appeared to be bin Laden. An agent reporting from Kandahar suggested that the Saudi had come to visit one of his wives. The camera showed a tall man in Arab robes surrounded by armed bodyguards walking from a building previously mapped by the CIA as bin Laden's residence to a tiny mud-brick mosque across the way. There was no way to be 100 percent certain that the man was bin Laden, but the evidence was very strong. On two other missions the Predator recorded images of a man who CIA analysts later concluded was probably bin Laden, but in these cases they were less certain than they were about the Tarnak case.[17]

Their arguments about the mission continued even as the Predator flew. One issue was security and secrecy. As Taliban radar tracked the flights, some at the CIA worried about Uzbekistan's exposure. They did not want to jeopardize their work with the Uzbek commando unit. A downed Predator would also be a propaganda coup for the Taliban. The drone carried little sensitive equipment—most of its sophisticated electronics were housed in the pilot's remote console. Yet nobody wanted a Predator to be captured, and CIA officers sometimes felt that the Pentagon overestimated the drone's ability to hide from enemy aircraft and ground fire. Richard Clarke discounted the strength of the Taliban air force: Its pilots never fired the few air-to-air missiles they carried on their MiGs, and if they tried, they would probably just blow themselves up, he said. He badgered the CIA not to worry so much about Predator accidents. "The pilot will return safely to base," he noted sarcastically.[18]

Their fights about money were even more pointed. When one Predator crashed on takeoff, the Air Force tried to bill the CIA for the replacement cost. Tenet, Pavitt, and Black protested. They had not budgeted money for broken $3 million drones. Aggravated, the Pentagon's officials battled back. Whit Peters at the Air Force felt that the CIA's managers wanted "to run everything and pay for nothing," as he recalled it. "They like to have sexy toys that do interesting things so they can claim credit . . . and of course, they don't want to pay for it." For their part the CIA's officers felt they were push-ing the Pentagon to innovate. Left to its own devices the Air Force would bury the Predator's development in excruciating testing schedules, reams of written specifications, and elaborate contracts. The CIA could move much faster, the agency's officers felt. The Air Force ought to pay for the Afghan operation, CIA officers believed, in part because the Pentagon was learning more about the drone's capabilities in a month than they could in half a year of sterile testing in Nevada. Memos and emails ricocheted around Virginia and back and forth to the White House, but still the funding question went unresolved.[19]

By mid-October fierce winds gathered in northern Afghanistan. On some flights the Predator's meek engine had trouble propelling the drone across the mountains. The Predator kept drifting back toward Uzbekistan. Tempera-tures plummeted, and wing icing became a more worrisome problem. They knew from Balkans experience that the Predator was a very difficult plane to fly in bad weather. The White House and the Counterterrorist Center halted the operation. The Afghan mission had always been designed as a finite ex-periment.[20]

During the winter hiatus Black and others at the CIA hoped the lawyers would resolve the treaty questions that had postponed testing of an armed version of the Predator. Having seen the images of bin Laden walking toward the mosque at Tarnak, Black was now a vocal advocate of affixing missiles to the drone. Here was the clean shot they had been seeking for more than two years: positive identification of their target, no questionable human agents, no delay.

At the White House and the Pentagon, too, those involved hoped to be fly-ing Predators again in the spring—if they could find the money.

THE DRONE IMAGERY had brought them back once again to Tarnak Farm on the sagebrush-strewn desert flats outside of Kandahar. Tarnak had been the target of the CIA's first secret plan to kidnap bin Laden, back in 1998. More than two years later the United States, an unchallenged global power with a military larger than all of its serious rivals combined, with aircraft carrier groups and B-2 bomber wings that could strike any target worldwide in twenty-four hours or less, still found itself stymied by this lightly defended mud-walled compound of several hundred acres, a fort that would not even have intimidated horsebacked Pashtun raiders several centuries before. Tarnak's water-streaked concrete office building—the onetime agricultural extension office of a doomed Afghan communist government—peeked over an empty plain that could be crossed from all directions. There were no mountains within miles, no rock walls, no gorges, no natural defenses of any kind. Yet Tarnak flummoxed Clinton and his closest national security advisers. To a great extent the problem was one of foreign policy: As Massoud's intelligence aides put it, the Americans insisted on capturing the king without disturbing the pawns. By refusing to declare the Taliban an enemy Clinton and his Cabinet made Tarnak a very complicated target. In another sense, however, the farm was a symbol of the political-military problem now commonly referred to in Washington as "asymmetric warfare," which described the advantages that terrorists and guerrillas can exploit against a superpower by virtue of being small, dispersed, and blended with civilian populations.

Clinton's national security and intelligence team spent many hours studying satellite photographs of Tarnak's flat-roofed, one-story residential buildings, clustered in several tiny villages behind the compound walls. At the Pentagon, targeters with the Joint Chiefs of Staff crunched trigonometry equations and blast calculations to determine which of Tarnak's little concrete boxes—no more than sheds, by American standards—would collapse on their inhabitants if one or two or three cruise missiles slammed into the particular house where bin Laden slept. One of the nearby sheds was a mosque. Another was a medical clinic. American military doctrine presumed the sanctity of such buildings. This was the purpose of the Pentagon's missile math: to determine which available munitions would be most likely to destroy the Tarnak house where bin Laden stayed while knocking down the fewest neighboring houses. Alone among the world's militaries, the United States had the capacity to ask and answer such questions. It was also the first military power in world history whose leaders argued day after day in conference rooms about the mathematical nuances of their destructive power.[21]

Then there was the child's swing. Families lived at Tarnak. The CIA estimated that the compound contained about one hundred women and children—bin Laden's family and family members of some top aides. There were laundry lines, and agent reporting and satellite imagery clearly showed a wooden swing near some of the residential buildings. There were no pictures of any kids actually swinging, but the children were officially presumed to be nearby.[22]

The swing made an impression on Clinton. The president recognized that his conflict with bin Laden was multidimensional. The propaganda war mattered. "It's almost like he was daring me to kill them," Clinton recalled of the women and children at Tarnak. He had learned through hard experience: "I do not care how precise your bombs and your weapons are, when you set them off, innocent people will die."[23]

Tarnak was now the visual locus of their elusive enemy. The Predator image of bin Laden in his flowing robes at the farm compound was copied onto videotape by the CIA. It was a startling loop, convincing and ominous. Tenet brought the tape to the White House and played it for Berger and Clinton. The video's eerie power seemed to convert Tenet to the Predator's cause. He carried the video to classified briefings on Capitol Hill and raved about the drone's achievements. They were getting closer to their mark, he hoped. Clinton, too, was encouraged by the Predator experiment. The president remained interested in the possibility of a Special Forces raid in Afghanistan against bin Laden. But the Pentagon and CIA's "strong and constant view," as Clinton recalled it years later, was that such operations were likely to fail without better intelligence and a great deal of lead time. The Predator images were intriguing, but they did not provide enough.[24]

A S   T H E   P R E D A T O R   F L E W above him, bin Laden pressed his two-front war below, against Massoud and the United States.

In September, al Qaeda's jihadist volunteers in Brigade 55, based at Rishikor, a former Afghan army camp on Kabul's southern outskirts, joined the Taliban's late-summer thrust against the Northern Alliance. The CIA estimated al Qaeda's annual budget at $30 million, much of it spent on the Taliban and war-fighting operations in Afghanistan. Thousands of Pakistani *madrassa* students, aided by ISI, joined Taliban forces on the outskirts of Taloqan, the ramshackle northern town that now served as Massoud's headquarters. Loaded with cash, they bribed Northern Alliance commanders to switch sides. Aided by unusually precise artillery fire—a bombardment that some American analysts interpreted as evidence of direct participation by Pakistani army officers—they stormed the town and sent Massoud and his men reeling into nearby Badakhshan province. Suddenly Massoud faced the loss of his overland supply lines to Tajikistan. It might take another summer of fighting for the Taliban to cut him off completely, but if they did, Massoud would have to either seek exile in Dushanbe or bottle himself up in the Panjshir, living off what he could capture and forage. The Taliban might be weakening politically among Pashtuns, but its resources—money for bribes, ammunition, and vehicles; volunteers from abroad; expert military advice from Pakistan—did not slacken.[25]

A month after Taloqan's fall, on October 12, a small tender boat packed with explosives glided alongside a 505-foot, American Arleigh-Burke class guided-missile destroyer docked at Aden, Yemen. The USS *Cole* was a billion-dollar command and attack ship equipped with computer-linked radar that could follow more than one hundred airplanes, ships, and missile targets at once. It had relatively little defense, however, against three suicide bombers in a thousand-dollar skiff. The attackers blew a hole twenty feet high and forty feet wide in the *Cole*'s hull, killed seventeen American sailors, and wounded thirty more. With just slightly more skilled execution, CIA analysts later concluded, the bombers would have killed three hundred and sent the destroyer to the bottom.[26]

There had been no specific tactical warning that the *Cole* was a target. The CIA had circulated a classified analysis the day before the attack that highlighted the growing al Qaeda threat in the region, but it provided no specific warning about the *Cole*. A Pentagon intelligence analyst resigned on October 13, declaring that his warnings about al Qaeda in the region had been ignored and suppressed by his superiors. None of his analysis involved specific threats against the *Cole,* however. Daniel Benjamin and Steven Simon, the former White House counterterrorism aides in Richard Clarke's office, who had left government by the time of the *Cole* attack, later accused the U.S. Navy of blatantly ignoring the al Qaeda threat. "A more telling display of the persistent disbelief" that bin Laden and his network posed a danger "would be hard to imagine," they wrote. They also blamed Anthony Zinni, the regional commander in chief, for permitting refueling operations in Yemen. Zinni defended his Yemen policy with arguments similar to those he called upon to advocate American engagement with General Musharraf in Pakistan. Even where Arab and Muslim governments were highly imperfect, Zinni argued, it was in America's best interests to deepen contacts and alliances despite the risks.[27]

The *Cole* attack hit officers and analysts in the CIA's Counterterrorist Center very hard. The millennium period had been a succession of terrifying near misses, but they had gotten through unscathed. Now they had taken the first big loss at bin Laden's hands since the Africa embassy attacks. In the initial weeks the center was consumed by searches for evidence about the attackers and their links to bin Laden. They found connections between the bombers and an al Qaeda operative who had recently spent time at a Kandahar guest house. But they could not prove bin Laden's personal responsibility for the attack—at least, the evidence would not meet the standards of a criminal indictment. Nor could they provide specific proof of bin Laden's role that Clinton could cite if he wished to publicly justify retaliation. Yet the CIA's officers told colleagues that they were dead certain of bin Laden's involvement.[28]

"We've got to change the rules," the CIA's bin Laden unit chief argued in the aftermath. It was time for the agency to try to break the policy stalemate about the Taliban. Al Qaeda was growing, and its sanctuary in Afghanistan allowed ever more ambitious operations. Within the CIA and at interagency White House sessions the Counterterrorist Center officers spoke starkly. "Al Qaeda is training and planning in Afghanistan, and their goal is to destroy the United States," they declared, as one official recalled it. "Unless we attack their safe haven, they are going to get continually stronger and stronger."[29]

Clarke was the only senior White House official who agreed. Clinton would be president of the United States for just three more months. His vice president, Al Gore, from whom Clinton had grown estranged, was locked in a close election campaign against the Republican governor of Texas, George W. Bush. Any military attack Clinton launched now would rebound on Gore one way or another. If the president fired at bin Laden and missed or if he killed Arab or Afghan women and children, he risked making the White House appear reckless or incompetent on the eve of the national vote. Undoubtedly Clinton would be accused by talk show conservatives, however absurdly, of launching the strike to boost Gore's chances. In any event, few of Clinton's senior national security aides supported a retaliatory attack. Even after the *Cole* bombing, Clarke could not persuade Defense Secretary William Cohen or his top uniformed officer, Hugh Shelton, to take an offensive strike against al Qaeda or the Taliban seriously. "Although we fully shared Mr. Clarke's anger and frustration," recalled Madeleine Albright, "it was not clear that air strikes directed at training camps would cause any significant disruption to al Qaeda." Shelton produced a paper after the attack describing thirteen options for the use of American military forces in Afghanistan, including several plans to conduct Special Forces raids to capture or kill bin Laden. Shelton's chief of operations later described the paper as essentially a primer designed to "educate" Sandy Berger and aides such as Clarke about the "extraordinary complexity" of actually going ahead with any of the options. Clarke had by now given up on the Pentagon. Their "overwhelming message," he said later, "was 'We don't want to do this.'" Even after a direct assault on American sailors aboard the *Cole,* the consensus among the Pentagon's civilian and uniformed leaders, Clarke remembered, was "that their capacity not be utilized for commando operations in Afghanistan." That left the CIA and the possibility of using Massoud's Northern Alliance as a proxy force to attack al Qaeda. Clarke had set aside his earlier skepticism about Massoud and now agreed on the need for infusions of guns and money. He encouraged Black and Rich, the bin Laden unit chief, to go ahead with a new Afghan plan.[30]

The bin Laden unit and the Afghan specialists in the Near East Division of the Directorate of Operations traded ideas. They had to confront a basic question: Were they willing to go in deeper with Ahmed Shah Massoud?

Gary Schroen, now the deputy chief in Near East, accepted the Counterterrorist group's ardent view that Massoud was the only game in town. The scattered Pashtun opposition to the Taliban—Hamid Karzai, Abdul Haq, and the rest—simply could not get anything done, Schroen and his colleagues argued. On the other hand, continuing with outreach to supposed Taliban moderates, as urged by the State Department, "is crap," Schroen said. Schroen had flown with a State team to Europe for secret meetings with supposed Taliban intermediaries that fall. It was all a game, he reported. The Taliban only sought to string the United States along and discourage them from launching military attacks. If the CIA was going to pressure the Taliban in a new and serious way, Schroen said, they had to work with Massoud.[31]

The purpose of CIA covert aid, they all decided, should be to strengthen Massoud, keep him in the fight after the loss of Taloqan, put more pressure on al Qaeda and Taliban troops, and create conditions for more effective counterterrorist work on the ground, directed at bin Laden and his lieutenants. "From an intelligence perspective," as Black recalled their thinking later, "to have a fighting chance" against bin Laden, the CIA "needed to attack the Afghan terrorist sanctuary protected by the Taliban."[32]

This meant a new and sizable covert action program to shore up Massoud's finances and supplies. They sat down at Langley in November and drew up a specific list of what Massoud needed based on the assessments of the Counterterrorist JAWBREAKER and NALT teams who had been traveling regularly to the Panjshir. They agreed that Massoud needed cash to bribe commanders, to counteract a Taliban treasury swollen with Arab money. He needed trucks, helicopters, light arms, ammunition, uniforms, food, and maybe some mortars and artillery. He did not need combat aircraft. Tanks were not a priority. The plan they had in mind was not designed to help Massoud conquer Afghanistan or challenge Taliban control of Kabul. The goal was to disrupt al Qaeda's safe haven and put the CIA into a better position to attack bin Laden. The list of covert supplies they proposed for Massoud would cost between $50 million and $150 million, depending on how aggressive the White House wanted to be.[33]

Under the plan, the CIA would establish a permanent base with Massoud in the Panjshir Valley. Rich, the bin Laden unit chief at the Counterterrorist Center, argued that the CIA had to show Massoud a more serious commitment. The agency's officers had to be down around the campfire with Massoud's men, drawing up plans and looking for opportunities to attack. They needed to be on the ground and on the front lines all the time, the CIA's proposal documents argued. To overcome the confusion and mistrust that had developed with Massoud about snatch operations, CIA officers would now be able to go directly into action alongside the Northern Alliance if they developed strong intelligence about bin Laden's whereabouts. There would be no more embarrassments like the episode where the CIA had attempted to call back Massoud's rocket attack on Derunta.

It took some time to develop a consensus around the Massoud plan among the CIA's leadership. There was still a sense in some quarters at Langley that the Counterterrorist Center's bin Laden unit—the Manson Family—was over the top. Tall and intense, Rich was seen by some of his colleagues as typical of the unyielding zealots the unit had seemed to produce one after another since about 1997. The bin Laden team talked about the al Qaeda threat in apocalyptic terms. And if you weren't with them, you were against them.

Cofer Black tried to keep the discussions in balance and tried to see the other side's point of view, but at the end of almost every argument, he backed the bin Laden unit. There was a continual undercurrent of bureaucratic tension between the Counterterrorist Center and the Directorate of Operations. The center was quasi-independent, with a direct line to Tenet, but it drew on D.O. resources and officers. There were always questions about where budget funds would come from and who would have operational control. These tensions were heightened by the emotion that seemed to surround the bin Laden issue. If Jim Pavitt, who ran the D.O., questioned details about the new covert plan to aid Massoud, somebody from the Counterterrorist Center would jump on him, arguing that he just didn't understand how serious this was. They bristled at each other, but soon they had a finalized plan of options for the White House. The "Blue Sky memo," as it was called, landed at the National Security Council in December. Yet Pavitt scribbled on one draft of the memo that he did not believe "a proposal of this magnitude should be on the table" so late in the Clinton Administration. This was the sort of ambivalence at what he called the "passive-aggressive" CIA that drove Richard Clarke to distraction.

They were worse than lame ducks now at the White House. The November presidential election had deadlocked and then devolved into a weeks-long national crisis over Florida recounts and constitutional disputes. It looked as if George W. Bush would prevail, but Clinton's White House aides were enduring the strangest postelection transition in a century as the CIA's options paper landed.

The national security cabinet met on December 20. Apart from Clarke there was hardly any support for the CIA's covert action proposals. The cabinet members raised old objections and new ones. Massoud was a drug trafficker; if the CIA established a permanent base in the Panjshir, it risked entanglements with the heroin trade. Pickering and others at the State Department still believed there was at least a 25 percent chance that, through patient negotiation, the Taliban could be persuaded to hand bin Laden over for trial. Berger believed that it would be a mistake to break with Pakistan by backing Massoud. In Islamabad in March, Musharraf had promised Clinton that he would deliver on the bin Laden problem. The general had not done much yet, but it would be rash to change horses now. Moreover, by sending covert aid to Massoud they would be handing the next administration a new proxy war in one of the most dangerous corners of the world. What if Pakistan responded to the Massoud aid by escalating its jihad attacks in Kashmir, provoking a nuclear crisis? Wasn't that the sort of risk the next administration should calculate for itself? They discussed other options to pressure al Qaeda that had been prepared by Clarke in a detailed strategy memo that sought to "roll back" al Qaeda over three to five years, in part through aid to Massoud. These included new efforts to secure cooperation from Pakistani intelligence and to seek bin Laden's expulsion. Clinton's Cabinet remained enticed by the promises of partnership with Pakistan's army and fearful of a total break.[34]

The word went back to the Counterterrorist Center: There would be no covert action program for Massoud. The CIA's continuing aid to Massoud—its relatively small payments and its intelligence collection and sharing program—could not be redesigned in any way that would "fundamentally alter" the Afghan battlefield.

The decision chilled the CIA's liaison with Massoud. Both the CIA's officers and Massoud's leadership group felt they were approaching the limits of cooperation under the existing White House ground rules. Massoud's contact with the CIA went "a bit" cold that winter, recalled one of the commander's intelligence aides. The Panjshir visits from Langley halted, but Massoud's men were not completely sure why. "I presume that they were searching for a clear demonstration of willingness from [our] side to conduct a capture operation" against bin Laden or one of his lieutenants, said the intelligence aide.[35]

A CIA team flew out to Uzbekistan early that winter. They inspected the agency's recently purchased Mi-17 helicopter and decided to prepare it for winter storage. "They kind of mothballed it," recalled Gary Schroen, speaking of the CIA helicopter but also of the agency's liaison with Massoud.[36]

The Clinton administration's eight-year struggle with Osama bin Laden, al Qaeda, and Afghanistan had ended. "You replay everything in your mind, and you ask, 'Was there anything else that could have been done?'" Clinton said later. "I tried to take Mr. Bin Laden out of the picture for the last four years-plus I was in office. . . . I don't think I was either stupid or inattentive, so he is a formidable adversary."[37]

"What Face Will Omar
Show to God?"

GEORGE W. BUSH NEVER SPOKE in public about Osama bin
Laden or al Qaeda during his campaign for the presidency. The Republican Party's foreign policy and defense platforms made no mention of bin
Laden or his organization. Terrorism barely registered as an issue during the
2000 contest. After the USS *Cole* attack in October, a reporter asked Bush
about Afghanistan: "If a country is hosting a terrorist cell, should that country also be subject to reprisals?" Bush answered that he would not "play his
hand" on that issue until he was president. "But I would tell the world that
we're going to hold people accountable.... There's going to be a consequence." Asked if the Clinton administration "had done enough to capture
the likes of Osama bin Laden or other suspected terrorist leaders," Bush demurred again. "I don't have enough intelligence briefings," he said.[1]

Reporters peppered him with pop quizzes about foreign policy. Bush's
intellect and qualifications had become campaign issues. He had traveled
abroad very little and had no direct experience in international affairs. He
could not spontaneously identify General Pervez Musharraf as Pakistan's
leader. His lapses prompted a writer from *Glamour* magazine to list a series of

names and ask Bush what came to mind: Christine Todd Whitman, Madonna, *Sex and the City,* the Taliban. Whitman was a "good friend." On the television show, Bush explained that he did not "get cable." About the Taliban, he shook his head in silence. The writer provided a hint: "Because of the repression of women—in Afghanistan." Bush lit up. "Oh, I thought you said some band. The Taliban in Afghanistan! Absolutely. Repressive."[2]

Bush relied heavily on Condoleezza Rice, his chief foreign policy adviser during his campaign. Rice was a self-described "Europeanist." She had written books on the communist-era Czechoslovak army and on the reunification of Germany. She had run the Soviet affairs directorate of the National Security Council under Bush's father. "I like to be around her," Bush explained, because "she's fun to be with. I like lighthearted people, not people who take themselves so seriously that they are hard to be around." Rice was a self-confident administrator with well-developed views about post–Cold War Europe. But she had to cram during the campaign about areas of the world she knew less well. At one point she described Iran as "the state hub for technology and money and lots of other goodies to radical fundamentalist groups, some will say as far-reaching as the Taliban." But Iran's Shiite regime and the Taliban's radical Sunni mullahs were blood enemies, and Iran actually sent arms and money to Ahmed Shah Massoud, to aid his war against the Taliban. Challenged by a reporter, Rice insisted that the Iranians were "sending stuff to the region that fell into the hands of bad players in Afghanistan and Pakistan." She did not explain what players. Asked about her statement once again, she said that of course she was aware of the enmity between Iran and the Taliban.[3]

None of the rest of Bush's closest foreign policy advisers had recent experience in South Asia, either. Vice President Richard Cheney and Defense Secretary Donald Rumsfeld had wide knowledge of global affairs but no personal acquaintance with Pakistan or Afghanistan. Paul Wolfowitz, appointed as deputy defense secretary after the election was resolved, was a specialist in Southeast Asia. Secretary of State Colin Powell and Deputy Secretary of State Richard Armitage had perhaps the most experience in the region. Each had worked closely with Pakistan's army and government during the 1980s and early 1990s. Armitage had been heavily involved from Washington in the last phase of the anti-Soviet jihad. Powell had worked with Pakistan's military during the 1990 run-up to the Gulf War. Their experiences, however, were rooted in the close ties between the United States and Pakistan's army and intelligence service during the Cold War years. Both men had been out of government during the 1990s as that alliance had frayed to the point of dysfunction, partly over bin Laden's terrorism and the related issue of jihadists fighting in Kashmir.

The son of a former CIA director, Bush was conditioned to believe in the agency's mission and people. During the long recount dispute in Florida he heard from family friends who urged him to consider leaving George Tenet in place for the good of the CIA's professionals. Tenet's most important mentor in the Senate, David Boren, the conservative Democrat from Oklahoma, was a Bush family friend. Boren and his daughter had belonged to the same secretive Yale fraternity, Skull and Bones, as had the two George Bushes. Boren's daughter later worked for George W. Bush in the Texas state government. In Boren's estimation, "The families trust each other." Just after New Year's Day, 2001, the former senator, now president of the University of Oklahoma, was in Miami to watch his Sooners play in the Orange Bowl football game. His cell phone rang in the midst of a boisterous pep rally. "I want to talk to you about George Tenet," president-elect Bush said over the noise, as Boren recalled it. "Tell me about this guy."[4]

Boren talked Tenet up enthusiastically. "I don't know if he's a Democrat or a Republican," Boren told Bush. "He's a straight shooter. . . . If there's anything a president needs, it's somebody who will tell him what he really thinks, have the courage to disagree with you, and look you in the eye and do so." These were among Tenet's great strengths, Boren said. "If you give him a chance to stay, I think it would be good for the agency because he's totally nonpolitical. . . . The agency has had so many directors, its morale is down. And I think it would be a great gesture for continuity and professionalism if you kept him on."

"I'm going to meet with him face-to-face," Bush replied. "I'll be able to judge this."[5]

For a president who valued "lighthearted people" who did not take themselves too seriously, Tenet was made to order. Like Bush he was salty, casual, and blunt. Tenet's emphasis on the CIA's traditional missions of warning and objective analysis had also appealed to the elder Bush, after whom Tenet had renamed the CIA's Langley headquarters. The White House announced on January 16 that Tenet had been asked to stay on at the CIA for "an undetermined period of time." President Bush would decide "at a later period" how long Tenet would remain at Langley.[6]

The CIA director had survived, but he was on a tryout. He now had to build steadily, meeting by meeting, an entirely new set of relationships with

Bush, Rice, and the national security cabinet. He began to brief Bush on intelligence matters each morning, face-to-face. The president agreed to make an early visit to CIA headquarters at Langley. "We are grateful to you for the active interest that you have demonstrated in our work from day one," Tenet declared before an overflow headquarters audience. Bush reflected on the differences between the CIA his father had run in 1976 and the agency now. His father's era had faced "an overarching threat" from Soviet communism, Bush said, but now "that single threat has been replaced by new and different threats, sometimes hard to define and defend against: threats such as terrorism, information warfare, the spread of weapons of mass destruction."[7]

Sandy Berger, who felt the first President Bush had failed to arrange adequate transition briefings on national security for the incoming Clinton team, vowed to run a handoff of the sort he would have wished to receive. The "number one" issue on his agenda, he recalled, "was terrorism and al Qaeda. . . . We briefed them fully on what we were doing, on what else was under consideration, and what the threat was." Berger ordered each directorate in the National Security Council to write an issues memo for Rice and her deputy, Stephen Hadley. The memos were then enhanced by oral briefings and slide show presentations. Berger himself attended only one, the session organized by Richard Clarke to talk about bin Laden and al Qaeda. "I'm here because I want to underscore how important this issue is," Berger explained to Rice. Later, in the West Wing of the White House, Berger told his successor, "You're going to spend more time during your four years on terrorism generally and bin Laden specifically than any issue."[8]

The warnings did not register. The CIA briefed Bush's senior national security team about al Qaeda, but its officers sensed no deep interest. Rice, Cheney, Rumsfeld, and Wolfowitz—the four with the strongest ideas and the most influence—had spent many months thinking and talking about what they would emphasize during their first one hundred days in the White House. They were focused on missile defense, military reform, China, and Iraq. Neither terrorism nor South Asia was high on the list.

In their early briefings, Clarke's office described bin Laden as an "existential" threat to the United States, meaning that the danger he posed went beyond the dozens or hundreds of casualties al Qaeda might inflict in serial bombing attacks. Bin Laden and his followers sought mass American fatalities and would use weapons of mass destruction in American cities if they could, Clarke and officers at the CIA's Counterterrorist Center firmly believed. Tenet and Pavitt briefed Bush, Cheney and Rice on intelligence issues, including the al Qaeda threat, which Pavitt recalled describing as one of the gravest threats to the country. Bush asked whether killing bin Laden would end the problem. Pavitt and Tenet replied that it would make an impact but not end the peril. When the CIA later elaborated on this point in assessments for Bush's White House, agency analysts argued that the only way to seriously hurt al Qaeda would be to eliminate its Afghan sanctuary. But they failed to persuade Bush or his top advisers. Throughout the 2000 campaign Bush and his team described missile defense as a central priority. They defined the most important security threat faced by the United States as hostile regimes that possessed or might soon acquire ballistic missiles that could strike American cities. In tandem they argued that China and to some extent Russia loomed as crucial security challenges. CIA briefers sensed that Bush's national security cabinet viewed terrorism as the kind of phenomenon it had been during the 1980s: potent but limited, a theatrical sort of threat that could produce episodic public crises but did not jeopardize the fundamental security of the United States. "I don't think we really had made the leap in our mind that we are no longer safe behind these two great oceans," Armitage said later.[9]

Clarke saw the early weeks of the Bush administration as an opportunity to win a more receptive audience for his ideas about bombing the Taliban and challenging bin Laden. He had on his desk analytical papers, recommendations, and discarded Cabinet agendas from the last weeks of the Clinton administration. Clarke and his aides composed a three-page memorandum to Rice dated January 25. Their package included Clarke's previous proposals from 1998 and late 2000. He urged covert aid to Massoud, new Predator flights, and other measures. A Cabinet-level meeting about al Qaeda's imminent threat was "urgently needed," he and his chief of staff, Roger Cressey, wrote. This was not "some narrow little terrorist issue." Suspected al Qaeda "sleeper cells" inside the United States were "a major threat in being."[10]

The Bush administration needed a new regional policy in South Asia, Clarke insisted. He emphasized several proposals that had earlier been blocked by Berger and the Clinton Cabinet. These included covert military aid to Massoud and bombing strikes on Taliban "infrastructure" such as Tarnak Farm. Clarke also highlighted in his memo the possibility of "making a deal" with Pakistan about bin Laden. His idea was that Bush should signal Musharraf that confronting al Qaeda was now America's number one priority. Moreover, the United States would stop pressuring Pakistan about a return to democracy if Musharraf's army and intelligence service would solve the bin Laden problem once and for all. Clarke also underscored proposals to deliver more money for the CIA's Counterterrorist Center to attack al Qaeda cells worldwide, more covert aid to Uzbekistan, and a tougher diplomatic assault on Islamic charity financing to terrorist groups. Clarke's memo blended into one agenda aggressive ideas from the previous administration—some partially approved and others that had been rejected.[11]

Clarke was in an awkward position. He had acquired a reputation as a uniquely powerful Washington mandarin. He was publicly described as the government's best expert on terrorism policy and the bin Laden threat. He was a hawkish nonpartisan civil servant known and respected by some members of Bush's team. Rice told Clarke she wanted him to stay on at the National Security Council. Yet it was obvious from the start that Clarke would lose some or most of his power in the Bush administration. Condoleezza Rice had strong ideas about how the National Security Council should be managed. Clarke's personal influence on terrorism issues did not fit Rice's model. In addition he was tainted by his Cabinet-level participation in the Clinton administration's policies, which in a season of partisan turnover at the White House looked innately suspect.

Clarke's January 25 memo went nowhere. No Cabinet meeting about al Qaeda, Afghanistan, or regional policy was scheduled. Weeks later Rice completed the first phase of her NSC reorganization, and Clarke formally lost his Cabinet-level status on terrorism issues. In response he asked Rice for a transfer. Clarke said he wanted to give up his work on bin Laden and concentrate instead on the threat of attacks against American computer systems. Rice agreed, promising to consult Clarke occasionally on terrorism questions.

Hugh Shelton, who stayed on as chairman of the Joint Chiefs of Staff, used the transition weeks to extricate the Navy from its obligation to maintain cruise missile submarines within striking distance of Afghanistan. The program had proved expensive; in addition, it disrupted deployments, and the CIA had never delivered intelligence precise enough to act upon. Besides, the strong-minded Rumsfeld, determined to pursue missile defense and an ambitious military reorganization, thought terrorism "was out there, but it didn't happen today," as Shelton recalled it, so "maybe it belongs lower on the list." Rumsfeld conceded later that he was focused on other priorities early in 2001, and said that the Pentagon at this time was not organized or trained to deal with an enemy like bin Laden.[12]

Cofer Black and the bin Laden unit chief at the CIA's Counterterrorist Center made no objection to the loss of the submarines. Their priority that winter was to accelerate Air Force testing of an armed version of the Predator, which the CIA could then fly over Afghanistan and use to shoot at bin Laden and his top aides. A lethal Predator would eliminate the problem of synchronizing perishable human agent reports from Afghanistan with cruise missile flight times, the CIA officers argued. An armed drone would reduce the "sensor to shooter" timeline, previously counted in hours, to mere seconds. By February the State Department's lawyers had waved off concerns that an armed drone might violate the Intermediate Nuclear Forces Treaty. But the Air Force had many technical questions yet to resolve. Air Force engineers had fitted the Predator with a modified version of the Hellfire anti-tank missile, but they did not know what impact its firing would have on the Predator's flight-worthiness. The Predator was such a light and unwieldy craft that some engineers feared the explosive propulsion of an igniting missile would send the drone reeling backwards, perhaps out of control. A February test in Nevada was encouraging: The drone's missile struck a target tank turret six inches right of center.[13]

But the Bush Cabinet had no policy about the novel idea of shooting terrorists with armed flying robots. The Cabinet had barely formed, and neither the principals nor their deputies had yet held a formal discussion of bin Laden. There was some talk of an interagency policy review on Afghanistan and al Qaeda, but none had been properly organized. Iraq, Iran, the Israeli-Palestinian conflict, China, Russia, and missile defense all stood ahead of Afghanistan in the security policy queue.

Black pressed the Air Force to certify that a Hellfire-armed, laser-aimed Predator could kill bin Laden if he spent the night at his Tarnak Farm residence—without taking out large numbers of bystanders. If the CIA was to propose a lethal Predator mission to President Bush or his Cabinet, the agency would need technical proof that it could succeed. But the Hellfire had never been designed to knock down mud-brick or concrete walls. All of the missile's manuals, specifications, and test results documented its ability to destroy tanks. In an era of expensive high-technology weapons systems, Pentagon culture emphasized precision, idiot-proof firing procedures, and the careful, scientific matching of weapons and targets. If the Pentagon was to make good on presidential orders to limit bystander deaths in a Tarnak missile strike, for example, the Air Force had to predict accurately how many rooms in a building struck by a Hellfire would actually be destroyed. This meant more tests. With CIA assistance an Air Force team built in Nevada a mockup of the Tarnak residence where bin Laden stayed. The Counterterrorist Center pushed for a speedy schedule, but there was no way to conduct such an elaborate test overnight.[14]

Meanwhile, Clarke argued with Black and others at the CIA over whether to send the Predator back to Afghanistan as the weather warmed, strictly for reconnaissance missions, with only cameras and sensors on board. Even though his role was waning, Clarke wanted the Predator in the air again; this had been the agreed plan back in October, he asserted. But Tenet, Black, and Pentagon officers argued that flying reconnaissance now would be a mistake. The Taliban had clearly identified the drone's radar signature during the autumn. At the beginning of that series of Predator flights, Black had been told in a briefing that the radar cross-section of the drone was no more noticeable than a small flock of birds. Now they were discovering, Black argued, that the Predator looked on enemy radar much more like a full-sized commercial airliner flying at a conspicuously slow speed, relatively easy to identify. The CIA's officers figured that at best they would be able to mount five or six Predator missions before the Taliban shot one down. They did not want to waste these flights, they said, before the Predator was armed. Under a new agreement with the Air Force, the CIA had agreed to shoulder half the cost of future Predator missions and losses. That meant the agency would be billed about $1.5 million for each drone that went down. Black and his colleagues also argued that a shootdown might jeopardize Uzbekistan's cooperation with the CIA. The agency formally asked government analysts whether the Predator's reconnaissance value justified all these risks. The analysts replied that satellite imagery and reconnaissance aircraft could do virtually as well. Clarke saw the CIA's position as more evidence of its aversion to risk. No Predators were sent to Afghanistan.[15]

The CIA was divided over Black's enthusiasm for armed drones. Some officers in the Near East Division of the Directorate of Operations remained skeptical. The feeling was "Oh, these harebrained CTC [Counterterrorist Center] ideas," recalled one official. "This is going to be a disaster." The internal debates and uncertainty ultimately slowed the pace of deployment.[16]

There was no foreign policy context for flying armed Predators in Central Asia that winter or spring. The South Asia bureau at the State Department remained leaderless until June. Al Eastham, a career foreign service officer and Clinton holdover, ran day-to-day regional affairs on an interim basis. Eastham continued to emphasize that America would not choose sides in the Afghan civil war. Neither Bush nor his senior advisers provided any contrary public signal. Clarke again pitched Rice on aid to the Northern Alliance in March, but Rice and her deputy Stephen Hadley wanted to wait for a broader program that would include Pashtun opponents of the Taliban. Clarke agreed that Pashtuns should be involved but insisted that Massoud needed help immediately. He lost the argument.[17]

Rice and Armitage received cables and memos offering diverse and sometimes contradictory advice about Afghanistan. The U.S. ambassador to Pakistan, Bill Milam, sent a long cable in early February titled "Options for dealing with Afghan terrorism problem," which suggested that Bush seize his fresh start to offer the Taliban a last chance grand bargain: large-scale economic aid in exchange for U.S. custody of bin Laden. If the Taliban refused, the U.S. could begin openly backing the militia's opponents, seeking Mullah Omar's overthrow. As always, the Islamabad embassy opposed any embrace of Massoud, but its political analysts thought the Bush administration could profitably support anti-Taliban Pashtuns such as Hamid Karzai if the grand bargain idea failed.[18]

Zalmay Khalilzad, an influential voice inside Bush's forming National Security Council, echoed some of this advice. The Afghan-born foreign policy analyst had helped oversee the Bush transition. Rice then appointed him to run her Middle East directorate. Khalilzad was an old acquaintance of Hamid Karzai. They had run into each other in Pakistan and elsewhere over the years, and they stayed in touch. After the murder of Karzai's father by the Taliban, Khalilzad had turned against the Taliban in the articles he published from his consulting office at the RAND Corporation in Washington. He urged Clinton to openly seek the movement's overthrow.

Among other things, Khalilzad feared the spread of Taliban ideology to Pakistan. "The prospect of a nuclear-armed Pakistan adopting the credo of the Taliban, while unlikely, is simply too risky to ignore," he had written a year before joining the National Security Council. Yet he also opposed any deep American alliance with Ahmed Shah Massoud. Fearful of a north-south ethnic split, Khalilzad argued adamantly that Pashtuns—exiles and royalists like Karzai—had to be the locus of any successful anti-Taliban strategy. If the goal was Mullah Omar's demise, "too close a relationship with the Northern Alliance will hinder rather than help this objective," he believed. Khalilzad wanted to help dissident Pashtuns who could "fracture the Taliban internally." These views placed him at odds with Cofer Black and the bin Laden unit at the Counterterrorist Center, who saw Massoud as by far their most valuable potential ally against al Qaeda. They also did not see how politically weak Pashtun exiles could be effective in fomenting a coup or splitting the Taliban from the inside.[19]

All this debate meant the Bush administration had no clear direction. It would take months to fashion a new approach. The Cabinet displayed little sense of urgency.

PAKISTAN'S ARMY had long enjoyed better relations with Republican administrations in Washington than with Democrats, yet it was not clear that tradition would hold this time. Musharraf's advisers in Islamabad knew that Bush's 2000 campaign had raised massive contributions from Indian-American businessmen. These donors pressed Bush and his advisers to tilt American policy toward India. The Republican Party platform, crafted in part to please financial supporters, emphasized relations with India over those with Pakistan. Conservative intellectuals on the Bush foreign policy team, such as Harvard University's Robert Blackwill, recommended a strategic shift toward India to counter the menace of a rising China.[20]

Musharraf and his advisers in Islamabad sent Bush a confidential three-page letter that outlined common ground between Pakistan and the United States and pressed for closer ties. Condoleezza Rice met with Musharraf's ambassador to Washington, Maleeha Lodhi, an accomplished female former journalist who like Rice had risen to the top of her male-dominated foreign policy establishment. The two governments could work together to isolate bin Laden, Lodhi pledged, but Pakistan's army still felt that the Taliban were misunderstood in Washington. The Taliban had recently cracked down on opium poppy production, Lodhi noted. "Yeah, Stalin also got a lot of things done," Rice answered.[21]

The White House delivered a confidential written reply to Musharraf early in 2001 that contained many encouraging signals about the future of the U.S.-Pakistan alliance, but the letter also linked the chances for an improved relationship—debt relief, sanction waivers, and security cooperation—with resolution of the bin Laden problem. "The continued presence of Osama bin Laden and his al-Qaida organization is a direct threat to the United States and its interests that must be addressed," Bush wrote. "I believe al-Qaida also threatens Pakistan's long-term interests."

The letter arrived in the midst of an intensifying debate within Pakistan's army and establishment over support for the Taliban. Musharraf had consolidated army rule by winning the allegiance of politically neutral civil servants such as the diplomats in Pakistan's British-style elite foreign service. Now the civilians in his government began to openly question the army's support for jihadists in Afghanistan. "We find practical reasons to continue with policies that we know are never going to deliver and the eventual costs of which we also know will be overwhelming. . . . Thus we are condemned to ride a tiger," wrote Pakistan's high commissioner in India, Ashraf Jehangir Qazi, in a confidential cable that January, prepared in advance of a meeting of ambassadors in Islamabad. Pakistan had "no choice," Qazi argued, but had to somehow "resolve the OBL [Osama bin Laden] problem before addressing any other issue." If the Taliban refused to cooperate, Pakistan should squeeze their supplies and "undermine the authority of those Taliban leaders who refuse to cooperate." Other key civilians around Musharraf—Lodhi; Arif Ayub, the ambassador to Kabul; and the country's civilian finance minister—weighed in with similar arguments. Mullah Omar refused to do the Pakistan army's bidding and refused to acquiesce even on the smallest issues, yet the United States and other world powers all adamantly believed that Pakistan pulled the Taliban's strings. Pakistan had achieved the "worst of both worlds," as one official recalled arguing.[22]

The dissidents in Pakistan's government supported a break with the Taliban because they thought it was in Pakistan's national interest. Mullah Omar and his jihadist allies had spooked former Soviet governments in Central Asia and alienated them from Pakistan, chilling trade. The economy sagged under debts, sanctions, and a poor investment climate. Some strains of the Taliban's violent radicalism had blown onto Pakistani soil. Al Qaeda harbored and trained anti-Shiite fanatics who mounted assassinations and touched off riots in Pakistani cities. All of this was tolerated by Pakistan's generals in the name of "strategic depth" against India. But what depth had they really won?

A few generals in Musharraf's cabinet sided with the civilians. One was Moinuddin Haider, a retired three-star appointed by Musharraf as interior minister, in charge of Pakistan's police and internal security. Haider's brother had been killed by sectarian terrorists with links to Afghanistan. "We are losing too much," he argued in closed gatherings with Musharraf and other generals. The Taliban "don't listen to us on matters of smuggling, narcotics, weapons," Haider said. "They're not serious about this." Even worse, the Taliban had taken to issuing threats against Musharraf. Omar wrote the Pakistani leader a private letter on January 16, 2001, urging him to "enforce Islamic law . . . step by step" in order to appease Pakistan's religious parties. Otherwise, there could be "instability" in the country. "This is our advice and message based on Islamic ideology," Omar warned. "Otherwise you had better know how to deal with it."[23]

But Pakistan's policy on Afghanistan ran largely on automatic pilot. Musharraf endorsed the alliance with the Taliban in part because he believed that Pakistan needed reliable Pashtun allies next door. Pakistani intelligence kept the jihadist combine churning. Even the civilian liberals in the government resented the constant pressure they received about the Taliban and bin Laden from the American government—the humiliating formal démarches and the endless sanctions and speeches. Even though they abhorred the Taliban's philosophy, some of the civilian Pakistani elite took a little pride in how Omar and bin Laden flustered and punished the Americans. Liberal Pakistani diplomats used all their wiles to protect the Taliban from international sanctions. They obfuscated, they dodged, they rationalized. It was just a matter of being professional, they believed. However distasteful his outlook, Mullah Omar helped defend Pakistan from the existential threat of Indian aggression. The liberal civilians around Musharraf believed they could work for change gradually from within their government.[24]

The Taliban kept spinning off in new and bizarre directions, however. On March 1 the movement announced its intention to destroy all the statues in Afghanistan that depicted human form. Militiamen armed with rockets and assault rifles began blasting two ancient sandstone statues of Buddha believed to have been hewn in the third and fifth centuries when a Buddhist community thrived in central Afghanistan. One statue rose 120 feet, the other 175 feet. Their jewels had long ago been stripped away, and their faces had been hacked off by previous Muslim rulers. But the figures remained, glorious and dignified, legs draped by folded robes. The Taliban's audacious vandalism provoked worldwide condemnation and shock that rarely followed the militia's massacres of Afghan civilians. Curators and government spokesmen pleaded that the demolitions be suspended. Mullah Omar seemed puzzled. "We do not understand why everyone is so worried," he said. "All we are breaking are stones."[25]

Wealthy Buddhist nations in Asia—many of them donors to Pakistan's sick treasury—pressured Musharraf to intervene before it was too late. The general asked Moinuddin Haider to fly to Kandahar and reason with Omar. Haider hurriedly consulted Islamic scholars to fashion detailed religious arguments that might appeal to the Taliban. Flanked by translators, note takers, and Islamic consultants, he flew by executive jet to Kandahar's airport, circling down over Tarnak Farm. The visitors drove to Mullah Omar's new walled suburban estate on Kandahar's outskirts, constructed in lavish style by Osama bin Laden. It lay nestled in pine trees on a rise beneath a sharp rock mountain. There was an ornate main palace, a house for servants, a lavish guest house, and a blue mosque with white trim.

"We deliberated for six months, and we came to the conclusion that we should destroy them," Omar explained when they were settled.

Haider quoted a verse from the Koran that said Muslims should not slander the gods of other religions. Allah would decide who was worthy on the day of judgment, Haider said.

He cited many cases in history, especially in Egypt, where Muslims had protected the statues and art of other religions. The Buddhas in Afghanistan were older even than Islam. Thousands of Muslim soldiers had crossed Afghanistan to India over the centuries, but none of them had ever felt compelled to destroy the Buddhas. "When they have spared these statues for fifteen hundred years, all these Muslims who have passed by them, how are you a different Muslim from them?" Haider asked.

"Maybe they did not have the technology to destroy them," Omar speculated.

Omar said he feared what Allah would say to him on the Day of Judgment. He talked about himself in the third person. "Allah will ask me, 'Omar, you have brought a superpower called the Soviet Union to its knees. You could not break two statues?' And what would Mullah Omar reply?"

Peering from his one healthy eye, the Taliban leader continued: "On the Day of Judgment all of these mountains will turn into sand and fly into the air. And what if these statues in this shape go before Allah? What face, then, will Mullah Omar show to God?"[26]

HAIDER RELAYED an account of Omar's visions to the U.S. embassy in Islamabad, which in turn cabled a report to Washington. The embassy had largely given up on the idea that the Taliban might be persuaded to voluntarily hand bin Laden over to the United States. Omar's rantings to Haider about the apocalypse only reinforced this analysis.

Yet Milam and others in the embassy continued to advocate close engagement with Musharraf's government. Their conversations with relative liberals like Haider persuaded them that Pakistan's attitude toward the Taliban might be shifting.

Diplomats, defense attachés, and CIA case officers in the Islamabad embassy reported continually on whether Taliban-style Islamic radicalism had begun to infect Pakistan's army or government elite. Among other things, with help from American and European exchange students at Pakistan's two prestigious colleges for army officers, the U.S. embassy conducted an annual "beard census" of Pakistani army officers, counting the number of officer graduates and serving generals who kept their beards in accordance with Islamic tradition.[27] The numbers seemed reassuring. Only two or three Pakistani generals at the rank of lieutenant general or higher kept beards in 2001. The rate was less than 10 percent among graduates of the elite officers' schools.

Anglophilic education, a vast and mobile business diaspora, satellite television, a free domestic press, and the lively, open traditions of Pakistan's dominant Punjabi culture still insulated its society from the most virulent strains of political Islam. The Punjabi liberals who mainly ran Pakistan's government resented the fearful, nattering lectures they heard from former Clinton administration officials such as Strobe Talbott, who spoke publicly about the dangers of a Taliban-type takeover in Pakistan. Yet even these liberals acknowledged readily by early 2001 that two decades of official clandestine support for regional jihadist militias had changed Pakistan. Thousands of young men in Quetta, Peshawar, and Karachi had now been inculcated in the tenets of suicide warfare. The country's main religious parties—harmless debating societies and social service agencies in the first decades after partition—had become permanent boards of directors for covert jihadist wars. They were inflamed by ambition, enriched with charity funds, and influenced by radical ideologies imported from the Middle East.

The U.S. embassy poured out cables and analytical papers about the potential for "Talibanization" in Pakistan. The embassy's defense and political analysts mainly concluded that while the danger was rising, it remained in check. Yet even a slight risk of a takeover by Islamic radicals argued for continued close engagement with Musharraf's government, these American analysts believed.[28]

GEORGE TENET INTRODUCED HIMSELF to the new Bush Cabinet by issuing dire warnings about an imminent threat of new terrorist strikes from bin Laden. CIA threat reporting surged during January and February, leading up to the *hajj* pilgrimage in March. There were "strong indications" that bin Laden was "planning new operations" and was now "capable of mounting multiple attacks with little or no warning," Tenet said. The CIA warned Prince Turki that it had reports of a planned terrorist strike in Mecca. Al Qaeda recruitment videos circulated in the Middle East, showing bin Laden reading poems in praise of the *Cole* bombers while touring martial Afghan training camps. For the first time since he was sworn into office, Tenet put terrorism first on his list as he reviewed the most important security challenges faced by the United States in his annual winter briefing to the Senate. The CIA director showed Rice and others the video of bin Laden at Tarnak Farm and outlined the agency's disruption efforts in Afghanistan and elsewhere. Rice asked

Tenet to prepare a memo on covert action authorities for Afghanistan that would expand the CIA's permissions in the field. When Tenet presented his draft, he and Rice's office decided to wait to implement the new authorities until the Bush Administration had developed new policies on al Qaeda and Central Asia. Bush himself recalled that Tenet told him the CIA had all the authority it needed.[29]

Zalmay Khalilzad, at the National Security Council, sought to use the Bush administration's leverage to establish credible Pashtun opposition to the Taliban on Pakistani soil. But Musharraf's government refused that spring to allow official Afghan opposition groups, as Khalilzad urged, "because we'd have a civil war," as one Pakistani official recalled. The discussions continued warily. The Pakistanis told the Americans they were being taken for a ride by self-aggrandizing Afghan exiles. They asked for names of America's favored "moderate" anti-Taliban Pashtuns. The CIA had to protect unilateral contacts and recruitments among anti-Taliban Pashtuns, however, some of whom lived in Pakistan.[30]

Tenet traveled secretly to Islamabad that spring of 2001. Mahmoud had remained cold and recalcitrant in the year since his CIA-escorted tour of the Gettysburg battlefield.

Tenet said he saw nothing to lose by keeping the lines open. Mahmoud had tightened up on American access to every sector of the Pakistani army and intelligence service. He had decided to enforce strict liaison rules that blocked American contacts with Pakistani corps commanders, division commanders, and other generals. CIA access to Pakistani intelligence officers remained limited. Inside the U.S. embassy, opinion about Mahmoud's motivations was divided. Accounts of the ISI chief's new religiosity had begun to circulate widely. Yet Mahmoud remained correct, formal, and condescending in one-on-one meetings.[31]

Mahmoud hosted a dinner for Tenet at the ISI mess in Islamabad. There was a numbing routine to these official liaison meals: starched uniforms, exotic headdresses, fruit juice, smiles, and stiff formality. The working sessions were little better. Mahmoud tried to reassure the Americans that he was on their side. Tenet asked for practical help. The CIA's objective was to penetrate bin Laden's security, arrest his aides, and break up his operations, Tenet said. The Americans continued to believe that Pakistani intelligence could do much more to help track bin Laden's location and disrupt his terrorist planning.

The CIA and the Drug Enforcement Administration had managed to maintain some cooperation with Pakistani police and intelligence services on drug trafficking issues. They talked about whether it would be possible to use the counternarcotics channel to get bin Laden.[32]

Tenet came and went quickly. After decades official liaison between the CIA and ISI had its own self-perpetuating momentum. One meeting followed another. High-level visits were reciprocated. As Tenet left, planning began for when Mahmoud might travel again to the United States. Early September 2001 looked as if it might be convenient.

"Many Americans
Are Going to Die"

AHMED SHAH MASSOUD retained a Washington lobbyist as the Bush administration took office. He wanted someone who could arrange meetings on Capitol Hill for his Panjshiri advisers. He wrote a letter to Vice President Cheney urging the new administration to reexamine its alliance with Pakistan. He traveled secretly to Russia and Iran to shore up supply arrangements. In Moscow, the tycoon-ruled capital of his former communist enemy, Massoud met quietly with Russian defense officials worried about bin Laden's drive into Chechnya and Central Asia. In the Panjshir, Massoud welcomed European visitors worried about his ability to hold his ground. A sympathetic Belgian politician invited him to travel in early April to Strasbourg, France, the seat of the European parliament, to deliver a speech about the al Qaeda threat. Massoud accepted. With the loss of his headquarters in Taloqan, his military prospects looked grave. He told his advisers and visitors that he knew he could not defeat the Taliban on the Afghan battlefield, not so long as they were funded by bin Laden and reinforced from Pakistani *madrassas*. He sought to build a new political and military coalition within Afghanistan and without that could squeeze the Taliban and break their grip on ordinary Afghans. For this, sooner or later, he would require the support of the United States, he said.[1]

His CIA liaison had slackened, but his intelligence aides still spoke and exchanged messages frequently with Langley. That spring they passed word that Massoud was headed to France. Gary Schroen from the Near East Division and Rich, the chief of the bin Laden unit, said they would fly to Paris.[2]

Massoud's reputation—his myth—depended on his tenacious refusal to leave Afghan territory even in the darkest hours. At midlife he allowed himself and his family many more comforts than he had known in the Panjshir during the early 1980s, but only to the extent that cities like Tehran or Dushanbe could provide them. Many of his senior advisers, such as Abdullah, circulated regularly in European and American cities. Massoud did not follow. His political strength among Afghans rested on his claim to be the most stalwart, consistent fighter on Afghan soil, a claim that had the virtue of truth. Yet Massoud had been educated at Kabul's *lycée*. He retained his French. At forty-nine, Paris in April was his well-chosen indulgence.

At the hotel Schroen discovered to his amusement that he had been officially registered as part of Massoud's Afghan delegation. Massoud Khalili, the aide to the commander who had accompanied Schroen on his maiden flight to Kabul in 1996, had made his arrangements. He innocently included his CIA friend on the delegation's official list. But Schroen had been "declared" or openly identified as a CIA officer to the French intelligence services. They surely were monitoring the guest lists and bugging the rooms. Now the French, so often irritating to the CIA's Near East Division, would have even more reason than usual to wonder what the CIA was up to with Massoud.[3]

They met in a sizable group. Massoud's back was plaguing him, and he did not look well. A streak of gray now ran through his hair. He had not slowed much; he still worked through the night and flew off jubilantly on reckless helicopter reconnaissance missions in the Panjshir. But he was an aging lion, regal but stiffening.

The Americans wanted to reassure him that even though there had been no recent CIA visits to the Panjshir, the agency was still going to keep up its regular payments of several hundred thousand dollars each, in accordance with their intelligence sharing deal. The CIA also wanted to know how Massoud felt about his military position as the spring fighting season approached in Afghanistan. Would he be able to hang in there?

Massoud said that he could. He believed he could defend his lines in the northeast of Afghanistan, but that was about all. Counterattacks against the

Taliban were becoming more difficult as his resources frayed. A drive on Kabul remained out of the question. The United States government had to do something, Massoud told the CIA officers quietly, or eventually he was going to crumble. The Americans told him that they would keep trying. There was a new administration in Washington, as they all knew. It would take time for the Cabinet to settle in and educate itself, but this was a natural opportunity to review policy.[4]

Massoud doubted they had time. "If President Bush doesn't help us," he told a press conference in Strasbourg a few days later, "then these terrorists will damage the United States and Europe very soon—and it will be too late."[5]

Massoud believed that the Taliban were seeking to destroy him or force him into exile. Then al Qaeda would attempt to link up with Islamist militants in remote areas of Uzbekistan and Tajikistan, to press forward into Central Asia, burnishing bin Laden's mystique as a conquerer of lost Islamic lands. Massoud's clanking helicopters, patchwork supply lines, and Panjshiri volunteers could not stop this juggernaut. He could only rebound, he believed that spring, if outside powers put enough pressure on Pakistan and the conservative Persian Gulf kingdoms to cut off or severely pinch the Taliban's supplies. Since Massoud could not strike these supply lines militarily, he had to attack them through politics. This is what had brought him to the European parliament. It was also why he pushed his aides to lobby the U.S. Congress that spring.[6]

At the same time Massoud hoped to exploit the Taliban's weaknesses inside Afghanistan. He called this part of his strategy "the new return." For a year now Massoud had been stitching a revived *shura,* or governing council, that united Taliban opponents from every major Afghan ethnic group and every major region. From Quetta, Pakistan, Hamid Karzai organized among the Kandahar area's Durrani tribes. Ismail Khan had entered western Afghanistan from Iran and was leading an uprising near Herat. Karim Khalili, the country's most prominent Shiite leader, had returned from exile to Bamian province to work against the Taliban. Haji Qadir, a former Pashtun warlord-politician in Jalalabad, had slipped into Kunar province to lead a local rebellion. Aburrashid Dostum, the Uzbek warlord, had come back to Afghanistan from exile and fought behind Taliban lines in the rough northern mountains.[7]

Many of Massoud's "new return" partners had been part of the failed mujahedin government in Kabul during the early 1990s, before the Taliban rose. Many had been discredited by their violent infighting during that earlier period. Yet they had all come back to Afghanistan. They had agreed, at least on paper, to share power and abide by common, quasi-democratic principles linked by Massoud's vision and charisma.

It baffled Massoud that the United States, in the midst of a life-and-death struggle against al Qaeda, as he was, could not see the political and military potential of the diverse anti-Taliban alliance he was forging on Afghan soil. That spring Massoud invited his new Washington advocate, Otilie English, a lobbyist who had worked for the Committee for a Free Afghanistan during the 1980s, to meet with him in northern Afghanistan. With his chief CIA liaison, Amrullah Saleh, providing translation, Massoud recorded a videotaped seminar for English about the changing landscape inside Afghanistan, al Qaeda's strengths and weaknesses, foreign involvement in the war, and his own strategy. Massoud and his aides hoped English would use the commander's ideas to change minds in Congress or the State Department.

The Taliban's "extreme actions now have cracked the Pashtuns," Massoud told her. "An average Pashtun mullah is asking—he knows the history and simply has a question: Why are there no schools? Why is there no education for women? Why are women not allowed to work?" The Taliban's religious tenets had been imported from Pakistan and applied inflexibly, Massoud said. Traditional Afghan religious leaders at the village level had now begun to challenge these decrees.[8]

The Arabs and the Pakistani Taliban were the key to the war's outcome, he continued. "It is a totally separate story whether Osama is a popular figure outside Afghanistan or not, but inside Afghanistan, actually, he is not," Massoud told English. "For myself, for my colleagues, and for us totally, he is a criminal. He is a person who has committed crimes against our people. Perhaps in the past there was some type of respect for Arabs. People would consider them as Muslims. They had come as guests. But now they are seen as criminals. They are seen as tyrants. They are seen as cruel. Similarly, the reaction is the same against the Pakistani Taliban." As a result, resentment was gathering against Taliban rule "from the bottom" of Afghan society, from "the grass roots, the *ulama*," or religious leaders.

"How do we counter them?" Massoud asked. He outlined a strategy of local military pressure and global political appeals. While his allies seeded small revolts around Afghanistan, Massoud would publicize their cause worldwide as one of "popular consensus and general elections and democracy." The Taliban and bin Laden "are pushing to establish their caliphate, and what they call their emirate. This is a total contradiction to what we want." Massoud insisted that he was not trying to revive the failed Kabul government of the early 1990s. "Everything should be shared," he told his lobbyist. "These are our slogans—what we believe in. We believe in a moderate Islam, and of course, they believe in extremism."

His visitors asked what Massoud wanted from the United States. "First, political support," he answered. "Let us reopen our embassy" in Washington. "This is issue one." Second, he needed "humanitarian assistance" that was not "wasted in Pakistan and for administration costs and in the U.N. system." He needed food and medical aid on the ground in northern Afghanistan to support his followers and his loose collection of rebel allies. "And, of course, financial assistance." With cash he could purchase most of the military supplies he needed from the Russians. But he was not getting enough by way of direct donations. Finally, he hinted to English about the tensions in his liaison with the CIA. "Our intelligence structure is preoccupied with tactical information that we need. That is our priority," he said. "We do not see any problem to working directly against the terrorists. But we have very, very limited resources."[9]

On her way back to Washington, English met with a CIA officer in Uzbekistan. She explained the message she would be carrying to Congress and the Bush administration.

"I hope you're successful," the CIA man said.

She was surprised. Her lobbying office had shaky relations with the agency. "Really? Do you mean that?"

"Yeah. I've been writing the same thing that you're saying, and I've been writing it for months, and I'm getting no response. I've been writing it for years, and I've been getting no response."[10]

Peter Tomsen, the former U.S. ambassador to the Afghan resistance, arrived in Dushanbe in June. Tomsen had retired from the foreign service. He now lectured and published articles denouncing Pakistani intelligence and the Taliban. Hamid Karzai and Abdul Haq tracked him down at a vacation villa in Tuscany that spring. They urged him to travel to Tajikistan to meet with Massoud and join their global political campaign. Tomsen agreed—if the meeting would develop a real political strategy. Ten years before, Tomsen had championed a "commanders' *shura*" with a central role for Massoud, a blend of military pressure and political appeals similar to Massoud's current plan. At the time, the CIA had opposed Tomsen, preferring to work with Pakistani intelligence. Now Tomsen revived his ideas, encouraged by Karzai and Abdul Haq, and he crafted a confidential strategy paper for Massoud.

Tomsen stayed in touch with former colleagues from his years in govern-

ment service, but he found the CIA more secretive than ever. Over the years
Tomsen had concluded that America's failed policies in Afghanistan flowed in
part from the compartmented, top secret isolation in which the CIA always
sought to work. The agency saw the president as its client. By keeping the
State Department and other policy makers at a distance, it preserved a certain
freedom to operate. But when the agency was wrong—the Bay of Pigs, Gulbuddin Hekmatyar—there was little check on its analysis. Conversely, when it
was on the right track—as with Massoud in the late 1990s—it often had trouble finding allies in political Washington.[11]

At his house in Dushanbe, Massoud lamented to Tomsen that the rebel-
lions by his scattered allies around Afghanistan were making limited progress.
Supplies were inadequate. The Karzais were under severe pressure around
Kandahar and in Pakistan. "Dostum was of the opinion that, with his return,
all Uzbeks would take up guns and start an uprising," Massoud told Tomsen.
But this had not happened. "I personally don't believe that the collapse of the
Taliban is that imminent."

Massoud said he wanted to build the broadest possible anti-Taliban coalition. For that he was willing to drop old grievances and link his Northern Alliance with the exiled King Zahir Shah in Rome. Massoud appealed to Tomsen
to bring the king into his alliance. "Talk to Zahir Shah," he urged. "Tell him
that I accept him as head of state."

This grand Pashtun-Tajik alliance might finally persuade the American
government to change its policy. "There are two shortcuts to stop the war,"
Massoud told Tomsen and Abdul Haq that spring afternoon. "One is military.
The other is American pressure on Pakistan."[12]

"I'M TIRED OF SWATTING FLIES," President Bush told Condoleezza
Rice in the Oval Office that spring after another in a series of briefings about
al Qaeda threats. "I want to play offense."[13]

Chaired by Stephen Hadley, the deputies committee held its first meeting
on bin Laden and Afghanistan on April 30. "There will be more attacks," CIA
briefing slides warned. Al Qaeda was the "most dangerous group we face."
They reviewed options left over from the last Clinton Cabinet session on the
subject, conducted more than four months earlier. Richard Armitage set the
outline for a new policy direction. He said that the destruction of al Qaeda
should be the number one American objective in South Asia, a higher priority even than nuclear weapons control. The goal Armitage outlined, as he re-

called it, was "not just to roll back al Qaeda, but to go after and eliminate them." The deputies asked the CIA to dust off its plan for large-scale covert aid to Massoud so that the shopping list and military objectives could be refined, integrated with other policy goals, and presented to the full Cabinet.[14]

The deputies also endorsed continued testing of an armed Predator, although there were many questions yet to be resolved about exactly how missiles would be fired if the drone was sent to Afghanistan. They asked the Pentagon yet again to develop contingency military plans to attack al Qaeda targets.

Paul Wolfowitz, Bush's influential deputy defense secretary, had concluded by now that "war against al Qaeda is something different from going after individual acts of terrorism." This was a change from how terrorism had been managed the last time the Republicans held power. Wolfowitz could see, as he recalled it, that "it really does involve all the elements of national power, that it's not just something for the intelligence community alone." As to the regional questions, he concluded it was impossible to destroy al Qaeda "without recognizing the role that the government of Afghanistan is playing."[15]

The deputies' decision to make bin Laden their top priority marked a change from the Clinton years when the president and his aides often listed terrorism second or third in their private talks with Musharraf and others. Yet the White House committee, slow to begin, now had to sort out many of the same old questions about Pakistan that had vexed Clinton. The country seemed extraordinarily dangerous. Wolfowitz concluded, as he recalled it, that "you can't go after the government of Afghanistan without recognizing the problems in your relationship, particularly with Pakistan, but with other neighboring countries" as well. By April State Department diplomats believed Pakistan simply did not intend to cut off aid to the Taliban. Would the United States try once again to issue diplomatic ultimatums to Islamabad? What if Pakistan failed to respond?[16] Above all, how could they attempt to destroy al Qaeda, which had insinuated itself with the Pakistani military and intelligence service, without undermining Pakistan?

The deputies decided to slow down and review these questions before they delivered any new covert arms or money to Massoud or his fledgling anti-Taliban alliance. In a late May meeting, Rice asked Tenet, Black, and Clarke about "taking the offensive" against al Qaeda. Reflecting Khalilzad's view, Rice did not want to rely exclusively on the Northern Alliance. Clarke again urged unsuccessfully that some money be funnelled to Massoud right away, to keep him in action. Meanwhile, the administration's publicly stated policy about Afghanistan remained unaltered. As he laid out budget priorities to the Senate two weeks after the deputies meeting on al Qaeda, Colin Powell mentioned Afghanistan only once, to ask for $7 million. The money would be used, he said, to promote regional energy cooperation and to attack child prostitution.[17]

THE CIA'S THREAT reporting about bin Laden surged that spring to levels the Counterterrorist Center had rarely seen. Tenet thought the threat intelligence from intercepts and human agents was as frightening as he had ever witnessed. Cofer Black said later that he became convinced in the spring that al Qaeda was about to strike hard. He could not tell where, but it seemed to him that the Arabian peninsula and Israel were the most likely targets. Intercepts of suspected al Qaeda members kept referring to multiple and spectacular attacks, some of which seemed to be in the late planning stages. He told Rice in late May that the threat was a "7" on a scale of ten, close to but not as intense as the "8" he felt during the Millennium. "What worries me," Black's deputy told a closed session of the House Intelligence Committee on June 4, "is that we're on the verge of more attacks that are larger and more deadly." These might include weapons of mass destruction. There were lots of ominous sports metaphors in the fragmentary intercept reports. The score was going to be 200 to nothing. The Olympics were coming.[18]

Between May and July the National Security Agency reported at least 33 different intercepts indicating a possible imminent al Qaeda attack. Classified threat warnings about terrorist strikes ricocheted through the government's secure message systems nearly every day. The FBI issued 216 secret, internal threat warnings between January 1 and September 10, 2001, of which 6 mentioned possible attacks against airports or airlines. The State Department issued 9 separate warnings during the same period to embassies and citizens abroad, including 5 that highlighted a general threat to Americans all over the world. The Federal Aviation Administration issued 15 notices of possible terrorist threats against American airlines.[19]

Bin Laden taunted them openly. He met near the Pakistan border in early June with Bakr Atiani, a reporter for a Saudi-owned satellite television network. "They said there would be attacks against American and Israeli facilities within the next several weeks," Atiani recalled of his interview with bin Laden and his Arab aides. "It was absolutely clear that they had brought me there to hear this message." He could sense that bin Laden was confident.

"He smiled. . . . It felt like bin Laden had his own Arab kingdom in southern Afghanistan." Following a mechanical ritual, State Department diplomats met Taliban representatives in Pakistan on June 26 and warned they would be held directly responsible if bin Laden attacked.[20]

A one-hundred-minute bin Laden recruitment video surfaced simultaneously in Kuwait City. "Blood, blood, and destruction, destruction," bin Laden crowed as the tape concluded. "We give you the good news that the forces of Islam are coming."[21]

"I want a way to bring this guy down," Bush told his advisers in the White House that month as he reviewed the threat reports. But when Rice met with Pakistan's foreign minister in late June, she only repeated the stale warning that Pakistan would ultimately be judged by the behavior of its allies. Clarke wrote a week later to urge that Bush officials think now about how much pressure they would put on Pakistan after the next al Qaeda attack, and then implement that policy immediately. His recommendation was ignored. Bush wrote Musharraf about the danger of terrorism a few weeks later, but his letter did not depart from past entreaties.[22]

The presidential policy document that would recast government-wide strategy against al Qaeda moved slowly through White House channels. When the final integrated plan—including tentative provisions for covert aid to Massoud—was ready for the full Cabinet to consider, it took almost two months to find a meeting date that was convenient for everyone who wanted to attend.

The CIA's Counterterrorist Center reported ominously that key operatives in bin Laden's network had begun to disappear. Others seemed to be preparing for martyrdom. "Sunni extremists associated with Al Qaeda are most likely to attempt spectacular attacks resulting in numerous casualties," warned a classified threat advisory issued in June by the Intelligence Community Counterterrorism Board. It mentioned Italy, Israel, and the Arabian peninsula as the most likely targets. A leader of the FBI's counterterrorism team declared he was "98 percent certain" that bin Laden would strike overseas. A later review found this was the "clear majority view" among intelligence analysts. Another advisory concluded that "al Qaeda is prepared to mount one or more terrorist attacks at any time." There were some reports that the attack was aimed at U.S. soil. An intelligence alert in early June said that Khalid Sheikh Mohammed was recruiting volunteers to undertake missions in the United States, where they would "establish contact with colleagues already living there." In July the CIA's Counterterrorist Center reported that it had interviewed a source who had recently returned from Afghanistan. The source had reported, "Everyone is talking about an impending attack."[23]

The CIA prepared a briefing paper on July 10 for senior Bush administration officials: "Based on a review of all-source reporting over the last five months, we believe that [bin Laden] will launch a significant terrorist attack against U.S. and/or Israeli interests in the coming weeks. The attack will be spectacular and designed to inflict mass casualties against U.S. facilities or interests. Attack preparations have been made. Attack will occur with little or no warning."[24]

Tenet brought huge wall charts to the White House in mid-July to show Condi Rice the web of threats and the al Qaeda members they were tracking from Pakistan to the Middle East. Tenet called spy chiefs in about twenty friendly countries to plead for help. Vice President Cheney called Saudi Crown Prince Abdullah. Tenet said later that "the system was blinking red" and that Bush's cabinet understood the urgency.[25] Yet the threat reports remained, as they often had been since 1998, vague and elusive. They were also part of a much wider tapestry of intelligence reporting that was routinely circulated to Cabinet-level officials. In June, only 18 out of 298 classified Senior Executive Intelligence Briefs sent to Bush administration officials referred to bin Laden or al Qaeda.[26]

Urged on by Tenet and Black, CIA stations worldwide collaborated that spring and summer with local police and intelligence services to arrest al Qaeda associates and interrogate them. The objective was "to drive up bin Laden's security concerns and lead his organization to delay or cancel its attacks," as Tenet recalled it. They recovered rockets and explosives in Jordan, broke up a group planning to hit American buildings in Yemen, learned of plans for various other small-scale attacks, and acquired many new names of suspects for American border watch lists. They chased reports of a bin Laden team supposedly trying to smuggle explosives into the United States from Canada. They picked up a report about a plot to crash a plane into the U.S. embassy in Nairobi or destroy it with car bombs. But they could not get a convincing handle on the big, spectacular attacks that the NSA's telephone intercept fragments showed were on the way. They considered whether al Qaeda was feeding them disinformation through these intercepts, but they concluded that the plots were authentic. They just could not get a line on the perpetrators.[27]

Officers in the CIA's Counterterrorist Center felt a rising sense of fatalism that summer. They worked long hours, exchanging Arabic translations across their office partitions, frequently "with a panic-stricken look" in their eyes, as one of the center's officers recalled. For every bin Laden operative they caught, another fifty were getting through their net, they feared. "We're going to miss stuff," they told one another, as this officer remembered it. "We *are* missing stuff. We can't keep up." CIA leaders such as deputy director John McLaughlin said later that some Bush Administration officials, who had not experienced prior surges of threat and panic, voiced frustrating skepticism about the validity of the threat intelligence, wondering aloud if it were disinformation. Hadley told Tenet in July that Paul Wolfowitz had doubts about the threat reports. One veteran CIA officer at the Counterterrorist Center said later that he so feared a disaster he considered resigning and going public.[28]

Some recipients of their classified reports felt equally frustrated. The CIA's unremitting flow of threat information remained in many cases nonspecific, speculative, or based on sources known to be unreliable. The Counterterrorist Center circulated a classified threat report that summer titled "Threat of Impending Al Qaeda Attack to Continue Indefinitely." Tenet agreed that the CIA's reporting was "maddeningly short on actionable details," as he put it later. Worst of all, the most ominous reporting that summer, which hinted at a large attack, "was also most vague."[29]

BIN LADEN DETERMINED TO STRIKE IN U.S. was the headline on the President's Daily Brief presented to Bush at his Crawford, Texas, ranch on August 6. The report addressed questions Bush had asked about domestic threats and included the possibility that bin Laden operatives would seek to hijack airplanes. The hijacking threat, mentioned twice, was one of several possibilities outlined. There was no specific information about when or where such an attack might occur. Tenet said the intelligence indicated that al Qaeda might have delayed a major attack.[30]

"We are going to be struck soon," Cofer Black told the Pentagon's classified annual conference on counterterrorism nine days later. "Many Americans are going to die, and it could be in the U.S."[31]

In mid-July Tenet ordered the Counterterrorist Center to search all its files for any lead or name that might take them toward bin Laden's biggest and most active plots. He wanted to find "linkages among the reports as well as links to past terrorist threats and tactics," as he recalled it.[32] CIA and FBI officers dug back through the surveillance images and cables generated in Kuala Lumpur, Malaysia, in January 2000. For the first time he saw that Khalid al-Mihdhar and Nawaf al-Hazmi, who had been photographed and tracked during that operation, had unrestricted visa access to the United States, had probably entered the country, and might still be resident. Yet neither man had ever been placed on a watch list.

The CIA apparently did not formally notify the FBI about this alarming discovery. Only the New York field office received a routine request to search for Mihdhar. Investigators later could find no evidence that anyone briefed Clarke, Bush's cabinet, or the president about the missing suspects.[33]

BY NOW THE TWO MEN were living in cheap motels in Laurel and College Park, Maryland, a dozen miles or so from the White House.

All nineteen of the attackers had safely entered the United States by mid-July. Fifteen were Saudi Arabians, including al-Mihdhar and al-Hazma. Two others were from the United Arab Emirates. Mohammed Atta was the only Egyptian, Ziad Jarrah the only Lebanese. The leaders among the group, those with pilot training, included the members of the Hamburg cell who had traveled from Germany to Kandahar late in 1999 and then applied successfully to American flight schools. Early in 2001 the conspirators trained as pilots were joined in the United States by their muscle, Saudi recruits with no flight training, who arrived in Florida and New Jersey between April 23, 2001, and June 29, 2001, then settled into short-term apartments and motels to await the go signal. The late-arriving Saudis mainly came from the restive southwest of the kingdom. A few of them had been to college, while others had no higher education. Some had histories of depression or alcoholism. Some had never displayed much religious zealotry before a sudden exposure to radical ideas changed their outlooks dramatically. Nearly all of the supporting hijackers visited Afghanistan for the first time in 1999 or 2000, as Mohammed Atef and Khalid Sheikh Mohammed began to organize the final version of their suicide airliner hijacking plan. Most of the Saudi muscle, George Tenet said later, "probably were told little more than that they were headed for a suicide mission in the United States."[34]

They lived openly and attracted little attention. They did not hold jobs. They moved frequently. Two and possibly as many as six of them passed American border posts carrying passports that showed signs of fraud or suspicious background, yet in only one case did a Customs and Immigration officer foil entry, unaware of the Saudi's intentions as he ordered his deportation. Among the plotters there were tensions, accusations, and apparent changes of heart as the launch date approached. Jarrah and Atta clashed as the former operated on his own and spent time with his girlfriend; a one-way ticket Jarrah bought to see her in Germany during the summer of 2001 suggests that he may have decided to drop out of the plot, but was talked back in. The two Saudi volunteers surveilled by the CIA in Malaysia had lived openly in southern California since early 2000. One of them, Nawaf al-Hazmi, was listed in the phone book, opened a local bank account, and even reported an attempted street robbery to police in suburban Fairfax, Virginia, on May 1, 2001, although he later decided not to press charges. The two Saudi veterans of the plot shirked their English and piloting studies and aggravated their colleagues. In Pakistan Khalid Sheikh Mohammed fretted like a harried mid-level corporate manager, pressured repeatedly by bin Laden to speed up the date of the attack, but unable to keep his front-line suicide pilots fully on track. He protected Atta from bin Laden's hectoring about timing and targets and tried to give the Egyptian the space and resources he needed to bring the project to completion. Atta selected early September after determining Congress would be in session. Although bin Laden continued to lobby for the White House as a target, Atta still favored the Capitol, believing it would be easier to strike; the evidence suggests the decision may have remained unresolved until the very end.[35]

The hijackers' money came from al Qaeda contacts living in the United Arab Emirates. One of these, Ali Abdul Aziz Ali, Mohammed's nephew, used Western Union and less formal currency exchange offices in Dubai and other Persian Gulf cities to send $119,500 to Mohammed Atta and others in his group while they attended school in Florida and elsewhere. A second money source, Mustafa Alhawsawi, a brother of one hijacker, sent them $18,000 via Western Union. He also received by return transfer all the group's leftover funds—about $42,000—when the hijackers wound up their affairs in late August 2001 and prepared to die.

Alhawsawi arranged to place the surplus funds on his Standard Chartered Bank Visa Card. Then he boarded a flight from the United Arab Emirates to Karachi, Pakistan, and disappeared.[36]

MASSOUD DISPATCHED his foreign policy adviser, Abdullah, to Washington in August. Their Northern Alliance lobbyist, Otilie English, scratched together a few appointments on Capitol Hill. It was difficult to get anyone's attention. They had to compete with Pakistan's well-heeled, high-paid professional lobbyists and advocates, such as the former congressman Charlie Wilson, who had raised so much money for Pakistan's government in Congress during the anti-Soviet jihad. Abdullah and English tried to link their lobbying effort with Hamid Karzai and his brother, Qayum, to show that Massoud was fighting the Taliban with multiethnic allies. But the members they met with could barely manage politeness. Guns or financial aid were out of the question. Some barely knew who Osama bin Laden was. With the Democrats they tried to press the issue of women's rights in Afghanistan, but even that seemed to be a dying cause now that the Clintons were gone. Both Massoud's group and the Karzais were "so disappointed, so demoralized" after a week of meetings on the Hill and at the State Department, Karzai's lobbyist recalled.[37]

"You're basically asking for the overthrow of the Taliban," an incredulous midlevel State Department officer told Qayum Karzai in one meeting that August. "I'm not sure if our government is prepared to do that."[38]

Abdullah bristled as he listened yet again to arguments about "moderate and nonmoderate Taliban. . . . It was ridiculous." But he also picked up encouraging hints from the White House and senior officials at State, including Richard Haas, director of policy planning. They invited Abdullah back in September. He sensed there might be a change of approach coming, but he could not be sure.[39]

While Abdullah was in Washington, an email arrived from Hamid Karzai in Pakistan. Karzai had been served with an expulsion order by Pakistani intelligence, and he reported that he could no longer delay its execution. He had to be out of the country by the end of September 2001 or he risked arrest.

The ISI had been monitoring Massoud's anti-Taliban campaign. Its Afghan bureau was determined to oppose any effort to foment rebellion against Mullah Omar from Pakistani soil.

Hamid Karzai was agitated. He wanted to slip inside Afghanistan to join Dostum, Ismail Khan, and the others fighting in alliance with Massoud. But he wasn't sure where to go, and he could not win military support from the Americans. He wondered what Massoud would advise.

Abdullah and Qayum Karzai huddled in a Starbucks off Dupont Circle to talk about Hamid's options. They were afraid that ISI was monitoring his communications and might already know of his plan to enter Afghanistan. That made his situation all the more dangerous. It had been just two years since the assassination of Hamid's father on a Quetta street.[40]

"Look, I no longer have a place to stay in Pakistan," Hamid Karzai told Massoud when he raised him a few days later on a satellite phone.[41] Should he try to cross secretly from Pakistan to Kandahar, despite the risks of encountering Taliban forces or bin Laden's Arab radicals? Or should he fly first to

Dushanbe, enter Afghanistan from the north, and then hope that Massoud's men could help him reach a mountainous Afghan province from where Karzai could challenge the Taliban?

Massoud felt strongly that Karzai should head around to the north. He would be most welcome in Northern Alliance country. He should not try to drive directly for Kandahar, as Karzai recalled Massoud's advice. The ground for nationwide war against the Taliban and al Qaeda, Massoud said, had not yet been prepared.[42]

32

"What an Unlucky Country"

E ARLY IN SEPTEMBER, Massoud's intelligence service transmitted a routine report to the CIA's Counterterrorist Center about two Arab television journalists who had crossed Northern Alliance lines from Kabul. The intelligence sharing liaison between Massoud and the CIA concentrated mainly on Arabs and other foreigners in Afghanistan. If Massoud's forces captured prisoners or if they learned about movements by Arab-led military units, they typically forwarded reports across the dedicated lines that linked the Panjshir Valley directly to Langley. In this case officers in the bin Laden unit at the Counterterrorist Center took note of the movement of the two Arab journalists. It did not seem of exceptional interest.[1]

The pair carried a television camera and other equipment, possessed Belgian passports, and claimed to be originally from Morocco. One was squat, muscular, and caramel-skinned. He cut his hair very short, shaved his face clean, and wore European clothes and glasses. His companion was tall and darker. One spoke a little English and French, the other only Arabic. Their papers showed they had entered Kabul from Pakistan after arriving from abroad.[2]

The conspiracy they represented took shape the previous May. On a Kabul computer routinely used by Ayman al-Zawahiri, the Egyptian doctor who was bin Laden's closest partner, an al Qaeda planner wrote a letter of introduction in patchy French. On behalf of the Islamic Observation Center in London, the letter explained, "one of our best journalists" planned to produce a television report on Afghanistan. He sought an interview with Ahmed Shah Massoud. A list of proposed questions written on the computer in French included one infused with dark irony: "How will you deal with the Osama bin Laden issue when you are in power, and what do you see as the solution to this issue?"[3]

Inserting disguised al Qaeda agents from Taliban-ruled Kabul into Massoud's headquarters near the Tajikistan border was a daunting operation. Massoud's troops were on continuous hostile alert against Arab volunteers. Al Qaeda had tried to smuggle agents carrying explosives into the Panjshir the year before, but the perpetrators had been arrested. This time bin Laden's planners prepared the deceptive legends of their assassins carefully and exploited the long history of Arab jihadists in Afghanistan to complete the infiltration.

Abdurrab Rasul Sayyaf, the white-bearded, Arabic-speaking Afghan Islamist first selected and promoted by Saudi intelligence in 1980, had aligned himself with Massoud in recent years. His military power had been much reduced since the late 1980s and early 1990s when he had been the favored recipient of hundreds of millions of dollars in aid and weaponry from Prince Turki al-Faisal's service and independent Persian Gulf proselytizers.

Aged and politically irrelevant, Sayyaf maintained a modest headquarters compound outside of the capital; he was no longer active in the war. Because of his long history as the host of Arab volunteers in Afghanistan and his wide contacts among Arab Islamist theologians, he provided a link between Massoud and Arab radicals. Massoud was chronically uncomfortable about his reputation in the wider world of political Islam. Just as he sought American and European aid to isolate the Taliban, he reached out to Arab and Islamic audiences to counter bin Laden's incendiary propaganda.[4]

Al Qaeda's planners tapped their connections to Sayyaf and played on Massoud's desire to be understood in the Arab world. An Egyptian who had fought with Sayyaf during the anti-Soviet years called him by satellite telephone to recommend the visiting Arab journalists. Sayyaf relayed an endorsement to Massoud. Through this and other channels the journalists emphasized that they intended to portray the Northern Alliance in a positive light, to help rehabilitate and promote Massoud's reputation before Arab audiences.

Massoud authorized a helicopter to pick up the pair just north of Kabul

and fly them to Khoja Bahuddin, a compound just inside the Tajikistan border where Massoud had established a headquarters after the loss of Taloqan.
The two Arabs checked into a guest house run by Massoud's foreign ministry
where a dozen other Afghan journalists and visitors were staying.

But Massoud was in no hurry to see them. Despite their letters and en-
dorsements, their interview request languished. Days passed, and still Massoud was too busy, the visitors were told. They shot video around Khoja
Bahuddin, but their interest slackened. They lobbied for their interview, bran-
dished their credentials again, and eventually declared to their hosts that if a
meeting with Massoud did not come through soon, they would have to leave.[5]

AFGHANISTAN AFTER 1979 was a laboratory for political and military visions conceived abroad and imposed by force. The language and ideas that
described Afghan parties, armies, and militias originated with theoreticians in
universities and seminaries in Europe, the United States, Cairo, and Deoband.
Afghans fought as "communists" or as "freedom fighters." They joined jihadist armies battling on behalf of an imagined global Islamic *umma*. A
young, weak nation, Afghanistan produced few convincing nationalists who
could offer an alternative, who could define Afghanistan from within. Ahmed
Shah Massoud was an exception.

Yet Massoud did not create the Afghanistan he championed. Partly, he
failed as a politician during the early 1990s. Partly, he was limited by his regional roots, especially as the Afghan war's fragmenting violence promoted
ethnic solidarity. Most of all, Massoud was contained by the much greater resources possessed by his adversaries in Pakistan and Saudi Arabia.

At the end of his life, as he fought the Taliban and al Qaeda, he saw the potential to recover his nationalist vision of Afghanistan through an alliance
with the United States. He saw this partnership primarily as a brilliant tactician
would—grounded not in ideology but in urgent and mutual interest, the need
to contain and defeat Osama bin Laden and his jihadist volunteers.

Massoud did fight also for political ideas. He was not a "democrat" in an
American or European sense, although conceivably he could have become
one in a peaceful postwar era. He was indisputably tolerant and forgiving in
the midst of terrible violence, patient, and prepared to work in coalitions.

Massoud frustrated bin Laden and the Taliban because of his extraordinary tactical skills, but also because he competed credibly for control of
Afghanistan's political identity. It was Massoud's unyielding independence
that earlier had enticed and stymied both the Soviet Fortieth Army and the

CIA. In the early years of the jihad the agency's station chiefs read British imperial history and managed Afghanistan more or less as Kipling recommended. They raised Pashtun tribes against their Russian adversaries and kept their distance behind the Khyber Pass. Later, between 1988 and 1992, presented with a chance to do the hard neo-imperial work of constructing a postwar, national, sustainable Afghan politics, Langley's leaders argued against any direct American involvement. Neither the CIA's managers nor any of the American presidents they served, Republican or Democrat, could locate a vision of Afghanistan to justify such an expensive and uncertain project. The Afghan government that the United States eventually chose to support beginning in the late autumn of 2001—a federation of Massoud's organization, exiled intellectuals, and royalist Pashtuns—was available for sponsorship a decade before, but the United States could not see a reason then to challenge the alternative, radical Islamist vision promoted by Pakistani and Saudi intelligence. Massoud's independent character and conduct—and the hostility toward him continually fed into the American bureaucracy by Pakistan—denied him a lasting alliance with the United States. And it denied America the benefits of his leadership during the several years before 2001. Instead—at first out of indifference, then with misgivings, and finally in a state of frustrated inertia—the United States endorsed year after year the Afghan programs of its two sullen, complex, and sometimes vital allies, Pakistan and Saudi Arabia.

And at the end of this twisted road lay September 2001 when the American public and the subsistence traders of the Panjshir Valley discovered in twin cataclysms that they were bound together, if not by the political ideas they shared, then at least by the enemies who had chosen them.

THE OPPORTUNITIES missed by the United States on the way to September 2001 extended well beyond the failure to exploit fully an alliance with Massoud. Indifference, lassitude, blindness, paralysis, and commercial greed too often shaped American foreign policy in Afghanistan and South Asia during the 1990s. Besides Massoud, the most natural American ally against al Qaeda in the region was India, whose democracy and civilian population also was threatened by radical Islamist violence. Yet while the American government sought gradually to deepen its ties to New Delhi, it lacked the creativity, local knowledge, patience, and persistence to cope successfully with India's prickly nationalism and complex democratic politics—a failure especially ironic given the ornery character of American nationalism and the great complexities of Washington's own democracy. As a result, America failed during the late 1990s to forge an effective antiterrorism partnership with India, whose regional interests, security resources, and vast Muslim population offered great potential for covert penetrations of Afghanistan.

Nor did the United States have a strategy for engagement, democratization, secular education, and economic development among the peaceful but demoralized majority populations of the Islamic world. Instead, Washington typically coddled undemocratic and corrupt Muslim governments, even as these countries' frustrated middle classes looked increasingly to conservative interpretations of Islam for social values and political ideas. In this way America unnecessarily made easier, to at least a small extent, the work of al Qaeda recruiters.

Largely out of indifference and bureaucratic momentum, the United States constructed its most active regional counterterrorism partnerships with Pakistan and Saudi Arabia, despite evidence that both governments had been penetrated by al Qaeda. Dependent upon Saudi oil and unwilling to reexamine old assumptions about the kingdom's establishment, Washington bounced complacently along in its alliance with Riyadh. Nor was the United States willing to confront the royal families of neighboring energy-rich kingdoms such as Qatar and the United Arab Emirates, even when sections of those governments also appeased and nurtured al Qaeda. In Pakistan, the hardest of hard cases, the Clinton administration allowed its laudable pursuit of nuclear stability and regional peace to cloud its eyesight about the systematic support for jihadist violence within Pakistan's army and intelligence service. Unwilling to accept the uncertainties and high political costs of a military confrontation with the Taliban, American diplomats also suspended disbelief and lazily embraced Saudi and Pakistani arguments that the Taliban would mature and moderate. Even by late 2000, when many members of Clinton's national security cabinet and his Joint Chiefs of Staff at last accepted that hopes for Taliban cooperation against bin Laden were absurd, the Clinton cabinet adamantly opposed military action in Afghanistan. This caution prevailed despite week after week of secret intelligence cables depicting active, advanced, but unspecified al Qaeda plans to launch mass attacks against American civilians.

President Clinton, weakened by impeachment proceedings and boxed in by a hostile Republican majority in Congress, proved unwilling or unable to force the astonishingly passive Pentagon to pursue military options. As an alternative he put the CIA's covert action arm in the lead against al Qaeda. Historically, the CIA has carried out its most successful covert actions when its main patron under American law, the president of the United States, has been eager to push the agency forward and has proven willing to stomach the risks and failures that accompany CIA operations. This was not Clinton. The president authorized the CIA to pursue al Qaeda and he supported the agency to some extent. Yet he did not fully believe that the CIA was up to the job, and he at times withheld from Langley the legal authorities, resources, and active leadership that a president more confident about the agency's abilities might have provided.

Was the president's evident skepticism about the CIA justified? Since the advent of spectacular modern terrorism in the late 1960s, the record of even the most accomplished intelligence agencies in preventing terrorist attacks has been mixed at best. The CIA in the 1990s was generally seen by intelligence specialists as strong on technology and mediocre at human intelligence operations against hard targets. Agent penetrations and covert action often work best where an intelligence service shares language, culture, and geographical space with its adversary—as with British operations in Northern Ireland, for example. Even then, it usually proves impossible to stop all terrorist attacks, and an intelligence service's efforts to maneuver a terrorist group into surrender or peaceful politics often requires decades of persistent, secret effort. The difficulty is compounded when the enemy are religiously motivated fanatics who see their violence as above politics and divinely sanctioned. The Israeli spy and security services, widely regarded as leaders in human intelligence, agent penetrations, and covert action, have been unable to thwart suicide bombings by Islamist radicals. In the case of the CIA's attempts to disrupt al Qaeda's leadership in Afghanistan, the severe inherent difficulties were extended by the vast cultural gaps and forbidding geographical distances that separated CIA operatives from their targets.

Still, even within these limits, the agency did not do all it might have done. George Tenet's discretionary, internal allocation of money and people did not fully reflect his rhetoric about an all-out war, as he later acknowledged. The Counterterrorist Center's failure early in 2000 to watch-list two known al Qaeda adherents with American visas in their passports appears, in hindsight, as the agency's single most important unforced error. If it had not occurred, the specific attacks that were to unfold with such unique destructive power in New York and Washington might well have been prevented. Some of the CIA's disruption operations in Afghanistan after 1998 were creative and resourceful, while others, such as the Pakistani commando plan in 1999, were naïve and ill-judged. In the end, however, it is difficult to evaluate fully the agency's performance in covert operations against bin Laden after 1998 because some significant ideas generated by CIA officers—notably their plan to partner more actively inside Afghanistan with Massoud—were never authorized by the White House.

EARLY IN SEPTEMBER CLARKE unloaded his frustrations in a memo to Rice. The previous spring she had declared the president was tired of "swatting flies" in his contest with bin Laden. Clarke felt that was all they were doing six months later. "Decision makers should imagine themselves on a future day when CSG has not succeeded in stopping al Qaeda attacks and hundreds of Americans lay dead in several countries, including the U.S.," Clarke wrote. "What would those decision makers wish that they had done earlier?" The CIA was "masterful at passive aggressive behavior" and would resist funding new policy initiatives. "You are left with a modest effort to swat flies," Clarke declared. "You are left waiting for the big attack, with lots of casualties, after which some major U.S. retaliation will be in order."[6]

The Bush Cabinet met at the White House on September 4. Before them was a draft copy of a National Security Presidential Directive, a classified memo outlining a new U.S. policy toward al Qaeda and Afghanistan. The stated goal of the draft document was to eliminate bin Laden and his organization. Its provisions included a plan for a large but undetermined amount of covert action funds to aid Massoud in his war against the Taliban. The CIA would supply Massoud with trucks, uniforms, ammunition, mortars, helicopters, and other equipment to be determined by the agency and the White House—the same rough shopping list drawn up the previous autumn. There was to be money as well for other anti-Taliban forces, although the full scope of covert action would unfold gradually, linked to renewed diplomatic efforts. Still, under the plan Massoud's coalition of commanders and scattered insurgents in Afghanistan would soon be better equipped than at any time since the early 1990s.[7] The Cabinet approved this part of the proposal, although there remained uncertainty about where the money would come from and how much would ultimately be available.

A long, inconclusive discussion followed about whether to deploy an armed Predator to Afghanistan. The CIA remained divided internally. Cofer Black and the bin Laden unit at the Counterterrorist Center wanted to go forward. James Pavitt at the Directorate of Operations worried about unintended consequences if the CIA suddenly moved back into the business of running lethal operations against targeted individuals—assassination, in the common usage. Such targeted killings carried out directly by the CIA could open agents in the field to retaliatory kidnappings or killings. The missions might also expose the agency to political and media criticism.

The CIA had conducted classified war games at Langley to discover how its chain of command, made up of spies with limited or no military experience, might responsibly oversee a flying robot that could shoot missiles at suspected terrorists. By early September of 2001 Tenet had reviewed a "concept of operations" submitted by his Counterterrorist Center that outlined how a CIA-managed armed Predator might be fielded and how a decision to fire would be made. At the September 4 Cabinet meeting, Tenet said he wanted the Bush policy makers to understand the proposal: The CIA would be operating a lethal fixed-wing aircraft of the sort normally controlled by the Air Force and its Pentagon chain of command. If Bush and his Cabinet wanted to entrust that operational role to the CIA, Tenet said, they should do so with their eyes wide open, fully aware of the potential fallout if there were a controversial or mistaken strike. Some at the meeting interpreted Tenet's comments as reluctance to take on the mission. There were differing recollections about how forceful Tenet was in outlining the potential risks. For his part, Tenet believed he was only trying to clarify and facilitate a presidential decision that would break recent precedent by shifting control of a lethal aircraft from the uniformed military to the CIA. The armed Predator was by now a CIA project, virtually an agency invention. The Air Force was not interested in commanding such an awkward, unproven weapon. Air Force doctrine and experience argued for the use of fully tested bombers and cruise missiles even when the targets were lone terrorists. The Air Force was not ready to begin fielding or commanding armed robots.[8]

Rice told the group that an armed Predator was needed, but that it obviously was not ready to operate. The principals agreed that the CIA should pursue reconnaissance Predator flights in Afghanistan while work continued—the same recommendation Clarke had made unsuccessfully the previous winter.

On Massoud, however, the CIA could at least start the paperwork. CIA lawyers, working with officers in the Near East Division and Counterterrorist Center, began to draft a formal, legal presidential finding for Bush's signature authorizing a new covert action program in Afghanistan, the first in a decade that sought to influence the course of the Afghan war.[9]

MASSOUD READ PERSIAN POETRY in his bungalow in the early hours of September 9. The next morning he prepared to fly by helicopter toward Kabul to inspect his forward lines and assess Taliban positions. A colleague told him that he ought to meet the two Arab journalists before he left; they had been waiting for many days. He said he would talk to them in the cement office used by his intelligence aide, Engineer Arif. Around noon he settled in the bungalow on a cushion designed to ease his back pain. Massoud Khalili, his friend and ambassador to India, sat next to him. As the more compact Arab journalist moved a table and set up his tripod at Massoud's chest level, Khalili joked, "Is he a wrestler or a photographer?"[10]

Massoud took a telephone call. Eight Arabs had been arrested by his troops near the front lines. He asked Engineer Arif to see if he could find out more about them, and Arif left the room.

The visiting reporter read out a list of questions while his colleague prepared to film. About half his questions concerned Osama bin Laden. Massoud listened, then said he was ready.

The explosion ripped the cameraman's body apart. It smashed the room's windows, seared the walls in flame, and tore Massoud's chest with shrapnel. He collapsed, unconscious.

His guards and aides rushed into the building, carried his limp body outside, lifted him into a jeep, and drove to the helicopter pad. They were close to the Tajikistan border. There was a hospital ten minutes' flight away.

Several of Massoud's aides and the lanky Arab reporter sitting to the side of the blast recovered from the noise, felt burning sensations, and realized they were not badly hurt. The Arab tried to run but was captured by Massoud's security guards. They locked the assassin in a nearby room, but he wiggled through a window. He was shot to death as he tried to escape.

On the helicopter Massoud's longtime bodyguard, Omar, held the commander's head and watched him stop breathing. Omar thought to himself, he said later, "He's dying and I'm dying."[11]

AMRULLAH SALEH CALLED the CIA's Counterterrorist Center from Tajikistan. He spoke to Rich, the bin Laden unit chief. Saleh was in tears, sobbing and heaving between sentences as he explained what had happened.

"Where's Massoud?" the CIA officer asked.

"He's in the refrigerator," said Saleh, searching for the English word for morgue.[12]

Massoud was dead, but his inner circle had barely absorbed the news. They were all in shock. They were also trying to strategize in a hurry. As soon as the Taliban learned that Massoud was gone, they would swarm up the Panjshir Valley in attack, Massoud's surviving aides felt certain. Based on the Taliban's past behavior in newly conquered lands, the valley faced devastation and atrocities. Massoud's aides had to get themselves organized. They had to choose a new leader and reinforce their defenses. They needed time.

They had already put out a false story claiming that Massoud had only been wounded. Meanwhile, Saleh told the Counterterrorist Center, the suddenly leaderless Northern Alliance needed the CIA's help as it prepared to confront al Qaeda and the Taliban.[13]

This looked to many of the CIA's officers like the end of the Northern Alliance. Massoud's death immediately called into question a central plank of the national security strategy designed to confront al Qaeda in Afghanistan, endorsed by Bush's Cabinet just five days earlier. There was no one in the wings who approached Massoud's stature. The CIA's quick assessment was that Massoud's coalition might not be viable either militarily or politically without him.[14]

Officers in the Counterterrorist Center alerted the White House to the news that Massoud was dead. Within hours the story had leaked to CNN. From Tajikistan, Saleh called Langley again, angry. The CIA was the only call he had made confirming Massoud's death. How had the agency let it leak so fast?

On the morning of September 10 the CIA's daily classified briefings to President Bush, his Cabinet, and other policy makers reported on Massoud's death and analyzed the consequences for America's covert war against al Qaeda. At the White House Stephen Hadley chaired a meeting of the Deputies Committee called to finalize new policies toward Afghanistan and Pakistan, decisions that would round out the National Security Presidential Directive approved by cabinet members six days earlier. Explaining the Bush Administration's deliberate pace in fashioning new policies toward al Qaeda, Paul Wolfowitz emphasized the need to think carefully about Afghanistan and Pakistan. Yet after five months of discussion and delay they had arrived at relatively cautious, gradual plans that departed from Clinton policies in their eventual goals, but not in many of their immediate steps. On the Taliban, the committee agreed to pursue initially a track of diplomatic persuasion: They would send an envoy to Afghanistan to urge Mullah Omar to expel bin Laden or face dire consequences, as Clinton's diplomats had done unsuccessfully for several years. In the meantime the Bush Administration would secretly provide enough covert aid to keep the Northern Alliance on life support, if possible, and would prepare for additional secret aid to anti-Taliban Pashtuns. If diplomacy failed, anti-Taliban forces would be encouraged to attack al Qaeda units inside Afghanistan. If that limited covert war failed, the Bush Administration would then move directly to overthrow the Taliban itself, providing enough aid to Afghan opposition forces to achieve victory. The deputies estimated on September 10 that the full project, if it all proved necessary, would likely take about three years. The group also agreed to try to improve relations with Pakistan; its departures from Clinton's approach on that score were subtle at best.

Officers in the CIA's Counterterrorist Center, still hopeful that they could maintain a foothold in northern Afghanistan to attack bin Laden, called frantically around Washington to find a way to aid the rump Northern Alliance before it was eliminated.

Massoud's advisers and lobbyists in Washington, aware of the truth, ducked media phone calls as best they could, trying to keep alive the speculation, still prominently featured in news accounts, that Massoud might still be alive. But privately, as September 10 wore on, phone call by phone call, many of the Afghans closest to the commander, in Dushanbe and Tehran and Europe and the United States, began to learn that he was gone.[15]

Hamid Karzai was in Pakistan when his brother reached him. With less than three weeks to go before Pakistani intelligence planned to expel him, Karzai was torn. He did not think southern Afghanistan was ripe for rebellion, yet he did not want to end up as just another Afghan exile in Europe. Karzai had talked to Massoud a few days earlier. He was considering a flight to Dushanbe, from where he might enter Afghanistan across Massoud's territory. From there Karzai could try to begin his quixotic rebellion among anti-Taliban Pashtuns.

Karzai's brother said it was confirmed: Ahmed Shah Massoud was dead.

Hamid Karzai reacted in a single, brief sentence, as his brother recalled it: "What an unlucky country."[16]

Afterword

In the year since I completed research for the first edition of *Ghost Wars,* the history it describes has been enlarged by the disclosure of previously classified U.S. government documents, mainly from the Clinton Administration's second term and the first nine months of the George W. Bush Administration. By far the greatest number of these memos, intelligence reports, emails and handwritten notes were obtained and published by the subpoena-brandishing investigative staff of the National Commission on Terrorist Attacks Upon the United States, more commonly known as the 9/11 Commission, a ten-member panel of former American politicians and lawyers co-chaired by Thomas H. Kean and Lee H. Hamilton. The commission was appointed to investigate "facts and circumstances relating to the terrorist attacks" of September 11 and to make recommendations about preventing such attacks in the future. It delivered a majestic 567-page final report in July 2004. Together with previously published interim statements by its investigative staff and voluminous testimony from Clinton, Bush, their cabinet officers, and CIA officials, the commission's final report placed before the public an unprecedented cache of secret documents and communications from inside the American government and intelligence community. These included the first published interrogation statements from captured al Qaeda leaders such as the architect of the September 11 operation, Khalid Sheikh Mohammed. In addition to the commission's work the non-governmental National Security Archive published during 2004 some new declassified American diplomatic cables about Afghanistan, Pakistan, and bin Laden.

My goal in crafting this edition of *Ghost Wars* has been to incorporate these new materials into the narrative where they enhance or correct the history I constructed in the first edition. The great majority of these additions and fixes occur in Part Three, covering the years from 1998 to 2001. Most of the new material in this edition adds direct quotations from documents, emails, and reports not previously available. In other cases I have been able to quote the recollections of cabinet and intelligence officers who had declined to speak for the record during my earlier research, but who testified under oath before the commission. I have also gone back to my own interview subjects and have convinced a few of them who declined to be named in the first edition to allow me to place some of their originally anonymous quotations "on the record" here. In doing so I have tried to make the book's sourcing and multiple points of view as transparent and complete as possible.

Newly disclosed material has also allowed me to make the narrative's chronology more precise. While conducting the original research, I attempted to persuade people to describe highly classified intelligence operations, especially in the period after 1998. Generally, I found that my sources were very confident about *what* had happened but less confident about *when* it had happened. Even for the best-placed sources, checking exact dates by going back to file rooms full of secret documents was often difficult, so I usually had to rely on a painfully laborious and imprecise process of cross-checking memories about dates and sequences among multiple sources. I did have the benefit of the Joint Inquiry Committee's published chronology, but the committee's investigators were unable to obtain and declassify material about some sensitive CIA operations in Afghanistan. Astute readers will have recognized my authorial wobbles in the first edition, where I sometimes turned into a controversial episode with an elastic phrase about time, such as, "Early that year. . . ."

Overall, I feel very fortunate that the documents and testimony obtained by the 9/11 Commission confirmed rather than contradicted my original narrative. In the end a journalist is only as good as his sources, and now that the commission has laid bare such a full record, I am more grateful than ever for the honesty, balance, and precision displayed by my most important sources during my original research. Still, there are a few significant chronological errors in the third part of the first edition. Some involve the exact timing of the several cases where President Clinton and his national security cabinet secretly considered firing cruise missiles at Osama bin Laden in Afghanistan. The commission's investigation shows that the last of these episodes occurred in the spring of 1999, not the autumn of 2000, as I had originally reported, relying on a published interview with Clinton for the date. The commission's work also makes clear that some of my sources, in talking to me about these incidents, occasionally conflated or combined in their memories episodes that had occurred separately. Beyond the intrinsic benefits of precision, these discrepencies are probably significant mainly because, now untangled, they locate specifically the political moments in which Clinton made his crucial decisions in his secret campaign against bin Laden—in one episode, for instance, the president had to decide whether to fire cruise missiles in the same week that he faced an impeachment trial in the U.S. Senate. The commission's efforts still leave a few small mysteries in the record. For instance, it is still not clear to me when the Pakistani government first proposed collaborating with the CIA to train a commando team to try to capture or kill bin Laden—in December of 1998, as my interview sources place it, or the following summer, when the training clearly began in earnest. On these and other chronology issues I have made adjustments in the main text and clarified sourcing in the notes. I have also corrected a dozen or so small, embarrassing unforced errors from the first edition, such as faulty spellings and garbled numbers.

A more subjective and interesting question, perhaps, is whether any of the history in *Ghost Wars* should be reinterpreted in light of the commission's disclosures. In at least one important area, recent revelations do clearly transform our understanding. The interrogation statements of Khalid Sheikh Mohammed, Ramzi Binalshibh, and Abu Zubaydah disclosed by the commission substantially alter our understanding of the origins of the specific plot carried out by the Hamburg cell on September 11. These interrogation statements were given by unreliable witnesses under duress in unknown circumstances, and should therefor be treated with caution. Yet the statements were taken separately and they do seem consistent about key issues, such as how the idea to turn hijacked airplanes into cruise missiles originated, the role played by bin Laden, and the internal dynamics among the hijackers as they prepared for their attack. I have incorporated these disclosures into the text of this edition. A fuller history of the specific September 11 plot may yet become available, if bin Laden or other al Qaeda leaders are eventually taken into custody.

On the broader questions of American foreign policy and intelligence operations during the two decades leading up to September 11, the commission's final report is perhaps generous toward the Saudi government and the Pakistan army, but many of these favorable judgments involve conspiracy theories that my book did not address at all, such as whether the Saudi embassy in Washington aided the September 11 hijackers while they were in the United States. Also, the commissioners saw themselves, as they wrote, "looking backward in order to look forward," and they may have managed their published criticisms of Riyadh and Islamabad with future American counterterrorism partnerships in mind.

In any event, it seems too early to radically reinterpret such a recent history, or to reallocate proportions of blame and responsibility. For those of us in Washington and New York, at least, the aftershocks of September 11 still rumble daily. We navigate to work past patrols of body-armored police dispatched by color-coded alert schemes that would seem fantastical even if encountered in science fiction. The pollsters' fever charts from America, Europe, the Middle East, and Central Asia depict an impassioned, sharply divided world in which, among other things, the standing of the United States in popular opinion has plummeted in a very short time. Holding their flag-draped ceremonies in secret, American military transport crews unload dead and wounded in twos and threes from Iraq and Afghanistan. In such a tempestuous present, an examination of the past seems a relative luxury. It is for now far easier for a researcher to explain how and why September 11 happened than it is to explain the aftermath.

Steve Coll
Washington D.C.
August 2004

Notes

PROLOGUE

1. The account in this chapter of Schroen's visit to Kabul, the details of his discussions with Massoud, and the history between them more than five years earlier is drawn from multiple interviews with U.S. government officials and Afghan government officials, including Gary Schroen, May 7 and September 19, 2002, Washington D.C. (SC).

2. Massoud's troops raged out of control against Hazaras, an Afghan Shiite group, in the Kabul neighborhood of Karte She in March 1995, committing rapes and looting stores. See "Afghanistan, Crisis of Impunity," Human Rights Watch, July 2001, p. 22.

3. CIA Operating Directives are derived from an annual assessment of American intelligence priorities as determined by a special interagency board meeting in Washington. The board's goal is to ensure that intelligence collection conforms to the priorities of White House foreign and defense policies. Each CIA station receives its own specific O.D. In theory, the performance of a station chief may be judged based on how well he or she recruits agents who can report on the issues listed in the O.D. In practice, CIA station chiefs traditionally have enjoyed substantial autonomy and are not strictly measured against the O.D.

4. That Afghanistan was assigned to Langley is from an interview with a U.S. government official.

5. Christopher, during prepared testimony for his confirmation hearings on January 25, 1993, devoted only four out of more than four thousand words to Afghanistan, saying that "restoring peace to Afghanistan" was in America's interest. Four months later, on May 28, Christopher told a CNN interviewer: "[W]e're very concerned about the situation in Afghanistan and the fact that it

does seem to be a breeding ground for terrorist activities around the world, and I think
that we're going to pay particular attention to
that there. Some countries, unfortunately, in
some areas of the world ... seem to be
sponsoring more terrorism as it leeches out
with its ugly spokes of the pitchfork into
other countries." According to a Lexis-Nexis
search, Christopher did not publicly mention
Afghanistan again during his term as Secretary of State except in four passing references, none of which addressed American
policies or interests there.

6.   That it was an Ariana Afghan plane: Barnett R. Rubin, *The Fragmentation of Afghanistan,*
p. xxvii. For a specific account of the Afghans
who greeted him, see Kathy Gannon, Associated Press, July 6, 2002.

7.   Peter L. Bergen, *Holy War, Inc.,* pp. 93–94.

8.   Interviews with U.S. government officials. See also "Usama bin Ladin: Islamic
Extremist Financier," publicly released CIA
assessment, 1996.

9.   Interviews with U.S. government officials. The unit's existence has also been described in numerous press reports.

10.   The numbers cited here are from interviews with U.S. government officials, as is
the description of the Stinger recovery program. For an early account of the program,
see Molly Moore, *The Washington Post,* March 7,
1994.

11.   The prices and commission system
cited are from interviews with U.S. government officials and Pakistani intelligence officials, including an interview with Lt. Gen.
Javed Ashraf Qazi (Ret.), who was director
general of Pakistan's Inter-Services Intelligence from 1993 to 1995, May 19, 2002,
Rawalpindi, Pakistan (SC). Qazi said the Pakistanis charged the Americans $80,000 per
returned missile, which he said is also what
ISI had to pay to buy a missile from the
Afghans.

12.   The quotations are from interviews
with Schroen, May 7 and September 19,
2002, confirmed by Afghan officials involved.

13.   Gannon, Associated Press, July 6, 2002.

14.   Anthony Davis, "How the Taliban Became a Military Force," in William Maley, ed.,
Fundamentalism Reborn, p. 68.

15.   Glyn Davies, State Department Regular Briefing, September 27, 1996, Federal
Document Clearing House. Davies also said
during the briefing that the Taliban had announced "that Afghans can return to Kabul
without fear, and that Afghanistan is the
common home of all Afghans and we [take]
those statements as an indication that the
Taliban intends to respect the rights of all
Afghans." When asked about the Taliban's
imposition of strict Islamic law in other areas
under their control, Davies responded,
"We've seen some of the reports that they've
moved to impose Islamic law in the areas that
they control. But at this stage, we're not reading anything into that. I mean, there's—on
the face of it, nothing objectionable at this
stage. ... Remember, we don't have any
American officials in Kabul. We haven't had
them since the Soviets left because we've
judged it too dangerous to maintain a mission there. So what we're reacting to for the
most part are press reports, reports from
others who, in fact, have sources there—in
other words, second-, third-hand reports."

16.   Interview with a U.S. government official. The circumstantial evidence of Schroen's
ill-timed trip also seems a powerful indicator
that the U.S. intelligence community did not
expect Massoud to collapse so quickly. The
U.S. ambassador to Islamabad at the time,
Tom Simons, said that the embassy did not
forecast the fall of Kabul in any of its reporting to Washington. Author's interview
with Tom Simons, August 19, 2002, Washington, D.C. (SC).

CHAPTER 1: "WE'RE GOING
TO DIE HERE"

1. Associated Press, November 22, 1979.

2. Associated Press, November 30, 1979.

3. The detailed account in this chapter of how the attack unfolded, and how embassy personnel responded, is drawn from multiple interviews with U.S. officials, including Lloyd Miller, November 18, 2002, Quantico, Virginia (GW), and Gary Schroen, August 29, 2002, Washington D.C. (SC). The account also draws from interviews given to reporters in Islamabad at the time. Among the latter were multiple eyewitness Associated Press dispatches of November 21 and 22, 1979; Stuart Auerbach's first-day narrative in *The Washington Post,* November 22, 1979; and Tom Morganthau, Carol Honsa, and Fred Coleman in *Newsweek,* December 3, 1979. Marcia Gauger, the only journalist to see the riot unfold from inside the embassy, wrote an account for the December 3, 1979, *Time* magazine in which she directly contradicted the Carter administration's claim that the Pakistani government had been instrumental in saving U.S. personnel. The man Gauger was supposed to meet for lunch that day, political counselor Herbert G. Hagerty, later provided a comprehensive reconstruction of the attack in a chapter for the book *Embassies Under Siege,* edited by Joseph G. Sullivan. See also Dennis Kux, *The United States and Pakistan, 1947–2000,* pp. 242–45.

4. Three Western reporters interviewed Jamaat student union officers at Quaid-I-Azam University immediately after the riots. The union officers appeared to accept responsibility for organizing the demonstrations, expressed regret over the loss of life, but adamantly defended their cause. Stuart Auerbach, "Politics and Religion: A Volatile Mix for Zia in Pakistan," *The Washington Post,* November 26, 1979. Michael T. Kaufman, "Students in Islamabad See a Growing Islamic Uprising," *The New York Times,* November 26, 1979. The most detailed account of Jamaat's role at the university during this period is in *The Economist,* December 1, 1979.

5. For a deep account of the impact of Saudi funding on Jamaat and other similar organizations at major universities in the Islamic world and elsewhere, see Gilles Kepel, *Jihad,* pp. 61–105.

6. Associated Press, November 21, 1979.

7. Alexei Vassiliev, *The History of Saudi Arabia,* pp. 395–96; *Fortune,* March 10, 1980; Joshua Teitelbaum, *Holier Than Thou,* pp. 20–21; *Newsweek,* December 3, 1979.

8. *The Muslim,* November 21, 1979. The day's paper, a special edition, offered some of the first signs that trouble was brewing. Below the first two stories on the front page— "Unidentified Armed Men Occupy Kaba" and "U.S. May Use Force"—was a third story titled "Anger in 'Pindi." The story reported that shopkeepers in Rawalpindi shuttered their stores "and came out in the streets in a spontaneous reaction. By midday all shops in the main bazaars and shopping centres were closed and large processions were forming to march. . . . They were shouting anti-Zionist and anti-Imperialist slogans."

9. Interview with a U.S. official familiar with the reports.

10. Interviews with U.S. officials. The CIA later reconstructed a comprehensive account of the Islamabad embassy attack that became the basis of a lecture course in embassy security taught to young case officers.

11. Associated Press, November 21, 1979.

12. That the company supplied Grand Mosque blueprints to security forces: *Financial Times,* August 22, 1998. Osama bin Laden's father, Mohammed bin Laden, the company's founder and patriarch, had earlier received a large contract from the Saudi royal family to renovate and extend the Grand Mosque. His company also constructed highways leading to Mecca.

13. *Newsweek,* December 3, 1979.

14. What Prince Turki concluded about the Mecca uprising: "Memorandum of Conversation Between HRH Prince Turki and Senator Bill Bradley," April 13, 1980, author's files. Quotations from Tehran: *The New York Times,* November 23, 1979; *The Washington Post,* November 23, 1979.

15. BBC Summary of World Broadcasts, distributed November 23, 1979.

CHAPTER 2: "LENIN TAUGHT US"

1. Robert G. Kaiser, *Why Gorbachev Happened,* pp. 53–56.

2. The figure of 3,725 military officers trained by the Soviets is from Larry P. Goodson, *Afghanistan's Endless War,* p. 51, and Barnett B. Rubin, *The Fragmentation of Afghanistan,* p. 71. The figure of twelve thousand political prisoners is from Martin Ewans, *Afghanistan,* p. 142. Rubin provides detailed accounts of early Afghan communist campaigns to destroy traditional tribal and religious leadership through mass imprisonments and murders.

3. Svetlana Savranskaya, working paper, "Afghanistan: Lessons from the Last War," October 9, 2001.

4. Robert Gates estimates "up to 20" Soviet officers killed in his unpublished manuscript, Chapter 11, pp. 36–37. Ewans cites the more typical estimate of "possibly one hundred." The Soviets never provided a specific accounting.

5. "Meeting of the Politburo of the Central Committee of the Communist Party of the Soviet Union," March 17, 1979, transcript of proceedings, originally classified Top Secret, translated and released by the National Security Archive, Washington, D.C. This and other original American and Soviet documents cited in this chapter were first assembled in English as "Toward an International History of the War in Afghanistan, 1979–1989," a notebook of documents compiled by Christian F. Ostermann and Mirceau Munteanu of the Cold War International History Project at the Woodrow Wilson Center. The documents were released at a conference organized by Ostermann on April 29–30, 2002. Also participating in the project were the Asia Program and the Kennan Institute for Advanced Russian Studies at the Woodrow Wilson Center; the George Washington Cold War Group at George Washington University; and the National Security Archive, Washington, D.C.

6. Ibid., March 18, 1979.

7. The original source for this transcript is in "Limited Contingent," by Boris Gromov, the Soviet general who led the Fortieth Army's retreat from Afghanistan, published in Russian by *Progress,* Moscow, 1994. The version here was translated into English and released by the Cold War International History Project, George Washington University, Washington, D.C.

8. The options paper and covering memo are in Robert M. Gates, *From the Shadows,* p. 144. The attitude of officers in the Near East Division is from the author's interviews.

9. Gates, *From the Shadows,* p. 131.

10. Interviews with multiple officers who served in the Directorate of Operations, and particularly the Near East Division, during this period.

11. Gates, *From the Shadows,* p. 144.

12. Ibid.

13. Goodson, *Afghanistan's Endless War,* p. 57. Mohammed Yousaf, a brigadier general in the Afghan bureau of the Pakistani intelligence service, later estimated that massive defections dropped the size of the Afghan army from about 100,000 to about 25,000 men by 1980. Goodson uses similar figures, estimating a collapse from 80,000 to 30,000 men during the same period, primarily due to desertions to the rebels.

14. "Afghanistan: Prospects for Soviet Intervention," AMEMBASSY Moscow to SECSTATE, Moscow 13083, released by the Cold War International History Project. The American government's system of document classification is richly complicated and constantly changing. Generally, "Confidential" is the lowest level of document classification, "Secret" is the next highest, then "Top Secret." A Top Secret document can be further compartmented by limiting circulation to a short list of readers cleared with a particular temporary code word—this designation is usually called Top Secret/Codeword. The gradations of secrecy persist because they provide a crude system to determine which classes of government employees need to be investigated, supervised, and cleared to read certain classes of secret documents.

15. "Report to the CPSU CC on the Situation in Afghanistan," June 28, 1979, Top Secret, Special Folder. Translated by the Cold War International History Project. The original Russian source was "The Tragedy and Valor of the Afghani" by A. A. Likhovskii, Moscow: GPI "Iskon," 1995.

16. "To the Soviet Ambassador," June 28, 1979, Top Secret, translated by the Cold War International History Project. Kremlin records make clear that Taraki continued to ask for Soviet troops, in disguise if necessary, through the summer of 1979.

17. The date of the finding is from Gates, *From the Shadows,* pp. 143 and 146. Years later Brzezinski would tell an interviewer from *Le Nouvel Observateur* (January 15 and January 21, 1998, p. 76) that he had "knowingly increased the probability" that the Soviets would intervene in Afghanistan by authorizing the secret aid. Brzezinski implied that he had slyly lured the Soviets into a trap in Afghanistan. But his contemporary memos—particularly those written in the first days after the Soviet invasion—make clear that

while Brzezinski was determined to confront the Soviets in Afghanistan through covert action, he was also very worried that the Soviets would prevail. Those early memos show no hint of satisfaction that the Soviets had taken some sort of Afghan bait. Given this evidence and the enormous political and security costs that the invasion imposed on the Carter administration, any claim that Brzezinski lured the Soviets into Afghanistan warrants deep skepticism.

18. The Hughes-Ryan Amendment to the Foreign Assistance Act of 1961, passed into law in 1974, established the need for a formal presidential "finding" for covert action. Several subsequent executive orders and presidential security directives provided for the detailed process by which presidential covert action findings are drafted, approved, and implemented within the executive branch, including at the CIA, which is identified by the law as the primary federal agency for covert action. (If the president wants another U.S. agency to participate in a covert action, this must be spelled out in a finding; otherwise, the CIA is the default agency for such programs.) The provisions of Hughes-Ryan were overtaken in U.S. law by the Intelligence Authorization Act for fiscal year 1991. This law spells out what had previously been a more informal standard, namely, that covert action must be "necessary to support identifiable foreign policy objectives" and also must be "important to the national security of the United States." For a definitive review of U.S. law governing covert action, see Michael W. Reisman and James E. Baker, *Regulating Covert Action,* from which these quotes and citations are drawn.

19. Gates, *From the Shadows,* p. 146.

20. "The KGB in Afghanistan," by Vasiliy Mitrokhin, English edition, Working Paper No. 40, Cold War International History Project, introduced and edited by Odd Arne

Westad and Christian F. Ostermann, Washington, D.C., February 2002. Mitrokhin, a KGB archivist who defected to Great Britain as Soviet communism collapsed, has provided in this paper detailed citations of KGB files and cables relevant to Afghanistan dating back to the early 1960s.

21. This account is drawn in part from recollections by American and Soviet participants in the events who appeared at the conference "Toward an International History of the War in Afghanistan, 1979–1989," in Washington, D.C., April 29–30, 2002. That the KGB planted stories that Amin was a CIA agent is from Mitrokhin, "KGB in Afghanistan," p. 50. The Indian document is from the recollection of a senior officer in the CIA's Directorate of Operations at that time. See also "Partners in Time" by Charles G. Cogan, *World Policy Journal,* Summer 1993, p. 76. Cogan ran the Near East Division of the Directorate of Operations beginning in mid-1979. He wrote that the Soviets had "unfounded" suspicions that Amin worked for the CIA because of "Amin's supposed American connections (he had once had some sort of loose association with the Asia Foundation)."

22. Mitrokhin, "KGB in Afghanistan," p. 93.

23. Amstutz offered his recollections at the April 2002 conference. Recollections of the Near East Division officers are from the author's interviews.

24. Account of the Kabul station's priorities and its failure to predict the 1978 coup is from the author's interview with Warren Marik, March 11, 2002, Washington, D.C. (SC). Marik served as a CIA case officer in Kabul from late 1977 until early 1980. The general outline of his account was confirmed by other U.S. officials familiar with the Kabul station during those years.

25. "What Are the Soviets Doing in Afghanistan?" memorandum is from Thomas

Thornton, assistant to the president for national security, to Zbigniew Brzezinski, September 17, 1979, released by the Cold War International History Project.

26. "Personal Memorandum, Andropov to Brezhnev," in early December 1979, is from notes taken by A. F. Dobrynin and provided to the Norwegian Nobel Institute, translated and released by the Cold War International History Project.

27. Multiple sources cite Politburo records of the tentative decision to invade on November 26, including Goodson, *Afghanistan's Endless War,* p. 51. The infiltration of Karmal on December 7 and the account of the attempts to poison Amin are from "New Russian Evidence on the Crisis and War in Afghanistan" by Aleksandr A. Lyakhovski, Working Paper No. 41, draft, Cold War International History Project. The KGB assault plans are from Mitrokhin, "KGB in Afghanistan," pp. 96–106.

28. Gates, *From the Shadows,* p. 133.

29. Mitrokhin, "KGB in Afghanistan," p. 106.

30. "Reflections on Soviet Intervention in Afghanistan," memorandum for the president from Zbigniew Brzezinski, December 26, 1979, released by the Cold War International History Project.

31. "Memorandum for the Secretary of State," January 2, 1980, released by the Cold War International History Project.

CHAPTER 3: "GO RAISE HELL"

1. Interviews with Howard Hart, November 12, 2001, November 26, 2001, and November 27, 2001, in Virginia, as well as subsequent telephone and email communications (SC). Abdul Haq was killed by Taliban troops inside Afghanistan in October 2001. He had entered eastern Afghanistan, against the advice of the CIA, in order to stir up opposition to the Taliban in the immediate af-

termath of the September 11 attacks. That Hart and the CIA maintained a close relationship with Haq until the late 1980s comes not only from Hart but from the author's interviews with several other U.S. officials.

2. Interviews with Hart, November 12, 26, and 27, 2001. His biography is also described in George Crile, *Charlie Wilson's War,* pp. 117–21, also based on interviews with Hart.

3. Interviews with former CIA officials from this period. That George was a postman's son is from Crile, *Charlie Wilson's War,* p. 62.

4. Lessard's conflict with Hart and the worries he expressed around the time of his death are from interviews with U.S. officials who knew Lessard.

5. Quotes and Hart's point of view are from interviews with Hart, November 12, 26, and 27, 2001.

6. Interviews with U.S. officials familiar with the 1979 presidential findings. See also Steve Coll, *The Washington Post,* July 19 and 20, 1992.

7. Charles G. Cogan, "Partners in Time," *World Policy Journal,* Summer 1993. Cogan has written that the first Lee Enfield rifles authorized for the mujahedin by Carter's amended finding arrived in Pakistan about ten days after the Soviet invasion. Details of other weapons supplied are from the author's interviews with Hart and other U.S. officials.

8. Martin Ewans, *Afghanistan,* p. 158. The KGB archivist Vasiliy Mitrokhin, in "The KGB in Afghanistan," cites KGB statistics, unavailable to the CIA at the time, showing more than five thousand reported rebel actions in 1981 and almost twice as many the next year. "Using the methods of terror and intimidation and playing on religious and national sentiments, the counterrevolutionaries have a strong influence on a considerable part of the country's population," the Soviet Fortieth Army's headquarters admitted to

Moscow in June 1980. See "Excerpt from a report of 40th Army HQ," released by the Cold War International History Project.

9. The Bangkok meeting and Hart's cabling are from interviews with Hart, November 12, 26, and 27, 2001. See also Crile, *Charlie Wilson's War,* pp. 125–26. The January 1982 cable is cited in Robert M. Gates, *From the Shadows,* p. 251. Gates reports that CIA director William Casey read this cable from Hart. Unbeknownst to the CIA, during the same month that Hart cabled seeking more and better weapons, the KGB Residency in Kabul reported to the Politburo that "the counter-revolutionary forces have managed to keep their zones of influence and to attract a considerable part of the population into the struggle against the existing regime." See Mitrokhin, "KGB in Afghanistan," p. 132.

10. Interviews with former CIA officials. Typical was the observation of Fred "Fritz" Ermath, a former CIA Soviet analyst, who said, "The Kermit Roosevelts, the Cord Meyers were gone. . . . The old guys were hearts and minds guys. . . . But they were gone, see? And I think this generational shift, again with the Vietnam experience as part of the saga . . . The new guys said, 'Well, we're going to stick to our operational meaning, and what we can do is deliver mules, money and mortars.'"

11. The bounty idea is from interviews with Hart, November 12, 26, and 27, 2001. It is not clear whether the system was ever implemented by ISI.

12. Mary Ann Weaver, *Pakistan,* p. 57.

13. Ibid., p. 61.

14. "Devout Muslim, yes," is from Mohammed Yousaf, *Silent Soldier,* pp. 99–100.

15. "Afghan youth will fight," is from "Memorandum of Conversation," President Reagan and President Zia-ul-Haq, December 7, 1982, released by the Cold War International History Project.

16. Mitrokhin, "KGB in Afghanistan," pp. 151–52. Mohammed Yousaf and Mark Adkin, *The Bear Trap,* p. 49.

17. Dennis Kux, *The United States and Pakistan, 1947–2000,* pp. 256–57.

18. "Your Meeting with Pakistan President . . ." Memo from Shultz to Reagan, November 29, 1982, and "Visit of Zia-ul-Haq," from Shultz, also dated November 29, 1982, both released by the Cold War International History Project.

19. The CIA's analysts understood Zia's ambivalence about the United States. In a special estimate prepared on November 12, 1982, the CIA reported, "Islamabad is aware that only the United States can offset Soviet pressures and provide Pakistan with the sophisticated weapons it believes it needs." Yet "the Pakistanis continue to doubt the reliability of U.S. commitments and U.S. steadfastness in time of crisis." See "Special National Intelligence Estimate on Pakistan," November 12, 1982, released by the Cold War International History Project.

20. Interviews with Hart, November 12, 26, and 27, 2001, and with Yousaf, June 1992, Dusseldorf, Germany (SC). A retired Pakistani brigadier general at the time of the interviews, Mohammed Yousaf is the coauthor of *The Bear Trap,* a detailed account of the ISI's Afghan operations between 1983 and 1987.

21. ISI telephone codes are from the author's 1992 interviews with Yousaf, June 1992. ISI rules about CIA contact with Afghans are from Hart, November 12, 26, and 27, 2001, and other U.S. officials familiar with the liaison. Yousaf said that he and Akhtar were blindfolded while visiting the United States. A U.S. official interviewed in 1992 said he "wouldn't steer you away from that. We do have sensitive facilities."

22. Yousaf, *Silent Soldier,* pp. 25–27. Akhtar's professional information is on pp. 27–32.

23. The size of the ISI Afghan bureau is from Yousaf and Adkin, *Bear Trap,* pp. 1–3. How ISI was perceived is from interviews with Yousaf and other ISI and Pakistan army generals.

24. Published estimates of U.S. covert aid between fiscal 1981 and 1984 include Barnett R. Rubin, *Refugee Survey Quarterly,* United Nations High Commissioner for Refugees, 1996. These estimates were confirmed in interviews with several U.S. officials. Fiscal year 1984 was an unusual, complicated year because surplus Pentagon funds were added to the pipeline at the last hour. The Soviet figures cited here are from Larry P. Goodson, *Afghanistan's Endless War,* p. 63.

25. Details of the weapons systems and financial details are from Yousaf, June 1992; Hart, November 12, 26, and 27, 2001; and other U.S. officials familiar with the pipeline during these years. Yousaf and Adkin describe many of these purchases in *The Bear Trap.* The Turkish incident comes from interviews with Yousaf. Hart recalled that the CIA paid the Chinese about $80 for a Kalashnikov copy that probably cost them about $12 or $15 to make. Because the Chinese enforced the greatest quality control in their manufacturing, over time most of the CIA's covert purchases shifted toward Beijing. State-owned Chinese ships always seemed to steam into Karachi on just the date they were due, and the assistant Chinese defense attaché from the Islamabad embassy would invariably be standing at dockside, clipboard in hand.

26. Interviews with Hart, November 12, 26, and 27, 2001, and Yousaf, June 1992.

27. See Chapter 7 for a more detailed account of this issue.

28. "The Secretary's Visit to Pakistan: Afghanistan," cable from U.S. embassy, Islamabad, to Secretary of State, June 1, 1983, released by the Cold War International History Project.

29. A copy of the letter was obtained by the author. Hart's trip into Afghanistan is from interviews with Hart, November 12, 26, and 27, 2001. He is the only source for the account of the trip. At least two other D.O. officers, including a later Islamabad station chief, also made unauthorized trips into Afghanistan during the Soviet phase of the war, according to U.S. officials familiar with the trips.

CHAPTER 4: "I LOVED OSAMA"

1. This account of Badeeb's trip to Pakistan and his meeting with Zia is from the author's interview with Ahmed Badeeb and Saeed Badeeb on February 1, 2002, in Jedda, Saudi Arabia (SC). The interview lasted approximately two hours and was conducted in English. Subsequently, Ahmed Badeeb supplied to the author videotapes of two days of interviews he gave early in 2002 to an Arabic-language satellite news service based in Lebanon, Orbit Television. The author employed a Washington, D.C.–based firm to translate these Orbit interviews from Arabic into English. Some of the quotations of Badeeb in this chapter, such as the account of his visit with boxes of cash to Pakistan, are from the author's interview. Other quotations are from the Orbit interviews, as rendered into English by the translation service. The distinctions are indicated in the footnotes. That Badeeb attended college in North Dakota is from an interview with a U.S. official.

2. Interview with Nat Kern, January 23, 2002, Washington, D.C. (SC). Kern maintains close contacts with the Saudi government as the editor of a newsletter about oil markets and Middle East politics. The quote from Turki is attributed by Kern to his business partner, Frank Anderson, a retired clandestine officer in the CIA's Near East Di-

vision and at one time director of the D.O.'s Afghanistan task force.

3. Nawaf Obaid, "Improving U.S. Intelligence Analysis on the Saudi Arabian Decision Making Process," master's degree thesis, John F. Kennedy School of Government, Harvard University, 1998. "Both believed fervently" is from Mohammed Yousaf, *Silent Soldier,* p. 87.

4. The Saudi air cover over Karachi is from the Badeeb interviews with Orbit.

5. The history of GID is from interviews with Saudi officials; with Nat Kern, January 23, 2002; a telephone interview with Ray Close, a former CIA station chief in Jedda who subsequently worked as a consultant to Prince Turki, January 10, 2002 (SC); and David Long, a former U.S. diplomat who also later worked for Prince Turki, January 22, 2002, Washington, D.C. (SC). By one account GID provided Sadat with a regular income during 1970 when Sadat was Egypt's vice president. See Bob Woodward, *Veil: The Secret Wars of the CIA, 1981–1987,* p. 352.

6. Alexei Vassiliev, *The History of Saudi Arabia,* p. 213, quoting the British Arabist Gertrude Bell. Vassiliev's history, translated from the original Russian, draws heavily on original Arabic and Ottoman sources as well as the accounts of travelers; it is the principal source of the pre-twentieth-century Arabian peninsula history in this chapter.

7. The author owes the observation that Saudi Arabia was the first modern nation-state created by jihad to the anonymous author of a survey of the kingdom published in *The Economist,* March 23, 2002.

8. The demographic statistics are from Vassiliev, *History of Saudi Arabia,* p. 421.

9. The quotations are from a speech Prince Turki gave on February 3, 2002, in Washington, D.C.; it was transcribed and published on the World Wide Web by the Center for Contemporary Arab Studies. Prince Turki also

spoke briefly about his time at Lawrenceville during an interview with the author, August 2, 2002, in Cancun, Mexico (SC).

10. That Clinton did not know Turki at Georgetown and only met him after taking office is from interviews with senior Saudi officials and with Kern, January 23, 2002.

11. Quotations are from Turki's speech on February 3, 2002.

12. Ibid. The assassination of Turki's father is from Vassiliev, *History of Saudi Arabia,* pp. 394–95.

13. Interviews with Saudi and U.S. officials. Government budget statistics are from *The Economist,* March 23, 2002. GID's computer expansion is from interviews with U.S. officials and *Business Week,* October 6, 1980.

14. Interviews with U.S. officials.

15. Author's interview with Ahmed Badeeb and Saeed Badeeb, February 1, 2002.

16. Interviews with Saudi officials. The George quote is from the author's interview with Clair George, December 21, 2001, Chevy Chase, Maryland (SC).

17. Interview with Saeed Badeeb, February 1, 2002. That their father was a modestly successful merchant in Jedda is from an interview with a Saudi newspaper editor.

18. That the Saudis arranged contacts for the CIA at the *hajj* is from interviews with former U.S. intelligence officials. The "Safari club" is from Turki's speech, February 3, 2002.

19. "Memorandum of Conversation between HRH Prince Turki and Senator Bill Bradley," April 13, 1980, author's files.

20. That the agreement with the Saudis to match funding dollar for dollar was reached in July is from the unpublished original manuscript of Robert Gates's memoir, p. 13/31. That Bandar used to hold on to the funds and that CIA officers speculated he was doing so to earn the interest is from interviews with three U.S. officials with direct knowledge. Hart, the Islamabad station chief from

1981 to 1984, said in interviews that the Saudis were frequently late in paying their bills, although he did not comment on Bandar's role.

21. Badeeb quotes are from the Orbit interview. Yousaf's quote is from Yousaf, *Silent Soldier,* p. 88.

22. The account of the Taif conference and Badeeb's encounters with the mujahedin leaders and with Sayyaf is from the author's interview with Badeeb, February 1, 2002, and so is the following account of the relationship between GID and Saudi charities.

23. That Turki sometimes controlled where the charity funds could be directed is from an interview with Turki and with other Saudi officials. The Badeeb quote is from the author's interview, February 1, 2002.

24. Peter L. Bergen, *Holy War,* pp. 41–48, provides a carefully sourced account of the bin Laden family's origins and business success.

25. Interview with Turki, August 2, 2002. That Faisal set up a trust to ensure the safe passage of the bin Laden firm to the older sons is also from that interview.

26. Bergen, *Holy War,* pp. 47–48. Bin Laden's allowance is reported in National Commission staff statement no. 15, p. 3–4.

27. Author's interview with Badeeb, February 1, 2002.

28. The Badeeb quote is from the author's interview, February 1, 2002.

29. Interviews with U.S. officials.

30. See, for instance, the testimony of Cofer Black, director of the CIA's Counterterrorist Center between 1999 and 2002, September 26, 2002, to Congress's Joint Inquiry into the September 11 attacks. "We had no relationship with him [bin Laden] but we watched a 22-year-old rich kid from a prominent Saudi family change from frontline mujahedin fighter to a financier for road construction and hospitals." CIA Director George Tenet

testified under oath on October 17, 2002, that during the 1980s, "While we knew of him, we have no record of any direct U.S. government contact with bin Laden at that time."

31.   "I loved Osama . . ." and "He was not an extremist at all . . ." are Badeeb quotes from the Orbit interviews.

32.   Ibid.

33.   Quotations are from Turki's speech in Washington, D.C., February 3, 2002. He provided this version of his interactions with bin Laden during the 1980s in several other interviews as well.

34.   Badeeb, Orbit interviews. (See p. 609, note 1.) It was during the first day's Orbit interview that Badeeb talked most openly and expansively about his relationship with bin Laden and about bin Laden's relationship with the Saudi government. At the the start of the second day's session, Badeeb interrupted his interviewer to volunteer a "clarification" that bin Laden was not a Saudi intelligence agent and that Badeeb met with him "only in my capacity as his former teacher." The sequence raises the possibility that Saudi government officials saw or heard about the first part of the interview, were displeased, and asked Badeeb to issue this "clarification."

CHAPTER 5: "DON'T MAKE IT OUR WAR"

1.   Contents of briefing to Reagan from Robert Gates's unpublished original manuscript, p. 23/33.

2.   Interviews with former CIA officials. Also Mohammad Yousaf and Mark Adkin, *The Bear Trap,* pp. 193–95.

3.   That McMahon wondered about the purpose of the covert war, Bob Woodward, *Veil,* p. 104. The Twetten quote is from Kirsten Lundberg, Philip Zelikow, and Ernest May, "Politics of a Covert Action," p. 12. The Directorate of Intelligence assessment is from "Afghanistan: The Revolution After Four Years," CIA, Directorate of Intelligence, July 1982; declassified July 1999; released by the National Security Archive.

4.   "The longest midlife crisis in history" is from George Crile, *Charlie Wilson's War,* p. 39. The book provides detailed and colorful accounts, mainly from Wilson and CIA officer Gust Avrakatos, of Wilson's role in the Soviet-Afghan conflict, which Crile regards as decisive. The book also describes in profane and painful detail Wilson's alcoholism, womanizing, self-infatuation, and extravagant, sometimes bullying global travel. The quotes from former Miss Northern Hemisphere are on p. 223.

5.   The congressional resolution is quoted in Lundberg, Zelikow, and May, "Politics of a Covert Action," p. 20. "The U.S. had nothing . . ." is from Crile, *Charlie Wilson's War,* p. 262.

6.   There have been multiple accounts of William Casey's covert dealings with the Catholic Church during the 1980s. Some of his efforts in Central America were described in testimony at Clair George's criminal trial arising from the Iran-Contra scandal. About the CIA and the Church in Poland see Carl Bernstein and Marco Politi, *His Holiness.*

7.   Interview with a former CIA official. See also Woodward, *Veil,* p. 130.

8.   The quote from Mrs. Casey is from Joseph E. Persico, *Casey: From the OSS to the CIA,* p. 26. The pre-CIA biographical material in this chapter draws heavily on Persico's strong work, which itself drew on access to Casey's papers and extensive interviews with his family and CIA colleagues. Also helpful was Casey's own scattered accounts of his war experiences and political outlook in *Scouting the Future,* an extensive collection of Casey's public speeches compiled by Herbert E. Meyer.

9.   "Goosing ship builders" is from Persico, *Casey,* p. 51, and "ex-polo players" is on p. 56.

10. "Never had I been in contact," ibid., p. 57.

11. Ibid., pp. 68–69.

12. Fifty-eight teams, Persico, ibid., p. 79. Success rate and "We probably saved" and "for the first time," ibid., p. 83. See also Casey's speech of September 19, 1986, in Casey, *Scouting the Future*, pp. 218–27.

13. "Had been permitted to run down" is from Robert M. Gates, *From the Shadows*, p. 210. The vodka martini scene and "He would demand something," ibid., p. 198.

14. "The Mumbling Guy" is from the author's interview with Ahmed Badeeb, February 1, 2002, Jedda, Saudi Arabia (SC). The Reagan note to Bush is from Persico, *Casey*, p. 228. The Buckley quote, ibid., p. 571. "I can tell you" is from a speech on June 29, 1984, in Casey, *Scouting the Future*, p. 289.

15. "As a legacy" is from Casey's speech of May 21, 1982, in Casey, *Scouting the Future*, p. 11. "The primary battlefield" is from his speech of July 30, 1986, ibid., p. 26. "The isthmus" and "the oil fields" is from his speech of October 27, 1986, ibid., p. 35.

16. The *Mein Kampf* comparison is from Casey's speech of May 1, 1985, in Casey, *Scouting the Future*, p. 183. "That two can play the same game" is from his speech of October 27, 1986, ibid., p. 36. "Far fewer people" is from his speech of September 19, 1986, ibid., p. 299. "Afghan freedom fighters" is from his speech of October 23, 1981, ibid., pp. 119–20.

17. "Realistic counter-strategy" is from Casey's speech of October 29, 1983, ibid., pp. 119–20. p. 144. His discussions with Ames about communism and traditional religion are from his speech of May 1, 1985, ibid., pp. 186–87.

18. Casey and King Khalid, Persico, *Casey*, pp. 310–11. Casey and oil, interviews with former CIA officers and U.S. officials.

19. "Is completely involved" is from Yousaf, *Silent Soldier*, pp. 80–81. The $7,000 carpet is from Persico, *Casey*, p. 507. He reported the gift and passed the carpet to the U.S. government.

20. Persico, *Casey*, p. 226.

21. Casey and Zia, and Zia's red template, are from Charles G. Cogan, "Partners in Time," *World Policy Journal*, p. 79. "Moral duty" is from Gates, *From the Shadows*, p. 252. The CIA map produced for Casey is from Gates's unpublished manuscript, pp. 18/63–65.

22. Persico, *Casey*, p. 313.

23. Interviews with Howard Hart, November 12, 26, and 27, 2001 (SC). His account is corroborated by several other sources, including Yousaf.

24. Memo quotation is from Gates's manuscript, pp. 23/37–38.

25. Interviews with former CIA officials.

26. Gates, *From the Shadows*, p. 320.

27. Funding numbers and December 6 memo quotations from Gates's manuscript, pp. 23/37–38.

28. That Casey insisted on seeing the border camps is from the author's 1992 interviews with Yousaf. "Kabul must burn!" is from the same interviews. What Casey and Akhtar wore is from a photograph taken during the visit and published in Yousaf, *Silent Soldier*.

29. Gates's manuscript, pp. 13/6–11.

30. The May 1984 lecture report is quoted in CIA, Directorate of Intelligence, "The Soviet Invasion of Afghanistan: Five Years After," May 1985, released by the National Security Archive. That U.S. diplomats traveled to Central Asia is from an interview with Edmund McWilliams, January 15, 2002, Washington, D.C. (SC). McWilliams was a political officer in the Moscow embassy during this period and traveled to Central Asia several times.

31. Interviews with Yousaf, 1992. Also Yousaf and Adkin, *Bear Trap*, pp. 189–95.

32. Yousaf's recollections from the author's 1992 interviews. The Gates quotations are from Gates's manuscript, pp. 26/13–14.

33. Interviews with officials at all three agencies during 1992.

34. Gates, *From the Shadows,* p. 199.

35. Interviews with U.S. officials. "Not authorize . . . which we did" is from a written communication to the author from Piekney, July 6, 2003.

CHAPTER 6: "WHO IS THIS MASSOUD?"

1. The account of Massoud's childhood and family life is based primarily on a lengthy series of interviews in Kabul in May 2002 with Yahya Massoud, Ahmed Shah's older brother by two years (GW). Yahya also provided a daylong tour of the Panjshir Valley during which he narrated his family's history in the region and discussed his brother's tactics for defending the valley from the Soviets. Throughout the 1980s, Yahya served in Ahmed Shah Massoud's army as an adviser and as a liaison between Massoud and the British intelligence service, MI6. There is a brief account of the young Massoud's war games in Sebastian Junger's 2001 book, *Fire,* which contains an essay on Massoud titled "The Lion in Winter," p. 213.

2. Interview with Ahmed Wali Massoud, May 7, 2002, Kabul, Afghanistan (GW).

3. Barnett R. Rubin, *The Fragmentation of Afghanistan,* pp. 83, 218, and 221.

4. Interview with Zia Mojadedi, May 14, 2002, Kabul, Afghanistan (GW). Mojadedi was an agriculture professor during the 1960s and 1970s at Kabul University. In 1969, future Afghan leader Gulbuddin Hekmatyar was among his students. Mojadedi recalls that his student was "highly volatile." For a detailed discussion of the growing chasm between the Islamists and the communists during the

1960s and 1970s in Afghanistan—and particularly at Kabul University—see Rubin, *Fragmentation of Afghanistan,* pp. 81–105.

5. Olivier Roy, *Afghanistan: From Holy War to Civil War,* p. 38.

6. This account of the origins of the Muslim Brotherhood and the group's early history is drawn in part from Mary Anne Weaver, *A Portrait of Egypt,* pp. 26–29, and Daniel Benjamin and Steven Simon, *The Age of Sacred Terror,* pp. 57–59.

7. Ayman al-Zawahiri, *Knights Under the Prophet's Banner.* Extracts from this book manuscript were published by Al-Sharq al-Awsat; FBIS translation, December 2001. Yasser Arafat was drawn to the Muslim Brotherhood while serving as a young lieutenant in the Egyptian army; he was arrested twice for Brotherhood activities. Later he turned toward secular leftist politics.

8. Benjamin and Simon, *Age of Sacred Terror,* p. 65.

9. Weaver, *Portrait of Egypt,* pp. 28–29.

10. Rubin, *Fragmentation of Afghanistan,* p. 83.

11. Interview with Ali Ashgar Payman, May 7, 2002, Kabul, Afghanistan (GW). Payman, a deputy planning minister in the interim government of 2002, was a contemporary of Hekmatyar's at Kabul University.

12. Michael Griffin, *Reaping the Whirlwind,* pp. 17–18.

13. Rubin, *Fragmentation of Afghanistan,* pp. 103–4.

14. There are accounts of Massoud's 1978 return to Afghanistan in William Branigin's October 18, 1983, dispatch from the Panjshir for *The Washington Post* and in Jon Lee Anderson's *The Lion's Grave,* pp. 218–19.

15. That the Soviets didn't initially intend to use their own troops against the mujahedin is from "The Tragedy and Valor of the Afghani," Moscow, GPI, "Iskon," 1995,

pp. 176–77, translated by Svetlana Savran-skaya, National Security Archive.

16. Edward Girardet, *The Christian Science Monitor,* September 23, 1981. Girardet was the first Western journalist to provide a detailed account of Massoud's war in the Panjshir.

17. Vasiliy Mitrokhin, "The KGB in Afghanistan," p. 134.

18. Sebastian Junger, *Fire,* p. 201.

19. William Dowell, *Time,* July 5, 1982. On his way into Afghanistan from Pakistan, Dowell was escorted by a group of Mas-soud's men. At one point, the mujahedin passed within a few feet of an Afghan army fort. To Dowell's astonishment, instead of opening fire, the soldiers inside the fort waved and smiled.

20. Girardet, *Christian Science Monitor,* September 24, 1981.

21. Rubin, *Fragmentation of Afghanistan,* pp. 234–37, describes Massoud's military and civil organization in the Panjshir, especially as it compared to Hekmatyar's organization in Pakistan. The quotations are from Roy, *Afghanistan,* pp. 63–64.

22. Rubin, *Fragmentation of Afghanistan,* p. 220.

23. United Press International, May 24, 1983.

24. Interview with Brig. Gen. Syed Raza Ali (Ret.), ISI, May 20, 2002, Rawalpindi, Pakistan (SC). Raza worked in ISI's Afghan bureau from the early 1980s through the Soviet withdrawal.

25. Rubin, *Fragmentation of Afghanistan,* p. 232.

26. Interview with an Arab journalist then in Peshawar.

27. Interview with Graham Fuller, 1992.

28. Interview with a U.S. official.

29. Interview with William Piekney, January 14, 2002, Tysons Corner, Virginia (SC).

30. Interview with Abdullah, May 8, 2002, Kabul, Afghanistan (GW).

31. Ibid. The assassination attempt is from *The Christian Science Monitor,* May 2, 1984, and *The Washington Post,* May 2, 1984.

32. Patricia I. Sethi, *Newsweek,* June 11, 1984.

33. Edward Girardet, *Christian Science Monitor,* October 2, 1984.

34. CIA, Directorate of Intelligence, "The Soviet Invasion of Afghanistan: Five Years After," Secret, May 1985.

35. This summary of Massoud's relations with the British and French is based on interviews with U.S. officials, Yahya Massoud (who handled the liaison with the British), May 2002, and Daoud Mir, who later served as Massoud's representative in France. See also George Crile, *Charlie Wilson's War,* pp. 199–200. Yahya Massoud reported regarding the British, "We had close contact. I can tell you that more than fourteen times I traveled back and forth to the U.K. seeking assistance. They assisted us very well. They gave us very special equipment. They gave us military training—not through Pakistan." The quotations regarding "penis envy" and "trying to find some liberator character" are from an interview with a former CIA officer.

36. Interview with Afghan ambassador to India Massoud Khalili, May 28, 2002, Kabul, Afghanistan (GW).

37. "Playing their own game" is from the interview with Syed Raza Ali, May 20, 2002. That the CIA began unilateral supplies to Massoud in 1984 is from the author's interview with former CIA Near East Division chief Thomas Twetten, March 18, 2002, Washington, D.C. (SC). Crile, *Charlie Wilson's War,* p. 202, cites Afghan task force chief Avrakatos and also dates the beginning of CIA aid to late 1984.

38. "He was never a problem" is from an interview with a U.S. official. "He cannot make a man stronger" is from an interview with Mohammed Yousaf, 1992.

39. Girardet, *Christian Science Monitor,* October 2, 1984.

CHAPTER 7: "THE TERRORISTS WILL OWN THE WORLD"

1. The Anderson quote is from Kirsten Lundberg, Philip Zelikow, and Ernest May, "Politics of a Covert Action," Kennedy School of Government Case Program. The account in this chapter about the internal deliberations surrounding NSDD-166 comes from this excellent case study as well as notes and transcripts from the author's original reporting about the decision directive for *The Washington Post* in July 1992 and more recent interviews by the author with participants.

2. Quotations in this and preceding paragraph are from Lundberg, Zelikow, and May, "Politics of a Covert Action."

3. NSDD-166 and its annex remain classified and have never been published. It remains unclear how specific the original authorizations in the annex were and how many of the new CIA practices evolved under interagency review after the decision directive was signed. In interviews conducted in 1992, Mohammed Yousaf dated the arrival of the first burst communications sets to late 1985. U.S. officials interviewed recently by the author authoritatively date the large-scale expansion of the CIA's unilateral recruitment of paid reporting agents on Afghanistan to 1985. A smaller number of such agents had been on the payroll earlier, according to interviews, but after 1985 the ranks grew to the dozens, and monthly stipends began to swell. It is not clear whether this expansion of unilateral agents was explicitly set in motion by NSDD-166's annex. As to the issue of shooting Soviets, Lundberg, Zelikow, and May, "Politics of a Covert Action," reports that the decision directive "endorsed direct attacks on Soviet military officers," p. 25. The author interviewed multiple participants who remember this issue being discussed at the CIA and by the interagency committee, but those interviews did not make clear whether the decision directive itself endorsed such targeted killings. The interviews underlying the Harvard case study do appear authoritative. George Crile's account of the issue, narrated from the perspective of Avrakatos, does not make clear precisely what legal authorities governed his work.

4. Lundberg, Zelikow, and May, "Politics of a Covert Action," p. 52.

5. Interviews with U.S. officials.

6. Humphrey's recommendation is from the author's interviews in 1992 with multiple U.S. officials involved in the debate over supplying sniper rifles to the mujahedin.

7. Joseph E. Persico, *Casey: From the OSS to the CIA,* pp. 428–29.

8. The Pillsbury quote is from Lundberg, Zelikow, and May, "Politics of a Covert Action," p. 32. Other details are from the case study and author's interviews with U.S. officials.

9. That the CIA recruited and paid European journalists and travelers to report on Afghanistan is from multiple interviews with U.S. officials, including an interview with Warren Marik, March 11, 2002, Washington, D.C. (SC). That Haq's relationship with Hart was passed to Piekney is from the author's interviews with U.S. officials. Haq was by now a celebrated and famous commander. President Reagan praised him at a black-tie dinner in Washington, and Haq later met British prime minister Margaret Thatcher. Although he was an increasingly outspoken critic of Pakistani intelligence and Hekmatyar, Haq did not openly break with the CIA until 1987.

10. Robert M. Gates, *From the Shadows,* p. 348.

11. "Death by a thousand cuts" is from Mohammed Yousaf and Mark Adkin, *The Bear Trap,* p. 1.

12. Interviews with Mohammed Yousaf in 1992.

13. Artyom Borovik, *The Hidden War*, p. 76. The booby trap examples from plastic explosives and "Hidden death" are on pp. 35–36.

14. Quotations in this and the preceding paragraph are from the author's interviews with Yousaf, 1992.

15. Najibullah's elevation to the Politburo is from Barnett R. Rubin, *The Fragmentation of Afghanistan*, p. 128. The size of Afghan intelligence service, ibid., p. 133. The location of foreign residencies and penetration of mujahedin headquarters is from Vasiliy Mitrokhin, "The KGB in Afghanistan," pp. 151–56.

16. The use of Spetsnaz tactics and "Omsk vans" is from interviews with U.S. officials in 1992. It is also described in detail in Lundberg, Zelikow, and May, "Politics of a Covert Action." Helicopter tactics along Pakistani border and that Spetsnaz troops commandeered pickup trucks and operated in disguise are from Timothy Gusinov, a former Soviet military adviser in Afghanistan, writing in *The Washington Times*, November 3, 2001. The KGB's use of false bands is from Mitrokhin, "The KGB in Afghanistan."

17. Interviews with U.S. officials.

18. That Afghan fighters rejected suicide missions uniformly is from interviews with Yousaf and with Howard Hart, November 12, 26, and 27, 2001, in Virginia (SC), and other U.S. officials.

19. "Most likely use" is from an interview with a U.S. official in 1992, addressing the specific question of sniper rifles, detonator packages, and other "dual use" covert supplies. "These aren't terrorist . . . ever again" is from George Crile, *Charlie Wilson's War*, p. 166. "Do I want . . . spreads fear," ibid., p. 318. Endorsed reward for belt buckles, ibid., p. 350.

20. The Vaughan Forrest quotation is from a telephone interview with Forrest, 1992.

"Shooting ducks" and "off Russian generals" are from an interview with a participant in the debates, 1992.

21. Interviews with multiple U.S. officials involved with the sniper rifle debate, 1992, as well as interviews with Yousaf, 1992, who received the guns and implemented the training.

22. Statistics about Americans abroad in 1985 are from Bruce Hoffman, *Inside Terrorism*, p. 150. Habash's quotation from 1970 is also cited in Hoffman, pp. 70–71. He dates Jenkins's seminal formulations to his article "International Terrorism: A New Mode of Conflict," in David Carlton and Carlo Schaerf, eds., *International Terrorism and World Security*.

23. "The incidents would become" is from Duane R. Clarridge, with Digby Diehl, *A Spy for All Seasons*, p. 320. The account of the Counterterrorist Center's birth, the memo, and the quotations in the following five paragraphs are from Clarridge, ibid., pp. 320–29, and from an interview with Clarridge, December 28, 2001, San Diego, California (SC).

24. A partially declassified version of NSDD-207 has been obtained and published by the National Security Archive.

25. "Pretty much anything he wanted" is from Robert Baer, *See No Evil*, pp. 84–85. "Hit teams" is from the author's interview with Clarridge, December 28, 2001.

26. Interview with Robert Gates, March 12, 2002, Cleveland, Ohio (SC).

27. The Baer quotation is from Baer, *See No Evil*, pp. 84–85. The Cannistraro quotation is from the author's interview with Vincent Cannistraro, January 8, 2002, Rosslyn, Virginia (SC).

28. The use of beacons in planted weapons is from an interview with Clarridge, December 28, 2001.

29. That the CIA had no sources in Hezbollah and "absolutely no idea" where the hostages were is from Baer, *See No Evil*,

pp. 86–92. That the Counterterrorist Center was inundated with hoaxes, some mounted by Hezbollah, is from the interview with Cannistraro, January 8, 2002.

30. The trucks and the development of the operation with Delta Force are from the interview with Clarridge, December 28, 2001.

31. The account of the Eagle Program, the prototypes, the effort to equip them with cameras, explosives, and rockets is from the interview with Clarridge, December 28, 2001.

32. Clarridge, with Diehl, *Spy for All Seasons,* p. 339.

33. Interview with Yousaf, 1992.

34. Bruce Hoffman, *Inside Terrorism,* p. 41.

35. Counterterrorist branches and priorities are from interviews with Clarridge, December 28, 2001; Cannistraro, January 8, 2002; and Stanley Bedington, a senior analyst at the center from its founding, November 19, 2001, Rosslyn, Virginia (SC).

36. Interview with Clarridge, December 28, 2001.

37. Bedington's recollection that bin Laden's activities were first reported in CIA cables around 1985 is supported by an unclassified profile of bin Laden released by the agency in 1996. Drawing on agency reporting, the profile says, "By 1985, Bin Laden had drawn on his family's wealth, plus donations received from sympathetic merchant families in the Gulf region, to organize the Islamic Salvation Front. . . ."

38. Gates, *From the Shadows,* p. 349.

CHAPTER 8: "*INSHALLAH,*
YOU WILL KNOW MY PLANS"

1. Interview with Milton Bearden, November 15, 2001, Tysons Corner, Virginia (SC). "I want you to go out there and win" is from Milt Bearden and James Risen, *The Main Enemy,* p. 214.

2. "Uncle Milty" is from Robert Baer, *See*

No Evil, p. 142. Other quotations and anecdotes are from interviews with U.S. officials.

3. Interview with Milton Bearden, March 25, 2002, Tysons Corner, Virginia (SC).

4. Robert M. Gates, *From the Shadows,* p. 429.

5. Published accounts of the first Stinger shot include Mohammed Yousaf and Mark Adkin, *The Bear Trap,* pp. 175–76, and Milton Bearden, "Afghanistan, Graveyard of Empires," *Foreign Affairs,* pp. 21–22. Also Milt Bearden and James Risen, *The Main Enemy,* pp. 248–52. The incoming cable quoted is from Bearden and Risen. That the attack was recorded by a KH-11 is from interviews with U.S. officials. The Bearden quote describing the video is from the interview, November 15, 2001, and Bearden and Risen, *Main Enemy,* p. 252. That Reagan screened biopics of foreign visitors is from Bob Woodward, *Veil,* p. 249. George Crile, in *Charlie Wilson's War,* argues that the crucial groundwork for the introduction of the Stinger was laid by Wilson and his supporters.

6. Cable quoted by Gates, *From the Shadows,* p. 430.

7. This account of the CIA's agent network is from the author's interviews with three former and current U.S. officials. Interviews conducted by the author with British officials in 1992 also described their liaison with Massoud but provided no dates. The British liaison appears to have begun very early in the war. According to still-classified records of the Afghan covert action program, the CIA received authority to expand its unilateral agent network after NSDD-166 was signed in March 1985, but the Islamabad station would have had standing authority to recruit some agents earlier for routine espionage purposes. That CIA assistance to Massoud began in 1984, see note 37 of chapter 6.

8. Interviews with U.S. officials.

9. Ibid.

10.   Interview with Bearden, November 15, 2001.

11.   That bin Laden's house was in the University Town section of Peshawar is from Peter L. Bergen, *Holy War, Inc.,* p. 56. The description of the neighborhood is from the author's visits.

12.   Quotations and dates are from al-Zawahiri, *Knights Under the Prophet's Banner.* The English version is from the FBIS translation. The manuscript appeared to represent an effort by al-Zawahiri to publish a personal memoir and political manifesto before he was captured or killed by U.S. or coalition forces in Afghanistan. Some of the recollections in the manuscript may be constructed to promote al-Zawahiri's contemporary political agenda, but many of the dates and details of the political and theological arguments he writes about are consistent with other accounts.

13.   Azzam's biography details are from *Nida'ul Islam,* July–September 1996, and interviews with Arab journalists and activists who asked not to be further identified. See also Bergen, *Holy War,* pp. 51–54; Roy, *Afghanistan: From Holy War to Civil War,* p. 85; Mary Anne Weaver, *The New Yorker,* January 24, 2000. That the Tucson office opened in 1986 is from Judith Miller and Dale Van Natta, *The New York Times,* June 9, 2002.

14.   The Gates quotation is from Gates, *From the Shadows,* p. 349. "We should try . . . see them as the enemy" is from an interview with a U.S. official. "Actually did some very good things . . . anti-American" is from Bearden's interview with *Frontline,* "Hunting Bin Laden," March 21, 2000. The description of how the issue was viewed and debated within the U.S. intelligence community is from interviews with former U.S. officials.

15.   The account here and following of debates between bin Laden, Azzam, and other Arabs in Peshawar is drawn primarily from interviews with Arab journalists and activists who were in Peshawar at the time. Prince Turki described bin Laden's relationship with Azzam and al-Zawahiri in similar terms in an interview on August 2, 2002, Cancun, Mexico: "Bin Laden, I think, liked very much Abdullah Azzam . . . and was taken by the man's eloquence and personality." Published accounts of the debates among Peshawar Arab activists during this period include *The New York Times,* January 14, 2001.

16.   "A place steeped in cussedness" is from an interview with Peter Tomsen, former special envoy to the Afghan resistance, May 8, 2003, Washington, D.C. (SC). "Know my plans" is from an interview with an Arab activist who was in Peshawar at the time.

17.   Published accounts of the November 13, 1986, Politburo meeting on Afghanistan, citing Politburo archives, include Michael Dobbs, *The Washington Post,* November 16, 1992. Gates describes the same meeting in less detail in *From the Shadows,* p. 430. The quotations here are from English translations of Politburo records provided by Anatoly Chenyaev of the Gorbachev Foundation in Moscow to the Cold War International History Project, George Washington University, Washington, D.C.

18.   U.S. officials interviewed by the author in 1992 described the VEIL intelligence as a significant factor in the decision to push the escalation ratified by NSDD-166. The intelligence reporting is described in detail in the case study "Politics of a Covert Action" by Kirsten Lundberg, Philip Zelikow, and Ernest May, Harvard University, 1999.

19.   Gates, *From the Shadows,* p. 386.

20.   Quotations are from "The Costs of Soviet Involvement in Afghanistan," Directorate of Intelligence, CIA, Office of Soviet Analysis; originally classified Secret, February 1987. Published by National Security Archive; released by the CIA. Sanitized and declassified

version, 2000, CIA Special Collections. "It still looked as though" is from Milt Bearden and James Risen, *The Main Enemy*, p. 217.

21. Gorbachev's meetings and conversations are from archives and Politburo documents translated into English by the Gorbachev Foundation, provided by Anatoly Chenyaev to the Cold War International History Project, George Washington University, Washington, D.C.

22. Ibid.

23. All quotations about Casey's seizure and hospital discussions are from Joseph E. Persico, *Casey: From the OSS to the CIA*, pp. 551–57.

24. Details about the three commando teams are from Mohammed Yousaf and Mark Adkin, *The Bear Trap*, pp. 200–205, and from interviews with Yousaf in 1992. The satellite photos of Kazakhstan riots are from Gates, *From the Shadows*, p. 385.

25. Bearden's conversation with Clair George is from interviews with U.S. officials and from Bearden and Risen, *Main Enemy*, pp. 290–91. Bearden's call to Yousaf is from Yousaf and Adkin, *Bear Trap*, p. 205. In his memoir Bearden is careful to absolve Casey from all knowledge of the attacks on Soviet soil. According to Bearden, when he first went out to Islamabad, Clair George told him that Casey had plans to make propaganda radio broadcasts into Soviet Central Asia and that this idea faced resistance from the State Department. In his memoir Bearden blames Yousaf for the attacks. The involvement of Akhtar, then head of Pakistani intelligence, "remained in doubt."

26. Milton Bearden, "Afghanistan, Graveyard of Empires"; Bergen, *Holy War*, p. 57, citing in part translations of a slim biographical portrait of bin Laden in Arabic first published in 1991.

27. Ayman al-Zawahiri, *Knights Under the Prophet's Banner*, FBIS translation.

28. Quotations are from Arab journalists and from activists.

29. "Up to $25 million per month" is an estimate from Bearden in "Afghanistan." The question of which of the Afghan mujahedin parties received what percentage of ISI weapons was debated at great length during the late 1980s and early 1990s. Hamid Gul, Yousaf, and more than half a dozen U.S. officials directly involved all asserted that by the late 1980s, ISI and the CIA operated the pipeline by a rough rule of thumb: Hekmatyar received about 20 to 25 percent; Rabbani a similar amount; Younis Khalis and Sayyaf somewhat less. The three "moderate" factions recognized by ISI received 10 percent or less each. After 1987, ISI moved with CIA encouragement toward a system of "operational packaging" in which commanders, rather than political leaders, sometimes received weapons directly. What do all these statistics and supply system variations add up to? By all accounts the four main Islamists in the resistance—Hekmatyar, Rabbani, Khalis, and Sayyaf—received the greatest share of the official ISI-CIA-GID supply line. Hekmatyar himself probably did not receive as much raw material as the CIA's critics sometimes asserted, although he and Sayyaf clearly had the most access to private Arab funding and supplies, and Hekmatyar received preferential treatment by ISI's Afghan bureau for training and operations, especially after 1989. No detailed statistics about CIA's covert supplies have ever been formally published by the U.S. government.

30. Interviews with U.S. officials, including former congressional aides who made visits to Pakistan while Bearden was station chief.

31. Interviews with U.S. officials familiar with ISI's Afghan bureau during this period.

32. Bearden's dialogue with Hekmatyar is from Bearden and Risen, *Main Enemy*, pp. 282–83. Anderson, "a pretty good com-

mander . . . as many scalps" and Bearden, "much, much more time . . . very angry with me," are from *Afghan Warrior: The Life and Death of Abdul Haq,* a film by Touch Productions broadcast by the BBC, 2003. In his memoir, Bearden recalls his dialogue with Hekmatyar as confrontational and unyielding. The author has heard another account of their meetings from a well-informed U.S. official. This version supports Bearden's published account but is slightly different in tone. In this version Bearden tells Hekmatyar, "You don't like me, and I don't like you. I'm accused of giving you the lion's share. I wouldn't give you a fucking thing, but you've got commanders that are good." Hekmatyar replies, "I didn't say I didn't like you."

33. The English translations are from Politburo records provided by Anatoly Chenyaev of the Gorbachev Foundation to the Cold War International History Project.

34. Barnett R. Rubin, *The Search for Peace in Afghanistan,* pp. 83–84, partially quoting Shultz's memoirs.

35. Interview with Gates, March 12, 2002, Cleveland, Ohio (SC).

36. Gates, *From the Shadows,* pp. 424–25.

37. Archives and Politburo documents, from Anatoly Chenyaev of the Gorbachev Foundation, Cold War International History Project.

38. Gates, *From the Shadows,* pp. 430–31.

CHAPTER 9: "WE WON"

1. Biography details and quotation are from interviews with Edmund McWilliams, January 15 and February 26, 2002, Washington, D.C. (SC).

2. The cable, "From Amembassy Kabul to Secstate WashDC," January 15, 1988, is in the author's files.

3. Robert M. Gates, *From the Shadows,* pp. 431–32.

4. Director of Central Intelligence, "USSR: Withdrawal from Afghanistan," Special National Intelligence Estimate, March 1988, originally classified Secret; published by National Security Archive, Washington, D.C.

5. Interview with Milton Bearden, November 15, 2001, Tysons Corner, Virginia (SC).

6. The Gul quotation is from an interview with Gul, May 23, 2002, Rawalpindi, Pakistan (SC). The Defense Intelligence Agency profile was declassified and provided to the author in 1992. That Gul was close to Saudi intelligence then and later is from the author's interviews with Ahmed Badeeb and Saeed Badeeb, February 1, 2002, Jedda, Saudi Arabia (SC). That Americans thought he was sympathetic is from interviews with U.S. officials at the Islamabad embassy between 1989 and 1992. "Moderate Islamist" is from Milt Bearden and James Risen, *The Main Enemy,* p. 292.

7. Interview with Gul, May 23, 2002. Bearden, "only real strength . . . strayed into Afghanistan," is from Bearden and Risen, *Main Enemy,* pp. 235 and 238. Bearden's support for sending high-tech weapons to eastern Afghanistan, ibid., pp. 278–79.

8. Original interview with Sig Harrison published in *Le Monde Diplomatique* and quoted in Charles G. Cogan, "Shawl of Lead," *Conflict.*

9. Interviews with Milton Bearden, March 25, 2002, Tysons Corner, Virginia (SC).

10. Martin Ewans, *Afghanistan: A Short History of Its People and Politics,* p. 170.

11. Interviews with Bearden, March 25, 2002, and other U.S. and Pakistani officials. "Tell them not" is from the interview with Bearden. "Big-chested homecoming . . . Arizona plates" is from Bearden and Risen, *Main Enemy,* p. 345.

12. Interviews with U.S. officials. Bearden and Risen, *Main Enemy,* pp. 350–51.

13. Interview with Robert Oakley, February 15, 2002, Washington, D.C. (SC).

14. Ibid. See also Dennis Kux, *The United States and Pakistan,* p. 292.

15. Ahmed Rashid, *Taliban: Militant Islam, Oil, and Fundamentalism in Central Asia,* p. 89, citing an intelligence report presented to Prime Minister Nawaz Sharif in 1992.

16. Who McWilliams saw and what they told him are from interviews with McWilliams, January 15, 2002.

17. Barnett R. Rubin, *Fragmentation of Afghanistan,* p. 249.

18. Interviews with U.S. officials.

19. Interviews with Yahya Massoud, May 9 and 21, 2002, Kabul, Afghanistan (GW).

20. Cable in author's files. "For God's sake" is from an interview with Hamid Gailani, May 14, 2002, Kabul, Afghanistan (GW).

21. Interview with McWilliams, January 15, 2002.

22. The account of the embassy's reactions and the controversy over the earlier episode in Kabul are from interviews with several U.S. officials, including McWilliams, on January 15, 2002. The internal investigation described two paragraphs later is from McWilliams. Bearden's quoted views about Massoud are from Bearden and Risen, *Main Enemy,* p. 279. That Bearden saw Hekmatyar as "an enemy," ibid., p. 283. In his memoir Bearden not only describes Hekmatyar "as an enemy, and a dangerous one," but he also discounts "allegations that the CIA had chosen this paranoid radical as its favorite." But the record shows no evidence of CIA pressure on Hekmatyar during this period, and other U.S. officials say that CIA records from these months show a persistent defense of Hekmatyar by the agency.

23. Artyom Borovik, *The Hidden War,* pp. 161–62. KGB chief's tennis, ibid., p. 242. Polish ambassador, ibid., p. 239. Officer reading from book about 1904 Japan war, ibid., p. 233. Gromov on Massoud, ibid., p. 246. Last fatality, ibid., p. 278.

24. Bearden, "Afghanistan, Graveyard of Empires," *Foreign Affairs,* pp. 22–23.

25. Interview with Bearden, November 15, 2001. Also Bearden and Risen, *Main Enemy,* pp. 358–59.

26. From Robert Gates's unpublished original manuscript, p. 31/20, quoting Shevardnadze's memoir.

CHAPTER 10: "SERIOUS RISKS"

1. The account of two stations inside the embassy and the details of payments to Afghan commanders are from interviews with U.S. officials.

2. Multiple published accounts of the failed attack on Jalalabad describe the role of ISI, discussions within the Pakistani government, and the problems of the Afghan interim government. See Dennis Kux, *The United States and Pakistan, 1947–2000,* pp. 298–99; Mohammed Yousaf and Mark Adkin, *The Bear Trap,* pp. 227–31; Barnett R. Rubin, *The Fragmentation of Afghanistan,* p. 250; and Olivier Roy, *Afghanistan: From Holy War to Civil War,* p. 72. As Roy writes, "The Pakistani soldiers who pressed the guerrillas to join the conventional war in 1989 looked on Afghanistan as a 'headquarters operations map' upon which one moves little blue, red and green flags over a space where units are interchangeable and objectives quantifiable. As seen by Afghans, this was [a space] of tribes, ethnic groups, zones of influence of one chief or another."

3. The figure of "about $25 million" is from Rubin, *Fragmentation of Afghanistan;* he quotes U.S. diplomats citing reports that Saudi intelligence spent $26 million. The Gul quote is from the author's interview with Hamid Gul during 1992.

4. The characterizations here and in preceding paragraphs are drawn from interviews with Robert Oakley, February 15, 2002, Washington, D.C. (SC); Benazir Bhutto, May 5, 2002, Dubai, United Arab Emirates (GW); Mirza Aslam Beg, May 23, 2002,

Rawalpindi, Pakistan (SC); and Hamid Gul, May 23, 2002, Rawalpindi, Pakistan (SC); as well as with other U.S. officials and Pakistani officers. The conversation between Bhutto and Akhund, "I wonder if . . . turn out" is from Iqbal Akhund, *Trial and Error,* p. 38.

5. "Not some Johnnies" and "prepared to allow" are from Kux, *The United States and Pakistan,* p. 298. "Eyes blazing with passion" and "one week" are from the interview with Bhutto, May 5, 2002. "There can be no ceasefire . . . becomes *Darul Amn*" is from Akhund, *Trial and Error,* p. 177. In his memoir Bearden writes that he traveled through the Khyber Agency during the Jalalabad siege and found the battle "a halfhearted effort that senselessly piled up casualties on both sides." Milt Bearden and James Risen, *The Main Enemy,* p. 362. Bearden also writes that as he left Pakistan that summer, he presented Hamid Gul with a U.S. cavalry sword and tried to help Gul choose a university in America for his oldest son to attend. Some years later, Bearden acknowledges, "the CIA would describe the plucky little general as 'the most dangerous man in Pakistan.' And that, too, would be right." Ibid., p. 367.

6. Information on the Sarobi plan, the Peshawar meeting, and the truck supplies are from interviews with U.S. officials.

7. Interview with Gary Schroen, July 31, 2002, Washington D.C. (SC).

8. The estimate of the dollar value of Soviet monthly aid during this period is from Larry P. Goodson, *Afghanistan's Endless War,* p. 70.

9. CIA Stinger and sludge operations are from interviews with U.S. officials.

10. Ibid.

11. Ibid. Some U.S. officials interviewed referred to the Bush administration's renewed finding as "the bridge finding," meaning that it bridged U.S. covert policy from the Soviet

occupation period, now ended, with the final defeat of Najibullah, a Soviet client. Besides setting Afghan "self-determination" as an objective of CIA covert action, the Bush finding also set out humanitarian objectives for U.S. policy, as NSDD-166 had done earlier. These included the voluntary return of Afghan refugees from Pakistan and Iran. The full scope of this finding is not known, but it seems to have been a fairly modest revision of Reagan-era objectives, undertaken mainly to account for the withdrawal of Soviet troops.

12. Interview with Edmund McWilliams, January 15, 2002, Washington, D.C. (SC).

13. "To SecState WashDC Priority, Dissent Channel," June 21, 1989.

14. While reporting in Pakistan during this period, and later in London, the author heard this argument repeatedly from British diplomats and intelligence officers involved in the Afghan program.

15. "Just because a few white guys" is from a written communication from Milton Bearden to the author, July 5, 2003.

16. The characterization of the view of CIA officers is from interviews with Milton Bearden, November 15, 2001, Tysons Corner, Virginia (SC), and several other U.S. officials.

17. Oakley said that his "problem with McWilliams" was that McWilliams had a naïve, unrealistic desire to change U.S. policy that had been endorsed by the White House. By 1991, Oakley's own views seem to have shifted more in McWilliams's direction, but by then McWilliams was long gone from the embassy.

18. Letter from McWilliams to Oakley, July 23, 1989.

19. Interviews with U.S. officials.

20. The account of the Anderson-Bearden trip is from interviews with several U.S. officials, including Bearden, March 25, 2002,

Tysons Corner, Virginia (SC). Bearden later wrote and published a novel in 1998, *Black Tulip: A Novel of War in Afghanistan,* based on his tour as station chief in Islamabad. Bearden's fictional hero, Alexander, has a close encounter with a group of Algerian volunteers in the same eastern area of Afghanistan. In the novel Bearden writes a fantasy of revenge. An anti-Arab Afghan mujahedin commander lures the Algerians to a feast around a campfire and supplies a goat with "two claymore mines packed neatly inside the chest cavity." Most of the Algerians are killed when the mines detonate, and a survivor is tortured and killed by Afghans.

21. Interviews with U.S. officials.

22. Ibid.

23. Richard MacKenzie, reporting for *The Washington Times,* broke the story of the massacre on July 11, 1989, to the author's chagrin. See also Barnett R. Rubin, *The Fragmentation of Afghanistan,* pp. 250–51.

24. Interview with an Arab activist familiar with Azzam's visit with Massoud that summer. Olivier Roy, *Afghanistan: From Holy War to Civil War,* p. 86, also describes Azzam's journey that summer. So did Daoud Mir, an aide to Massoud, in interviews, July 31 and August 8, 2002, Washington, D.C. (GW). That Azzam compared Massoud to Napoleon is from Mir interviews. After meeting with Massoud, Roy writes, Azzam "endeavored to strike a balanced attitude" between Massoud and Hekmatyar.

25. The summary of the debates is drawn largely from interviews with two Arab participants. Al-Zawahiri's published writings make clear where he and bin Laden stood on theological questions.

26. Azzam is quoted by his son-in-law, Abdullah Anas, in *The New York Times,* January 14, 2001.

27. Multiple published accounts, including from Anas, ibid., describe a split among the Arab volunteers then in Peshawar after Azzam's death, and most accounts date to this period of bin Laden's emergence as the new head of al Qaeda, as he called the successor organizaton of Azzam's Office of Services. But the sequence of this split and takeover remains unclear. American intelligence dates al Qaeda's founding to 1988. Peter L. Bergen, *Holy War, Inc.,* p. 60, quotes the British military journalist and inveterate Afghan traveler Peter Jouvenal as seeing bin Laden rebuilding his base in Jaji in February 1989, months before Azzam's murder. "I witnessed them digging huge caves, using explosives and Caterpillar digging equipment," Jouvenal said. At the same time multiple accounts, including from the chief of staff of Saudi intelligence, Ahmed Badeeb, describe bin Laden leaving Pakistan with his family at some point during 1989 for his home in Jedda, Saudi Arabia. By late 1990, bin Laden is clearly back in Jedda, fomenting jihad in South Yemen. How all of these movements and activities by bin Laden overlap with the takeover and rebirth of al Qaeda under his leadership is not fully clear.

CHAPTER 11: "A ROGUE ELEPHANT"

1. Interviews with U.S. officials. Interview with Peter Tomsen, January 21, 2002, Omaha, Nebraska (SC). Also "Special Envoy to the Afghanistan Resistance," State Department action memorandum, April 19, 1989, declassified and released, March 23, 2000.

2. Interview with Tomsen, January 21, 2002, and with other U.S. officials.

3. Ibid. The CIA was under pressure from mujahedin supporters in Congress because of complaints from Afghan commanders about a sharp slowdown in weapons supplies. A Chinese factory dedicated to making rockets for Pakistani intelligence had burned down, and a major weapons depot in

Rawalpindi had been destroyed, either by accident or sabotage. As a result, large shipments to Pakistan had been delayed at a time when the carnage at Jalalabad was draining ordnance supplies.

4. The author has seen a copy of the document.

5. The account of the shift in U.S. policy is drawn primarily from interviews with U.S. officials, including Tomsen, January 21, 2002. The policy is outlined in State Department cables from late 1989 and early 1990 that were reviewed by the author. Tomsen began to discuss his plans for the commanders' *shura* publicly in early 1990. Barnett R. Rubin, *The Fragmentation of Afghanistan,* pp. 247–80, provides a detailed, carefully reported account of Afghan political-military developments and U.S. policy gyrations during this period.

6. Tomsen's travel to Pakistan, briefings to officials, and arguments with Harry are from interviews with U.S. officials. Harry: "Coming back" and "Why are you so anti-Hekmatyar?" are from interviews with U.S. officials. Twetten had participated in the interagency meeting and had signed off on the new policy on behalf of the CIA, according to Tomsen. He and others at the State Department saw the CIA's reversal as an effort to appease Pakistani intelligence, which was upset by the new policy direction.

7. Interview with Thomas Twetten, March 18, 2002, Washington, D.C. (SC).

8. Rubin, *Fragmentation of Afghanistan,* pp. 261–62.

9. The account in this chapter of the CIA's role in the winter offensive of 1989–90, including the details of the agency's payments to Massoud, are from interviews with U.S. officials.

10. That CIA unilateral agents reported to Islamabad that bin Laden was funding a

Hekmatyar coup attempt is from interviews with U.S. officials.

11. Rubin, *Fragmentation of Afghanistan,* p. 253. The author was in Pakistan at the time of the coup attempt and interviewed Pakistani, American, and, later, Afghan government officials and military officers about the events.

12. That the CIA had reports at the time that bin Laden had funded the Tanai coup attempt is from interviews with U.S. officials. The agency had sources among Afghan commanders and within Pakistani intelligence at the time, but it is not clear exactly where the reports about bin Laden's role came from.

13. Interview with Benazir Bhutto, May 5, 2002, Dubai, United Arab Emirates (GW). The no-confidence vote against Bhutto failed, but the army did forcibly remove her from office nine months later. According to Oakley, the American embassy in Islamabad concluded that Pakistani intelligence participated that winter and spring in conspiracies aimed at ousting Bhutto from power. Interview with Robert Oakley, February 15, 2002, Washington, D.C. (SC).

14. Rubin, *Fragmentation of Afghanistan,* p. 253, cites reports that funding for the Tanai coup attempt came from "ISI and Saudi intelligence."

15. Interview with Thomas Twetten, March 18, 2002. Twetten said he had no recollection of any "piece of paper" coming into Langley from the Islamabad station providing advanced word or planning about the Tanai coup, and he felt certain that he would remember that "if they had told us" about the coup attempt. "They never were honest with us on Hekmatyar," Twetten said. "When we insisted, they would arrange for a meeting with Hekmatyar, but it wasn't very often and it wasn't very productive, even in the best of times."

16. Interviews with U.S. officials. While serving as ambassador to the Afghan resistance, Tomsen met with Prince Turki seventeen times.

17. Interviews with Saudi officials.

18. The meeting of Massoud's representative Prince Bandar and Turki's funding for the commanders' *shura* are from interviews with U.S. officials and an aide to Massoud.

19. Funding levels and estimates of private Gulf money are from Rubin, *Fragmentation of Afghanistan,* p. 182.

20. Gorbachev Foundation, documents presented at "Towards an International History of Afghanistan," Cold War International History Project, Washington, D.C.

21. Interviews with U.S. officials.

22. That the CIA reported on the trucks rolling to arm Hekmatyar is from interviews with U.S. officials. Tomsen's meeting and the quotations from the cable to Washington: "SE Tomsen Meeting with Shura of Commanders Oct. 6," cable dated October 10, 1990, author's files.

23. Barnett R. Rubin, *The Search for Peace in Afghanistan,* p. 115, and interview with Tomsen, January 21, 2002. Lunch meeting between Tomsen and Harry is from interviews with U.S. officials. "Not only a horribly bad . . . Afghan political context," ibid.

24. Rubin, *Fragmentation of Afghanistan,* p. 254. Rubin, *Search for Peace,* p. 121.

25. The meeting between Turki and Massoud's representatives is from an interview with Daoud Mir, July 31, 2002, Washington, D.C. (GW). Mir recalled that when he finally met Turki at a palace in Jedda, he began complaining vociferously that Saudi intelligence had misunderstood Massoud for many years. He talked, he recalled, until a frustrated Turki covered his ears with his hands, indicating that he had heard enough.

26. The increase in Massoud's stipend and the struggle to ship weapons to the Panjshir are from interviews with U.S. officials.

27. "Sore on our backside" is from an interview with Maj. Gen. Mahmud Ali Durrani (Ret.), May 20, 2002, Rawalpindi, Pakistan (SC).

28. Dennis Kux, *The United States and Pakistan, 1947–2000,* p. 309.

29. Interview with Robert Oakley, February 15, 2002.

30. While traveling in Kashmir during this period, the author met with Kashmiri Islamist guerrillas who talked of their training in Afghanistan and displayed weapons clearly manufactured in China. The warning to Indian officials about sniper rifles is from interviews with U.S. officials in India during 1991.

31. Ahmed Badeeb interview with Orbit satellite network, early 2002; translated from original Arabic. See note 1 of chapter 4.

32. Ibid.

33. This account of bin Laden's meeting with Khalil and the senior prince is from an interview with Khalil A. Khalil, January 29, 2002, Riyadh, Saudi Arabia (SC). Khalil declined to identify the prince by name but said that "King Fahd is his direct uncle." This may have been Prince Turki.

34. Douglas Jehl, *The New York Times,* December 27, 2001.

35. Prince Turki, MBC television and *Arab News,* November 7, 2001. In an interview with ABC's *Nightline* on December 10, 2001, Turki cited bin Laden's proposals to lead an anti-Iraqi jihad as "the first signs of a disturbed mind, in my view." The implication is that Turki was untroubled by bin Laden prior to the autumn of 1990.

36. "Whereas before . . . as well as beyond" is from the memo "Démarche to Pakistan on Hekmatyar and Sayyaf Gulf Statements," January 28, 1991; excised and released April 6, 2000. The memo urges a

"strong approach to the GOP [Government of Pakistan], preferably by both the U.S. and Saudi Arabia," and also urges making the same points to Prince Bandar, the Saudi ambassador in Washington. Badeeb's trip is from an interview with Ahmed Badeeb, February 1, 2002, Jedda, Saudi Arabia (SC).

CHAPTER 12: "WE ARE IN DANGER"

1. The account in this chapter of the CIA covert action program to ship captured Iraqi armor, artillery, and other equipment to Pakistan for the Afghan rebels is drawn from interviews with multiple U.S. and Saudi officials. While working as a correspondent in Pakistan and Kabul, the author also reported on the program a few months after it began. Steve Coll, *Washington Post,* October 1, 1991.

2. Interviews with U.S. officials, including Peter Tomsen, January 21, 2002, Omaha, Nebraska (SC).

3. Charles Cogan, former chief of the Near East Division in the Directorate of Operations, wrote in 1990 that the Tanai coup "revealed, once again, that Gulbuddin, whatever his negative public image, leaves the other resistance leaders far behind in terms of tactics and maneuvering." Cogan acknowledged, however, that this "still did not make Gulbuddin a credible alternative to Najibullah." Not all of his former colleagues at the CIA accepted the second point. See Charles G. Cogan, "Shawl of Lead," *Conflict,* p. 197.

4. Barnett R. Rubin, *The Fragmentation of Afghanistan,* p. 255.

5. This account of CIA and State Department reporting about Arab radicals is from interviews with U.S. officials.

6. Interview with Milt Bearden, March 25, 2002, Tysons Corner, Virginia (SC).

7. "It is not the world" is from Joshua Tei-

telbaum, *Holier Than Thou,* p. 30. "Crusaders," ibid., p. 29. "Member of the establishment . . . against the regime" is from *Frontline,* "Hunting bin Laden," March 21, 2000. Mary Anne Weaver in *The New Yorker,* January 24, 2000, sees bin Laden increasingly "under the sway" of Hawali and another "awakening sheikh," Salman Awdah, during this period.

8. Teitelbaum, *Holier Than Thou,* pp. 32–36.

9. The spending of the Ministry of Pilgrimage and Religious Trusts and numbers of religious employees are from Teitelbaum, *Holier Than Thou,* p. 101. Fahd's offer of free Korans is from Alexei Vassiliev, *The History of Saudi Arabia,* p. 473. Saudi foreign minister Prince Saud al-Faisal traveled to Uzbekistan, Turkmenistan, Tajikistan, and Azerbaijan within weeks of the Soviet Union's formal dissolution early in 1992, opening Saudi embassies in Uzbekistan and Kazakhstan. Saud emphasized that Islam provided the foundation for Saudi relations in the Central Asian region. See Saleh al-Khatlan, "Saudi Foreign Policy Toward Central Asia," *Journal of King Abdulaziz University,* 2000.

10. Interviews with U.S. officials. Schroen's exchange with Prince Turki from interview with Gary Schroen, July 31, 2002, Washington D.C. (SC).

11. Interview with Prince Turki, August 2, 2002, Cancun, Mexico (SC).

12. Interviews with U.S. officials. That Hekmatyar, Sayyaf, and Haqqanni had offices in Saudi Arabia for mosque fund-raising is from written communication to the author from Peter Tomsen, May 3, 2003.

13. The account of the Saudi escort telling bin Laden that the Americans were out to kill him is from an interview with Vincent Cannistraro, January 8, 2002, Rosslyn, Virginia (SC). Cannistraro was chief of operations and analysis at the CIA's Counterterrorist Center during this period. He said the ac-

count had been provided to him by a long-time Saudi intelligence officer directly involved. A *New York Times* account published on January 14, 2001, based on extensive interviews with U.S. and Arab sources, reported that bin Laden later told "associates" that Saudi Arabia had hired the Pakistani intelligence service to kill him, although there was no evidence, the *Times* story said, that such a plot ever existed. There are various published accounts of bin Laden's forced departure from Saudi Arabia, which is generally dated to mid-1991, around the time of the Letter of Demands controversy within the kingdom. The former U.S. counterterrorism officials Daniel Benjamin and Steven Simon report that bin Laden first traveled to Afghanistan, then to Sudan. See their book, *The Age of Sacred Terror,* p. 110. Other accounts have him traveling initially to Pakistan. Peter L. Bergen, in *Holy War, Inc.,* p. 29, quotes trial testimony by former associates reporting that bin Laden arrived in Sudan with family and followers in his personal jet. For the interrogation statements of two bin Laden associates, see National Commission final report, p. 57.

14. Rubin, *Fragmentation of Afghanistan,* pp. 266–67.

15. Peter Tomsen, "An extremist seizure," is from "Afghan Policy—U.S. Strategy," September 26, 1991, excised and declassified March 23, 2000, author's files. "Scramble for power" is from "Afghanistan: Trends for 1992," December 16, 1991, excised and declassified March 23, 2000, author's files. Charles Cogan, reflecting a widely held outlook at the CIA, wrote in 1993 that "the partnership, if you will, between the United States and the Afghan resistance was of limited duration and could only have been so. The long-range aims of a country in which Islamists were at last beginning to have a say would not be, could not be, wholly compatible with the aims of a Western nation."

16. Interview with a U.S. official. The estimate of the number of tanks is uncertain. ISI officers interviewed by the author acknowledged being pressed by the CIA to destroy leftover Afghan equipment.

17. Interview with Edmund McWilliams, February 26, 2002, Washington, D.C. (SC) The size of Dostum's militia is from Rubin, *Fragmentation of Afghanistan,* p. 270. Rubin provides a definitive account of the internal collapse of the Najibullah regime and the fruitless negotiations by the United Nations early in 1992.

18. Michael Griffin, *Reaping the Whirlwind,* p. 5, quoting the *International Herald Tribune.*

19. The account of Hekmatyar's operations at Charasyab in April 1992 is drawn largely from an interview with an Arab journalist who was there. The author was in Kabul at the time and heard similar accounts from travelers in the region. The author visited Charasyab in 2002. Abdullah Anis, the son-in-law of Abdullah Azzam, an Algerian Islamist activist who was close to Massoud, has also published an account of the Massoud-Hekmatyar negotiations. His recollections of the radio exchange from Massoud's side are similar to those of the Arab journalist in Charasyab.

20. Interview with an Arab journalist then with Hekmatyar. Prince Turki has also acknowledged that bin Laden was in Peshawar at the time and participated in the peace talks. Turki told the Arab television network MBC on November 7, 2001, speaking of bin Laden, "He went there to work with other Islamic personalities who were trying to reconcile the Afghan mujahedin, who differed on the setting up of a government. I saw him among those personalities."

21. William Maley, "Interpreting the Taliban," in William Maley, ed., *Fundamentalism Reborn,* p. 9.

22. The author was in Kabul at the time and watched Massoud's forces rout Hek-

matyar over several days of intensive street fighting.

23. Interview with Yahya Massoud, May 9, 2002, Kabul, Afghanistan (GW).

24. Personal weapons: Rubin, *Fragmentation of Afghanistan*, p. 196. Estimates of total outside aid: Larry P. Goodson, *Afghanistan's Endless War*, p. 99.

25. Abdul Haq's letter to Tomsen is from *Afghan Warrior: The Life and Death of Abdul Haq*, Touch Productions, aired by the BBC, 2003. Tomsen memos: "Afghanistan—U.S. Interests and U.S. Aid," December 18, 1992, excised and declassified April 4, 2000, author's files; and "Central Asia, Afghanistan and U.S. Policy," February 2, 1993, excised and declassified March 23, 2000, author's files.

CHAPTER 13: "A FRIEND OF YOUR ENEMY"

1. "The heartbreak" is from Associated Press, June 17, 1992. "141 words" and "very much apart" are from David Halberstam, *War in a Time of Peace*, pp. 193 and 22. "A small blip" is from an interview with Anthony Lake, May 5, 2003, Washington, D.C. (GW).

2. "The biggest nuclear threat" is from the *Arkansas Democrat-Gazette*, September 27, 1991. "Strong special operations" is from *The Boston Globe*, February 2, 1992.

3. It had not been a major issue: Interview with Lake, May 5, 2003. Clinton's views about terrorism and Afghanistan are from interviews with senior U.S. officials close to the president.

4. Interview with Robert Gates, March 12, 2002, Cleveland, Ohio (SC).

5. Woolsey's trip to Little Rock and that he had met Clinton only once are from an interview with James Woolsey, February 20, 2002, Washington, D.C. (SC). His antiwar activities

and professional history are from Michael Gordon, *The New York Times*, January 11, 1993.

6. Interview with Woolsey, February 20, 2002.

7. Ibid. For a similar account of this scene, see Halberstam, *War in a Time of Peace*, p. 192.

8. Interview with Thomas Twetten, March 18, 2002, Washington, D.C. (SC).

9. What Clarridge concluded is from an interview with Duane Clarridge, December 28, 2001, Escondido, California (SC).

10. How Woolsey was perceived at the White House is from interviews with Clinton administration officials.

11. Interview with Woolsey, February 20, 2002.

12. Interviews with Clinton administration officials.

13. Kasi's background is from John Ward Anderson and Kamran Khan, *The Washington Post*, February 17, 1993. "Something big" is from Patricia Davis, *The Washington Post*, November 14, 2002.

14. Davis, *The Washington Post*, November 14, 2002. See also the *Post* coverage of the shootings by Bill Miller, Patricia Davis, D'Vera Cohn, Robert O'Harrow Jr., and Steve Bates, January 26, 1993.

15. The core source of nearly all published biographies of Yousef is the FBI witness statement produced from handwritten notes by FBI special agent Charles B. Stern and United States Secret Service officer Brian G. Parr. The notes were taken during their six-hour conversation with Yousef while flying back to the United States from Pakistan on February 7 and 8, 1995. According to Parr's testimony at Yousef's trial, Yousef refused to allow them to take notes while they spoke in a makeshift interview room at the back of the plane, so Stern and Parr each got up periodically and took summary notes out of

Yousef's sight, in another part of the plane. The notes were dictated on February 9. The details about his uncle, Khalid Sheikh Mohammed, and his great-uncle, Mohammed's father, are from Finn et al., *The Washington Post,* March 9, 2003.

16. During one of his FBI interviews, Yousef acknowledged that after the World Trade Center bombing, while he was a fugitive, his parents knew that he was responsible for the attack and on the run from American authorities. Yousef said that his parents had moved to Iran. Certainly they would have been safer there than in Pakistan, less vulnerable to police or government pressure. While in Iran, Yousef said, his parents received a phone call from a woman purporting to be from an American phone company who was looking to locate Yousef about a billing issue. Yousef told the story to indicate that he and his parents had assumed the caller was from the FBI and that they had dodged the inquiry.

17. Yousef complained repeatedly during his interviews with the FBI about his lack of funds. He said that he had "borrowed" money from friends in Peshawar who did not know about his plans. The World Trade Center attack was a threadbare operation in many respects. Yousef, however, was able to purchase a first-class ticket to Pakistan when he made his escape after the bombing.

18. "Attack a friend" is from the statement by FBI special agent Stern and Secret Service officer Parr, February 7 and 8. They placed the phrase in quotes.

19. A photocopy of the letter was introduced as evidence at Yousef's trial. The brief narrative of the attack is from transcripts of opening statements delivered at the trial.

20. Daniel Benjamin and Steven Simon, *The Age of Sacred Terror,* p. 13. The authors were counterterrorism officials at the Na-

tional Security Council during Clinton's second term.

21. Interview with Woolsey, February 20, 2002; interview with Stanley Bedington, senior intelligence analyst at the Counterterrorist Center during this period, November 19, 2001, Rosslyn, Virginia (SC); and interviews with other U.S. officials.

22. That the personal histories of Yousef and Kasi were murky and that Iranian-sponsored terrorism "was *the* priority" are from the interview with Lake, May 5, 2003. "Sudafed" is from the interview with Bedington, November 19, 2001.

23. This account of the center's budgetary pressures is from interviews with U.S. officials. By this account the pressure eased after 1996 when domestic terrorist attacks led Congress to open its purse for counterterrorism programs governmentwide. Since the September 11 attacks there have been contradictory assertions about how aggressively counterterrorism efforts were funded by Clinton and Congress. Benjamin and Simon assert, for instance, that the White House provided budget increases to the CIA's Counterterrorist Center. CIA officials have been quoted in news reports as saying they did not do well in budgetary struggles even during the second term. Since the relevant budgets are all highly classified, it is difficult to resolve the contradictions with any confidence. Clearly the second Clinton term was better for counterterrorism budgets than the first. A separate issue is whether other cuts at the CIA during this period in the Directorate of Operations, on which the center heavily depended, merely shifted the burden of the budget problems from one CIA office to another. This, too, is a difficult question to resolve without fuller access to the classified budgets.

24. That the center had no more than one

hundred personnel during this time and its branch structure are from·the interview with Bedington, November 19, 2001.

25. Interview with Larry Johnson, deputy director of the State Department's counter-terrorism office during this period, January 15, 2002, Bethesda, Maryland (SC). Clinton signed two important policy documents on terrorism, Presidential Decision Directive-35 and Presidential Decision Directive-39, during the first six months of 1995. See chapter 16.

26. This history draws from the staff report of Eleanor Hill, staff director of the Joint Intelligence Committee Inquiry into the events of September 11, issued October 8, 2002.

27. Benjamin and Simon are especially forceful in their criticisms of the FBI's internal culture. They quote Clinton's former national security adviser, Samuel Berger, and deputy national security adviser James Steinberg complaining that they could not extract crucial information from the FBI about a wide variety of subjects including terrorism. Benjamin and Simon write, "For the NSC staff working on counterterrorism, this was crippling—but how crippling was also something they could not know. Every day a hundred or more reports from the CIA, DIA, the National Security Agency, and the State Department would be waiting in their computer queues when they got to work. There was never anything from the FBI. The Bureau, despite its wealth of information, contributed nothing to the White House's understanding of al-Qaeda. Virtually none of the information uncovered in any of the Bureau's investigative work flowed to the NSC." *Age of Sacred Terror,* p. 304.

28. Eleanor Hill, Joint Intelligence Committee Inquiry staff report, October 8, 2002.

29. The record of a Woolsey and Lake discussion about bin Laden is from two former senior Clinton administration officials. One of the officials recalled that the memo of the conversation had been prepared by either George Tenet or Richard Clarke, who both later figured heavily in the Clinton administration's covert campaign against bin Laden. This official also believed that the discussion concerned evidence that bin Laden was funding violence by Somali militiamen against American troops. The quotations from and descriptions of CIA reports and cables about bin Laden are from the Joint Inquiry Committee's final report, Appendix, pp. 5–6.

30. "Did we screw up ... Of course" interview with Lake, May 5, 2003.

CHAPTER 14: "MAINTAIN A PRUDENT DISTANCE"

1. After working first as chief of analysis and then as deputy director of the CIA's Counterterrorist Center from 1993 until 1999, Pillar spent a year as a visiting scholar at the Brookings Institution in Washington, where he completed a book, *Terrorism and U.S. Foreign Policy,* that was published shortly before the September 11 attacks. The book is a thorough and scholarly review of the modern terrorist threat and American policy instruments for containing it, and it provides a rich archive of Pillar's own analytical outlook. The account of Pillar's views in this chapter is based partially on his book and other published journal articles, as well as on multiple interviews with U.S. officials familiar with CIA Counterterrorist Center analysis during this period. Among those who spoke on the record about the 1993–94 period were former CIA director James Woolsey; Stanley Bedington, a senior analyst at the center until 1994; and Thomas Twetten, chief of the CIA's Directorate of Operations during this period.

2. Mary Anne Weaver, *A Portrait of Egypt,* provides a richly reported account of the rise of the Islamic Group and its roots in the Upper Nile. Human Rights Watch and Amnesty

International have accumulated thorough records of the atrocities in the Algerian conflict after the elections were canceled.

3. This summary of the muddled debates in Washington over the challenge of Islamist insurgencies in North Africa is drawn from interviews with multiple participants, some located at the White House and others at the State Department and the CIA.

4. One issue in the liaison was the routine use of torture against detainees by Egyptian counterterrorist units. The CIA and the State Department tried to calibrate their funding to encourage Egyptian reforms without breaking off the liaison, according to officials involved. At one stage during the mid-1990s the CIA suspended funding to a certain Cairo unit because of its repeated human rights abuses, two officials involved said in interviews. The details of these counterterrorist aid programs and human rights policy decisions remain highly classified, and the extent of American pressure on Egyptian security units is difficult to describe with any confidence. In any event, according to human rights monitors, Egyptian police continued to make widespread use of torture. That the U.S. sent its first declared CIA station chief to Algiers in 1985 is from the author's interview with Whitley Bruner, February 26, 2002, Washington, D.C. (SC). Bruner was the declared station chief. He left Algiers in 1989 and afterward served in the Tunis and Tel Aviv stations before retiring in 1997.

5. Interview with Bruner, February 26, 2002.

6. Ibid.

7. Interviews with former CIA officials in the Near East Division.

8. Interviews with U.S. officials, including officials who consumed CIA intelligence from Saudi Arabia and others familiar with its collection. In an interview, a former British intelligence official who worked in his government's Saudi Arabia station and later in the Middle East department at headquarters said he was told by CIA colleagues in Riyadh during this period that station policy heavily limited their ability to recruit sources in the kingdom on sensitive subjects, including Islamic radicalism.

9. The information concerning Turki's exchange of letters with Clinton is from interviews with Saudi officials. The White House meeting is from interviews with Saudi and U.S. officials. A similar account of the meeting is in the *Los Angeles Times,* July 14, 1996.

10. *The New York Times,* August 23, 1993.

11. For an account of the January–February massacres in Kabul, see Michael Griffin, *Reaping the Whirlwind,* p. 30. The estimate of ten thousand civilian deaths from fighting during 1993 is from Ahmed Rashid, *Taliban: Militant Islam, Oil, and Fundamentalism,* p. 226. See also Larry P. Goodson, *Afghanistan's Endless War,* pp. 74–75.

12. That Prince Turki worked with Hamid Gul during this period is from Charles Cogan, former CIA Near East Division chief in the Directorate of Operations, writing in "Partners in Time," *World Policy Journal,* p. 78, as well as from interviews with Saudi, Pakistani, and U.S. officials. The portrait of Javed Nasir's Islamist outlook is from interviews with multiple Pakistani officials, including his successor as ISI director-general, Lt. Gen. Javed Ashraf Qazi (Ret.), May 19, 2002, Rawalpindi, Pakistan (SC).

13. To: SECSTATE Washington, D.C., February 5, 1993, "Implications of Continued Stalemate . . . ," author's files.

14. That the White House did no policy review on Afghanistan during the first Clinton term is from multiple interviews with former Clinton White House and State Department officials. Christopher's outlook and Raphel's background are from interviews with former Clinton administration officials. David Halberstam's *War in a Time of Peace* provides a deep

account of foreign policy formation during the first Clinton term and the heavy priorities accorded to Clinton's domestic policy agenda.

15. What Raphel argued is from interviews with former Clinton administration officials. Quotations are from the author's interviews with officials who declined to be further identified.

16. "A place where" is from the interview with Woolsey, February 20, 2002, Washington, D.C. (SC).

17. Interview with Thomas Twetten, March 18, 2002, Washington, D.C. (SC).

18. "Just really background," ibid.

19. Cogan, "Partners in Time," *World Policy Journal,* p. 82.

CHAPTER 15: "A NEW GENERATION"

1. Cofer Black's biography and Khartoum station profile in 1993 are from interviews with U.S. officials. Black testified before the Joint Inquiry Committee on September 26, 2002. He referred to his service in Sudan in passing during his testimony. Later he became the State Department's counterterrorism coordinator.

2. That the Operating Directive was limited to intelligence collection and did not authorize covert action to disrupt bin Laden is from the author's interviews with U.S. officials. In prepared testimony for the Joint Inquiry Committee on October 17, 2002, CIA director George Tenet said, "As early as 1993, our units watching [bin Laden] began to propose action to reduce his organization's capabilities." The statement suggests that case officers may have proposed specific covert action plans from Khartoum to their superiors at Langley that were turned down.

3. Interviews with U.S. officials.

4. The Saudi-Egyptian intelligence report is from "Usama bin Ladin: Islamic Extremist

Financier," publicly released CIA assessment, 1996.

5. Evidence later showed that bin Laden had by now paid for terrorist and paramilitary operations in Yemen, against a hotel occupied by American soldiers, and in Somalia, against U.S. Army Rangers fighting Somali Islamic militias. The CIA and FBI did not learn of bin Laden's involvement in these plots until several years later. A key breakthrough came in the summer of 1996 when a close bin Laden aide, Jamal al-Fadl, who had been embezzling funds, defected from al Qaeda and walked into the U.S. embassy in Eritrea to provide testimony in exchange for asylum.

6. The general portrait of bin Laden's business activities and his $50 million bank investment are from "Usama bin Ladin: Islamic Extremist Financier," the CIA assessment released in 1996. Specific land purchases and office details are from testimony of Jamal al-Fadl in the federal trial of al Qaeda members who attacked the U.S. embassies in Nairobi, Kenya, and Dar es Salaam, Tanzania, February 6, 2001.

7. Fadl testimony, February 6, 2001.

8. "Talk about jihad," ibid. Bin Laden's movements and wariness are from Fadl testimony and author's interviews with U.S. officials.

9. The Khartoum assassination attempt has been described in many published accounts, although sometimes the details vary slightly. The version here is from interviews with U.S. officials with access to CIA reporting.

10. Jamal al-Fadl was the embezzler. How bin Laden treated him is from his 2001 court testimony, February 6, 2001.

11. "Insatiable carnal desires" is from Joshua Teitelbaum, *Holier Than Thou,* p. 58. By the CIA's count in "Usama bin Ladin: Islamic Extremist Financier," 1996, his Advi-

sory and Reformation Committee issued "over 350 pamphlets critical of the Saudi government." Greater Hijaz and Greater Yemen are from Teitelbaum, *Holier Than Thou,* pp. 77–78.

12. Interviews with U.S. and British officials.

13. Prince Turki discussed the effort in an interview with ABC's *Nightline* on December 10, 2001: "His mother went to see him. His uncle—his uncle was eighty years old. He went to see him in Sudan to try to convince him to come back." Bin Laden's quotations are from Peter L. Bergen, *The Holy War,* p. 89. His $1 million allowance is from National Commission staff statement no. 15, p. 3–4.

14. Bakr quotation is from Bergen, ibid. How senior Saudi princes thought of bin Laden in this period is from interviews with Saudi officials.

15. In his congressional testimony on September 26, 2002, Black referred to bin Laden's attempt to kill him but provided no details. This account is from interviews with U.S. officials.

16. Daniel Benjamin and Steven Simon, *The Age of Sacred Terror,* pp. 242–43.

17. Five contemporaneous witness interview reports, produced as evidence in Yousef's trial, document in detail the conversations between Yousef and U.S. federal agents immediately after his arrest. See note 15 in chapter 13. In addition, Parr testified twice at federal trials about his rendition of Yousef and their conversations aboard the jet that brought Yousef from Islamabad to New York. Parr testified on August 12, 1996, in the Manila airline bombings case and on October 22, 1997, in Yousef's World Trade Center bombing case. The description of Yousef's shackling and examination aboard the plane is from Parr's testimony. Quotations are used only where the reports themselves indicate exact quotations.

18. Interview with Fred Hitz, CIA inspector general during this period, March 8, 2002, Princeton, New Jersey (SC). Stephen Dycus et al., *National Security Law,* provides a detailed account of the legal issues.

19. Witness interview report by FBI Special Agent Bradley J. Garrett, dictated February 7, 1995, transcribed February 10, 1995.

20. Witness interview report by FBI special agent Bradley J. Garrett, "Pakistan to U.S. Airspace," dictated and transcribed February 8, 1995.

21. Discussions of motive and quotations, ibid.

22. Witness interview report by FBI Special Agent Charles B. Stern and Brian G. Parr, United States Secret Service, "Aircraft in Flight," dictated February 9, 1995, transcribed February 28, 1995.

23. Yousef's comments about his flight to Pakistan, who aided him in Manila, and bin Laden, ibid.

24. The information about the guest house owned by bin Laden is from multiple published sources, including Benjamin and Simon, *Age of Sacred Terror,* p. 237. Yousef had also spent many hours at the International Islamic University in Islamabad where Abdullah Azzam first lectured when he came to Pakistan, according to Mary Anne Weaver, *A Portrait of Egypt,* p. 196.

25. Stern and Parr witness interview report, "Aircraft in Flight," February 9, 1995.

26. Khalid Sheikh Mohammed has recently been described by U.S. officials as a suspected mastermind of the September 11 attacks. He was arrested in Rawalpindi, Pakistan, on March 1, 2003, by Pakistani police and intelligence officers. Most accounts sketch his life in tracks that run parallel to Ramzi Yousef's: of Pakistani origin but raised in Kuwait and educated in engineering in the West. Mohammed briefly attended a Baptist

college in North Carolina before transferring to North Carolina A&T, a historically black university, where he studied mechanical engineering. He reportedly told American interrogators that he joined the Muslim Brotherhood at age 16.

27. *The New York Times,* June 9, 2002.

28. Morocco attack, *The New York Times,* January 14, 2001. Air France hijacking and Eiffel Tower kamikaze plan from Eleanor Hill, Joint Inquiry Staff Statement, September 18, 2002. Belgian manual, *The New York Times,* January 14, 2001. Mindanao attack, *Asiaweek,* May 5, 1995. For a thorough account of the Mubarak assassination attempt, see Weaver, *A Portrait of Egypt,* pp. 174–77. Threat to Lake, Benjamin and Simon, *Age of Sacred Terror,* p. 244. Among the multiple published accounts of the Riyadh bombing, Teitelbaum, *Holier Than Thou,* pp. 73–74, has substantial detail. Among the multiple accounts of the bombing of the Egyptian embassy in Islamabad, al-Zawahiri, *Knights Under the Prophet's Banner,* provides the perspective of one of the conspirators.

29. Eleanor Hill, Joint Inquiry Staff Statement, September 18, 2002.

30. Woolsey's December visit and CIA reporting on Shiite threats during 1995 are from "Senate Select Committee on Intelligence Staff Report on the Khobar Towers Terrorist Attack," September 12, 1996. That Hezbollah was the reported source of the threat against Lake is from an interview with a Clinton administration official. "Out of nowhere" is from the author's interview with Prince Turki, August 2, 2002, Cancun, Mexico (SC). Saudi Shiites with links to Iranian intelligence services detonated a truck bomb near a U.S. Air Force apartment compound called Khobar Towers in eastern Saudi Arabia on June 25, 1996, killing nineteen American airmen and wounding hundreds of others. The CIA's Riyadh station, the Defense Intelligence Agency, and Saudi intelligence detected the Shiite terrorist threat in the kingdom many months before the Khobar bombing occurred. The September 12 staff report describes intelligence reporting and protection planning in Saudi Arabia during 1995 in some detail. After the Khobar bombing, Saudi Arabia's Interior Ministry was slow to cooperate with FBI investigators, creating new tensions in the U.S.-Saudi relationship.

31. Federal Register, Executive Order 12947, January 25, 1995. The failure to list al Qaeda in 1995 is difficult to understand, given the steady stream of reporting then in hand at the CIA about bin Laden's contacts in Khartoum with anti-Israeli groups such as Hamas, Hezbollah, Algeria's Armed Islamic Group, Egypt's Islamic Group, and some even more radical Egyptian factions. At that point, however, al Qaeda had not formally declared war on the United States or Israel, and it had not been directly implicated in any terrorist attacks. Later, in 1997, the State Department released its first list of officially designated Foreign Terrorist Organizations, and it did not include al Qaeda on that list, either. By then the evidence about al Qaeda's global terrorism was far more substantial and far more widely available on the public record. The State Department's counterterrorism coordinator at the time, Philip C. Wilcox, said in February 1995 that while "there are informal contacts among Islamists . . . there is little hard evidence of a coordinated international network or command and control apparatus among these groups." Benjamin and Simon, in *Age of Sacred Terror,* quote Robert Blitzer, who was in charge of the FBI's international terrorism division until 1996, as saying that until his departure, "the community kept saying ad hoc terrorists and loosely affiliated terrorists and I didn't agree. . . . I thought this was some kind of major network. We just didn't have

enough of an intelligence base, didn't know how bin Laden and others were commanding it, how they moved people and how they moved money. We didn't have that information sorted out."

32. Interviews with Saudi officials and U.S. officials. Among the former Riyadh CIA station chiefs who were consultants for Prince Turki was Ray Close, who had run the station during the 1970s. Another station chief from a later period retired to Spain on a Saudi consultancy, according to his former colleagues. A number of Middle East specialists from Britain's MI6 intelligence service also acquired retainer contracts. Frank Anderson, the CIA's Near East Division chief, who had argued that the jihadists from Afghanistan were not a major factor in North African Islamist insurgencies, left the agency in 1995. He soon joined a Washington consultancy that maintained close ties with the Saudi government.

33. The author is grateful to Walter Pincus who first reported on this document in *The Washington Post* on June 6, 2002, and who provided a copy of the passages analyzing Sunni Islamic terrorism.

34. Ibid. All quotations are from the document.

35. The estimate remains classified, but CIA director George Tenet quoted from it at length in his October 17, 2002, prepared testimony to the Joint Inquiry Committee investigating the September 11 attacks. Eleanor Hill also quoted portions of the estimate in her September 18, 2002, Joint Inquiry Staff Statement. The quotations here are from Tenet's testimony, except for "new breed," which is from the Joint Inquiry Committee's final report, p. 4, and "As far as . . . his associates," from the final report, p. 313.

36. Ibid. "New terrorist phenomenon" from National Commission, staff statement no. 5, p. 1–2. Estimate title from staff statement no. 11, p. 4.

CHAPTER 16: "SLOWLY, SLOWLY SUCKED INTO IT"

1. The account of Durrani's ascension is drawn primarily from Olaf Caroe, *The Pathans,* pp. 254–55, and Martin Ewans, *Afghanistan: A Short History of Its People and Politics,* pp. 22–23. A former British officer in the tribal areas of Pakistan and Afghanistan, Caroe draws on multiple original and imperial sources.

2. Caroe, *The Pathans.* He attributes the story of Durrani's selection at the *jirga* to the 1905 autobiography of the "Iron Amir" of Afghanistan, Abdur Rahman, who recorded the story as it was recounted "in the Kabul annals." Whatever its basis in fact, the story's themes—Durrani's humble silence and the attempt by more powerful khans to choose a weak king—became an oft-repeated, shaping narrative of Afghan politics.

3. Ibid., pp. 251–85. The first dynasty of Durrani royals passed from Ahmed Shah through his son Timur, located in the Saddozai Popalzai tribal branch. The second and third dynasties, terminating with King Zahir Shah in 1973, drew its leaders from the Mohammedzai Barakzai tribal branch.

4. The Naqibullah quotation is from Jon Lee Anderson, *The New Yorker,* January 28, 2002. Anderson had traveled in southern Afghanistan during the anti-Soviet jihad and had spent weeks in a mujahedin encampment overseen by Naqibullah. After the Taliban lost Kandahar in December 2001, Anderson met up with Naqibullah again and spent several days in his company. He saw that the warlord was carrying a prescription written in Germany for antipsychotic medication and asked him about it, prompting Naqibullah's explanation.

5. Interview with Spozhmai Maiwandi, a Pashtun broadcaster with Voice of America who chronicled the Taliban's rise and spoke regularly with Mullah Omar and other Tal-

iban leaders, March 28, 2002, Washington, D.C. (GW). Maiwandi's frequent interviews with the Taliban on VOA's Pashto-language service led some other Afghans, especially those loyal to Ahmed Shah Massoud, to denounce the U.S.-funded radio service as pro-Taliban. VOA's reputation in turn fueled suspicions in the region that the Taliban was an instrument of U.S. policy.

6. The account of the rural roots of the Taliban is mainly from Olivier Roy, "Has Islamism a Future in Afghanistan?," in William Maley, ed., *Fundamentalism Reborn,* pp. 204–11, as well as from interviews with Maiwandi and other Kandahar Pashtuns. Ahmed Rashid's *Taliban: Militant Islam, Oil, and Fundamentalism in Central Asia* is the definitive book-length account of the movement. Michael Griffin, *Reaping the Whirlwind,* and Larry P. Goodson, *Afghanistan's Endless War,* also provide detailed accounts of the movement's origins and rise.

7. Rashid, *Taliban,* pp. 90–91, reports that the *madrassa* long funded about four hundred places for Afghan students. In 1999 it had fifteen thousand applicants. Rashid quotes the Haqqannia's leader, Pakistani politician Samiul Haq, complaining that Pakistani intelligence ignored his *madrassa* during the anti-Soviet jihad, favoring a network of Muslim Brotherhood– linked religious schools affiliated with Jamaat-e-Islami and Hekmatyar. Jamaa-e-Islami was the Islamist political rival to Haq's political party.

8. Martin Ewans, *Afghanistan: A Short History of Its People and Politics,* p. 204. For deeper accounts of the roots of the School of Islamic Studies at Deoband and its role in Muslim theology and anticolonial movements, Ewans recommends A. A. Rizvi, *A History of Sufism in India,* two volumes, 1978 and 1983, and Rizvi's *History of Dar al-Ulum Deoband,* 1980.

9. Rashid, *Taliban,* pp. 87–94.

10. Interview with Hashmat Ghani Ahmadzai, May 12, 2002, Kabul, Afghanistan (GW).

11. Interview with Qayum Karzai, May 19, 2002, Kabul, Afghanistan (GW), and with Hamid Karzai, October 21, 2002, Kabul, Afghanistan (SC).

12. This account of Karzai's detention by Fahim, his interrogation, and the circumstances of his escape is drawn from interviews with multiple sources involved in the episode, including Qayum Karzai, May 19, 2002, and Afghan vice president Hedayat Amin-Arsala, May 21, 2002, Kabul, Afghanistan (GW). Amin-Arsala was foreign minister at the time of Karzai's detention. Amin-Arsala was never certain who ordered Karzai's arrest: "I'm not really quite sure if [then Afghan president Rabbani] ordered his arrest. But certainly the intelligence people, who were headed by Fahim, they knew."

13. Interview with Hamid Karzai, October 21, 2002.

14. That Karzai provided $50,000 in cash and a large cache of weapons is from Karzai's interview with Ahmed Rashid, *The Daily Telegraph,* December 8, 2001. Why Karzai supported the Taliban and that many Pashtuns hoped they would lead to the king's return are from interviews with Qayum Karzai, May 19, 2002; Hedayat Amin-Arsala, May 21, 2002; Hashmat Ghani Ahmadzai, May 12, 2002; and Zalmai Rassoul, May 18, 2002, Kabul, Afghanistan (GW).

15. Even Omar's birth year is uncertain. Rashid, *Taliban,* p. 23, places Omar's birth "sometime around 1959." An undated CIA biographical fact sheet about Omar describes his birth as "circa 1950." Each of these dates has been used in various press accounts to estimate Omar's age, compounding the confusion. The account given to U.S. diplomats is from the declassified State Department cable "Finally, a Talkative Talib,"

from Islamabad to Washington, February 20, 1995, released by the National Security Archive.

16. CIA fact sheet, ibid. Omar's ties to Bashar and "charismatic nor articulate" are from "Finally, a Talkative Talib," ibid.

17. Taliban legend, Associated Press, September 20, 2001. Red Cross, *Sunday Times,* September 23, 2001.

18. *The Washington Post,* December 27, 2001.

19. *Toronto Star,* December 9, 2001.

20. "A simple band . . . goal" is from *Time,* October 1, 2001. "The Taliban . . . our people" is from the Associated Press, September 20, 2001.

21. Roy, "Has Islamism a Future in Afghanistan?," p. 211. "Of course, the problem with the Taliban is that they mean what they say," Roy wrote three years after their initial emergence. "They do not want a King, because there is no King in Islam. . . . The Taliban are not a factor for stabilization in Afghanistan."

22. Interview with Benazir Bhutto, May 5, 2002, Dubai, United Arab Emirates (GW). This section is also drawn in part from interviews with Pakistani officials close to Bhutto.

23. The Bhutto quotations are from the Benazir Bhutto interview, May 5, 2002.

24. Ibid.

25. All quotations, ibid.

26. Interview with Lt. Gen. Javed Ashraf Qazi (Ret.), May 19, 2002, Rawalpindi, Pakistan (SC). Qazi was the director-general of Pakistani intelligence at the time. "This was seventeen tunnels!" he said. "Seventeen tunnels full of arms and ammunition. Enough to raise almost half the size of Pakistan's army." The dump had been created just before the end of the anticommunist phase of the Afghan war. "Both sides, they pumped in an immense amount of weapons. . . . And dumps were created." Other detailed accounts of the seizure of the Spin Boldak dump include Anthony Davis, "How the Taliban Became a Military Force," in Maley, ed., *Fundamentalism Reborn,* pp. 45–46, Rashid, *Taliban,* pp. 27–28, and Rashid, "Pakistan and the Taliban," in Maley, ed., *Fundamentalism Reborn,* p. 81. Rashid, citing interviews with Pakistani military officials and diplomats, estimates the dump held about eighteen thousand AK-47 assault rifles and 120 artillery pieces.

27. The extent of Babar's involvement with the Taliban at the time of their emergence remains unclear. A boastful man, Babar fueled suspicion that he had created and armed the movement by introducing Taliban leaders to the likes of Prince Turki, the Saudi intelligence chief, and calling them "my children." But several associates of Babar said these quotes have been blown out of proportion and they mainly reflect Babar's habits of blustery speech.

28. Mullah Naqibullah, one of Kandahar's dominant warlords at the time, said that as the Taliban swept into the city, he and other local Pashtun powers were urged by Hamid Karzai, other Pashtun leaders, and President Rabbani in Kabul not to fight against the Taliban. For Rabbani and Massoud the Taliban initially looked like a Pashtun force that could hurt their main enemy, Hekmatyar.

29. Davis, "How the Taliban Became a Military Force," pp. 48–49.

30. Interview with Qazi, May 19, 2002.

31. Interview with Bhutto, May 5, 2002. The CIA reported on the links between ISI's Afghan training camps and the Kashmir insurgency during this period, at one point threatening to place Pakistan on the U.S. list of nations deemed to be terrorist sponsors.

32. All quotations from "chap in Kandahar" through "all of them" are from the interview with Qazi, May 19, 2002.

33. All quotations from "I became slowly"

through "carte blanche" are from the interview with Bhutto, May 5, 2002.

34. Rashid, "Pakistan and the Taliban," p. 86, describes the internal ISI debate about the Taliban during 1995. "The debate centered around those largely Pashtun officers involved in covert operations on the ground who wanted greater support for the Taliban, and other officers who were involved in longer term intelligence gathering and strategic planning who wished to keep Pakistan's support to a minimum so as not to worsen tensions with Central Asia and Iran. The Pashtun grid in the army high command eventually played a major role in determining the military and ISI's decision to give greater support to the Taliban."

35. Interview with Bhutto, May 5, 2002.

36. Interview with Ahmed Badeeb, February 1, 2002, Jedda, Saudi Arabia (SC).

37. Scene and quotations, ibid.

38. Ibid. See note 27.

39. Turki's interview with MBC, November 6, 2001.

40. After Hekmatyar was forced into exile by the Taliban, he visited Prince Turki in Saudi Arabia, hoping for assistance, according to Saudi officials. When a stunned Turki asked Hekmatyar why the kingdom should help him when he had denounced the royal family in its time of need in 1991, Hekmatyar shrugged obsequiously. His speeches then had been "only politics," he said, according to the Saudi account.

41. That Saudi intelligence paid cash bonuses to ISI officers is from an interview with a Saudi analyst. That Saudi Arabia subsidized Pakistan with discounted oil is from multiple interviews with Saudi officials. That Saudi intelligence preferred to deal directly with Pakistani intelligence is from the interview with Badeeb, February 1, 2002.

42. "Situation reports" and development

of the liaison are from an interview with a senior Saudi official.

43. Prince Turki has said publicly that the Taliban "did not receive a single penny in cash from the kingdom from its founding," only humanitarian aid. None of the kingdom's records are transparent or published, so it is impossible to be sure, but Turki's claim, even if interpreted narrowly, seems unlikely to withstand scrutiny. Nawaf Obaid, a Saudi intelligence analyst, wrote in a 1998 master's thesis, "Improving U.S. Intelligence Analysis on the Saudi Arabian Decision Making Process," that most of the Saudi aid to the Taliban was funneled by the kingdom's official religious establishment. Obaid quotes a "high-ranking official in the Ministry of Islamic Guidance" as saying that after the Soviet Union was defeated in Afghanistan, the kingdom's religious leaders "focused on funding and encouraging the Taliban." Human Rights Watch quoted journalists who saw white-painted C-130 Hercules transport aircraft which they identified as Saudi Arabian at Kandahar airport in 1996 delivering artillery and small arms ammunition to Taliban soldiers. There were subsequent reports of strong arms supply links between the Taliban and commercial dealers operating from the United Arab Emirates as well. Taliban religious police, Human Rights Watch concluded, were "funded directly by Saudi Arabia; this relatively generous funding . . . enabled it to become the most powerful agency within the Islamic Emirate."

44. Interview with Prince Turki, August 2, 2002, Cancun, Mexico (SC). Turki also said, "We had taken a policy, since the civil war started in Afghanistan, that we're not going to support any group in Afghanistan, financially or otherwise, from the government but that humanitarian aid [from Saudi Arabia] could continue. And it was mostly through

these [charity] organizations that the humanitarian aid went to Afghanistan. . . . Now, I can't tell you that individuals did not go and give money to the Taliban. I'm sure that happened. But not the institutions themselves."

45.   See note 43.

46.   Interviews with senior Saudi officials.

47.   Interviews with U.S. officials. All of the quotations are from State Department cables between November 3, 1994, and February 20, 1995, declassified and released by the National Security Archive.

48.   Interview with Bhutto, May 5, 2002. Quotations from Talbott meeting are from a State Department cable of February 21, 1996, declassified and released by the National Security Archive. Bhutto's comments to Wilson and Brown are from a State Department cable, April 14, 1996.

49.   Interview with former senator Hank Brown, February 5, 2003, by telephone (GW). Brown was one of the very few elected politicians in Washington to pay attention to Afghanistan during this period. "I just get a lump in my throat every time I think about it, but Afghanistan really is the straw that broke the camel's back in the Cold War," he recalled. "If there ever was a people in this world that we're indebted to, it would be the people of Afghanistan. And for us to turn our backs on them, it was just criminal. Who's done more to help us? It really is a disgrace what we did."

CHAPTER 17: "DANGLING THE CARROT"

1.   Miller's background, outlook, and involvement with the Turkmenistan-Afghanistan-Pakistan pipeline deal are from the author's interview with Miller, September 23, 2002, Austin, Texas (SC and GW).

2.   In Unocal's 1994 10-K, the company explained its losses by saying that "the 1994 operating earnings reflected higher natural gas production, higher foreign crude oil production, stronger earnings from agricultural products, and lower domestic oil and gas operating and depreciation expense. However, these positive factors could not make up for the lower crude oil and natural gas prices, and lower margins in the company's West Coast refining and marketing operations." Two years later, in 1996, the company sold its refining and marketing operations to focus more exclusively on international exploration and development.

3.   The company's 1996 annual report was titled "A New World, A New Unocal," and it detailed a major turnaround in the company's business strategy.

4.   For a detailed discussion of the stranded energy reserves of the Caspian region and the dilemma faced by Turkmenistan in particular, see Ahmed Rashid's *Taliban: Militant Islam, Oil, and Fundamentalism in Central Asia,* pp. 143–56.

5.   Ibid., p. 168.

6.   Interview with Miller, September 23, 2002.

7.   That the control tower was built on the wrong side is from Steve LeVine, *The Washington Post,* November 11, 1994. LeVine quotes a Western diplomat as saying, "The builders warned them, but the Turkmen said, 'It looks better this way.'" Other colorful depictions of Niyazov's post-Soviet rule include Alessandra Stanley, *The New York Times,* November 23, 1995; Daniel Sneider, *The Christian Science Monitor,* March 25, 1996; and Robert G. Kaiser, *The Washington Post,* July 8, 2002.

8.   The numbers on trade between the United States and the Central Asian republics are from the testimony of James F. Collins, the State Department's senior coordinator for the new independent states,

before the House International Relations Committee, November 14, 1995.

9. "Promote the independence . . ." is from the testimony of Sheila Heslin, former National Security Council staffer, before the Senate Governmental Affairs Committee, September 17, 1997. The assistance of the U.S. ambassador and others in the government to Unocal is from the interview with Miller, September 23, 2002, and American government officials. For an examination of U.S. energy strategy in the region, see Dan Morgan and David Ottaway, *The Washington Post,* September 22, 1997.

10. Interview with a senior Saudi official.

11. Author's interview with Benazir Bhutto, May 5, 2002, Dubai, United Arab Emirates (GW). Bhutto would only say that Bulgheroni's Bridas visited her "through one of the Muslim Arab leaders." In a separate interview, however, Turki said that he was the one who made Bulgheroni's introductions with the Pakistani leadership.

12. *Platt's Oilgram News,* October 23, 1995.

13. Dan Morgan and David Ottaway, *The Washington Post,* October 5, 1998. Kissinger quoted Dr. Samuel Johnson, who was commenting on a man who had wed for a second time immediately after the end of a miserable first marriage.

14. Robert Baer, *See No Evil,* pp. xix and 244.

15. Raphel's views on the pipeline and her activities in support of it are from interviews with a senior Clinton administration official. "We were all aware that business advocacy was part of our portfolio," the official said. "We were doing it for that reason, and we could choose Unocal because they were the only American company."

16. Simons's background, his tenure as ambassador, and his perspective on the pipeline are from the author's interview with Tom Simons, August 19, 2002, Washington, D.C. (SC).

17. Ibid. More than half a decade after the fact, Bhutto spoke with indignation about those who invoked her husband's name to get her to change sides: "They started saying my husband is interested [in Bridas] and that's why I'm not going to [cancel the MOU with Bridas], which made me really, really upset because I felt that because I am a woman, they're trying to get back at me through my husband. But nonetheless, the fact of the matter was that it had nothing to do with my husband. It had to do with an Arab leader. It had to do with the country he represented. And the fact that [Bridas] had come first. I mean, they're wanting us to break a legal contract . . ."

18. Interview with a Pakistani government official.

19. Interviews with Bhutto, May 5, 2002, and Simons, August 19, 2002. Despite the contentious nature of the meeting, Bhutto and Simons provided similar accounts, with neither one attempting to mask just how poorly it had gone. Simons described it as "a disastrous meeting," and Bhutto called it "a low point in our relations with America."

20. The account of the Unocal-Delta expedition into Afghanistan is based on the author's interview with Miller, September 23, 2002, interviews with Delta's American representative, Charlie Santos, in New York on August 19 and 23, 2002, and again on February 22, 2003 (GW).

21. A copy of the Unocal support agreement was provided to the author. The agreement contained the caveat that "a condition for implementation of the pipeline projects is the establishment of a single, internationally recognized entity authorized to act on behalf of all Afghan parties." The word *entity* was deliberately used instead of *government* to give Unocal some wiggle room down the line.

22. In June, Santos returned to Kandahar without Miller and stayed for more than a

week, to try one more time to get the Taliban to sign the support agreement. Finally, Santos got fed up and tore into one of the Taliban negotiators: "We've been sitting here for ten days, and you keep saying, 'Wait another day. Wait another day. Wait another day.' I'm going! This is bullshit! Forget this project!" With that he went out to his car and started to drive away. As he did, he saw one of the Taliban in his rearview mirror yelling for him not to go. After several more hours of negotiations, the Taliban at last agreed to sign a handwritten two-sentence statement saying that they supported the concept of the pipeline, but nothing more.

CHAPTER 18: "WE COULDN'T INDICT HIM"

1. Interview with Marty Miller, September 23, 2002, Austin, Texas (SC and GW).

2. Interview with Tom Simons, August 19, 2002, Washington, D.C. (SC).

3. Interviews with several U.S. officials familiar with the CIA-ISI liaison during this period. Rana's professional background is from Pakistani journalist Kamran Khan. Rana's outlook is from interviews with U.S. officials and also an interview with his predecessor, Lt. Gen. Javed Ashraf Qazi (Ret.), May 19, 2002, Rawalpindi, Pakistan (SC). He recalled that ISI had come under "tremendous fire" in Pakistan because of the raid in Quetta in search of Kasi that had been based on faulty information.

4. Interviews with U.S. officials.

5. "All the way down to the bare bones" is from *The New York Times,* April 27, 1995. The portrait of Deutch here is drawn from multiple published sources and interviews with former colleagues of Deutch at the White House and the CIA. Moynihan's legislation was introduced in January 1995: *Los Angeles Times,* October 8, 1995.

6. "A technical guy" is from *The New York*

Times Magazine, December 10, 1995. "From what I know" is from his confirmation hearing, *The New York Times,* April 27, 1995.

7. Twelve case officers in training and eight hundred worldwide is from Bob Woodward, *The Washington Post,* November 17, 2001, confirmed by interviews with U.S. officials. That this represented about a 25 percent decline from the Cold War's peak is from interviews with U.S. officials. See also testimony of George Tenet before the Joint Inquiry Committee, October 17, 2002. "California hot tub stuff" is from an interview with a Directorate of Operations officer who retired during this period.

8. Interview with Fritz Ermath, January 7, 2002, Washington, D.C. (SC).

9. Portrait of White House terrorism analysis, Clinton's interest in biological terrorism, and policy review in the first half of 1995 are from interviews with former Clinton administration officials.

10. "U.S. Policy on Counterterrorism," June 21, 1995, redacted version declassified and publicly released. Context for the decision directive's issuance can be found in Daniel Benjamin and Steve Simon, *The Age of Sacred Terror,* pp. 229–30. Benjamin and Simon arrived in the White House counterterrorism office soon after the new policy took effect.

11. The UBL acronym as the ultimate sign of importance is from an interview with Anthony Lake, May 5, 2003, Washington, D.C. (GW). That the bin Laden unit was formally known as the bin Laden Issue Station is from the testimony of George Tenet, Joint Inquiry Committee, October 17, 2002. That the Counterterrorist Center's bin Laden unit began with about twelve people is from the National Commission's final report. That it was a "virtual station" and a management prototype is from interviews with U.S. officials. That the NSA had tapped bin Laden's

satellite telephone during this period is from James Bamford, *The Washington Post,* June 2, 2002. The bin Laden issue station's startup was accompanied by classified White House directives that delineated the scope of its mission. Whether this initial document authorized active disruption operations against bin Laden's network is not clear. At least some authorities beyond normal intelligence collection may have been provided to the CIA by President Clinton at this stage, but the precise scope is not known.

12. "One of the most significant" is from "Usama bin Ladin: Islamic Extremist Financier," CIA assessment released publicly in 1996. Clarke quotations from his written testimony to the National Commission, March 24, 2004. See also National Commission staff statement no. 7, p. 4. "Let's yank on this bin Laden chain" is from the author's interview with a former Clinton administration official.

13. The account in this chapter of internal U.S. deliberations surrounding bin Laden's expulsion from Sudan is based on interviews with eight senior American officials directly involved as well as Saudi and Sudanese officials. Among those who agreed to be interviewed on the record was former U.S. ambassador to Sudan Timothy Carney, July 31, 2002, Washington, D.C. (SC). Carney provided the chronology of the Emergency Action Committee's decision-making and cables to Washington. Benjamin and Simon, strongly defending White House decision-making during this episode, provide a detailed account in *Age of Sacred Terror,* pp. 244–45. "He says that . . . to kill him either" is from an interview with a former Clinton administration official. The plot against Lake probably originated with Hezbollah, not bin Laden, according to former officials. At one stage the plot became so serious that Lake moved out of his suburban home and authorized a countersurveillance effort aimed at detecting his assassins. This security effort required Lake to authorize secret wiretaps of all his telephones. In 1970, Lake was subject to a secret FBI wiretap by the Nixon administration after he resigned his job as Henry Kissinger's special assistant and then went to work for Democratic presidential candidate Edmund Muskie. In 1995, Lake sat at Kissinger's old desk in the Old Executive Office Building as he signed the papers authorizing wiretaps of his own phones. He looked up at the FBI agents, according to one account, and said, "You know, there's a certain irony to all this." The FBI agent reportedly replied in a deadpan tone, "Oh, we know, sir."

14. Interview with Carney, July 31, 2002.

15. Ibid.

16. Interviews with former Clinton administration officials directly involved in the discussions.

17. "An embassy is a tool" is from the interview with Carney, July 31, 2002.

18. That the dinner was on February 6, 1996, is from Barton Gellman, *The Washington Post,* October 3, 2001. Carney, writing with Mansoor Ijaz, has also published a brief account of his participation, in *The Washington Post,* June 30, 2002.

19. Gellman, *The Washington Post,* October 3, 2001, and Carney, *The Washington Post,* June 30, 2002; also Benjamin and Simon, *Age of Sacred Terror,* pp. 246–47. The original document was published by *The Washington Post* in October 2001. Clinton administration officials confirmed its authenticity in interviews and described the document's origins in a series of working group meetings led by the National Security Council.

20. *Time,* May 6, 1996.

21. "We told the Americans" is from an interview with a Sudanese official. No "reliable evidence" is from the National Commission, staff statement no. 5, p. 3.

22. Interviews with U.S. officials involved. See also, National Commission staff statement no. 5, p. 4.

23. Ibid.

24. The contact with Egypt and Jordan is from an interview with a U.S. official. "To keep him moving" is from the interview with Lake, May 5, 2003. "[W]ere afraid it was . . . done anything to us" is from a speech by Clinton in October 2001 to the Washington Society of Association Executives, quoted in *USA Today*, November 12, 2001.

25. Interview with Prince Turki, August 2, 2002, Cancun, Mexico (SC).

26. "Never mentioned . . . send him away" is from "Hunting bin Laden," *Frontline*, March 21, 2000. The Sudanese official's account from an interview with the author.

27. BBC Summary of World Broadcasts, excerpts from *Al-Sharaq al-Awsat*, June 18, 1996. BBC translation.

28. Badeeb Orbit interview, early 2002. Original Arabic language tape supplied to the author by Badeeb. See notes to chapter 4.

29. Interviews with former Clinton administration officials. Benjamin and Simon, *Age of Sacred Terror*, pp. 463–64. In June 1996, Carney visited Deutch and Tenet at CIA headquarters to discuss reopening the Khartoum embassy. By this time Carney was based in Nairobi and traveling occasionally to the Sudanese capital. Carney recalls that Deutch and Tenet were now ready to support reopening the embassy. Tenet said, by Carney's account, that "it was time to get the U.S. government back in, and we need to do it now." Carney said that in an election year, "I can't imagine the administration would want to take a chance that Sudan would somehow become a campaign issue" by taking the risk to reopen the embassy. Carney said, "Let's hold off until after the election and then do it." But Tenet, by Carney's account, replied, "No, we need to do it now." The embassy, however, remained closed.

30. Interview with a Sudanese official.

31. "Sudan is not a good . . ." is from "Hunting bin Laden," *Frontline*, March 21, 2000. The information from the Sudanese official is from the author's interview. This account tracks with multiple published accounts, including some drawing on Afghan sources in Jalalabad where the flights landed.

32. Badeeb Orbit interview, early 2002. Turki confirmed Badeeb's account of the Qatar stopover in an interview with the author, August 2, 2002. Turki blamed Qatar's decision on the tiny emirate's history of nipping at the heels of its larger Saudi neighbor. For the conclusion of American investigators, see National Commission staff statement no. 5, p. 4, and the final report, p.63.

33. Interviews with U.S. officials involved.

34. Robert Fisk, *The Independent*, July 10, 1996.

35. This account of the failed attempt to arrest Khalid Sheikh Mohammed in Qatar is drawn mainly from the interviews with U.S. officials. See also the Joint Inquiry Committee's final report, pp. 310–13 and the National Commission's staff statement no. 5, pp. 2–3. For how Mohammed was assigned within CTC, see the commission's final report, p. 276. James Risen and David Johnston published an excellent account of the episode in *The New York Times*, March 8, 2003. The quotations from Freeh's letter are from their account.

36. Kathy Gannon, Associated Press, July 11, 1996. Sudan's government formally reported to the United Nations on June 3, 1996, that bin Laden had left that country for Afghanistan. Initial press reports from Pakistan quoted Pakistani intelligence and religious party leaders as saying that bin Laden's arrival in Afghanistan had been facilitated in part by his former allies from the anti-Soviet jihad, Gulbuddin Hekmatyar and the Islamist political party Jamaat-e-Islami.

37. Interview with Kenneth Katzman, Congressional Research Service terrorism analyst, August 27, 2002, Washington, D.C. (GW).

38. United Press International, June 7, 1996.

39. Ahmed Rashid, *Taliban: Militant Islam, Oil, and Fundamentalism in Central Asia,* pp. 41–42; Barnett R. Rubin, *The Fragmentation of Afghanistan,* p. xv; Michael Griffin, *Reaping the Whirlwind,* p. 65.

40. Quotations from Raphel's meetings and Simons's cables from "A/S Raphel Discusses Afghanistan," declassified cable, April 22, 1996, released by the National Security Archive. Massoud's perspective is from interviews with aides to Massoud.

41. "Has become a conduit for drugs" is from Robin Raphel's testimony before the Senate Subcommittee on Near Eastern and South Asian Affairs, June 6, 1996. "Concerned that economic opportunities" and "will be very good" are from Rashid, *Taliban,* pp. 45 and 166. Raphel's comment to a Russian counterpart from State Department cable of May 13, 1996, declassified and released by the National Security Archive.

42. Life expectancy is from Benjamin and Simon, *Age of Sacred Terror,* p. 135. That Afghanistan was 173 is from Raphel, Senate Subcommittee testimony, June 6, 1996.

43. Interview with Benazir Bhutto, May 5, 2002, Dubai, United Arab Emirates (GW). That all the while Bhutto continued to lie: In meetings in Islamabad in the spring of 1996 with one of their strongest supporters in the U.S. Congress, Senator Hank Brown, Bhutto and her aides denied providing any aid to the Taliban. On June 26, 1996, Bhutto's ambassador to the United States, Maleeha Lodhi, testified at a congressional hearing: "Pakistan, let me state emphatically, does not provide arms or ammunition to any faction."

44. Interview with Simons, August 19, 2002.

45. Interviews with U.S. officials. Steve LeVine of *Newsweek* first reported publicly on bin Laden's large payments to the Taliban, on October 13, 1997. National Commission investigators describe bin Laden's 1996 financial problems in staff statement no. 15, although they provide no assessment of any payments to the Taliban. Given his $1 million allowance for more than ten years, $3 million would not be an exorbitant sum for bin Laden even in tight times. But it is not clear what contributions he made, if any, or where they came from.

46. Peter L. Bergen, *Holy War, Inc.,* p. 28. Benjamin and Simon, *Age of Sacred Terror,* p. 134.

47. The Massoud quotes and tactical details are from Davis, "How the Taliban Became a Military Force," in William Maley, ed., *Fundamentalism Reborn,* pp. 65–67. Ahmed Rashid writes in the same volume, p. 87, on the role of Pakistani intelligence during this period: "The ISI played a leading role in helping the Taliban's capture of Jalalabad and Kabul, first by helping subvert the Jalalabad *Shura* and offering its members sanctuary in Pakistan, and then allowing the Taliban to reinforce their assault on Kabul by fresh troops drawn from Afghan refugee camps on the border."

48. Ibid.

49. Najibullah's translation and comment are from *The Guardian,* October 12, 1996, and from an interview with a U.N. official who visited Najibullah.

50. Griffin, *Reaping the Whirlwind,* p. 3.

51. Quotations ibid., pp. 6–7.

52. Nancy Hatch Dupree, "Afghan Women Under the Taliban," in Maley, ed., *Fundamentalism Reborn,* p. 156, citing United Nations human rights reporting.

53. All quotations are from "Dealing with the Taliban in Kabul," a State Department cable from Washington to Islamabad and other embassies, September 28, 1996, declassified and released by the National Security Archive.

54. Simons's remarks from "Ambassador Meets the Taliban," State Department cable of

November 12, 1996, declassified and released by the National Security Archive. Simons also discussed the meeting in an interview. Christopher's letter and Raphel-Karzai from "U.S. Engagement with the Taliban on Osama bin Laden," State Department memo declassified and released by the National Security Archive.

55. Rashid, *Taliban,* p. 178, and Richard MacKenzie, "The United States and the Taliban," in Maley, ed., *Fundamentalism Reborn,* p. 91.

CHAPTER 19: "WE'RE KEEPING THESE STINGERS"

1. Schroen's trip to Kabul and his discussions with Massoud are described in detail in the Prologue.

2. Interviews with U.S. officials.

3. Interviews with U.S., Pakistani, Saudi, and Afghan intelligence officials involved with the Stinger program.

4. Interviews with U.S. officials.

5. "The U.S. does not support," *Agence France Presse,* October 24, 1996. "Impossible to justify" is from Dupree, in William Maley, ed., *Fundamentalism Reborn,* p. 149.

6. "Fanatically neutral" is from *The New York Times,* October 23, 1996.

7. *The Washington Post,* October 7, 1996.

8. This account of Schroen's visit to Kandahar is from interviews with U.S. officials.

9. "We're keeping these Stingers" is from an interview with Gary Schroen, May 7, 2002, Washington D.C. (SC).

10. Peter L. Bergen, *Holy War, Inc.,* p. 93. Michael Griffin, *Reaping the Whirlwind,* p. 137. Quotations are from Vernon Loeb, *The Washington Post,* August 23, 1998.

11. Bergen, *Holy War, Inc.,* pp. 1–23. Loeb, *The Washington Post,* August 23, 1998.

12. The Prince Turki quotations are from *Nightline,* December 10, 2001. "Mistaken policy or accident of history—take your pick," the Saudi foreign minister Saud al-Faisal, Turki's brother, said in an interview with *The Washington Post* during the same period. "The stability of Afghanistan seemed a bigger concern than the presence of bin Laden. . . . When the Taliban received him, they indicated he would be absolutely prevented from taking any actions. We had unequivocal promises." During this same period the Clinton White House was struggling to win cooperation from the Saudis for investigations of Iranian involvement in the terrorist bombing of June 1996 at Khobar Towers in eastern Saudi Arabia. But the Saudis, under the initiative of Crown Prince Abdullah, were in the midst of trying to construct a negotiated rapprochement with newly elected Iranian president Mohammad Khatami. The Saudis did not want the Americans to destroy this détente by prosecuting Iranian operatives involved in the bombing or launching retaliatory military strikes against Iran. Sandy Berger met repeatedly with Prince Bandar to try to win Saudi cooperation, but later he described the talks as a Saudi "ritual of evasion."

13. Interviews with Charlie Santos, August 19 and 23, 2002, New York City (GW). Also interview with Marty Miller, September 23, 2002, Austin, Texas (SC and GW), and interviews with U.S., Pakistani, and Afghan officials who traveled through Kandahar during this period.

14. Ibid. Also, interview with Thomas Goutierre, September 18, 2002, Omaha, Nebraska (GW). A center run by Goutierre at the University of Nebraska was retained by Unocal to train Pashtuns in Kandahar as oil pipeline workers in order to show the Taliban the potential economic benefits of the pipeline.

15. Bin Laden's death threat against Brown is from an interview with former senator Hank Brown, February 5, 2003, by telephone

(GW). In August 1996, Brown visited Kandahar on a multistop trip to Afghanistan designed to stir interest in peace talks. In Kandahar he met with senior Taliban officials. The Taliban had captured and imprisoned several Russian pilots who were running arms to Massoud's government. Brown, a former Navy pilot in Vietnam, visited with the prisoners. They asked Brown to pass along to the Taliban a request that they be permitted to run the engines on their plane once a month so that it would be in condition to fly if they were ever released. Brown did pass along the request, and a few weeks later the Taliban took their prisoners to the airport to check the engines on their plane. The Russians overpowered their guards, hopped into their plane, and flew away. The Taliban angrily blamed Brown for this fiasco. That the United States did not seriously begin to plan covert action to capture or kill bin Laden until the end of 1997 is from interviews with multiple U.S. officials. From their perspective at the White House, Daniel Benjamin and Steven Simon acknowledge in *The Age of Sacred Terror* that there was little sense of urgency about bin Laden among counterterrorism planners there until December 1997. The sense remained that bin Laden was a financier of Islamist extremists, not a major terrorist operator himself.

16. Ahmed Rashid, *Taliban: Militant Islam, Oil, and Fundamentalism in Central Asia,* pp. 201–2.

17. Ibid., p. 54, quoting Omar's interview with Rahimullah Yousufzai in the Pakistani English-language newspaper *The News*.

18. Reuters, April 10, 1997.

19. "Massoud felt cheated" is from an interview with Haroun Amin, September 9, 2002, Washington, D.C. (GW).

20. "He never thought for a second" is from an interview with Ahmed Wali Massoud, May 7, 2002, Kabul, Afghanistan (GW).

21. Massoud's trusted intelligence aide Engineer Arif was dispatched to sell gems in Las Vegas at one point, according to a U.S. official who met with him on the visit. "Day by day" is from an interview with Mohammed Neem, May 27, 2002, Kabul, Afghanistan (GW).

22. "No way" is from an interview with Daoud Mir, July 31 and August 8, 2002, Washington, D.C. (GW). "He could have an understanding" is from the author's interview with Mohiden Mehdi, May 27, 2002, Kabul, Afghanistan (GW). The earlier quotations from State Department reports about Pakistani aid to the Taliban are from declassified cables released by the National Security Archive.

23. Interview with a senior intelligence aide to Massoud.

24. The account of this trip is drawn from the interviews with U.S. officials and with aides to Massoud.

25. Quotations ibid. In recounting the history of their secret contacts with Massoud during the late 1990s, U.S. officials tend to emphasize the role of counterterrorism in the early meetings more than Massoud's aides do. Abdullah, then Massoud's foreign policy adviser, said in an interview that in 1997 "the discussions on terrorism had not really started." While there were general talks with the CIA about bin Laden, "what I can say is that it started with this narrow thing, Stingers. But it gradually developed." The Americans, on the other hand, saw the Stinger recovery program as a way to supplement Massoud's income and strengthen his military potential, and as a way to develop trust and regular communication for intelligence reporting about bin Laden.

26. Interview with Neem, May 27, 2002, and with other aides to Massoud, including several senior intelligence officers.

27. The Rashid quotation is from "Pakistan

and the Taliban," in Maley, ed., *Fundamentalism Reborn,* p. 88. Rashid continues: "Pakistan's strategy towards the Taliban was characterized as much by drift as by determination. Islamabad's policy was as much driven by corruption, infighting and inefficiency as it was a concerted attempt to push forward a Pashtun agenda in Afghanistan."

28. Interview with Mushahid Hussain, May 21, 2002, Islamabad, Pakistan (SC).

29. "They asked that we recognize" and "had no clue of how to run a country" are from Badeeb's interview with Orbit, early 2002, translated by the Language Doctors, Inc., Washington, D.C. "They are very religious people" is from the author's interview with Ahmed Badeeb, February 1, 2002, Jedda, Saudi Arabia (SC). "So as to fill the obvious vacuum" is from Badeeb's interview with Orbit.

30. Interview with Yar Mohabbat, September 20, 2002, St. Louis, Missouri (GW).

31. Ibid.

32. Ibid., and an interview with a congressional aide who toured the embassy during this period.

33. Ibid., and interviews with State Department officials. Rick Inderfurth, then the newly arrived assistant secretary of state for South Asia, recalled satisfaction over the State Department's ability to prevent the Taliban from taking control of the embassy, which might have increased their influence. The only way to prevent the Taliban takeover, Inderfurth argued, was to shut the embassy altogether.

34. The number fifty thousand widows is from a January 1997 survey by the International Committee for the Red Cross, cited in Nancy Hatch Dupree, "Afghan Women Under the Taliban," in Maley, ed., *Fundamentalism Reborn,* p. 155. U.N. appeal figures are from Rashid, *Taliban,* p. 108.

35. Tomsen cable: "Afghanistan Settlement— Analysis and Policy Recommendations,"

June 1997, excised and declassified April 4, 2000, author's files.

CHAPTER 20: "DOES AMERICA NEED THE CIA?"

1. "The ultimate staff guy" is from *The New York Times,* March 20, 1997.

2. "Remarks of the Director of Central Intelligence George J. Tenet on Strategic Direction," declassified transcript, May 5, 1998, released by CIA Office of Public Affairs.

3. Family history is from Tenet's account in two speeches, "Acceptance of the Ellis Island Medal of Honor Forum Club Lunch," November 6, 1997, and "Remarks by DCI George J. Tenet at Swearing-In Ceremony by Vice President Gore," July 31, 1997, CIA Office of Public Affairs.

4. "Always talking" is from the *New York Daily News,* March 21, 1997. "To the future editorial page editor" is from *Newsday,* March 21, 1997.

5. "Guy's guy" is from an interview with Cliff Shannon, former aide to Heinz, March 8, 2002, by telephone (GW). "He was the only person . . . hard work" is from an interview with Bill Reinsch, former aide to Heinz, March 5, 2002, by telephone (GW).

6. Interview with Gary Sojka, August 8, 2002, Washington, D.C. (GW).

7. Rudman quotation is from *The News Hour with Jim Lehrer,* March 19, 1997. The Newsom quotation is from an interview with Eric Newsom, March 8, 2002, Washington, D.C. (GW).

8. Interview with former senator David Boren, September 16, 2002, Norman, Oklahoma (GW).

9. Ibid. Interview with Clair George, December 12, 2001, Chevy Chase, Maryland (SC). Interview with Thomas Twetten, March 18, 2002, Washington, D.C. (SC).

10. Interview with John Despres, February 28, 2002, by telephone (GW).

11. Interviews with former senate Select Committee on Intelligence staff members.

12. Interview with Newsom, March 8, 2002.

13. "Streak of eccentric genius" is from "Acceptance of Ellis Island Medal," November 6, 1997. "Nowhere in the world" is from "Remarks by DCI George J. Tenet at Swearing-In Ceremony," July 31, 1997.

14. "Does America Need the CIA?" November 19, 1997, CIA Office of Public Affairs.

15. "Does America Need the CIA?," November 19, 1997. "George J. Tenet on Strategic Direction," May 5, 1998.

16. "Does America Need the CIA?," November 19, 1997.

17. "George J. Tenet on Strategic Direction," May 5, 1998.

18. "Does America Need the CIA?," November 19, 1997. "George J. Tenet on Strategic Direction," May 5, 1998. "Should never be the last resort" is from Senate Select Committee on Intelligence, "Hearing on the Nomination of George Tenet as Director of Central Intelligence," May 6, 1997.

19. This habit of personality extended even to his religious faith. Tenet and his family worshiped at a Greek Orthodox church. He also routinely attended Catholic mass with his best friend, Jack DeGioia, a philosopher and academic administrator who had risen to become president of Georgetown University, Tenet's alma mater. Without any discomfort he could move "back and forth between the two," as DeGioia put it. Interview with Jack DeGioia, March 26, 2002, Washington, D.C. (GW).

20. Senate Select Committee on Intelligence, "Hearing on the Nomination of George Tenet," May 6, 1997, and Senate Select Committee on Intelligence, Hearing on "World Threat Assessment," January 28, 1998. That Clinton's guidance to the intelligence community about collection priorities was a classified presidential decision directive is from author's interviews with former Clinton administration officials. Clinton's quotes about those priorities are from "Remarks by the President to Staff of the CIA and the Intelligence Community," July 14, 1995, White House, Office of the Press Secretary.

21. "Remarks by DCI George J. Tenet to the University of Oklahoma," September 12, 1997, CIA Office of Public Affairs.

22. Senate Select Committee on Intelligence, "Hearing on the Nomination of George Tenet," May 6, 1997.

23. "George J. Tenet on Strategic Direction," May 5, 1998.

24. The Albright quotation is from Dennis Kux, *The United States and Pakistan*, p. 342. "We're opposed to their [the Taliban's] approach on human rights," Albright said. "We're opposed to their despicable treatment of women and children and their lack of respect for human dignity. . . . It is impossible to modernize a nation if half or more of a population is left behind." Hillary Clinton's quotations are from "Remarks by First Lady Hillary Rodham Clinton, United Nations Economic and Social Council," December 10, 1997, White House Press Office.

25. Leonard Scensny, *Chicago Tribune,* October 21, 2001.

26. Interview with Abdullah, May 8, 2002, Kabul, Afghanistan (GW). Interview with Rick Inderfurth, February 20, 2002, Washington, D.C. (SC).

27. Interview with Marty Miller, September 23, 2002, Austin, Texas (SC and GW). Unocal's strategy, Robert Oakley said in an interview, had to be one of moderating the Taliban, drawing them out. "We felt it was worth a try. Most Afghans said, 'Look, they brought order. It's so much better than it was,'" Oakley said. Phyllis Oakley took over

at the Bureau of Intelligence and Research in the fall of 1997 and was involved with discussions about how to handle the Taliban. The Taliban were constantly searching for approval from the United States, she said. She described the Taliban's basic position in talks with the U.S. government in this way: "If you recognize us and build an embassy, we'll be glad to work with you—except on these issues." The off-limits issues were women's rights and terrorism, however, so the conversations never made progress. Robert Oakley described Unocal's attempts to moderate the Taliban as "frustrating" and cited the influence of bin Laden and other Arab extremists as the major reason. Bin Laden and others showered the Taliban with money, weapons, and volunteers. "It was a lot more than Unocal could give."

28. Interview with Miller, September 23, 2002. Interview with Thomas Goutierre, September 18, 2002, Omaha, Nebraska (GW).

29. "Afghanistan: Meeting with the Taliban," State Department cable, December 11, 1997, released by the National Security Archive.

30. Interview with Goutierre, September 18, 2002.

31. Interview with Miller, September 23, 2002. Miller is the source of the dinner scene at his house.

32. Senate Select Committee on Intelligence, "World Threat Assessment," January 28, 1998. The 105-page transcript of Tenet's May 1997 confirmation hearing contains a serious discussion of terrorism only on page 103, and then only briefly, with no mention of bin Laden.

33. Al-Fadl testified about his efforts to purchase uranium for bin Laden in open court early in 2001 during the trial of defendants accused of acting on bin Laden's behalf in the August 1998 terrorist strikes against U.S. embassies in Kenya and Tanzania. The question of contacts between al Qaeda and Iraq is highly controversial, and the evidence about such contacts at this writing remains at best uncertain. In interviews with U.S. officials throughout the intelligence community, the author heard repeated accounts of evidence collected in Sudan during the period of bin Laden's exile there, which showed meetings between visiting midlevel Iraqi officers and Islamists in bin Laden's circle. This was in the context of many meetings among multinational radicals in Khartoum with varying secular and Islamist agendas. The purpose and seriousness of these contacts, if they did occur, is difficult to gauge. U.S. intelligence believed and reported at the time, according to some of these officials—long before the events of September 11 or the debate over Iraqi links to bin Laden—that bin Laden's group may have solicited these meetings to explore development of a chemical weapons expertise. Both Sudan's government and Iraq's government clearly were interested in chemical weapons capabilities, and bin Laden, for his part, was close to the Khartoum regime. Stanley Bedington, a senior analyst in the CIA's Counterterrorism Center until 1994, said in an interview, "The Iraqis were active in Sudan giving bin Laden assistance. A colleague of mine was chief of operations for Africa and knew it extremely well. He said the relationship between Sudan and the Iraqis was very, very close indeed. . . . Basically, the Iraqis were looking for anti-American partners and targets of opportunity in places like Sudan. . . . But his [Saddam's] regime is essentially secular. If al Qaeda has established links with Iraq, it's entirely opportunistic." Later, after bin Laden relocated to Afghanistan and al Qaeda grew in strength, bin Laden clearly did engage in chemical weapons experiments at

camps there, although the extent of his progress and outside technical resources remain uncertain. The staff of the National Commission on Terrorist Attacks Upon the United States reported in the spring of 2004 that Sudan arranged contacts between Iraq and al Qaeda during the mid-1990s, including a meeting between an Iraqi intelligence officer and bin Laden in 1994. These and other sporadic, mid-level contacts "do not appear to have resulted in a collaborative relationship," the staff reported. "We have no credible evidence that Iraq and al Qaeda cooperated on attacks against the United States."

CHAPTER 21: "YOU ARE TO CAPTURE HIM ALIVE"

1. This chapter's account of the CIA's tribal agents, how they were first recruited, how their plans evolved, how they interacted with CIA officers, and how their operations were debated at the White House and at Langley is drawn from interviews with eight American officials knowledgeable about the plans. Many cables and documentation of these episodes remain classified and were unavailable to supplement the recollections of officials. As best the author could discover, the earliest accurate public reference to the plans described in this chapter was a very brief mention in a September 6, 1998, *New York Times* article by James Risen. Barton Gellman, writing in *The Washington Post* on December 19, 2001, provided a fuller sketch of their activities. Bob Woodward first described the team's makeup and intelligence collection role in *The Washington Post* on December 23, 2001. None of these articles described the origin of the unit as a team to arrest Kasi, the plan to attack Tarnak Farm, the plan to kidnap bin Laden and hold him in a cave, or the extended debate

over risks and casualties. On October 17, 2002, George Tenet testified at a Joint Inquiry Committee hearing that by 1998 the CIA was "pursuing a multi-track approach to bring bin Laden himself to justice, including working with foreign services, developing a close relationship with U.S. federal prosecutors, increasing pressure on the Taliban, and enhancing our capability to capture him."

2. "It's a match" is from Patricia Davis and Maria Glod, *The Washington Post,* November 14, 2002. Other background is from Davis and Thomas, *The Washington Post,* June 20, 1997, and Dennis Kux, *The United States and Pakistan,* p. 340. The account here of how the CIA received the tip about Kasi, how the fugitive was betrayed by a business partner, how the arrest operation was planned, and the "Red Light Zulu" radio message to Langley are from interviews with U.S. officials.

3. CNN, June 18, 1997.

4. Here as elsewhere in the book the author has published the full names of active CIA officers in the clandestine service only if those names have already been made public. In a few cases elsewhere in the book only the first name of an officer is used or no name at all in order to protect the officer's professional and personal security.

5. See note 1. The quotations are from interviews with Gary Schroen, September 19 and November 7, 2002, Washington D.C. (SC). Clinton aides' approval from National Commission final report, p. 110.

6. The public record about the grand jury investigation of bin Laden is limited. Press accounts date the origins of the investigation to 1996, around the time the CIA opened its bin Laden unit. Former National Security Council counterterrorism officials Daniel Benjamin and Steven Simon, in *The Age of Sacred Terror,* p. 239, confirm what court

records seem to indicate: that an indictment against bin Laden by the U.S. attorney in the Southern District of New York, then Mary Jo White, was first filed under seal in June 1998. CIA officers probably learned informally of the investigation because of their close interaction with FBI agents who were gathering evidence against bin Laden for the grand jury.

7. This account is from interviews with U.S. officials involved in the Egyptian rendition program. Some of those rendered to Egypt during this period were placed on trial by Egyptian authorities in 1999. Islamist violence against tourists and foreign interests in Egypt climaxed during 1997. In November, Islamic Group gunmen shot to death about seventy tourists, mainly Swiss and Japanese, at the Hatshepsut Temple in Luxor, Egypt.

8. Michael W. Reisman and James E. Baker, *Regulating Covert Action,* pp. 123–30. Paul R. Pillar, *Terrorism and U.S. Foreign Policy,* pp. 116–17. During the 1980s, under a ruling by the Justice Department's Office of Legal Counsel, U.S. agents had "no law enforcement authority in another nation unless it is the product of that nation's consent." In 1989 this standard was overturned by the Justice Department in favor of a new rule that authorized the executive branch to "violate the territorial sovereignty of other states" while making certain arrests abroad. As Reisman and Baker write, "Notwithstanding executive regulations and international norms against extraterritorial kidnapping, federal courts, until now, [have held] that once custody is obtained, the Court will not examine how a defendant was brought to the dock unless it involved conduct that 'shocks the conscience.'" These standards continue to evolve as fresh cases of fugitives abducted overseas and returned to American courts are reviewed on appeal.

9. Quotations are from interviews with Gary Schroen, September 19 and November 7, 2002 (SC).

10. Benjamin and Simon, *Age of Sacred Terror,* p. 26.

11. Vernon Loeb, *The Washington Post,* August 23 and 25, 1998. Peter L. Bergen, *Holy War, Inc.,* pp. 95–96.

12. The most thorough and balanced biography of al-Zawahiri yet published in English appeared as a long article in *The New Yorker* by Lawrence Wright on September 16, 2002.

13. Higgins and Cullison, in *The Wall Street Journal,* July 2, 2002, drawing from draft letters from al-Zawahiri to fellow Islamists that were discovered on the hard drive of a computer left behind in Kabul. The article makes plain the Egyptian's disputatious nature and growing isolation. So does a careful reading of al-Zawahiri's own post–September 11 memoir, *Knights Under the Prophet's Banner*; extracts were published in the Arabic newspaper *Al-Sharq al-Awsat.* In his memoir al-Zawahiri takes credit for a number of lethal terrorist operations prior to his formal alliance with bin Laden, including the 1995 bombing of the Egyptian embassy in Islamabad.

14. Higgins and Cullison, *The Wall Street Journal,* July 2, 2002, describe al-Zawahiri's itinerant travels and his fortunate escape from Russian custody in Dagestan. If the Russians had identified him correctly while he was in jail, it is possible that al Qaeda might have developed during the late 1990s in a different way.

15. Al-Zawahiri, *Knights Under the Prophet's Banner.*

16. Ibid.

17. Ibid.

18. The memo was released by the office of Senator Jon Kyl and was described by Walter Pincus in *The Washington Post,* February 25, 1998.

19. "Report of the Accountability Review Board," January 8, 1999. This was the commission led by Adm. William Crowe (Ret.) that reviewed the bombings of U.S. embassies in Kenya and Tanzania in August 1998 and the warnings that had preceded them.

20. March 9 meeting and quotation from "Afghanistan: [Redacted] Describes Pakistan's Current Thinking," State Department cable declassified and released by the National Security Archive.

21. Interview with Bill Richardson, September 15, 2002, Albuquerque, New Mexico (GW).

22. All quotations, ibid. Richardson's recollections are supported by Rick Inderfurth and the U.S. ambassador to Islamabad at the time, Tom Simons, both of whom accompanied him.

23. Ibid.

24. Ibid.

25. All quotations, ibid. Inderfurth and Simons were also at the table with Rabbani and recall the discussion similarly.

26. Interview with Rick Inderfurth, March 6, 2002, Washington, D.C. (SC).

27. Interview with Tom Simons, August 19, 2002, Washington, D.C. (SC).

28. Ibid.

29. Quotation from Jonathan Landay, *Christian Science Monitor,* July 1, 1998.

30. Timothy Weiner, *The New York Times,* February 1, 1999.

31. "To the extent of brainwashing" and other details are from the interview with Richard Clarke, July 9, 2003, Washington, D.C. (SC). Useful profiles of Clarke's career include Landay, *Christian Science Monitor;* Weiner, *The New York Times;* and Michael Dobbs, *The Washington Post,* April 2, 2000. The descriptions of Clarke's character and style are also drawn from interviews with about a dozen colleagues who worked closely with him during the late 1990s.

32. Interviews with former Clinton administration officials.

33. "Paranoid" and "facilitate" are from *USA Today,* May 22, 1998. That his status as a principal was unprecedented for an NSC staffer is from Benjamin and Simon, *Age of Sacred Terror,* p. 233. An account of PDD-62's provisions and significance is offered by Perl, "Terrorism, the Future, and U.S. Foreign Policy," Congressional Research Service, September 13, 2001, and is described in the Joint Inquiry Committee's final report, p. 234.

34. Clinton's bioterrorism session in April is from Benjamin and Simon, *Age of Sacred Terror,* p. 252. "Electronic Pearl Harbor" is from Weiner, *The New York Times,* February 1, 1999. "Pile driver" from National Commission staff statement no. 8, p. 3.

35. Michael Dobbs, *The Washington Post,* April 2, 2000.

36. Jonathan Landay, *Christian Science Monitor,* July 1, 1998.

37. Descriptions are from the author's visit, October 2002, and interviews with local residents.

38. Interview with Gary Schroen, September 19, 2002. Clarke email and Schroen cable from National Commission, final report, p. 112.

39. Ibid.

40. National Commission final report, pp. 112–114.

41. The nuclear weapons quotations are from Peter L. Bergen, *Holy War, Inc.,* p. 100. The ABC News quotations are from *The Washington Post,* April 23, 1998, and September 16, 2001.

42. Benjamin and Simon, Clarke's principal deputies for counterterrorism, write in their memoir that "there was nothing like a workable plan."

43. National Commission final report, p. 114.

CHAPTER 22: "THE KINGDOM'S
INTERESTS"

1. Quotation from Prince Sultan bin Salman, son of the governor of Riyadh, from
Ahmed Rashid, *Taliban: Militant Islam, Oil,
and Fundamentalism in Central Asia,* p. 138.

2. Bin Laden described the January arrests
of his Saudi followers at his May 1998 press
conference. He said they possessed an American Stinger missile and a number of SA-7
surface-to-air missiles. See Peter L. Bergen,
Holy War, Inc., pp. 100–101. The defection of
Moisalih and the arrests in Saudi Arabia it
produced are from "Afghanistan: Crisis of
Impunity," Human Rights Watch, July 2001,
p. 33. Turki has given half a dozen press interviews about his mission to Kandahar in
June 1998. He provided an early detailed account to the *Los Angeles Times,* August 8, 1999.

3. Abdullah's routine is from interviews
with senior Saudi officials. His demeanor,
palaces, and appearance are from an interview with Crown Prince Abdullah, January
28, 2002, Riyadh, Saudi Arabia (SC).

4. Interviews with senior Saudi officials.

5. One American counterterrorism official
called Naif's Interior Ministry a "black hole"
into which requests for names, telephone
numbers, and other details usually disappeared, never to reemerge. Turki's tent
accident was described by several U.S. officials.

6. Sheikh Turki's presence is from interviews
with senior Saudi officials. His presence was
also described by *Intelligence Newsletter,* October 15, 1998.

7. Turki's assessment of Mullah Omar, al
Qaeda membership, and bin Laden's leader-
ship role are from an interview with Prince
Turki, August 2, 2002, Cancun, Mexico (SC).

8. "Briefed . . . kingdom's interests" is from
the Associated Press, December 23, 2001,
quoting Turki's interview with the Arabic-
language satellite television network MBC.

"We made it plain" is from *Los Angeles Times,*
August 8, 1999.

9. The Turki interview was on ABC News
Nightline, December 10, 2001.

10. Rashid, *Taliban,* p. 72, describes Turki's
meeting with Omar as focused entirely on
the upcoming Taliban military thrust against
Northern Alliance forces in Mazar-i-Sharif.
Saudi officials denied this was a subject of
discussion. The only publicly available accounts of the meeting are from Turki and
Mullah Omar. The Taliban leader told *Time*
magazine on August 24, 1998, that Turki had
told him to keep bin Laden quiet. Omar
made no reference to a Saudi request to hand
bin Laden over for trial. Instead, after hearing from Turki, Omar said he told bin Laden
"that as a guest, he shouldn't involve himself
in activities that create problems for us."

11. Biographies and Afghan training of el
Hage, Odeh, and Mohammed are from opening statements by their defense lawyers at
their trial in the Southern District of New
York, February 5, 2001.

12. Casualty statistics and attack sequences
are from "Report of the Accountability Review Boards: Bombings of the U.S. Embassies in Nairobi, Kenya, and Dar es Salaam,
Tanzania, on August 7, 1998," released on
January 8, 1999.

13. Ibid. The July 29 CTC warning is from
the Joint Inquiry Committee's final report,
Appendix, p. 20. The review board's investigators examined classified intelligence and
threat warnings circulated prior to the attacks and found "no immediate tactical
warning" about the embassy bombings. The
board did not blame either the CIA or the
FBI for failing to discover bin Laden's Africa
cells. They did criticize the heavy dependence on fragmentary and often inaccurate
threat warnings as the primary guidance system for security measures at U.S. embassies.
"We understand the difficulty of monitoring

terrorist networks and concluded that vulnerable missions cannot rely upon such warning," the board wrote. "We found, however, that both policy and intelligence officials have relied heavily on warning intelligence to measure threats, whereas experience has shown that transnational terrorists often strike without warning at vulnerable targets in areas where expectations of terrorist acts against the U.S. are low." In the Africa cases, the earlier CIA and FBI efforts to track and disrupt el Hage's activities in Nairobi had lulled the agencies into a false belief that they had broken up the local cells. Also, the State Department ignored repeated warnings from the U.S. ambassador to Nairobi, beginning in December 1997, that the chancery building was too close to a major street and was therefore vulnerable to just the sort of truck bombing that eventually occurred.

14.   Interviews with U.S. officials. Tracking the African cells, ibid.

15.   Interview with a U.S. official with direct knowledge of the woman's reaction.

16.   Interviews with multiple senior Clinton administration officials.

17.   Interviews with participants. "Intelligence from a variety" is from Paul R. Pillar, *Terrorism and U.S. Foreign Policy,* pp. 100–101. "Spoke pretty clearly . . . confidence" is from an interview with a Clinton administration official. "The first compelling . . . Americans" is from an interview with a senior Clinton administration official who spoke to Clinton about the incident in 2003.

18.   Interviews with Clinton administration officials. Berger's view about military options is from testimony before the Joint Inquiry Committee, September 19, 2002. "I don't think there was anybody in the press calling for an invasion of Afghanistan" in August 1998 or at any point afterward, Berger testi-

fied. "I just don't think that was something [where] we would have diplomatic support; we would not have had basing support." Clinton's quotation, "As despicable . . . support us" is from an interview with a senior Clinton administration official.

19.   Tenet's briefing that day is from Vernon Loeb, *The Washington Post,* October 21, 1999. See also the chronology provided on the day the missile strikes were announced by Madeleine Albright, transcript of press conference, August 20, 1998, Federal News Service.

20.   Daniel Benjamin and Steven Simon, *The Age of Sacred Terror,* p. 358. National Commission staff investigators later reported that they found "no evidence that domestic political considerations entered into the discussion or decision-making process" during this period.

21.   Interviews with two Clinton administration officials familiar with the Pentagon's targeting work, which seems to have begun around the time of bin Laden's May press conference and his threat-filled interview with ABC News, which was broadcast in the United States a few weeks later.

22.   Interviews with multiple Clinton administration officials. The Zinni quotation is from Bob Woodward and Thomas Ricks, *The Washington Post,* October 3, 2001. In *Terrorism and U.S. Foreign Policy,* p. 107, the CIA's Pillar wrote, "Intelligence about a scheduled meeting of bin Laden and other terrorist leaders . . . determined the timing of the attack." See also the Joint Inquiry Committee's final report, p. 297.

23.   Gul's claim from National Commission, staff report no. 6, p. 6. Hussain's account from interview with Mushahid Hussain, May 21, 2002, Islamabad, Pakistan (SC).

24.   Ibid.

25.   Interviews with U.S. and Pakistani offi-

cials involved in the episode, including the U.S. ambassador to Pakistan at the time, Tom Simons, August 19, 2002, Washington, D.C. (SC). Some published accounts have suggested that Ralston told Karamat directly at dinner that the cruise missiles were in the air. But one U.S. official familiar with the event said that in fact Ralston was not so forthcoming, telling Karamat only in general terms that a "retaliatory action" was being planned by the United States. By this account Ralston left Pakistani airspace before the missiles arrived, infuriating Karamat who felt the Americans had failed to take him adequately into their confidence. Sharif, meanwhile, was angry that the United States talked directly to the army about the attack rather than to Pakistan's supposedly supreme civilian authority, and he was also angry at Karamat, believing that the general had deceived him or let him down. When Pakistani authorities learned that two of the missiles had fallen short and hit inside Pakistani territory, they denounced the attack in public and in private.

26. Interviews with Clinton administration officials. Also Pillar, *Terrorism and U.S. Foreign Policy.*

27. Quotation from an interview with a senior Clinton administation official. The secret Blair House exercise in July is from Benjamin and Simon, *Age of Sacred Terror,* pp. 254–55.

28. "Terrorist war" is quoted by Eleanor Hill, Joint Inquiry Staff Statement, September 18, 2002. "I think it's very important" is from *The Washington Post,* August 22, 1998. "You left us with the baby" is from *The Washington Post,* September 2, 1998.

29. Pillar, *Terrorism and U.S. Foreign Policy,* pp. 103 and 107.

30. Tenet's quotations are from the Joint Inquiry Committee's final report, Appendix, p. 21. Slocombe memo and Clarke forecast

from National Commission, staff statement no. 6, p. 3.

31. That Rana came along and an ISI officer translated is from an interview with a senior Saudi official.

32. Ibid.

33. The Omar quotations are from Prince Turki, ABC News *Nightline,* December 10, 2001.

34. Interview with a senior Saudi official. Speaking to the Associated Press on November 23, 2001, Turki quoted himself similarly: "I told him, 'You will regret it, and the Afghan people will pay a high price for that.'" See also National Commission, staff statement no. 5, pp. 9–10, which reports that Turki returned to Kandahar in June 1999 on a similar mission, "to no effect."

35. Interviews with U.S. officials.

CHAPTER 23: "WE ARE AT WAR"

1. In an early speech after becoming DCI, written to answer the question "Does America Need the CIA?," Tenet described the agency as the country's "insurance policy" against strategic surprise. Text of the speech from November 19, 1997, CIA Office of Public Affairs.

2. Interviews with Clinton administration officials. One recalled his reaction to the Africa bombings this way: "I'm at the White House, so I'm thinking two things: One is the venal thought that it is not good for the president to have embassies blowing up, so probably we want to limit that. And the other is that deterrence really depends on these kinds of things not happening, and that's really important for the exercise of U.S. power."

3. "A tendency . . . attention and resources" is from Paul R. Pillar, *Terrorism and U.S. Foreign Policy,* pp. 115–16.

4. Interviews with U.S. officials. David

Benjamin and Steven Simon highlighted the White House complaints about unedited intelligence in their book, *The Age of Sacred Terror*. The East Africa bombings, they wrote, "had a catalytic effect on CIA stations, foreign intelligence services, and it seemed, everyone who had ever peddled information" (p. 261). The CIA "gave Clinton substantial amounts of threat information that did not require presidential attention" (p. 265).

5. "No double standards" is from interviews with U.S. officials. Benjamin and Simon estimate that "scores" of embassies were closed for at least brief periods during the last months of 1998 and the first months of 1999.

6. Summaries of classified aviation threat reports in the fall of 1998 are from Eleanor Hill, Joint Inquiry Staff Statement, September 18, 2002.

7. Ibid., and interviews with U.S. officials. See also the Joint Inquiry Committee's final report, Appendix, p. 23.

8. Joint Inquiry Staff Statement, September 18, 2002.

9. That the submarine order was closely held, that Tarnak coordinates were preloaded, what Clinton made clear to his senior aides, and that exercises reduced decision-to-target time to about four hours are all from interviews with U.S. officials involved. Delenda Plan and Steinberg quotation from National Commission, staff statement no. 6, pp. 3–4, and no. 8, p. 4.

10. The account that follows is based mainly on interviews with multiple participants. Staff investigators from the National Commission have helpfully corrected two errors in the account of this episode in the first edition of *Ghost Wars*: It occurred in December 1998, not September; and decisionmakers feared hitting a mosque, not a hospital. See staff statement no. 6, p. 7.

11. Clinton's outlook and Clarke's advice from interviews with multiple senior Clinton administration officials involved in the discussions.

12. The Berger quotation is from testimony before the Joint Inquiry Committee, September 19, 2002.

13. That Berger's standard was "significant" or "substantial" probability of success is from interviews with Clinton administration officials.

14. The account in this section of the MONs signed by Clinton is from interviews with multiple officials familiar with the documents. Barton Gellman published the first account of the memos in *The Washington Post*, December 19, 2001. The account here differs from his in a few details. According to officials interviewed by the author, Clinton signed at least four MONs related to bin Laden. The first predated the Africa embassy bombings and authorized the use of force to detain or arrest bin Laden's international couriers, according to these officials. The second was drafted immediately after the embassy bombings and authorized snatch operations against bin Laden and certain of his lieutenants. The third was signed later that autumn and involved bin Laden's aircraft, as described in this chapter. A fourth was signed in late 1999 or early 2000 and involved the CIA's liaison with Massoud, as described in Chapter 25 and following. In addition to authorizing snatch operations by Massoud, Clinton specifically authorized the CIA's tribal team in southern Afghanistan, a Pakistani commando team, and an Uzbek commando team to carry out snatch operations using lethal force against bin Laden and his lieutenants. Whether the authorizations for each of these different strike forces required a separate MON or were handled by some other form of legal documentation is not clear to the author. All the documents re-

main highly classified. "As smart as bin Laden . . . equally ruthless" is from Clinton's speech to the Democratic Leadership Council at New York University, December 6, 2002.

15. Baker is the coauthor of a legal book on these issues, *Regulating Covert Action*.

16. Interviews with U.S. officials.

17. Ibid.

18. Interviews with U.S. officials involved. "We wanted . . . be possible" is from the Joint Inquiry Committee's final report, p. 283.

19. The Hitz quotation is from an op-ed article he published in *The Washington Post*, September 15, 1998. Goss called the Directorate of Operations "gun-shy," according to the Associated Press, September 15, 1998.

20. Clinton's national security adviser, Sandy Berger, confirmed the existence and conclusions of these opinions in testimony before the Joint Inquiry Committee on September 19, 2002. "We received rulings in the Department of Justice," Berger said, "not to prohibit our ability—prohibit our efforts to try to kill bin Laden, because [the assassination ban] did not apply to situations in which you're acting in self-defense or you're acting against command and control targets against an enemy, which he certainly was."

21. The summary of the debate over law enforcement approaches to bin Laden is from interviews with multiple Clinton administration officials. Albright and Cohen quotations are from their written testimony to the National Commission, March 23, 2004.

22. Ibid. See note 14. Pentagon order from National Commission, staff statement no. 6, p. 5.

23. "Written word . . . kettle of fish and much easier" is from an interview with a U.S. official involved. In testimony before the Joint Inquiry Committee investigating the

September 11 attacks, Cofer Black, who led the Counterterrorist Center after 1999, said in a statement, "Operational flexibility: This is a highly classified area. All I want to say is that there was a 'before' 9/11 and 'after' 9/11. After 9/11 the gloves come off." Divided planning in Pentagon from National Commission, staff statement no. 6, p. 5. Clinton's changing language from final report, pp. 126–133.

24. "Unless you find him . . . get the job done" is from an interview with a Clinton administration official involved.

25. "It was no question" is from Berger's testimony before the Joint Inquiry Committee, September 19, 2002. "Any confusion" is from National Commission staff statement no. 7, p. 9.

26. Douglas Frantz, *The New York Times*, December 8, 2001.

27. Michael Griffin, *Reaping the Whirlwind*, p. 207.

28. Ibid., p. 208. The letter was solicited by the Senate Foreign Relations Committee's subcommittee on South Asian affairs.

29. Interviews with multiple State Department officials from this period. Inderfurth summed up the department's policy in an interview: "The United States had been very involved, as had others, during the period of '79 through '89, choosing sides. What was needed now was not to choose sides but to get all parties to talk, and if we had chosen sides, our ability to press all sides to actually sit down would have been impaired. A lot of people that had dealt with Afghanistan over the years said, look, the Northern Alliance and those involved are virtually no better than those they're opposing." Inderfurth said he personally had the view that Massoud's alliance could not possibly be as bad as the Taliban, and among his colleagues "there would be people who would concede the point." The consensus within the State Department was,

according to Inderfurth, "Look, we've gone down that road before. We do not want to become an active participant in the civil conflict; we want to try to bring them together."

30. Statement by Karl F. Inderfurth, Senate Foreign Relations Committee, Subcommittee on Near Eastern and South Asian Affairs, October 8, 1998.

31. Quotations in this paragraph are from Clinton's speech at Georgetown University, November 7, 2001. "Painful and powerful . . . community" is from Clinton's speech to the British Labour Party conference at Blackpool, England, October 3, 2002. Arguably, both the Irish Republican Army and the Zionist movement that emerged after World War II achieved important political goals through terrorist violence—as did the Palestine Liberation Organization.

32. "Fanatics . . . value of life" is from Clinton's Blackpool speech, October 3, 2002.

33. "Take Mr. bin Laden" is from *USA Today*, November 12, 2001. "Reduce the risks . . . in the future" is from Clinton's Blackpool speech, October 3, 2002.

34. Pillar, *Terrorism and U.S. Foreign Policy.* "A challenge . . . solved," p. vii. "A war that cannot be won . . . to some degree controlled," pp. 217–18. The account in this section of the debates between Pillar on the one hand and Clarke's aides Simon and Benjamin on the other is drawn in part from multiple officials in several departments. Skepticism is due when participants seek to characterize their positions about a catastrophe like September 11 in the light of hindsight. In this case, however, it is possible to document the views of Pillar, Simon, and Benjamin without such colorizing. After he left the CIA's Counterterrorist Center in 1999, Pillar spent a year at the Brookings Institution where he synthesized his views and experiences into a book that was written and published just before the events of September 11. In the same

period, after they left the White House, Simon and Benjamin collaborated on an article in the security journal *Survival* about terrorism and al Qaeda. In documenting their competing views here, I have relied solely on language composed by the participants before they had the benefit of knowing about September 11.

35. Pillar, *Terrorism and U.S. Foreign Policy,* p. 120.

36. Ibid. "Often sensational public," p. 4. "Skewed priorities and misdirected resources," p. 203.

37. Paul R. Pillar, "Intelligence and the Campaign Against International Terrorism," in *The Campaign Against International Terrorism,* Georgetown University Press, forthcoming at the time of this writing. This article, unlike his work while at Brookings, was written after the September 11 attacks.

38. All of the quotations in this paragraph are from Pillar, *Terrorism and U.S. Foreign Policy,* p. 56.

39. Steven Simon and Daniel Benjamin, "America and the New Terrorism," *Survival,* Spring 2000, pp. 59–75.

40. Ibid.

41. That Tenet called the White House regularly to highlight specific bin Laden threat reports is from interviews with several Clinton administration officials.

42. Tenet's memo was cited and quoted by Eleanor Hill, Joint Inquiry Staff Statement, September 18, 2002. In congressional testimony that same day, Hill said Tenet's declaration of war inside the CIA was not widely known outside of Langley. "It was the DCI's decision," she said. "It was circulated to some people, but not broadly within the community." Awareness of the gravity of the bin Laden threat, she said, was greater among senior officials than among agents operating in the field. This was especially true at the FBI.

43. That bin Laden became a "Tier 0" priority is from the Joint Inquiry Committee's final report, p. 40. "In hindsight . . . there sooner," p. 42. "We never . . . Directorate of Intelligence," p. 41. "Never got to first base," p. 46.

CHAPTER 24: "LET'S JUST BLOW THE THING UP"

1. Interviews with senior Pakistani government officials.

2. Ziauddin's meetings with Sharif's father in Lahore and his reputation as a political general are from interviews with both senior Pakistani and U.S. officials.

3. The CIA's plan to use ISI to set up bin Laden for ambush or capture is from interviews with U.S. officials. There are varying accounts of how American newspaper reporting caused bin Laden to stop using his satellite telephone in the autumn of 1998. The White House counterterrorism aides Benjamin and Simon cite a *Washington Times* story that reported bin Laden "keeps in touch with the world via computers and satellite phones" as the triggering event. But there were other stories from the same period, including one in *The Washington Post* that quoted former CIA officials and other analysts talking about bin Laden's use of telecommunications.

4. Interviews with U.S. officials.

5. Ibid.

6. "That those ISI individuals . . . didn't know what they were doing" is from an interview with a Clinton administration official. "The policy of the government . . . the overall policy of the government" is from an interview with a second U.S. official. "An incredibly unholy alliance . . . nuclear war in Kashmir" is from an interview with a third senior Clinton administration official.

7. Interviews with U.S. and Pakistani officials.

8. The specific proposal to Ziauddin and his response are from an interview with a U.S. official.

9. Pakistan had paid for but never received American-made F-16 fighter jets at the time economic sanctions were imposed by the congressionally mandated Pressler Amendment in 1991. The original amount frozen was $658 million, but various forms of relief had reduced the amount to $501 million by December 1998, according to the United States. See Associated Press, December 2, 1998.

10. The time and duration of the Oval Office meeting, the Riedel quotation, and the order of Clinton's talking points are from the Federal Document Clearing House transcript of a briefing provided that afternoon by Riedel and Karl F. Inderfurth.

11. Ibid., and interviews with U.S. and Pakistani officials.

12. Details about the Pakistani proposal are from interviews with U.S. officials. One U.S. official and one Pakistani official present vividly recall a discussion about a commando team at this White House meeting. However, evidence assembled by the National Commission suggests the plan was hatched only later, when Sharif met Clinton in July 1999. Either way, it seems clear that training did not begin in earnest until the summer of 1999.

13. Interviews with U.S. and Pakistani officials present. "We tried to get the Pakistanis . . . political risk in getting him" is from *USA Today,* November 12, 2001.

14. What Sharif said at the lunch, including the joke about cruise missiles and the intelligence report on bin Laden's health, is from an interview with Mushahid Hussain, Sharif's information minister during the visit, who was present at the luncheon, May 21, 2002, Islamabad, Pakistan (SC). U.S. officials also recall the report about bin Laden's health.

15. What Sharif, Albright, and Berger said

over lunch is from the Riedel-Inderfurth briefing hours later. The words quoted are Inderfurth's.

16.　Interviews with multiple U.S. officials.

17.　"Since just telling us" is from an interview with a Clinton administration official.

18.　"Had neither the ability nor the inclination" is from interviews with U.S. officials.

19.　Interviews with Haji Habib Ahmadzai and Sayed Khaled Ishelwaty, aides to Abdul Haq, May 14, 2002, Kabul, Afghanistan (GW).

20.　Ibid. Interview with Peter Tomsen, January 21, 2002, Omaha, Nebraska (SC).

21.　The account of the desert camp episode is based on interviews with seven U.S. officials familiar with the event. Several of the officials were interviewed multiple times about the episode. The National Commission's staff statement no. 6, p. 8, adds important public confirmation and precise dates. Barton Gellman, writing in *The Washington Post* of December 19, 2001, was the first to make public reference to the episode.

22.　Mary Anne Weaver, "Of Birds and Bombs," *APF Reporter,* online at www.aliciapatterson.org.

23.　That the U.A.E. effectively maintained a secret air base in northern Pakistan for hunting is from the author's interview with a U.S. official. After the events of September 11, Pakistan made the base available to the United States for clandestine use in its 2001 military campaign against al Qaeda and the Taliban, this official said. It was only then that the U.S. learned of the arrangement between Pakistan and the U.A.E., the official said.

24.　Ahmed Rashid, *Taliban: Militant Islam, Oil, and Fundamentalism in Central Asia,* p. 201, describes the early contacts between Taliban leaders and Arab hunters in the winter of 1994–95. Unocal employees and consultants who watched bin Laden settle in Kandahar

in the winter of 1996–97 said he had a local reputation as an avid falcon hunter.

25.　Interviews with U.S. officials.

26.　Ibid. The quotation is from an interview with Gary Schroen, November 7, 2002, Washington, D.C. (SC).

27.　Ibid.

28.　AAP Newsfeed, May 13, 1998. Vice President Al Gore announced the agreement with Sheikh Zayed at the White House. Also, interviews with Clinton administration officials.

29.　Interviews with U.S. officials.

30.　Interview with Schroen, November 7, 2002.

31.　"Wanted to cooperate . . . were properly understood" is from an interview by the author.

32.　Interview with Schroen, November 7, 2002.

33.　Interviews with U.S. officials. The quotation from Mike, although he is not identified even by his first name, appears on p. 237 of the Joint Inquiry Committee's final report.

34.　Prepared testimony of George Tenet before the Joint Inquiry Committee, October 17, 2002. Mike's cable quotation from National Commission final report, p. 140. Clinton quotations from *Newsweek,* April 18, 2002.

CHAPTER 25: "THE MANSON FAMILY"

1.　Statement of the Director of Central Intelligence, Senate Armed Services Committee, "Current and Projected National Security Threats," February 2, 1999.

2.　"Like two-year-olds" is from an interview with a U.S. official.

3.　Ninety-seven-paragraph statement: "Current and Projected National Security Threats," February 2, 1999.

4.　"Daunting impediments . . . pressure on bin Laden" is from the prepared testimony of George Tenet before the Joint Inquiry Committee, October 17, 2002. Cofer Black made the same retrospective argument at these hearings: "Frankly, from an intelligence perspective, in order to have a fighting chance to protect this country from al Qaeda, we needed to attack the Afghan terrorist sanctuary protected by the Taliban. CIA appreciated this all too well. That is also why on 11 September we were ready and prepared to be the first boots on the ground."

5. "A new comprehensive plan ... principal lieutenants" is from the prepared testimony of George Tenet before the Joint Inquiry Committee, October 17, 2002; details about intelligence collection goals are from interviews with U.S. officials.

6. Interviews with U.S. officials.

7. Ibid. During the Joint Inquiry Committee hearings, a dispute erupted between the committee's staff director, Eleanor Hill, and the CIA press office over the number of agency analysts who had been assigned to follow bin Laden and other terrorists prior to September 11. Hill said the CIA had only 3 analysts assigned to al Qaeda full-time at the Counterterrorist Center, a number that rose to 5 during 2000. The CIA argued that this selection of statistics vastly understated the number of analysts working on the bin Laden and terrorism target in other departments. In a press statement the agency said that 115 analysts throughout the agency worked on terrorism during this period and that the bin Laden unit directed 200 officers worldwide. It is hard to know how to evaluate this argument since all of the underlying statistics and personnel records remain classified. The estimate of 25 professionals working in the bin Laden unit in 1999, from interviews with U.S. officials, would include personnel assigned to the CIA from other agencies such as the FBI and the National

Security Agency. The Joint Inquiry Committee's final report estimated there were "about 40 officers from throughout the Intelligence Community" assigned to the unit prior to September 11, 2001. The statistics about average experience and "take direction from the ladies" is from the final report, p. 64.

8. Ibid. All quotations are from the author's interviews.

9. Ibid.

10. Ibid. "We are at war ... his operations" from the Joint Inquiry Committee's final report, Appendix, pp. 26–27.

11. The 30 percent cut in operating budget and the statistics about Directorate of Operations personnel during the 1990s are from the testimony of Cofer Black before the Joint Inquiry Committee, September 26, 2002. Black said he had to allocate only "as many people as three infantry companies" across all the targets tracked by the Counterterrorist Center. Some of these groups, such as Hezbollah, which in 1999 had killed more Americans than al Qaeda, required substantial resources, Black said. Overall, Black testified, "We did not have enough people, money, or sufficiently flexible rules of engagement." Congressional investigators later criticized Black's plan to confront bin Laden for "an absence of rigor in the planning process."

12. The account of the Tashkent bombing and its aftermath is from *The Washington Post,* February 17, 1999, and Ahmed Rashid, *The New Yorker,* January 14, 2002. Rashid reported in this excerpt from his book *Jihad* that the Tashkent bombings allegedly were organized in the United Arab Emirates.

13. Interviews with U.S. officials.

14. Details of Karimov's cooperation and the attitude of the CIA, ibid. Clinton administration officials from the Pentagon and State were equally enthusiastic about the liaison. General Anthony Zinni, the Marine

general who then ran Central Command, led the Pentagon's charge into Central Asia, flying there repeatedly for meetings with his counterparts and developing military-to-military cooperation. Albright and FBI Director Louis Freeh also traveled to Tashkent within a year of the February 1999 car bombings.

15. Interviews with Clinton administration officials. Quotations are from interviews with two different officials.

16. Interview with Qayum Karzai, May 21, 2002, Kabul, Afghanistan (GW).

17. Interview with Hamid Karzai, October 21, 2002, Kabul, Afghanistan (SC).

18. Ibid., and interviews with U.S. officials.

19. Ibid.

20. Inderfurth testimony before Senate Appropriations subcommittee on foreign operations, "Afghanistan Today: The U.S. Response," March 9, 1999.

21. Interviews with State Department officials involved in the discussions.

22. Pickering's argument, ibid.

23. Massoud's outlook during this period, phone calls with Mullah Omar, and back-channel meetings with Taliban representatives are from multiple interviews with Massoud aides and relatives. Interviews with his foreign policy adviser, Abdullah, May 8, 2002, Kabul, Afghanistan, and February 26, 2003, Washington, D.C. (GW), and Ahmed Wali Massoud, May 7, 2002, Kabul, Afghanistan (GW). Also multiple interviews with senior intelligence aides to Massoud during this period.

24. Interviews with State Department officials. Interview with Karl "Rick" Inderfurth, May 7, 2002, Washington, D.C. (SC). Defending this policy, Inderfurth said, "It was very clear in the discussions that we had with other countries that we would never support a Taliban regime taking control of the country, never recognize it until all of these vari-

ous concerns were addressed—including terrorism, including human rights, including narcotics. . . . We also made it clear—whether it would be with the Russians or indeed with the Iranians—that it was important Massoud remain a viable opposition force. And that's all we needed to say."

25. "Statement by Karl Inderfurth," Tashkent, July 19, 1999. Also, "Tashkent Declaration on Fundamental Principles for a Peaceful Settlement of the Conflict in Afghanistan."

26. Interview with Inderfurth, May 7, 2002.

27. Interviews with Massoud's advisers and aides; see note 23.

28. Interviews with multiple State Department and Clinton administration officials. Sheehan wrote a thirty-page classified memo during this period urging more pressure on U.S. allies such as Saudi Arabia, the United Arab Emirates, and Pakistan over the terrorism problem. The memo called Pakistan central to the problem and suggested that terrorism should be elevated as the primary issue in U.S.-Pakistan relations. The memo was ignored by senior State Department officials who believed nuclear proliferation and economic development had to remain near the top of the agenda with Pakistan. See *The New York Times,* October 29, 2001, and *The Washington Post,* December 20, 2001. Clinton's outlook on Pakistan is from a senior administration official who reviewed the subject with Clinton in 2003.

29. The account of the CIA's opening to Massoud and the Counterterrorist Center's initial trip to the Panjshir are from interviews with multiple U.S. officials as well as multiple interviews with intelligence and foreign policy advisers to Massoud.

30. Previous CIA payments to Massoud, after 1996, had been authorized from the Stinger recovery program. The October 1999 visit inaugurated a counterterrorism pro-

gram that also produced cash stipends to Massoud from the CIA. Agency officers carried cash on multiple official visits after 1999. One official estimated the typical payment at $250,000; another recalled it was $500,000.

31. All quotations are from author's interviews. These sorts of exchanges reinforced a pattern of mutual suspicion between the Clinton White House and the CIA.

32. The language quoted is from interviews with U.S. officials. Without prompting, several officials in different areas of government used the same phrase in interviews when they described the policy guidance. A declassified sentence in a redacted section of the Joint Inquiry Committee's final report asserts: "The CIA was not authorized to upset the political balance in Afghanistan." What Clinton said about Massoud and what he recalled about the analysis he received at the time is from a senior administration official who reviewed the subject with Clinton in 2003. For the February memo, see National Commission final report, p. 139.

33. Interviews with U.S. officials and Massoud aides. As part of this network the CIA installed a secure phone in the suburban basement of Daoud Mir, Massoud's envoy in Washington. The network effectively put the CIA in real-time contact with Massoud agents who placed radio sets as far forward into Taliban territory as Kabul and Jalalabad, according to Massoud intelligence aides.

34. The quotation is from author's interview.

35. "American solution" is from an interview with a U.S. official.

36. Interview with Abdullah, February 26, 2003.

37. Ibid.

38. Ibid.

39. Interview with a senior intelligence aide to Massoud.

CHAPTER 26: "THAT UNIT DISAPPEARED"

1. The Taliban's role is inferred from court testimony provided by a Hamburg cell member who traveled to Kandahar immediately after the four described here. Mounir el-Motassadeq testified that Atta told him in February 2000 how to travel to Afghanistan for training and that his only instructions were to go to the Taliban office at an address in Quetta that Atta provided. When he got there, Motassadeq said, the Taliban did not ask why he had come; they arranged for him to travel to Kandahar.

2. The Atta biography is from McDermott, *Los Angeles Times,* January 27, 2002. Jarrah's biography is from Laabs and McDermott, *Los Angeles Times,* January 27, 2003. Binalshibh's background is from *The New York Times,* February 10, 2003; *Los Angeles Times,* October 24, 2002; and Associated Press, September 14, 2002.

3. Interviews with U.S. officials. Testimony of George Tenet, Senate Intelligence Committee, February 2, 2000.

4. Interviews with U.S. officials.

5. The trial of Mounir el-Motassadeq and his conviction as an accessory in the September 11 attacks, held in Germany during the winter of 2003, produced the first courtroom evidence and witness statements documenting the birth and growth of the Hamburg cell. McDermott (see note 2) and Peter Finn in *The Washington Post* have published rich interview-based biographies of Atta, Jarrah, Zammar, and others. CIA and FBI reporting about Zammar is from the Joint Inquiry Committee's final report, pp. 29–30.

6. Swanson and Crewdson, *Chicago Tribune,* February 20, 2003, reported that "police records" they obtained showed that "among the numbers called were three belonging to radical Saudi clerics. . . . The calls occurred soon after the three clerics—Nasser

al-Omar, Safar al-Hawali, and Saman al-Auda—were freed in 1999." The calls were reportedly placed from a phone belonging to Motassadeq.

7. "A house of study . . . attached to his mother" is from McDermott, *Los Angeles Times,* January 27, 2002. "Raising him as a girl" is from *The New York Times,* October 10, 2001. "Almost tricked him" and "embodied the idea of drawing" are from McDermott.

8. "Danger" is from *The Washington Post,* July 15, 2002. "The victors will come . . . paradise is rising" is from Laabs and McDermott, *Los Angeles Times,* January 27, 2003.

9. National Commission staff statement no. 16, pp. 2–4, 13–14, 18–19.

10. Ibid.

11. *Chicago Tribune,* February 26, 2003.

12. The information on Musharraf's family is from *The New Yorker,* August 12, 2002. Musharraf's attitude toward the Taliban is from an interview with Pervez Musharraf, May 25, 2002, Islamabad, Pakistan (SC), and interviews with Pakistani and U.S. officials who talked regularly with Musharraf.

13. "He took off his commando jacket" and "Down to earth" are from *The New Yorker,* August 12, 2002.

14. What the embassy pieced together is from interviews with U.S. officials. Also, Bruce Riedel, "American Diplomacy and the 1999 Kargil Summit at Blair House," Center for Advanced Study of India, University of Pennsylvania, Policy Paper Series 2002.

15. That Musharraf briefed Sharif and that Sharif approved is from multiple sources including U.S. officials. This remains a subject of controversy among some Pakistani commentators and political figures.

16. That the information was obtained from cables from Islamabad and a dozen secret letters from interviews with U.S. officials. Reports of Pakistan preparing its nuclear arsenal for possible use is from Riedel, "American Diplomacy and the 1999 Kargil Summit."

Riedel, then at the National Security Council, cites one "well-informed assessment" which concluded that a Pakistani strike on Bombay alone with a small weapon "would kill between 150,000 and 850,000." Clinton's June 19 letter is from Madeleine Albright's written testimony to the National Commission, March 23, 2004.

17. Riedel, ibid. "Sharif seemed to be hedging his bet on whether this would be a round trip."

18. Ibid.

19. Interview with Mushahid Hussain, May 21, 2002, Islamabad, Pakistan (SC).

20. "I want to help you" is from an interview with a U.S. official. "A pretty good standard . . . intelligence for action" is from an interview with a second U.S. official.

21. Riedel, "American Diplomacy and the 1999 Kargil Summit."

22. Ziauddin with Pickering is from an interview with a U.S. official. The October 7 meeting between Ziauddin and Omar is from Michael Griffin, *Reaping the Whirlwind,* p. 233, and interviews with U.S. and Pakistani officials.

23. That Ziauddin ordered the CIA-trained commandos to protect Sharif from a coup is from an interview with a U.S. official familiar with detailed American intelligence reporting on the incident.

24. The account here of Ziauddin, the Tenth Corps, and the end of the CIA-funded commando unit is from interviews with seven U.S. officials. Some accounts of the coup published in South Asia and elsewhere have speculated that Musharraf moved against Sharif to block Ziauddin from ending ISI's support for the Taliban—that it was ISI, in effect, that created the coup. But Ziauddin was too weak a figure to be much of a threat. Besides, the evidence makes clear that Musharraf was not actively planning a coup in early October. Otherwise, he would not have

taken a working vacation to Sri Lanka. It was Sharif who brought his own reign down by misjudging his support in the army and with ISI's rank and file when he tried to fire Musharraf.

25. *The New Yorker,* August 12, 2002.

26. Interview with a U.S. official.

27. Interview with a senior Pakistani official close to Musharraf.

28. Interview with Thomas Pickering, April 24, 2002, Rosslyn, Virginia (SC). "Diverted the discussion . . . return to democracy" is from an interview with a second Clinton administration official. A central player in the U.S. relationship with Musharraf, both during the Kargil crisis and after the coup, was the American Marine Corps general Anthony Zinni, then commander-in-chief of CENTCOM. Early in 2000, while traveling in Central Asia, Zinni told Dana Priest of *The Washington Post,* "If Pakistan fails, we have major problems. If Musharraf fails, hardliners could take over, or fundamentalists, or chaos. We can't let Musharraf fail."

29. Interview with David Boren, September 16, 2002, Norman, Oklahoma (GW).

30. Testimony of George Tenet, Joint Inquiry Committee, October 17, 2002, and the committee's final report, Appendix, p. 29.

31. "So great was the fear" is from Daniel Benjamin and Steven Simon, *The Age of Sacred Terror,* p. 311.

32. Judith Miller, *The New York Times,* January 15, 2001.

33. The information regarding Berger's meetings is from his testimony before the Joint Inquiry Committee, September 19, 2002. "Operations we knew . . . early January 2000" is from testimony of an unidentified "senior officer" of the CIA's Counterterrorist Center before the Joint Inquiry Committee, September 20, 2002.

34. The account of the cash and course notes is from *The Seattle Times,* June 28, 2002.

35. Clinton's call to Musharraf is from an interview with a senior U.S. official who reviewed notes of the conversation. Milam is from National Commission final report, p. 176.

36. Benjamin and Simon, *Age of Sacred Terror,* pp. 31–32.

37. Interview with Cofer Black, September 13, 2002 (SC).

38. "Provided a kind of tuning fork . . . what they were doing" is from testimony of the Counterterrorist Center officer, September 20, 2002.

39. Eleanor Hill, Joint Inquiry Staff report, September 20, 2002.

40. Interview with Cofer Black, September 13, 2002. National Commission, Staff Statement no. 2, p. 4.

41. Eleanor Hill report, September 20, 2002.

42. Ibid.

43. Tenet's testimony, October 17, 2002. In her independent review of this failure, Eleanor Hill concluded that the CIA's "practice for watch listing was often based upon an individual officer's level of personal experience with, and understanding of, how other government agencies received and used this information. There also may have been too much emphasis on making certain there was a minimum fixed amount of information on an individual before he or she was watch listed."

44. Eleanor Hill report, September 20, 2002.

45. For a full account of how the Malaysia plotters were connected to the plans eventually carried out on September 11, see National Commission staff statement no. 16, which draws on interrogation statements of al Qaeda leaders in U.S. custody.

46. Testimony of George Tenet, Senate Select Committee on Intelligence, February 2, 2000.

47. Tenet testimony, October 17, 2002.

48. Ziad Jarrah was detained by authorities in the United Arab Emirates in January 2000 for an irregularity in his passport. But the CIA was not involved in this incident in any way, and the detention did not lead to any surveillance or further action, according to Eleanor Hill of the Joint Inquiry Staff.

CHAPTER 27: "YOU CRAZY WHITE GUYS"

1. Interviews with multiple U.S. officials and aides to Massoud familiar with the intelligence collection efforts at Derunta. After September 11, documentary evidence surfaced that confirmed al Qaeda's interest in chemical weapons. The hard drive of a computer used by Ayman al-Zawahiri in Kabul showed that around the summer of 1999 he exchanged notes with bin Laden's military commander, Mohammed Atef, about how to build a laboratory for what they called the "yogurt" program. This was a modest effort with an initial budget of only $2,000. Documents found by journalists at Rishikor, an al Qaeda camp used by Uzbeks and others outside of Kabul, described a curriculum with a section on the manufacture of "major poisons and gases," including ricin and cyanide. See *The Wall Street Journal,* July 2, 2002, and *The New York Times,* March 17, 2002.

2. "What do you think this is?" is from an interview with a U.S. official. "We're on mules" is from an interview with a second U.S. official.

3. Interviews with two U.S. officials.

4. Ibid.

5. Interview with a senior aide to Massoud who was involved with the CIA liaison. Speaking of the events of September 11, the adviser continued: "Those who criticize the security agencies in the United States for the loss of life, property, and suffering, they are wrong. They have to criticize the law, they

have to criticize the people who really restricted, people with knowledge to do something." All quotations from American officials in the previous four paragraphs are from the author's interviews with senior officials directly involved. After September 11, Clinton's White House aides and CIA officers at Langley offered almost opposite views about the impact of the legal guidance on covert operations with Massoud and others. National Security Adviser Sandy Berger, who was primarily responsible for the classified legal authorizations, testified to the Joint Inquiry Committee: "We were not pursuing a law enforcement model. . . . We were trying to kill bin Laden and his lieutenants." Berger cited the president's willingness to fire cruise missiles at bin Laden—if the Saudi could be reliably located—as evidence of this intent. But at the same hearings Cofer Black emphasized that White House rules had inhibited CIA operations, especially those with proxy forces such as Massoud. "We did not have . . . sufficiently flexible rules of engagement," he said. Asked if the United States should "consider revoking the prohibition against the use of lethal force" in counterterrorist operations, Black replied, "Yes."

6. "Relationship . . . minor issue," from an interview with an intelligence aide to Massoud. The perception of a double standard in American policy toward Massoud is from interviews with multiple aides and advisers.

7. Interviews with multiple U.S. officials. Quotations from Black's briefing documents are from the Joint Inquiry Committee's final report, pp. 387–88. That unilateral reports outstripped liaison reports in 1999: Tenet's testimony before the Joint Inquiry Committee, October 17, 2002. "By 9/11, a map would show that these collection programs and human networks were in place in such numbers as to nearly cover Afghanistan,"

Tenet testified. That CIA never penetrated bin Laden's leadership group prior to September 11 is from the Joint Inquiry Committee's final report, p. 91. "If the Drug Enforcement Administration can put actual, salaried *American* officers undercover in clannish narcotrafficking organizations in foreign countries, surely the CIA can learn to penetrate aggressively proselytizing Islamic fundamentalist organizations," Senator Richard Shelby complained of this failure in 2003.

8. Interviews with U.S. officials. Albright quotation from her written testimony to the National Commission, March 23, 2004.

9. Ibid. "Anytime . . . next day at noon" is from an interview with a U.S. official.

10. Ibid. Abdullah recalled receiving CIA satellite maps of the Uruzgan camp: interview with Abdullah, February 26, 2003, Washington, D.C. (GW).

11. Interviews with multiple U.S. officials. Details about the aborted attacks are in National Commission staff statement no. 7, p. 4.

12. Interview with Zekrullah Jahed Khan, May 28, 2002, Kabul, Afghanistan (GW). "Bin Laden's too hard" is from an interview with a U.S. official.

13. Quotations from interviews with U.S. officials.

14. Interviews with multiple U.S. officials and multiple intelligence aides to Massoud.

15. Ibid.

16. Ibid.

17. Interview with Hugh Shelton, October 31, 2002, Reston, Virginia. (SC). David Halberstam, *War in a Time of Peace,* p. 414.

18. Daniel Benjamin and Steven Simon, *The Age of Sacred Terror,* pp. 294–96. "We don't have Pakistan . . . likely to fail" is from Berger's testimony to the Joint Inquiry Committee, September 19, 2002.

19. "All we had . . . sheikh is coming" is from an interview with a Pentagon official. Cohen quotations from National Commission, staff statement no. 6, p. 5, and his written testimony, March 23, 2004.

20. That planners saw political and tactical problems operating near Pakistan is from the interview with Shelton, October 31, 2002.

21. "A standard military position . . . cannon fodder" is from Benjamin and Simon, *Age of Sacred Terror,* pp. 294–96. "It would scare the shit," ibid., p. 318. And interviews with U.S. officials.

22. Interview with Shelton, October 31, 2002.

23. Ibid.

24. Ibid., and interviews with Clinton administration officials.

25. Interviews with U.S. officials.

26. Ibid.

27. Ibid. The quotation is from an interview with a Clinton administration official.

28. Ibid. The quotation is from the interview with Shelton, October 31, 2002.

29. Interview with Shelton, October 31, 2002. Also based on interviews with multiple Clinton administration officials. "We had a force . . . predicate to do it" is from an interview with Thomas Pickering, April 24, 2002, Rosslyn, Virginia (SC). That Berger noted sixty-seven Americans dead from terrorism during Clinton's presidency and that he saw no political context or support for an American war in Afghanistan is from his testimony to the Joint Inquiry Committee, September 19, 2002. Clarke memo and March meeting from National Commission staff statement no. 8, pp. 5–6.

30. Shelton quotation is from interview, October 31, 2002.

31. Interviews with U.S. officials.

32. The account of this meeting is from multiple American and Afghan officials present or familiar with reports of the discussion.

33. Interview with Abdullah, February 26, 2003.

CHAPTER 28: "IS THERE ANY POLICY?"

1. Hired Lanny Davis: *The Washington Post,* February 6, 2000. Mahmoud's role is from interviews with Pakistani and U.S. officials. See also Michael Griffin, *Reaping the Whirlwind,* pp. 234–35.

2. Interviews with U.S. officials. Mahmoud's biography is also from Pakistani journalist Kamran Khan and Pakistani officials who worked with him.

3. Interviews with U.S. and Pakistani officials.

4. The information about the renditions of Arab Islamists is from interviews with U.S. and Pakistani officials. Officials from both sides recall that one of the suspects was a Jordanian with an American passport who eventually had to be released for lack of charges. "Actively considering" is from *The Washington Post,* February 4, 2000.

5. That Clinton overruled the Secret Service is from Daniel Benjamin and Steven Simon, *The Age of Sacred Terror,* pp. 317–18. Also, interview with Rick Inderfurth, May 7, 2002, Washington, D.C. (SC). The State Department itself documented the extraordinary expansion of al Qaeda–linked Kashmiri militants during Musharraf's first year in office, in its report "Patterns of Global Terrorism 2000," released in April 2001.

6. "First since Nixon" is from Dennis Kux, *The United States and Pakistan, 1947–2000,* p. 356.

7. "We're going to show them . . . up in the air" is from the interview with Inderfurth, May 7, 2002.

8. Clinton on the plane is from Inderfurth, ibid. The scene on the tarmac is from Inderfurth, ibid.; and *The Washington Post,* March 26, 2000; and interviews with a Pakistani official who was present.

9. Interview with the Pakistani official quoted; all of the dialogue is from this official's recollection.

10. "Uncertain loyalties" is from Benjamin and Simon, *Age of Sacred Terror,* pp. 317–18.

11. Berger's recollections, ibid. Also, interview with a Pakistani official, and National Commission staff statement no. 5, pp. 13–14.

12. "Danger that Pakistan . . . no one can win" is from *The Washington Post,* March 26, 2000.

13. Interviews with U.S. officials.

14. Ibid. The quotation is from the author's interview with an official.

15. "Vacillated" is from the interview with Hugh Shelton, October 31, 2002, Rosslyn, Virginia (SC). "May hold the key" is from Anthony Zinni's testimony before the Senate Armed Services Committee, February 29, 2000.

16. "People who do that . . . that position" is from Barton Gellman, *The Washington Post,* December 19, 2001, and from interviews with a U.S. and a Pakistani official. Reports about Taliban and bin Laden from National Commission, staff statement no. 5, p. 10.

17. Tim Judah, "The Taliban Papers," *Survival,* pp. 69–80. Judah's important article makes use of Pakistani foreign ministry papers discovered in that country's looted embassy in Kabul immediately after the fall of the capital in the autumn of 2001.

18. Ibid. If the Pakistani documents are accurate—and Judah's reporting leaves little doubt that they are—then some or all of the CIA, National Security Council, and State Department officials Mahmoud met in April must have delivered these threats to endorse Russian aerial attacks and U.S. missile strikes against Taliban targets.

19. Ibid.

20. Ibid. Written testimony of Louis Freeh to the National Commission, April 13, 2004.

Tenet and Musharraf from National Commission final report, p. 503.

21. Interview with a Pakistani official who talked with Mahmoud during the spring of 2000. U.S. officials said they did not start to pick up on Mahmoud's reported religious conversion until the next year.

22. From an interview with the same Pakistani official.

23. Interviews with U.S. officials.

24. Ibid.

25. At least $3 million from accounts of the National Commercial Bank is from testimony of Vincent Cannistraro, House International Relations Committee, October 3, 2001; *Boston Herald,* October 14, 2001. That IIRO gave the Taliban $60 million is from its secretary-general, Adnan Basha, quoted in *The Washington Post,* September 29, 2001.

26. Sheehan's cable suppressed is from Benjamin and Simon, *Age of Sacred Terror,* pp. 294–95.

27. "Allegations . . . enforced consistently" is from the State Department's report "Patterns of Global Terrorism 2000," April 2001. The conclusions of American investigators are from National Commission staff statement no. 15, p. 10.

28. Interview with Prince Turki, August 2, 2002, Cancun, Mexico (SC). "Did not effectively . . . liaison services" is from the Joint Inquiry Committee's final report, p. xvii.

29. What Massoud believed in the summer of 2000 is from interviews with several of his senior aides. Massoud's supply lines are described in detail in "Afghanistan, Crisis of Impunity," Human Rights Watch, July 2001. The figure of $10 million from India is from an interview with a U.S. official familiar with detailed reporting about Massoud's aid. That figure is an estimate for one year of assistance from India in the 2000 time period. Ismail Khan's escape from a Kandahar prison is from Larry P. Goodson, *Afghanistan's End-*

less War, p. 84. He had been held by the Taliban since 1997. Assistant Secretary of State Rick Inderfurth, testifying before a Senate Foreign Relations subcommittee in July 2000, also cited the April assassination of the Taliban-appointed governor of Kunduz as evidence of gathering dissent.

30. Interview with Abdullah, May 8, 2002, Kabul, Afghanistan (GW). Also, interview with a senior intelligence aide to Massoud.

31. Interview with Danielle Pletka, March 27, 2002, Washington, D.C. (GW). Earlier in 2000, Secretary of State Madeleine Albright presented Congress with a twenty-four-page statement titled "America and the World in the 21st Century." She devoted one sentence to Afghanistan and did not mention bin Laden by name.

32. Interviews with U.S. officials. The State Department provided several hundred thousand dollars during 2000 to aid efforts at political negotiations organized from exiled King Zahir Shah's offices in Rome. Squabbling among royal factions and slow progress disillusioned State officials, however, and the stipend was reduced the following year.

33. "Remarks by Karl F. Inderfurth," at a hearing of the Senate Foreign Relations Committee, Subcommittee on Near Eastern and South Asian Affairs. Tellingly, the hearing was entitled "The Taliban: Engagement or Confrontation?" The Congress as well as the Clinton administration could not make up its mind about that question.

34. Interviews with U.S. officials, including Gary Schroen, November 7, 2002, Washington D.C. (SC).

35. Ibid.

36. Interview with Hamid Karzai, October 21, 2002, Kabul, Afghanistan (SC).

37. Interview with Afrasiab Khattak, May 23, 2002, Islamabad, Pakistan (SC).

38. Interviews with U.S. officials.

39. Ibid. The accounts of internal debates

about travel to the Panjshir in this section are drawn primarily from interviews with four officials familiar with them.

40. Interview with a senior intelligence aide to Massoud.

41. Ibid.

CHAPTER 29: "DARING ME TO KILL THEM"

1. Details of discussions about new options in the hunt for bin Laden are from interviews with multiple U.S. officials. Berger testified about the memo he wrote to Clinton and dated it as February before the Joint Inquiry Committee on September 19, 2002.

2. Interviews with multiple U.S. officials. Clarke operated in a series of bureaucratic coalitions, and his ability to create policy or programmatic change on his own was limited. George Tenet was exceptionally alert to the al Qaeda threat, aggressively warned the White House about specific threat intelligence, and pushed for strong disruption efforts from the CIA's Counterterrorist Center. Tenet's role in key policy debates after 1998—whether to covertly arm the Northern Alliance, whether to arm the Predator—is less clear. Allen's comment is from National Commission staff statement no. 7, p. 5.

3. Details of the Eagle program are from an interview with Dewey Clarridge, December 28, 2001, Escondido, California (SC). Other CIA officials confirmed his account. A search of electronic news databases turned up no previously published account of the Eagle. Clarridge does not discuss it in his memoir.

4. Karem's background and role are from an interview with James Woolsey, February 20, 2002, Washington, D.C. (SC). See also *Aviation Week and Space Technology,* December 14, 1987; May 23, 1988; and June 20, 1988, for details of Amber's early history and

design characteristics. *Popular Science,* September 1994, provides a history of the Predator to that point, including an account of Karem's role.

5. Interview with Thomas Twetten, March 18, 2002, Washington, D.C. (SC). Interview with Woolsey, February 20, 2002. The information on Navy funding is from *Aerospace Daily,* January 28, 1994. Between its birth as Amber and its operational debut as Predator, the prototype drone was also called the Gnat.

6. Interviews with Woolsey, February 20, 2002, and Twetten, March 18, 2002. Interview with Whit Peters, May 6, 2002, Washington, D.C. (SC). The Air Force announced that the Eleventh Reconnaissance Squadron would operate Predators in July 1995, *Aerospace Daily,* July 31, 1995.

7. Twenty-four hours, five hundred miles, twenty-five thousand feet, and the Sony camera are from *Popular Science,* September 1994. The pilot profiles and roles of payload specialists in the van are from *Air Force Magazine,* September 1997, which profiled the Eleventh Reconnaissance Squadron. Also, interview with Peters, May 6, 2002.

8. Interview with Woolsey, February 20, 2002.

9. Debate about intelligence collection versus the kill chain is from interview with Peters, May 6, 2002, and interviews with multiple other U.S. officials. Navy test to link Predator to attack submarines is from *Defense Daily,* June 7, 1995. Laser targeting in Kosovo but not used is from the interview with Peters.

10. Interview with Thomas Pickering, April 24, 2002, Rosslyn, Virginia (SC). Interviews with multiple U.S. officials. What Clarke said is from an interview with a U.S. official.

11. Quotations from interviews with U.S. officials.

12. Barton Gellman first described the

INF treaty debate in *The Washington Post,* December 19, 2001. The account here is also from interviews with U.S. officials.

13. Interviews with U.S. officials.

14. Interview with Peters, May 6, 2002. Interviews with other U.S. officials. Daniel Benjamin and Steven Simon, *The Age of Sacred Terror,* pp. 322–23.

15. This account of the Predator proof of concept mission, including the scenes in the Langley flight center, is drawn from interviews with five U.S. officials familiar with the operation. All quotations are from author's interviews, except Clarke's exchange with Berger, from National Commission staff statement no. 8, p. 7.

16. Ibid. Benjamin and Simon provide an account of the autumn mission that includes the MiG incident, although they make no reference to the location of the flight center or the size and nature of the audience.

17. Ibid.

18. Ibid. "The pilot will return" is from an interview with a U.S. official.

19. Interview with Peters, May 6, 2002. Interviews with multiple U.S. officials. Benjamin and Simon report that Peters resolved the problem in December 2000 by locating enough money to keep the Predator program going in Afghanistan.

20. Interviews with U.S. officials. Recalled one of these officials of the wind problem: "No matter how fast it was going, it would go backwards. So we had to stop. And the thought was, okay, we would begin again in March or April."

21. That there were long discussions of blast fragmentation patterns at Tarnak is from interviews with multiple U.S. officials. Tarnak's layout is from interviews and author's visit, October 2002.

22. Ibid. In 2001 the CIA watched as bin Laden moved his family and other civilians out of Tarnak and began to turn the compound into a military training camp. U.S. analysts concluded that bin Laden had finally realized he was being closely watched at Tarnak and it was not safe. In place of the laundry lines and children's swing he erected a military obstacle course and firing range.

23. *Newsweek,* April 8, 2002. Clinton made his comments in an interview with Jonathan Alter. "I don't care . . . people will die" is from Clinton's speech to the British Labour Party conference, October 3, 2002.

24. Interviews with U.S. officials. Also, Gellman, *The Washington Post,* December 19, 2001, and Benjamin and Simon, *Age of Sacred Terror.* Said one White House official of Tenet's enthusiasm for the Predator images, "George, eventually, seeing the videotapes, decided this was the greatest thing since sliced bread. And [now] it was his idea in the first place." Clinton's outlook and "strong and constant view" from an interview with a senior administration official who reviewed the subject with Clinton in 2003.

25. Larry P. Goodson, *Afghanistan's Endless War,* p. 84. Human Rights Watch, "Crisis of Impunity," July 2001. The Human Rights Watch researchers reported that "the U.S. government was sufficiently concerned about the possibility of Pakistani involvement" in the capture of Taloqan "that it issued démarche to the Pakistani government in late 2000, asking for assurances that Pakistan had not been involved. The démarche listed features of the assault on Taloqan that suggested the Taliban had received outside assistance . . . including the length of preparatory artillery fire [and] the fact that much of the fighting took place at night." The CIA's $30 million estimate is from National Commission staff statement no. 15, p. 11.

26. *The Washington Post,* October 13, 2000; October 15, 2000; and June 19, 2001. What the CIA later concluded is from interviews with U.S. officials.

27. No specific tactical warning is from "Terrorist Attack on USS *Cole*: Background and Issues for Congress," Congressional Research Service, January 30, 2001. The Pentagon analyst resignation is from *The Washington Post,* October 26, 2000; and *The New York Times,* October 26, 2000. Benjamin and Simon are from *Age of Sacred Terror,* p. 324. Zinni defended himself in testimony before a Senate subcommittee on October 19, 2000; see *The Washington Post,* October 20, 2000.

28. Sandy Berger testified to the Joint Inquiry Committee on September 19, 2002, that "when we left office, neither the intelligence community nor the law enforcement community had reached a judgment about responsibility for the *Cole.* That judgment was reached sometime between the time we left office and 9/11." National Commission staff reported that "the highest officials" of the Bush Administration received "essentially the same analysis" as the Clinton Cabinet did late in the year, showing that individuals linked to al Qaeda had been involved, but that proof of bin Laden's role was lacking. The State Department's annual report on global terrorism, culled from CIA and other intelligence community reports and published in April 2001, found "no definitive link" between the *Cole* attack and "bin Laden's organization." Berger and other Clinton officials cite the lack of a proven link as one reason that they did not launch military action against bin Laden or the Taliban before leaving the White House. However, interviews about the Massoud covert action proposal and other subjects debated during the late autumn of 2000 seem to make clear that for a variety of reasons, including unsettled national pol-

itics and a desire not to preempt the next president's options, Clinton and Berger had little interest in a parting military shot. Even without the establishment of definitive responsibility for the *Cole* attack, they might have found other ways to justify an attack if they had wanted to launch one. The Bush administration's early hesitancy about bin Laden and its causes are described in chapters 30 and 31.

29. Interviews with U.S. officials. All quotations are from the author's interviews.

30. The thirteen options and the quotations from Clarke and Shelton's operations chief are from the Joint Inquiry Committee's final report, pp. 279 and 305–6. Albright quotation from her written testimony to the National Commission March 23, 2004.

31. Ibid.

32. From Black's testimony to the Joint Inquiry Committee, September 26, 2002.

33. Interviews with five U.S. officials familiar with the CIA's plan. The account of the plan's development in the next seven paragraphs is from those interviews.

34. *The New York Times,* January 16, 2001, first described the December 20 principals' meeting. That account emphasized discussions at the meeting about who was responsible for the *Cole* bombing. That the meeting also formally rejected the plan backed by Clarke and the CIA for covert aid to Massoud is from interviews with U.S. officials. "Roll back" from National Commission staff statement no. 8, p. 8.

35. "A bit . . . a capture operation" is from an interview with an intelligence aide to Massoud.

36. According to the interview with Schroen, September 19, 2002, Washington D.C. (SC), the seventh and last CIA liaison team to reach the Panjshir before September 11 exited during the early winter of 2001 when the helicopter was put into storage.

37. "You replay . . . formidable adversary" is from Clinton's response to a question during a speech at the Washington Society of Association Executives in October 2001, as quoted in *USA Today,* November 12, 2001.

CHAPTER 30: "WHAT FACE WILL OMAR SHOW TO GOD?"

1. That Bush never spoke in public about bin Laden or al Qaeda is from a search of the Lexis-Nexis electronic news database. It is conceivable that the author missed something, but the database is very extensive. The party platform is from www.rnc.org. "If a country is hosting . . . intelligence briefings" is from Bulletin Broadfaxing Network, Inc.'s transcript of a Fox News interview with Bush, October 12, 2000.

2. *National Journal,* May 4, 2000. Also recounted by Elaine Sciolino in *The New York Times,* June 16, 2000.

3. All quotations in this paragraph are from Sciolino, *The New York Times,* June 16, 2000.

4. Interview with former senator David Boren, September 16, 2002, Norman, Oklahoma (GW).

5. Ibid. All quotations are from Boren's conversation with Bush.

6. "An undetermined period . . . a later period" is from *The New York Times,* January 19, 2001.

7. "We are grateful . . . weapons of mass destruction" is from a Federal News Service transcript. The visit took place on March 20, 2001.

8. "Number one . . . the threat was" is from Berger's testimony to the Joint Inquiry Committee, September 19, 2002. What Berger said to Rice is from interviews with U.S. officials. See also Barton Gellman, *The Washington Post,* January 20, 2002, and Daniel Benjamin and Steven Simon, *The Age of Sacred Terror,* pp. 328–29.

9. That Clarke's office described the al Qaeda threat as "existential" is from Benjamin and Simon, *Age of Sacred Terror,* pp. 328–29. The CIA's annual threat assessment, delivered by Tenet, had also emphasized the primacy of the missile threat from rogue and hostile regimes; until 2001 this was the danger Tenet listed first in his public briefing. In testimony delivered on February 7, 2001, for the first time the CIA director listed al Qaeda first. Armitage's quotation is from the Joint Inquiry Committee's final report, p. 39.

10. Excerpts from this January 25 memo have been quoted in at least three published reports. Gellman, *The Washington Post,* January 20, 2002, cites "sleeper cells" and "a major threat in being." Benjamin and Simon, in *Age of Sacred Terror,* cite "urgently needed" and "this is not some little terrorist issue." See also National Commission staff statement no. 8, p. 9.

11. See note 10. The idea of "making a deal" with Musharraf and trading military rule for help on bin Laden was not described in the other published accounts of these exchanges; it is from interviews with U.S. officials.

12. "Was out there . . . lower on the list" is from Benjamin and Simon, *Age of Sacred Terror,* pp. 335–36. Rumsfeld's recollection is from National Commission, staff statement no. 6, p. 11.

13. Discussions of armed Predator testing and the "sensor to shooter" quotation are from interviews with U.S. officials. The missile struck the turret is from *The New York Times,* November 23, 2001, quoting a General Atomics Aeronautical Systems, Inc., press release issued at the time of the test.

14. Interviews with U.S. officials. See also Gellman, *The Washington Post,* January 20, 2002.

15. Interviews with U.S. officials. See also National Commission staff statement no. 7, p. 6.

16. Ibid. "Oh these harebrained . . . a disaster" is from an interview.

17. In an extensive interview about U.S. policy toward Afghanistan on March 27, 2001, Eastham was asked to summarize U.S. policy toward the Taliban. "We have contacts with all the factions in Afghanistan," he said. "That includes the Taliban. We talk to the Taliban when we get the opportunity and when we have things to say, just as we talk to the representatives of the Northern Alliance, and just as we talk to representatives of the former king, of Afghan groups outside Afghanistan. We try to maintain contacts with all parts of Afghanistan." *The News Hour with Jim Lehrer,* March 27, 2001. Clarke, Rice, and Hadley from National Commission, staff statement no. 5, p. 15.

18. Interviews with U.S. officials.

19. Ibid. "The prospect . . . fracture the Taliban internally" is from "Afghanistan: The Consolidation of a Rogue State" by Zalmay Khalilzad and Daniel Byman, *The Washington Quarterly,* Winter 2000.

20. The Republican platform said that the United States "should engage India" while being "mindful" about its relationship with Pakistan. Bush appointed Blackwill as his ambassador to India. Once in New Delhi, Blackwill pushed for a tougher U.S. policy toward Musharraf.

21. Letter exchange and Stalin quote are from an interview with a Pakistani official.

22. "We find practical reasons . . . refuse to cooperate" is from documents recovered in Pakistan's embassy in Kabul, Afghanistan, after September 2001 and reported as "The Taliban Papers" by Tim Judah in *Survival,* Spring 2002, pp. 69–80. "Worst of both worlds" is from an interview with a Pakistani official. Quotations from Bush's letter from written testimony of Colin Powell to the National Commission, March 23, 2004.

23. Interviews with Pakistani officials in-

volved in the discussions. "We are losing too much . . . serious about this" is from an interview with a Pakistani participant in the discussions. Omar's letter to Musharraf is from Judah, "The Taliban Papers," *Survival.*

24. After the United Nations passed another round of economic sanctions against the Taliban late in December 2000, Pakistan's foreign minister sat down with his Taliban counterpart to work out how to evade the sanctions without calling too much attention to themselves. According to minutes of the meeting discovered by Tim Judah in Kabul, Mullah Omar's foreign envoy, Muttawakil, confessed that "the Taliban are not very optimistic of the new Bush administration," because they believe that Bush and Clinton are "like two hands of one person." The Pakistani minister mentioned his nervousness about Zalmay Khalilzad who had suggested Pakistan "should be declared a terrorist state." The Pakistani envoy assured the Taliban that his government "had no intention of downgrading the Afghan embassy" in Islamabad as U.N. sanctions required, although "it would be desirable to show some superficial reduction to exhibit compliance." In another cable discovered by Judah, which provided talking points for Pakistani ambassadors to use in defending the Taliban, the foreign ministry urged, "We should avoid any statements that may be offensive to the Taliban." Judah, "The Taliban Papers," *Survival.*

25. Statue descriptions are from Jason Elliot, *An Unexpected Light,* pp. 336–37. "We do not understand . . . are stones" is from Molly Moore, *The Washington Post,* March 2, 2001. According to Ramzi Binalshibh, several Saudis who were to become "muscle" hijackers on September 11 participated in the destruction. See National Commission final report, p. 527.

26. This account of Haider's visit to Kan-

dahar is from interviews with Pakistani and U.S. officials. All quotations are from an interview with a Pakistani official. *Time,* August 12, 2002, provides a similar account of the meeting, which lasted about two hours, according to those interviewed.

27. Interviews with U.S. officials.

28. Ibid.

29. The surge in threat reporting during the first three months of 2001 is from interviews with U.S., Pakistani, and Saudi officials. Tenet's quotations are from the Joint Inquiry Committee's final report, Appendix, p. 38. Turki said in an interview that he was "inundated by warnings from the Americans. January, February, March. We'd get reports telling us, 'We suspect something is going to happen. Please keep on the lookout.'" Pakistani officials quoted Tenet similarly. Bin Laden's remarks about the *Cole,* videotaped that winter at an Afghan wedding where one of his sons married a daughter of his Egyptian commander Mohammed Atef, binding their families, were broadcast on al Jazeera on March 2, 2001. "In Aden, the young man stood up for holy war and destroyed a destroyer feared by the powerful." He described *Cole* as having sailed "to its doom" along a course of "false arrogance, self-conceit, and strength." Rice and Tenet's exchanges on draft CIA covert action authority is from National Commission staff statement no. 7, p. 7. Bush's recollection from the final report, p. 199.

30. Interviews with Pakistani officials. "Because we'd have a civil war" is from an interview.

31. Interviews with U.S. officials.

32. Tenet's visit to Islamabad is from interviews with U.S. and Pakistani officials. Some of the sources who described the visit did not attend all the meetings. The full agenda and scope of the discussions with Mahmoud remain unclear, but it is certain that Mah-

moud did little in the aftermath to change ISI's policies and practices in Afghanistan. The exact date of Tenet's travel is also uncertain. His visit appears to have occurred in late March or April.

CHAPTER 31: "MANY AMERICANS ARE GOING TO DIE"

1. Otilie English began paid work as a Northern Alliance lobbyist on February 15, 2001. The letter to Cheney is from an interview with Haroun Amin, chargé d'affaires at the Afghan embassy in Washington, September 9, 2002 (GW). Information on Massoud's travels is from interviews with his aides. What Massoud believed that spring is from videotaped conversation with English and Elie Krakowski, June 2001 (hereafter "English video"), and transcript of videotaped conversation among Massoud, Peter Tomsen, Hamid Karzai, and Abdul Haq, also from June 2001 (hereafter "Tomsen video").

2. Interviews with U.S. officials and aides to Massoud.

3. Ibid.

4. Ibid.

5. *Los Angeles Times,* June 12, 2002.

6. English video, interviews with multiple aides to Massoud.

7. English video and Tomsen video.

8. All quotations are from the English video. The translation from Dari is by Massoud's aide Amarullah Saleh.

9. All of Massoud's quotations, ibid.

10. Interview with Otilie English, September 3, 2002, Washington, D.C. (GW).

11. Interview with Peter Tomsen, January 21, 2002, Omaha, Nebraska (SC), and subsequent written communications from Tomsen.

12. All quotations are from an English transcript of the Tomsen video. Abdul Haq's role in the meeting was a source of some tension. Haq did not want to meet with Massoud inside Northern Alliance territory. Haq

and Hamid Karzai also disagreed somewhat about strategy toward the Taliban, according to Massoud and Karzai aides. Haq believed it was possible to negotiate with Taliban leaders and secure defections. Karzai favored talks but also was ready to participate in military action. Ultimately, Haq died because he believed he could rally Pashtuns in eastern Afghanistan to his cause in October 2001 simply by calling on their tribal and personal loyalties. The CIA also remained deeply skeptical about Haq. Even as the agency embraced Karzai, its officers dismissed Haq as someone who could not produce results.

13.   Bart Gellman, *The Washington Post,* January 20, 2002. *Time,* August 12, 2002, dates the conversation to the first days of spring 2001. Also, interview with a White House official.

14.   Gellman, *The Washington Post,* January 20, 2002, and *Time,* August 12, 2002, have described the agenda and some of the discussion at this meeting. Armitage and Wolfowitz testified about aspects of the meeting before the Joint Inquiry Committee. Armitage quotations are from his testimony, Federal News Service, September 19, 2002. CIA slides from National Commission final report, p. 203.

15.   Testimony of Paul Wolfowitz before the Joint Inquiry Committee, September 19, 2002. Wolfowitz defended the deliberate pace of the deputies committee's work by arguing that since the September 11 hijackers had already entered the United States by July, even if the Bush administration had advanced its plans to support Massoud or attack al Qaeda, they probably would not have prevented the New York and Pentagon attacks. Of course, it could be argued equally that a robust disruption of bin Laden's Afghanistan sanctuary might have delayed or altered the course of the attacks. Both sides of the argument rest almost entirely on speculation.

16.   Wolfowitz quotation, ibid. State offi-

cials' conclusions from National Commission, staff statement no. 5, p. 10.

17.   State Department transcript, testimony of Colin Powell before the Senate Appropriations Subcommittee on Foreign Operations, May 15, 2001. Late May meeting is from National Commission staff statement no. 7, p. 7.

18.   Testimony of George Tenet, Joint Inquiry Committee, October 17, 2002. Testimony of Cofer Black, Joint Inquiry Committee, September 26, 2002. "What worries . . . more deadly" from the Committee's final report, Appendix, p. 43. Interviews with U.S. officials. Black's "7 . . . 8" is from National Commission staff statement no. 10, p. 2.

19.   Information about NSA intercepts is from Eleanor Hill, Joint Inquiry Staff Statement, September 18, 2002. FBI threat reports from the testimony of Michael Rolince, FBI special agent in charge, Washington, D.C., Joint Inquiry Committee, September 24, 2002. State warnings are from the testimony of Richard Armitage, Joint Inquiry Committee, September 19, 2002. FAA warnings are from *The New York Times,* May 21, 2002.

20.   Atiani quotations are from Pamela Constable, *The Washington Post,* July 8, 2001. The June 26 démarche is from the Joint Inquiry Committee's final report, p. 120.

21.   Bin Laden quotations are from Associated Press, June 19, 2001.

22.   "I want a way" from *The New York Times,* May 17, 2002. Rice, Clarke, and Bush letter from National Commission, staff statement no. 5, p. 16.

23.   All quotations are from Eleanor Hill, Joint Inquiry Staff Statement, September 18, 2002, except "98 percent certain" and "clear majority view," which are from the Joint Inquiry Committee's final report, p. 8. "Establish contact" is from the final report, p. 29.

24.   Ibid.

25. *Time,* August 12, 2002. National Commission staff statement no. 10, p. 3.

26. Eleanor Hill, Joint Inquiry Staff Statement, September 18, 2002.

27. Ibid., and testimony of George Tenet, Joint Inquiry Committee, October 17, 2002. The Tenet quotations are from his testimony.

28. Testimony of unidentified CIA Counterterrorist Center officer, Joint Inquiry Committee, September 20, 2002. McLaughlin's view and CTC officer's fears from National Commission staff statement no. 7, p. 8. What Hadley said about Wolfowitz from the final report, p. 259.

29. "Threat . . . to Continue Indefinitely" is from "Counterterrorism Intelligence Capabilities and Performance Prior to 9/11," House Permanent Select Committee on Intelligence, July 17, 2002. The Tenet quotation is from his Joint Inquiry testimony, October 17, 2002.

30. A copy of this section of the PDB was published by the National Commission. Tenet on delay is from staff statement no. 7, p. 8.

31. Testimony of Cofer Black, Joint Inquiry Committee, September 26, 2002.

32. Tenet's Joint Inquiry testimony, October 17, 2002.

33. Hill, Joint Inquiry statement, September 18, 2002. Also, Joint Inquiry Committee final report, p. 15. National Commission staff statement no. 10, p. 4. Final report, p. 267.

34. Statement of FBI director Robert S. Mueller, Joint Inquiry Committee, September 26, 2002. Backgrounds of the supporting hijackers and Tenet quotation from the Joint Inquiry Committee final report, p. 138.

35. Statement of Robert S. Mueller, Joint Inquiry Committee, September 26, 2002. National Commission staff statement no. 16, based on interrogation statements by Mohammed and Binalshibh, pp. 5–19. Their statements describe debate among al Qaeda

leaders about whether it was wise to attack the United States. By Mohammed's account, bin Laden argued that the attack should go forward to support anti-Israel insurgents and to protest American troops in Saudi Arabia.

36. All financial details and flight to Karachi, from Mueller's Joint Inquiry Committee statement, September 26, 2002.

37. Interviews with aides to Massoud and Karzai. "So disappointed" is from an interview with Daoud Yaqub, adviser to Karzai and former executive director of the Afghanistan Foundation, May 27, 2002, Kabul, Afghanistan (GW).

38. Quotation is from interview with Yaqub, ibid.

39. Abdullah quotations are from *Los Angeles Times,* June 12, 2002.

40. Interview with Yaqub, May 27, 2002, and with several other aides to Karzai and Massoud.

41. Interview with Hamid Karzai, October 21, 2002, Kabul, Afghanistan (SC).

42. Ibid.

CHAPTER 32: "WHAT AN
UNLUCKY COUNTRY"

1. That the Counterterrorist Center knew about the journalists as they crossed Massoud's lines is from interviews with U.S. officials.

2. These details about the assassins, as well as other aspects of the plot described in this chapter, draw on two comprehensive journalistic investigations of Massoud's death: Jon Anderson, *The New Yorker,* June 10, 2002, and Pyes and Rempel, *Los Angeles Times,* June 12, 2002. *Time,* August 12, 2002, also added fresh details to the record through interviews. In addition, this chapter's account is based on interviews in Kabul with seven aides to Massoud, several of them witnesses to the attack, and on interviews with U.S. officials who later debriefed Massoud's aides.

3. *The Wall Street Journal,* December 31, 2001. The draft letter was discovered on a computer hard drive acquired by *Journal* reporters in Kabul during the autumn of 2001.

4. Anderson, *The New Yorker,* June 10, 2002, raises the possibility that Sayyaf conspired with al Qaeda to kill Massoud. Witting or unwitting, Sayyaf was a key facilitator in the operation.

5. Interviews with aides to Massoud; Anderson, ibid.; Pyes and Rempel, *Los Angeles Times,* June 12, 2002.

6. National Commission final report, pp. 212–213.

7. Daniel Benjamin and Steven Simon, *The Age of Sacred Terror,* pp. 345–46, provide the most detailed account of this meeting available to date. Barton Gellman, *The Washington Post,* January 20, 2002, also described the agenda, and some participants made partial references to the discussion in Joint Inquiry Committee testimony. Benjamin and Simon raise doubts about the Cabinet's commitment to the covert aid for Massoud and his anti-Taliban allies. "The issue of funding the hundreds of millions of dollars to finance the effort was given to the OMB and CIA to figure out," they write, describing this as "the kind of decision that leaves much undecided, since a government agency that is told to finance a program 'out of hide,' out of the existing budget, frequently argues back that the issue is not a high enough priority."

8. Benjamin and Simon, *Age of Sacred Terror,* pp. 345–46. The authors say that Tenet "intervened forcefully" during the discussion and said it would be a "terrible mistake . . . for the director of Central Intelligence to fire a weapon like this." That would happen, he reportedly said, "over his

dead body." Other officials deny that Tenet was so categorical. They describe him as trying to explain the risks, not argue for a particular outcome. Within weeks after September 11, the CIA did field and operate armed Predators, as did the Air Force, drawing on procedures developed in the summer of 2001. After September 11 the armed Predator was used successfully on the Afghan battlefield and later to shoot and kill a traveling party of accused terrorists in Yemen.

9. Interviews with U.S. officials. The September 4 decision on the Predator is from National Commission staff statement no. 7, p. 7. Hadley formally tasked Tenet to draft a finding for covert aid to Massoud on September 10.

10. Interviews with aides to Massoud; Anderson, *The New Yorker,* June 10, 2002; Pyes and Rempel, *Los Angeles Times,* June 12, 2002. "Is he a wrestler" is from Pyes and Rempel.

11. How the assassination unfolded, from interviews with aides to Massoud; Anderson, *The New Yorker,* June 10, 2002; Pyes and Rempel, *Los Angeles Times,* June 12, 2002. "He's dying" from *Los Angeles Times.* The full quotation provided from Omar is "I saw my commander's face and thought to myself, 'He's dying and I'm dying.'"

12. The exchange with Saleh is from interviews with U.S. officials.

13. Interviews with aides to Massoud and with U.S. officials.

14. Ibid.

15. Interviews with three aides and advisers to Massoud then in Washington. September 10 deputies meeting from National Commission, staff statement no. 5, pp. 15–16.

16. Interview with Qayum Karzai, May 19, 2002, Kabul, Afghanistan (GW).

Bibliography

This book is based primarily on about two hundred interviews conducted between the autumn of 2001 and the summer of 2003 with American, Afghan, Pakistani, and Saudi participants in the events described. Many of these interviews were conducted entirely or partially on the record. Many others were held under ground rules designed to protect the identity of the source interviewed. Where these "background" rules were used, they were necessary usually because the material under discussion was highly classified or otherwise sensitive. All the interviews relied upon are indicated in the chapter notes. Where an interview was on the record, the chapter notes also indicate when and where it took place, and whether it was conducted by the author, Griff Witte, or both of us. The chapter notes also attempt to connect background interview sourcing with open material such as declassified documents and congressional hearings, as well as with previously published work by journalists and scholars. That material is inventoried below. Most of the American government documents describing the CIA's role in Afghanistan and its campaign against al Qaeda are likely to remain classified for many years, however. Saudi and Pakistani documents may never be available. In the chapter notes and here, my aim is to make as much material as possible transparently available to readers and researchers, given the constraints, in the hope that future writers will be able to correct and add to the preceding narrative.

BOOKS

Abir, Mordechai. *Saudi Arabia: Government, Society and the Gulf Crisis.* London: Routledge, 1993.
Ahmad, Hazrat Mirza Tahir. *The Gulf Crisis: The New World Order.* Trans. Mubarak Ahmad Nazir. Surrey, England: Islam International, 1992.

Akhund, Iqbal. *Trial and Error: The Advent and Eclipse of Benazir Bhutto.* Oxford, England: Oxford University Press, 2000.

Ali, Tariq. *Pakistan: Military Rule or People's Power?* London: Jonathan Cape, 1970.

Amirahmadi, Hooshang, and Nader Entessar, eds. *Reconstruction and Regional Diplomacy in the Persian Gulf.* London: Routledge, 1992.

Anderson, Jon Lee. *The Lion's Grave: Dispatches from Afghanistan.* New York: Grove Press, 2002.

Arnold, Anthony. *Afghanistàn: The Soviet Invasion in Perspective.* Stanford, Calif.: Hoover Institution Press, 1981.

Badeeb, Saeed M. *The Saudi-Egyptian Conflict over North Yemen, 1962–1970.* Boulder, Colo.: Westview Press; Washington, D.C.: American-Arab Affairs Council, 1986.

———. *Saudi-Iranian Relations 1932–1982.* London: Centre for Arab and Iranian Studies and Echoes, 1993.

Baer, Robert. *See No Evil: The True Story of a Ground Soldier in the CIA's War on Terrorism.* New York: Crown, 2002.

Bamford, James. *The Puzzle Palace: Inside the National Security Agency, America's Most Secret Intelligence Organization.* New York: Houghton Mifflin, 1983.

Bearden, Milt. *The Black Tulip: A Novel of War in Afghanistan.* New York: Random House, 1998.

Bearden, Milt, and James Risen. *The Main Enemy: The Inside Story of the CIA's Final Showdown with the KGB.* New York: Random House, 2003.

Benjamin, Daniel, and Steven Simon. *The Age of Sacred Terror.* New York: Random House, 2002.

Bergen, Peter L. *Holy War, Inc.: Inside the Secret World of Osama bin Laden.* New York: The Free Press, 2001.

Bernstein, Carl, and Marco Politi. *His Holiness: John Paul II and the Hidden History of Our Time.* New York: Simon & Schuster, 1997.

Beschloss, Michael R., and Strobe Talbott. *At the Highest Levels: The Inside Story of the End of the Cold War.* London: Little, Brown, 1993.

Bhutto, Benazir. *Daughter of Destiny: An Autobiography.* New York: Simon & Schuster, 1989.

Borovik, Artyom. *The Hidden War: A Russian Journalist's Account of the Soviet War in Afghanistan.* New York: Grove Press, 1990.

Brisard, Jean-Charles, and Guillaume Dasquié. *Forbidden Truth: U.S.-Taliban Secret Oil Diplomacy and the Failed Hunt for bin Laden.* New York: Thunder's Mouth Press/Nation Books, 2002.

Burki, Shahid Javed. *Pakistan: A Nation in the Making.* Boulder, Colo.: Westview Press; Karachi, Pakistan: Oxford University Press, 1986.

Cannon, Lou. *President Reagan: The Role of a Lifetime.* New York: Simon & Schuster, 1991.

Carlton, David, and Carlo Schaerf, eds. *International Terrorism and World Security.* London: Croon Helm, 1975.

Caroe, Olaf. *The Pathans.* Karachi, Pakistan: Oxford University Press, 1958.

Casey, William J. *Scouting the Future: The Public Speeches of William J. Casey.* Comp. Herbert E. Meyer. Washington, D.C.: Regnery Gateway, 1989.

Clarridge, Duane R., with Digby Diehl. *A Spy for All Seasons: My Life in the CIA.* New York: Scribner, 1997.

Coll, Steve. *On the Grand Trunk Road: A Journey into South Asia.* New York: Random House, 1994.

Collins, Aukai. *My Jihad: The True Story of an American Mujahid's Amazing Journey from Usama Bin*

Laden's Training Camps to Counterterrorism with the FBI and CIA. Guilford, Conn.: Lyons Press, 2002.

Cooley, John K. *Unholy Wars: Afghanistan, America, and International Terrorism.* 2d ed. London: Pluto Press, 2000.

Cordesman, Anthony H. *After the Storm: The Changing Military Balance in the Middle East.* Boulder, Colo.: Westview Press; London: Mansell, 1993.

Crile, George. *Charlie Wilson's War: The Extraordinary Story of the Largest Covert Operation in History.* New York: Atlantic Monthly Press, 2003.

Cronin, Audrey K., and James M. Ludes, eds. *The Campaign Against International Terrorism.* Washington, D.C.: Georgetown University Press, 2003.

Dobbs, Michael. *Down with Big Brother: The Fall of the Soviet Union.* New York: Knopf, 1997.

Duncan, Emma. *Breaking the Curfew: A Political Journey Through Pakistan.* London: Arrow Books, 1989.

Durrani, Mahmud Ali. *India and Pakistan: The Cost of Conflict, the Benefits of Peace.* Baltimore, Md.: Johns Hopkins University Foreign Policy Institute, 2000.

Dycus, Stephen, et al. *National Security Law.* Boston: Little, Brown, 1990.

Edwards, David B. *Before Taliban: Genealogies of the Afghan Jihad.* Berkeley and Los Angeles, Calif.: University of California Press, 2002.

Elliot, Jason. *An Unexpected Light: Travels in Afghanistan.* New York: St. Martin's Press, 1999.

Ewans, Martin. *Afghanistan: A Short History of Its People and Politics.* New York: HarperCollins, 2002.

Fandy, Mamoun. *Saudi Arabia and the Politics of Dissent.* New York: St. Martin's Press, 1999.

Farr, Grant M., and John G. Merriam, eds. *Afghan Resistance: The Politics of Survival.* Lahore, India: Vanguard, 1988.

Fullerton, John. *The Soviet Occupation of Afghanistan.* Hong Kong: Far Eastern Economic Review, ca. 1983.

Ganguly, Sumit. *The Crisis in Kashmir: Portents of War, Hopes of Peace.* Cambridge, England: Woodrow Wilson Center Press and Cambridge University Press, 1997.

Gates, Robert M. *From the Shadows: The Ultimate Insider's Story of Five Presidents and How They Won the Cold War.* New York: Simon & Schuster, 1996.

Gauhar, Altaf, ed. *The Challenge of Islam.* London: Islamic Council of Europe, 1978.

Goodson, Larry P. *Afghanistan's Endless War: State Failure, Regional Politics, and the Rise of the Taliban.* Seattle: University of Washington Press, 2001.

Grau, Lester W., and Michael A. Gress, trans. and ed. *The Soviet-Afghan War: How a Superpower Fought and Lost: The Russian General Staff.* Lawrence, Kans.: University Press of Kansas, 2002.

Griffin, Michael. *Reaping the Whirlwind: The Taliban Movement in Afghanistan.* London: Pluto Press, 2001.

Gunaratna, Rohan. *Inside Al Qaeda: Global Network of Terror.* New York: Columbia University Press, 2002.

Halberstam, David. *War in a Time of Peace: Bush, Clinton, and the Generals.* New York: Scribner, 2001.

Hiro, Dilip. *The Longest War: The Iran-Iraq Military Conflict.* London: Grafton, 1990.

Hoffman, Bruce. *Inside Terrorism.* New York: Columbia University Press, 1998.

Horwitz, Tony. *Baghdad Without a Map and Other Misadventures in Arabia.* New York: Plume, 1991.

Hourani, Albert. *A History of the Arab Peoples.* London: Faber and Faber, 1991.

Huntington, Samuel P. *The Clash of Civilizations: Remaking of World Order.* New York: Simon & Schuster, 1996.

Jalali, Ali Ahmad, and Lester W. Grau. *Afghan Guerrilla Warfare: In the Words of the Mujahideen Fighters.* St. Paul, Minn.: MBI, 2001.

Jones, Owen Bennett. *Pakistan: Eye of the Storm.* New Haven, Conn.: Yale University Press, 2002.

Junger, Sebastian. *Fire.* New York: W. W. Norton, 2001.

Kaiser, Robert G. *Why Gorbachev Happened: His Triumphs and His Failures.* New York: Simon & Schuster, 1991.

Keddie, Nikki R., and Mark J. Gasiorowski, eds. *Neither East nor West: Iran, the Soviet Union, and the United States.* New Haven, Conn.: Yale University Press, 1990.

Kepel, Gilles. *Jihad: The Trail of Political Islam.* Cambridge, Mass.: Belknap Press, 2002.

Korany, Bahgat, Paul Noble, and Rex Brynen, eds. *The Many Faces of National Security in the Arab World.* London: Macmillan, 1993.

Kux, Dennis. *The United States and Pakistan, 1947–2000: Disenchanted Allies.* Washington, D.C.: Woodrow Wilson Center Press, 2001.

Lacey, Robert. *The Kingdom: Arabia and the House of Sáud.* New York: Avon Books, 1981.

Lake, Anthony. *6 Nightmares: Real Threats in a Dangerous World and How America Can Meet Them.* Boston: Little, Brown, 2000.

Laquer, Walter. *The New Terrorism: Fanaticism and the Arms of Mass Destruction.* Oxford, England: Oxford University Press, 1999.

Loeffler, Reinhold. *Islam in Practice: Religious Beliefs in a Persian Village.* Albany: State University of New York Press, 1988.

McChesney, R. D. *Central Asia: Foundations of Change.* Princeton, N.J.: Darwin Press, 1996.

Macrory, Patrick. *Kabul Catastrophe: The Invasion and Retreat, 1839–1842.* London: Prion, 1966.

Maley, William, ed. *Fundamentalism Reborn? Afghanistan and the Taliban.* London: Hurst, 1988.

Maraniss, David. *First in His Class: The Biography of Bill Clinton.* New York: Simon & Schuster, 1995.

Masters, John. *Bugles and a Tiger: A Volume of Autobiography.* New York: Viking, 1956.

Miller, Charles. *Khyber: British India's North West Frontier.* New York: Macmillan, 1977.

Miller, John, and Michael Stone, with Chris Mitchell. *The Cell: Inside the 9/11 Plot, and Why the FBI and CIA Failed to Stop It.* New York: Hyperion, 2002.

Mylroie, Laurie. *The War Against America: Saddam Hussein and the World Trade Center Attacks, a Study of Revenge.* 2d ed., rev. New York: HarperCollins, 2001.

Persico, Joseph E. *Casey: From the OSS to the CIA.* New York: Viking, 1990.

Pillar, Paul R. *Terrorism and U.S. Foreign Policy.* Washington, D.C.: Brookings Institution Press, 2001.

Prendergast, John. *Prender's Progress: A Soldier in India, 1931–1947.* London: Cassell, 1979.

Rashid, Ahmed. *Taliban: Militant Islam, Oil, and Fundamentalism in Central Asia.* New Haven, Conn.: Yale University Press, 2000.

————. *The Resurgence of Central Asia: Islam or Nationalism?* Karachi, Pakistan: Oxford University Press; London: Zed Books, 1994.

Raza, M. Hanif. *A Souvenir of Peshawar.* Islamabad, Pakistan: Colorpix, 1994.

Reisman, Michael W., and James E. Baker. *Regulating Covert Action: Practices, Contexts, and Policies of Covert Coercion Abroad in International and American Law.* New Haven: Yale University Press, 1992.

Roy, Olivier. *Afghanistan: From Holy War to Civil War.* Princeton, N.J.: Darwin Press, 1995.

————. *Islam and Resistance in Afghanistan.* Cambridge, England: Cambridge University Press, 1986.

————. *The New Central Asia: The Creation of Nations.* New York: New York University Press, 1997.

Rubin, Barnett R. *The Search for Peace in Afghanistan: From Buffer State to Failed State.* New Haven, Conn.: Yale University Press, 1995.

————. *The Fragmentation of Afghanistan: State Formation and Collapse in the International System.* 2d ed. New Haven, Conn.: Yale University Press, 1995.

Rubin, Barry. *Islamic Fundamentalism in Egyptian Politics.* London: Macmillan, 1990.

Scales, Robert H., Jr. *Future Warfare Anthology.* Rev. ed. Carlisle Barracks, Penn.: U.S. Army War College, 2001.

Sinclair, Gordon. *Khyber Caravan: Through Kashmir, Waziristan, Afghanistan, Baluchistan, and Northern India.* Lahore, Pakistan: Sang-E-Meel Publications, 1978.

Singh, Khushwant. *Train to Pakistan.* New Delhi, India: Ravi Dayal, 1988.

Stewart, James B. *Blood Sport: The President and His Adversaries.* New York: Simon & Schuster, 1996.

Sullivan, Joseph G., ed. *Embassies Under Siege: Personal Accounts by Diplomats on the Front Line.* Washington, D.C.: Brassey's, 1995.

Swinson, Arthur. *North-West Frontier: People and Events, 1839–1947.* London: Corgi Books, 1967.

Tanner, Stephen. *Afghanistan: A Military History from Alexander the Great to the Fall of the Taliban.* New York: Da Capo Press, 2002.

Teitelbaum, Joshua. *Holier Than Thou: Saudi Arabia's Islamic Opposition.* Washington, D.C.: Washington Institute for Near East Policy, 2000.

Vassiliev, Alexei. *The History of Saudi Arabia.* New York: New York University Press, 2000.

Weaver, Mary Anne. *A Portrait of Egypt: A Journey Through the World of Militant Islam.* New York: Farrar, Straus and Giroux, 1999.

————. *Pakistan: In the Shadow of Jihad and Afghanistan.* New York: Farrar, Straus and Giroux, 2002.

Wilkinson-Latham, Robert. *North-West Frontier, 1837–1947.* London: Osprey, 1977.

Woodward, Bob. *Shadow: Five Presidents and the Legacy of Watergate.* New York: Simon & Schuster, 1999.

————. *Veil: The Secret Wars of the CIA, 1981–1987.* New York: Simon & Schuster, 1987.

Yergin, Daniel. *The Prize: The Epic Quest for Oil, Money and Power.* New York: Simon & Schuster, 1992.

Yousaf, Mohammad. *Silent Soldier: The Man Behind the Afghan Jehad, General Akhtar Abdur Rahman Shaheed.* Lahore, Pakistan: Jang, 1991.

Yousaf, Mohammad, and Mark Adkin. *The Bear Trap: Afghanistan's Untold Story.* Lahore, Pakistan: Jang, 1992.

JOURNAL ARTICLES AND MANUSCRIPTS

"Afghanistan, Crisis of Impunity: The Role of Pakistan, Russia, and Iran in Fueling the Civil War." *Human Rights Watch* 13, no. 3 (July 2001): 3–58.

Al-Khatlan, Saleh M. "Saudi Foreign Policy Toward Central Asia." *Journal of King Abdulaziz University* 14, no. 1 (2000): 19–31.

Al-Zawahiri, Ayman. *Knights Under the Prophet's Banner.* Excerpts as printed in *Al-Sharq al-Awsat,* trans. FBIS. December 2, 2001.

Azzam, Maha. "Islamic Oriented Protest Groups in Egypt 1971–1981: Theory, Politics, and Dogma." Thesis, Oxford University, 1989.

Bearden, Milton. "Afghanistan, Graveyard of Empires." *Foreign Affairs* 80, no. 6 (November/December 2001): 17–30.

Beg, Mirza Aslam. "Taliban's Military Successes, 1995–2000." *National Security* (ca. 2001): 1–44.

Benjamin, Daniel, and Steven Simon. "A Failure of Intelligence?" *The New York Review of Books* (December 20, 2001): 76–80.

———. "America and the New Terrorism." *Survival* 42, no. 1 (Spring 2000): 59–75.

Cogan, Charles G. "Partners in Time: The CIA and Afghanistan Since 1979." *World Policy Journal* 10, no. 2 (Summer 1993): 73–82.

———. "Shawl of Lead: From Holy War to Civil War in Afghanistan." *Conflict* 10 (1990): 189–204.

Deutch, John, Ashton Carter, and Philip Zelikow. "Catastrophic Terrorism: Tackling the New Danger." *Foreign Affairs* 77, no. 6 (November/December 1998): 80–94.

Dowell, William. "With Massoud's Rebels." *The Washington Quarterly* 5, no. 4 (Autumn 1982): 209ff.

Gates, Robert. "From the Shadows Manuscript." Vols. 1 and 2. Kennedy School Library. Examined and typed April 27, 2002.

Hyman, Anthony. "Propaganda Posters of the Afghan Resistance." *Central Asian Survey Incidental Papers Series,* no. 3 (January 1985): 1–55.

Jalali, Ali A. "Afghanistan: The Anatomy of an Ongoing Conflict." *Parameters* 31, no. 1 (Spring 2001): 85–98.

Judah, Tim. "The Taliban Papers." *Survival* 44, no. 1 (Spring 2002): 69–80.

Katzman, Kenneth. "Counterterrorism Policy: American Successes." *The Middle East Quarterly* 5, no. 4 (December 1998): 45–52.

Khalilzad, Zalmay. "Anarchy in Afghanistan." *Journal of International Affairs* 51, no. 1 (Summer 1997): 37–56.

Khalilzad, Zalmay, and Daniel Byman. "Afghanistan: The Consolidation of a Rogue State." *The Washington Quarterly* 23, no. 1 (Winter 2000): 65–78.

Kline, David. "The Conceding of Afghanistan." *The Washington Quarterly* 6, no. 2 (Spring 1983): 130ff.

Kuperman, Alan J. "The Stinger Missile and U.S. Intervention in Afghanistan." *Political Science Quarterly* 114, no. 2 (Summer 1999): 219–63.

Lundberg, Kirsten, Philip Zelikow, and Ernest May. "Politics of a Covert Action: The U.S., the *Mujahideen,* and the Stinger Missile." Kennedy School of Government Case Program, Harvard University, 1999.

Obaid, Nawaf E. "Improving U.S. Intelligence Analysis on the Saudi Arabian Decision Making Process." Master's degree thesis, Harvard University, 1998.

Riedel, Bruce. "American Diplomacy and the 1999 Kargil Summit at Blair House." Center for Advanced Study of India, University of Pennsylvania, Policy Paper Series, 2002.

Rubin, Barnett. "Afghanistan: The Forgotten Crisis." *UNHCR Refugee Survey Quarterly* 15, no. 2 (1996).

Saikal, Amin. "The Role of Outside Actors in Afghanistan." *Middle East Policy* 7, no. 4 (October 2000): 50–57.

Tomsen, Peter. "A Chance for Peace in Afghanistan." *Foreign Affairs* 79, no. 1 (January/February 2000): 179–82.

———. "Geopolitics of an Afghan Settlement." *Perceptions, Journal of International Affairs* 5, no. 4 (December 2000/February 2001): 86–105.

Weaver, Mary Anne. "Of Birds and Bombs." *APF Reporter* 20, no. 4 (2001): http://www.alicia patterson.org.

CONGRESSIONAL HEARINGS

Armitage, Richard. *Joint House and Senate Select Intelligence Committee Hearing on Events Surrounding the Terrorist Attacks of September 11, 2001 ("Joint Inquiry Committee").* September 19, 2002.

Berger, Samuel. *Joint Inquiry Committee.* September 19, 2002.

Black, Cofer. *Joint Inquiry Committee.* September 26, 2002.

Cannistraro, Vincent M. *Senate Foreign Relations Committee: Near East and South Asian Affairs Subcommittee Hearing on Terrorism and the Middle East Peace Process.* March 19, 1996.

———. *House International Relations Committee Hearing on al Qaeda and the Global Reach of Terrorism.* October 3, 2001.

Collins, James F. *House International Relations Committee Hearing on Central Asia.* November 14, 1995.

Freeh, Louis. *Joint Inquiry Committee.* October 8, 2002.

Gee, Robert W. *Statement to House International Relations Committee: Subcommittee on Asia and the Pacific.* February 12, 1998.

Hayden, Michael. *Joint Inquiry Committee.* October 17, 2002.

Heslin, Sheila. *Senate Governmental Affairs Committee Hearing on Finance Reform.* September 17, 1997.

Hill, Eleanor. *Hearings: Joint Inquiry Committee.* September 18, 2002; September 20, 2002; September 24, 2002; October 1, 2002; October 8, 2002; October 17, 2002.

———. *Staff Statements: Joint Inquiry Staff Statement.* September 18, 2002.

———. *The Intelligence Community's Knowledge of the September 11 Hijackers Prior to September 11, 2001.* September 20, 2002.

———. *The FBI's Handling of the Phoenix Electronic Communication and Investigation of Zacarias Moussaoui Prior to September 11, 2001.* September 24, 2002.

————. *Counterterrorism Information Sharing with Other Federal Agencies and with State and Local Governments and the Private Sector.* October 1, 2002.

————. *Proposals for Reform Within the Intelligence Community.* October 3, 2002.

————. *On the Intelligence Community's Response to Past Terrorist Attacks Against the United States from February 1993 to September 2001.* October 8, 2002.

————. *Joint Inquiry Staff Statement.* October 17, 2002.

Inderfurth, Karl F. *Senate Foreign Relations Committee: Near Eastern and South Asian Affairs Subcommittee Hearing on Afghanistan.* July 10, 1997.

————. *Senate Foreign Relations Committee: Near Eastern and South Asian Affairs Subcommittee Hearing on Events in Afghanistan.* October 22, 1997.

————. *Senate Foreign Relations Committee: Near Eastern and South Asian Affairs Subcommittee Hearing on Events in Afghanistan.* October 8, 1998.

————. *Senate Appropriations Committee: Foreign Operations Subcommittee Hearing on Afghanistan.* March 9, 1999.

————. *Senate Foreign Relations Committee: Near Eastern and South Asian Affairs Subcommittee Hearing on the Crisis in Afghanistan.* April 14, 1999.

————. *Senate Foreign Relations Committee: East Asian and the Pacific Affairs Subcommittee Hearing on Pakistan.* October 14, 1999.

————. *House International Relations Committee: East Asian and the Pacific Affairs Subcommittee Hearing on Regional Security in South Asia.* October 20, 1999.

————. *Senate Foreign Relations Committee: Near Eastern and South Asian Affairs Subcommittee Hearing on Afghanistan.* July 20, 2000.

Karzai, Hamid. *Senate Foreign Relations Committee: Near Eastern and South Asian Affairs Subcommittee Hearing on Afghanistan.* July 20, 2000.

Khalilzad, Zalmay. *Senate Foreign Relations Committee: Near Eastern and South Asian Affairs Subcommittee Hearing on Events in Afghanistan.* October 22, 1997.

————. *Senate Foreign Relations Committee: Near Eastern and South Asian Affairs Subcommittee Hearing on Events in Afghanistan.* October 8, 1998.

Lake, Anthony. *Joint Inquiry Committee.* September 19, 2002.

Leno, Mavis. *Senate Appropriations Committee: Foreign Operations Subcommittee Hearing on Human Rights Abuses Against Women in Afghanistan.* March 9, 1999.

Massoud, Ahmed Shah. *Letter Submitted to the Senate Foreign Relations Committee: Near Eastern and South Asian Affairs Subcommittee Hearing on Events in Afghanistan.* October 8, 1998.

Mueller, Robert S. *Joint Inquiry Committee.* September 26, 2002; October 17, 2002.

Pillar, Paul. *Joint Inquiry Committee.* October 8, 2002.

Powell, Colin. *Senate Appropriations Committee: Foreign Operations Subcommittee Hearing on Afghanistan.* May 15, 2001.

Raphel, Robin. *Senate Foreign Relations Committee: Near Eastern and South Asian Affairs Subcommittee Hearing on Current Events in South Asia.* February 4, 1994.

————. *Senate Foreign Relations Committee: Near Eastern and South Asian Affairs Subcommittee Hearing on Afghanistan.* June 6, 1996.

Rolince, Michael. *Joint Inquiry Committee.* September 24, 2002.

Rubin, Barnett. *Senate Foreign Relations Committee: Near Eastern and South Asian Affairs Subcommittee Hearing on Events in Afghanistan.* October 8, 1998.

————. *Senate Foreign Relations Committee: Near Eastern and South Asian Affairs Subcommittee Hearing on the Crisis in Afghanistan.* April 14, 1999.

Santos, Charles. *House International Relations Committee Hearing on al Qaeda and the Global Reach of Terrorism.* October 3, 2001.

Scowcroft, Brent. *Joint Inquiry Committee.* September 19, 2002.

Tenet, George. *Senate Select Intelligence Committee Hearing on the Nomination of George Tenet as Deputy Director of Central Intelligence.* June 14, 1995.

————. *Senate Select Intelligence Committee Hearing on Current and Projected National Security Threats.* February 5, 1997.

————. *Senate Select Intelligence Committee Hearing on the Nomination of George Tenet as Director of Central Intelligence.* May 6, 1997.

————. *Senate Appropriations Committee Hearing on Counterterrorism.* May 13, 1997.

————. *Senate Select Intelligence Committee Hearing on Current and Projected National Security Threats.* January 28, 1998.

————. *Senate Armed Services Committee Hearing on Current and Projected National Security Threats.* February 2, 1999.

————. *Senate Select Intelligence Committee Hearing on Current and Projected National Security Threats.* February 2, 2000.

————. *Senate Armed Services Committee Hearing on Current and Projected National Security Threats.* February 3, 2000.

————. *Senate Select Intelligence Committee Hearing on Current and Projected National Security Threats.* February 7, 2001.

————. *Senate Armed Services Committee Hearing on Current and Projected National Security Threats.* March 8, 2001.

————. *Senate Select Intelligence Committee Hearing on Current and Projected National Security Threats.* February 6, 2002.

————. *Joint Inquiry Committee.* October 17, 2002.

Tomsen, Peter. *Senate Committee on Foreign Relations: Near Eastern and South Asian Affairs Subcommittee Hearing on Afghanistan.* July 20, 2000.

————. *House Committee on International Relations Hearing on the Future of Afghanistan.* November 7, 2001.

Watson, Dale. *Senate Foreign Relations Committee Hearing on the Report of the National Commission on Terrorism.* June 15, 2000.

————. *Joint Inquiry Committee.* September 26, 2002.

White, Mary Jo. *Joint Inquiry Committee.* October 8, 2002.

Wolfowitz, Paul. *Joint Inquiry Committee.* September 19, 2002.

Zinni, Anthony. *Senate Armed Services Committee Hearing on Afghanistan.* February 29, 2000.

CONGRESSIONAL REPORT

Senate Select Committee on Intelligence and House Permanent Select Committee on Intelligence, "Joint Inquiry into Intelligence Community Activities Before and After the Terrorist Attacks of September 11, 2001," final report prepared December 2002, redacted and released August 2003.

COMMISSION REPORT

"The 9/11 Commission Report: Final Report of the National Commission on Terrorist Attacks Upon the United States," released July 2004. Also, interim staff statements no. 1–17.

SPEECHES

Al-Faisal, Turki, Prince. "Special Address at Georgetown University." February 3, 2002, Washington, D.C.

Berger, Samuel. "Remarks to the National Academy of Sciences." January 22, 1999, Washington, D.C.

Clinton, Bill. "Remarks to Staff of the CIA and Intelligence Community." July 14, 1995, McLean, Virginia.

———. "On the Work Force Investment Act of 1998." August 7, 1998, Washington, D.C.

———. "Remarks to the National Academy of Sciences." January 22, 1999, Washington, D.C.

———. "Speech at Georgetown University." November 7, 2001, Washington, D.C.

———. "Speech at Labour Party Conference." October 3, 2002, Blackpool, England.

———. "Remarks to Democratic Leadership Council at New York University." December 6, 2002, New York, New York.

Clinton, Hillary. "Remarks to United Nations Economic and Social Council." December 10, 1997, New York, New York.

Inderfurth, Karl F. "Statement by Karl Inderfurth." July 19, 1999, Tashkent, Uzbekistan.

Simons, Thomas W., Jr. "The Evolving American Approach to World Affairs and the Emerging Pakistan-U.S. Relationship: Works in Progress." (Speech presented to Association of Retired Ambassadors.) September 22, 1996, Islamabad, Pakistan.

———. "Regional Stability in South Asia: U.S. Views." (Speech presented to United Service Institution.) November 27, 1996, New Delhi, India.

———. "Pakistan-U.S. Relations: A Personal Perspective." (Speech presented to English Speaking Union of Karachi.) June 3, 1998, Karachi, Pakistan.

Tenet, George. "Remarks at Swearing-in Ceremony by Vice President Gore." July 31, 1997, Washington, D.C.

———. "Speech at the University of Oklahoma." September 12, 1997, Norman, Oklahoma.

———. "Acceptance of the Ellis Island Medal of Honor." November 6, 1997, New York, New York.

———. "Does America Need the CIA?" November 19, 1997, Ann Arbor, Michigan.

———. "Remarks at Intelligence Community Awards Ceremony." December 11, 1997, McLean, Virginia.

———. "Remarks to CIA Employees on Strategic Direction." May 5, 1998, McLean, Virginia.

———. "Oscar Iden Lecture at Georgetown University." October 18, 1999, Washington, D.C.

SELECTED U.S. GOVERNMENT DOCUMENTS

"Afghan Policy—U.S. Strategy." State Department Cable, September 26, 1991.

"Afghanistan Settlement—Analysis and Policy Recommendations." State Department Cable, June 1997.

"Afghanistan: The Revolution After Four Years." CIA, Directorate of Intelligence, July 1982. Released July 1999 by the National Security Archive.

"Afghanistan: Trends for 1992." State Department Cable, December 16, 1991.

"Afghanistan—U.S. Interests and U.S. Aid." State Department Memorandum, December 18, 1992.

"Biography of Mohammed Omar." CIA fact sheet, December 21, 1998.

"Central Asia, Afghanistan and U.S. Policy." State Department Memorandum, February 2, 1993.

"The Costs of Soviet Involvement in Afghanistan." CIA, Office of Soviet Analysis, February 1987. Released 2000.

"Démarche to Pakistan on Hekmatyar and Sayyaf Gulf Statements." State Department Action Memorandum, January 28, 1991. Released April 6, 2000.

"Executive Order 12947." Federal Register, January 25, 1995.

"Implications of a Continued Stalemate in Afghanistan." State Department Cable, February 5, 1993.

"Memorandum of Conversation Between HRH Prince Turki and Senator Bill Bradley." Memorandum, April 13, 1980.

"Ramzi Ahmed Yousef: A New Generation of Sunni Islamic Terrorists." FBI assessment, 1995.

"Report of the Accountability Review Boards: Bombings of the U.S. Embassies in Nairobi, Kenya and Dar es Salaam, Tanzania on August 7, 1998." Released January 8, 1999.

"SE Tomsen Meeting with Shura of Commanders Oct. 6." State Department Cable, October 10, 1990.

"The Soviet Invasion of Afghanistan: Five Years After." CIA, Directorate of Intelligence, May 1985.

"Special Envoy to the Afghan Resistance." State Department Action Memorandum, April 19 1989. Released March 23, 2000.

"Terrorism, the Future, and U.S. Foreign Policy." Congressional Research Service, September 13, 2001.

"Terrorist Attack on USS *Cole*: Background and Issues for Congress." Congressional Research Service, January 30, 2001.

"To SecState WashDC Priority, Dissent Channel." State Department Cable, June 21, 1989.

"Usama bin Laden: Islamic Extremist Financier." CIA Assessment, 1996.

"U.S. Policy on Counterterrorism." Presidential Directive-39, June 21, 1995.

"USSR: Withdrawal from Afghanistan." Director of Central Intelligence, Special National Intelligence Estimate, March 1988.

DOCUMENT SETS

The Cold War International History Project at the Woodrow Wilson Center. "Toward an International History of the War in Afghanistan, 1979–1989." Comp. Christian F. Ostermann and Mircea Munteanu. Conference in association with The Asia Program and The Kennan Institute for Advanced Russian Studies at the Woodrow Wilson Center, The George Washington Cold War Group at The George Washington University, and the National Security Archive. Washington, D.C.: April 29–30, 2002.

———. "Excerpt from a report of 40th Army HQ."

———. Gromov, Boris. "Limited Contingent." *Progress,* Moscow, 1994.

———. Likhovskii, A. A. "The Tragedy and Valor of the Afghani." GPI "Iskon," Moscow, 1995.

———. Lyakhovski, Aleksandr A. "New Russian Evidence on the Crisis and War in Afghanistan." Working paper no. 41.

———. Mitrokhin, Vasiliy. "The KGB in Afghanistan." English ed., working paper no. 40.

———. Politburo records provided by Anatoly Chenyaev and translated by the Gorbachev Foundation.

———. "Special National Intelligence Estimate on Pakistan." November 12, 1982.

The National Security Archive. "The September 11th Sourcebooks: National Security Archive Online Readers on Terrorism, Intelligence and the Next War."

———. *Volume I: Terrorism and U.S. Policy.* Jeffrey Richelson and Michael L. Evans, eds. September 21, 2001.

———. "The Soviet Experience in Afghanistan: Russian Documents and Memoirs." *Volume II: Afghanistan: Lessons from the Last War.* John Prados and Svetlana Savranskaya, eds. October 9, 2001.

———. *Volume IV: The Once and Future King?: From the Secret Files of King Zahir's Reign in Afghanistan, 1970–1973.* William Burr, ed. October 26, 2001.

———. *Volume VII: The Taliban File.* Sajit Gandhi, ed. September 11, 2003.

COURT DOCUMENTS

United States of America v. Ibrahim A. el-Gabrowny et al., S(2) 93 Cr. 181 (S.D. New York, 1993).

United States of America v. Ramzi Ahmed Yousef et al., S 93 Cr. 180 (S.D. New York, 1993).

United States of America v. Ramzi Ahmed Yousef et al., S(10) 93 Cr. 180 (S.D. New York, 1995).

United States of America v. Ramzi Ahmed Yousef et al., S(12) 93 Cr. 180 (S.D. New York, February 1996).

United States of America v. Ramzi Ahmed Yousef et al., S(12) 93 Cr. 180 (S.D. New York, August 1996).

United States of America v. Ramzi Ahmed Yousef et al., S(12) 93 Cr. 180 (S.D. New York, August 1997).

United States of America v. Ramzi Ahmed Yousef et al., S(12) 93 Cr. 180 (S.D. New York, October 1997).

United States of America v. Usama bin Laden et al., S 98 Cr. 539 (S.D. New York, 1998).

United States of America v. Ali Mohamed, S(7) 98 Cr. 1023 (S.D. New York, 2000).

United States of America v. Usama bin Laden et al., S(7) 98 Cr. 1023 (S.D. New York, February 5, 2001).

United States of America v. Usama bin Laden et al., S(7) 98 Cr. 1023 (S.D. New York, February 6, 2001).

NEWSPAPERS, MAGAZINES, AND BROADCAST NEWS

Newspapers: *Aerospace Daily, Al-Sharq al-Awsat, Arab News, The Arkansas Democrat-Gazette, The Boston Herald, Chicago Tribune, The Christian Science Monitor, The Daily Telegraph, Defense Daily, The Financial Times, The Guardian, The Independent* (London), *Los Angeles Times, The Muslim* (Islamabad), *New York Daily News, The New York Times, The News* (Islamabad), *Newsday* (New York), *Platt's Oilgram News, The Seattle Times, The Toronto Star, USA Today, The Wall Street Journal, The Washington Post, The Washington Times.*

Magazines: *Air Force Magazine, Asiaweek, Aviation Week and Space Technology, Business Week, The Economist, Financial Times, Fortune, Le Monde Diplomatique, Le Nouvel Observateur, National Journal, The New York Times Magazine, The New Yorker, Newsweek, Nida'ul Islam, Popular Science, Time.*

News Agencies: AAP Newsfeed, Agence France Presse, Associated Press, Bulletin Broadfaxing Network, Federal News Service, Intelligence Newsletter, MBC, Reuters, United Press International.

Broadcast News: ABC News, ABC's *Nightline, al Jazeera,* BBC, CNN, *Fox News, The News Hour With Jim Lehrer, Orbit,* PBS's *Frontline.*

FILMS, TELEVISION, AND VIDEOTAPES

Afghan Warrior: The Life and Death of Abdul Haq, Touch Productions, London, 2003.

Ahmed Badeeb 2002 Interview with Orbit Television, supplied to the author by Badeeb, translated by The Language Doctors, Inc. See note 1, chapter 4.

Ahmed Shah Massoud with Abdul Haq and Peter Tomsen, June 24, 2001, Dushanbe, Tajikistan, informal video and transcript of meeting.

Ahmed Shah Massoud with Otilie English, April 27, 2001, Khoja Bahuddin, Afghanistan, informal video of meeting.

Hunting bin Laden, produced and directed by Martin Smith, aired as an episode of *Frontline,* Public Broadcasting System, March 21, 2000.

Acknowledgments

This book belongs first to my sources. During the course of my research, scores of people—Americans, Afghans, Pakistanis, Saudis—agreed to sit for long and sometimes repeated interviews about sensitive subjects, without any guarantees about how I would handle the material. Many of them are listed by name in the notes. I am deeply grateful for their time and trust. I also accept full responsibility for any errors of fact and interpretation in what I have written; those who helped me should not be blamed. Unfortunately, some of the people to whom I owe the most cannot be named here. They know who they are; they have my sincere and lasting thanks.

More than any individual, Len Downie, the executive editor of *The Washington Post,* my partner and friend for the last five years, granted this book its life. His sincere, unflagging support and encouragement of the project, despite the varied burdens it placed on him, made all the difference.

Many others at the *Post,* my professional home since 1985, contributed greatly to the book. Bo Jones supported the project and much else. Don Graham provided a helpful manuscript reading, among many other things. Cyndy Zeiss kept me in order and on time. David Hoffman and Phil Bennett took time they did not possess to read early drafts and provided crucial encouragement, support, edits, and suggestions. Brigit Roeber and the entire research department helped in many ways. Walter Pincus and Bob Woodward offered important documents from their personal archives. Barton Gellman, Dana Priest, Tom Ricks, and Glenn Kessler blazed journalistic paths that I followed, and also contributed ideas and practical assistance. Michael Keegan and Dick Furno made the book's maps possible. Mike Abramowitz, Joann Armao, Bob Barnes, Milton Coleman, Jackson Diehl, Jill Dutt, Doug Feaver, David Finkel, Emilio Garcia-Ruiz, Deb Heard, Fred Hiatt, Steve Hills, Anne Hull, Bob Kaiser, Kevin Merida, Larry Roberts, Gene Robinson, Chris Schroeder, Maralee Schwartz, Liz Spayd, and Matt Vita offered friendship and humor through a relentlessly paced period of news. They and other reporters and editors too many to list have made the *Post* not only a great newspaper but a creative and exciting place to work. In important ways, this book belongs to the newsroom.

One of my purposes in this project was to provide Afghans with reliable, transparent access to hidden strands of their own history. Especially when I worked as a correspondent in the region between 1989 and 1992, I was aided, befriended, and protected in extraordinary ways by many Afghans. In particular I would like to remember here my late friend, communist-era minder, driver, and translator, Najibullah, who was killed in a rocket attack on Kabul in 1992. In Afghanistan this more recent time around, my colleague Pam Constable, her Kabul housemates, and the exceptional translator Dr. Najib offered hospitality and crucial reporting help in the capital and Kandahar. In Pakistan, Karl Vick and Kamran Khan were invaluable. I am grateful as well to Maleeha Lodhi for her friendship and cheerful arguments. Asad Hayuddin helped arrange important meetings in Washington and Islamabad. David Long and Nat Kern made helpful introductions in Saudi Arabia. None of these people should be held responsible for my writings or interpretations in this book.

One of the greatest research challenges I faced was to connect recollections from interviews (inevitably selective) with authenticating, contemporaneous documents. I am grateful to Robert Gates for directing me to his unedited manuscript, held at Harvard University. Peter Tomsen generously shared declassified State Department cables from his vast personal archive on Afghanistan. Otilie English provided a very helpful taped interview with Ahmed Shah Massoud from early 2001. Karl Inderfurth provided important travel calendars and other documents that added precision to my account of U.S. diplomatic history in Afghanistan between 1997 and 2000. Bill Harlow, Mark Mansfield, and Jenny in the CIA's office of public affairs helpfully directed me to open source material. Other sources consulted diaries, calendars, official histories, archives, and other government documents to ensure that my narrative was as accurate and complete as possible. I am grateful to all of them. Excerpts from classified documents published by the congressional Joint Inquiry Committee on the September 11 attacks provided important insight about the 1998–2001 period. *The Age of Sacred Terror,* by Daniel Benjamin and Steven Simon, former White House counterterrorism officials, also offered helpful inside documentation about those years. Finally, Christian Ostermann and his colleagues at the Cold War International History Project collected and, where necessary, translated an enormously valuable archive of Soviet and American documents about Afghanistan from the 1980s, adding to the earlier good work by the National Security Archive at George Washington University. The National Security Archive worked its declassification magic again during 2003 and added useful new material about U.S. policy toward the Taliban.

As the source notes indicate, I also sought to connect my original interviews with other previously published journalism and scholarship on Afghanistan, the CIA, and terrorism in

South Asia. My colleague Pam Constable wrote early and intrepidly about the Taliban. So did John Burns and Barry Bearak of *The New York Times*. Vernon Loeb of the *Post* wrote extensively about bin Laden prior to September 11; I have drawn from his work. Peter Finn broke extensive ground about al Qaeda more recently. I have relied also on the early, in-depth journalism of Douglas Frantz, James Risen, and Judith Miller of the *Times* about bin Laden, U.S. counterterrorism policy, and aspects of Pakistani and Saudi intelligence. *The Wall Street Journal* produced major breakthroughs from their investigations into the life of Ayman al-Zawahiri. I am also grateful to the team at the *Los Angeles Times* for their matchless biographical work on the members of the Hamburg cell. Among American scholars, Barnett Rubin's writing, especially *The Fragmentation of Afghanistan,* lays a very important foundation for anyone writing about Afghanistan's post-1979 traumas. Ahmed Rashid's book *Taliban* was not only a great feat of journalism, but an act of personal bravery. I have relied also on Olivier Roy's enduring insights into Afghanistan and political Islam. I owe many other professional debts to previously published work; the notes provide a full accounting.

Thanks to Jean Cleary for finding me a room of my own. Thanks to Adam Holzman for his friendship, sounds, humor, and ideas.

From our first conversation shortly after September 11 to our last edit two years later, Ann Godoff supported this book's highest possible ambitions and nurtured them at every turn. She is a great editor and a remarkable person. Her assistant at The Penguin Press, Meredith Blum, was a terrific correspondent and an encouraging partner. Rose Ann Ferrick's meticulous, thoughtful work on the manuscript improved it immeasurably. Ryu Spaeth's work on the bibliography and chapter notes, and his careful copyediting, also made a major contribution. As she has for nearly two decades now, Melanie Jackson, my literary agent, provided sound counsel throughout, steering us all through a few unusual bumps with confidence and skill.

Thanks above all to my family, especially to Alexandra, Emma, and Max for their love, tolerance, and encouragement.

Index

Rahman, Akhtar Abdur, 63–66, 132, 178
  on Afghan war strategy, 103, 104, 105
  background of, xvii, 64, 164
  CIA contacts with, 63, 64, 65, 69, 99,
    105, 148, 149
  funding channeled through, 67
  Islamic politics of, 73
  Saudi links with, 71, 72, 73, 81, 180
  U.S. delegations received by, 129
  on weapons distribution, 67–68, 129
Rahman, Jamil al-, 83
Rahman, Omar Abdal, 250, 251, 258
Ralston, Joseph, 411
Rana, Naseem, xvii, 315, 331, 374, 414
Raphel, Arnold, 178, 179, 180
Raphel, Robin, xv, 264, 299, 308–9, 310,
    328–30, 335, 338
Rashid, Ahmed, 348
Reagan, John, 23, 31
Reagan, Ronald, 56, 58, 62, 92, 122, 125,
    126, 198, 267, 388
  on Afghan-Soviet conflict, 70, 89, 90, 97,
    102, 105, 127, 136, 149–50, 159, 165,
    168, 169, 176–77, 195, 264, 407
  anti-Soviet stance of, 90, 91, 93, 159, 195
  antiterrorist policies under, 138, 139,
    140, 272, 318, 377–78, 409
  on Casey's speaking style, 96–97
  Libyan targets bombed by, 409
  Pakistan aided by, 62
  presidential campaign of, 95
reconnaissance drones, 527–28
  see also Predator reconnaissance drones
Red Brigades, 142
Regan, Donald T., 161
Reinsch, Bill, 356
rendition process, 272, 377–78
Reno, Janet, 406, 426–28
Republican Party, 264, 307, 352, 543, 552
Ressam, Ahmed, 486–87, 491
Revere, Paul, 387
Rice, Condoleezza, 544, 546, 547–48,
    550–51, 552, 564, 568
Rich (bin Laden unit chief), xiv, 456, 459,
    461, 469, 539, 540, 560, 582
Richardson, Bill, 383–86
Riedel, Bruce, 384, 442, 481
rocket-propelled grenade launchers, 58

Roosevelt, Franklin D., 74–75, 94
Roy, Oliver, 118, 120, 289
Rubin, Bennett, 119
Rudman, Warren, 356
Rumsfeld, Donald, 544, 546, 548
Russia:
  Massoud aided by, 335, 345, 464, 465,
    514, 519, 559
  pipelines controlled by, 302, 305
  Taliban-sponsored incursions on, 345
  see also Soviet Union
Rutskoi, Alexander, 178

Sadat, Anwar, 154, 423
Safari Club, 81
Sakharov, Andrei, 177
Salang Highway, 8, 13, 115–16
Saleh, Amrullah, xvi, 464, 562, 582–83
Salman (American Taliban member), 312
Salman, Prince, 84
Santos, Charlie, 312, 313, 342, 343
satellite photography, 149, 150, 245, 447,
    448, 449, 527
Saud, Abdul Aziz ibn, King of Saudi Ara-
    bia, xvii, 73, 74–75, 76, 77, 78, 79, 84,
    265
Saudi Arabia:
  al Qaeda members from, 489, 570
  anti-Soviet Afghan effort aided by,
    65–66, 67, 72
  bin Laden expelled from, 231, 267, 270,
    323–24
  bin Laden sympathizers in, 397–98,
    400–401
  Casey's visits to, 93, 98–99
  charity organizations of, 154, 278–79,
    517
  clerical establishment of, 83, 216–17, 228
  conservative religious movement in, 26,
    75–77, 93, 152, 296–97
  counterterrorism recalcitrance of,
    516–18
  external spy service of, see General Intel-
    ligence Department
  history of, 75–77, 297
  Iran as rival of, 216, 297, 399
  Iranian-sponsored terrorist threats in,
    276